R97
18 Aug

4   93rd   Street   5   6   1st

East   oi
       nf
Jewish Museum
91st   Street   East   91st Street
ast
Cooper-Hewitt Museum
       ne
Solomon R. Guggenheim   89th   Street   East   89th   Street
Museum   Gracie Mansion   Carl

YORKVILLE   Schurz   A
                                            End   Avenue   River   Drive
86TH STREET
East   no   86th M   Street   East   86th   Street   Park   Schurz

VO Institute for
ewish Research   of   East   Street

East   83rd   Street   East   ow   83rd   Street   Coler Mem.
                          ok   oy   na   Hospital
                                     ov   and Home   B
East   of   on   81st   Street   oj   81st   Street
j   oi   80th   Street   ou   80th   Street
om
East   UPPER   oe   79th   Street   East   79th   Street
       EAST   78th   Street   oz   78th   Street
       SIDE   John
Ukrainian Institute   Jay
of America   77TH STREET   op   Park
East   bs   M   76th   Street   East   ox   76th   Street
Harkness House
East   75th   Street   East   75th   Street
or   Whitney Museum of   os   ROOSEVELT
       American Art
East   73rd   Street   East   73rd   Street   Island Bridge   C
                          ol   oq
rick   72nd   Street   East   72nd   Street   Channel
ollection   East   71st   oo   Street   og   71st   Street   ISLAND
Asia House   od   East
br   Channel
East   69th   Street   East   69th   Street
Consolato generale   Ist. Italiano di Cultura   West
d'Italia   68th   Street   East   68th   Street   Correction
       68TH STREET   Drive   Hospital
       HUNTER COLLEGE
Temple   66th   Street   East   66th   Street
Emanu-El   St. Vincent
East   Py   Ferrer   Rockefeller
       65th   China House   East   65th   University
bn   bq   oc   ob   pv
ba   px
East   bm   oa   nb   63rd   Street   East   63rd   Street
ps   pz   bo
nickerbocker Club   pr   West
otel Pierre   East   LEXINGTON   61st   Abigail Adams   East
EastMetropolitan   AVENUE   Smith House   Channel
Club   60th M   Street   E   60th   Street
ok   59TH ST.   pu   pt   Roosevelt   Queensboro Bridge
I.C.E.   Bloomingdale's
eneral Motors   xd   xa
uilding   xb   xt   xp
East   57th   Street   E. 57th   Street   Goldwater
Trump Tower   Memorial
AT & T   Hospital   E
Headquarters   Delano
East   55th   Street   East   55th   Street   Sutton
                                            City
TH AVENUE   LEXINGTON   Citicorp   Hospital
       AVENUE   Center   xc
East   M   Seagram Building   East   52nd   xm
Park Avenue   Street   Street   Street
Plaza   51ST STREET   Roosevelt
       M   General Electric   xw   Memorial
t. Patrick's   Building   xj   ao   NEW YORK COUNTY
athedral   xu   QUEENS COUNTY   F
East   48th   Street   East   48th   Street   Franklin
East   D O W N   East River
46th   Street   E. 46th St   Second
United Nations   United Nations
Headquarters
Vanderbilt Avenue   General Assembly
Madison   United Nations Plaza   Building
East   44th   St One & Two   af   Conference
       4   5   United Nations Plaza   Building   6

"Being situated on a harbor, which attracted the first Dutch settlers, made New York's fortune. Its exceptional vitality was also a contributory factor. Wealth, poverty, liberty, violence, a melting pot of races and cultures . . ."
Hélène Trocmé

"The subway often generates prolific ideas, due to the movement, the busy throng, the traveler's alert state of mind, as he clatters under streets and rivers, under the foundations of enormous buildings . . ."
Saul Bellow

"My memory of Manhattan is that of a simpler, friendlier city. . . . There was no underground subway but, on the other hand, outings on the elevated railway represented, for a young boy, the height of enjoyment."

Mirwin Edman

THIS IS A BORZOI BOOK
PUBLISHED BY ALFRED A. KNOPF, INC.

Copyright © 1994 Alfred A. Knopf, Inc., New York

*Originally published in France by Nouveaux-Loisirs, a subsidiary of
Gallimard, Paris, 1994. Copyright © 1994 by Editions Nouveaux-Loisirs*

*Endpapers cartography originally printed in Guide del mondo: New York -
Washington © Touring Club Italiano, Milan 1992. Reprinted with permission of TCI.*

New York. English
New York/ [Gallimard editions].
p. cm.-- (Knopf guides)
Includes bibliographical references and index.
ISBN 0-679-75065-7 : $25.00
1. New York (N.Y.) -- Guidebooks.
I. Gallimard (Firm) . II. Title. III. Series
F128.18. N35   1994
917.47'10443 -- dc20
CIP 94-8367

First American Edition

NUMEROUS SPECIALISTS AND ACADEMICS HAVE CONTRIBUTED TO THIS GUIDE:
AUTHORS AND EDITORS: David Abrahamson, Delphine Babelon, Laurence de Bélizal, Sophie Body-
Gendrot, Paule du Bouchet, Norman Brouwer, Béatrice Coron, Leah Dickerman, Philippe J.
Dubois, Cécile Dutheil, Sarah Elliott, Élisabeth de Farcy, Catherine Fouré, Walter A. Friedman, Mr
G., Isabelle Gournay, Nina Gray, Nancy Green, Benoît Heimermann, Doris Hering, Catherine
Hodder, Denis Hollier, Kim Hopper, Sidney Horenstein, Seth Kamil, Michael Kerker, Louise Kerz,
Rod Knox, Sophie Lenormand, Brooks McNamara, Anne Magniant, Peter D. Meltzer,
Frédéric Morvan, Anka Muhlstein, Edward O'Donnell, Katherine Palmer, Janette Sadik-Khan,
Michelle de Rosset, Ken Sheppard, Christine Silva, Cassie Springer, Ed Stancik, Hélène Trocmé,
Elisa Urbanelli, Béatrice Viterbo, John Waldman, Peter Watrous, Jonathan Weinberg.
ILLUSTRATORS AND ICONOGRAPHERS: Christine Adam, Philippe Biard, Jean Chevallier,
Paul Coulbois, Tanguy Cuzon du Rest, Claire Cormier, François Desbordes, Stéphanie Devaux,
Bernard Duhem, Hubert Gauger. Alain Gouessant, Donald Grant, Jean-Marie Guillou,
Gilbert Houbre, Marc Lacaze, Yann Le Duc, Bruno Lenormand, Valérie Malpart,
Patrick Merienne, Claude Quiec, Alexandra Rose, Jean-Claude Senec, Jean Torton,
Catherine Totems, Pierre-Marie Vallat, Olivier Verdy, Jean Wilkinson.
PHOTOGRAPHERS: Laurence de Bélizal, Ted Hardin, John C. Fletcher.

WE WOULD ALSO LIKE TO THANK:
MUSEUM OF MODERN ART: Richard Oldenburg, Jeanne Collins, Lucy O'Brien ; FRICK COLLECTION:
Edgar Munhall, Jack Kennedy; METROPOLITAN MUSEUM: Philippe de Montebello, Barbara Burn,
Kent Lydecke, Mary Doherty , Lina Komaroff; THE CLOISTERS: Mary Shepard; SOLOMON R. GUGGENHEIM:
Thomas Krens, Lisa Denison, Samar Qandil, Joan Young; WHITNEY MUSEUM: David Ross and
Jack Kennedy.

WE WOULD LIKE TO GIVE SPECIAL THANKS TO:
Barry Bergdoll, Luis R. Cancel (Commissioner, City of New York Department of Cultural Affairs),
Alain Dister, Seymour Durst, Gordon McCollum, Henri Peretz, Carole Sorelle (Assistant Commissioner
for Public Affairs)

TRANSLATED BY SUE ROSE;
EDITED AND TYPESET BY BOOK CREATION SERVICES, LONDON.
PRINTED IN ITALY BY EDITORIALE LIBRARIA.

NEW YORK

KNOPF GUIDES

CONTENTS

NATURE, *15*

Climate, *16*
Geology, *18*
Hudson River, *20*
Central Park, *22*
City flora and fauna, *24*

HISTORY AND LANGUAGE, *25*

Chronology, *26*
From New Amsterdam to New York, *30*
American-style town planning, *32*
The first public services, *34*
Transportation, *36*
Trial by fire, *38*
Crime and corruption, *40*
The port, *42*
In the melting pot, *44*
The homeless, *46*
Languages, *48*

LIFESTYLES, *49*

Religions, *50*
Festivals and parades, *52*
The Written Press, *54*
Radio and television, *56*
The musical, *58*
Jazz, *60*
Dance, *62*
Sports, *64*
Interior design and furniture, *66*
Cheesecake, 68
Specialties, *70*

ARCHITECTURE, *71*

Manhattan from 1664 to 1994, *72*
Colonial style and Federal style, *82*
Greek Revival style, *84*
Gothic Revival and High Victorian Gothic styles, *86*
Italianate and Second Empire styles, *88*
Queen Anne style and Romanesque Revival, *90*
"Beaux Arts" style, *92*
The birth of the skyscraper, *94*
The eclecticism of the first skyscrapers, *96*
Art Deco style, *98*
International style, *100*
Postmodernism, *102*
Major projects, *104*

NEW YORK AS SEEN BY PAINTERS, *105*

Canyon streets, *106*
Urban landscapes, *108*
Above, below, *110*
Skyline, *112*

NEW YORK AS SEEN BY WRITERS, *113*

Around the World Trade Center, *135*

World Trade Center to Battery Park, *136*
The Statue of Liberty, *144*
Ellis Island, *148*
World Trade Center to the Financial District, *158*

Around City Hall, *167*

South Street Seaport, *172*
Woolworth Building, *180*
Brooklyn Bridge, *186*

Lower East Side, *189*

Chinatown, *190*
Jewish neighborhood, *194*
Little Italy, *196*

Around Washington Square, *197*

Washington Square to SoHo-TriBeCa, *198*
Washington Square to Gansevoort Meat Market, *210*
Washington Square to Chelsea, *216*

Around Union Square, *221*

Union Square to East Village, *222*
Union Square to Gramercy Park, *228*
Union Square to Madison Square, *232*

Around Grand Central Terminal, *235*

Grand Central Terminal, *236*
Empire State Building, *242*
Theater district, *258*
Chrysler Building, *266*

Around Rockefeller Center, *273*

Rockefeller Center, *274*
MOMA, *290*

Around Central Park, *307*

Upper East Side, *308*
Central Park, *314*
Frick Collection, *322*
Whitney Museum, *326*
Metropolitan Museum, *328*
Guggenheim Museum, *338*
Upper West Side, *342*

Off the Beaten Track, *349*

Morningside Heights and Harlem, *350*
The Cloisters, *362*
Brooklyn Heights, *366*

Practical Information, *367*

Index, *439*

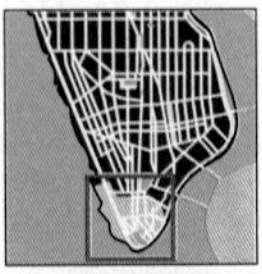

WORLD TRADE
CENTER

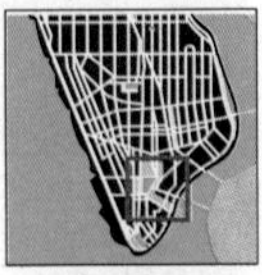

CITY HALL

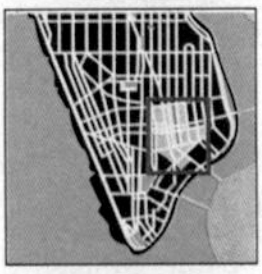

LOWER EAST SIDE

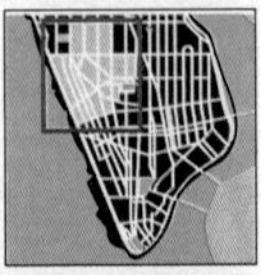

WASHINGTON SQUARE

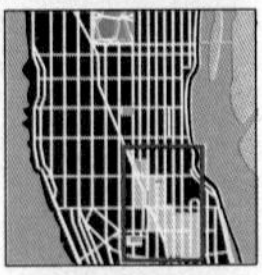

UNION SQUARE

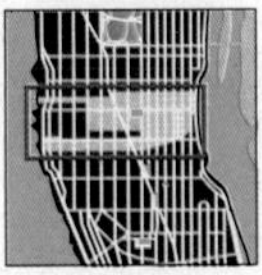

GRAND CENTRAL
TERMINAL

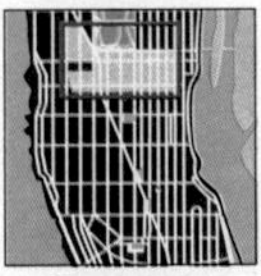

ROCKEFELLER
CENTER

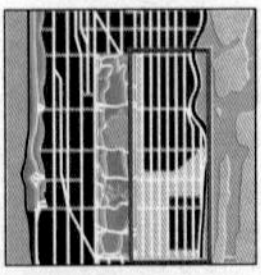

AROUND
CENTRAL PARK

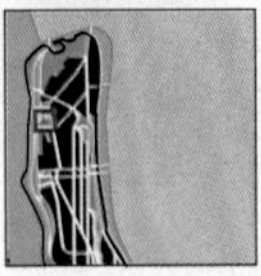

HARLEM AND UPPER
MANHATTAN

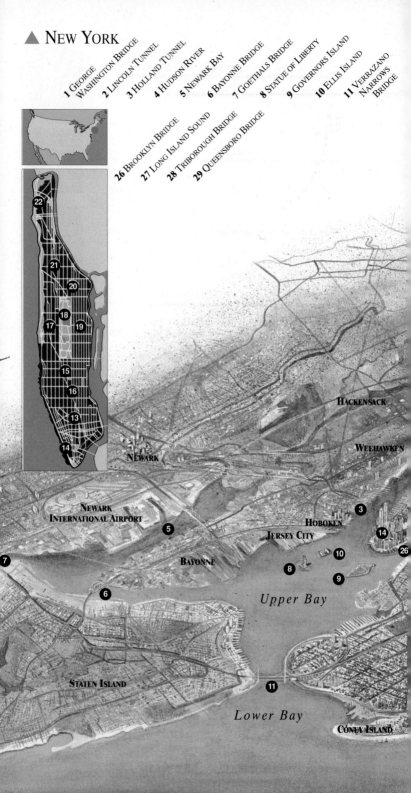

1 GEORGE WASHINGTON BRIDGE
2 LINCOLN TUNNEL
3 HOLLAND TUNNEL
4 HUDSON RIVER
5 NEWARK BAY
6 BAYONNE BRIDGE
7 GOETHALS BRIDGE
8 STATUE OF LIBERTY
9 GOVERNORS ISLAND
10 ELLIS ISLAND
11 VERRAZANO NARROWS BRIDGE

26 BROOKLYN BRIDGE
27 LONG ISLAND SOUND
28 TRIBOROUGH BRIDGE
29 QUEENSBORO BRIDGE

HACKENSACK

WEEHAWKEN

NEWARK

NEWARK INTERNATIONAL AIRPORT

HOBOKEN

JERSEY CITY

BAYONNE

Upper Bay

STATEN ISLAND

Lower Bay

CONEY ISLAND

Atlantic Ocean

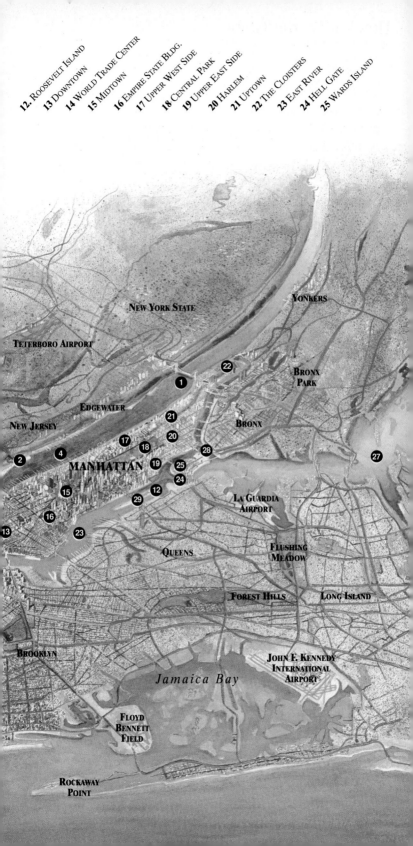

12. ROOSEVELT ISLAND **13** DOWNTOWN **14** WORLD TRADE CENTER **15** MIDTOWN **16** EMPIRE STATE BLDG. **17** UPPER WEST SIDE **18** CENTRAL PARK **19** UPPER EAST SIDE **20** HARLEM **21** UPTOWN **22** THE CLOISTERS **23** EAST RIVER **24** HELL GATE **25** WARDS ISLAND

NEW YORK STATE

YONKERS

TETERBORO AIRPORT

22

BRONX PARK

EDGEWATER

1

21

NEW JERSEY

2

4

17

18

20

BRONX

MANHATTAN

19

28

15

25

24

27

16

12

29

LA GUARDIA AIRPORT

13

23

QUEENS

FLUSHING MEADOW

FOREST HILLS

LONG ISLAND

BROOKLYN

Jamaica Bay

JOHN F. KENNEDY INTERNATIONAL AIRPORT

FLOYD BENNETT FIELD

ROCKAWAY POINT

HOW TO USE THIS GUIDE
(Sample page shown from the guide to Venice)

The symbols at the top of
each page refer to
the different parts
of the guide.

■ NATURAL ENVIRONMENT

● KEYS TO UNDERSTANDING

▲ ITINERARIES

◆ PRACTICAL INFORMATION

The itinerary map
shows the main points
of interest along the
way and is intended
to help you find
your bearings.

The mini-map
locates the particular
itinerary within
the wider area
covered by
the guide.

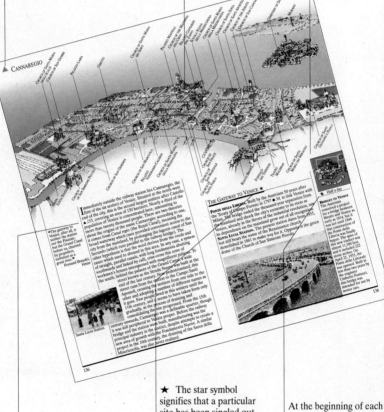

★ The star symbol
signifies that a particular
site has been singled out
by the publishers for its
special beauty,
atmosphere or cultural
interest.

● ▲ ■ ◆

The symbols alongside a
title or within the text
itself provide cross-
references to a theme
or place dealt with
elsewhere in the guide.

At the beginning of each
itinerary, the suggested
means of transport to be
used and the time it will
take to cover the area are
indicated:

🚣 By boat
🚶 On foot
🚲 By bicycle
🕐 Duration

THE GATEWAY TO VENICE ★

PONTE DELLA LIBERTA. Built by the Austrians 50 years after
the Treaty of Campo Formio in 1797 ● *34,* to link Venice with
Milan. The bridge ended the thousand-year separation from
the mainland and shook the city's economy to its roots as
Venice, already in the throes of the industrial revolution, saw

🚶 Half a day

BRIDGES TO VENICE

NATURE

CLIMATE, *16*
GEOLOGY, *18*
HUDSON RIVER, *20*
CENTRAL PARK, *22*
CITY FLORA AND FAUNA, *24*

New York City's climate is typical for northeastern areas of the Atlantic coast and resembles the weather conditions that prevail along the northeast coast of Asia. Frontal systems and the close proximity of the ocean combine to accentuate great fluctuations in temperature. This means that although New York is in a temperate latitude, hurricanes, heat waves, blizzards and spectacular weather changes can occur almost overnight. During some years the temperature can vary considerably from -13°F in winter to 106°F in summer, in other words by as much as 119°F.

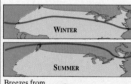

WINTER

SUMMER

POSITION OF THE JET STREAM IN WINTER AND SUMMER
Jet stream: strong winds traveling from west to east at very high altitudes and generated by the interplay between hot and cold air masses and the coriolis force.

ARCTIC AIR
Arctic air from Siberia crosses central Canada and sweeps into the city, bringing bitterly cold weather in its wake.

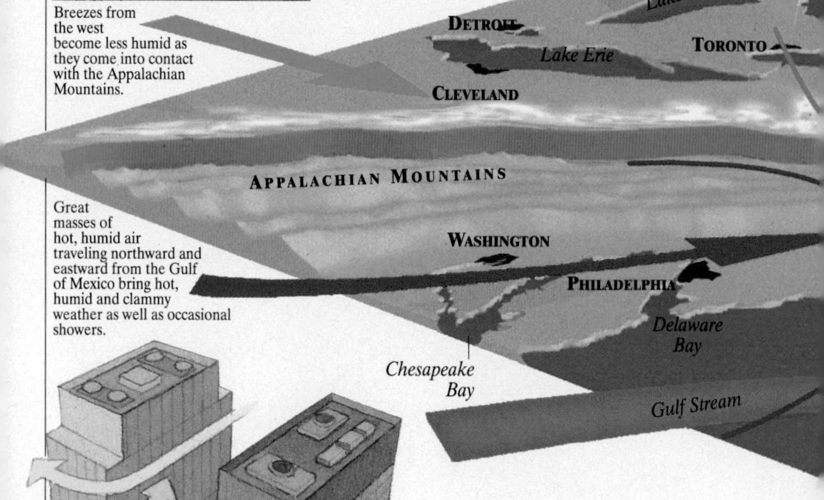

Breezes from the west become less humid as they come into contact with the Appalachian Mountains.

Lake Huron

DETROIT

Lake Erie

TORONTO

CLEVELAND

APPALACHIAN MOUNTAINS

Great masses of hot, humid air traveling northward and eastward from the Gulf of Mexico bring hot, humid and clammy weather as well as occasional showers.

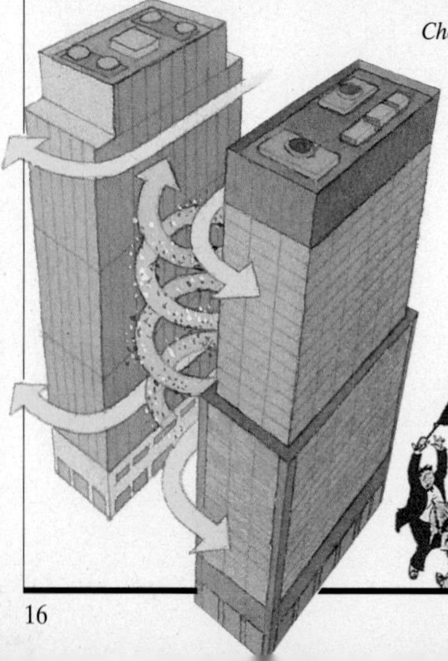

WASHINGTON

PHILADELPHIA

Delaware Bay

Chesapeake Bay

Gulf Stream

THE "CANYON" EFFECT
In Manhattan high-rise buildings have unpredictable effects on the wind. The "canyon" effect – typically found in Downtown and Midtown – is produced when the wind bounces off the ground and the sides of the skyscrapers to form columns of rising air.

During extremely cold snaps, the Hudson River can become partially blocked with ice.

The ocean is responsible for violent storms in this area. At times the east coast of North America has some of the world's most changeable weather.

Temperatures can hit, and occasionally soar above, 100°F in the summer. Hoses, fountains, even fire hydrants, are urban solutions to cooling off at times like these.

When the city is beset by thick fog, the tops of Manhattan's highest skyscrapers disappear – as the Woolworth Building has done here – transforming the skyline.

In March 1993, a blizzard swept the east coast, from the Gulf of Mexico to Canada. A mass of cold air (-20°F) collided with a mass of hot air (85°F) and the difference in temperature caused snowstorms and tornados.

LAKE ONTARIO

NEW YORK

BOSTON

ATLANTIC OCEAN

Coastal regions enjoy milder weather in the winter and cooler weather in summer than areas farther inland.

THE CAUSE OF A DEPRESSION
When hot, humid air coming in from the Gulf of Mexico and cold air coming down from Canada collide, they generate a coastal storm.

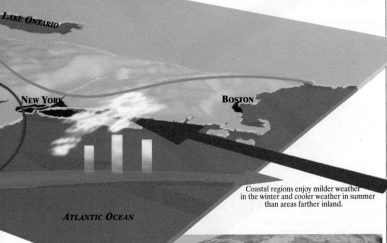

17

GEOLOGY

The islands at the top of New York Bay, which form one of the
main indentations along the eastern coast of the United States,
were created by geological conditions in the region's distant
past. Because the coastline's navigable waterways are wide, deep
and fairly long, ships can be easily piloted down them and
moored. New York's location, at the mouth of the Hudson
River, on a sheltered bay that opens into several other navigable
waterways, has played a crucial role in stimulating the city's port
growth, contributing to its status as one of the major ports in the
United States. Of the five boroughs that make up Greater New
York, only the Bronx is
connected to the
mainland.

**17,000 YEARS
AGO.** During the
height of glaciation,
the site of New York was
covered with an ice sheet 1000
feet thick and the shoreline was 600
feet farther back to the east.

**10,000
YEARS AGO**
When the
glaciers melted, the
terminal moraine acted
as a dike and the valleys
hollowed out by glaciation (the
Hudson, East and Harlem
rivers) filled up.

**10,000
YEARS AGO
TO PRESENT**
The sea reached its
present level 4,000–
6,000 years ago, and the

The bare face of a marble mass, 500 million years old, can be found in Isham Park, at the north end of Manhattan.

Hudson River

Landfills

Mudbank

Terminal moraine, composed of boulders deposited by the glaciers

Rocky substratum or granite bed

Since building work started in Manhattan, the landscape has altered and the shoreline has been modified. Certain sites in Manhattan are built on landfills – among them Battery Park, South Street Seaport, the World Trade and the World Financial centers.

The fresh waters of the Hudson
River and the salt waters of New York Bay
converge along the western shore of Manhattan. Despite being
one of the busiest ports in the world, New York harbor remains
home to many species of wildlife. Here the resident marine
fauna mingles with seasonal fauna; certain migratory fish (bass,
sturgeon) spawn farther upstream in the Hudson. Paradoxically,
many species are abundant here; because of the pollution they
are in no danger of being caught for mass consumption. Crabs,
lobsters and shrimp live on the sea bed, while the peregrine
falcon dives from the dizzy height of the bridges.

Many of the piers of New York Harbor are in
varying stages of decay and form an
extraordinary micro-habitat in themselves.

LAUGHING GULL
This bird
migrates south
in winter
anywhere from the
Carolinas to South
America. It is a
familiar sight in the
harbor in spring and
summer.

Great black-backed gull

Herring gull

Ring-billed gull

**FOUREYE
BUTTERFLYFISH**
The Gulf Stream
provides the bay with
an annual influx of
tropical fish such as
groupers, snappers
and butterfly fish.

BLUE CRAB
Large numbers of this
crab are found in
New York Harbor,
where it is still
frequently fished.

GULLS AND SEAGULLS
Certain species, such as the great black-
backed gull and the herring gull, live here all
year round, as does the ring-billed gull.

AMERICAN SHAD
Every spring, shad navigate the harbor on
their way to their breeding grounds farther
inland.

STRIPED BASS
Fishing for this
predator takes
place around the
Statue of Liberty
in the fall.

AMERICAN EEL
New York's waters are a paradise for the
young eels spawned in the Sargasso Sea. They
swim up the Hudson River and its tributaries.

Aquatic fauna is
plentiful around the
harbor's piers, which
are covered with
starfish, while sea
horses play hide and
seek among the
fronds of seaweed.
Predatory fish (bass,
eel) come here to
hunt.

MONARCH
This butterfly spends every fall in the park on its way to Mexico.

For most migrating birds New York is between their winter quarters and their breeding ground.

Central Park was created in the mid-19th century, so that New Yorkers without access to the countryside could enjoy some of its benefits on a small scale. The park, which extends over 840 acres, not only provides New Yorkers with somewhere to go for a breath of fresh air but also is of considerable importance to many species of wildlife, including birds, butterflies and dragonflies. This lush haven in a forest of concrete is a stopover, for several hours or several days, for various migrating birds.

AMERICAN REDSTART
With its outspread tail this bird resembles a huge butterfly. It is one of the most common passerines in North America.

SCARLET TANAGER
This bird, which prefers to feed on caterpillars, leaves South America in the spring and nests in May in the oak trees of Central Park.

The cardinal has extended its range northward but can be found here year round.

CARDINAL
The male has bright red plumage, whereas the coloring of the female is drab brown.

BALTIMORE ORIOLE. This bird builds its nest in the shape of a ball suspended from a branch, occasionally using such materials as fishing twine.

BLUE JAY
The blue jay lives in the park all year round and can easily be distinguished by its call, from which it derives its name: "dchay-dchay-dchay". The jay is fairly tame and extremely fond of corn or peanuts in the winter.

CAPE MAY WARBLER
Regarded as one of the most beautiful species of its family, the striped warbler is always found near spruce trees. Its migratory path takes it through Central Park.

YELLOW-RUMPED WARBLER
This is the only representative of the warbler family to spend winter in the region of New York.

MOURNING DOVE
This dove derives its name from its rather melancholy call, which is similar to that of the owl.

COMMON GRACKLE
These birds breed alone but feed in flocks in the winter.

CITY FLORA AND FAUNA

GERMAN COCKROACH
This insect is perfectly suited to city life. In 18 months a pair can produce 130,000 offspring.

Although it consists mainly of concrete, steel and glass, Manhattan provides a home for various animals and plants which, over time, have grown accustomed to their man-made environment. Not surprisingly, this unpromising habitat has attracted mainly adaptable species, especially those that were introduced by man, such as sparrows, starlings and pigeons. These animals and birds, some of which were brought over from the Old World, quickly multiplied in the absence of direct competition, creating fresh problems for the city's inhabitants.

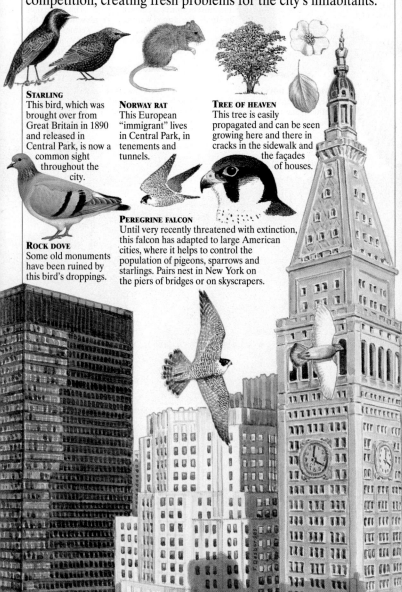

STARLING
This bird, which was brought over from Great Britain in 1890 and released in Central Park, is now a common sight throughout the city.

NORWAY RAT
This European "immigrant" lives in Central Park, in tenements and tunnels.

TREE OF HEAVEN
This tree is easily propagated and can be seen growing here and there in cracks in the sidewalk and the façades of houses.

ROCK DOVE
Some old monuments have been ruined by this bird's droppings.

PEREGRINE FALCON
Until very recently threatened with extinction, this falcon has adapted to large American cities, where it helps to control the population of pigeons, sparrows and starlings. Pairs nest in New York on the piers of bridges or on skyscrapers.

An Algonquin Indian and a Dutchman flanking the New York City seal, crowned with the American eagle.

THE STAMP ACT. In 1765, representatives from nine of the thirteen British colonies met in New York to protest against the imposition of a stamp duty on commodities; the act was repealed the following year. Tradesmen played a vital role in the initial phase of the struggle for independence by boycotting English produce. But the city was taken by the English in 1776 and became a stronghold of the Loyalists. After the end of the hostilities, in 1783, George Washington made a victorious entry into New York.

NEW YORK AS CAPITAL OF THE UNITED STATES. This chapter in New York's history lasted from 1789 to 1790. The first president, George Washington, swore his oath of office on the balcony of Federal Hall ● *85* ▲ *162*, which had been reconstructed after the revolution by the French architect Pierre Charles L'Enfant. The following year the seat of the federal government was moved to Philadelphia. In 1797 Albany became the capital of the State of New York, and New York City's growth from that time onward depended purely on its economic role.

1776
Declaration of Independence by the thirteen British colonies in America.

Washington making a triumphal entry into New York in 1783.

1783
The War of Independence ends in 1783 with the Treaty of Paris, which recognizes the existence of the United States.

THE 19TH CENTURY

BOOM TOWN. By 1800 the city's population was more than 60,000. Over the next few decades, port activity escalated and New York's harbor became the busiest in the country ● *42*. In 1807 on the Hudson, Robert Fulton launched the first commercially successful steamboat. In 1818 the first regular shipping line between New York and Liverpool was established. Shipyards spread out along the East River, and the food and textile industries flourished. In 1820, the Stock Exchange replaced the open-air money market that had operated on Wall Street since 1792 ▲ *160*. In anticipation of further growth, a commission drew up a grid street plan for the city extending over the entire island of Manhattan ● *32*.

1803
Napoleon sells Louisiana to the United States.

1860
Election of Lincoln.

Warehouses and factories, such as this sugar refinery, were built along the East River.

THE OPENING OF THE ERIE CANAL. This canal connected the Great Lakes and the Atlantic, and it consolidated New York's supremacy as a port. By 1830 Manhattan had more than 200,000 inhabitants. The first horse-drawn buses appeared and a railroad running between New York and Harlem was opened ● *36*.

NEW YORK TAKES THE LEAD. By 1860 the city was the largest in the U.S. The population had been swelled by the arrival of numerous immigrants, especially Irish and German. Brooklyn's population had increased ten times in the space of thirty years, while that of Manhattan had quadrupled.

1861
Outbreak of the Civil War, which ended in 1865 with victory for the North and the abolition of slavery.

1865
Lincoln is assassinated.

1876
Philadelphia Centennial Exposition.

● History of New York

During the Civil War, New York remained in the Union and sent a great many men to fight for the North; the departure of troops leaving for the front was marked by rousing parades.

1889
Construction of the Eiffel Tower in Paris.

1898
Spanish-American War in Cuba and the Philippines. The United States annexes Hawaii.

$10,000 Reward

After years of impunity, Boss Tweed was brought to trial and convicted of theft; he died in a New York prison.

1901
Death of Queen Victoria, who had reigned over the British Empire since 1837.

1914–18
World War One. The United States enters the war in 1917.

1917
The Communists seize power in Russia.

Cast-iron structures ● *94* – office buildings with cast-iron façades – and "proto-skyscrapers" fitted with elevators, began to appear in the 1870's in downtown Manhattan, notably on Park Row. In 1856, 840 acres in the center of Manhattan were earmarked for a huge park ■ *22*, ▲ *314*. The Metropolitan Museum of Art was founded in 1870 ▲ *328*. During the Civil War, violent draft riots broke out in protest against conscription, claiming several hundred victims. In the post-war years the city government was controlled by the "Tweed Ring" under William "Boss" Tweed; he was convicted of corruption and removed from office in 1873 ● *40*.

THE CONSTRUCTION OF THE BROOKLYN BRIDGE.
Completed in 1883, the bridge joined the two most densely populated areas of the city ▲ *186*. Increasingly New York was the gateway to the New World, and the Statue of Liberty ▲ *144*, given to the U.S. by France in 1886, welcomed immigrants as they entered the harbor. The city grew to such an extent that there was an urgent need for improved public transportation. Streetcars dating from the beginning of the century, and the elevated railway ● *36*, built in 1867, were electrified between 1890 and 1905, and a subway system was added in 1904 ▲ *236*.

NEIGHBORING BOROUGHS ANNEXED. By 1898 the city consisted of five districts: Manhattan, a commercial and residential area with over 1.5 million inhabitants; Brooklyn, a busy town with 900,000 inhabitants; and the less populous boroughs of the Bronx, to the north, Queens, adjacent to Brooklyn on Long Island, and Staten Island, to the south. Together, they created Greater New York, the most densely populated city in the United States, with 3.5 million inhabitants. The upper and middle classes had already started to move uptown in Manhattan, and in some cases to leave the city for the suburbs of New Jersey and Long Island.

THE 20TH CENTURY

THE SKYSCRAPER ERA. The Flatiron Building ● *96*, ▲ *233*, dating from 1902 and 312 feet high, is one of the many skyscrapers built in the heart of Manhattan at the turn of the century.

> **"THIS IS THE FIRST SENSATION ... YOU FEEL THAT THE AMERICANS HAVE PRACTICALLY ADDED A NEW DIMENSION TO SPACE. ... WHEN THEY FIND THEMSELVES A LITTLE CROWDED, THEY SIMPLY TIP A STREET ON END AND CALL IT A SKYSCRAPER."** WILLIAM ARCHER

They soon threatened to overshadow the streets and in 1916 the city government drew up a "Zoning Resolution", a set of regulations controlling the design of office buildings. This ordinance required architects to design towers with setbacks, establishing the characteristic shape of the skyscraper ● 96. By this time, Manhattan was connected to Long Island by bridges, and two new railroad stations had been built in the center: Pennsylvania Station ▲ 249, in 1910, and Grand Central Station ▲ 236.

THE WALL STREET CRASH. In the crash of October 24th, 1929, stock prices which had been overvalued by rash speculation plummeted. The Depression of the 1930's hit New York hard, but this period saw the completion of major projects such as the first bridge over the Hudson (the George Washington Bridge), the Empire State Building ▲ 242, and the Chrysler Building ▲ 266, as well as the start of work on Rockefeller Center ▲ 274. Fiorello La Guardia, the high-principled mayor elected in 1933, used federal aid as best he could to mitigate the devastating effects of the Depression.

THE WORLD CAPITAL. Many intellectuals and artists (including Albert Einstein, Marc Chagall, Piet Mondrian and Artur Rubinstein) took refuge in New York from a war-stricken Europe. After the victory of 1945 New York became the seat of the newly created United Nations. The organization's headquarters were opened in 1953 ▲ 264. Although by 1950 New York's population had reached almost 8 million, Manhattan had already begun to see a decline in the number of its own residents: some port activities were transferred to New Jersey and some manufacturing moved out of the city, which was handicapped by traffic congestion and inadequate maintenance. A new influx, of poor immigrants increased the city government's financial burden ● 44.

FINANCIAL CRISIS. In 1975 New York teetered on the brink of bankruptcy, partly because of mayor John Lindsay's lavish spending on social services. The banks refused to lend the city further funds and the state government offered a solution by establishing, in collaboration with the banks, the Municipal Assistance Corporation (Big MAC). This body imposed various austerity measures on the city, leading to deteriorating public services. However New York remained unrivaled as a financial center and cultural capital and several new skyscrapers were added to Manhattan: the twin towers of the World Trade Center ● 103 in 1973, Battery Park City ▲ 141 and its development program for the banks of the Hudson ● 104, ▲ 138, in the 1980's. The bay, relatively deserted by shipping, has witnessed dazzling celebrations: the bicentennial of American Independence in 1976 and, in 1992, the gathering of large yachts in honor of Christopher Columbus, who, despite never having set foot on the North American continent, is considered its discoverer.

Panic in Wall Street. The Crash in October 1929 marks the start of the Great Depression.

1933
Franklin Roosevelt launches the New Deal, intended to boost the flagging American economy in the grip of recession since 1929.

1941
The Japanese attack Pearl Harbor and the United States goes to war.

1949–53
Proclamation of the People's Republic of China and war in Korea. Also the beginning of the cold war and McCarthyism.

Fiorello La Guardia greets Albert Einstein in 1936.

1963
John F. Kennedy is assassinated in Dallas.

1969
American astronauts Neil Armstrong and Edwin Aldrin walk on the Moon.

1974
Nixon resigns following the Watergate scandal.

1989
Berlin Wall falls and the Communist bloc begins to crumble.

1993
Bill Clinton succeeds George Bush.

● FROM NEW AMSTERDAM TO NEW YORK

New Amsterdam was a small, prosperous, peaceful town that slowly covered the southern tip of Manhattan, a site bought from the Indians in 1626. With its windmills and brick houses, it resembled Amsterdam, its parent city. In 1650 its population numbered barely one thousand people – mainly Dutch and English settlers, plus a sprinkling of Jews from Brazil and even then, some Blacks. New Amsterdam was annexed by the English in 1664 and renamed New York.

A TRADING POST
The Dutch who settled on the island were employed by the new West India Company, founded in Amsterdam in 1621.

FOR A HANDFUL OF GUILDERS
Some historians maintain that Peter Minuit's purchase of Manhattan from the Canarsie Indians in exchange for some glass jewelry and trinkets worth 60 guilders (the equivalent of $24) was the first case in North America of Europeans' exploiting the Indians. However, it has never been determined whether Minuit intentionally took advantage of the natives' gullibility, or whether they felt at all cheated, since for several years they continued to visit the area to trade valuable skins with the Dutch.

THE SKIN TRADE
The prosperity of New Amsterdam was based on the sale of beaver skins, otter skins and mink. Between 1629 and 1635 the skin trade escalated: the number of beaver skins traded nearly doubled from 7,520 to 14,891 and the number of seal skins soared from 370 to 1,413.

A CULTURAL CENTER IN THE MAKING
In the 18th century intellectual life in New York was not as brilliant as in Boston or Philadelphia. However, King's College (below), the forebear of Columbia University, was founded in 1754, and a free-thinking press developed. By 1775 New York already numbered 25,000 inhabitants.

NIEUW AMSTERDAM op 't eyland Manhattans.

PETER STUYVESANT, GOVERNOR OF NEW NETHERLAND
This highly intelligent but difficult man, who had lost a leg during a battle at sea, was intensely disliked by the Dutch settlers, both for his authoritarian ways and for his rigorous government of New Amsterdam, which was going rapidly downhill (above, a satirical depiction of his arrival in May 1647). He decreed that the taverns should close at 9 o'clock in the evening and remain shut on Sunday mornings and, in the interest of public health, ordered that the pigs overrunning the streets were to be shot on sight.

TOLERATION
The Dutch merchants made the best of the British, and the British respected Dutch culture and language and left people free to choose their own religion. Trinity (Episcopal) Church, as it appeared in 1737 was built for English colonists. It was replaced in 1846 by a new church in neo-Gothic style ● *86.*

MELTING POT
As the city grew it became more cosmopolitan: French Huguenots took refuge here after the revocation of the Edict of Nantes in 1685; German Protestants joined the Dutch, English, Scottish, Irish, Jewish and Black settlers.

New York's commercial origins made it the most heterogeneous colony in North America.

New Amsterdam's first streets were laid out by the settlers along routes already used by people and livestock. At the beginning of the 19th century, as the city continued to spread northward, a coherent town planning program became an urgent priority and the state governor appointed a commission to design a "definitive" plan for Manhattan. Between 1807 and 1811, this commission perfected the existing grid system, which makes it simple for people to find their bearings and move easily from north to south and east to west.

NEW AMSTERDAM
The earliest plan parceling out Manhattan, shows the allocation of plots of land to the Dutch settlers, the fort, several streets, the swamps and pasture land ● 74.

A LOGICAL USE OF SPACE
After Independence the city spread out in an anarchic sprawl, at the mercy of projects initiated by private property developers. The members of the 1807 commission, who were wealthy merchants, took four years to make their recommendations. Since New York was primarily a business center, the grand designs that were a feature of older European cities and which the French engineer L'Enfant had followed in designing the federal capital of Washington were deemed pointless. New York needed a simple plan that would facilitate the sale of land as well as movement around the island and, most important, from one shore to another. The darker colored area on the *Commissioner's Map* of 1811 (opposite) indicates the size of the city at that time. la ville à cette époque.

CONTROVERSY
Although the grid system was efficient and fairly easy to apply, town planners began in the mid-19th century to criticize its undue inflexibility which worked against Manhattan's topography. Their dream was to achieve a perfect symbiosis between city life, with all its advantages, and a more rural setting. Frederick Law Olmsted, the "father" of Central Park ■ 22 ▲ 314 (right), designed the park that William Cullen Bryant had campaigned for, feeling that the people of New York should enjoy open spaces similar to those in European cities.

At the beginning of the 20th century the major thoroughfares devised by Olmsted and his colleagues were finally laid: Riverside Drive and the future Henry Hudson Parkway, ▲ *356* (above, a view at the turn of the century) in Manhattan, and also Eastern Parkway and Ocean Parkway in Brooklyn. Various means of locomotion were accommodated by an assortment of slip roads and footbridges. These were later replaced by highways, which were better suited to motor vehicles.

A GEOMETRIC GRID

There were to be 12 avenues running north to south, 100 feet wide, with numbering starting in the east, bisected by 155 streets running east to west, 60 feet wide, with numbering starting in the south. These blocks were then subdivided into plots all roughly the same size (25 by 100 feet). Not many public squares and open spaces were provided because, in the opinion of the Commissioners, the vast expanses of water surrounding the city made them unnecessary. A market, several squares and a huge parade ground for military drills did, however, appear on the 1811 plan. But these were soon allocated and built over, hence the campaign led by the press for a large park.

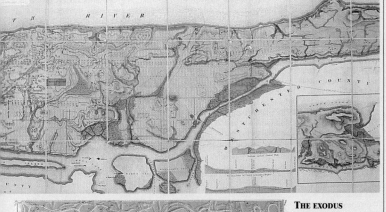

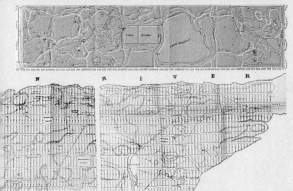

THE EXODUS NORTHWARD
The new grid system was to be applied north of Houston St. as far as 155th St. Not a tree, stream, or hill was spared (above, a topographical map). Around 1850 the grid had reached 60th St. Central Park (opposite) ■ *22*, ▲ *314* was not created until 1858.

The notion of public services first appeared at the beginning of the 19th century, when the municipal government was faced with the inevitable problems caused by the expansion of a large city. However, the authorities were not completely free to act: they were often hampered by private companies unwilling to relinquish their share of some very lucrative markets. The authorities also had difficulty persuading the state of New York to allow them to create special departments to run their public services and undertake any necessary work.

GAS AND ELECTRICITY

At the start of the 19th century, gas was the main source of power for lighting (below, a gas lamplighter in front of St. Thomas Church). In 1880 Broadway was equipped with an electric lighting system using the arc lamp. After inventing the incandescent bulb, Edison set up his own electricity company in New York in 1881. Buildings were first supplied

with electricity in 1882 and electric street lighting then became much more common. Below, men installing underground cabling around 1900.

SUPPLY OF WATER

Although water supply was one of the most pressing problems – being vital for sanitation and fire fighting – it was not until 1837 that work began on the Croton Reservoir (above), between 5th and 6th aves. and 40th and 42nd sts., on the site now occupied by the New York Public Library and Bryant Park. Completed in 1842, the reservoir was supplied by an aqueduct from Westchester County. Private homes had running water after the 1860's.

POLICING

In 1844 a single police force comprising 200 men replaced the disparate units operating at the beginning of the century, which had consisted mainly of volunteers and part-time policemen. In 1853, the wearing of uniforms was made compulsory, which caused a great deal of dissatisfaction. But, from then on, the New York police force became a model for other American cities.

TELEPHONE

The New York telephone system was inaugurated in 1878. Seven years later, the first long-distance trunk lines – New York–Boston, followed by New York–Chicago – were opened, the latter for the World's Columbian Exposition of 1893.

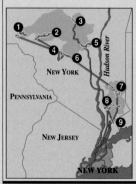

The waterways of New York City.

1 : Cannonsville Reservoir
2 : Pepacton Reservoir
3 : Schoharie Reservoir
4 : Neversink Reservoir
5 : Ashokan Reservoir
6 : Rondout Reservoir
7 : West Branch Reservoir
8 : Croton Reservoir
9 : Kensico Reservoir

This underground section of New York at the corner of 6th Ave. and 50th St. was drawn in 1939. It shows the astonishing network of underground pipes that keeps the city alive. The orange cables supply power to the subway, the mauve cables are for the telephone and telegraph system, the green pipes supply water, the pink pipes supply steam for the district heating and the blue pipes carry gas. On the level below, the passageway to the subway can be seen, and to the left of that, the yellow sewage disposal pipe. Below that, the subway tunnels and, at the very bottom, 500–600 ft below the surface, the City Tunnel, supplying drinking water to the city.

SANITATION AND PUBLIC HEALTH

In 1866 New York reorganized its Board of Health (opposite, inside a 19th-century ambulance), providing a team of health inspectors whose job was to enforce regulations. Some regulations were unrealistic, such as the one stipulating that every room in a building must have a window.

STATE EDUCATION

Education was mostly private in 1842, when a department run by the Board of Education (composed of thirty-four elected members), which distributed the city's funds among the wards was created. The Board was also responsible for appointing teachers, choosing textbooks and syllabuses and building schools. Free public education was begun statewide in 1849 and, by 1860, 90 percent of all elementary school students attended public school. The main priority of state schools for many years was to teach immigrants' children how to read and write and instill in them the values underlying democracy.

35

Ferries started running in the 18th century; horse-drawn buses appeared in the 1830's, then, from 1870, by the elevated railroad (the "elevated" or the "El"). A solution to the problems caused by pollution and traffic congestion in the city was provided by the subway: the IRT (Interborough Rapid Transit) opened its first line in 1904. In 1955 the New York City Transit Authority, which had just been set up, became responsible for all the city's public transportation.

FERRIES

These were the main method of transportation to and from Manhattan until the bridges were built at the end of the last century ▲ *188*. The first ferry started running in 1712, and many lines were opened during the steam era. In 1810 Cornelius Vanderbilt, the future railway magnate, laid the foundations of his fortune with the Richmond Turnpike Ferry, which ran between Staten Island and Manhattan. Since two of New York's five boroughs are islands, there is still a ferry service (notably the Staten Island ferry which operates a 24-hour service); 75,000 people use these ferries daily.

TAXIS

It was not until 1907 that taxis were brought under regulation by the city authorities, who enforced meter inspection and set a minimum fare for each journey. The granting of licenses increased to such an extent that by 1937 the number of taxis had to be reduced from 21,000 to 14,000 (there are currently 11,787 taxis in New York) and a badge was designed for the hood (which is the origin of the name "medallion cab"). These official taxis have been painted yellow since 1970, and although there are a great many of them in Manhattan, they are not so easy to find in the other boroughs. Since there are still not enough of them, the number of unofficial taxis has increased to some 50,000. Their drivers are drawn mainly from the city's ethnic minorities.

The "El" traces sweeping curves high above 110th St.

City Hall Subway Station, New York

FROM THE "EL" TO THE SUBWAY SYSTEM

The elevated rail system had four routes which ran along 2nd, 3rd, 6th and 9th aves.,

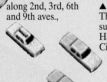

making it possible to get from Harlem ▲ 350 to the Battery ▲ 142 in 40 minutes. The first pneumatic subway line, the City Hall Line, ran from City Hall ▲ 168 to 145th St., via the West Side ▲ 342. Since then, the New York system, with 722 miles of track and 469 stations, has become the largest in the world. The City Hall station (above), which has been closed for the past fifty years, is still in its original condition. On the other hand, nothing now remains of the elevated railway over the Bowery, which, with its two tracks, completely overshadowed the street (above). The last section of the 3rd Ave. line was not dismantled until 1955.

"The subway rolls and rumbles underground
The bridges are shaken by railway lines.
The city trembles.
Shouts, fire and smoke,
Steam sirens sounding like raucous hoots."
Blaise Cendrars

BAROUCHES AND HORSE-DRAWN BUSES

From 1831 privately owned vehicles, had to share the streets with public transportation. The new horse-drawn buses created huge traffic jams, not to mention the problems caused by the horses themselves (there were 80,000 in New York around 1880). This is why the El, despite its attendant noise and pollution, was seen as a great improvement.

37

The numerous fire escapes that have disfigured the façades of many New York apartment buildings for over a century (to the amazement of foreign visitors) are a legacy of several catastrophic blazes in the early 20th century which made their construction obligatory. In the past, attracted by the bells and sirens of the fire engines, onlookers used to flock to the raging fires.

FIRE AT THE TRIANGLE SHIRTWAIST COMPANY
On March 25, 1911, fire broke out in this factory near Washington Square, which employed 500 workers, mainly Jewish and Italian women. The garment workers' union had called, in vain, for additional fire escapes and for workshop doors to be left unbolted. Women, young girls and children died from suffocation or from jumping out of the windows (above, painting by Victor Joseph Gatto). The death toll was severe: 146 victims.

CONSUMED BY FIRE
During the war of Independence New York was devastated in 1776 and 1778, by arson attacks, attributed by turns to the Loyalists and to the Patriots. In December 1835, at the very time when the city was beginning to spread northward, a fire caused by a burst gas main broke out in Hanover Square ▲ 166 and in the narrow alleyways behind the docks. A strong wind carried the flames as far as South St., Broad St. and Wall St. For two days the flames raged Downtown, while the severe cold hindered the firemen; water froze in their hoses. In total, nearly seventeen blocks in the financial district were destroyed, including all the buildings from the Dutch period.

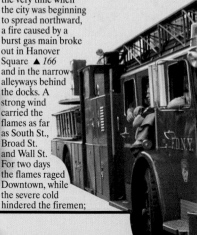

FIRE AT CRYSTAL PALACE

Built for the Exposition of 1853, this huge building, thought to be fireproof, was totally destroyed by fire in 1858. Fortunately, there were no victims.

THE FIRE DEPARTMENT

Though impressive, with their gleaming red paint and clanging speed, fire engines could be rendered totally useless by adverse weather conditions. In March 1908, at a fire at the Equitable Building ● 97, ▲ 153 on Broadway, the water froze as it came out of the pumps.

FIREMEN

It was not until 1865 that New York City created a professional, paid fire department. Until then, as was the case everywhere, fire fighting had been left to rival groups of volunteers (it was not unusual for them to come to blows at a fire), who were proud of their shiny equipment, their badges and their traditional parades. From the end of the 19th century, the meticulous organization, efficiency and the continually modernized equipment of the FDNY (Fire Department of New York City) were held up as a model for other cities. The department now employs more than 11,000 firefighters who deal with nearly 360,000 emergency calls per year, of which at least 100,000 are fires.

For lovers of "whodunits" New York is the metropolis where Ed McBain's cops use all means at their disposal to fight crime. Or there is the legendary Harlem of the 1960's policed by Ed Cercueil and Fossoyeur Johnson, the two black cops created by Chester Himes. New York has always acted as a magnet for white-collar criminals highly skilled in the fields of administration and finance, and for the underworld, earning it the reputation of being a violent, dangerous city.

CHARLES LUCIANO
"Lucky" Luciano (above, the photos for his criminal record) became the godfather of all godfathers by arranging for the bosses of two rival gangs to be assassinated.

THE SAINT SYLVESTER AT THE W. 47TH STREET POLICE STATION
Drunkards, busy policemen and, in the foreground, a makeshift coffin containing the corpse of a woman who has just thrown herself out of the window of a nearby hotel. This 1939 illustration by Robert Riggs shows the police station for the area around Times Square, one of the most volatile parts of the city.

PROHIBITION
Adopted in 1920 (and repealed in 1933), this law was an unlooked-for bonus for New York's criminal elements. Instances of large quantities of contraband alcohol being destroyed by the police (below, on the docks of New York) did nothing to stop bootleggers from amassing huge illicit fortunes.

"MEAN STREETS"
In his film *Mean Streets*, Martin Scorsese evokes his experiences as an adolescent in one of New York's Italian neighborhoods with its bums and dropouts. Crime has permeated the local community to such an extent that it has become impossible to distinguish it from everyday life.

BOSS TWEED
In the mid-19th century, William Tweed, nicknamed "Boss" Tweed, made Tammany Hall, New York's Democratic machine, a byword for corruption. His consummate skill in electoral fraud and intimidation enabled him to control and systematically loot public funds.

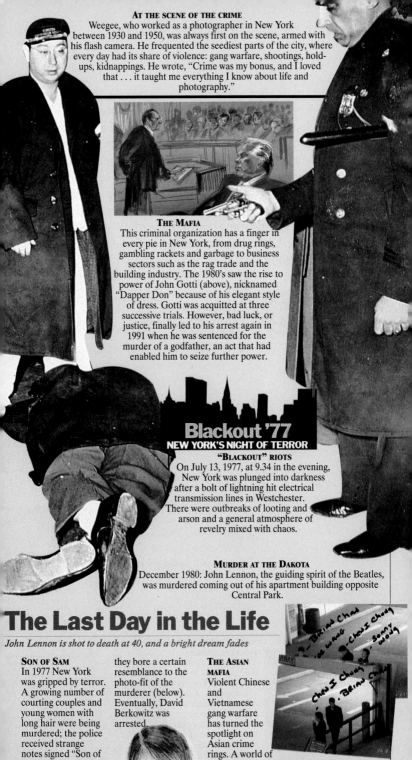

AT THE SCENE OF THE CRIME

Weegee, who worked as a photographer in New York between 1930 and 1950, was always first on the scene, armed with his flash camera. He frequented the seediest parts of the city, where every day had its share of violence: gang warfare, shootings, hold-ups, kidnappings. He wrote, "Crime was my bonus, and I loved that . . . it taught me everything I know about life and photography."

THE MAFIA

This criminal organization has a finger in every pie in New York, from drug rings, gambling rackets and garbage to business sectors such as the rag trade and the building industry. The 1980's saw the rise to power of John Gotti (above), nicknamed "Dapper Don" because of his elegant style of dress. Gotti was acquitted at three successive trials. However, bad luck, or justice, finally led to his arrest again in 1991 when he was sentenced for the murder of a godfather, an act that had enabled him to seize further power.

Blackout '77
NEW YORK'S NIGHT OF TERROR

"BLACKOUT" RIOTS

On July 13, 1977, at 9.34 in the evening, New York was plunged into darkness after a bolt of lightning hit electrical transmission lines in Westchester. There were outbreaks of looting and arson and a general atmosphere of revelry mixed with chaos.

MURDER AT THE DAKOTA

December 1980: John Lennon, the guiding spirit of the Beatles, was murdered coming out of his apartment building opposite Central Park.

The Last Day in the Life

John Lennon is shot to death at 40, and a bright dream fades

SON OF SAM

In 1977 New York was gripped by terror. A growing number of courting couples and young women with long hair were being murdered; the police received strange notes signed "Son of Sam". Some innocent New Yorkers were denounced to the police by over-zealous neighbors because they bore a certain resemblance to the photo-fit of the murderer (below). Eventually, David Berkowitz was arrested.

THE ASIAN MAFIA

Violent Chinese and Vietnamese gang warfare has turned the spotlight on Asian crime rings. A world of secret societies and syndicates, involved in all kinds of illegal trafficking, is gradually coming to light and there is a danger that the Asian community as a whole may suffer unjustly as a result of this adverse publicity.

41

● THE PORT, SOURCE OF A CITY'S WEALTH

Giovanni da Verrazano, the first European to enter New York Bay, in 1524, immediately appreciated its natural advantages. The wide outer harbor (Lower Bay), itself sheltered from the ocean, opens out north of the Narrows into the magnificent Upper Bay, which also branches out into several secondary bays and channels washed by the tides. Although since the middle of the 20th century New York is no longer the leading international port (Rotterdam having moved into the lead), it is still the largest port in the United States with an average annual traffic of forty million tons.

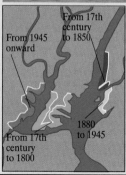

From 17th century to 1850

From 1945 onward

1880 to 1945

From 17th century to 1800

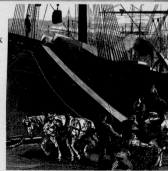

DOCKERS AT WORK
The completion of the Erie Canal in 1825 linked New York with the Great Lakes and the Midwest: a ton of wheat now took six days instead of twenty to reach New York from Buffalo and the cost of the journey plummeted from $100 to $10.

A THRIVING HARBOR

The successive localization of port activities gives an idea of this site's enormous potential. In the 17th and 18th centuries everything was centered around the tip of Manhattan, especially its West Side. Gradually, during the 19th century, piers built perpendicular to the shoreline extended along the East River and the Hudson River (as far as 70th St.), on the New Jersey shoreline and in Brooklyn.

VIEW FROM SATELLITE

This shows every part of the coastline which has been developed to handle New York port traffic – that is Manhattan, Brooklyn ▲ 366, Staten Island and New Jersey.

THE DEATH OF A GIANT

In February 1942, the *Normandie*, the most famous liner of its time, went up in flames while berthed on the Hudson River. It was capsized by the firemen, who deluged it with tons of water. In twelve hours, all that remained was a wreck.

THE LARGE TRANSATLANTIC LINERS

In 1818, some New York shipowners created the Black Ball Line, the first regular service between New York and Liverpool. Thirty years later the British Cunard Line set an example by replacing its large

sailing ships with steamers. Today after more than a century of heavy traffic, the New York City Passenger Ship Terminal welcomes fewer than 500,000 passengers per year.

LEADING THE FIELD

At the end of the 19th century nearly half the United States' foreign trade passed through New York. The city exported timber, meat, cereals, flour and cotton from the South and imported tropical foodstuffs and manufactured products.

THE PORT AUTHORITY

In 1921 the states of New York and New Jersey created the Port Authority of New York and New Jersey to centralize port activities and coordinate essential large-scale projects. At the end of World War Two, due to cramped conditions and restricted movement, most of the port activities

were transferred from Manhattan to Brooklyn ▲ 366, to Newark Bay and as far as Perth Amboy, on the coast of New Jersey.

43

In 1870, 83 percent of New Yorkers had one relative born abroad. This was true in 1993 for 40 percent of New Yorkers, of which 25 percent are Black and 25 percent of Hispanic origin. Soviet Jews and people from China, Korea, the Dominican Republic, Cuba and other Latin-American countries form the most recent wave of immigrants. From Chinatown to Little Odessa, the city is in a constant state of ethnic flux. New immigrants arrive as others leave and the neighborhoods change their identity: Harlem was Jewish before being Black, the Lower East Side was Jewish and Italian before becoming Chinese.

THE IRISH

By 1790 Irish settlers in New York were as numerous as those of Dutch origin. More arrived between 1820 and 1853, having been forced to leave Ireland for the New World by terrible famines, and by 1860 they constituted one-quarter of the city's population. Mainly Catholic, they celebrate St. Patrick's Day with a splendid parade.

THE JEWS

An initial immigration of Sephardic Jews in the 17th century was followed by the influx of many German Jews in the mid-19th century. Then came the massive exodus of Jews from Eastern Europe in the last three decades of that century. The collapse of the Communist bloc has led to the arrival of a new wave of Russian Jews.

PUERTO RICANS AND OTHER HISPANICS

Before the Cubans, who started to arrive in the 1960's, immigrants from Puerto Rico, an American territory, began to flock to East Harlem, "El Barrio", between 1921 to 1924. In 1970 they numbered 810,000 (over 10 percent of the population).

THE CHINESE.

Recent waves of Chinese immigrants from Shanghai, Taiwan and Hong Kong, following the Cantonese who arrived in the 19th century, have made

New York's Chinese community the largest in the U.S., surpassing that of San Francisco. Since quotas were scrapped by the Immigration and Nationality Act of 1965, this Asian immigration has become less well documented because it is not so rigorously controlled.

> "... OF THIS MODERN ELDORADO, WHERE, LITTLE EUROPEAN CHILDREN WERE TOLD, THE STREETS WERE PAVED WITH GOLD, AND THE LAND SO VAST AND ABUNDANT THAT EVERYONE COULD FIND A PLACE IN IT."
>
> FRANZ KAFKA

THE GERMANS. The first Germans arrived around 1710 and in 1790 accounted for 10 percent of the population. By 1860 they numbered 118,000, many of them shopkeepers. The major concentration of Germans was in a quarter called Deutschlandle, east of the Bowery, between Houston and 12th streets.

THE BLACKS
There were only 24,000 African Americans in New York in 1890 and 460,000 in 1940 – that is 6 percent of the population. Since then, a demographic shift has taken place, bringing many Blacks from the South to New York, and from the agricultural sector to the manufacturing sector and small-scale industry. In 1970, the Black community – swelled by black immigrants from the Caribbean – accounted for 21 percent of New York's population.

THE ITALIANS
The Italians arrived later, primarily in the 20th century, and unlike earlier immigrants they came to the U.S. with the intention of returning to their homeland. This is why the men emigrated alone; once they had decided to stay, they brought over their families. By 1930 the Italians numbered 1,070,355; they shared the Lower East Side with the Jews working alongside them in the garment industry.

THE OTHER COMMUNITIES
Poles, most of them Catholic, are united by strong national traditions and demonstrate this cohesion in the big Pulaski Day Parade around October 5. In Astoria, Queens, there is an established Greek community, and The Bronx is home to many Armenians. Since 1964 many Haitians, Latin Americans and Asians (Japanese, Koreans and Indians) have settled in New York.

STREET NEWS

New York City, which is by turns repressive and hospitable, even occasionally aggressively charitable, has always been unpredictable in its aid to tramps and the homeless. During the 1980's the numbers of homeless rose alarmingly. For more than fifty years their presence on the streets had not been so obvious. Some new laws managed to increase the capacity of adult shelters tenfold, resulting in more than twenty-four thousand available beds.

BLACKWELL'S ISLAND
This Welfare Island on the East River (above), now known as Roosevelt Island, seemed a suitable place for the detention of dropouts, the infirm and the destitute. Some thirty charitable institutions, hospices, asylums, hospitals, prisons and shelters for single women were built here in 1935.

THE FIRST SHELTER
In 1734, on the site of what is now City Hall ▲ 168, New York constructed a building intended to function simultaneously as a prison, a hospice and a workhouse. This provided care for the dying, a home for orphans and shelter for social misfits, the poor, criminals, even runaway slaves.

EVANGELICAL MISSIONS
After the Civil War, various Protestant missions sprang up in the city. Some, like the McAuley Mission (now situated at 90 Lafayette St.), still survive. Unlike the few existing night shelters, the missions are free of charge, but regular attendance at prayers is essential and strict discipline is still enforced in the dormitories.

REHOUSING REPORT
In July 1993, the Department of Homeless Services was created to respond to the problems of homelessness. The department currently houses about 5,500 families (a large majority of whom are young single mothers and their children) and 6,500 single people. It is estimated that one third of the latter are suffering from serious mental illness, aggravated by alcohol and drug abuse.

> " . . . the tramps, the down-and-outs, the shopping-bag ladies, the drifters and drunks. They range from the merely destitute to the wretchedly broken. Wherever you turn, they are there, in good neighbourhoods and bad. "
>
> Paul Auster

JACOB RIIS

The Dane Jacob Riis (1849–1914) arrived in New York in 1870. As a journalist on the *New York Tribune* he denounced the poverty of immigrants, and with his photographs (left) campaigned for social reform.

IN THE STREET

Thousands of New Yorkers of no fixed abode live in the streets, in the parks, on patches of wasteland and in the subway. At times these living quarters acquire a distinctive identity and a community spirit. The authorities will turn a blind eye if there are no complaints from the neighbors but a "settlement" always represents a fire hazard.

PUBLIC SHELTERS

In December 1979 a law was passed requiring New York City to provide public shelters for all "destitute and needy" homeless men. It took a second ordinance for women to benefit from the same law. The refuge (below) was set up in an armory of the National Guard (W. 168th St., between Broadway and Fort Washington Ave.). Around 1985 the number of men housed never dropped below 1,200 per night.

POTTER'S FIELD

Since 1869 tramps and poor people were buried in Potter's Field, to the northeast of the city, on Hart Island. The pine coffins arrived by ferry and the gravediggers were prisoners.

I AM HOMEL AND HUNGRY, ANYTHING WILL HELP!!!

"THE BIG APPLE"
New York is popularly called the "Big Apple", a custom dating from at least the 1930's, when jazz musicians took the name of a Harlem nightclub and extended it to the whole neighborhood and then to the city in general. In the mid 1970's, the New York Convention and Visitors Bureau used the phrase in an ad campaign to boost tourism.

English was increasingly spoken in the colony after the Duke of York succeeded the Dutch as its owner in 1664 ● 26, although as late as 1760 a Manhattan lady could still write, "The English language is beginning to be more universally understood here." All kinds of languages and dialects gradually entered the city, due to trade and immigration, enriching the brand of English spoken in New York.

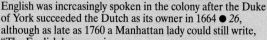

A POLYGLOT CITY

More than eighty languages are now spoken in New York. Spanish is the second most common language, after English, reflecting the high number of residents from Puerto Rico, the Caribbean, and Central and South America. Various other languages are currently used in daily business transactions: Yiddish in the diamond merchants' quarter (West 47th Street) ▲ 299, Moroccan Arabic, Farsi and Bengali among newspaper vendors, Korean in the fruit and vegetable stores, and Wolof between Senegalese peddlers. Different languages can also be heard in all the ethnic enclaves scattered around the city: Cantonese in Chinatown ▲ 190, Haitian Creole on the Upper West Side ▲ 342, Ukrainian and Polish in the East Village, Hungarian in Yorkville, Armenian in Murray Hill and Spanish in East Harlem ▲ 350. It is not unusual for children to learn English concurrently with their mother tongue.

STREET AND PLACE NAMES

Many street and place names still bear linguistic traces of New York's successive generations of settlers. Such is the case with the name "Manhattan" (formerly "Manhatta"), which owes its name to the Delaware Indians. There are many theories about the original meaning of "Manhattan", but it probably meant something like "island" or "island with hills". The Dutch legacy can be seen in the names of Harlem and Gramercy (which came from the Dutch word *krum-martsje*, meaning "crooked little swamp"). *Spuyten Duyvil* ("the Devil's waterspout") may possibly have been named after the

A street in Chinatown (below).

treacherous waters at the confluence of the Hudson ● 20 and Harlem rivers, the Bowery (from *bouwerie*, "farm" ● 82) and Brooklyn ▲ 366 (*breukelen*, reclaimed land). The English names of some Lower Manhattan streets ▲ 158 are derived from the Dutch: "*De Wall*" was translated into "Wall Street", and "*Maagde Paetje*" into "Maiden Lane".

ART OF LIVING

RELIGIONS, *50*
WALTER A. FRIEDMAN
FESTIVALS AND PARADES, *52*
BROOKS MCNAMARA
THE WRITTEN PRESS, *54*
DAVID ABRAHAMSON
RADIO AND TELEVISION, *56*
LOUISE KERZ
THE MUSICAL, *58*
MICHAEL KERBER
JAZZ, *60*
PETER WATROUS
DANCE, *62*
DORIS HERING
SPORTS, *64*
BENOÎT HEIMERMANN
INTERIOR DESIGN
AND FURNITURE, *66*
NINA GRAY
CHEESECAKE, *68*
CASSIE SPRINGER
SPECIALTIES, *70*
CASSIE SPRINGER

● RELIGIONS

ELIZABETH SETON
Elizabeth Seton (1774–1821), the first American-born saint, was canonized in 1975. She founded the order of the Sisters of Charity in New York.

In 1656 Peter Stuyvesant, the governor of New Amsterdam and a devout Protestant, tried to force the colony to embrace one religion. The West India Company was opposed to this move; it was afraid it might damage trade as New York was already a patchwork of different religions. Modern-day New York is home to more than one hundred religious denominations. Catholicism is the main religion, while the Jewish community is the largest outside Israel.

JEHOVAH'S WITNESSES
This is one of the largest evangelical movements in New York and is based in Brooklyn. Their two magazines *Awake!* and *The Watchtower* are published in at least 80 languages and boast a circulation of more than ten million copies. They are distributed door to door or in the street.

ST. PATRICK'S CATHEDRAL. This cathedral, the seat of the city's Roman Catholic archbishop, is on 5th Ave., between 50th and 51st sts., and was completed in 1906 ▲ *283*. It is consecrated to the patron saint of Ireland. The number of Catholics currently living in New York is estimated at 2.5 million.

LUBAVITCHER COMMUNITY
The Lubavitcher Chassidic Movement, based in Brooklyn, is a mystical branch of Judaism. Its members, who are all men and can be recognized by their black apparel, beards and sidecurls, include some eminent Talmud experts.

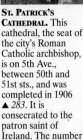

NATIVIST PROTESTANTS
Protestantism was the main religion until the mid-19th century. But by 1864, following the immigration of Irish and German Catholics, half the population were Catholics. This cartoon by Thomas Nast, which depicts some parents protecting their children from the invading Catholic bishops, conveys Protestant distrust of Catholics, whom they criticized for their proposed changes to the educational system such as discontinuing Bible-readings and attempting to obtain state subsidies for their own schools.

> **"IT WAS CLEAN, BUT NOT BRISK, NOTHING LIKE THE URGENCY OF NEW YORK, RUDE OFTEN, PREMISED ON A NOTION THAT TIME WAS FLYING."**
>
> JANET HOBHOUSE

ISLAM

This religion became widespread in New York only in the second half of this century. The Islamic Center of New York, opened in 1991, sits on the corner of 96th St. and 3rd Ave. Its axis forms an angle of 29 degrees with the street, so that the building is facing Mecca.

JUDAISM

Over a million Orthodox Jews from Eastern Europe emigrated to America between 1880 and 1910. Many of them settled in New York. They started daily newspapers, theater companies, socialist political groups and unions. After World War Two, New York Jews gave their support to the creation of a Jewish state in Palestine and lobbied the government for economic and military aid to Israel.

BUDDHISM

The impressive statue of Shinran-Shonin, who founded the Buddhist sect Jodo Shinshu, watches over the New York temple, built in 1938 on Riverside Drive. This statue, originally erected in Hiroshima, 1½ miles from the center of the explosion, was brought to New York in 1955 as a reminder of the horrors of

atomic warfare and a symbol of hope for lasting peace in the world.

THE UNIFICATION CHURCH

The Unification Church, founded in 1954 in Korea by Sun Myung Moon, decided on Manhattan as its base. In 1982, in Madison Square Garden ▲ *249*, the Reverend Moon made a great show of his church's impressive number of disciples (the Moonies) by celebrating a mass marriage which joined 2,075 couples in matrimony.

THE BLACK CHRISTIAN COMMUNITIES

At the end of the 18th century, in response to discrimination and racial segregation, a group of Black New Yorkers formed their own denomination, the African Methodist Episcopal Zion Church. Today most of the Black churches in New York, including the famous Abyssinian Baptist Church ▲ *359*, can be found in Harlem. The largest Black denominations are the Baptists, the Methodists and the Pentecostalists.

Since the 18th century, Manhattan has hosted countless political, civic, religious and military events. These celebrations, most of which are annual but in some cases one-time events, reflect New York City's fundamental concerns. The first well-known festival took place in 1788; it celebrated the ratification of the American Constitution with a huge parade and a banquet for five thousand guests.

DISTINGUISHED GUESTS
These have included the French hero of the American Revolution the Marquis de Lafayette, who was received in 1824 with a profusion of speeches and parades. A lavish ball was held in his honor.

THE CIVIL WAR
The armed forces have often been involved in noteworthy festivals in the city's history. In 1865 thousands of soldiers marched through Manhattan to celebrate the end of the Civil War.

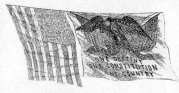

TICKER TAPE PARADES
At the end of the 19th century, in the Financial District ▲ 158, official guests used to be bombarded with ticker tape thrown from the office buildings. Despite the fact that the practice of holding these parades has declined somewhat, due to the traffic and prohibitive cleaning costs, it nevertheless continues to this day, only now with shredded computer paper. The most recent ticker tape parade took place in 1991 to celebrate the return of the troops from the Gulf War.

ST. PATRICK'S DAY PARADE
The St. Patrick's Day Parade takes place unfailingly every year on March 17th. This cultural event was organized for the first time in the 1760's by Irish soldiers stationed in New York. Since 1838, the parade has been sponsored by the Ancient Order of Hibernians, an Irish Catholic brotherhood. This major festival, which has become extremely popular, symbolizes the solidarity of the Irish community.

GAY AND LESBIAN PRIDE MARCH
Every year this march commemorates the first major protest in favor of gay rights, the Stonewall Inn Riots ▲ 212, which broke out on June 30, 1969, in Greenwich Village. As many as 10,000 people have attended this event over the past few years.

FEAST OF SAN GENNARO
In September, Mulberry St., in Little Italy ▲ 196, hosts the parade for San Gennaro, the patron saint of Naples.

MACY'S THANKSGIVING DAY PARADE
This parade, which has taken place at the end of November since the 1920's, celebrates the Plymouth Colony's first harvest on American soil in 1621 with numerous floats, giant balloons of cartoon characters and brass bands. It is sponsored by Macy's ▲ 249, the city's largest department store.

CHINESE NEW YEAR
A fireworks display is one of the attractions of this lavish celebration that takes place in late winter in Chinatown ▲ 190. For thirty-six hours, dragons with huge heads weave their way through the quarter, animated by groups of men hidden beneath them.

GREENWICH VILLAGE HALLOWEEN PARADE
Several thousand people don elaborate fancy dress costumes for this Halloween celebration.

● THE WRITTEN PRESS

THE "PENNY PRESS"
The first mass-circulation newspapers emerged in the early 1830's and early 1840's with the founding of the *New York Sun*, the *New York Herald* and the *New York Tribune*.

The New Y

Copyright 1941, by T

Entered as Second-Class Matter,
Post Office, New York, N. Y.

NEW YORK MON

For more than 250 years, New York's vibrant and occasionally unruly press has played a central role in the life of the nation. One of the earliest battles over press freedom was fought, and won, by a New York printer, and the city has long been the home of many of the most influential newspapers and magazines. The New York press's robust contribution to the uniquely American cultural milieu, as well as to the nation's continuing impulse for political and social reform, endows it with a rich and varied history.

THE ZENGER TRIAL

Charged by New York's colonial governor with spreading "Scandalous, Virulent, False and Seditious Reflections upon the Government" in his *New York Weekly Journal*, colonial printer John Peter Zenger's acquittal in 1735 helped to establish a central tenet of the freedom of the press: the right to publish criticism of government officials.

"YELLOW JOURNALISM"

In the 1890's, intense competition for readers between William Randolph Hearst's *New York Journal* and Joseph Pulitzer's *New York World* led to unparalleled levels of journalistic sensationalism and chauvinism. Featuring sex, sin and violence, the result came to be termed "yellow journalism", a name derived from the Yellow Kid, a popular character in Richard F. Outcault's *Sunday World* comic strip "Hogan's Alley", about life in tenements.

THE TABLOID NEWSPAPERS

The *New York Post* and the *New York Daily News*, direct descendants of the Penny Press, did not merely deal with the most sordid aspects of life in the city; they also tackled political issues of national concern.

ork Times.

w York Times Company:

, DECEMBER 8, 1941.

THE POWER AND THE GLORY

In most countries, one newspaper, published in the capital city, serves as the "journal of record", defining much of the nation's public agenda. Only *The Washington Post*, and particularly during Watergate, has come close to challenging the role of *The New York Times* as the most influential national newspaper since World War Two.

THE "MUCKRAKERS"

For the first dozen years of the 20th century, *McClure's* and other crusading magazines exposed many of society's ills. Called "muckrakers" by Theodore Roosevelt (after the Man with the Muckrake in *Pilgrim's Progress*), Ida Tarbells' *History of Standard Oil*, Lincoln Steffen's *The Shame of the Cities*, and Ray Stannard Baker's reports on working conditions shaped much of the Progressive agenda of the period and fostered needed urban and industrial reforms.

MAGAZINES

The United States' most famous magazines, which are read throughout the country and abroad, include *Time*, *Vogue*, *Harper's Bazaar*, *Esquire*, *Vanity Fair*, *People*, *Ebony* and *Rolling Stone*.

THE NEW YORKER

For nearly seventy years, this urbane, intellectual, weekly magazine has focused on society and culture in the city. Its contributors have included such well-known writers as James Thurber, Dorothy Parker, Kenneth Tynan and John Updike as well as the artist Saul Steinberg.

In 1907 Lee De Forest patented the Audion, an amplifier that was the precursor of the cathode ray tube. This invention heralded the advent of the crystal set, which was sold during the 1920's in Manhattan by mail order and in kit form. A decade later, people in New York witnessed the beginnings of television. Today Manhattan is home to three major national private networks (ABC, CBS and NBC) and receives more than 75 other stations and cable channels.

LEE DE FOREST'S AUDION
Lee De Forest used this device to broadcast the voice of the famous tenor Enrico Caruso from the stage of the old Metropolitan Opera House. This feat of technology amazed the entire world. De Forest started the first amateur radio station at his home in the Bronx.

DAVID SARNOFF
Sarnoff saw the potential of radio as big business. As early as 1916 he stated that this "music box" would rapidly become useful around the home. In 1921 he became general manager and later president of RCA (the National Broadcasting Company).

FELIX THE CAT
Following the invention of the electronic movie camera by Vladimir Zworykin and of the cathode ray tube, RCA (the Radio Corporation of America) decided, in 1923, to use the famous comic strip hero Felix the Cat for their first experiments in animation.

GEORGE BURNS AND GRACIE ALLEN
For seventeen years this pair of vaudeville actors were a great success in a popular comedy broadcast on the NBC radio network. In 1950 the program was transferred to television.

WALTER CRONKITE
A newscaster of the evening news at CBS (the Columbia Broadcasting System) from 1962 to 1981, Cronkite ended all of his programs with his own distinctive catchphrase, "And that's the way it was."

"SESAME STREET"
Since 1969, this program and its star, Big Bird, have taught innumerable children how to read and count.

IMPORTANT DEBATES
In 1960 John F. Kennedy and Richard M. Nixon, both presidential candidates, took part in the first series of televised election debates. After the last one, which took place in New York, Kennedy was elected president. Since then, television has become a key platform for political confrontations.

SPORTS PROMOTION THROUGH THE MEDIA
In the 1960's and 1970's an ABC sportscaster, Howard Cosell, used to broadcast live game coverage and interview sports personalities in the locker rooms. He brought sports into everyone's home, sharing his infectious enthusiasm with his viewers.

HOME BOX OFFICE AND MUSIC TELEVISION
HBO was the first fee-paying cable network and the first to make use of satellite broadcasting. MTV has given the rock industry a new lease on life with its stylized pop videos and special effects.

BARBARA WALTERS
In 1964 Barbara Walters made her debut as an interviewer on the *Today Show* for NBC; then she became co-anchor of the ABC evening news broadcast before finally making it as a star in her own right with her own programs. Her success helped to promote the role of women in the profession.

"THE WAR OF THE WORLDS"
"Poisonous black smoke, death rays, an army wiped out, people dropping like flies. Monstrous Martians landing all over the country . . ." In 1938 a tidal wave of panic swept New York when Orson Welles broadcast, on CBS, his hyper-realistic description of a Martian invasion, inspired by H. G. Wells' famous novel *The War of the Worlds*.

● THE MUSICAL

The musical, the form of theater that best evokes Broadway, has its origins in operetta, which was introduced to New York by European composers in the early 20th century. These light operas – in which crowned heads acted out their dramas in exotic settings – caused some lovers of vaudeville and burlesque sketches to develop a taste for more refined entertainment.

SHOW BOAT

"SHOW BOAT"
Show Boat (1927), based on the novel by Edna Ferber and created by Jerome Kern and Oscar Hammerstein II, is an outstanding example of musical theater. The libretto displays genuine dramatic intensity and the well-loved songs (most of which have become standards) complement the plot perfectly. The show tackles certain taboo subjects, such as living conditions of Blacks in the South, mixed marriages, and marital strife.

GEORGE AND IRA GERSHWIN
The two brothers, George, the composer, and Ira, the lyricist (above), born into a humble Jewish family, created several Broadway hits. In 1930 their *Girl Crazy* made a name for Ethel Merman and Ginger Rogers.

"OKLAHOMA!"
This musical by Rodgers and Hammerstein did not use showgirls or chorus lines. The innovative choreography by Agnes de Mille was given as much importance as the music and the plot. The show, which opened in 1943, ran for 2,248 performances.

"KISS ME KATE"
Cole Porter composed some of the most successful hits including *Kiss Me Kate, Anything Goes, Panama Hattie* and *Can Can*.

> **"NEW YORK WAS A YUKON–SALEM WHERE YOU COULD GET SPIRITUAL RICHES, SAVE YOURSELF, AND FLEE, ONE WAY OR ANOTHER, A KIND OF POVERTY AND DEATH."**
>
> JANET HOBHOUSE

"A CHORUS LINE"
This show directed by Michael Bennett holds the record for the longest running show on Broadway, with 6,137 performances. This is a perfect example of a musical that is about show business itself. Set in modern-day New York, its main characters are a producer and a choreographer.

PRICES
In 1927 the cost of a ticket for *Showboat* hit an all-time high of $4.50. Today, one can often pay as much as $65 to see a Broadway hit musical.

BOB FOSSE
Fosse was one of the rare Broadway choreographers and producers to make movies as well. In addition to his resounding stage success of *Dancin'*, he made the movies *Cabaret*, and *Lenny*, followed by an autobiographical movie, *All That Jazz*.

LAVISH PRODUCTIONS
Sophisticated machinery, dramatic lighting and sets and eye-catching costumes are now integral parts of the musical. In *Les Misérables*, the audience watches a barricade being built (center); in *Cats*, the audience watches a spaceship appear; in *Phantom of the Opera*, a huge chandelier; in *Miss Saigon*, a helicopter.

59

THIRD EDITION
COTTON CLUB PARADE

Although jazz was born in New Orleans, it came of age in New York. During the 1920's, Harlem was the capital of the Black American world, a mecca for the Black intelligentsia. In the prevailing climate of creative activity – both intellectual and financial – many new clubs sprang up, providing more opportunities for jazz musicians. They flocked to Harlem, and new styles of jazz were created by the many bands formed in this period.

DUKE ELLINGTON
Duke Ellington was one of the major jazz composers of the century. While resident at the Cotton Club, between 1927 and 1931, where he was a star attraction, he developed "jungle music", an exotic style of jazz to accompany the sinuous dancing of chorus girls.

COTTON CLUB
The Cotton Club opened in Harlem in 1922. Blacks were barred from the audience, as its gangster owners wanted the club to be a gathering place for the city's (White) *glitterati*. However all the bands and acts performing there were Black.

BIG BANDS
The popularity of the big bands, which were aimed primarily at dance audiences, hit an all-time high between the two world wars. Above, the Fletcher Henderson band in 1925, with Coleman Hawkins on tenor saxophone (bottom, second left) and Louis Armstrong on cornet (top, third left).

Duke Ellington

SMALL BANDS: BEBOP
This inaccessible, provocative style with its insistent, fiendish beat and piercing dissonances, was well suited to small bands. It was very popular during the 1940's with young jazz "intellectuals", including the saxophonist Charlie Parker, the trumpeter Dizzy Gillespie, and the pianist Thelonius Monk. Their younger colleague, the trumpeter Miles Davis, created "cool", an introverted style in marked contrast to the aggressive exuberance of bebop. From left to right, Tommy Potter, Charlie Parker, Dizzy Gillespie and John Coltrane at Birdland in 1951.

"FREEDOM AND JAZZ GO HAND IN HAND."

THELONIUS MONK

CAB CALLOWAY

This dancer-singer-conductor was nicknamed the "Hi-De-Ho Man" because of his strange way of mixing slang and yodeling in performance. Calloway and his swinging jazz orchestra used to perform in Harlem. In the 1930's, he wrote the *Hipster's Dictionary*, a work that revealed the secrets of his new mode of expression.

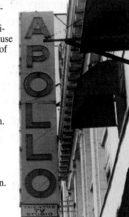

APOLLO THEATER ▲ 358

Ella Fitzgerald and Sarah Vaughan (opposite) made their debut performing in the Apollo Theater's "amateur nights". Fitzgerald carried off first prize at the Apollo in 1934. Four years later she had her first hit with *A Tisket a Tasket*. Vaughan was discovered in 1942.

SUN RA

At the end of the 1970's a frenzied, expressionistic style of music emerged. The conductor Sun Ra, headed a carnivalesque big band that included singers and dancers as well as instrumentalists. Among the latter was the saxophonist John Gilmore.

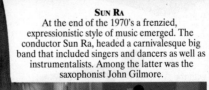

In the 20th century New York has been a fertile breeding ground for daring essays in choreography. Ballet has explored new dimensions and the city has witnessed the birth of many companies. Three great pioneers of modern dance, Isadora Duncan, Ruth St. Denis

MARTHA GRAHAM
Her powerful, abrupt, angular style was resolutely innovative. After her debut as a soloist in 1926 she stated, "My dance is urban, not pastoral".

and Martha Graham, began their careers in New York. Martha Graham, the only one to remain here, stimulated and influenced this art, both in the works she created and through her teaching methods.

THE NEW YORK CITY BALLET
In 1934, in response to a request by Lincoln Kirstein, George Balanchine (1904–83) founded the School of American Ballet. Realizing that the classical ballet he had been performing in St. Petersburg was in need of fresh inspiration, he then formed the New York City Ballet to achieve this.

PAUL TAYLOR
This former swimmer formed his own company which first performed in 1957. His bold, flowing choreography is often informed by a sense of humor.

MERCE CUNNINGHAM
Cunningham founded his troupe in 1953 and soon became famous for his avant-garde creations. For some forty years he collaborated with the composer John Cage on ballets in which music and dance are equally important, neither being reduced to a supporting role. Their collaborative work profoundly influenced young choreographers such as Trisha Brown, Douglas Dunn and Randy Warshaw.

"THE NUTCRACKER"

In 1954, George Balanchine created a new version of this great classical ballet. Since then, *The Nutcracker* has become an American tradition. During the Christmas season, the New York City Ballet gives as many as thirty-two performances of this ballet.

"GISELLE"

The multi-ethnic Dance Theater of Harlem set the action of this classical ballet in New Orleans, while preserving the original choreography. The company was founded in 1969 in the crypt of a Harlem church by Arthur Mitchell, the first Black dancer to perform with the New York City Ballet.

DANCE AT ALL LEVELS

The Broadway Dance Center located on Broadway between 55th and 56th sts., offers classes in all styles of dance.

"REVELATIONS"

This is the best-known creation by the Alvin Ailey American Dance Theater, a mainly Black company formed in 1958. The exciting work produced by this troupe draws its inspiration from the Black American tradition, Alvin Ailey's own roots and traditional gospel music.

THE SIXTIES

This turbulent decade produced many talented dancers. Two names in particular stand out: Twyla Tharp, whose style has breathed new life into the repertoire of many companies, and Meredith Monk (opposite) who has acquired a wide following.

New York has always been closely involved with the world of sports. On June 19, 1845, just across the Hudson River in Hoboken, the first baseball game was organized. New York also boasts two of the country's most famous stadiums: Yankee and Shea.

ALEXANDER JOY CARTWRIGHT (1820–92)

Although Abner Doubleday was long regarded as the father of baseball, the credit was subsequently given to Cartwright; he adapted the rules of cricket, designed a new field and organized the first game in America.

BABE RUTH (1895–1948)

Babe Ruth, considered the greatest of all baseball players, moved from the Baltimore Orioles, where he started in 1914, to the Boston Red Sox to the Yankees. With the Yankees, in 1927 he set the existing record of 60 home runs for one season. He hit 714 home runs in major league play, a record that held until 1974. He also led the Yankees to seven pennants (1921–3, 1926–8, 1932).

At any moment, a great moment.

MADISON SQUARE GARDEN

Built then rebuilt four times between 1879 and 1968, the most famous sports center in New York has virtually never been closed. Among the many celebrities

JOE NAMATH

His amazing skill as a quarterback at the University of Alabama earned him a three-year no-cut contract of over $400,000 from the New York Jets before he had ever played as a professional. Years before carrying off the Super Bowl in 1969, this high-spirited, charismatic player figured prominently in the New York tabloids as well as being the idol of football fans.

NEW YORK YACHT CLUB

The New York Yacht Club, one of the oldest sailing clubs in the world, is situated in the heart of Manhattan ● *93*, ▲ *251*. This venerable institution manned the *America*, the first holder of the cup of that name. This trophy, which is

competed for every three years, left the premises of the New York Yacht Club only in 1983, after 132 years of American invincibility.

JOHN McENROE

Brought up in Queens, trained on Long Island and a Manhattan habitué, John McEnroe is more closely associated

NEW YORK MARATHON

The New York Marathon, which usually takes place at the end of October, was first organized in 1970, when the vogue for jogging was at its peak. In the space of only a few years, this race has acquired an international reputation, not only due to its setting, but also to the caliber and popularity of its winners.

who have appeared in the Garden are Sarah Bernhardt, Marilyn Monroe, the tennis player Suzanne Lenglen and Muhammad Ali. The Garden's home teams are the Knicks ▲ *249* (above) and the Rangers (below, left).

with New York than any other sports personality. Having won the U.S. Open four times between 1979 and 1984, McEnroe has helped to make the two weeks at Flushing Meadows Park a highlight of international tennis.

● INTERIOR DESIGN AND FURNITURE

At the end of the 18th century, New York's master craftsmen – mainly European-born – satisfied their customers' desire for the latest fashions by copying and adapting the styles of the Old World. In the last few years of the 19th century, they adopted a showy, luxurious style of interior design which complemented the city's extraordinary growth. The single-story mansion on Fifth Avenue belonging to multi-millionaire William H. Vanderbilt perfectly symbolized these excesses: its decoration cost $1,800,000.

640 FIFTH AVENUE

This was the home of Vanderbilt ▲ 284. The dining room was decorated in the so-called "aesthetic" style, which was then all the rage. The Parisian interior designer Pierre Victor Galland made the *trompe l'oeil* design of the ceiling in this room, combining an unusually rich blend of Chinese, Japanese and Turkish influences. The house was crammed with works of art which, on the whole, reflected the tastes of the time. Once a week Vanderbilt opened his art gallery to the public, showing off its 19th-century European painting. The house was demolished in 1925.

GOTHIC REVIVAL STYLE

Style followed style in the 19th century, each more eclectic than the last. This piece by A. J. Davis reveals the considerable influence of architecture ● *86* on furniture design. The chair's pointed arches romantically suggest the ogive windows of medieval cathedrals.

THE CLASSICAL PERIOD

A neo-classical style, which emphasized harmony and symmetry, prevailed between the end of the American Revolution and the beginning of the 19th century. The carved eagle on the back of this dining room chair symbolizes the new American republic.

"SKYSCRAPER" BOOKCASE

The rising set-back design of this work by Paul Frankl reflects the silhouette of 1920's skyscraper architecture in New York ● *97*.

CHIPPENDALE-STYLE CARD TABLE

This table displays three features of furniture made in New York: the fifth leg, which permits the extension of the table-leaf, the ornamental design of the legs and the gadrooning just below the table top.

ROCOCO REVIVAL STYLE

This style is distinguished by its luxuriant floral ornamentation. A typical example is the dining room table, by John Henry Belter, which is encrusted with a tangle of branches, leaves and bunches of grapes.

● CHEESECAKE

Founded in New York in 1921, *Lindy's* restaurant is famous for its cheesecake.

The two recipes (Jewish and Italian) for the American cheesecake originated in New York at the turn of the century. What is now called New York cheesecake by out-of-towners is closer to the Jewish recipe. It is heavier than the Italian recipe, whose main ingredient is *ricotta* cheese, and has a smooth texture which comes from the cream and cream cheese used.

2. Melt the butter then mix in a bowl with the graham crackers. Place the mixture in a mold lined with waxed paper.

3. Press down with a glass to obtain a base a scant ½ inch thick. Place in the refrigerator for about 45 minutes.

6. Gradually add the cream cheese to the mixture.

7. Then pour in the heavy cream and add the vanilla and the orange zest.

11. Leave to rest for an hour and a half, then unmold and decorate with the strawberries.

12. To make the syrup cook the strawberries, the sugar and the water over a low heat.

INGREDIENTS

Topping: 1 cup sugar, 3 tbsp/4½ tbsp cornstarch, 3½ cups cream cheese, 2 eggs, ½ cup heavy cream, 1 sachet of vanilla, orange zest, 18 oz strawberries.
Syrup: ¼ lb strawberries, ¼ cup sugar, 1½ tbsp water.
8½-inch mold.

Base: 4 tbsp butter, 9 oz graham crackers.

1. To make the base, first crush the graham crackers.

4. Cream the sugar and the cornstarch.

5. Add the whole eggs.

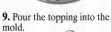

8. Mix the ingredients well.

9. Pour the topping into the mold.

10. Cook in a hot oven (400°–450°F) for 45 mins.

13. Strain the mixture and use to glaze the cheesecake.

BAGELS
These small ring-shaped rolls, often served with smoked salmon and cream cheese, are a Jewish specialty.

You can buy large, chewy pretzels, hot and salted, from sidewalk venders or pretzel sellers (above, a pretzel seller in the 1940's).

A set of placemats depicting the presidents of the U.S., glasses illustrating the establishment's ideals of service and, in more exotic vein, the spices sold on 9th Ave. at International Food.

The Rear of the Best
With Love from
CARNEGIE
DELICATESSEN & RESTAURANT
212-757-2245
854 Seventh Avenue, New York, NY at 55th St.
Chicago, Illinois
Tysons Corner, Va

The traditional doggy bag in which customers at some restaurants used to take home the leftovers from their meal. They are given to customers at the Carnegie Delicatessen, a typical New York establishment specializing in Jewish food from Central Europe, famous for its gargantuan servings of pastrami.

WALDORF SALAD
The ingredients of this dish, created in the 1930's at the Waldorf-Astoria Hotel, include apples, nuts and celery.

Certain pubs – New York institutions such as McSorley's Old Ale House, Pete's Tavern and the Peculiar Pub – serve locally brewed beer.

Jigsaw puzzles and ties are among New York's souvenirs.

ARCHITECTURE

MANHATTAN FROM 1664
TO 1994, *72*
COLONIAL STYLE
AND FEDERAL STYLE, *82*
GREEK REVIVAL STYLE, *84*
GOTHIC REVIVAL AND HIGH
VICTORIAN GOTHIC STYLES, *86*
ITALIANATE AND
SECOND EMPIRE STYLES, *88*
QUEEN ANNE STYLE AND
ROMANESQUE REVIVAL, *90*
"BEAUX ARTS" STYLE, *92*
ISABELLE GOURNAY
THE BIRTH OF
THE SKYSCRAPER, *94*
ISABELLE GOURNAY
THE ECLECTICISM OF
THE FIRST SKYSCRAPERS, *96*
ISABELLE GOURNAY
ART DECO STYLE, *98*
ISABELLE GOURNAY
INTERNATIONAL STYLE, *100*
ISABELLE GOURNAY
POSTMODERNISM, *102*
ISABELLE GOURNAY
MAJOR PROJECTS, *104*

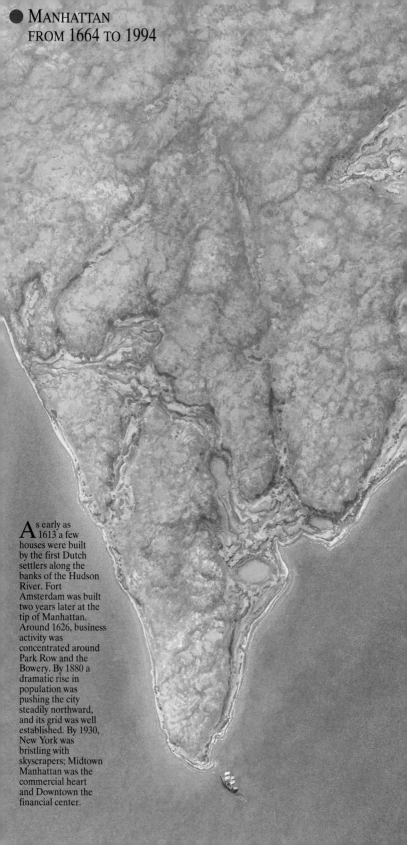

MANHATTAN
FROM 1664 TO 1994

As early as 1613 a few houses were built by the first Dutch settlers along the banks of the Hudson River. Fort Amsterdam was built two years later at the tip of Manhattan. Around 1626, business activity was concentrated around Park Row and the Bowery. By 1880 a dramatic rise in population was pushing the city steadily northward, and its grid was well established. By 1930, New York was bristling with skyscrapers; Midtown Manhattan was the commercial heart and Downtown the financial center.

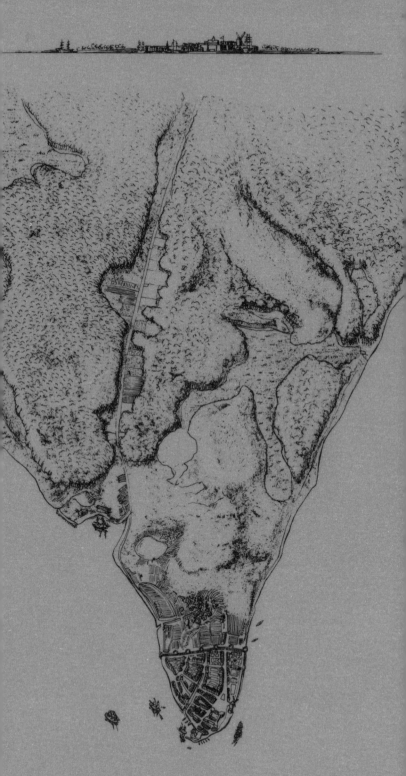

1664

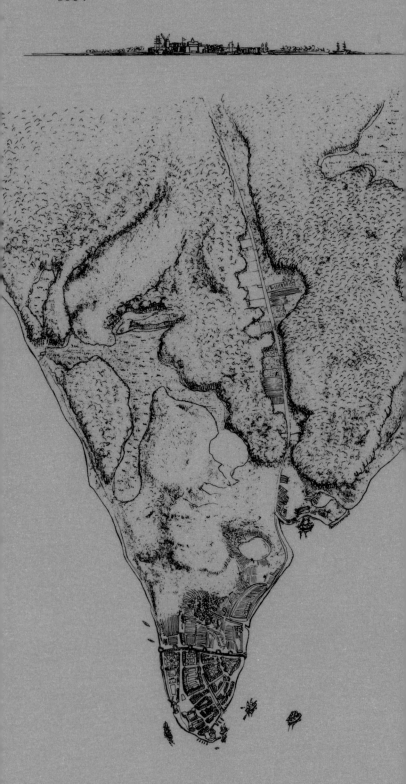

1664

1774

1774

1880

1930

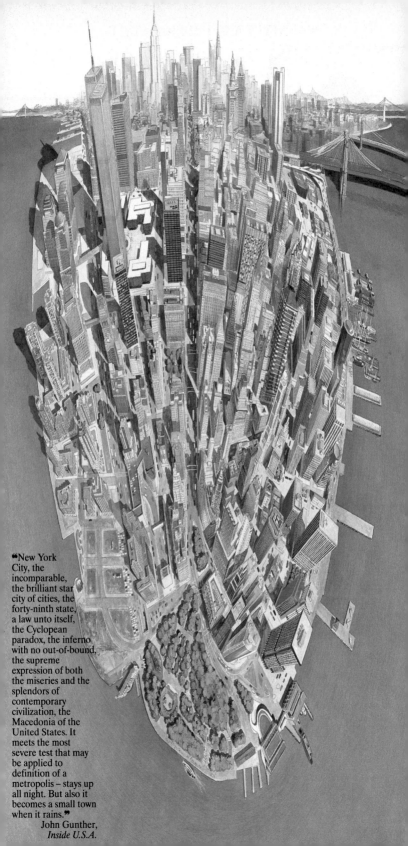

"New York City, the incomparable, the brilliant star city of cities, the forty-ninth state, a law unto itself, the Cyclopean paradox, the inferno with no out-of-bound, the supreme expression of both the miseries and the splendors of contemporary civilization, the Macedonia of the United States. It meets the most severe test that may be applied to definition of a metropolis – stays up all night. But also it becomes a small town when it rains."
John Gunther,
Inside U.S.A.

Vestiges of colonial New York, whether Dutch or English, are few and far between, although several remaining old Colonial houses in Manhattan hint at the look of the city in the late 18th century. Much more common are the early 19th-century houses built in the Georgian style dubbed "Federal" which developed in the early years of Independence.

DYCKMAN HOUSE, 1783 (204th St. and Broadway) ▲ *361*
Dyckman House is the only surviving example of the type of farmhouse built in Manhattan up until the mid-19th century by settlers of Dutch origin. Its double-sloped gambrel, or mansard, roof is typical of Dutch colonial houses.

Splayed stone lintels above windows, with or without keystone, are typical features of the Georgian style.

MORRIS-JUMEL MANSION, 1765 (W. 160th St. and Jumel Terrace) ▲ *361*
This is the only Georgian country house remaining in New York from the English colonial period. The grand Corinthian portico and corner quoins are reminiscent of the English Palladian style, which was widely adopted by wealthy Americans in the mid-18th century. The carved balustrade on the crest of the roof is a more typically American feature.

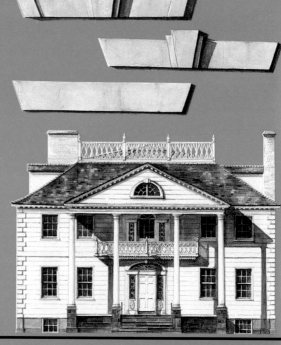

"Birdcages" decorate the wrought-iron railings of some Federal-style staircases.

THE ROOF
Some Federal-style houses have pitched roofs pierced with dormer windows.

THE ENTRANCE
The most striking feature of Federal-style houses is the main entrance. The doorway of 59 Morton Street, with its engaged colonettes, is crowned with a fanlight and flanked by sidelights.

Typical Federal-style lintels.

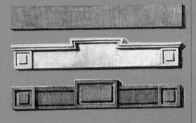

EDWARD MOONEY HOUSE, 1785–9 (18 The Bowery). The Edward Mooney House is an example of transitional architecture. Its façade, overlooking the Bowery, displays Georgian elements, while the gable end (on Pell Street), with its top-story quarter round windows, anticipates the Federal style.

ROMAN CATHOLIC ORPHAN ASYLUM, 1825–6 (32 Prince St.)
This former Catholic orphanage, a typical structure from the Federal period, now houses a convent and a school. Its features – so-called Flemish bond brickwork, dormer sash windows and fanlight – are reminiscent of domestic architecture.

● GREEK REVIVAL STYLE

The cast-iron railings of 10 Washington Square display a combination of Grecian geometric and floral motifs and classical scrolls.

The 1830's were prosperous years for New York. They witnessed the flowering of the Greek Revival style, which was widely applied to large civic, religious and commercial buildings, as well as houses. Although a development of late 18th-century European neo-classicism, the Greek Revival style also represented a tribute to ancient Greek democracy by the fledgling American nation.

COLONNADE ROW, 1833, Seth Greer (428–34 Lafayette St.) ▲ 227
Four houses remain out of the nine that originally made up LaGrange Terrace (the name was derived from the French country home of the Marquis de Lafayette). The Greek architectural features of this residential structure were modified to suit domestic typology: from the restrained decoration to the giant Corinthian-order portico.

VILLAGE COMMUNITY CHURCH, 1847, Samuel Thomson (143 West 13th St.) ▲ 219
In the 19th century many New York parishes commissioned new buildings modeled on the classical Greek temple. A typical example is this old church in Greenwich Village. Such buildings were constructed of brick, granite, polished marble or limestone; softer materials, such as sandstone or wood, were used for the columns. These austere exteriors often conceal richly decorated interiors.

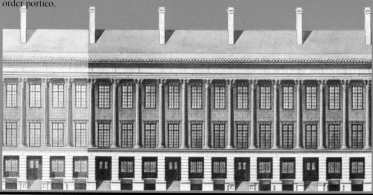

An attic story is a characteristic feature of Greek Revival houses, like this one in Cushman Row, with its regular small square windows surrounded by laurel wreaths.

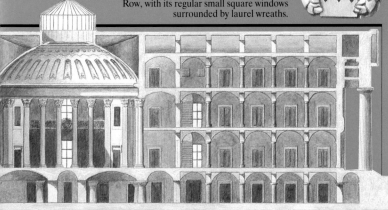

FEDERAL HALL, 1834–42, Town & Davis (28 Wall St.) ▲ *162*

The most imposing examples of Greek Revival style in Manhattan are public buildings, and among these the most eye-catching is the former Federal Customs House. The restraint of its marble Doric exterior, modeled on the Parthenon, belies the sumptuous interior, which boasts a domed, coffered ceiling resting on marble Corinthian columns and adorned with elegant classical ironwork.

PORCHES

Porches were set back within the façade so as not to encroach on the narrow New York streets. The main entrance, typically framed in solid granite, was illuminated by side lights and a fanlight.

WAREHOUSES

After the conflagration of December 1835, many warehouses were built to the same basic design: granite ground floor, brick upper stories and a façade sometimes totally made of granite, as here, at 170–6 John Street.

The bays and the cornice are the only form of decoration. Here, wealth goes hand in hand with austerity.

CUSHMAN ROW, 1940 (406–418 W. 20th St.) ▲ *220*

This is a group of identical row houses. The two most characteristic features of this style of house are the cornices and the attic story, concealing a flat roof.

GOTHIC REVIVAL AND HIGH VICTORIAN GOTHIC STYLES

The arches of Grace Church, ▲ 224, on Broadway, are adorned with figurative reliefs.

The Gothic Revival style appeared in New York in the 1830's. Although it was applied primarily to religious structures, elements found their way into civic architecture. The early form of Gothic Revival, with its rural medieval architecture, gave way, in the 1860's, to a more complex style, High Victorian Gothic, and later, at the end of the century, to Neo-Gothic, whose idiom was closer to that of 14th-century Gothic; St Thomas's, on Fifth Avenue, is an outstanding example.

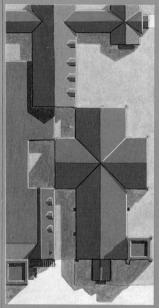

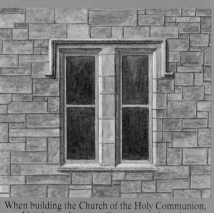

When building the Church of the Holy Communion, Upjohn made every effort to reproduce the appearance of English rural churches down to the smallest detail, even to the point of choosing uneven blocks of stone, in different shades, to give the church the weathered look of old stone.

The Church of the Holy Communion is typical of American parishes in combining the place of worship with a building devoted to social activities.

CHURCH OF THE HOLY COMMUNION, 1846, Richard Upjohn (6th Ave.) ▲ 220
In 1846, Upjohn, the architect of Trinity Church ▲ 154, designed the first asymmetrical Gothic Revival church in America, similar to those built in the English countryside. This church became the model for many others in the United States.

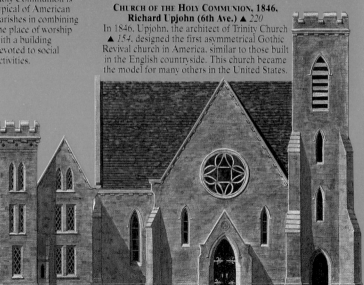

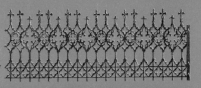

The Gothic Revival grillwork of
Grace Church on Broadway.

High Victorian Gothic, inspired by Italian and
French Gothic architecture, showed the
influence of John Ruskin's theories. It became
very fashionable in New York in the 1860's.

For a short time
during the 1840's the
property developers
of rowhouses applied
Gothic elements to
their buildings, as can
be seen on the doors
of 135 E. 12th Street
▲ 85.

**THOMAS STREET INN, 1875, J. Morgan
Slade (8 Thomas St.) ▲** *209*
This is an example of High Victorian Gothic
as applied to a commercial building. The
rational use of the materials – brick
and stone – and the polychrome
decoration are distinctive features
of this style.

A decorative arcade on
Governor Tilden's house.

**DECORATIVE
IRONWORK**
One of the most
striking features of
neo-Gothic style is
the use of cast iron
for screens and
balconies, which
boasted pointed
quatrefoil and trefoil
motifs.
**MEDIEVAL
INSPIRATION**
Some granite façades
had medieval features
such as lancet arch
doorways and ogee
arches.

**NATIONAL ARTS CLUB,
formerly GOVERNOR
TILDEN'S HOUSE,
1884, Calvert Vaux
(15 Gramercy Park
South) ▲** *230*
Here the architects
combined sculpture
and polychrome
decoration in the
purest Ruskinian
tradition. Note the
stringcourses under
the windows and the
curved arcading,
suggestive of
northern Italian
Gothic architecture.

● ITALIANATE AND SECOND EMPIRE STYLES

The doorway of the Salmagundi Club (47 5th Avenue), crowned with a semicircular fanlight, has double doors. The lavishly carved architrave is topped with a pediment.

As early as 1845, but primarily in the 1850's and 1860's, two new styles took Manhattan by storm – one inspired by the Italian Renaissance and the other by Second Empire French architecture. The two styles could be combined, crowning "Florentine" façades with mansard roofs. It was during these years of heady economic and urban growth that architects began to make use of new materials such as cast iron.

THE ITALIANATE CORNICE
The Italianate façade is articulated by deeply recessed windows with ledges. The building is crowned by a projecting cornice supported by corbels, often made of galvanized iron.

CARY BUILDING, 1857, King and Kellum (105–107 Chambers St.) ▲ *209*
Italianate-style commercial buildings were often constructed of cast-iron elements, bolted onto conventional brick or wooden structures. The façades of these cast-iron buildings were painted to resemble stone – which was too expensive – as on the Haughwout Building ● *94*, ▲ *204*, or here, on the Cary Building.

ANALOGY
Features common to both Italianate and Second Empire styles are strong horizontal divisions, grouped columns, deeply recessed window arches and projecting cornices, as seen on the Cary Building (left) and Gilsey House (above, right).

BROWNSTONES
Thousands of Italianate-style rowhouses were constructed between 1845 and 1870, a period of great economic growth. They were built of brownstone, a type of rich brown sandstone quarried in Connecticut and New Jersey. This material became so popular that New Yorkers still call these houses "brownstones". This (right) is the Langston Hughes House, at 20 E. 127th Street, in Harlem.

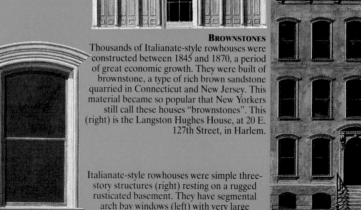

Italianate-style rowhouses were simple three-story structures (right) resting on a rugged rusticated basement. They have segmental arch bay windows (left) with very large windowpanes.

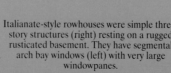

The ironwork on the roof of 881 Broadway is reminiscent of that on Napoleon III's addition to the Louvre.

GILSEY HOUSE, 1871
(1200 Broadway) ▲ *234*

Several New York buildings, such as the Gilsey House, with its cast-iron façade, built by Stephen Decatur Hatch, were directly inspired by Haussmann's neo-Baroque style. The double-slope, so-called mansard roof, a key feature of this style, marks the first significant influence of French architecture in New York.

The Gilsey House's façade (below) overlooking Broadway, and a detail (left) of the pyramidal pavilion roof at the corner. Geometric and scattered polychrome patterns are created by the slates.

Another example of slate patterns at 19 Gramercy Park ▲ *230.*

70 PERRY ST., 1867

The popular mansard roof had begun to replace flat roofs in the 1830's. Adding a mansard roof to an Italianate façade gave the owner an additional story to rent out.

Queen Anne Style and Romanesque Revival

A stylistic change took place in the years following the depression of the 1870's. The Italianate style was replaced by two picturesque modes: Queen Anne and Romanesque Revival. The first combined Medieval, Renaissance, classical and even Japanese features to create an occasionally eccentric architecture. The second, a pragmatic, weighty style introduced by H. H. Richardson, combined Romanesque and Byzantine influences.

Brick was commonly used in the Queen Anne style for its formal and decorative potential, in combination with other materials. This varied effect is seen to good advantage in the Potter Building, Park Row ▲ *170*.

The Japanese-style glazing bars of the Century Building ▲ *223* and the floral-motif ironwork of the Chelsea Hotel ▲ *220* – are typical of the Queen Anne style.

The sunflower became the archetypal motif of Queen Anne decoration.

Most Queen Anne structures in New York are polychromatic, with brick façades enhanced with stone and terracotta trimmings.

Queen Anne-style row houses, 1894, W. Holman Smith (35–45 W. 94th St.)
These houses still have their eccentric gables, a galvanized metal cornice, punctuated alternately by small triangular pediments and scrolled pediments, decorated with pinecones. The regularity of the façades is interrupted by picturesque bow windows.

Stone, terracotta and brick used together in a Romanesque Revival lintel.

GILBERT KIAMIE HOUSE formerly the Grolier Club, 1895 (29 E. 32nd St.)

Romanesque Revival façades are typically articulated by bold semicircular bays, divided by thick mullions and transoms, occasionally embellished with leaded glass panes. The bonding is richly varied, incorporating rubble stone, terracotta and reliefs featuring carved plant forms, strapwork and grotesque motifs.

WALLACE BUILDING, 1893–4, Oscar Wirz (56–8 Pine St.). This is one of the few examples of Romanesque Revival being applied to skyscraper architecture. Note the intricate Byzantine detailing of the semicircular bays (opposite).

On the Wallace Building Romanesque Revival decoration has been adapted to suit the proportions of the skyscraper.

The juxtaposition of rustication and dressed stone is typical of Romanesque Revival (seen here at 112 E. 17th St.). The contrast is accentuated by the use of bas-relief elements.

The grilles of the DeVinne Press Building employ a motif similar to those used on Rouen Cathedral in France.

DEVINNE PRESS BUILDING, 1885–6, Babb, Cook and Willard (393–9 Lafayette St.) ▲ *227* In the prosperous 1880's, many Romanesque Revival factories and warehouses, including this printing works, were built in New York. Tall round-arched bays such as these were to influence commercial architecture at the end of the century.

● "BEAUX ARTS" STYLE

Between 1846 and 1914, more than four hundred American architects studied in Paris at the École des Beaux-Arts. In fact, the United States had no architectural school until 1867. The prestige enjoyed by Paris-trained architects prompted their younger colleagues to follow in their footsteps, and nearly half of these graduates practised in New York. "Beaux-Arts"-style buildings are now coming back into favor among certain Postmodern architects.

NEW YORK PUBLIC LIBRARY, 1911, Carrère & Hastings (5th Ave., between 40th and 42nd sts.) ▲ *252.* The key feature of this monumental building is the clearly organized and

balanced plan (below), a fundamental lesson of Beaux-Arts training found in major public commissions. The wide corridors, punctuated by columns, are conducive to circulation and make every department of the New York Public Library easily accessible. The triple arcade, accentuated by columns and surmounted by groups of carved figures (above), gives the main entrance the status of a triumphal arch.

HENRY VILLARD HOUSES, 1884, McKim, Mead and White (451–5 Madison Ave., between 50th and 51st sts.) ▲ *284.* This group of six private residences, arranged around a central courtyard, is a replica of a traditional Italian palazzo. The south wing was intended for Henry Villard, one of America's wealthiest railway magnates, who commissioned the project. The houses now form part of a hotel.

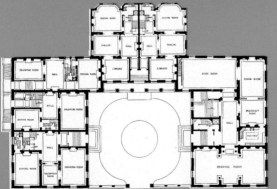

The main source of inspiration for the Henry Villard Houses was the Palazzo della Cancelleria in Rome, whose decoration was simplified and limited to the window frames, the balconies and the quoins.

THE PIERPONT MORGAN LIBRARY, 1906, McKim, Mead & White (33 E. 36th St.) ▲ 241

"I want a gem": these were the words of the financier J. Pierpont Morgan, an ardent admirer of Italian Renaissance architecture, when he commissioned a private library-cum-museum from McKim. The three rooms are linked by a vestibule extended by an apse. The allegorical paintings on the walls are adapted from Raphaël's frescoes in the Vatican.

The decoration of the cornice on the Racquet and Tennis Club of New York ▲ 286 sets up a subtle balance between picturesque and monumental elements.

NEW YORK YACHT CLUB, 1900, Warren and Wetmore (37 W. 44th St.) ▲ 251

The architects of this sailing club turned the narrow site to account by devising three classical bays decorated with galleon sterns, which could have come straight out of *Peter Pan*; they overhang 44th Street, bringing dolphins, seaweed and shells in their wake.

LOW MEMORIAL LIBRARY, 1897, McKim, Mead & White (Columbia University) ▲ 352

Between 1894 and 1903 Charles McKim designed the general plan for the Columbia campus, located between West 116th and 120th streets. The overall scheme, dense and homogeneous, is one of the most characteristic examples of the "City Beautiful" movement, the urban design equivalent of the "Beaux-Arts" style. The focal point of the composition is this library, with its awe-inspiring peristyle and dome. However, the proportions remain on a human scale and the steps, which serve as a podium, have become a popular student gathering place.

THE BIRTH OF THE SKYSCRAPER

The birth of the skyscraper, in the 1860's, was a response to the spatial constraints imposed by the tight urban fabric of Lower Manhattan. It was made possible by the design of light steel frames, the invention of the electric passenger elevator and the fact that the rocky terrain lent itself to the laying of foundations. But there was another reason: the desire to go one better than the competition. However, although the techniques were new, the forms and the decoration remained eclectic.

In 1913 the Woolworth Building, dubbed the "eighth wonder of the world", was its tallest building at 792 feet ▲ 180.

Decorative elements were cast in factories and then bolted onto the structure.

HAUGHWOUT BUILDING, 1857, J. P. Gaynor (488 Broadway, at Broome St.) ▲ 204. This forebear of the skyscraper was built by Daniel D. Badger, to plans by Gaynor, with prefabricated cast-iron elements which made it possible to incorporate large areas of glass. The Haughwout Building was originally a department store selling glass, china, clocks and watches.

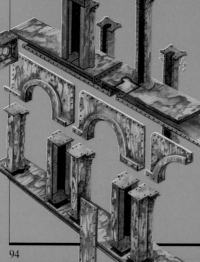

CAST-IRON ASSEMBLY
Standardized cast-iron parts were assembled and bolted on at the construction site. This job did not require skilled workmen and the process was cheaper than stone construction. But the cast iron was not initially strong enough to be used for buildings with a large number of stories; in addition, its low resistance to fire represented a very real danger for the building's occupants. Behind the metal façade, the load-bearing structures continued to be made of wood or conventional masonry: it was not until the invention of the Bessemer process (1856) and the popularization of high-resistance steel, that a homogeneous frame was developed ▲ 203.

BAYARD BUILDING, formerly CONDICT BUILDING, 1898, Louis Sullivan and Lyndon P. Smith (65 Bleecker St.) ▲ *209*
This is the only building in New York designed by the master of the Chicago School. A projecting cornice stabilizes the rhythm of the decorative pilasters, alternately thick and thin, and achieves an innovative balance between horizontal and vertical elements.

Detail from the terracotta decoration of the Bayard Building. Here Sullivan was exploiting the geometrical interlaced motifs which were a hallmark of his style.

In 1857, in the Haughwout Store, Elisha Otis installed the first passenger elevator fitted with a safety device.

ANSONIA HOTEL, 1904, Paul E. M. Duboy and Michael Graves (2109 Broadway) ▲ *347*. The French-born architect endeavored to give this apartment building a Parisian look. This was no easy task, as it entailed maintaining a harmonious sense of proportion in a huge apartment building with disparate façades, combining a whole spectrum of materials, whose height was three times that of its Parisian counterparts.

● THE ECLECTICISM OF THE FIRST SKYSCRAPERS

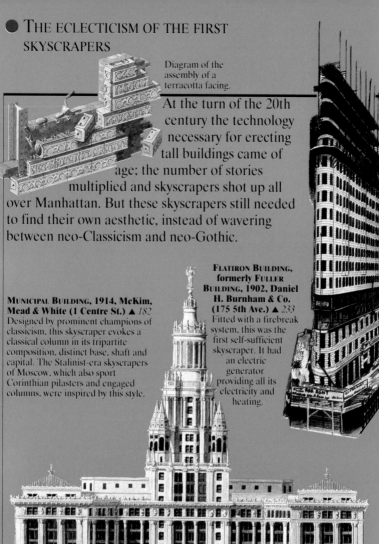

Diagram of the assembly of a terracotta facing.

At the turn of the 20th century the technology necessary for erecting tall buildings came of age; the number of stories multiplied and skyscrapers shot up all over Manhattan. But these skyscrapers still needed to find their own aesthetic, instead of wavering between neo-Classicism and neo-Gothic.

MUNICIPAL BUILDING, 1914, McKim, Mead & White (1 Centre St.) ▲ 182
Designed by prominent champions of classicism, this skyscraper evokes a classical column in its tripartite composition, distinct base, shaft and capital. The Stalinist-era skyscrapers of Moscow, which also sport Corinthian pilasters and engaged columns, were inspired by this style.

FLATIRON BUILDING, formerly FULLER BUILDING, 1902, Daniel H. Burnham & Co. (175 5th Ave.) ▲ 233
Fitted with a firebreak system, this was the first self-sufficient skyscraper. It had an electric generator providing all its electricity and heating.

THE TOPS
The tops of the Bankers Trust ▲ *163*, Woolworth ▲ *180* and Metropolitan Life Insurance Company ▲ *234* buildings were inspired respectively by classical mausoleums, Gothic steeples and the campanile in Saint Mark's square in Venice. This was not for ideological reasons but served, rather, to give each building a distinctive identity on the Manhattan skyline.

The plans drawn up in 1922 by the Viennese architect Adolf Loos for the headquarters of the *Chicago Tribune* (left) were a literal reference to the tripartite division of the skyscraper and suggest a giant Doric column.

ZONING RESOLUTION
In 1916 a set of building regulations was passed to prevent the "canyon" effect ■ *16*. Skyscrapers could be built with a height relative to the width of the street. Successive setbacks were then employed to make them narrower and allow light into the street. When the building size had been reduced to a quarter of the site at street level, the tower could continue to rise ad infinitum.

EQUITABLE BUILDING, 1912–15 (120 Broadway) ▲ *153*
Designed before the zoning law, the Equitable Building (left) should, according to its criteria, have been built in the shape of a pyramid (right).

97

During the property boom of the 1920's, New York architects drew their inspiration from European movements – Viennese Secession, German Expressionism, French Art Deco – and even transcended them. The Chrysler Building ▲ 266 is one of the most striking examples of this trend. The geometric, streamlined aesthetic of Art Deco was ideally suited to the tapering shape of the new skyscrapers.

FRIEZES IN ABUNDANCE
An abundance of decorative friezes appeared during the Art Deco period. Here, a detail of one at 2 Park Ave. built by Ely Jacques Kahn.

THE FIRST ART DECO SKYSCRAPER
The main entrance of the Barclay-Vesey Building, 1923–6 ▲ *140* (140 West St.) is decorated with bells, the logo of the Bell Telephone Company.

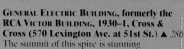

GENERAL ELECTRIC BUILDING, formerly the RCA VICTOR BUILDING, 1930–1, Cross & Cross (570 Lexington Ave. at 51st St.) ▲ *286*
The summit of this spire is stunning in its originality and exuberance. The lacy ornamental stonework, brickwork and glazed ceramic veneer, gilded in places, suggest Flamboyant Gothic; yet, apart from the stylized pinnacles, none of these varied motifs had any precedents; the chevrons and bolts of lightning symbolize the Hertzian waves broadcast by the Radio Corporation of America, the original owner of this tower.

DYNAMIC COMPOSITIONS
The radiator grilles in the Chanin Building, 1929 (122 E. 42nd St.) ▲ *272*. These grilles, the work of the sculptor René Chambellan, combine rays and chevrons, spirals and ripples.

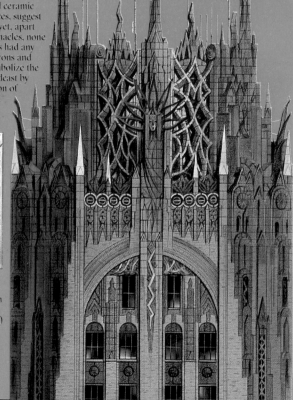

THE SKYLINE

In 1929 the Multiple Dwelling Act authorized the construction of very tall apartment houses and hotels. Central Park West was subsequently endowed with a number of soaring residences, some with twin towers. On the East Side, the double profile of the Waldorf-Astoria Hotel (1930–1, Schultze & Weaver) rose to challenge the Chrysler and General Electric buildings on the Midtown skyline.

AMERICAN STANDARD BUILDING, formerly AMERICAN RADIATOR BUILDING, 1924, Hood & Fouilhoux (40 W. 40th St.) ▲ *254.* This has one of the earliest pyramidal silhouettes. The black brick facing employed by Raymond Hood, a former pupil at the École des Beaux-Arts, was an innovative step. It enabled him to minimize the contrast between the building's solid masses and the windows.

FILM CENTER BUILDING, 1928–9, Buchman & Kahn (630 9th Ave.) ▲ *256*
The entrance hall of this building, designed by one of the masters of the Modern Jazz style, is a prime illustration of this style's typical features. Certain motifs, like those of the mosaics, were directly inspired by Mayan art.

The Gothic pinnacles on the setbacks of the American Standard Building are enhanced with gold.

TWO NEW DECORATIVE ELEMENTS
The horizontal bands of blue-green glazed terracotta and the giant stylized letters, which form part of the decoration of the entrance and the top of the McGraw-Hill Building, were introduced by the architect Raymond Hood.

Former MCGRAW-HILL BUILDING, 1930–1, Hood, Godley & Fouilhoux (330 W. 42nd St.) ▲ *256*. This skyscraper, whose use of horizontal lines and rounded corners at the top creates a dynamic effect, doubled as headquarters and printing works for a large publishing company. An early example of streamlining, this building displays a functionalism akin to that of the International Style.

The term "international style" was first used, in 1932, by the architect Philip Johnson and the art historian Henry-Russell Hitchcock to describe the exhibition of modern European architecture held at MOMA in the same year. However, New York architects were not ready to embrace European modernism and the city did not become a testing ground for modern architecture until around 1950.

W. LESCAZE HOUSE, 1934 (211 E. 48th St.) ▲ *262*
This townhouse was the architect's home and place of work and one of the first International Style buildings in New York. It contrasts sharply with the neighboring brownstone residences. Ribbon windows and glass block panes let the light filter in while maintaining privacy.

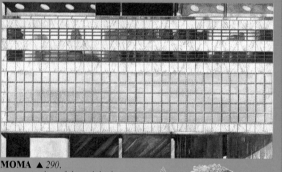

MOMA ▲ *290*, reconstruction of the original façade, 1939, Philip Goodwin and Edward Durell Stone (11 W. 53rd St.)
The original building to house the Museum of Modern Art formed a marked contrast with the adjacent rowhouses.

THE INITIAL COMPOSITION
The emphasis is on horizontal and vertical lines. The façade expresses the building's various functions: a welcoming, glazed ground floor, two levels of windowless exhibition rooms, two office stories and a roof terrace. The geometric severity of the building is tempered by the curve of the canopy and the round openings in the roof.

LEVER HOUSE, 1952, Skidmore, Owing & Merrill (390 Park Ave.) ▲ *286*. The generation of "minimalist" skyscrapers, with their pared down lines, came of age with this building. It uses only a quarter of the available area and its main vertical structure is set at right angles to Park Avenue. Under threat in 1983, Lever House is now listed as a landmark.

A NEW APPROACH TO PUBLIC OPEN SPACES. Because Lever House rests on stilts, a pedestrian area opens up at street level. Trees grow up through the opening in the roof terrace (left). The airy effect breaks the uniformity of the avenue.

Narrow decorative bronze I-beams punctuate the windows of the Seagram Building and accentuate the vertical thrust of the metal frame.

SEAGRAM BUILDING, 1958, Ludwig Mies van der Rohe in collaboration with Philip Johnson (375 Park Ave.) ▲ *286*
The German-born architect was already an established name in Chicago when he received the commisssion for this building. A rectangle composed of three times five bays, 38 stories high, it is proportioned according to classical canons. The building is set back from Park Avenue, creating space for a plaza from which this example of the minimalist skyscraper can be admired. Its austere lines were realized in rich materials, however; and the Seagram Building topped all records for cost per square meter.

DECORATIVE BRONZE
The vertical structure is accentuated by decorative bronze I-beams; the corner posts are also clad in bronze.

The top is sliced off at a 45° angle, making Citicorp easy to distinguish on the Manhattan skyline.

CITICORP CENTER, 1978, Hugh Stubbins & Assoc. (Lexington Ave., between 53rd and 54th Sts.) ▲ *286*
This 46-story tower, sheathed in aluminum panels, sits on four pillars and a central column. A sunken plaza occupies the area which has been liberated at ground level.

FORD FOUNDATION, 1967, Kevin Roche, John Dinkeloo & Assocs. (321 E. 42nd St.) ▲ *264*. The technical and stylistic innovation of this building is its brick and glass façade. It was built using girders made of exposed steel (Cor-ten) which is resistant to atmospheric corrosion.

A BETTER BALANCE BETWEEN PUBLIC AND PRIVATE SPACES
At the end of the 1960's, architects endeavored to improve the relationship between public and private spaces. The Ford Foundation is one of the most successful examples of this attempt; two office wings open onto an immense enclosed atrium-garden which can be seen from the street.

● POSTMODERNISM

Detail of the polished steel elevator
door-plaques inside the Sony Building.

In the 1980's, the prosperity enjoyed
by big business gave the skyscraper a
new lease on life. In New York, one of
the hotbeds of Postmodernism since
the 1970's, architects and real estate
developers viewed the revival of past
forms as an antidote to the
International Style, and a means of
restoring to larger corporate buildings
a symbolic dimension.

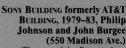

**SONY BUILDING formerly AT&T
BUILDING, 1979–83, Philip
Johnson and John Burgee
(550 Madison Ave.)**
The era of the Postmodern
skyscraper dawned with this
building. To make his "small"
37-story building more
monumental, Johnson revived
tripartite composition. His
Chippendale-style pediment
aroused great controversy.

**THE RISE OF
POSTMODERNISM**
With its AT&T headquarters
(now the Sony Building),
which appeared on the
covers of *Time* and *The
New Yorker*, Johnson's
firm launched a new
fashion; and Johnson –
once an exponent of
the International Style
– maintained his
position as an arbiter of
taste in New York.
    The place of honor in
the main lobby was
held by a statue,
the *Spirit of
Communication*,
brought from the
previous headquarters.

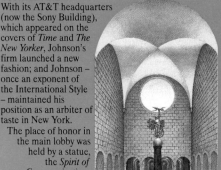

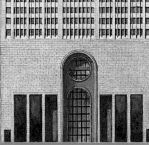

WASHINGTON COURT, 1986, James Stewart Polshek & Partners ▲ *212*
(6th Ave., between Waverly Place and Washington Square)
Postmodernism has also had its effect on residential architecture: these rowhouses,
with their harmonious façades, reflect the spirit of Greenwich Village.

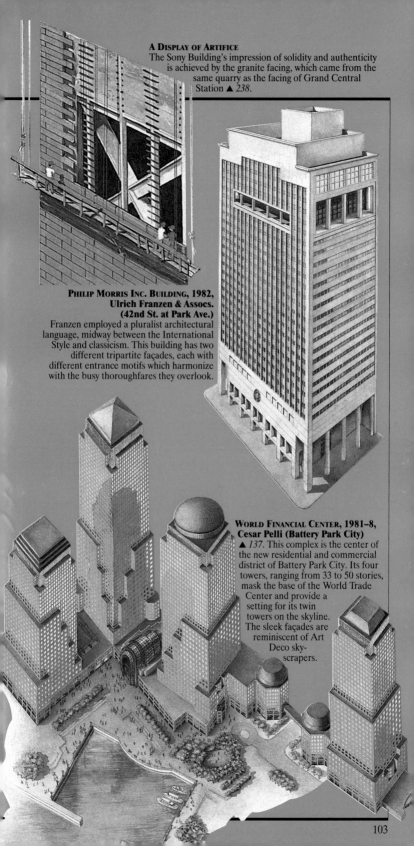

A DISPLAY OF ARTIFICE
The Sony Building's impression of solidity and authenticity is achieved by the granite facing, which came from the same quarry as the facing of Grand Central Station ▲ *238*.

PHILIP MORRIS INC. BUILDING, 1982, Ulrich Franzen & Assocs. (42nd St. at Park Ave.)
Franzen employed a pluralist architectural language, midway between the International Style and classicism. This building has two different tripartite façades, each with different entrance motifs which harmonize with the busy thoroughfares they overlook.

WORLD FINANCIAL CENTER, 1981–8, Cesar Pelli (Battery Park City)
▲ *137*. This complex is the center of the new residential and commercial district of Battery Park City. Its four towers, ranging from 33 to 50 stories, mask the base of the World Trade Center and provide a setting for its twin towers on the skyline. The sleek façades are reminiscent of Art Deco skyscrapers.

Because of the recession, some projects designed in the 1980's never saw the light of day. Neither the skyscrapers scheduled to be built on Columbus Circle nor Donald Trump's 150-story dream tower were realized. However, on the West Side, the redevelopment of the banks of the Hudson reveals a new approach to urban design.

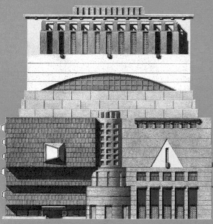

WHITNEY MUSEUM, 1966, Marcel Breuer & Assocs. (Madison Ave. at 75th St.) ▲ *326*

This building, built by a former professor at the Weimar Bauhaus to house a collection of modern American art, quickly became too cramped. The plans for enlarging it, designed in 1986 by Michael Graves, rekindled the "quarrel of the Moderns and the Postmoderns". In order to treble the effective area, Graves planned to demolish some apartment buildings on Madison Avenue and to build, on top of the new red granite base and the existing museum – disregarding the character of the original building – a huge exhibition hall illuminated by a lunette, and, on top of that, a colonnaded restaurant.

The plans for a tower by Pederson and Fox at 383 Madison Avenue were abandoned.

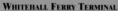

WHITEHALL FERRY TERMINAL
In 1992 the Postmodernist architect Robert Venturi was commissioned to build a new maritime terminal on the tip of Manhattan. He reproduced the proportions of the façade from the neighboring Battery Maritime Terminal and topped the building with a startling clock over 98 feet in diameter, which called to mind the slogan "Time is Money". This approach follows the tradition of large American neo-Classical railroad stations.

NEW YORK
AS SEEN BY PAINTERS

JONATHAN WEINBERG

CANYON STREETS, *106*
URBAN LANDSCAPES, *108*
ABOVE, BELOW, *110*
SKYLINE, *112*

"What a sight these towers of Manhattan are, glittering with millions of golden specks, soaring endlessly, as if they were going to touch the sky!"

Langston Hughes

Wherein lies New York's quintessential nature? Georgia O'Keeffe (1887–1986) who painted *Radiator Building* (2; detail in 3) in 1927, felt that the skyscraper was the enduring symbol of the city. O'Keeffe painted what she saw from her own windows. She professed to be as interested in the spaces between the buildings, the "canyons", as in their architecture. Robert Henri (1865–1929) held that the real city was not to be found at the tops of the temples to Mammon but at the very bottom; in 1902, he painted *New York in Winter* (1).

| 1 | 2 |
| | 3 |

> **"A LOVE OF ART IS NOT ENOUGH TO PERCEIVE THE STRENGTH, MEANING AND SPARK OF BEAUTY IN A GANG OF URCHINS FROM THE EAST SIDE."**
>
> ROBERT HENRI

Maurice Prendergast (1859–1924) and Robert Henri ● *107*, members of "The Eight", specialized in painting scenes of American city life. Prendergast's fondness for the city is clearly visible in the 1901 paintings *East River* (2) and *Central Park* (1). In his photograph *Flatiron* (3), taken in 1909, Edward Steichen (1879–1973) captured this early skyscraper in a wintry twilight. A more mundane portrait of a skyscraper is *Chrysler Building under Construction* (1931) by Earl Horter.

| 1 | 3 |
| 2 | 4 |

"I REGARDED THIS MODERN CITY AS A SORT OF HELL. THE SUBWAY, HIDDEN IN THE BOWELS OF THE EARTH, SEEMED TO SYMBOLIZE AN ENVIRONMENT THAT CONFOUNDS THE SENSES AND DESTROYS LIFE."

GEORGE TOOKER

Edward Hopper (1882–1967; below), the most outstanding of Robert Henri's pupils, visited Paris where he began his career by painting in an impressionist style. He returned to New York in 1910, to devote himself to

more familiar American subjects. The works for which he became famous depicted lonely figures in typically American settings, such as cinemas, service stations, and hotel rooms. Hopper stated that his favorite subject was "sunlight striking the wall of a house". *Roofs of Washington Square*, 1926 (1), is the view from the roof of his studio. This canvas, a dazzling composition of light and airy distances, seems to offer an escape from the artificial lighting of the New York subway system, depicted in George Tooker's painting *Subway* (2; detail in 3). In this oppressively claustrophobic canvas, completed in 1950, the characters are lost in the alienating maze of technology. Hopper and Tooker both desired to expose what they saw as the banality of the American way of life.

1

2	3

111

These two paintings, *View of Manhattan West from Philip Morris at Park Avenue and 41st Street* (1982), by Richard Haas, with its jumble of buildings and erratic spaces, and – even more so – Joseph Stella's *Brooklyn Bridge, Variation on an Old Theme* (1939), with its Gothic arches, rigid steel cables and heavy traffic, enshrine the city in its own mythology.

New York
AS SEEN BY WRITERS

NEW YORKERS

TALENT

Does the character of a city come principally from its buildings or its people? According to Timothy Dwight (1752–1817), writing in 1811, the city acts as a magnet for people of talent and is thus shaped by them.

❝In every large city there will always be found a considerable number of persons who possess superior talents and information; and who, if not natives, are drawn to it by the peculiar encouragement which it holds out to their exertions. The field of effort is here more splendid, and the talents are more needed, honored, and rewarded than in smaller towns. New York has its share of persons sustaining this character: men really possessing superior minds and deserving high esteem. Together with these, there is not a small number, here as elsewhere, who arrogate this character to themselves, and some of whom occasionally acquire and lose it: men accounted great through the favorable influence of some accident, the attachment of some religious or political party during a fortunate breeze of popularity, or the lucky prevalence of some incidental sympathy, or the ardent pursuit of some favorite public object in which they have happened to act with success. These meteors, though some of them shine for a period with considerable luster, soon pass over the horizon, and are seen no more.

The citizens at large are distinguished as to their intelligence in the manner alluded to above. To this place they have come with the advantages and disadvantages of education found in their several native countries. Some of them are well informed, read, converse, and investigate. Others scarcely do either, and not a small number are unable to read at all. Most of these are, however, Europeans.❞

TIMOTHY DWIGHT, *TRAVELS IN NEW ENGLAND AND NEW YORK*,
HARVARD UNIVERSITY PRESS, 1969

GILDED YOUTH

F. Scott Fitzgerald (1896–1940) glamorized the 1920's as a decade belonging to "gilded youth". In this autobiographical piece, he feels like an observer of the city rather than a participant because his future wife, Zelda, is in Alabama.

❝New York had all the iridescence of the beginning of the world. The returning troops marched up Fifth Avenue and the girls were instinctively drawn East and North toward them – this was the greatest nation and there was gala in the air. As I hovered ghost-like in the Plaza Red Room of a Saturday afternoon, or went to lush and liquid garden parties in the East Sixties or tippled with Princetonians in the Biltmore Bar I was haunted always by my other life – my drab room in the Bronx, my square foot of the subway, my fixation upon the day's letter from Alabama – would it come and what would it say? – my shabby suits, my poverty, and love. While my friends were launching decently into life I had muscled my inadequate

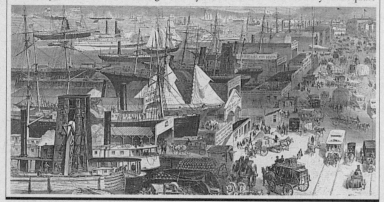

bark into midstream. The gilded youth circling around young Constance Bennett in the Club de Vingt, the classmates in the Yale-Princeton Club whooping up our first after-the-war reunion, the atmosphere of the millionaires' houses that I sometimes frequented – these things were empty for me, though I recognized them as impressive scenery and regretted that I was committed to other romance.**99**

F. SCOTT FITZGERALD, *THE CRACK UP*, © FITZGERALD ESTATE, 1932

STRANGERS AND NEIGHBORS

Edmund B. White (1899–1985), an American journalist, was very conscious of the city's previous illustrious inhabitants.

66On any person who desires such queer prizes, New York will bestow the gift of loneliness and the gift of privacy. It is this largess that accounts for the presence within the city's walls of a considerable section of the population; for the residents of Manhattan are to a large extent strangers who have pulled up stakes somewhere and come to town, seeking sanctuary or fulfillment or some greater or lesser grail. The capacity to make such dubious gifts is a mysterious quality of New York. It can destroy an individual, or it can fulfill him, depending a good deal on luck. No one should come to New York to live unless he is willing to be lucky.

New York is the concentrate of art and commerce and sport and religion and entertainment and finance, bringing to a single compact arena the gladiator, the evangelist, the promoter, the actor, the trader and the merchant. It carries on its lapel the unexpungeable odor of the long past, so that no matter where you sit in New York you feel the vibrations of great times and tall deeds, of queer people and events and undertakings. . . . I am twenty-two blocks from where Rudolph Valentino lay in state, eight blocks from where Nathan Hale was executed, five blocks from the publisher's office where Ernest Hemingway hit Max Eastman on the nose, four miles from where Walt Whitman sat sweating out editorials for the Brooklyn Eagle, thirty-four blocks from the street Willa Cather lived in when she came to New York to write books about Nebraska, one block from where Marceline used to clown on the boards of the Hippodrome . . . and for that matter I am probably occupying the very room that any number of exalted and somewise memorable characters sat in, some of them on hot, breathless afternoons, lonely and private and full of their own sense of emanations from without.**99**

E. B. WHITE, *HERE IS NEW YORK*, HARPER BROS., 1949

LABORERS

First-generation immigrants add color and diversity to the masses thronging the streets of the city. Charles Dickens (1812–70) described some Irish laborers.

66 . . . let us see what kind of men . . . are . . . those two labourers in holiday clothes, of whom one carries in his hand a crumpled scrap of paper from which he tries to spell out a hard name, while the other looks about for it on all the doors and windows.

Irishmen both! You might know them, if they were masked, by their long-tailed blue coats and bright buttons, and their drab trousers, which they wear like men well used to working dresses, who are easy in no others. It would be hard to keep your model republics going, without the countrymen and countrywomen of those two labourers. For who else would dig, and delve, and drudge, and do domestic work, and make canals and roads, and execute great lines of Internal Improvement! Irishmen both, and sorely puzzled too, to find out what they seek. Let us go down, and help them for the love of home, and that spirit of liberty which admits of honest service to honest men, and honest work for honest bread, no matter what it be.

That's well! We have got at the right address at last, though it is written in strange characters truly, and might have been scrawled with the blunt handle of the spade the writer better knows the use of, than a pen. Their way lies yonder, but what business takes them there? They carry savings: to hoard up? No. They are brothers, those men. One crossed the sea alone, and working very hard for one half year, and

living harder, saved funds enough to bring the other out. That done, they worked together side by side, contentedly sharing hard labour and hard living for another term, and then their sisters came, and then another brother, and lastly, their old mother. And what now? Why, the poor old crone is restless in a strange land, and yearns to lay her bones, she says, among her people in the old graveyard at home: and so they go to pay her passage back: and God help her and them, and every simple heart, and all who turn to the Jerusalem of their younger days, and have an altar-fire upon the cold hearth of their fathers.**

CHARLES DICKENS, *AMERICAN NOTES*,
LONDON, 1842

RAGING TORRENTS

Theodore Dreiser (1871–1945), the American novelist, writes here of the sheer masses of people going about their business in the city.

**Take your place on Williamsburg Bridge some morning, for instance, at say three or four o'clock, and watch the long, the quite unbroken line of Jews trundling pushcarts eastward to the great Wall-about Market over the bridge. A procession out of Assyria or Egypt or Chaldea, you might suppose, Biblical in quality; or, better yet, a huge chorus in some operatic dawn scene laid in Paris or Petrograd or here. A vast, silent mass it is, marching to the music of necessity . . . And they are New York, too – Bucharest and Lemberg and Odessa come to the Bowery, and adding rich, dark, colorful threads to the rug or tapestry which is New York.

Since these are but a portion, think of those other masses that come from the surrounding territory, north, south, east and west. The ferries – have you ever observed them in the morning? Or the bridges, railway terminals, and every elevated and subway exit?

Already at six and six-thirty in the morning they have begun to trickle small streams of human beings Manhattan or cityward, and by seven and seven-fifteen these streams have become sizable affairs. By seven-thirty and eight they have changed into heavy, turbulent rivers, and by eight-fifteen and eight-thirty and nine they are raging torrents, no less. They overflow all the streets and avenues and every available means of conveyance. They are pouring into all available doorways, shops, factories, office-buildings – those huge affairs towering so significantly above them. Here they stay all day long, causing those great hives and their adjacent streets to flush with a softness of color not indigenous to them, and then at night, between five and six, they are going again, pouring forth over the bridges and through the subways and across the ferries and out on the trains, until the last drop of them appears to have been exuded, and they are pocketed in some outlying side-street or village or metropolitan hall-room – and the great, turbulent night of the city is on once more.**

THEODORE DREISER,
THE COLOR OF A GREAT CITY,
THE DREISER TRUST, 1923 © 1923 BY
BONI & LIVERIGHT, INC.

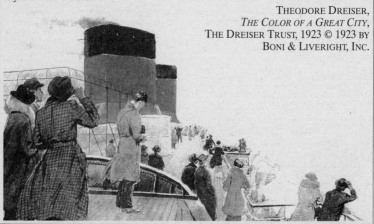

A TRANSIENT POPULATION

Don DeLillo (b. 1936) picks some individuals out of the crowd – not celebrities but anonymous characters or people on the streets.

❝Harbors reveal a city's power, its lust for money and filth, but strangely through the haze what I distinguished first was the lone mellow promise of an island, tender retreat from straight lines, an answering sea-mound. This was the mist's illusion and the harbor's pound of flesh. Skippy tugged at licorice with her teeth, the black strands expanding between hand and jaw. She had a shaded face and she was ageless, a wanderer in cities, one of those children found after every war, picking in the rubble for scraps of food the gaunt dogs have missed. Such minds are unreclaimable but at the same time hardly dangerous and governments acknowledge this fact by providing millions of acres of postwar rubble. On our way to find a bus stop we saw the subway crowds drop into openings in the earth, on their way up the length of Manhattan or under rivers to the bourns and orchards, there to be educated in false innocence, in the rites of isolation. Perhaps the only ore of truth their lives possessed was buried in this central rock. Beyond its limits was their one escape, a

dreamless sleep, no need to fear the dare to be exceptional. Dozens of pigeons swarmed around a woman tossing bread crumbs. She was in a wheelchair held at rest by a young boy, both on fire with birds, the pigeons skidding on the air, tracing the upward curve of the old woman's arm. I watched her eyes climb with the birds, all her losses made a blessing in a hand's worth of bread. Pigeons and meningitis. Chocolate and mouse droppings. Licorice and roach hairs. Vermin on the bus we took uptown. I wondered how long I'd choose to dwell in these middle ages of plague and usury, living among traceless men and women, those whose only peace was in shouting ever more loudly. Nothing tempted them more than voicelessness. But they shouted. Transient population of thunderers and hags. They dragged through wet streets speaking in languages older than the stones of cities buried in sand. Beds and bedbugs. Men and lice. Gonococcus curling in the lap of love. We rode past an urban redevelopment project. Machine-tooth shovels clawed past half-finished buildings stuck in mud, tiny balconies stapled on. All spawned by realtor-kings who live in the sewers. Skippy coughed blood onto the back of her hand. The bus panted over cobblestones and I studied words drawn in fading paint on the sides of buildings. Brake and front end service. Wheel alignment. Chain and belt. Pulleys, motors, gears. Sheet-metal machinery. Leather remnants. Die cutting and precision measuring. Cuttings and job lots. Business machines. Threads, woolens, laces. Libros en español. We left by the back door and Skippy went back to whatever she was doing (or dealing) in that hotel. Rain blew across the old streets. The toothless man was still at his cart, a visitation from sunken regions, not caring who listened or passed, his cries no less cadenced than the natural rain. YOU'RE BUYING I'M SELLING YAPPLES YAPPLES YAPPLES.❞

DON DELILLO, *GREAT JONES STREET*,
RANDOM HOUSE INC., NEW YORK, 1989

"TALL BUILDINGS"

AMERICAN BEAUTY

In "The American Scene", Henry James (1843–1916) wrote of his impressions of a visit in 1906 after an absence of almost twenty years.

❝Memory and the actual impression keep investing New York with the tone, predominantly, of summer dawns and winter frosts, of sea-foam, of bleached sails and stretched awnings, of blanched hulls, of scoured decks, of new ropes, of

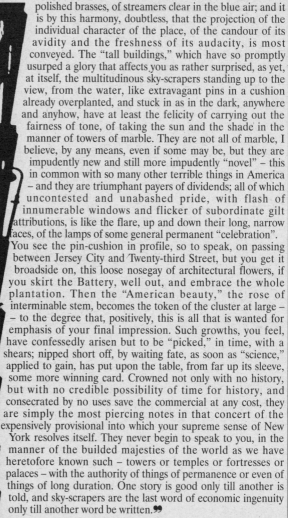

polished brasses, of streamers clear in the blue air; and it is by this harmony, doubtless, that the projection of the individual character of the place, of the candour of its avidity and the freshness of its audacity, is most conveyed. The "tall buildings," which have so promptly usurped a glory that affects you as rather surprised, as yet, at itself, the multitudinous sky-scrapers standing up to the view, from the water, like extravagant pins in a cushion already overplanted, and stuck in as in the dark, anywhere and anyhow, have at least the felicity of carrying out the fairness of tone, of taking the sun and the shade in the manner of towers of marble. They are not all of marble, I believe, by any means, even if some may be, but they are impudently new and still more impudently "novel" – this in common with so many other terrible things in America – and they are triumphant payers of dividends; all of which uncontested and unabashed pride, with flash of innumerable windows and flicker of subordinate gilt attributions, is like the flare, up and down their long, narrow faces, of the lamps of some general permanent "celebration".

You see the pin-cushion in profile, so to speak, on passing between Jersey City and Twenty-third Street, but you get it broadside on, this loose nosegay of architectural flowers, if you skirt the Battery, well out, and embrace the whole plantation. Then the "American beauty," the rose of interminable stem, becomes the token of the cluster at large – – to the degree that, positively, this is all that is wanted for emphasis of your final impression. Such growths, you feel, have confessedly arisen but to be "picked," in time, with a shears; nipped short off, by waiting fate, as soon as "science," applied to gain, has put upon the table, from far up its sleeve, some more winning card. Crowned not only with no history, but with no credible possibility of time for history, and consecrated by no uses save the commercial at any cost, they are simply the most piercing notes in that concert of the expensively provisional into which your supreme sense of New York resolves itself. They never begin to speak to you, in the manner of the builded majesties of the world as we have heretofore known such – towers or temples or fortresses or palaces – with the authority of things of permanence or even of things of long duration. One story is good only till another is told, and sky-scrapers are the last word of economic ingenuity only till another word be written.**99**

HENRY JAMES, *THE AMERICAN SCENE*,
INDIANA UNIVERSITY PRESS, BLOOMINGTON
AND LONDON, 1968

RAPID RUINS

G.K. Chesterton (1874–1936), the English journalist, novelist and short-story writer, was impressed by the industry of the city's builders.

66There is one point, almost to be called a paradox, to be noted about New York; and that is that in one sense it is really new. The term very seldom has any relevance to the reality. . . . But there is a sense in which New York is always new; in the sense that it is always being renewed. A stranger might well say that the chief industry of the citizens consists of destroying their city; but he soon realises that they always start it all over again

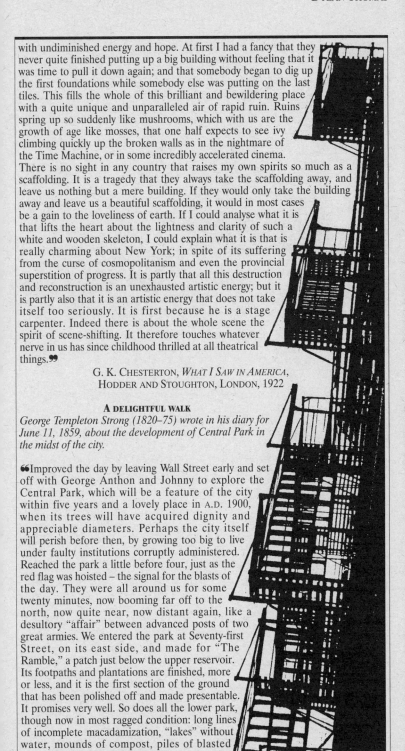

with undiminished energy and hope. At first I had a fancy that they never quite finished putting up a big building without feeling that it was time to pull it down again; and that somebody began to dig up the first foundations while somebody else was putting on the last tiles. This fills the whole of this brilliant and bewildering place with a quite unique and unparalleled air of rapid ruin. Ruins spring up so suddenly like mushrooms, which with us are the growth of age like mosses, that one half expects to see ivy climbing quickly up the broken walls as in the nightmare of the Time Machine, or in some incredibly accelerated cinema. There is no sight in any country that raises my own spirits so much as a scaffolding. It is a tragedy that they always take the scaffolding away, and leave us nothing but a mere building. If they would only take the building away and leave us a beautiful scaffolding, it would in most cases be a gain to the loveliness of earth. If I could analyse what it is that lifts the heart about the lightness and clarity of such a white and wooden skeleton, I could explain what it is that is really charming about New York; in spite of its suffering from the curse of cosmopolitanism and even the provincial superstition of progress. It is partly that all this destruction and reconstruction is an unexhausted artistic energy; but it is partly also that it is an artistic energy that does not take itself too seriously. It is first because he is a stage carpenter. Indeed there is about the whole scene the spirit of scene-shifting. It therefore touches whatever nerve in us has since childhood thrilled at all theatrical things.**

G. K. CHESTERTON, *WHAT I SAW IN AMERICA*,
HODDER AND STOUGHTON, LONDON, 1922

A DELIGHTFUL WALK
George Templeton Strong (1820–75) wrote in his diary for June 11, 1859, about the development of Central Park in the midst of the city.

**Improved the day by leaving Wall Street early and set off with George Anthon and Johnny to explore the Central Park, which will be a feature of the city within five years and a lovely place in A.D. 1900, when its trees will have acquired dignity and appreciable diameters. Perhaps the city itself will perish before then, by growing too big to live under faulty institutions corruptly administered. Reached the park a little before four, just as the red flag was hoisted – the signal for the blasts of the day. They were all around us for some twenty minutes, now booming far off to the north, now quite near, now distant again, like a desultory "affair" between advanced posts of two great armies. We entered the park at Seventy-first Street, on its east side, and made for "The Ramble," a patch just below the upper reservoir. Its footpaths and plantations are finished, more or less, and it is the first section of the ground that has been polished off and made presentable. It promises very well. So does all the lower park, though now in most ragged condition: long lines of incomplete macadamization, "lakes" without water, mounds of compost, piles of blasted stone, acres of what may be greensward hereafter but is now mere brown earth; groves of slender young transplanted maples and locusts, undecided between life and death, with here and there an arboricultural experiment that has failed utterly and is a mere broomstick with ramifications. Celts, caravans of dirt carts, derricks, steam engines, are the elements out of which our future Pleasaunce is rapidly developing. The work seems pushed with vigor and system, and as far as it has gone, looks thorough and substantial. A small army of Hibernians is distributed over the ground. Narrowness is its chief drawback. One sees quite across this *Rus in Urbe* at many points. This will be less felt as the trees grow. The tract seems to have been judiciously laid out. Roads and paths twist about in curves of artistic tortuosity. A broad avenue, exceptionally straight (at the lower end of the park) with a quadruple row of elms, will look Versailles-y by A.D. 1950. On the Fifth Avenue side, the hideous State Arsenal building stares at students of the picturesque, an eyesore that no landscape gardening can alleviate. Let us hope it will soon be destroyed by an accidental fire. From the summit of the rock mount in which "The Ramble" culminates, and from the little wooden framework of an observatory or signal flag tower thereon erected, the upper reservoir (lying on the north) is an agreeable object, notwithstanding the formalism of its straight lines. Johnny was delighted with his walk . . . 99

THE DIARY OF GEORGE TEMPLETON STRONG,
THE MACMILLAN PUBLISHING COMPANY, NEW YORK, 1952

BROADWAY

The Russian futurist poet Vladimir Mayakovsky (1893–1930) was often out of favor with government regimes in his homeland but after his suicide, he was acclaimed by Stalin as "the best and most talented poet of our Soviet epoch".

66Tarmac like glass.
                    A clang with each step.
Trees,
        and blades of grass,
                        with crew-cuts.
Avenues
           run
               from North to South,
and streets
           from East to West.
Between –
           who could have stretched them that far! –
buildings
           a good mile high.
Some houses seem to touch
                 the stars,
while others
            reach for the sky.
Most Yanks are too idle
                to go out walking.
They ride express
             elevators
                  throughout.

At seven hundred hours
 the human tide rolls in.
And at seventeen hundred
 rolls out.
Machines
 rattle
 clatter
 chink
pedestrians
 go deaf and dumb,
while past them more
 dumb people sprint
only stopping
 to spit out their chewing gum.
Yelling at a friend:
 'Make money!'
A mother suckles her child:
 'Don't holler!'
And the kid,
 with its nostrils runny
looks less like it sucks a breast than
 a dollar
and like everyone else,
 in a hurry.
The workday done,
 now all around
you're battered by
 electric hurricanes.
You take the subway,
 vanish underground,
or climb
 on the elevated
 train.
You can ride as high
 as a chimney stack
or dart
 between the feet of a house.
On Brooklyn Bridge, a tram
 snakes its back
or under the Hudson,
 sneaks like a mouse.**"**

VLADIMIR MAYAKOVSKY, *BROADWAY*

THE VILLAGE
The development of Greenwich Village is described by Edmund Wilson (1895–1972) in his novel "I Thought of Daisy".

"Among those tangled irregular streets to the west of Washington Square, I caught occasionally, from the taxi, a glimpse, almost eighteenth-century, of a lampless, black-windowed street-end where the street-urchins, shrieking in the silence, were stacking up bonfires in the snow – those lost corners of the old provincial city, where the traffic of the upper metropolis no longer gnashed iron teeth, no longer oppressed the pavements with its grindings and its groans – where those soft moans and hoots of the shipping washed the island from the western shore. There they had come, those heroes of my youth, the artists and the prophets

of the Village, from the American factories and farms, from the farthest towns and prairies – there they had found it possible to leave behind them the constraints and self-consciousness of their homes, the shame of not making money – there they had lived with their own imaginations and followed their own thought. I did not know that, with the coming of a second race, of which Ray Coleman, without my divining it, had already appeared as one of the forerunners – a mere miscellaneous hiving of New Yorkers like those in any other part of town, with no leisure and no beliefs – I did not know that I was soon to see the whole quarter fall a victim to the landlords and the real-estate speculators, who would raise the rents and wreck the old houses – till the sooty peeling fronts of the south side of Washington Square, to whose mysterious studios, when I had first come to live in the Village, I had so much longed some day to be admitted, should be replaced by fresh arty pinks – till the very guardian façades of the north side should be gutted of their ancient grandeurs and crammed tight with economized cells – till the very configuration of the streets should be wiped out, during a few summer months when I had been out of New York on vacation, by the obliteration of whole blocks, whole familiar neighborhoods – and till finally the beauty of the Square, the pattern of the park and the arch, the proportions of everything, should be spoiled by the first peaks of a mountain-range of modern apartment-houses (with electric refrigerators, uniformed elevator boys and, on the street-level, those smartly furnished restaurants in which Hugo was soon to be horrified at finding copies of *Town and Country*), dominating and crushing the Village, so that at last it seemed to survive as a base for those gigantic featureless mounds, swollen, clumsy, blunt, bleaching dismally with sandy yellow walls that sunlight which once, in the autumn, on the old fronts of the northern side, still the masters of their open plaza – when the shadows of the leafless trees seemed to drift across them like clouds – had warmed their roses to red.**

EDMUND WILSON, *I Thought of Daisy*,
W. H. ALLEN, LONDON, 1920

FERRYBOAT RIDE

The novel "Manhattan Transfer" by John dos Passos (1896–1970) is a collection of hundreds of fictional and atmospheric episodes that take place in New York. The following extract describes a trip on the Ellis Island Ferry.

**It was blowing cold in his face and he was sitting on the front of a ferryboat when he came to. His teeth were chattering, he was shivering . . . .

Across the zinc water the tall walls, the birchlike cluster of downtown buildings shimmered up the rosy morning like a sound of horns through a chocolatebrown haze. As the boat drew near the buildings densened to a granite mountain split with knifecut canyons. The ferry passed close to a tubby steamer that rode at anchor listing towards Stan so that he could see all the decks. An Ellis Island tug was alongside. A stale smell came from the decks packed with upturned faces like a load of melons. Three gulls wheeled complaining. A gull soared in a spiral, white wings caught the sun, the gull skimmed motionless in whitegold light. The rim of the sun had risen above the plumcolored band of clouds behind East New York. A million windows flashed with light. A rasp and a humming came from the city. . . .

In the whitening light tinfoil gulls wheeled above broken boxes, spoiled cabbageheads, orangerinds heaving slowly between the splintered plank walls, the green spumed under the round bow as the ferry skidding on the tide, gulped the broken water, crashed, slid, settled slowly into the slip. Handwinches whirled with jingle of chains, gates folded upward. Stan stepped across the crack, staggered up the manuresmelling wooden tunnel of the ferryhouse out into the sunny glass and benches of the Battery. He sat down on a bench, clasped his hands round his knees to keep them from shaking so. His mind went on jingling like a mechanical piano.

There was Babylon and Nineveh, they were built of brick. Athens was goldmarble columns. Rome was held up on broad arches of rubble. In Constantinople the minarets flame like great candles round the Golden Horn. . . . O there's one more river to cross. Steel, glass, tile, concrete will be the materials of the skyscrapers. Crammed on the narrow island the millionwindowed buildings will jut, glittering pyramid on pyramid, white cloudsheads piled above a thunder storm . . .
Kerist I wish I was a skyscraper.**99**

JOHN DOS PASSOS, *MANHATTAN TRANSFER*,
HARPER AND BROTHERS, NEW YORK AND LONDON, 1925

RAMSHACKLE STREETS
Joseph Heller, the novelist, was born in New York in 1923. His novel "Good As Gold" satirizes the politics of the city and this particular extract describes a drive along the southern rim of Brooklyn.

66Following the smooth parkway as it curved with the shoreline to the east, he soon saw in the distance on his right the gaunt structure of the defunct Parachute Jump standing on the narrow spit of land across Gravesend Bay and recalled, with some pride in his upbringing, how that Parachute Jump, the hit of the World's Fair in New York in 1939 or '40, was moved to the Steeplechase boardwalk afterward but had never proved adequately perilous for success to an indigenous population trained on the Cyclone and the Thunderbolt and on the Mile Sky Chaser in Luna Park. Now it looked forlorn: no one owned it and no one would take it away. Like those haunted, half-completed luxury apartment houses in Manhattan whose builders had run out of money and whose banks would not supply more, gaping with dismal failure and aging already into blackest decrepitude before they ever shone spanking new. A moment later came the skeletal outline of the giant Wonder Wheel, idled for the year by the chilly season, the only Ferris wheel left in Coney Island now that Steeplechase, the Funny Place, was bankrupt and gone. Hard times had descended there as in other places. Where Luna Park had last whirred in bright lights on summer evenings over thirty years earlier there now rose a complex of

high, honeycombed brick dwellings that looked drabber than ordinary against the lackluster sky. On the overpass spanning Ocean Parkway Gold turned his head for a speeding glimpse of Abraham Lincoln High School and bemoaned for the thousandth time the vile chance that had located him in classes there the same time as Belle and gulled him into a mismanaged destiny of three dependent children and a wife so steadfast. If a man marries young, he reasoned aristocratically in the self-conscious mode of a Lord Chesterfield or a Benjamin Franklin, as Gold himself had been minded to do, it will likely be to someone near him in age; and just about the time he learns really to enjoy living with a young girl and soars into his prime, she will be getting old. He would pass that precious homiletic intelligence on to both sons, if he remembered. If only Belle were fickle, mercenary, deceitful. Even her health was good.
He turned off the parkway past Brighton at the exit leading toward Sheepshead Bay and Manhattan Beach. The slender crescent on the southern rim of Brooklyn through which he'd driven was just about the only section of the area with which he was familiar. Almost all of the rest was foreign to him and forbidding. His thoughts went back to a ramshackle street he'd passed minutes before on which stood the same moldering antique police station to which he'd been brought as a small child

the day Sid had abandoned him and gone off with his friends. What a heartless thing to have done. Gold must have been numb as he waited in the precinct house. If they asked him his address he might not have known it. The nearest telephone to his house then was in a candy store at the trolley stop on the corner of Railroad Avenue. Just a few years later he was earning two-cent tips for summoning girls from the flats for calls from boys phoning for dates. Brooklyn was a big fucking borough.**99**

JOSEPH HELLER, *GOOD AS GOLD*, JONATHAN CAPE, LONDON, 1979

BAYMEN
Joseph Mitchell (b. 1908) reminds us that New York is situated on the ocean and many make their living from fishing.

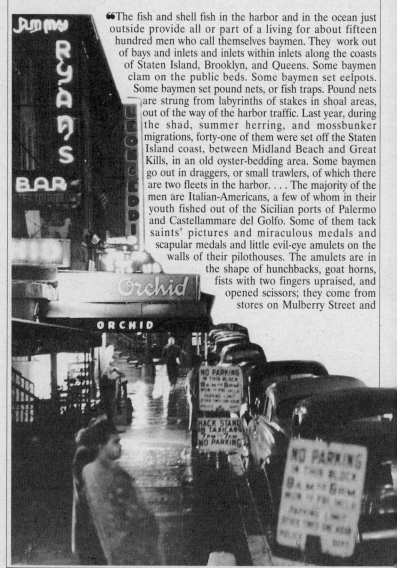

66The fish and shell fish in the harbor and in the ocean just outside provide all or part of a living for about fifteen hundred men who call themselves baymen. They work out of bays and inlets and inlets within inlets along the coasts of Staten Island, Brooklyn, and Queens. Some baymen clam on the public beds. Some baymen set eelpots. Some baymen set pound nets, or fish traps. Pound nets are strung from labyrinths of stakes in shoal areas, out of the way of the harbor traffic. Last year, during the shad, summer herring, and mossbunker migrations, forty-one of them were set off the Staten Island coast, between Midland Beach and Great Kills, in an old oyster-bedding area. Some baymen go out in draggers, or small trawlers, of which there are two fleets in the harbor. . . . The majority of the men are Italian-Americans, a few of whom in their youth fished out of the Sicilian ports of Palermo and Castellammare del Golfo. Some of them tack saints' pictures and miraculous medals and scapular medals and little evil-eye amulets on the walls of their pilothouses. The amulets are in the shape of hunchbacks, goat horns, fists with two fingers upraised, and opened scissors; they come from stores on Mulberry Street and

are made of plastic. The harbor draggers range from thirty to fifty feet and carry two to five men. According to the weather and the season, they drag their baglike nets in the Lower Bay or in a fishing ground called the Mud Hole, which lies south of Scotland and Ambrose lightships and is about fifteen miles long and five to ten miles wide. The Mud Hole is the upper part of the Old Hudson River Canyon, which was the bed of the river twenty thousand years ago, when the river flowed a hundred and twenty-five miles past what is now Sandy Hook before it reached the ocean. The draggers catch lower-depth and bottom feeders, chiefly whiting, butterfish, ling, cod, porgy, fluke, and flounder. They go out around 4 A.M. and return around 4 P. M., and their catches are picked up by trucks and taken to Fulton Market.**99**

JOSEPH MITCHELL, *UP IN THE OLD HOTEL*,
PANTHEON BOOKS, NEW YORK, 1992

LIFE IN THE CITY

WALKING ON MIRRORS

Wallace Stevens (1879–1955), the American poet, made the following entries in his journal in the year 1900, during a visit to New York.

66Took dinner in a little restaurant – poached eggs, coffee and three crusts of bread – a week ago my belly was swagging with strawberries. Bought a couple of newspapers from a little fellow with blue eyes who was selling *Journals* and *Worlds* & who had to ransack the neighborhood for the ones I wanted. As I came back to my room the steps of the street for squares were covered with boarders etc. leaning on railings and picking their teeth. The end of the street was ablaze with a cloud of dust lit by the sun. All around me were tall office buildings closed up for the night. The curtains were drawn and the faces of the buildings looked hard and cruel and lifeless. This street of mine is a wonderful thing. Just now the voices of children manage to come through my window from out it, over the roofs and through the walls.

All New York, as I have seen it, is for sale – and I think the parts I have seen are the parts that make New York what it is. It is dominated by necessity. Everything has its price – from Vice to Virtue. I do not like it and unless I get some position that is unusually attractive I shall not stay. What is there to keep me, for example, in a place where all Beauty is on exhibition, all Power a tool of Selfishness, and all Generosity a source of Vanity? New York is a field of tireless and antagonistic interests – undoubtedly fascinating but horribly unreal. Everybody is looking at everybody else – a foolish crowd walking on mirrors. I am rather glad to be here for the short time that I intend to stay – it makes me appreciate the opposite of it all. Thank Heaven the winds are not generated in Yorkville, or the clouds manufactured in Harlem. What a price they would bring!

The carpet on the floor of my room is gray set off with pink roses. In the bathroom is a rug with the figure of a peacock woven in it – blue and scarlet, and black, and green, and gold. And on the paper on my wall are designs of fleur-de-lis and forget-me-not. Flowers and birds enough of rags and paper – but no more. In this Eden, made spicey with the smoke of my pipe which hangs heavy in the ceiling in this Paradise ringing with the bells of streetcars and the bustle of fellow boarders heard through the thin partitions, in this Elysium of Elysiums I now shall lay me down.**99**

66June 17, Sunday.

Last night I sat in an open square near the Washington Arch. A man passed me with his coat tightly buttoned, his hands in his trousers pockets, his head bent and his hat well pulled-down. His clothes were in rags. As he started to cross Fifth Avenue a 'bus drove by and he stopped to let it pass. On the top of the 'bus was a group of girls in neat Spring jackets and bonnets covered with cherries and roses.

This morning the church bells are ringing.

New York is the most egotistical place in the world.**"**

FROM HOLLY STEVENS, *SOUVENIRS AND PROPHECIES*,
ALFRED A. KNOPF INC., NEW YORK, 1977

THE JANITOR

The Russian politician Lev Trotsky (1879–1940) was expelled from his homeland in 1924. He and his family wandered from country to country for a while before settling in Mexico. The following extract from his autobiography describes a spell in New York.

"We rented an apartment in a workers' district, and furnished it on the instalment plan. That apartment, at eighteen dollars a month, was equipped with all sorts of conveniences that we Europeans were quite unused to: electric lights, gas cooking-range, bath, telephone, automatic service-elevator, and even a chute for the garbage. These things completely won the boys over to New York. For a time the telephone was their main interest; we had not had this mysterious instrument either in Vienna or Paris.

The janitor of the house was a negro. My wife paid him three months' rent in advance, but he gave her no receipt because the landlord had taken the receipt-book away the day before, to verify the accounts. When we moved into the house two days later, we discovered that the negro had absconded with the rent of several of the tenants. Besides the money, we had intrusted to him the storage of some of our belongings. The whole incident upset us; it was such a bad beginning. But we found our property after all, and when we opened the wooden box that contained our crockery, we were surprised to find our money hidden away in it, carefully wrapped up in paper. The janitor had taken the money of the tenants who had already received their receipts; he did not mind robbing the landlord, but he was considerate enough not to rob the tenants. A delicate fellow indeed. My wife and I were deeply touched by his consideration and we always think of him gratefully. This little incident took on a  symptomatic significance for me – it seemed as if a corner of the veil that concealed the "black" problem in the United States had lifted.**"**

LEV TROTSKY, *MY LIFE*, CHARLES SCRIBNER'S SONS, NEW YORK, 1930

BEAUTIFUL GIRLS

Ogden Nash (1902–71) was famous for his light verse, of which the following is a good example.

"In New York beautiful girls can become more beautiful
by going to Elizabeth Arden,

> **"A HUNDRED TIMES I HAVE THOUGHT, NEW YORK IS A CATASTROPHE, AND FIFTY TIMES: IT IS A BEAUTIFUL CATASTROPHE."**
>
> LE CORBUSIER

And getting stuff to put on their faces and waiting for
        it to harden,
And poor girls with nothing to their names but a letter
        or two can get rich and joyous
From a brief trip to their loyous.
So I can say with impunity
That New York is a land of opportunity.
It also has many fine theatres and hotels,
And a lot of taxis, buses, subways and els,
Best of all, if you don't show up at the office or at a
        tea nobody will bother their head,
They will just think you are dead.
That's why I really think New York is exquisite.
And someday I'm going to pay it a visit. **"**

OGDEN NASH, *A BRIEF GUIDE TO NEW YORK*,
FROM *"VERSES FROM 1929 ON"*, 1940

THE HARLEM RENAISSANCE

Langston Hughes (1902–67) was one of the most important figures of the Harlem Renaissance. Discovered by the poet Vachel Lindsay, he wrote poetry, plays, and novels whose language resonated with dialect and jazz rhythms. In "The Big Sea" (1940), his autobiography, Hughes recounts a fascinating life in Paris and Harlem when "the Negro was in vogue".

"White people began to come to Harlem in droves. For several years they packed the expensive Cotton Club on Lenox Avenue. But I was never there, because the Cotton Club was a Jim Crow club for gangsters and monied whites. They were not cordial to Negro patronage, unless you were a celebrity like Bojangles. So Harlem Negroes did not like the Cotton Club and never appreciated its Jim Crow policy in the very heart of their dark community. Nor did ordinary Negroes like the growing influx of whites toward Harlem after sundown, flooding the little caberets and bars where formerly only colored people laughed and sang, and where now the strangers were given the best ringside tables to sit and stare at the Negro customers – like amusing animals in a zoo.

The Negroes said: 'We can't go downtown and sit and stare at you in your clubs. You won't even let us in your clubs.' But they didn't say it out loud – for Negroes are practically never rude to white people. So thousands of whites came to Harlem night after night, thinking the Negroes loved to have them there, and firmly believing that all Harlemites left their houses at sundown to sing and dance in cabarets, because most of the whites saw nothing but the cabarets, not the houses.

Some of the owners of Harlem clubs, delighted at the flood of white patronage, made the grievous error of barring their own race, after the manner of the famous Cotton Club. But most of these quickly lost business and folded up, because they failed to realize that a large part of the Harlem attraction for downtown New Yorkers lay in simply watching the colored customers amuse themselves. And the smaller clubs, of course, had no big floor shows or a name band like the Cotton Club, where Duke Ellington usually held forth, so, without black patronage, they were not amusing at all. **"**

LANGSTON HUGHES, *THE BIG SEA*, 1940

A COLLAPSING CITY

The following piece by John Updike (1932–), the American novelist, short-story writer and poet, comes from an essay entitled "Is New York City Inhabitable?"

127

66New York is of course many cities, and an exile does not return to the one he left. I left, in April of 1957, a floor-through apartment on West Thirteenth Street, and return, when I do, to midtown hotels and the Upper East Side apartments of obliging friends. The Village, with its bookstores and framer's shops, its bricked-in literary memories and lingering bohemian redolence, is off the track of a professional visit – an elevator-propelled whirl in and out of high-rise offices and prix-fixe restaurants. Nevertheless, I feel confident in saying that the disadvantages of New York life which led me to leave have intensified rather than abated, and that the city which Le Corbusier described as a magnificent disaster is less and less magnificent. Always, as one arrives, there is the old acceleration of the pulse – the mountainous gray skyline glimpsed from the Triboro Bridge, the cheerful games of basketball and handball being played on the recreational asphalt beside the FDR Drive, the startling, steamy, rain-splotched intimacy of the side streets where one's taxi slows to a crawl, the careless flung beauty of the pedestrians clumped at the street corners. So many faces, costumes, packages, errands! So many preoccupations, hopes, passions, lives in progress! So much human stuff, clustering and streaming with a languid colorful impatience like the pheromone-coded mass maneuvers of bees! But soon the faces and their individual expressions merge and vanish under a dulling insistent pressure, the thrum and push of congestion. As ever more office buildings are heaped upon the East Fifties – the hugest of them, the slant-topped white Citicorp building, clearly about to fall off its stilts onto your head – and an ever-greater number of impromptu merchants spread their dubiously legal wares on the sidewalks, even pedestrian traffic jams. One is tripped, hassled, detoured. Buskers and beggars cram every available niche. The sidewalks and subway platforms, generously designed in the last century, have been overwhelmed on both the minor and major entrepreneurial scales. The Manhattan grid, that fine old machine for living, now sticks and grinds at every intersection and the discreet brownstones of the side streets look down upon a clogged nightmare of perpetual reconstruction and insolent double parking. Even a sunny day feels like a tornado of confusion one is hurrying to get out of, into the sanctum of the hotel room, the office, the friendly apartment. New York is a city with virtually no habitable public space – only private spaces expensively maintained within the general disaster. While popular journalism focuses on the possible collapse of Los Angeles and San Francisco into chasms opened by earthquakes, here on the East Coast, on its oblong of solid granite, the country's greatest city is sinking into the chasm of itself.99

JOHN UPDIKE, *ODD JOBS*, ALFRED A. KNOPF INC.,
NEW YORK, 1991

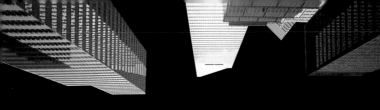

New York
ITINERARIES

AROUND THE WORLD TRADE CENTER, *135*
STATUE OF LIBERTY, *144*
ELLIS ISLAND, *148*
NEW YORK STOCK EXCHANGE, *164*
AROUND CITY HALL, *167*
SOUTH STREET SEAPORT MUSEUM, *172*
WOOLWORTH BUILDING, *180*
FOLEY SQUARE, *182*
BROOKLYN BRIDGE, *186*
LOWER EAST SIDE, *189*
AROUND WASHINGTON SQUARE, *197*
GREENWICH VILLAGE, *210*
AROUND UNION SQUARE, *221*
AROUND GRAND CENTRAL TERMINAL, *235*
EMPIRE STATE BUILDING, *242*
THEATER DISTRICT, *258*
THE UNITED NATIONS, *263*
CHRYSLER BUILDING, *266*
AROUND ROCKEFELLER CENTER, *273*
MOMA, *290*
AROUND CENTRAL PARK, *307*
CENTRAL PARK, *314*
FRICK COLLECTION, *322*
WHITNEY MUSEUM, *326*
METROPOLITAN MUSEUM, *328*
GUGGENHEIM MUSEUM, *338*
MORNINGSIDE HEIGHTS AND HARLEM, *350*
ST. JOHN THE DIVINE, *354*
THE CLOISTERS, *362*
BROOKLYN HEIGHTS, *366*

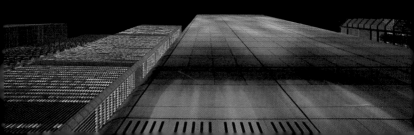

▲ The World Trade Center   90 West St., with the World Trade Center in the background ▼

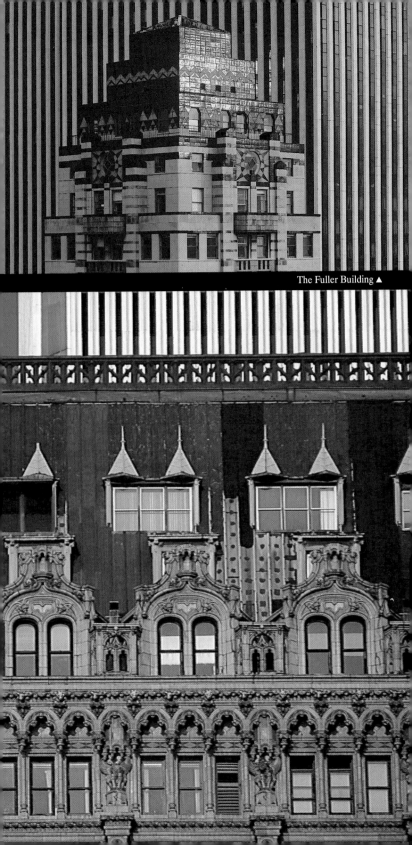

The Fuller Building ▲

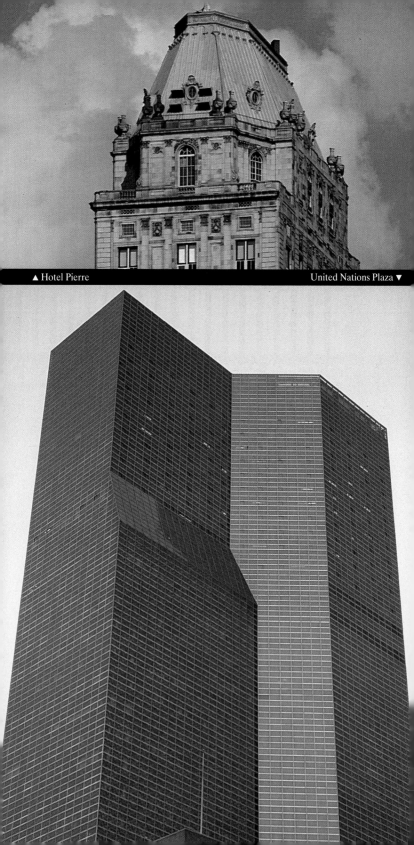

▲ Hotel Pierre

United Nations Plaza ▼

▲ World Financial Center

The American Standard Building ▼

▲ 3 Park Ave.

The Waldorf-Astoria Hotel ▼

AROUND THE
WORLD TRADE CENTER

WORLD TRADE CENTER
TO BATTERY PARK,
VIA THE SEA FRONT, *138*
ROD KNOX
THE STATUE OF LIBERTY, *144*
Catherine Hodeir
ELLIS ISLAND, *148*
Nancy Green
WORLD TRADE CENTER
TO BATTERY PARK
VIA BROADWAY, *152*
ROD KNOX
WORLD TRADE CENTER
TO THE FINANCIAL DISTRICT, *158*
ROD KNOX
NEW YORK STOCK EXCHANGE, *164*
ROD KNOX

▲ WORLD TRADE CENTER

1 CASTLE CLINTON
2 PIER A
3 MARINE MEMORIAL
4 1 BROADWAY
5 BROOKLYN TUNNEL
ENTRANCE
6 DOWNTOWN
ATHLETIC CLUB
7 CUNARD BLDG.
8 29 BROADWAY
9 TRINITY CHURCH
10 90 WEST ST.
11 THAMES TWINS
12 1 LIBERTY PLAZA

13 EAST RIVER SAVINGS
BANK
14 WORLD FINANCIAL
CENTER
15 WORLD TRADE
CENTER
16 ROCKEFELLER BLDG.
17 EMPIRE STATE BLDG.
18 WOOLWORTH BLDG.
19 BATTERY MARITIME
BLDG.
20 U.S. CUSTOM HOUSE
21 FRAUNCES TAVERN
22 BOWLING GREEN

23 85 BROAD ST.
24 26 BROADWAY
25 67 BROAD ST.
26 INDIA HOUSE
27 N.Y. STOCK
EXCHANGE
28 55 WALL ST.

BROOKLYN BRIDGE

EAST RIVER

STATE ST.

WATER ST.

HELIPORT

32 40 Wall St.
33 60 Wall St.
34 South Street
Seaport
35 Equitable Bldg.
36 Federal Reserve
Bank
37 70 Pine St.
38 Chase Manhattan
Bank
39 Liberty Tower
40 Federal Hall
41 Delmonico's
42 Municipal Bldg.

29 20 Exchange
Place
30 63 Wall St.
31 48 Wall St.

▲ WORLD TRADE CENTER
TO BATTERY PARK VIA THE SEA FRONT

Downtown Manhattan, the southern tip of the island, includes the Financial District, the World Trade Center, Battery Park and Battery Park City. Its early settlers – first the Dutch then the English – laid out narrow, winding streets here. The oldest of these, whose names date back as far as the 17th century, as well as their plan – borrowed from that of Amsterdam – testify to this initial occupation. And, as was the case in the parent city, some of these streets, notably Broad Street, started life as a canal ● *32*. Others, built later, reflect the well-known Dutch practice of reclaiming land from the sea by drainage; in fact, over the centuries, Manhattan has expanded well beyond its original boundaries ■ *18*, ● *72*. When the Dutch settled there, the shape of the shoreline differed greatly from its present one. It ran alongside WATER STREET to the east, along GREENWICH STREET to the west and along STATE STREET to the south. The acres of land that were gradually gained – due to a buildup of abandoned ships, detritus, earth from excavation work for the construction of buildings and subway lines – are now some of the most expensive in the world. Among the few remaining traces in Downtown of the English colonial period is the cemetery of TRINITY CHURCH, where some of the most famous names in American colonial history are buried. Just opposite, on the other side of Broadway, is Wall Street, the heart of the Financial District, which bankers and stockbrokers call simply "The Street". A harbor city, New York has grown through trade and shipping. Offshore in the distance stand the Statue of Liberty ▲ *144* and Ellis Island ▲ *148*, witnesses to the arrival of immigrants in their thousands. Over the centuries architects have ceaselessly rebuilt the city on top of this piece of original territory, where all the different layers of its history are now superimposed. The best time to visit Lower Manhattan is during the week; on weekends it is deserted.

AROUND THE WORLD TRADE CENTER

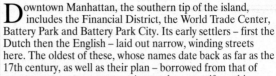

WORLD TRADE CENTER. BETWEEN CHURCH, LIBERTY, WEST AND VESEY STS. (1976, arch. Minoru Yamasaki & Assocs.; Emery Roth & Son). The World Trade Center is a complex of seven buildings grouped around a vast PLAZA, dominated by the 110-story TWIN TOWERS ★. It is the property of the port authorities of the states of New York and New Jersey and was designed to attract international companies to Lower Manhattan, which was experiencing a massive exodus of jobs to Midtown. The beginnings of the complex were problematic, and in order to avoid financial disaster, the State of New York rented out most of the buildings. Today it is a flourishing business center, a base for five hundred international companies which provide jobs for 50,000 people. The Center has

> **"THE WORLD TRADE CENTER LIKE AN ILLUMINATED COMPUTER, WITH ITS TWO TOWERS LIKE TALL VISUAL DISPLAY UNITS..."**
> PHILIPPE SOLLERS

"KING KONG"
Unlike the original legendary movie by Merian Cooper and Ernest B. Schoedsack (1933), in which the giant gorilla takes refuge at the top of the Empire State

Building ▲ *242*, the remake of 1976, by John Guillermin, uses the even-dizzier heights of the World Trade Center as the backdrop for the gorilla-hero's escape and death.

The World Trade Center seen from Brooklyn.

LOBBY OF THE WORLD TRADE CENTER
Thanks to a new structural design, the exterior walls of the towers bear most of the load, creating vast interior spaces. The lobby, on two levels, serves as a transition between the plaza and the lower street level.

also become one of the city's main tourist attractions, with 80,000 visitors per day. The towers of the World Trade Center, 1,350 feet high, are the highest points in the city and the second-highest in the world, after the Sears Tower in Chicago. The view over Manhattan from the top is not to be missed; it can be enjoyed from the observation deck of Tower Two. (The restaurant Windows on the World, at the top of Tower One, is closed at least until 1995.) From either vantage point you can see Manhattan spreading off to the north, cradled in the arms of the Hudson and the East River. The most famous skyscrapers can easily be pinpointed: in the distance, the graceful spire of the Empire State Building and the playful Chrysler Building are easily distinguished. Farther into the distance you have a panoramic view over the bay, the four other boroughs of New York and the surrounding countryside. On a clear day, you can even discern the curvature of the Earth! Looking downward, you plumb the depths of the "canyons" of the Financial District, with its own idiosyncratic building tops. In 1974 the French tightrope walker Philippe Petit crossed the gap between the towers on a high wire without a safety net. The following year the mountaineer George Willig scaled these giants, by designing a special tool that fit into the window washing tracks. In 1993 the parking garage and the lower ground floor, which has its own subway station and a shopping concourse including 70 stores, were badly damaged by a bomb attack which claimed six victims.

Because 90 West St. was designed to be seen from a distance, its crown is dramatically illuminated at night.

Interior of the New York Telephone Building.

SAINT NICHOLAS PROCESSION
On January 6 (the feast of Epiphany, the Greek Orthodox parishioners of St. Nicholas' Church process to Battery Park, where divers perform the ritual of searching for a wooden cross in the harbor waters.

BARCLAY–VESEY/NEW YORK TELEPHONE CO. BUILDING ★. 140 WEST ST., BETWEEN BARCLAY AND VESEY STS. (1923–6, arch. Ralph Walker, McKenzie, Voorhees & Gmelin) ● *98*. When this Art Deco building, located north of the World Trade Center, was completed, it was considered so striking an expression of the new industrial age that its designers were awarded the Architectural League of New York's gold medal of honor for 1927. The lobby, which runs the length of the building and which can be entered via Washington Street, is well worth a visit. The lobby floor is covered with bronze plates, which depict the workers laying the New York telephone system and the ceiling frescoes retrace the history of communication. To see the whole building at its best, you need only walk back to West Street then head toward the Hudson.

90 WEST STREET ★. (1905, arch. Cass Gilbert). This 23-story building was one of the first New York skyscrapers constructed using a fire-resistant frame. The lavish decoration of the neo-Gothic façade becomes increasingly more intricate as the building rises, culminating in an extravaganza of stalactites dripping from a cornice supported by consoles.

ST. NICHOLAS GREEK ORTHODOX CHURCH. 155 CEDAR ST. (1832). This Greek Orthodox chapel is a reminder that the district was once home to a Greek community. In 1920, the Hellenic Orthodox Church of Saint Nicholas bought this building, which was originally a private house, then a bar. Its upkeep is now seen to by a handful of parishioners, who stubbornly reject repeated offers from real estate developers. The fact that it sits in the middle of a parking lot, in close proximity to the Twin Towers, makes it one of the most incongruous sights in Downtown Manhattan.

West St., looking toward Liberty St., in 1900.

BATTERY PARK CITY

BATTERY PARK CITY. (1979, arch. Cooper Eckstut Associates). This vast complex of 112 acres, comprising offices, apartment buildings and open spaces, is located west of WEST STREET between BATTERY PARK to the south and CHAMBERS STREET to the north. It was built on top of landfill ■ *19* which was supplied partly by excavation work when the foundations of the World Trade Center were laid. The architects at Cooper Eckstut, who designed Battery Park City, did their utmost to respect the surrounding architecture and the natural environment. The World Financial Center consists of four stocky polished granite and glass towers, crowned with geometrically shaped roofs which identify their owners: a stepped pyramid (Merrill Lynch), a solid pyramid (American Express), a mastaba (Dow Jones and Oppenheimer). The luxurious, showy lobbies of the Center, with their wealth of materials, including polychromatic marble flooring and shiny black columns, are connected to the World Trade Center by two walkways, called North Bridge and South Bridge which cross West Street. The WINTER GARDEN, a pavilion that sits at the entrance to the World Financial Center, acts as a focus for the groups of buildings and thoroughfares that make up the Battery Park City complex. This building is a huge glass house planted with giant palm trees.

THE WORLD FINANCIAL CENTER. (1985, design arch. Cesar Pelli) ● *103.* The center consists of four towers which surround NORTH COVE MARINA, forming what one critic has enthusiastically described as a "Saint Mark's Square on the Hudson". The guardrail along the marina's esplanade is engraved with quotations from WALT WHITMAN and THOMAS O'HARA, former inhabitants of Lower Manhattan, celebrating the history and beauty of this site.

THE HOBOKEN FERRY. The landing stage for the ferry – whose nickname, the "Penguin Boat", is derived from the number of sober-suited executives ferried daily between the Financial District and Hoboken – is situated at the northernmost tip of North Cove. The crossing affords a wonderful view of Manhattan. Hoboken is the birthplace of Frank Sinatra. It also served as the setting for Elia Kazan's film *On the Waterfront* (1954) starring Marlon Brando.

A UTOPIAN PROJECT
An extensive redevelopment program for Manhattan's West Side waterfront proposed to cover the riverside walkway with a vast park which would have run alongside the Hudson from Battery Park to the George Washington Bridge. The then governor of New York, Nelson Rockefeller, talked of swimming once again in the "purified" waters of the river and of a reduction in the levels of air pollution in Manhattan. Battery Park City is a later manifestation of this aborted project.

ON THE WATERFRONT
Marlon Brando in a scene (below) from Elia Kazan's movie *On the Waterfront*. New York Harbor provides a realistic backdrop for a story of union corruption and for the private drama of a weak man who, in his search for happiness, is plagued by his conscience.

On The Waterfront

View of New York Harbor in 1878.

COMMEMORATIVE MONUMENTS
A number of memorials have been built in the vicinity of Battery Park. The American Merchant Mariners' Memorial. This sculpture (1991) by Marisol, inspired by a news photo from World War Two, is southeast of Pier A. In the park there is

the John Ericsson Memorial, dedicated to the designer of the *Monitor* ▲ *174*, the Netherlands Memorial Monument, commemorating the purchase of Manhattan from the Indians, and the Verrazano Memorial in honor of the first European to sail into the bay.

STUYVESANT HIGH SCHOOL. 345 CHAMBERS ST. (1992, arch. Gruzen Stanton Steinglass). This high school (not shown on the map) is situated just north of Battery Park City. Founded in 1904, it is a still-thriving institution, with a sterling reputation which enables it to recruit 3,000 of the brightest students in the city by means of extremely competitive examinations. The school has recently taken up residence in this monumental Postmodern building.

ESPLANADE AND SOUTH COVE ★. The esplanade (built in 1983) was the first seafront park project to be created in New York since that of Brooklyn Heights ▲ *366*. It affords magnificent views of the harbor. South Cove, with its rocks, wooden piers and wild grasses, evokes Manhattan's shoreline at the beginning of the colonial period. The OBSERVATION DECK is an abstract replica of the crown worn by the Statue of Liberty, which it faces.

DOWNTOWN ATHLETIC CLUB. 19 WEST ST. (1930, arch. Starrett & Van Vleck). The architects of this building were members of a very exclusive club for male WASPs (White Anglo-Saxon Protestants). With a height of 535 feet, this 36-story building was one of the tallest in Manhattan for its time. Its glazed-tile and glass Art Deco ● *98–9* ornamentation is greatly admired. Every year the club awards the Heisman Trophy for the best college football player in the nation. To visit the Trophy Hall, lined with the portraits of prizewinners since 1935, take the elevator; press the button marked "H".

BATTERY PARK

The southern tip of Manhattan, once of paramount strategic importance, was until the early 1800's the site of batteries of artillery. Today the public gardens of Battery Park are now arranged around Castle Clinton, the old fort where tickets for Ellis Island and the Statue of Liberty ▲ *144* are sold.

A "NEW" FORT. In 1635, on the site of what is now the U.S. Custom House, the Dutch built FORT AMSTERDAM later re-named by the British FORT GEORGE. In addition, the British built another fort on a man-made island 295 feet offshore. Between 1807 and 1811, in anticipation of war with Britain, a new fort, designed by JOHN MCCOMB was erected on the island. This fortification, called West Battery, formed a pair with East Battery on Governor's Island at the entrance to the East River. In 1815 West Battery was demilitarized and renamed CASTLE CLINTON, probably in honor of the mayor of New

On September 11, 1850, Jenny Lind, the "Swedish Nightingale", made her American debut at Castle Garden, promoted by P. T. Barnum. The latter staged a controversy in the New York press by praising the diva in public while panning her singing performance in the press using various pseudonyms. This ruse pushed the ticket price up to $25 for her first night. Within several years the soprano was just a memory.

York, De Witt Clinton, who later as governor of the state instigated the construction of the Erie Canal ● *27*. Foreign dignitaries visiting New York were officially welcomed at Castle Clinton; among them was Lafayette who received a warm reception here in 1824. Earlier that year the fortress had been renamed Castle Garden and remodeled. Later, it became a concert hall seating 6,000 people. Here New Yorkers could attend opera for 50 cents. After it was declared bankrupt in 1855, Castle Garden was transformed into the main immigrant landing depot, where immigrants could obtain information, medical care, currency and job offers. By the time the center was transferred to Ellis Island ▲ *148,* in 1892, eight million people had already passed through its doors. The land between Castle Clinton's island and Manhattan was gradually filled in, and in 1896 the fort was transformed into the New York Aquarium, which attracted millions of visitors. The aquarium was closed in 1941 to permit the construction of the BROOKLYN-BATTERY TUNNEL, then was moved to Coney Island. The fort was saved from demolition by ELEANOR ROOSEVELT, restored and listed as a National Historic Monument in 1946.

PIER A ★. S. W. CORNER OF WEST ST. AND BATTERY PLACE (1886, eng. George Sears Green, Jr.). This is the oldest pier in Manhattan. In 1919, in homage to the victims of World War One, a clock tower was added. Its bells used to signal the watches that were kept on shipboard. Until 1959 the pier was used as a headquarters for the harbor police and the maritime fire department – whose flotilla used to greet steamships landing for the first time with fantastic volleys of water.

A FORT-AQUARIUM
The aquarium had numerous species on display to the public. It also served as a breeding farm for fish which were later released into the state's rivers.

Tip of Lower Manhattan (below) with Battery Park.

▲ THE STATUE OF LIBERTY

In 1886, the people of France presented the people of the United States with a huge statue, "Liberty Enlightening the World". The idea for the monument was conceived by Edouard-René Laboulaye, the champion of liberalism, as a symbol of Franco-American friendship. In discussion with the statue's sculptor, Bartholdi, Laboulaye declared: "This will not be the revolutionary Liberty wearing a red bonnet and carrying a pike but the American Liberty, who brandishes not an incendiary torch, but one that lights the way." Erected in New York Harbor the statue has become a symbol of both freedom and the United States itself.

A TRIP THROUGH THE BODY OF A GIANT

The Statue of Liberty's colossal heel is the first sight to greet the visitor's eye. Once inside the base, you can visit a museum (renovated in 1986), that relates the statue's history. An elevator will take you to the top of the pedestal, then a metal spiral staircase leads to the crown with a view out over the ocean. Entrance to the torch is now prohibited for reasons of safety. The cartoon (right) from *The World*, May 16, 1885, shows Uncle Sam congratulating Miss Liberty.

BARTHOLDI: A SCULPTOR'S APPRENTICESHIP

Frédéric Auguste Bartholdi was born on April 2, 1834, in Colmar, Alsace. Family connections introduced the sculptor to a network of influential republican contacts.

The statue's stern facial features have been likened to the portrait of Mme Bartholdi, the sculptor's mother, by Ary Scheffer. Although the sculptor may have used his mother as a model, there is no reference to this in the exchange of letters between them.

EIFFEL TO THE RESCUE OF LIBERTY
At a height of 145 feet, the statue was vulnerable to high winds. The engineer Gustave Eiffel was hired to solve this

problem. The 1/10-inch-thick copper gown is riveted onto a flexible steel frame, which allows the statue a measure of give.

"LIBERTY" EXHIBITED IN PARIS
At the Paris Universal Exposition of 1878, visitors could climb inside a life-size model of the statue's head. For a time it towered above the roofs of Paris; for 50 centimes, one could climb as far as the crown and the torch. Although the Parisians, led by Victor Hugo, did not want to allow "their" statue of Liberty to leave Paris, it was nevertheless dismantled, packed in 214 crates, and shipped to America on the frigate *Isère*.

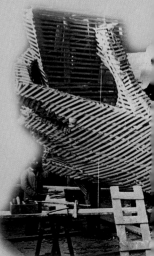

RICHARD MORRIS HUNT, ARCHITECT OF THE PEDESTAL
Hunt designed a high pedestal, a Doric base topped with a neo-classical loggia made of reinforced concrete and granite, to accentuate the size of the statue. The first stone was laid – following Masonic rites – in spring 1884.

The statue, which has been administered by the National Park Service since 1937, was given a facelift for her centennial in 1986. A Franco-American team was given the task of correcting the right arm and the head, which were slightly askew due to an error made when the statue was originally assembled. With a

new torch, its flame gilded in gold leaf, and her freshly cleaned gown, Miss Liberty was ready to take up her duties again for another century. Many people forget her French origins – so thoroughly has she come to symbolize the United States.

DEDICATION

On October 28, 1886, the statue, her face veiled by the Tricolor, was dedicated (above). Apart from her symbolic role at the entrance to New York, she has become a universally recognized figure, the subject of all sorts of products, from jam to pasta (top); she has "posed" for painters (Andy Warhol made multiple portraits of her) and appeared in films, such as Hitchcock's *Saboteur (*1942) and Schaffner's *Planet of the Apes* (1968).

ISLE OF TEARS, ISLE OF HOPE

Arrival of immigrants at Ellis Island circa 1900.

The history of the United States is to a great extent a drama of immigration. The drama has had some grim moments. By the end of the 19th century, immigrants were being attacked, even murdered, due to a rising tide of xenophobia in American society. The weight of public opinion, which had turned against Central and Southern European nationals, forced the Federal Government to assume responsibility for immigration, which had hitherto been left to the discretion of individual states. Institutions were restructured and centralized, various central committees were set up, strict immigration quotas were imposed. In 1892 the United States Immigration Station was established on Ellis Island. For millions of immigrants this was the waiting room for the Promised Land.

Immigrants alighting in New York harbor during the era of the great sailing ships (opposite), painting by Samuel Waugh.

HOW TO GET THERE. To get to Ellis Island from Manhattan, take the ferry from Castle Garden Dock (Battery Park ▲ *142*). After a crossing lasting some twenty minutes you will alight at the impressive redbrick landing stage, topped by a glass canopy, which leads to the Main Building.

MUSEUM OF IMMIGRATION. Within the building's precincts,

"Rumour had it . . . that some of us would be refused entry into the United States and would be sent back to Europe. The very thought brought me out in a cold sweat . . . Later, having mastered these anxieties, I was gripped by the fear that I would catch the mumps, smallpox, or some other disease . . . I didn't sleep a wink. I shook all night, listening to all those passengers snoring and dreaming aloud in a dozen different languages.**"**
Louis Adamic, describing his crossing in 1913

facing the sea, a wall of honor has been erected. It is some 98 feet long and is covered with a sheet of engraved copper bearing the names of 200,000 immigrants. A museum has recently been opened inside the building. The BAGGAGE ROOM on the ground floor, with its collection of trunks, suitcases, baskets and assorted belongings, all of which accompanied the immigrants on their journey, has been reconstructed on the ground floor, where various signboards indicate the route to follow. If you are in a hurry, you can take the elevator directly to the second story; but visitors with plenty of time may wish to begin their visit with an overview of the history of American immigration, which is provided in the main hall on the ground floor. This exhibition takes the form of individual

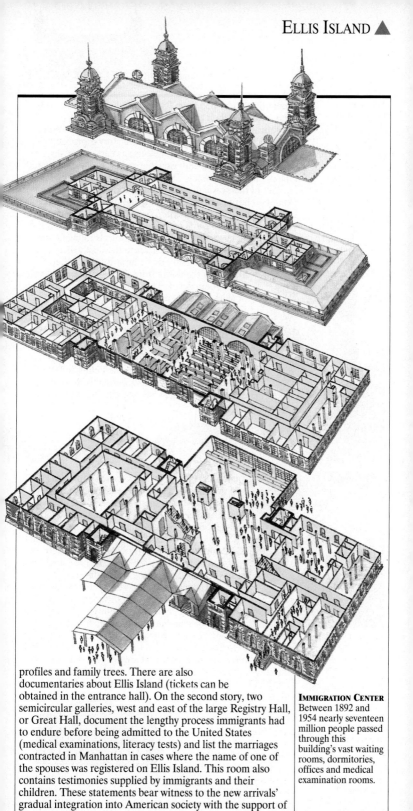

profiles and family trees. There are also documentaries about Ellis Island (tickets can be obtained in the entrance hall). On the second story, two semicircular galleries, west and east of the large Registry Hall, or Great Hall, document the lengthy process immigrants had to endure before being admitted to the United States (medical examinations, literacy tests) and list the marriages contracted in Manhattan in cases where the name of one of the spouses was registered on Ellis Island. This room also contains testimonies supplied by immigrants and their children. These statements bear witness to the new arrivals' gradual integration into American society with the support of

IMMIGRATION CENTER
Between 1892 and 1954 nearly seventeen million people passed through this building's vast waiting rooms, dormitories, offices and medical examination rooms.

149

Main entrance to
Ellis Island.

THE MEDICAL EXAMINATION
All the immigrants to the United States (below in the 19th century and in 1914) had to undergo a medical examination. Those suffering from contagious diseases such as trachoma (inflammation of the eyes), were rejected. Between 6 and 11 percent were deported for health reasons

networks that helped them find jobs and acquire new skills and facilitated their children's rapid assimilation into American life. There is a second movie theater for visitors wanting further information. The third story is probably the most fascinating part of the museum; its east gallery displays a collection of objects, both valuable and everyday, that shared the immigrants' odyssey. They illustrate the wide-ranging origins of their owners – a Scottish teapot, an Austrian pipe – and their hopes and dreams – wedding shoes, religious books, a sewing machine, a typewriter, flatirons, tools for a new life in a new land. The room of "Forgotten Voices", which is just as moving, focuses on the abandoned objects found before Ellis Island was restored. This leads to the west gallery where display cases detail the entry procedures for the United States, via the dormitories. Another doorway leads into a room devoted to small temporary exhibitions of works by contemporary artists depicting Ellis Island.

A HISTORICAL SITE, THE HISTORY OF A SITE

THE COST OF ASYLUM. Immigration laws were successively tightened to prohibit entry into the United States by anyone suffering from contagious diseases, by polygamists, prostitutes, the indigent,

anarchists, the Chinese (1882), the Japanese (1907) and the illiterate (1917). Despite being a narrow strip of land (it was soon doubled in size) Ellis Island was the ideal site for weeding out, detaining and deporting possible candidates for immigration. The original structure, which was far too small and was destroyed by a fire in 1897, was ultimately replaced by thirty-five buildings. In 1907, a record year, the Island processed a total of one million people. The majority of these hopeful candidates, who had often reached their destination after a grueling voyage, had only to endure another five or six hours of examination and interviews before reaching freedom, but approximately 20 percent were held in dormitories to await money from relatives or further medical examination. Each dormitory probably slept about three hundred immigrants and the hospital had room for as many as five hundred patients. About half of the detained were ultimately deported.
Some 3,500 people died on Ellis Island, and 350 were born there.

AT THE GATES OF OBLIVION. The 1924 laws regarding immigration quotas were the start of Ellis Island's slow decline. In 1933, for the first time, immigrants returning to their homeland outnumbered those who were just arriving. In 1937 the center

"A stranger who greeted us,
a hard man, asked:
'And how's your health?'
He examined us. His eyes
Like a dog's scrutinized us . . .
One thing is certain,
If he could have plumbed the depths of our hearts
He would have seen–
the wound.**"**
Avrom Reisen

dealt with only 160 deportees and thirty prisoners. During World War Two Ellis Island became a detention center for "enemies of the United States". The occasional Jewish refugee rubbed shoulders with Nazis and Communists from all over America. Finally, as Ellis Island was no longer

cost-effective, given the meager service it provided, it was permanently closed in 1954.

THE RESTORATION OF ELLIS ISLAND. Neglect brought decay: the decorated buildings, the historic objects left in storage there, the surrounding land were all left to the mercy of vandals, looters and the elements. Nature reclaimed the rooms that once had thronged with countless immigrants; all that remained were walls decayed by damp, gaping roofs, crumbling ceilings and parquet floors. In 1965 President Johnson's administration took action, making Ellis Island a National Monument, affiliated with the Statue of Liberty. The sea wall was strengthened and rebuilt in places. From 1976, when it was opened to the public, fifty thousand people have visited this site every year. In 1982, a campaign alerted public opinion to the dilapidated condition of the monument. Donations flooded in from all over the nation to save this part of its cherished heritage. The site was closed in 1983 for restoration. A detailed inventory was drawn up of everything worth salvaging: the registry hall ceiling, which had been constructed and covered with terracotta tiling in 1918, using Catalan technique, was restored; the walls were repaired, saving some of the messages that had been carved into the plaster at the turn of the century – moving testimonies of the immigrants' hopes and fears. The restoration of Ellis Island has been the most expensive project of its kind ever undertaken in the history of the United States ($156 million). However, the museum, opened on September 10, 1990, receives two million visitors every year.

HYPER–REALISM
In fine weather, bankers and stockbrokers sit on the steps of Liberty Plaza, their ties flicked over their shoulders, eating sandwiches bought in one of the Broadway delis. One of them,

seated on a bench, is checking the contents of his briefcase, sifting through documents from the Merrill Lynch brokerage firm. This is actually a startlingly lifelike statue, entitled *Double Check* (J. Seward Johnson Jr., 1982); the documents are perfectly legible. Another interesting sight is the clock set in the sidewalk at 174 Broadway. This belongs to a nearby jewelry store, William Barthman Jewelers.

LANDMARKS PRESERVATION LAW
The Singer Building (right), destroyed in 1970, is one of New York's most sorely missed masterpieces. Since then, the New York Landmarks Preservation Commission has consolidated its power of veto and widened its sphere of influence: it also has the right to preserve building interiors that are open to the public. There are more than 50 designated landmarks in New York today.

This route runs from the World Trade Center down Broadway, the most famous thoroughfare in Manhattan, which crosses the island from north to south. It was originally an old Indian trail that curved around forests and hills. During the building of Fort Amsterdam the Dutch widened it south of what is now Bowling Green and named it "Breede Wegh" (Broadway). "Lower Broadway" is now so densely lined with buildings that you cannot see their tops from street level: the disorderly layout of old New York and the heavy traffic hem you in. Many of the buildings have spacious lobbies covering an entire block.

AROUND LIBERTY PLAZA

EAST RIVER SAVINGS BANK BUILDING. 26 CORTLANDT ST., BETWEEN CHURCH, DEY AND CORTLANDT STS. (1934, arch. Walker & Gillette). The East River Savings Bank Building, which now houses a large store and leads from Cortlandt Street to Dey Street, is an Art Deco gem. The breathtaking scale of the red, black and brown marble former banking hall, with its barrel-vaulted ceiling and its floor patterned with optical geometrical motifs, makes the building well worth a visit.

1 LIBERTY PLAZA/165 BROADWAY. (1974, arch. Skidmore, Owings & Merrill). The construction of this glass box, which occupies the block bounded by Broadway, Church, Cortlandt and Liberty streets, was to blame for the demolition, in 1970 of the Singer Building – doomed because its usable floor space was five times smaller than that of the proposed new building. A Beaux Arts masterpiece, designed by ERNEST FLAGG, the Singer Building was the world's tallest building at the time of its completion (1908). Sixty years later it was the

The circular brass seal of the East River Savings Bank, flanked by two eagles, used to adorn the parapet overhanging the side entrances.

The Sky Lobby (left) of the Equitable Building.

"Before me stretches an avenue which would have looked wide if it had been lined with European houses; but it seems little more than a lane, dominated by buildings thirty and forty stories high. The sun only slants in fleetingly when it is at its zenith . . . These massive pieces of architecture weigh down on passersby, very nearly crushing them. These skyscrapers, who belong to a brotherhood of giants, help each other to rise, to prop each other up, to soar until all sense of perspective disappears. You try to count the stories one by one, then your weary gaze starts to climb in tens; you tilt your head, you crane your neck, and you realize that the topmost story is actually no more than the first of a sequence of set-back terraces, that can only be seen only from the side, or from the air."

Paul Morand, *New York*

tallest building ever to be pulled down. It could withstand wind pressure of 350 tons. It also anticipated the Zoning Resolution of 1916 ● *97* for its slender, elegant tower formed a setback in relation to the larger mass below, thereby allowing sunlight to reach the street. At the time of its demolition, the New York City Landmarks Commission, only five years old, was not sure enough of its powers to halt the plans of the new landlord, U.S. Steel.

MARINE MIDLAND BANK. 140 BROADWAY, BETWEEN LIBERTY AND CEDAR STS. (1967, arch. Skidmore, Owings & Merrill). This flat-roofed monolith, a typical example of the International Style ● *100*, is devoid of all decoration. Conventional ornamentation has taken the form of a separate work of art: the red cube sculpture (below) by Isamu Noguchi (1973).

EQUITABLE BUILDING ● *97* ★. 120 BROADWAY (1915, arch.

Ernest R. Graham of Graham, Anderson, Probst & White). Stone eagles and lions adorn the lower part of the façade of this neo-Renaissance building which covers a surface area thirty times larger than that of the original building of the same name. The construction of this building raised a general outcry, as New Yorkers were concerned that Lower Manhattan should not be entirely smothered by such "monsters". The Equitable Building is, however, a designated landmark and boasts one of New York's most impressive lobbies, with its vaulted, coffered ceiling adorned with gilded ceiling rosettes, its floor of pink marble, quarried in Tennessee, and its sandy-colored marble walls. It has four entrances, one for each of the adjacent streets. The lower part of the building occupies a whole block, while the body of the building, with its five thousand windows, is H–shaped. The "Sky Lobby", the former headquarters of the exclusive Banker's Club, can be visited by appointment. From here, you can enjoy a panoramic view over the neighboring roofs.

The Equitable Building in 1914.

The Trinity Building, as seen by a reveler, takes on a strange appearance. . . .

THAMES TWINS/TRINITY AND REALTY BUILDINGS ★. 111–115 BROADWAY (1905 and 1907, arch. Francis H. Kimball). These twin buildings, linked by a walkway that straddles Thames Street, are one of New York's architectural gems and make for a pleasant surprise deep in the heart of the bustling Financial District. The façades call to mind the Gothic lines of Trinity Church, and the interiors are treated in a similar style, with stained glass windows and gilded elevator doors, grotesques and gilded ornaments.

AROUND TRINITY CHURCH

IRVING TRUST BUILDING
The ground-floor banking hall of this building glows with red and gold mosaics.

AN ENGLISH CHURCH
Trinity Church (right, as rebuilt in 1846) was the first Manhattan parish established by the Church of England. When it was built, in the 1690's, all residents, whatever their religion, had to pay a tax for its construction.

BANK OF NEW YORK, FORMERLY IRVING TRUST BUILDING ★. 1 WALL ST., S. E. CORNER OF BROADWAY (1932, arch. Voorhees, Gmelin & Walker). The Greek practice of fluting columns to enhance the illusion of height and delicacy was adapted for the walls of this building. The plain limestone cladding and the abstract Art Deco motif of the façade enhance the building's monolithic appearance. Although built during the Great Depression, the Irving Trust Building, exudes a feeling of confidence. The company's name is derived from the American author, Washington Irving, who used to live at 3 Wall Street. To view the building as a whole, walk back to Rector Street.

TRINITY CHURCH ★. BROADWAY AT WALL ST. (1846, arch. Richard Upjohn). Trinity Parish, founded by a charter granted by William III in 1697, was given extensive pasture lands in Manhattan, which made it eventually the richest church in the United States. This is the third building of the same name to be built on this site; the first church, built in 1698, was destroyed by a fire in 1776 and the second was demolished in 1839 due to a defective roof frame. Completed in 1846, the present Gothic Revival church is clad in brownstone and boasts a bell tower whose slender spire soars to 280 feet. Until the end of the 19th century Trinity Church was the tallest building in New York; it used to serve as a landmark for ships. The stained glass window over the choir is one of the earliest made in the United States. The three bronze porch doors, designed by Richard Morris Hunt and constructed by Karl Bitter, Charles Niehaus, and J. Massey Rhind illustrate Adam and Eve's expulsion from Paradise. The hundred-year-old oak trees in the church burial ground shelter the graves of Alexander Hamilton, the first Secretary of the Treasury, Robert Fulton, inventor of the steam warship ▲ *174*, Captain

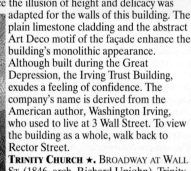

"I'VE SAID TO MYSELF A HUNDRED TIMES THAT NEW YORK IS A
CATASTROPHE, AND FIFTY TIMES THAT IT IS A SPLENDID
CATASTROPHE."

LE CORBUSIER

James Lawrence, a hero of the War of 1812, William
Bradford, the founder of the first newspaper in New York,
and Albert Gallatin, statesman and a founder of New York
University ▲ *200*. The oldest tombstone dates from 1681. An
ossuary contains the ashes of two thousand prisoners who
died during the War of Independence.

29 BROADWAY. (1931, arch. Sloan & Robertson). This Art
Deco building has several interesting features, notably the
stringcourses that coil around its gable, creating the effect of a
console. The lobby, with its wealth of jade marble, engraved
glass doors and radiator grills, is a perfect example of Art
Deco style. Cross the street to appreciate the overall design of
the building.

AROUND BOWLING GREEN

FORMER CUNARD BUILDING. 25 BROADWAY (1921, arch.
Benjamin Wistar Morris; Carrère and Hastings). In the
1920's, after its merger with the White Star Line, Cunard
became the leading steamship company to provide a
passenger service. With the exception of the luxury liners,
QUEEN MARY, QUEEN ELIZABETH and QUEEN ELIZABETH II,
most of their ships had names ending in "ia"
(MAURETANIA, for example) – as did the company's first
ship, BRITANNIA, which berthed in
New York on July 4, 1840. A post
office now occupies part of
Cunard's former headquarters.
The sumptuous main entrance, set in a neo-
Renaissance façade, leads into an immense lobby,
illuminated by antique chandeliers, with a vaulted
ceiling and walls lined with polychromatic terracotta.

**AN AMERICAN
CHURCH**
After the fire of 1776
the original Trinity
Church (above)
remained in ruins
throughout the War
of Independence. A
second church was
built after the war.
Like other Anglican
Churchs in the
United States, it
became part of
the new,
independent
Protestant
Episcopal Church.

**LOBBY OF THE
CUNARD BUILDING**
Above the octagonal
main hall, 65 feet
high, rise three
domes. The interior
walls of the building
are decorated with
charts showing
Cunard's lines and
illustrated by flags
from former French
and English colonial
empires (by the artist
Ezra Winters). The
pendentives
supporting the main
dome are decorated
with paintings of the
ships of four famous
sailors: Christopher
Columbus, Leif
Eriksson, John Cabot
and Sir Francis
Drake.

155

▲ WORLD TRADE CENTER TO BATTERY PARK, VIA BROADWAY

Government House in 1797, on the site of the future U.S. Custom House.

1 BROADWAY. This was the first office building to be built (in 1884), along the longest and most famous street in New York. It was originally called the Washington Building. In 1922 it was refurbished to house the headquarters of the United States Line, one of the many shipping companies based on Steamship Row. The reservation and ticket sales office (now converted into a bank) is on the ground floor. Note the compass dial set in the floor and the words "First-Class tickets" which still appear outside.

FORMER STANDARD OIL BUILDING. 26 BROADWAY (1922, arch. Carrère & Hastings and Shreve, Lamb & Blake). The neo-Renaissance façade of the former Standard Oil Building (left) cunningly curves here in a fan shape to follow the contour of Broadway. The names of the founders of the oil company, including John D. Rockefeller, grace the lobby which is lined with pilasters and columns. Note the STANDARD OIL CLOCK, on which the "S" indicates the minutes and the "O" the hours. As you approach Bowling Green, you can see the top of the building's pyramidal tower, whose main axis is aligned east-west, at an oblique angle to the main part of the building. This building now houses THE MUSEUM OF AMERICAN FINANCIAL HISTORY.

BOWLING GREEN. (rest. 1978, landscape architect, Paul Friedberg). Created in 1733, Bowling Green is the oldest park in the city. It occupies the site of a former Dutch parade ground, which had originally been adjacent to a cattle market. The new park consisted of a green where gentlemen could play bowls (hence its name) for an annual fee of one peppercorn, paid to the municipal government. It was here that PETER MINUIT bought Manhattan from the Indians ● *30*. At the center of the green, in 1766, New Yorkers raised a gilded statue of George III to show their gratitude at the repeal of the Stamp Act, which had placed a tax on all written documents. Although the 18th-century railings that surrounded the park are still there, the statue was melted down for making bullets during the War of Independence. In 1842 a fountain was built in the park. It was supplied by fresh water from the Croton Reservoir, thus giving New Yorkers, for the first time, access to clean water, unlike the well water that caused so many epidemics ● *34* in the city.

"BOWLING GREEN BULL". This enormous bronze bull (Arturo di Modica, 1989), stands for the time being at the entrance to the Financial District ▲ *158*, at the northernmost end of Bowling Green. The bull and the bear represent the two trends of the stock market: rising and declining.

U.S. CUSTOM HOUSE ★. 1 BOWLING GREEN (1907, arch. Cass Gilbert). The U.S. Custom House was established in 1842 at 28 Wall Street, the building now housing the present Federal Hall National Memorial. Twenty years later it was moved to 55 Wall Street, within the walls of the former Merchants' Exchange, and then in 1907 to 1 Bowling Green. When this Beaux Arts style ● *92* building was completed, there was no

income tax, so customs duties were the Federal Government's primary source of income. The lion's share of this revenue was provided by New York City, and therefore the U.S. Custom House accounted for most of the money vital to the American economy. Its importance is reflected in this imposing building. The marble hall leads into a sumptuous oval rotunda 48 feet high, illuminated by an elliptical skylight. The walls are decorated by eight frescoes (Reginald Marsh, 1937) depicting the arrival of a transatlantic steamship in New York Harbor; one of them shows Greta Garbo disembarking and being met by the press. In 1973 the Custom House moved to the World Trade Center. The National Museum of the American Indian is to take over these premises in 1994, when it leaves Harlem.

TOWARD THE SEA

CHURCH OF OUR LADY OF THE ROSARY. 7–8 STATE ST. (1793–1806, arch. John McComb, rest. 1965, Shanley & Sturges). This church can be found in a house with a Georgian-style east wing (1793) and a Federal-style west wing (1806) ● *82*. It belonged to the shipowner JAMES WATSON who would spend long hours watching the harbor activity from his house, whose columns were made from ships' masts.
BATTERY MARITIME BUILDING. 11 SOUTH ST. (1909, arch. Walker & Gillette). Until 1938 the MUNICIPAL FERRY PIERS served as landing stages for the various Brooklyn ferryboat lines. They are now used by the GOVERNOR'S ISLAND ferry. The inland side of this building, which gives access to the piers, has a colonnade and arches facing the water.

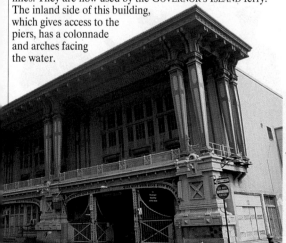

ALLEGORICAL ORNAMENTS
The steps of the main entrance to the U.S. Custom House are adorned with statues by Daniel Chester French, symbolizing four continents. The building's front-facing windows bear the heads of the eight races of mankind (Caucasian, Hindu, Latin, Celtic, Mongolian, Eskimo, Slavic and African); above the cornice are twelve statues representing the great commercial centers in Western history.

SAINT ELIZABETH ANN SETON
In 1809 Elizabeth Seton (1774–1821), who lived at 7–8 State St., founded the Sisters of Charity, the first American order of nuns. A member of the New York aristocracy, she was ostracized for her conversion to Catholicism. She was canonized in 1975, becoming the first female American saint ● *50*. There is a statue of her in the Shrine of St. Elizabeth Ann Seton.

157

The Financial District, which dates back to 1792 with the creation of the first Stock Exchange, was once dominated by the spire of Trinity Church ▲ *154*. With the advent of the skyscraper, the area's appearance changed radically.

"ONCE UPON A TIME IN AMERICA"
A scene (below) for the movie, *Once Upon a Time in America*, made in 1984 by Sergio Leone and filmed in the Federal Reserve

Bank. In this movie the director explores another face of the "American dream": the birth of great cities and the stranglehold of mob rule.

AROUND THE FEDERAL RESERVE BANK

JOHN STREET UNITED METHODIST CHURCH AND MUSEUM. 44 JOHN ST. (1841, arch. William Hurry). This church (the third on this site) was the home of the first Methodist congregation in America. Founded by the Englishman JOHN WESLEY (1703–91), Methodism rejected the ecclesiastical authority of the English crown and it became very popular in the United States. This building, contemporary with the Greek Revival style ● *84,* anticipates the Italianate style ● *88* in its central Venetian window, flanked by two other tall arched windows. The interior displays a refined elegance with its unostentatious stained glass windows and its horseshoe-shaped gallery. There is a MUSEUM on the lower ground floor.
FEDERAL RESERVE BANK. 33 LIBERTY ST. (1924, arch. York & Sawyer). The Federal Reserve Bank was founded in 1913 by President Woodrow Wilson to centralize the American banking system. The New York Reserve Bank, a key part of the Federal Reserve System, is where monetary policy is implemented for the Federal Reserve, influencing interest rates and economic activity throughout the nation.

The gold reserves from eighty countries and some foreign banks and international organizations, over one quarter of the world's stock, are stored 80 feet below ground in this massive rectangular fortress built of limestone and sandstone. Its impregnable appearance is modeled on Florentine Renaissance palaces. The strong rooms can be visited by appointment, and it used to be possible to watch old banknotes being destroyed. LOUISE NEVELSON PLAZA, farther east, at the intersection of Maiden Lane and Liberty and William streets, affords the best view of the crenelated turret that tops this building. This pedestrian area contains an abstract sculpture, *Shadows and Flags*, created by Louise Nevelson in 1977.

LIBERTY TOWER Situated at 55 Liberty St., this neo-Gothic tower decorated with finials and gargoyles once housed the Standard Oil Company ▲ *156*. The

CENTRAL BANK OF CHINA, FORMER NEW YORK CHAMBER OF COMMERCE. 65 LIBERTY ST. (1901, arch. James B. Baker). This architectural gem is one of the finest Beaux Arts style ● *92* buildings in New York and a product of the "City Beautiful" movement. The three pedestals on the façade used to bear statues, which did not survive the ravages of pollution. The wonderful lobby is worth a visit.

CHASE MANHATTAN BANK. 1 CHASE MANHATTAN PLAZA (1960, arch. Skidmore, Owings & Merrill). This building marked a watershed in the postwar development of Lower Manhattan, being the first International Style ● *100* office building to be constructed in this part of the city. It expressed the confidence of the bank's president, David Rockefeller, in the future of Downtown, at a time when businesses were moving Uptown. The tower's plain rectangular shape contrasts markedly with the slender spires surrounding it. The Chase Manhattan Bank boasts a superb art collection and its huge plaza contains work by Isamu Noguchi – a sunken Japanese garden with an arrangement of seven rocks – as well as a sculpture by Dubuffet (above), *Group of Four Trees*, created in 1972. The plaza affords a spectacular view of the neighboring buildings, especially 70 Pine Street.

frescoes in its lobby depict the building in 1909, as well as the Singer Building ▲ *152*, which stood on the site of the present Liberty Plaza.

AMERICAN INTERNATIONAL BUILDING ★. 70 PINE ST. (1932, arch. Clinton and Russell; Holton and George). This Art Deco ● *98* skyscraper, which originally housed the CITIES SERVICE COMPANY, responsible for the

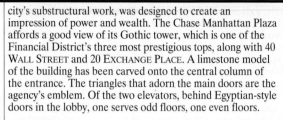

The French franc, which was hard currency at the time, is carved on the pediment (above) of the main door of 20 Exchange Place.

60 WALL STREET Built in 1988, the Morgan Bank's new building, is a heavy Postmodern tower, contrasting sharply with its more graceful neighbors. However, the lower part of the building is composed of a colonnade, echoing the one at 55 Wall St., just opposite. It houses a

vast atrium (above), open to the public in accordance with city-planning regulations.

The deeply recessed main entrance to Citibank behind its colonnade.

city's substructural work, was designed to create an impression of power and wealth. The Chase Manhattan Plaza affords a good view of its Gothic tower, which is one of the Financial District's three most prestigious tops, along with 40 WALL STREET and 20 EXCHANGE PLACE. A limestone model of the building has been carved onto the central column of the entrance. The triangles that adorn the main doors are the agency's emblem. Of the two elevators, behind Egyptian-style doors in the lobby, one serves odd floors, one even floors.

WALL STREET

The financial world's most famous street once marked the northernmost boundary of New Amsterdam. In 1653 the Dutch erected a wooden palisade as a form of protection, first against the Indians, then against the English ● 32. From 1792, when the first stock exchange was organized in this neighborhood ▲ 164, Wall Street began to establish its reputation as a financial center.

WILLIAMSBURGH SAVINGS BANK, FORMERLY SEAMEN'S BANK FOR SAVINGS. 72–74 WALL ST. (1926, arch. Benjamin Wistar Morris). The ships and anchors that adorn the ashlar façade are a reminder of this building's previous occupant. The lobby of no. 72, with its decorative brass grilles, paneled doors and gilded ceiling, is a masterpiece. The central door, opposite the elegant bank of elevators, is crowned with a brass bas-relief depicting a lighthouse.

63 WALL STREET. (1929, arch. Delano and Aldrich). The building rises in a series of setbacks to a top decorated with ornamental gargoyles, a better view of which can be obtained farther back up Wall Street. Note the coins adorning the façade and take a look at the corner lobby.

22 WILLIAM STREET BETWEEN BEAVER STREET AND EXCHANGE STREET ★. (1931, arch. Cross & Cross). Built for the CITY BANK FARMERS' TRUST COMPANY, this office tower fills a trapezoid-shaped block and has a façade with bevelled quoins. Take a look at the bronze doors decorated with trains, boats, planes and airships, typical Art Deco ● 98 motifs. On the cornice of the lower part of the building, huge helmeted centurions seem to watch the passersby. There is a better view of the lofty, slender tower farther west from William Street. The lobby offers a profusion of marble, mosaics, paintings and tin. Note the central dome, vaulted ceilings, elevator doors, floor and glass telephone booths.

CITIBANK. 55 WALL ST. (1836–42, arch. Isaiah Rogers; 1907, arch. McKim, Mead & White). This classical-inspired building, with its two-story colonnades, was built on the site of the first Merchants' Exchange, which had been destroyed by fire in 1835. The lower part of the building, which dates from 1836, served as the U.S. Custom House from 1863 ▲ 157 until 1899. After the departure of that tenant, "55 Wall Street" was enlarged to house Citibank (then called the First National City Bank). A Corinthian-order colonnade was added to the Ionic one by the architects McKim, Mead & White. The huge lobby measures 198 by 132 feet in height. The building now

> "THIS IS A DISTRICT OVERFLOWING WITH GOLD, A TRUE MIRACLE,
> AND YOU CAN EVEN HEAR THE MIRACLE THROUGH THE DOORS
> WITH ITS SOUND OF DOLLARS BEING COUNTED . . . "
>
> LOUIS-FERDINAND CÉLINE

stands empty; it has been closed to the public since 1992.

BANK OF NEW YORK BUILDING. 48 WALL ST. (1927, arch. Benjamin Wistar Morris III). Cross the street to appreciate the setbacks of this skyscraper which draws its inspiration from the Italian Renaissance and whose topmost aedicula is crowned with an eagle. The Bank of New York, the first bank in the newly independant state, was founded in 1784 by Alexander Hamilton ▲ *154*, Washington's former aide-de-camp and first Secretary of the Treasury. Alexander Hamilton died after being shot in a duel on July 11, 1804 by Aaron Burr, a rival in politics as well as in business.

MANUFACTURERS' HANOVER TRUST, FORMERLY BANK OF MANHATTAN CO. BUILDING ★. 40 WALL ST. (1929, arch. H. Craig Severance and Yasuo Matsui). This 69-story skyscraper (left) bears a certain resemblance to the Empire State Building ▲ *242* (like the latter, it was even hit by a plane in the 1940's). It was the tallest building in the world for just a few days before it was overtaken by the Chrysler Building ▲ *266*. The top, a Gothic Revival green pyramid, similar to the top of the Woolworth Building ▲ *180*, can easily be recognized on the Lower Manhattan skyline. The northeast corner of Broad and Beaver streets provides a good vantage point. The Bank of Manhattan Company, which was initially called the Manhattan Water Company, was New York's first public services company; it was founded by Aaron Burr in 1799 to supply drinking water. In 1842, when the Croton Aqueduct was opened, the company, which had also engaged in banking activities, dropped its water supply function and officially took the name of the Bank of Manhattan.

SEAMEN'S BANK FOR SAVINGS. 30 WALL ST. (1919, arch. York and Sawyer). This building was built on the site of the United States Assay Office which was designed by Martin E. Thompson and completed in 1823; it was demolished in 1915. Its façade is displayed in the American Wing of the Metropolitan Museum of Art.

161

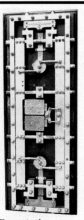

Former subtreasury vaults.

In 1883, a statue of George Washington by John Quincy Adams Ward was placed outside the entrance Federal Hall, at the approximate spot where he took his oath of office and where (right) President Benjamin Harrison made a speech.

26 Wall Street
Built in 1842, the U.S. Custom House displays a Doric austerity contrasting with the Stock Exchange (1903) façade, with its profusion of

figures and Corinthian opulence. Here, architecture mirrors the development of the United States, showing how the nation had evolved in sixty years from a modest, idealistic infancy to powerful and affluent maturity.

Federal Hall National Memorial ★. 26 Wall St. (1834–42, arch. Town & Davis). In 1701, the second New York City Hall was built on this site ▲ *176*. Remodeled in 1788 by Pierre-Charles L'Enfant (architect and city-planner for Washington, D. C.) the building, now renamed Federal Hall, served briefly as the headquarters of the American government until the capital was moved to Philadelphia in 1790. This building, later demolished, housed the first meeting, in March 1789, of the new Congress, and was the site of George Washington's inauguration as the first President of the United States, on April 30 of that year. The present Greek Revival ● *84* building was built in 1842 to house the first U.S. Custom House ▲ *157*, then, between 1862 and 1920, it became the headquarters of a U.S. subtreasury. Exhibits in the museum retrace the origins and history of the United States.

Morgan Guaranty Trust Company. 23 Wall St. at s. e. corner of Broad St. (1913, arch. Trowbridge & Livingston). In 1907, the financier and businessman J. Pierpont Morgan managed to stem the tide of panic then threatening Wall Street by locking the leading city bankers in his 5th Avenue home and forcing them to come up with a plan to rebuild people's confidence. While the "prisoners" were working, Morgan played solitaire – which indicates his status

> "ALL THE MAJOR FINANCIAL MARKETS HAVE GROWN UP IN THE HEART OF A CAPITAL CITY. THE AMERICAN STOCK EXCHANGE IS AN EXCEPTION: IT WAS CREATED IN A PORT, ON THE OUTSKIRTS OF A CITY WHICH IS NOT EVEN THE CAPITAL." M. TURIN

among them. His bank at 23 Wall Street was the last building to be built at this key intersection, around which were grouped the U.S. subtreasury (now the FEDERAL HALL NATIONAL MEMORIAL), to the north: the NEW YORK STOCK EXCHANGE, to the west; and, opposite, BANKERS TRUST, a rival occupying, in 1912, the tallest building in the world. By building this low, four-story structure, Morgan intended to create the impression that "Less is more". The bank had no identifying sign – the Morgan establishment did not need one! The Morgan family's highly reactionary stance brought them many enemies: a bomb exploded outside the building on September 16, 1920, killing thirty-three people and wounding hundreds of others. Those responsible were never traced.

BROAD STREET AND NEW YORK STOCK EXCHANGE

BROAD STREET. This street, which runs from Wall Street down to the tip of Manhattan, was originally a canal dug by the Dutch in 1660. In 1676, it was filled in ● *76.* Although "Wall Street" is famous the world over as shorthand for the U.S. stock market, the New York Stock Exchange, the focal point for most of the district's financial activity, is actually on Broad Street.

NEW YORK STOCK EXCHANGE ★. 8 BROAD ST. (1903, arch. George B. Post). The largest stock exchange in the world had its beginnings on May 17, 1792 under a buttonwood tree, near the intersection of Wall and William streets. Here twenty-four American brokers met to impose some sort of order on a chaotic market and signed the "Buttonwood Agreement". The tree was felled in 1865 by a storm, but a commemorative plaque was laid in front of 8 Broad Street. On March 8, 1817, the market adopted a constitution and a name, the New York Stock and Exchange Board, and moved into 40 Wall Street. In 1863, the Board shortened its name to the New York Stock Exchange and moved into larger premises at 10–12 Broad Street. Thirty-five years later, in 1903, it settled in its present home at 8 Broad Street. The history of the New York Stock Exchange is filled with eccentric figures. One of the most famous was Hetty Green, nicknamed the "Witch of Wall Street", who, in the 1880's, transformed her inheritance into a fortune worth more than $100 million. She achieved this without ever showing her face in the stockbroker central enclosure. The classical façade of the New York Stock Exchange conceals a vast and highly sophisticated trading floor, which can be visited during the week. Don't miss the opportunity to view this frenetic spectacle, with its hundreds of shouting stockbrokers and flashing annunciator boards.

"WALL STREET" The façade of the New York Stock Exchange bears a pediment enlivened with a group of sculpted figures entitled *Integrity Protecting the Works of Man* (John Quincy Adams Ward). In the center, the winged figure of Integrity looms over Science, Industry and Invention on the right, Agriculture and on the left, the Mining Industry.

The pyramid that tops the Bankers Trust (14–16 Wall St.) is one of the most distinctive sights on the Manhattan skyline and the only sign of eccentricity in the architecture of this building.

A hard currency – the dollar – a buoyant economy and a well-established banking system have made the New York Stock Exchange the leading money market in the world. Since its founding in 1792 it has survived many crises, including the crash of 1929. "Wall Street" has been instrumental in generating many of the technical innovations and new financial products used in trading halls since the beginning of the 20th century. It has created a new generation of stockbrokers.

"BLACK FRIDAY" AT THE NEW YORK STOCK EXCHANGE
On September 24, Jay Gould's attempt to corner the market having collapsed, the price of gold dropped nearly 20 percent. A panic in the securities market quickly followed.

"CURB EXCHANGE"
Early in this century small-scale stockholders carried out transactions at cash desks in stockbrokers' offices located along Broad St., and even in the street itself (below, in 1918).

After World War Two, while European stockbrokers waited for the recovery, on the other side of the Atlantic, records were being broken! However, in New York, people were wary of a new tool that had just appeared on the stockmarket: information technology.

ON TICKER TAPE
In order to send the rates on the Stock Exchange's Big Board to stockbrokers all over the country, Wall St. began, in 1867, to use teletype.

12,894,650

The New York Times.

"All the News That's Fit to Print."

VOL. LXXIX...No. 26,207...★★★★

NEW YORK, FRIDAY, OCTOBER 25, 1929.

TWO CENTS New York City | THREE CENTS Within 200 Miles | FOUR CENTS Elsewhere

GRUNDY SAYS LOBBY IS NEEDED TO UPHOLD PARTY TARIFF VOWS

HUMBERT ESCAPES ANTI-FASCISTS SHOT AT BRUSSELS TOMB

**WORST STOCK CRASH STEMMED BY BANKS;
12,894,650-SHARE DAY SWAMPS MARKET;
LEADERS CONFER, FIND CONDITIONS SOUND**

PANIC ON WALL STREET

"Worst Stock Crash Stemmed By Banks" ran the headline in *The New York Times* on Friday October 25, 1929. The day before, the share prices of the big names in American industry had plummeted and 12,894,650 stocks and shares had changed hands. America was about to plunge into the Great Depression. In 1934, to prevent a catastrophe of this scale from recurring, Congress instituted the Securities and Exchange Commission, which established strict regulations to prevent violent market fluctuations.

BATTLE OF THE "BEARS" AND THE "BULLS"

"On the Stock Exchange's coat of arms, the bull and the bear, hostile brothers, face each other." This animal metaphor, which originated in America, is now used to describe speculators' activity. The behavior of the "bears" – who sell stocks and shares because they believe the market is falling – and of the bulls – who buy stocks and shares at a certain price because they are gambling on a rising market – generate the Stock Market prices
▲ 156.

MICHAEL MILKEN
The "Golden Boy", inventor of junk bonds, being sworn in, in 1987.

The aggressive climate of the 1980's led to a series of illegal schemes: there was a rise in hostile takeover bids – the targeted company would be shut and stripped of its assets – and junk bonds. Unscrupulous businessmen such as Michael Milken built up huge fortunes in this way. In 1990 he was imprisoned for fraud.

The writings on the memorial (above) to soldiers who fought in the Vietnam War (Vietnam Veterans' Plaza, S.E. Water St.), include extracts from letters, military dispatches and newspaper clippings.

The sign in front of the Fraunces Tavern.

INDIA HOUSE
This building, at 1 Hanover Square, housed the Hanover Bank, the N.Y. Cotton Exchange and the W. R. Grace & Co., in quick succession. India House is a classic example of an Italianate-style ● *88* brownstone

residence. It is now occupied by a businessmen's club and contains a collections of art and naval objects.

INTERNATIONAL TELEPHONE AND TELEGRAPH BUILDING. 67 BROAD ST. (1928, arch. Buchman & Kahn). The best view of the spectacular verticality of this 35-story Gothic Revival ● *86* building is from the corner of Beaver Street and Broadway. The allegorical frescoes of the lobby, which take communication as their theme, depict mythological figures. The alcove of what used to be the main entrance, on the corner of William Street, is embellished with a mosaic (right).

MARITIME EXCHANGE BUILDING. 80 BROAD ST. (1930, arch. Sloan & Robertson). The entrance of this Art Deco ● *98* building, topped with four silver sea horses, leads into the lobby, whose ceiling is covered with paintings of ships, illustrating the history of ship-building. The building has Tiffany-style ● *66* stained glass windows, depicting cars, trains, boats and planes.

85 BROAD STREET. (1983, arch. Skidmore, Owings & Merrill). A brass plaque bearing a map of Lower Manhattan c. 1660 is placed below the archway leading into this building. The lobby follows the curve of the intersection with Stone Street. When the foundations were being laid, objects from the Dutch era were found; these are now exhibited in Pearl Street.

FRAUNCES TAVERN BLOCK HISTORIC DISTRICT

The Fraunces Tavern Block, located between Broad, Pearl and Water streets and Coenties Slip, occupies land salvaged from the sea by the Dutch in 1689.

FRAUNCES TAVERN. 54 PEARL ST. This house is an architectural conjecture of one built in 1719 for a wealthy merchant, Étienne (or Stephen) de Lancey. It was bought in 1762 by Samuel Fraunces who opened a restaurant, the Queen's Head Tavern, in it. After Independence, he changed its royalist name to his own. The tavern was frequented by members of the New York élite. George Washington was one of the establishment's patrons, and it was here, in 1783, that he gave a farewell dinner for his officers. In 1785, his business on the wane, Fraunces sold the tavern and became Washington's steward. The building, in Georgian style, was bought in 1904 by the *Sons of the Revolution* and restored in 1907 by William Mersereau. It contains a museum on early New York history and American decorative arts.

HANOVER SQUARE. This square was originally called Printing House Square in homage to William Bradford ● *54*, who founded the first American printing works here in 1693. It was renamed "Hanover" by the English, in honor of the reigning dynasty. Many streets in the district followed suit, taking the names of members of the royal family. After Independence, only Hanover Square retained its name. A statue of Abraham De Peyster, Mayor of New York between 1691 and 1693, stands in this square.

DELMONICO'S. 56 BEAVER ST. (1891, arch. James Brown Lord). This restaurant was founded in 1827 by two Italian immigrants, the Delmonico brothers. It has a white marble portico, possibly an antique from Pompeii. The interior contains photos, engravings and tapestries of old New York.

AROUND
CITY HALL

Civic Center, New York City.

CITY HALL TOWARD
SOUTH STREET SEAPORT, *168*
ROD KNOX
SOUTH STREET SEAPORT, *172*
NORMAN BROUWER
CITY HALL TOWARD
WOOLWORTH BUILDING, *176*
ROD KNOX
WOOLWORTH BUILDING, *180*
ISABELLE GOURNAY
NORTH OF CITY HALL, *182*
ROD KNOX
BROOKLYN BRIDGE, *186*
HÉLÈNE TROCMÉ
BRIDGES OF MANHATTAN, *188*
HÉLÈNE TROCMÉ

▲ City Hall toward South Street Seaport

1 City Hall
2 City Hall Park
3 Printing House Square
4 Pace University
5 Potter Bldg.

T he area now occupied by the Civic Center, the nation's second largest administrative center after that of Washington, employing 50,000 people, was a tranquil patch of countryside covered with fields and marsh lands. To the south stands City Hall, the offices of the mayor of New York since 1812, and Park Row, once the center of the theater district and also known as "Newspaper Row" because of the many newspapers based here. Farther southeast lies South Street Seaport, a remnant of the city's commercial, maritime past. To the west towers the Woolworth Building, while to the northeast administrative buildings and courthouses for the city and the State of New York are grouped around Foley Square.

CITY HALL
In paying homage to the Georgian and Louis XVI styles, the architects who designed City Hall (above, in 1826) were deliberately rejecting the monumental form of neo-classicism favored for the new capital, Washington. On top of City Hall's clock tower (below) stands a statue of Justice.

AROUND CITY HALL

CITY HALL ★. Between PARK ROW and BROADWAY (1803–12, arch. Joseph François Mangin and John McComb, Jr). This was New York's third City Hall. The first, built in 1641 during the Dutch occupation, was situated at about 71 Pearl Street, opposite the site where the Fraunces Tavern block ▲ 166 now stands. The second, built in 1701 on the corner of Broad and Wall streets, was demolished in 1812. On the same site, the U.S. CUSTOM HOUSE, now the FEDERAL HALL NATIONAL MEMORIAL ▲ 162 was constructed. City Hall served as the seat of Manhattan's administrative offices until the creation of "Greater New York" in 1898, which brought together the five boroughs – the Bronx, Queens, Brooklyn, Staten Island and Manhattan – following which the MUNICIPAL BUILDING ▲ 182 was built. It still houses the Mayor's office and is used for official ceremonies. The courtrooms and the office (open to the public) used by "Hizzoner" (the traditional New York nickname for the mayor) are reached by the building's main staircase.

Center, the cupola of City Hall.

CITY HALL PARK. The apple trees of this former public grazing ground (1686) were once used as gallows by the British. JACOB LEISLER, a Dutch merchant who was proclaimed "leader of Free New York" during the city's rebellion against excessive taxation by JAMES II, was hanged here for treason in 1691. The statue of another legendary convict – although executed elsewhere – also stands in the park ▲ 262: NATHAN HALE, a hero of the American Revolution, was summarily hanged by the British for spying. His last words were, "I only regret that I have but one life to lose for my country." The

6 PARK PLACE TOWER
7 PARK ROW BLDG.
8 TITANIC MEMORIAL LIGHTHOUSE
9 PECK SLIP
10 EX-ATT BLDG.
11 ST. PAUL'S CHAPEL
12 N.Y. COUNTY LAWYERS ASSN.
13 EX-N.Y. EVENING POST BLDG.
14 FEDERAL OFFICE BLDG.
15 ST. PETER'S CHURCH
16 WOOLWORTH BLDG.
17 FOLEY SQUARE
18 MUNICIPAL BLDG.
19 U.S. COURTHOUSE
20 N.Y. COUNTY COURTHOUSE
21 N.Y.C. CRIMINAL COURT BLDG.
22 THOMAS PAINE PARK
23 N.Y.C. DEPARTMENT OF HEALTH

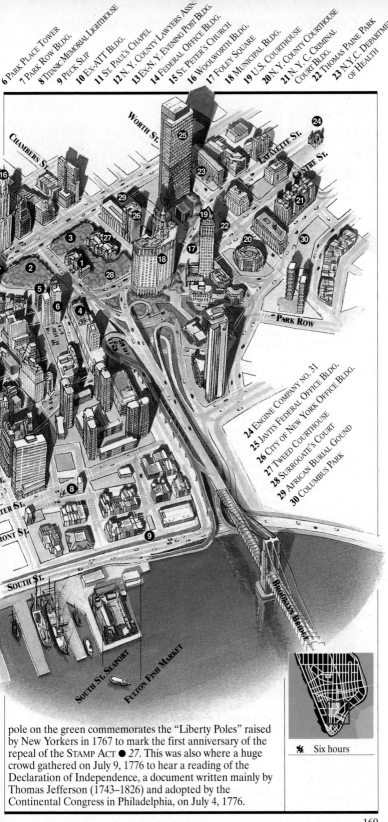

24 ENGINE COMPANY NO. 31
25 JAVITS FEDERAL OFFICE BLDG.
26 CITY OF NEW YORK OFFICE BLDG.
27 TWEED COURTHOUSE
28 SURROGATE'S COURT
29 AFRICAN BURIAL GOUND
30 COLUMBUS PARK

✺ Six hours

pole on the green commemorates the "Liberty Poles" raised
by New Yorkers in 1767 to mark the first anniversary of the
repeal of the STAMP ACT ● 27. This was also where a huge
crowd gathered on July 9, 1776 to hear a reading of the
Declaration of Independence, a document written mainly by
Thomas Jefferson (1743–1826) and adopted by the
Continental Congress in Philadelphia, on July 4, 1776.

169

THE CROTON FOUNTAIN
In 1842 a fountain was built on the site of the ornamental pond in City Hall Park (above) to celebrate the city's first supply of piped drinking water from the Croton Reservoir. The fountain was demolished in 1875.

FORMER POST OFFICE
This post office (opposite), which replaced the Croton Fountain, stood in front of City Hall. It was demolished in 1939 when the General Post Office was built on 8th Ave. ▲ 249.

NEWSPAPER ROW
In 1895 around fifteen daily newspapers were located near Park Row (below), including the *Times, World, Tribune, Sun, Post, Journal* and *Staats Zeitung*. Children used to sell

BENJAMIN FRANKLIN. PRINTING HOUSE SQUARE (1872, Ernst Plassman). In this square, east of City Hall, stands a statue of BENJAMIN FRANKLIN, printer, writer, scientist, statesman and signatory of the Declaration of Independence. From 1729 Franklin was editor of the *Pennsylvania Gazette*. Between 1732 and 1757 he published *Poor Richard's Almanack*.

PARK ROW, FORMERLY "NEWSPAPER ROW"

This area was the center of journalism during the second half of the 19th century. The proximity of City Hall and of the theater district around Theater Alley, was ideal for the newspapers, which took advantage of the inexhaustible supply of scandal afforded by these establishments. Although some of the buildings are still standing, the newspapers and the theaters have moved uptown to the vicinity of Times Square.

PACE UNIVERSITY, FORMERLY THE NEW YORK TIMES BUILDING. 41 PARK ROW (1889, arch. George B. Post). This building, occupied by Pace University since 1952, has such sturdy foundations (to accommodate the printing presses) that it was able to bear the extra weight when the height of the building was raised in 1905. The *New York Times* moved in 1903 to offices on what became Times Square ▲ 255.

POTTER BUILDING. 38 PARK ROW (1883, arch. Nathan Starkweather). This replaced the NEW YORK WORLD BUILDING, which had been destroyed by a fire. It was said to be fireproof due to its terracotta construction. The ornamental treatment of the façade was a first for an office building. The *Daily News*, the *New York Press* and the *Daily Observer* subsequently occupied

the morning and evening editions on the street with the familiar shout "Extra! Read all about it!". The office buildings had cavernous basements which housed heavy printing presses.

this building in their turn.

THE FORMER AMERICAN TRACT SOCIETY BUILDING. 150 NASSAU ST. (1896, arch. R. H. Robertson). The COLONNADE on top is all that remains of a penthouse suite built on top of the sloping copper roof. It was demolished when the height of the TIMES BUILDING was raised, thereby blocking its view. Visit the semicircular lobby, with its original marble moldings and coffered ceiling. This building has some of the last manually operated elevators in New York.

"THE MUSE WHO NOW RULES THE PRESS."

ANTHONY TROLLOPE

The riot quelled by the police in front of the Tribune Building, July 11, 1863.

PARK ROW BUILDING. 15 PARK ROW (1899, arch. R. H. Robertson). This building was the tallest skyscraper in the world when it was opened. The twin-domed crown used to dominate the skyline. The balconies thrusting away from the façade at intervals seem to be secured by magnetization. Four stone goddesses watch over the entrance. Make sure to see the reception area and the lobby, with its semicircular elevators. The lobby still has its original decoration: solid brass ramps, delicate marble trim and coffered ceiling.

TOWARD THE SOUTH STREET SEAPORT

TITANIC MEMORIAL LIGHTHOUSE. FULTON ST., between PEARL and WATER STS. This monument, erected in memory of those who went down with the *Titanic*, once sat on top of the Seamen's Church Institute Building (on State Street). The *Titanic* Memorial Lighthouse was moved to this site in 1976 and marks the entrance to South Street Seaport. Its clock is highly original: every day, at noon exactly, a black ball slides down from the top of a post.

PECK SLIP ★. PECK SLIP at FRONT ST. In the 18th century this neighborhood boasted many Federal-style houses belonging to the élite. In 1973 the Con Edison company demolished several blocks to build a sub-station, despite the angry protests of residents. Its wall is decorated with a trompe l'oeil painting by Richard Haas, which depicts the demolished site, the arches of the South Street Viaduct and the Brooklyn Bridge ▲ 186.

DRAFT RIOTS, JULY 11, 1863
The protesters converged on City Hall. They also attacked certain newspapers, especially Horace Greeley's *New York Tribune*, which "dared" to print the comment that "a negro is worth as much as an Irishman". They attempted to charge Tribune Tower, but the riot was quelled by the police.

JOURNALISM AND LITERATURE
The press, which had been free from the beginning, tended to favor journalistic methods that appealed to a mass market. The Civil War (1861–5) confirmed this trend and, during the 19th century, many writers who published their work in the newspapers gave rise to a type of journalism that appropriated the techniques of literature.

Since 1967 South Street Seaport Historic District, which covers seven blocks in Lower Manhattan and extends along three piers on the East River, has managed to preserve some of the last buildings to house shipowners' and merchants' offices during the golden age of the clipper ships. Schermerhorn Row, built in 1811 (opposite), was preserved in this way. The old Fulton Ferry Hotel, which faces the river, dates back to the 1860's. South of the block, the A. A. Low warehouse (1850) still stands.

Lettie G. Howard

Pioneer

Peking

Wavertree

A fleet of historic ships evokes the hustle and bustle of this neighborhood during the 19th century, when the long booms virtually touched the façades of the buildings – and when oysters (left) were cheap.

1 Pier 17 2 Fulton Fish Market 3 F.D.R. Drive 4 "Ambrose" 5 Pier 16 6 "Peking" 7 Pier 15 8 "Wavertree" 9 "Lettie G. Howard" 10 "Pioneer" 11 Fulton Ferry Hotel 12 A. A. Low Warehouse

PIER 15, PIER 16
Along pier 15 (above right) lies the *Wavertree*, built in England in 1885. In the center is the *Peking* (made in Germany in 1911); to the left of Pier 16 is the *Ambrose* (1907), a bright red lightship serving at the entrance to the Ambrose Channel, excavated in 1899, which enabled New York Harbor to accommodate the giant transatlantic liners of the 20th century.

Behind the poop of the *Peking* are the *Pioneer*, the *Andrew Fletcher*, which offers excursions around the harbor in the summer, and the *Lettie G. Howard*, a fishing schooner of 1893 (moored between the prows of the two square-rigged schooners).

FULTON FERRY HOTEL
This establishment's varied clientele included captains of trading vessels, farmers with produce to sell at the local markets, traders and businessmen.

A. A. LOW WAREHOUSE
The warehouse, designed by A. A. Low, a clipper owner and merchant involved in the China trade, now houses an exhibit of maritime artifacts.

SOUTH STREET SEAPORT MUSEUM
★ BOAT BUILDING SHOP ★

173

During the 19th century New York was the scene of several of the greatest technological advances in shipbuilding made possible by the industrial revolution. It was in New York in 1807 that Robert Fulton built the first profit-making steamboat; in 1814 he designed and launched the first steam battleship.

SHIPBUILDING IN NEW YORK
During the era of steel shipbuilding, New York's shipyards, in Brooklyn (above, in 1883) launched several of the country's great warships, including the *Maine* (above, left), whose sinking in Havana harbor in 1898 was one of the main causes of the Spanish-American War.

THE "MONITOR"
Built in 1862 by the Swedish engineer John Ericsson, the *Monitor* was the first battleship in the world to have its cannons housed in an armor-plated turret. It is here shown in battle with the Confederacy's own ironclad, the *Virginia*.

The New York shipyards, which are located in Brooklyn, Staten Island and on the Jersey shore, still do a lively business repairing and refitting all types of ships including the ocean liners, small tugs and barges that use the harbor.

Seafaring paraphernalia in local shop window (left) and fish signboard (right).

FULTON FISH MARKET
This original market (for produce) opened in 1821; eventually benefiting from the busy harbor activity, it became the city's wholesale fish market.

THE FISH MARKET
The flat-roofed Fulton Fish Market is located right on the East River front. The fish are no longer delivered by fishing boats; they arrive at night in refrigerated trucks from all over the country. Fish is for sale from midnight until 9 in the morning.

NEW YORK CENTRAL NO. 31
The pilothouse on exhibit on pier 13 at the South Street Seaport Museum was taken from a steam tug boat built in 1923.

Oysters and clams are two of New York's natural resources and for a long time were a local tradition in the city. Here and there you can still find "oyster bars" ▲ 238, where you can savor the famous Manhattan clam chowder.

South Street Seaport's two oldest restaurants are on Schermerhorn Row: Sloppy Louie's (early 1900's) is opposite on South St., and Sweet's Restaurant (mid-19th century) is in the old Fulton Ferry Hotel.

SOUTH STREET SEAPORT HISTORIC DISTRICT
Various temporary and permanent photographic exhibitions are mounted in the historic district, which is bounded by Fulton, Front, Beekman and Water sts. The Trans-Lux Seaport Theater (133 Beekman St.) shows films retracing the history of this area.

An exhibition of model ships (above) in the Fish Market.

SOUTH STREET SEAPORT MUSEUM

The huge cathedral of commerce that is Woolworth Building along with Saint Paul's Chapel, which in 1776 marked the city's northernmost boundary, are both situated to the west of the Civic Center. Another local landmark is the former AT&T Building.

FORMER AT&T BUILDING ★. 195 BROADWAY (1915–22, arch. William Welles Bosworth). This building conveys a feeling of strength. The huge Doric columns, 40 feet high, with their purity of line, are echoed by those in the lobby (below, left). One element strikes a false note with the classical Greek decoration: the vertical joins of the columns reveal that the stone is merely a covering. Against the lobby's west wall a monument to the glory of communication trumpets the vocation of the building's previous occupant, AT&T: "Service to the Nation in peace and war". The lobby also boasts a statue of *Adonis*. Another sculpture, by E. B. LONGMAN, was erected on the roof of the building. This statue, called *Spirit of Communication*, or more affectionately, *Golden Boy*, was moved in 1984 to the lobby of the new AT&T building at 550 Madison Avenue ▲ *289*, but was removed from there when Sony bought the building in 1993.

ST. PAUL'S CHAPEL ★

St. Paul's Chapel, at the intersection of Broadway and Fulton streets, is a part of Trinity parish. Having miraculously escaped unscathed from the many fires that

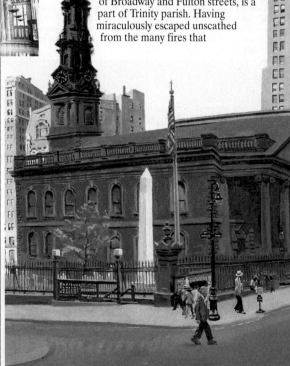

TELECOMMUNICATIONS
For more than a century AT&T provided virtually all the telephone services in the United States. In the 1970's, the company, which still owns the *Bell Laboratories* for research and development facilities, was the largest privately owned company in the world. In 1981 AT&T had more than one million employees, a turnover of 60 billion dollars, and over three million shareholders. An AT&T investment was the archetypal "gilt-edged investment" – risk-free. In 1982 the company lost its monopoly.

devastated most of Lower Manhattan ● *38*, this building is the only monument in the neighborhood predating the War of Independence. Completed in 1766, it is the oldest church in New York. The building, designed by Thomas McBean, was constructed of regular-sized blocks of Manhattan schist. It resembles St. Martin's-in-the-Fields, in London, whose architect, James Gibbs, taught McBean. Entry to St. Paul's used to be through the churchyard on Church Street. Above the present-day entrance, on Broadway, there is a NICHE containing a statue of St. Paul armed with a sword. Just below, in the middle of the porch, there is the tomb and monument of Brigadier General Richard Montgomery, who died in 1775 during the American Revolution at the battle of Quebec. The interior, painted in pastel colors, is graced by a barrel vaulted ceiling and an exquisite organ loft. The church service following George Washington's inauguration as President, on April 30, 1789, was held here. His PEW, as well as that of New York State's first governor, George Clinton, can still be seen. Free concerts are given in the chapel twice a week at noon. Its churchyard is a true haven of peace for employees who come from the Financial District to unwind. Seen from City Hall Park, the church spire forms a marked contrast with the twin towers of the World Trade Center.

GEORGE WASHINGTON IN ST. PAUL'S CHAPEL
Above George Washington's pew hangs the first oil painting of the Great Seal of the United States, designed in 1789, shortly after the election of the first president. George Washington's regimental flag is displayed at the rear of the nave.

Saint Paul's Chapel (center), a painting (1940) by Saul Berman.

THE CHURCHYARD OF ST. PAUL'S CHAPEL
This churchyard is even more of an oasis than the one at Trinity Church. Its trees – a riot of blossom in spring – its squirrels and its tombstones, most of them dating back to

the 18th century, present a striking contrast with the surrounding neighborhood. It is no longer used as a cemetery.

WEST OF BROADWAY

NEW YORK COUNTY LAWYERS' ASSOCIATION. 14 VESEY ST. (1930, arch. Cass Gilbert). This austere neo-Georgian building ● *82*, constructed of Vermont marble and limestone, was designed by the

Façade of the Federal Office Building.

"With an astonishing sense of harmony, [the city] crammed all of them together, the arched solid masses, the square towers, the terraces . . . and the stepped levels . . ., the pyramidal ziggurats, creating an ever-thickening forest of spires, obelisks, cones and turrets."
Elie Faure,
Mon Périple

architect of the Woolworth Building ▲ *180*, the Custom House ▲ *157* and the U.S. Courthouse. It is the headquarters of the New York County Lawyers' Association and has been dubbed "the house of law". The retrospective style of this building, designed for a conservative body concerned with projecting a traditional image, made it conspicuous at a time when architecture in the United States was going through a more bold, forward-looking phase. Its large auditorium (which is open to the public on request) is modeled on the main hall of Philadelphia's Independence Hall.

FORMER GARRISON BUILDING. 20 VESEY ST. (1906, arch. Robert D. Kohn, sculptor Gutzon Borglum). At one time, this building housed the *New York Evening Post*. In 1801 Alexander Hamilton, who is buried not far from here in Trinity churchyard, founded the newspaper which is now published as the *New York Post*, but was then a mouthpiece for conservative Federalist opinions. Later, another famous writer, William Cullen Bryant, who edited the *Post* from 1829 to 1878, gradually moved it toward a more working-class ethic. The building's façade is structured by limestone piers which rise in unbroken lines to the fine curb roof. The side walls were left plain, as future plans included other buildings on either side. Cross to the opposite side of the street to admire the ornamental Art Nouveau sculptures on top of the building, allegorical figures representing the "Four Periods of Publicity". They are the joint work of Estelle Rumbald Kohn (the architect's wife) and Gutzon Borglum. The latter also created the famous NATIONAL MEMORIAL in South Dakota where the gigantic heads of Presidents WASHINGTON, JEFFERSON, LINCOLN and ROOSEVELT are carved into the side of Mount Rushmore.

FEDERAL OFFICE BUILDING & U.S. POST OFFICE. 90 CHURCH ST. (1935, arch. Cross & Cross, Pennington Lewis & Mills Inc., Lewis A. Simon). There is no doubt that this building, complete with majestic eagles and occupying the entire block, is the property of the federal government, even if the main entrance, rather than being a triumphal focus of attention, is minimized by the sides of the building. The architects of this building combined architectural forms alternating vertical and horizontal lines: the stocky twin towers rise from a setback which sits above a sturdy neo-classical temple, a desperate attempt to marry the characteristic verticality of New York with the horizontality of Washington. Enter the building on Church Street to discover one of the finest post office interiors in the city, with its intricately worked grilles and monumental black Doric columns echoing the ones on the façade. Be sure to make a detour to see the stunning Art Deco stained glass windows and the inlaid work of the floor and ceiling – from which light is diffused through square panels, creating the effect of coffering. The building also boasts a magnificent lobby.

ST. PETER'S CHURCH. 22 BARCLAY ST. (1838, arch. John R. Haggerty and Thomas Thomas). This church was built on the site of an earlier St. Peter's Church, erected in 1785, the year after a ban on Roman Catholicism in New York was lifted. This was the parish church of the first Black American saint, Pierre Toussaint, whose ashes now lie in a crypt in St. Patrick's Cathedral on 5th Avenue ▲ *283*.

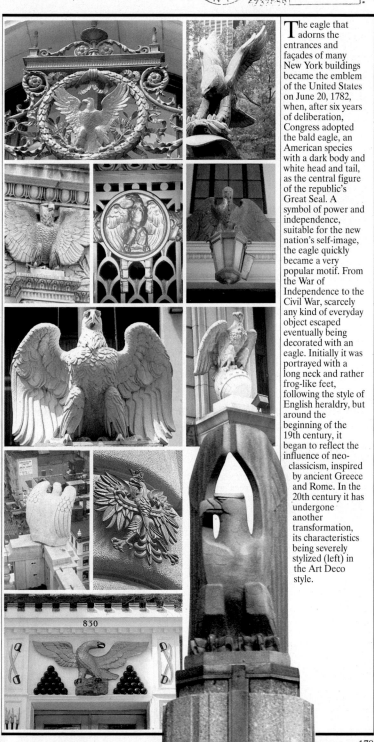

The eagle that adorns the entrances and façades of many New York buildings became the emblem of the United States on June 20, 1782, when, after six years of deliberation, Congress adopted the bald eagle, an American species with a dark body and white head and tail, as the central figure of the republic's Great Seal. A symbol of power and independence, suitable for the new nation's self-image, the eagle quickly became a very popular motif. From the War of Independence to the Civil War, scarcely any kind of everyday object escaped eventually being decorated with an eagle. Initially it was portrayed with a long neck and rather frog-like feet, following the style of English heraldry, but around the beginning of the 19th century, it began to reflect the influence of neo-classicism, inspired by ancient Greece and Rome. In the 20th century it has undergone another transformation, its characteristics being severely stylized (left) in the Art Deco style.

179

A RECORD TO BEAT
With its 60 stories
and a height of 792
feet, this was the
world's tallest
building – 92 feet
taller than the
Metropolitan Life
Tower. It was
relegated
to third
place by the
Chrysler
Building
▲ 266 and
40 Wall St.
in 1929.

In 1909 Frank Woolworth, the "king" of two
hundred five-and-ten-cent stores, embarked on
the creation of a headquarters for the company
which had made him a household name. He bought a plot
of land on Broadway. Cass Gilbert, the epitome of the eclectic
architect, urged his client to build the tallest building in the
world. The foundations of this "cathedral of
commerce" were laid in August 1911 and
work proceeded at the rate of one and a
half stories a week. Woolworth paid for
his skyscraper in cash: $15.5 million.

SIGNED IN STONE
Traces of the sort of
humor sometimes
found in cathedrals
can be seen in the
building's sculptures:
one of the consoles
(left) depicts Frank
Woolworth counting
the nickels and dimes
that made his fortune.

**THE "EIGHTH
WONDER OF THE
WORLD"**
Official opening of
the building took
place in April 1913
with a gala for 800
people, during which
President Woodrow
Wilson switched on
the building's lights
from the White
House.

A COPPER PINNACLE ON TOP OF A "TERRACOTTA" CATHEDRAL

Influenced by his travels in Europe, Woolworth insisted that his architect employ a Gothic style ● 86, reminiscent of French cathedrals and of London's Houses of Parliament.

Labor

THE LOBBY

The lobby, with entrances on Broadway, Barclay St. and Park Place, is a vast shopping arcade in the shape of a Latin cross. The walls are sheathed in marble and the vaulted ceilings in mosaics of Byzantine inspiration (above), which extol the virtues of labor and commerce. The Woolworth Building was one of the first buildings to provide direct access to the subway.

At the beginning of the 19th century, a new wave of immigrants in search of cheap accommodation settled on the intersection of Baxter, Park and Worth streets. This small triangular park, which was the setting for all kinds of entertainment, soon came to be called "Paradise Park". During the 1820's, the neighborhood began to deteriorate, becoming the haunt of gangsters and prostitutes. In 1845 the Five Points Mission (above) was set up.

❝Was there such a thing as an American style? Yes, if you saw it as an incredible juxtaposition of every architectural form imaginable. In one hundred metres, you could savour Renaissance-style columns with drums; Doric shafts; Corinthian capitals with peculiarly intricate designs, and even the odd allusion to the Egyptian Litiform Order. As for the buildings themselves, they fluctuate from gable to dome, from crenel to terrace roof, with relentless variety.❞
Victor Segalen,
Journal des Îles

The Municipal Building (right).

Most of the buildings of the Civic Center can be found to the north of the City Hall. They represent a host of architectural styles, their construction having spanned more than a century. Some of them were built in neo-classical styles inspired by Greco-Roman democratic tradition, frequently favored in the United States for government buildings. Architects and their clients, however, who were keen to build higher, often used neo-classical temples as bases on which to erect loftier structures. As the 20th century progressed, New York, whose architecture had been influenced previously by London, then Paris, began to create its own distinctive identity.

FOLEY SQUARE

This square occupies the site of what was once COLLECT POND ● 74, which had disappeared by 1811. Before Independence, a gallows stood on the island in the center. In 1854 the FIVE POINTS MISSION was founded in this section of New York to help the poor in the nearby slums of Five Points ● 191, who were being decimated by cholera. Thomas Foley (1852–1923), whose name was given to the square in 1926, had run a bar in the neighborhood before going into politics: he became alderman and sheriff of the County of New York and played a key role in getting Al Smith elected governor. Foley used to say that he enjoyed being involved in political intrigue for its own sake. He attributed his success to the fact that he always told the truth, adding: "People don't like it, but they come back six months later."

MUNICIPAL BUILDING ★. 1 CENTRE ST. AT 4 CHAMBERS ST. (1914, arch. McKim, Mead & White) ● 96. When the Bronx, Queens, Brooklyn and Staten Island were linked to Manhattan in 1898 to create Greater New York, it was decided that new administrative offices were needed. This building, which looks like a square-shouldered giant guarding City Hall, made such an impression on Stalin that the University of Moscow was later modeled on it. The architects, who were searching for a style of administrative architecture that best symbolized America and the 20th century, were influenced by the "City Beautiful"

movement which sprang up after the 1893 World's Columbian Exposition in Chicago and which focused on the creation of grand public buildings in elegantly landscaped parks. Their building consists of a fourteen-story u-shaped block crowned with a "Renaissance palace" rising from a monumental base with a neo-classical colonnade. The building is topped with three tiered drums, the bottom of which is flanked by four pinnacle turrets symbolizing the four boroughs joined to Manhattan. On the top stands a statue, *Civic Fame*, by Adolph A. Weinman. The building straddles Chambers Street with a central arch, through which vehicles crossing the Brooklyn Bridge ▲ *186* could formerly pass; thus the building became known as the "Gate of the City". A pedestrian walkway, over the bridge, starts here and is well worth following, as it affords an extraordinary view over Manhattan and leads to Brooklyn Heights ▲ *366*.

U.S. COURTHOUSE ★. 40 CENTRE ST. AT S. E. CORNER OF PEARL ST. (1936, arch. Cass Gilbert and Cass Gilbert, Jr) This was the last of Cass Gilbert's New York buildings. Here neo-classicism seems to be played out: a marble platform supports a CLASSICAL TEMPLE, pierced by a modern twenty-four-story tower with a gold top. During the week, one can attend hearings in the various courtrooms. The basement houses a SHOOTING GALLERY for F.B.I. agents.

NEW YORK COUNTY COURTHOUSE. 60 CENTRE ST. (1913–27, arch. Guy Lowell). The New York County Courthouse is an imposing Corinthian temple approached by a monumental staircase. At the center this hexagon-shaped building is a domed circular area, which is linked to each of the six wings by corridors. Thirty years later, this layout was adapted by the architects of the Pentagon. This central area is decorated with fine murals and a polychrome marble floor inlaid with brass medallions representing the signs of the zodiac. Outside, statues entitled *Law, Truth and Equity* stand on the pediment of the main entrance.

CRIMINAL COURTS BUILDING, FORMERLY THE DETENTION CENTER FOR MEN. 100 CENTRE ST. BETWEEN WORTH AND LEONARD STS. (1939, arch. Harvey Wiley Corbett and Charles B. Meyers). This building houses the City of New York's Courthouse and, formerly, a men's prison. It is the third municipal prison: the esplanade opposite stands on the site of the two previous buildings. The first, dating from 1838, was built in the Egyptian Revival style, which gave the building its nickname of "The Tombs", a nickname also applied to its two successors. One of the most famous anecdotes relating to the original prison concerns John Colt. This man, sentenced to be hanged in 1842, was allowed to marry and enjoy an hour-long honeymoon. At the end of the allotted hour he was found dead, stabbed through the heart with a knife. A second,

"In New York, everyone is afraid of the burly Irish cop: he only has to blow on his whistle to commandeer vehicles or to obtain help from everyone. Like ambulances and fire engines, the police have right of way on the road and priority use of the telegraph system and the telephone. This peace force whose job is to send people to Sing-Sing", as described by Paul Morand in *New York*, was divided into different specialist squads concentrating on areas such as robbery or bootlegging.

THE "TOMBS"
In *Ragtime*, a novel based on real characters which takes place in New York at the turn of the century, the writer E. L. Doctorow tells the story of a multi millionaire in a cell in The "Tombs". Above, the first, Egyptian-style prison.

Bas-reliefs from the Paine St. façade of the N.Y.C. Department of Health.

THE FIREHOUSES
When horses were first used to pull fire engines, they were kept in stables on the ground floor of firehouses (above, Engine Company no. 31). The men, who slept on the second floor, above, protested violently, so it was decided to move the stables to the back of the building. However, the firemen soon changed their mind about this because by the time they had harnessed up the horses to the vehicles, the fire had, in many cases, destroyed everything. Many horses who had spent their early working lives with the fire department found it very hard to adjust to a more tranquil life as carriage horses: whenever they heard a fire engine's siren, they would gallop off, putting their new owner in grave danger.

French Renaissance-style prison was built on the ruins of the first which was demolished in 1893. This in turn was destroyed in 1947. The present building, in Art Deco style, no longer contains a prison (moved to Rikers Island in 1974), but its court attracts visitors who attend trials held here.

DEPARTMENTS OF HEALTH, HOSPITAL AND SANITATION. 125 WORTH ST. (1935, arch. Charles B. Meyers). This Art Deco ● *98* temple was built to celebrate the victory of medicine over cholera, smallpox and tuberculosis. Previously, the department had occupied run down premises, inadequate for the task of trying to control the health and hygiene of 6 million inhabitants. Note the bas-reliefs depicting the medical sciences (above) and the splendid torchères (below, right) that grace the south and east entrances.

ENGINE COMPANY NO. 31. 87 LAFAYETTE ST. AT N. E. CORNER OF WHITE ST. (1895, arch. Napoleon Le Brun & Sons). The architect, who specialized in building firehouses, designed this building like a Loire Valley chateau, a style then very popular for the houses of the rich. Firemen used to live virtually full-time in the firehouse. This building, which is no longer used for its original purpose, is now a designated landmark.

JACOB K. JAVITS FEDERAL BUILDING AND CUSTOMS COURTHOUSE. 26 FEDERAL PLAZA (1967, arch. Alfred Easton Poor, Kahn & Jacobs, Eggers & Higgins). This International Style ● *100* building is clad in a facing whose motifs are designed to disguise its massive frame. Every day long lines of hopeful citizenship candidates stretch back from the checkpoint.

CITY OF NEW YORK OFFICE BUILDING, FORMER EMIGRANT INDUSTRIAL SAVINGS BANK. 51 CHAMBERS ST. (1912, arch. Raymond F. Almirall). This precursor of the Municipal Building is a mixture of styles: its Renaissance Revival twin towers with Art Deco tops stand on a neo-classical base. It was once the headquarters of the Emigrant Savings Bank, founded in 1851 by the Irish to help their fellow countrymen who were living in the slums of Five Points ▲ *191*. In time it became one of

EMIGRANT · INDVSTRIAL SAVINGS · BANK

the most powerful banks in the country. Enter through the west door to admire the gilded elevator cages.

"TWEED COURTHOUSE", OLD NEW YORK COUNTY COURTHOUSE. 52 CHAMBERS ST. (1858–78, arch. John Kellum, Leopold Eidlitz). The former New York County courthouse stands as a monument to the heights of corruption reached by William Marcy, TAMMANY HALL'S "Boss" Tweed ● *40*. Until his arrest in 1871, Boss Tweed pocketed huge amounts of city funds. A total of $14 million was eventually spent on the construction of this building, which was completed twenty years later and whose original cost had been estimated at $250,000. The municipal government then paid for an order – which was never delivered – of enough carpeting to cover City Hall Park three times over. The campaign led by George Jones, editor of *The New York Times*, and Thomas Nast, the cartoonist, finally led to Tweed's downfall. He was tried and sentenced, and died behind bars in 1878. The building, which was completed without the dome or

marble facing originally planned, has a CENTRAL ROTUNDA (above).

HALL OF RECORDS, SURROGATE'S COURT ★. 31 CHAMBERS ST. AT N. W. CORNER OF CENTRE ST. (1899–1911, arch. John R. Thomas, Horgan & Slattery). This impressive building, which serves both as surrogate's court and a home for the city archives, was intended to be the Municipal Building, but was deemed too small for this purpose. Work on the building was stopped, only to be restarted to build the Hall of Records. The architect used the popular Beaux Arts style ● *92* to reproduce the affluence of the Paris Opera House.

Detail from the façade of the Emigrant Savings Bank.

TWEED COURTHOUSE
The scandal surrounding the construction of the old New York Courthouse (below left) clearly demonstrates the type of methods that "Boss" Tweed stooped to as early as 1852 when he was an alderman. He would inflate costs on orders issued by the municipal government and pocket the difference. No one ever knew just how much Tweed and his ring embezzled.

UNDER THE HALL OF RECORDS
This building occupies, in part, the site of an old cemetery for Blacks; recently discovered, it was designated a landmark. Several hundred bodies have been exhumed, some of them still wearing 18th-century British uniforms; the British offered freedom to slaves who fought on their side in the War of Independence.

The neo-Baroque rotunda (left) of the Hall of Records and Surrogate's Court, designed by John R. Thomas.

185

▲ BROOKLYN BRIDGE

FERRYBOATS REPLACED BY A BRIDGE
In the mid-19th century, 50 million people a
year crossed the East River on the slow,
overcrowded ferryboats.

Manhattan, cut off from the mainland by a wide estuary and a
great river, the Hudson, needed bridges if it was to grow; but it
took many years before engineers
were able to construct bridges of
the required length. The oldest is
the Brooklyn Bridge, completed
in 1883.

A COSMOPOLITAN BUILDING SITE
The work force employed was a mixture of
old American stock and newly arrived
immigrants from Ireland, Germany and Italy.

A STEEL AND GRANITE MONSTER

This was the longest, highest bridge of the 19th century, with its two granite towers and steel cables and its metal roadway with a span of 1,595 feet, towering 148 feet above the water.

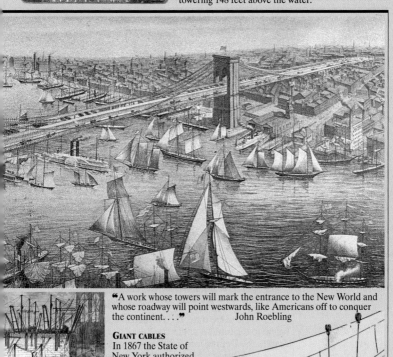

"A work whose towers will mark the entrance to the New World and whose roadway will point westwards, like Americans off to conquer the continent. . . .**"**   John Roebling

GIANT CABLES

In 1867 the State of New York authorized the construction of the suspension bridge in line with plans drawn up by John Roebling (1806–69), who arrived from Germany in 1831.

...took 14 years to build and ...st $16 million, exceeding all expectations.

A FAMILY OF ENGINEERS

Due to an accident at work, Roebling developed tetanus and died in 1869. His son Washington took over but was

The Manhattan skyline seen from Brooklyn.

disabled by "caisson disease"; Washington's wife, Emily, then became a liaison between Washington and the crew.

The New Harlem Bridge over the Harlem River (here in 1868) linked Harlem and the Bronx.

STATISTICS OF SOME NEW YORK BRIDGES
(1) Brooklyn: span 1,595 feet
(2) Manhattan: span 1,470 feet
(3) Williamsburg: span 1,597 feet
(4) Queensboro: max. span 1,182 feet
(5) Verrazano: span 4,260 feet
(6) George Washington: span 3,500 feet

THE BRIDGES OF MANHATTAN

For twenty years the Brooklyn Bridge remained the only link (apart from ferries) between Manhattan and Long Island, which – along with its beauty and virtuoso engineering – accounted for its popularity. Then, in the first decade of the 20th century, to satisfy the demands of a growing city, three other bridges were built over the East River.

ACROSS THE EAST RIVER. These were the Williamsburg Bridge in 1903, followed by the Queensboro bridge (commonly called the 59th Street Bridge) in 1909, and the Manhattan Bridge, in

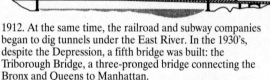

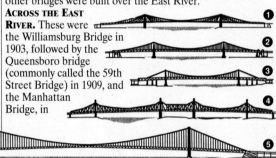

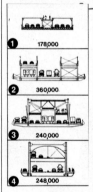

ANNUAL TRAFFIC
Number of people crossing the bridges each year:
(1) Brooklyn
(2) Manhattan
(3) Williamsburg
(4) Queensboro

WILLIAMSBURG BRIDGE
The Brooklyn Bridge (1883), then the Williamsburg Bridge (1903), shown (right) at the beginning of the century, made it much easier for New Yorkers who lived in Brooklyn to travel daily to their offices in Manhattan.

1912. At the same time, the railroad and subway companies began to dig tunnels under the East River. In the 1930's, despite the Depression, a fifth bridge was built: the Triborough Bridge, a three-pronged bridge connecting the Bronx and Queens to Manhattan.

ACROSS THE HUDSON. The George Washington Bridge, designed by Othmar Ammann and completed in 1931, remains the city's only bridge over the Hudson River. It is a suspension bridge, linking Manhattan, at 178th Street, to Fort Lee in New Jersey. Its span is over 3,500 feet – twice as long as that of the Brooklyn Bridge. This was the first major project to be completed by the Port of New York Authority, an interstate body created in 1921 to coordinate transportation in the metropolitan region. Although originally conceived as a railroad bridge, it was finally designed for automobile traffic; a lower level was added in 1962.

ACROSS THE NARROWS. At one time the longest suspension bridge in the world, the Verrazano-

Narrows Bridge (1964) spans the strait dividing Brooklyn from Staten Island at the mouth of the Upper Bay. This bridge, also designed by Ammann, has a span of 4,260 feet and a total length of 13,700 feet. In addition to its practical value in easing traffic congestion in Manhattan by providing a direct route from New Jersey to Long Island and its airports, the bridge serves as a spectacular gateway to the city.

LOWER EAST SIDE

SETH KAMIL

CHINATOWN, *190*
THE JEWISH NEIGHBORHOOD, *194*
LITTLE ITALY, *196*

▲ LOWER EAST SIDE

1 COLUMBUS PARK   2 TRANSFIGURATION CATHOLIC CHURCH   3 QUONG YEUN SHING & CO.   4 KAOSHEN CLUB   5 ASSN. SUN WEI   6 HIP SING TONG   7 CHATHAM SQUARE   8 SHEARITH ISRAEL GRAVEYARD   9 ST. JAMES CHURCH   10 MARINERS' TEMPLE BAPTIST CHURCH

The Lower East Side is one of Manhattan's liveliest, most historical neighborhoods. From the city's very beginnings this has been an immigrant neighborhood. An astonishing variety of ethnic groups have chosen to live here: Dutch, Irish, Black, Jewish, Italian, Chinese, German and Latin American, to mention only a few. Each of these groups has tried to form a self-sufficient community, creating its own social organizations as a bulwark against the demands of city life. These mutual aid institutions have played a vital role in finding work and accommodation for new immigrants and introducing them to the ways of the "New World". Religious and ethnic subgroups were formed within each community, so that there were organizations not simply for Jews, but for Russian Jews, Romanian Jews and Hungarian Jews, for example. Similarly Italian immigrants settled on the Lower East Side not as Italians but as Neapolitans, Sicilians and Milanese. This continual influx of immigrants also imported its share of marvelous national recipes – some of the best and cheapest restaurants in New York can be found on the Lower East Side.

"THE BIG ONION"
During the 1870's, the Lower East Side was called "The Big Onion". Although at the time this was a pejorative term, it has now acquired a new significance. In a sense, this neighborhood does resemble an onion: every time a layer is peeled away, there is another underneath, each representing a part of the neighborhood or another ethnic group.

CHINATOWN

COLUMBUS PARK. BAYARD AND MULBERRY (1892) was originally a patch of cultivated land belonging to the Bayard family, at the corner of Bayard Street and Mulberry Street. In the 19th century, the curved part of Mulberry Street was known as Mulberry Bend. This street led to Five Points, deep in the heart of the Sixth District, called by many

1970, THE CHANGING FACE OF A NEIGHBORHOOD
Above the modern sign for "New Jeannie's Restaurant", at 32 Mulberry St., there is still an old wooden sign for the establishment in its former Italian incarnation: "Moneta's". This exemplifies how the ethnic make-up of Mulberry St. has changed. Until the 1970's, this sector was exclusively Italian (right, at the beginning of the century) but it has now become almost exclusively Chinese: the restaurant is now identified in Chinese as well as English.

11 Khal Adath Jerushun Synagogue

12 Jarmulowsky Bank

13 Garden Cafeteria

14 Forward Bldg.

15 Seward Park

16 Beth Hamedrash Hagodol Synagogue

17 Banca Stabile

18 240 Centre Street

20 Old St. Patrick's Cathedral

MOTT ST. — **THE BOWERY** — **CHRYSTIE ST.** — **ELDRIDGE ST.** — **ALLEN ST.** — **ORCHARD ST.** — **ESSEX ST.** — **NORFOLK ST.**

LITTLE ITALY

DELANCY ST.

BROOME ST.

GRAND ST.

STRAUS SQUARE

EAST BROADWAY

CHINATOWN

PELL ST.

CONFUCIUS PLAZA

MANHATTAN BRIDGE

CHATHAM SQUARE

OLIVER ST.

ST. JAMES PLACE

🚶 Four hours

people the "Bloody old Sixth". This was the worst slum area in the history of New York. Until the mid-19th century, it was predominantly Irish; then Italians flocked here in search of cheap accommodation, cramming themselves into tiny apartments and living on top of each other, sometimes twelve or more to a room. In 1892 the slums of Five Points were demolished and replaced by Columbus Park. Almost as soon as it was built the park became a favorite site for open-air concerts and patriotic ceremonies. On Columbus Day and other public holidays, local musicians would gather in the park to play Italian melodies; street peddlers sold refreshments and the festive mood was heightened by fireworks displays.

CHURCH OF THE TRANSFIGURATION. 25 MOTT ST. This Georgian-style church, built in 1801 by the community of the First Episcopal Church of Zion, has seen some extraordinary

CHINATOWN HISTORY MUSEUM
The Chinatown History Museum occupies one floor of the public school on the corner of Bayard and Mulberry sts. It contains a collection of documents and personal letters written by the local inhabitants.

191

changes. In 1853, the Catholic Church bought the building for its thriving Italian and Irish communities. Then, in the 1950's, an increasing number of Chinese joined the parish, which is now almost exclusively Chinese. Under the times of services posted at the entrance to the church, there is a notice explaining that Mass is celebrated in Mandarin, Cantonese and English.

QUONG YEUN SHING & CO. 32 MOTT ST. This store is opposite the Church of the Transfiguration. It was founded in 1877 by the Lee family three generations ago and is the oldest store in Chinatown. This establishment started life as a grocery store, which doubled variously as a post office, a social center, a message service and a bank. It still has its original interior and façade and is a remnant of old Chinatown.

KAOSHEN CLUB. 12 MOTT ST. The headquarters of a secret political organization used to be based in this building (Kaoshen means "high mountain"). In 1895, Doctor Sun Yat-sen (founder and first president of the Republic of China) set

THE STREETS OF CHINATOWN
In the 19th century Doyers St. and Pell St. (above, in 1927) were dotted with Irish bars. A Chinese restaurant, Pell's Dinty (at 25 Pell St.) retains the name of the previous establishment. The Chinatown post office now occupies the site where one of the most popular bars of the time, Callahan's, used to stand. These bars used to employ scantily dressed waitresses and singers to draw in customers. Al Jolson and Irving Berlin were two very popular Jewish performers who used to work in Callahan's.

GREETINGS FROM C

up the New York branch of the secret revolutionary party Hsing Chung Hui in this building. This party brought about the demise of the Ch'ing imperial dynasty and established a republican government in China.

SUN WEI ASSOCIATION. 24 PELL ST. The exterior of this building offers an interesting example of Chinese symbolism. It is topped with an intricately carved wood pagoda, decorated with two carved fish representing financial profit. The association's colors are red, gold and green. Red symbolizes luck, gold symbolizes wealth and green symbolizes success in business.

HIP SING TONG. 16 PELL ST. This was one of the fraternal Chinese organizations, whose name, "tong", originally meant "hall" or "meeting place". Membership of these societies is shrouded in mystery and their money-making "activities" are frequently the subject of controversy. The tongs were secret fraternal societies created in China several hundred years ago and known then as "Triads". They were established in New York at the end of the 1870's to protect their members' interests. Over the years some tongs became involved in criminal activities including drug trafficking, embezzlement, prostitution, gambling and usury. However, today most tongs remain social organizations, helping new immigrants to find accommodation and employment

CHATHAM SQUARE. CORNER PARK ROW, BOWERY and EAST BROADWAY. This part of the city, which has been a prosperous center for trade since 1800, owes its name to the first Earl of Chatham, William Pitt the Elder. Lord & Taylor and Brooks Brothers opened their first clothing stores here. The arch in the center of the square was erected in 1962 as a memorial to Benjamin Ralph Kim Lau, a resident of Chinatown who died during World War Two, and to all the other Chinese soldiers who served under the American flag during the war. It is also sometimes called Kim Lau Square.

FIRST SHEARITH ISRAEL GRAVEYARD. 55 ST. JAMES PLACE. Half a block from Chatham Square, the first graveyard of the Spanish and Portuguese synagogue Shearith Israel, runs the length of St. James Place. This site, designated a "National Historic Landmark" and a "New York City Landmark" dates back to 1682. It is the oldest Jewish cemetery in the United States and one of the oldest cemeteries in New York.

ST. JAMES CHURCH. 132 JAMES ST. (1837). Although the parish was created in 1827 by Irish immigrants, St. James Church, now designated a "New York City Landmark", was not built until 1837. As can be seen from the plaque to the right of the entrance, its first pastor was Father Felix Valera (1788–1853), who was born in Cuba. To the left of the entrance, another plaque commemorates the formation, in 1836, of the Ancient Order of Hibernians, Hibernia being the Latin name for Ireland. The A.O.H. helped Irish immigrants to find work and gave them legal and occasional financial aid, as required.

MARINERS' TEMPLE. 12 OLIVER ST. (1842, arch. Minard Lafever). This Ionic-order, Greek Revival church was built by a Baptist congregation to serve the spiritual needs

DOYERS STREET
At the end of the 18th century this street served as a cart lane for a distiller, Anthony H. Doyer. A hundred years later, the bend half way down Doyers St. was nicknamed "Bloody Angle" during a "tong war" which raged in Chinatown at the time. The Hip Sing and the On Leong used to battle here for control of local criminal activities.

of mariners, a purpose commemorated by the huge ship bell to the right of the porch. A similar function was served by the SEA AND LAND CHURCH (61 Henry Street), renamed the First Chinese Presbyterian in 1866. Today the Mariners' Temple belongs to an Afro-American Baptist Congregation and boasts an excellent gospel choir.

BROAD AVENUES
At the end of the 19th century, the Bowery (right), which in the 17th century led to Dutch farmland, was populated by the homeless, and the neighborhood also had a high concentration of bars dealing in all kinds of illegal activities. In 1884, 27 percent of arrests in New York were made in the Bowery. That year, the neighborhood numbered 82 bars, an average of six per block.

THE JEWISH NEIGHBORHOOD

THE EDUCATIONAL ALLIANCE
The Educational Alliance, on the southeast corner of East Broadway and Jefferson St., was founded in 1891 by German Jews from Uptown to help Eastern European immigrants adjust to the American way of life. It offered lessons in English, civics and health education.

KHAL ADATH JERUSHUN AND ANSHEI LUBZ SYNAGOGUE. 12–16 ELDRIDGE ST. (1886, arch. Herter Brothers) This Moorish-style building was built by Russian-Polish Jews. The building's religious identity is not that clear from its façade, which sports a rose window similar to those found on some churches, but the interior is that of a fine Orthodox synagogue, with women's galleries and an ark for holding the Torah scrolls. The building is currently being restored under the auspices of the Eldridge Street Synagogue Project. It is open to the public on Sundays and on request.

JARMULOWSKY BANK. Southwest corner of CANAL and ORCHARD STS. (1912). This eleven-story building was built by Sender Jarmulowsky, a Polish Jew who arrived in America in 1856 and opened his bank in 1873. His customers were mainly immigrant Jews who were sending money back to the Old World to help their families to cross the Atlantic. By 1913 the bank was doing well, a state of affairs that continued until the outbreak of World War One, when a large number of the bank's Jewish customers withdrew their money to send it immediately to their families in Europe. Because they did not trust paper money, they demanded gold and silver coins. There was such a rush on the counters that the federal controller shut the Jarmulowsky bank on August 4, 1914 – too late, however, to save its founder from bankruptcy.

GARDEN CAFETERIA. Corner of EAST BROADWAY and RUTGERS ST. The Wing Shoon Restaurant stands on the site once occupied by the Garden Cafeteria, a famous rendezvous of the local intelligentsia. Some of the United States' most eminent socialists, communists and anarchists used to meet here for a cup of tea. Among them were the Russian anarchists Emma Goldman, Alexander Berkman, Leon Trotsky, and Nikolay Bukharin.

> "NOT TO HAVE SEEN THOSE HUCKSTERS AND THEIR CARTS, AND THEIR MERCHANDISE, AND THEIR EXTRAORDINARY ZEST FOR BARGAINING IS TO HAVE MISSED A SIGHT THAT ONCE SEEN DECLINES TO BE FORGOTTEN." *HARPER'S WEEKLY*

Isaac Bashevis Singer is said to have written many of his books at the Garden Cafeteria.

FORWARD BUILDING. 175 EAST BROADWAY (1912, arch. George A. Boehm). The former Forward Building stands southeast of Nathan Straus Square. The Jewish community still regards this apartment building, with its huge clock and the Yiddish word "Forvets" carved into the stone at the top, as a symbol of the power of socialism and the workers. Until 1975 it was the headquarters of the Jewish *Daily Forward*, once one of the major socialist Yiddish publications in the world. The building now houses a church and a Bible-making works, the New York Ling Liang Church. On the west façade of the building a Mandarin slogan that translates, "Through Christ you will find salvation" points up the changes that have taken place in the neighborhood's ethnic make-up.

SEWARD PARK. Corner of EAST BROADWAY and ESSEX ST. This park, which dates from 1901, was designed to provide an open space in New York's most densely populated neighborhood. One of the memorable moments in the history of Seward Park occurred during the Cloakmakers' Strike in 1910. About sixty thousand striking workers from many different trades thronged the corner of East Broadway and Essex, opposite the Forward Building. This was also where immigrant workers used to congregate with their signs in Yiddish, Italian and English, calling for better pay and work conditions.

BETH HAMEDRASH HAGODOL SYNAGOGUE. 60 NORFOLK ST. This is the synagogue of the oldest Orthodox Ashkenazic community in the United States. It was founded in 1852 and used to be situated on Allen Street. The Ashkenazic community bought the building, originally the Norfolk Baptist Church, in 1885. The synagogue, open to the public during daily prayers, has retained the fine Gothic interior of the original Baptist church.

GUSS'S PICKLES
Essex St. is the heart of the old Jewish business district. The famous Guss's Pickles can be found at no. 35. On Sundays New Yorkers come to buy his famous gherkins at 25 cents apiece, a good deal more than the 5 cents they once used to cost.

AT THE MARKET
Around 1910 hundreds of thousands of Jews lived in this neighborhood, many working as street vendors. Hester St. was the busiest, liveliest part of the Lower East Side, especially on Thursday evenings, when women came to buy provisions for the Sabbath.

195

Washday on Monday, c. 1900, in the tenements of Little Italy.

LITTLE ITALY

BANCA STABILE. 189 GRAND ST. Corner of S.W. MULBERRY and GRAND STS. (1885). This building used to house an Italian bank, a family business founded in 1865 to help immigrant Italians. The Stabile offered various other services in addition to banking, including translation and steamship reservations. This can be seen from the gilt lettering above one of the counters, where tickets for transatlantic crossings could be bought. Note the tin ceilings, the terrazzo floor, the huge vault and the original brass grilles.

240 CENTRE STREET. (1909, arch. Hoppin, Koen & Huntington) This huge stone building in French-Baroque style was originally built for the New York police headquarters. At the time, this neighborhood was a hive of criminal activity. The headquarters were deliberately situated near the city's main prison, called "The Tombs" ▲ *183*, itself not far from the insalubrious "Five Points" area ▲ *191*. The building was converted into condominiums in the late 1980's.

MOST HOLY CRUCIFIX CHURCH. 378 BROOME ST. This Neapolitan Catholic church was consecrated in 1926. At that time, so the story goes, a group of Neapolitans had established a community in the neighborhood. When they wrote home, they told their families that they worshipped together, so their wives decided to dispatch a priest to New York from the village of their birth. The only land they could build on within a radius of three blocks was this plot, between Mott and Mulberry streets. The church was built extremely swiftly, so that when he arrived the priest would find a parish in which he could preach and hold services.

OLD SAINT PATRICK'S CATHEDRAL. MULBERRY ST. at PRINCE ST. (1809–15, arch. Joseph Mangin). This building was New York's first Catholic cathedral before the construction, Uptown, of the present St. Patrick's on 5th Avenue. A fire in 1868 destroyed much of it, and restoration costs proved so prohibitive that its rose window was walled over and the damaged Gothic decorative elements were covered.

SICILIANS, MILANESE, NEAPOLITANS
The Italian stretch of Mulberry St. (also known as Via San Gennaro) is still lined with shops selling fresh pasta, freshly baked bread and cheese made on the premises (above, at the turn of the century). The Caffè Roma is on this street. In the 1930's it was a haunt of Italian actors. Migliaccio, a popular performer of Neapolitan folk songs who appeared in theaters in the Bowery under the name of Farfariello (meaning "little butterfly"), lived nearby. His act consisted of making good-humored fun of the people living in the neighborhood.

AROUND WASHINGTON SQUARE

WASHINGTON SQUARE
TO SOHO-TRIBECA, *198*
WASHINGTON SQUARE TOWARD
GANSEVOORT MEAT MARKET, *210*
WASHINGTON SQUARE
TO CHELSEA, *216*

▲ WASHINGTON SQUARE TO SOHO-TRIBECA

1 WASHINGTON SQUARE 2 N.Y. UNIVERSITY 3 ASCH BLDG. 4 E. HOLMES BOBST LIBRARY 5 JUDSON MEMORIAL CHURCH 6 MILLS HOUSE NO. 1 7 MACDOUGAL-SULLIVAN GARDENS 8 MUSEUM FOR AFRICAN ART 9 NEW MUSEUM OF CONTEMPORARY ART 10 GUGGENHEIM MUSEUM 11 LITTLE SINGER BLDG. 12 HAUGHWOUT BLDG. 13 ROOSEVELT BLDG.

✹ Seven hours

WASHINGTON SQUARE ★

This square has been the artistic and intellectual hub of Greenwich Village ▲ *210* since the turn of the century. Until the end of the 18th century, it was simply a vast tract of marshland with a stream, the MINETTA BROOK ▲ *202*, running through it. It was then converted into a potter's field, for the interment of victims of the great cholera and yellow fever epidemics. In the early 1800's it also served as the site of public hangings – events commemorated by the great elm that stands at the

A FORMER MILITARY PARADE GROUND
Washington Square sits on former marshland which was drained and converted into a military parade

northwest corner of the park, which was used as a gallows. During his trip to New York in 1824, Lafayette was invited to watch the hanging of twenty highwaymen. In 1826, when the streets were being laid and the surrounding lands were developed for sale as building lots, the municipal government drained the swamp and built the WASHINGTON MILITARY PARADE GROUNDS, which

ground in 1826 (above, in 1851). When it was not an arena for military parades, it was used as a park where various entertainments were staged. This park, which was dearly loved by New Yorkers, gave the neighborhood a new lease on life. When the park was redesigned in 1971, the central island, which sports a fountain and was once used by buses for turning round, was closed to traffic by the municipal government.

Washington Square (right) in the early 1900's.

were inaugurated on July 4, 1828. The area around Washington Square soon became popular with wealthy New Yorkers, who built imposing residences around the park. Henry James, who was born in 1843 at 27 Washington Place, not far from the Square, immortalized this neighborhood in his novel *Washington Square*. The WASHINGTON ARCH, which has stood at the north of the park since 1895, perfectly encapsulates the main cultural trend of the time, which has

14 100 6TH AVE. **15** N. Y. MERCANTILE EXCHANGE **16** HOUSE OF RELIEF, NEW YORK HOSPITAL **17** SCHEPP BLDG. **18** DUANE PARK **19** WESTERN UNION BLDG. **20** HIGH PRESSURE SERVICE HEADQUARTERS **21** CARY BLDG. **22** CONDICT STORE **23** AT&T BLDG. **24** N. Y. LIFE INSURANCE COMPANY BLDG. **25** JAMES BOGARDUS WAREHOUSE **26** DAVID BROWN STORE

been described as the "American Renaissance". The statues that grace its piers were added later; these are "Washington in War", by Hermon A. MacNeil (1916) and "Washington in Peace", by A. Stirling Calder (1918). The second half of the 19th century brought a fresh influx of European immigrants into Greenwich Village, a neighborhood lying west and south of Washington Square, which became a French and Italian enclave. At that time most of the houses were converted into apartments or replaced by tenements. Many artists chose to live in this part of the city, lured by its beauty and sense of history, while the gentry, who lived north of the square, gradually moved Uptown, deserting the district.

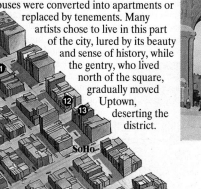

WASHINGTON ARCH
To commemorate the centenary of George Washington's inauguration ● 27, on April 30, 1889, the architect Stanford White was commissioned to create a temporary wooden triumphal arch. It stood at the north of the park at the bottom of 5th Ave. and was garlanded

From the beginning of the 20th century this neighborhood was largely bohemian in atmosphere, attracting those who wanted to mix with avant-garde artists. The writers Eugene O'Neill, Edna St. Vincent Millay and Theodore Dreiser followed in the footsteps of their famous forebears, Edgar Allan Poe, Herman Melville, Mark Twain and Henry James. Painters, including the members of the Ashcan school ▲ 217, set up their studios in some of the old houses. You have only to look upward when crossing certain streets to see the large skylights that crown these buildings. The former speakeasies, theaters, cafés and jazz clubs are still haunted by the memory of the celebrities who used to frequent them.

with strings of lights. The arch was such a resounding success that the city arts council asked White to build another, this time in marble, modeled on those in Rome and Paris.

SAMUEL F.B. MORSE (1791–1872)
Although he is primarily known as the inventor of the electric telegraph and the alphabet of audible signals that bears his name, Morse was also a highly esteemed painter. He was a founder and first president of the

National Academy of Design, opened in 1826. Nine years later he became a lecturer in art at N.Y.U., where he also set up a laboratory in its Main Building for his scientific experiments. He patented his telegraph system in 1837.

JUDSON MEMORIAL CHURCH
This church, which is dominated by the Romanesque-style campanile, is decorated with Italian Renaissance motifs adorned with terracotta moldings.

SOUTH VILLAGE

NEW YORK UNIVERSITY, MAIN BUILDING. 100 WASHINGTON SQUARE EAST (1894–5, arch. Alfred Zucker). New York University (N.Y.U.), founded in 1831 by ALBERT GALLATIN, a member of Thomas Jefferson's cabinet, is the largest private university in the United States. The MAIN BUILDING, at the center of a campus which is spread throughout the Village, occupies the site of the first university building, completed in 1833. This created a furore, as the administrators, eager to cut costs, had employed convicts from Sing Sing prison – a virtually cost-free work force – on the building. Local construction workers staged a union demonstration, one of the first of its kind organized in New York. When it degenerated into violence, the "Stone Cutter's Guild Riot", as it became known, had to be quelled by the

National Guard. This building is also famous for occupants such as SAMUEL F. B. MORSE, the inventor of the telegraph, and SAMUEL COLT, the designer of the famous revolver. All that remains of this building, destroyed in 1894, is a turret on Washington Square East.

THE BROWN BUILDING, FORMERLY THE ASCH BUILDING. 29 WASHINGTON PLACE. In 1911 this manufacturing loft, later converted into lecture halls for N.Y.U., was devastated by a fire that claimed 146 victims, all of them young women employed by the TRIANGLE SHIRTWAIST CO., one of the "sweatshops" in the clothing industry ● *38*. At the request of the *International Ladies' Garment Workers' Union*, founded in 1900, a plaque was fixed to the building to commemorate this tragedy.

ELMER HOLMES BOBST LIBRARY. 70 WASHINGTON SQUARE SOUTH (1972, arch. Philip Johnson and Richard Foster). This library, built for New York University, owes its nickname of "Redskin" to its red sandstone façade. The interior boasts a fine atrium and a checkerboard floor of gray, white and black marble based on one in the church of San Giorgio Maggiore in Venice.

JUDSON MEMORIAL CHURCH. 55 WASHINGTON SQUARE SOUTH (1888–93, arch. McKim, Mead & White) ● *90*. This church was built in homage to Adinoram Judson, the first American Baptist missionary in Burma, and financed partly by JOHN D. ROCKEFELLER ▲ *276*, who devoted some of his fortune to the city's Baptist congregations.

Program cover for an
Off-Broadway show in
Greenwich Village.

THE "LATIN QUARTER". In the 1850's,
"Frenchtown" was the nickname given to the area
south of Washington Square inhabited by a
community of French immigrants. However, most
of the French families moved out of the
neighborhood by 1875 because the many brothels
and sleazy dance halls had lowered the tone of the
area. Toward the end of the 19th century, a new
wave of Italian immigrants settled in the
neighborhood. They opened cafés and restaurants
next door to the French stores that were still in
business and the sector was named the "Latin Quarter". The
neighborhood, which was very popular with intellectuals at
the beginning of this century, became a magnet for jazz
musicians and, later, in the 1950's, for "beat generation
poets". In the 1960's Bob Dylan and other folk singers
transformed it into a center for folk music. It is still the place
to go if you want to catch the up-and-coming stars or linger
over an espresso on a Sunday afternoon. Bleecker Street is
lined with numerous picturesque bars: the Bitter End, the
Peculiar Club, Kenny's Castaways, the Back Fence; as well as
the famous Village Gate and the Circle in the Square, one of

the best Off-
Broadway theaters. On
MACDOUGAL STREET you will find the Caffè
Dante, the Caffè Reggio, opened in 1927, the Café
Borgia and Le Figaro Café.

PROVINCETOWN PLAYHOUSE. 133 MACDOUGAL ST. The
Provincetown Players, an improvisational theater company,
made their debut in New York at no. 139 MacDougal Street
before moving into this former stable (below). They were
responsible for launching the young playwright Eugene
O'Neill, by giving the first performance of his play *Bound
East for Cardiff*, in 1916. The writer later received the Pulitzer
Prize and became one of America's most celebrated
playwrights. The company disbanded in 1930 but the theater
was rebuilt around 1940 and is still in use today, keeping the
spirit of the legendary company alive.

**SAMUEL COLT
(1814–1862)**
In 1831, Colt
invented the "six-
shooter", a revolver
whose main
innovation was the
revolving breech
containing six
chambers for
cartridges, which
allowed the weapon
to be automatically
recharged after every
shot was fired. This
technique gave the
revolver its name.
The colt soon became
a favorite with
cowboys, and this
legendary weapon
played its part in
winning the West.
Colt, who began his
career as a wandering
comic actor, finished
life in the lap of
luxury due to this
invention, which
made him an
international
celebrity.

**PROVINCETOWN
PLAYERS**
This theater company
derived its name from
Provincetown, in
Cape Cod, where the
troupe was formed by
a group of Villagers
on their summer
holidays. It was the
journalist, John Reed,
who persuaded the
group to continue to
perform on their
return to New York.

201

At the end of the 1850's the engineers James Bogardus and Daniel Badger produced the first sales catalogue of cast-iron architectural decorative pieces ● *84*. The catalogue contained details of ready-made models, with understated ornamentation in the latest styles. It was possible to buy a façade by the foot.

The clothes market on Spring St. (opposite).

RICHMOND HILL HOUSE
In 1831, the manor house on the Richmond Hill estate was converted into a theater (below in 1832). In 1849 it was destroyed to build offices and workshops to meet the needs of a neighborhood going through a period of intense commercial growth.

MINETTA STREET. This street follows the erstwhile course of Minetta Brook, filled in around 1820, and was home to a large population of Blacks in the 18th century, hence its former nickname of "Little Africa". In the mid-19th century, the neighborhood deteriorated, becoming squalid and dangerous because of the brawls that regularly broke out there, especially at the time of the Draft Riots ● *28*. The following decades saw the street gradually fill up with Italian, French and then German immigrants ● *44*. Nearby, at 113 MacDougal Street, is the MINETTA TAVERN, a real "drinkers' museum", its walls covered with caricatures of Village personalities.

THE ATRIUM, ORIGINALLY MILLS HOUSE No. 1. 160 BLEECKER ST. (1896, arch. Ernest Flagg). At the end of the 19th century, many tenements were built south of Washington Square. The architect Ernest Flagg, who was interested in this type of housing, designed this Renaissance-style building. It was composed of 1,500 units, arranged around a grassy court. These rooms were mostly for newly arrived immigrants who could spend the night there for the modest sum of 20 cents. Subsequently, the courtyard was paved over, then covered, and the building became a shabby hotel, the Greenwich, before being converted into a private residence complete with ATRIUM in 1976.

MacDOUGAL-SULLIVAN GARDENS ★. Designated a "Historic District", this neighborhood consists of twenty-four Greek Revival ● *84* houses built back-to-back on two streets. Its layout served as a model for similar housing plans in New York in the 1920's. By 1923 the houses were badly run-down. They were bought and renovated by property developer, William Sloane Coffin. He removed the entrance steps, standardized the façades, using a style influenced by colonial architecture, and linked the backyards together to create a private common garden.

CHARLTON-KING-VANDAM HISTORIC DISTRICT. Between 6TH AVE. and VARICK ST. This historic enclave, which abuts on an industrial area, is a fine example of New York residential town planning in the last century. It boasts the longest unbroken row of Federal-style ● *82* townhouses in the city, dating from the 1820's, and a number of Greek Revival houses built between 1830 and 1850, the most eye-catching examples of which are nos. 37 and 39 Charlton Street and no. 203 Spring Street. This district occupies the former site of Richmond Hill, an estate of some 25 acres, whose Georgian manor house served as George Washington's headquarters in 1776 ● *27*. The lands were subsequently bought by Aaron

Burr, who laid out the present network of roads in 1797 in order to divide up the estate into building lots. He unfortunately had to sell the estate to JOHN JACOB ASTOR, who completed the task of parceling it out.

SoHo Cast-Iron Historic District ★

Around 1850, the area now called SoHo (a contraction of "South of Houston Street") was the major industrial and commercial center of New York. This historic district contains the highest concentration of cast-iron structures ● *94* in the United States, presenting an amazingly homogeneous urban landscape. These palaces of commerce were built for grocers, textile merchants and furniture store owners who, above all, needed vast interior spaces and attractive shop fronts. Initially, architects tried to give the cast iron the appearance of stone, by covering it with paint mixed with sand (the HAUGHWOUT BUILDING, of 1857 ▲ *204* is a typical example). Then, in the light of its success, they began to exploit the properties of cast iron, creating new motifs, including the slender colonnettes called "Sperm candles". This craze for the new material brought about a volte-face, and stone began to imitate the appearance of cast iron, as at 502 Broadway. (A foolproof way of telling the difference is to use a magnet.) By the

CAST IRON
The bolting process can be seen in the old and new façade of this factory in TriBeCa.

beginning of the 1960's, SoHo had lost its commercial importance and many former warehouses and industrial premises stood empty. Consequently, artists looking for large, bright reasonably priced studios began to move in. A special artists' statute, responding to tenants' requirements, authorized the conversion of these buildings into studios and apartments. SoHo is now a lively neighborhood with many avant-garde galleries, fascinating shops and charming restaurants. Moreover, the presence of three new museums – the Museum for African Art, the New Museum of Contemporary Art and the Guggenheim Museum of SoHo – grouped together along Broadway and called MUSEUM ROW – has enhanced the area's status as a cultural enclave.

MUSEUM FOR AFRICAN ART. 593 BROADWAY (1993, interior design Maya Lin). This museum, which moved here in 1993, is one of only three in the United States to

Bemba Figure, below, a sculpture exhibited at the Museum for African Art.

RICHARD MORRIS HUNT
Richard Morris Hunt was the first American architect trained at the École des Beaux Arts and a founder of the American Institute of Architects. He represented a whole generation of architects inspired by the Old World. His work includes the Roosevelt Building (below) as well as mansions for the élite.

specialize in ancient and modern African art, the others being the Maryland Museum of African Art and the Smithsonian's National Museum of African Art in Washington, D.C.

NEW MUSEUM OF CONTEMPORARY ART. 583 BROADWAY (1896–7, arch. Cleverdon & Putzel). This museum, which has been at this address since 1983, represents a complete break with tradition, as it exhibits only works less than ten years old, placing the emphasis on artists who have not yet acquired a wide following.

GUGGENHEIM MUSEUM OF SOHO. 575 BROADWAY (1881–2, arch. Thomas Stent). This companion to the museum on 5th Avenue ▲ *338* was opened at the end of 1992 and symbolizes the neighborhood's renaissance. The warehouse, with its red-brick façades and cast-iron window frames was given a completely new image by the architect ARATA ISOZAKI, who created an interior exhibition area of nearly 3,600 square yards, large enough to exhibit part of the collections from the Uptown Guggenheim. The metal signs gracing the museum's façades are replicas of the ones that used to appear on all workshops and warehouses at the height of the district's commercial success.

FORMER LITTLE SINGER BUILDING ★. 561–563 BROADWAY (1904, arch. Ernest Flagg). This L-shaped Art Nouveau building was designed for the famous sewing machine manufacturer. When Flagg designed a larger Singer Tower ▲ *152* in 1908, he called this one the "Little Singer". Flagg's aesthetic sense, developed at the École des Beaux Arts in Paris, can be seen in the building's prefabricated metal frame and interlaced floral motifs.

HAUGHWOUT BUILDING. 488–492 BROADWAY at BROOME ST. (1856–7, arch. John P. Gaynor). ● *94*. When Eder V. Haughwout, a specialist in tableware, commissioned this building, he got one of the very first cast-iron masterpieces, complete with open-cage elevator, installed by ELISHA OTIS.

ROOSEVELT BUILDING. 478–482 BROADWAY (1873–4, arch. Richard M. Hunt). This building shows how much could be achieved with cast iron. Three wide bays with colonnettes give the structure a sense of grace and lightness. When it was first built the building boasted superb brightly colored ornamental motifs. The ground floor and the basement, like several of the other buildings in the neighborhood, are occupied by stores – in this case, a fabric store (left).

GREENE STREET ★. This street has the most remarkable assortment of cast-iron buildings and its cobblestone paving, recently repaired, is an unusual sight in New York. Between nos. 8 and 34, a collection of cast-iron façades sets up a subtle, regular rhythm of alternating solid and hollow forms, light and shadow, as a counterpoint to the fire escapes. Built between 1872 and 1896, these buildings are the work of Warner, Wright, Duckworth and Snook.

N.Y. CITY FIRE MUSEUM. 278 SPRING ST. (1904, arch. Edward P. Casey). This small, fascinating and little-known museum is housed in a neo-classical fire station built just after the turn of the century. It retraces the history of fire fighting in the city, and boasts a superb collection of exhibits, including wooden firemarks dating from the 17th century and old fire engines.

THE EAR INN, FORMERLY THE JAMES BROWN RESIDENCE. 326 SPRING ST. (1817). This Federal-style house originally stood on the edge of the Hudson. As port traffic became heavier, the river was filled in as far as West Street, so that more docks could be constructed. The house was then converted into a distillery, then, during Prohibition, a brothel with a speakeasy upstairs. It is now a slightly timeworn, but lively, bar.

ISAAC MERRITT SINGER
The American Dream came true for this inventor, who began his career as a humble laborer. While repairing one of the early sewing machines, Singer was struck by the idea for his revolutionary, simplified model. He designed the machine in barely twelve hours, but he then had to borrow $40 to complete his prototype and apply for a patent (1851). He went into partnership with Edward Clark, founded the Singer Manufacturing Company and built up an enormous industrial empire.

"DAYLIGHT FACTORIES"
The façade of this Art Deco industrial building (1928) is decorated with bas-reliefs depicting laborers and craftsmen. This is a typical example of what was called a "daylight factory", several of which were built during the 1930's near the Holland Tunnel.

HOLLAND TUNNEL
The mouth of the tunnel, which was built in 1927 to link Manhattan with New Jersey, is adjacent to the site of a former railroad depot. Until 1850, this was a stylish residential area around St. John's Park. In 1869 Cornelius Vanderbilt bought the park and built the depot there. The freight trains had to run alongside the Hudson on West St. to reach St. John's Park. The depot was demolished in 1936, two years after a new terminal had been constructed a few blocks south.

The former headquarters of the New York Life Insurance Company boasts one of the last mechanical clocks in New York. It is worth a visit to admire the machinery.

TRIBECA WEST HISTORIC DISTRICT

TriBeCa – a recent coinage derived from "TRIangle BElow CAnal" – is bounded by CANAL STREET to the north, BROADWAY to the east and the HUDSON RIVER to the west. It falls into two distinct areas; the eastern part, which sports Italianate palaces of commerce with their marble façades, and the western part, with its Romanesque Revival warehouses and factories ● *90*, as well as two influential skyscrapers of the 1920's – the Western Union Building and the New York Telephone Company Building.

THE HISTORY OF THE NEIGHBORHOOD. During the English colonial period, the land belonged to Anthony Lispenard and the parish of Trinity Church ▲ *154*, which had been given this grant of land by Queen Anne in 1705. When the lands were later mapped for development and sold off, the streets were given the names of these landowners – Lispenard and his children Leonard, Thomas and Anthony (today Worth Street) – or of key figures in the parish such as Chambers, Murray, Duane, Reade and Watts. Between

1850 and 1920 the western part of the present TriBeCa was the trading center for wholesale fruit and vegetables and dairy products and supplied Washington Market, which covered part of the site now occupied by the World Trade Center.

INDUSTRIAL ARCHITECTURE. The sector's trading activities were given a boost by the new piers and warehouses and by the extension of rail facilities thanks to the NEW YORK CENTRAL & HUDSON RIVER RAILROAD FREIGHT DEPOT, built in 1869 for Cornelius Vanderbilt ▲ *260*. This huge freight depot stood on the site of ST. JOHN'S PARK (a residential public square with landscaped garden) and was demolished in 1936 when the HOLLAND TUNNEL, linking Manhattan and New Jersey, was built. TriBeCa is mainly a neighborhood for warehouses ● *85*, whose utilitarian function is still apparent from their loading ramps, metal canopies and security gates. The district boasts a whole range of styles, from the starkest lines, represented by the minimalism of the WAREHOUSE AT 135 HUDSON STREET (1886–7, arch. Kimball & Ihnen, right), to the most elaborate, such as the FLEMING SMITH WAREHOUSE (1891–2, arch. Stephen Decatur Hatch) in Flemish style, at nos. 451–453 Washington Street. There are still some wholesale stores around the small triangle of DUANE PARK but the rest of TriBeCa has become a residential area. Buildings are being restored and businesses are constantly springing up.

FORMER NEW YORK MERCANTILE EXCHANGE. 6 HARRISON ST. (1886, arch. Thomas R. Jackson). In 1872 the dairy farmers founded the BUTTER AND CHEESE EXCHANGE on Greenwich Street. Some ten years later, this Queen Anne-style building was built, and business carried out in the huge hall paved with polychromatic flags. After the Mercantile Exchange moved to the World Trade Center in 1977, this building was converted into apartments; one of New York's finest restaurants, the Chanterelle, now occupies the ground floor.

HARRISON STREET ROW. 25–41 HARRISON ST. (1796–1828). Most of the houses in this residential neighborhood were demolished during the second half of the 19th century to allow Washington Market to expand and to make way for the development of the docks. In 1975 it was decided to save the few remaining houses that now form this row. Two of them (nos. 31 and 33) stood here originally, while the others came from adjacent Washington Street. At the end of the street,

The New York Central & Hudson River Railroad Freight Depot in 1869.

WASHINGTON MARKET
After the Civil War and the development of steamship traffic, the narrow straits of the East River were abandoned for the wider stretches of the Hudson. Docks gradually sprang up all along the bank, and as a result, the part of southwest Manhattan now called TriBeCa underwent a period of intense commercial growth. Products were unloaded and taken to Washington Market (above, in 1888).

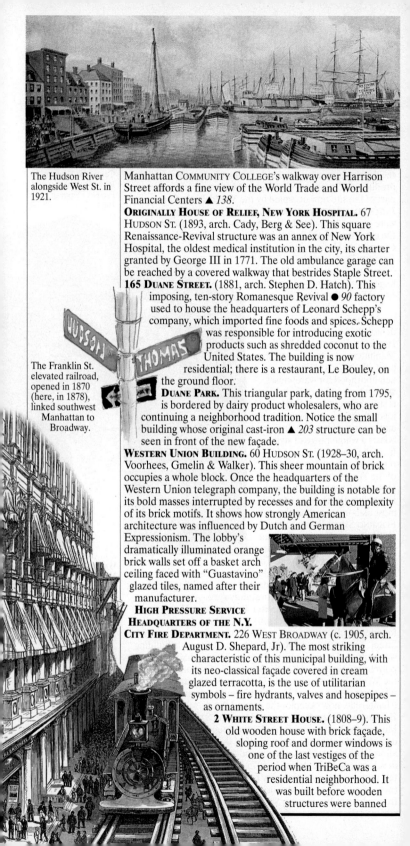

The Hudson River alongside West St. in 1921.

Manhattan COMMUNITY COLLEGE's walkway over Harrison Street affords a fine view of the World Trade and World Financial Centers ▲ *138*.

ORIGINALLY HOUSE OF RELIEF, NEW YORK HOSPITAL. 67 HUDSON ST. (1893, arch. Cady, Berg & See). This square Renaissance-Revival structure was an annex of New York Hospital, the oldest medical institution in the city, its charter granted by George III in 1771. The old ambulance garage can be reached by a covered walkway that bestrides Staple Street.

165 DUANE STREET. (1881, arch. Stephen D. Hatch). This imposing, ten-story Romanesque Revival ● *90* factory used to house the headquarters of Leonard Schepp's company, which imported fine foods and spices. Schepp was responsible for introducing exotic products such as shredded coconut to the United States. The building is now residential; there is a restaurant, Le Bouley, on the ground floor.

The Franklin St. elevated railroad, opened in 1870 (here, in 1878), linked southwest Manhattan to Broadway.

DUANE PARK. This triangular park, dating from 1795, is bordered by dairy product wholesalers, who are continuing a neighborhood tradition. Notice the small building whose original cast-iron ▲ *203* structure can be seen in front of the new façade.

WESTERN UNION BUILDING. 60 HUDSON ST. (1928–30, arch. Voorhees, Gmelin & Walker). This sheer mountain of brick occupies a whole block. Once the headquarters of the Western Union telegraph company, the building is notable for its bold masses interrupted by recesses and for the complexity of its brick motifs. It shows how strongly American architecture was influenced by Dutch and German Expressionism. The lobby's dramatically illuminated orange brick walls set off a basket arch ceiling faced with "Guastavino" glazed tiles, named after their manufacturer.

HIGH PRESSURE SERVICE HEADQUARTERS OF THE N.Y. CITY FIRE DEPARTMENT. 226 WEST BROADWAY (c. 1905, arch. August D. Shepard, Jr). The most striking characteristic of this municipal building, with its neo-classical façade covered in cream glazed terracotta, is the use of utilitarian symbols – fire hydrants, valves and hosepipes – as ornaments.

2 WHITE STREET HOUSE. (1808–9). This old wooden house with brick façade, sloping roof and dormer windows is one of the last vestiges of the period when TriBeCa was a residential neighborhood. It was built before wooden structures were banned

El International Restaurant.

FORMER CARY BUILDING
This building, at 105–107 Chambers St. (left), built in 1857 by the architects King & Kellum ● *88*, is a perfect example of a "first generation" cast-iron building, with its two Italianate façades (which imitate stone). It was built for the grocery store Cary, Howard & Sanger and remains a monument to the commercial prosperity around City Hall in the mid-19th century.

as a fire hazard and probably always housed a shop on the ground floor.

AT&T (AMERICAN TELEPHONE & TELEGRAPH COMPANY). 32 6TH AVE. (1930–2, arch. Ralph Walker). This Art Deco building originally housed the technical offices for transatlantic communications. In 1984, after the new headquarters building at 550 Madison Avenue was sold to Sony, the company moved its head offices into the 6th Avenue building. The linear quality of the façades and their ornamentation, the vast tiled map of the world on the wall of the lobby, as well as the mosaic allegories on the ceiling, endow the building with an industrial aesthetic in keeping with its function.

NEW YORK LIFE INSURANCE COMPANY BUILDING "THE CLOCKTOWER" ★. 346 BROADWAY (1894–9, arch. Stephen D. Hatch and McKim, Mead & White). This neo-Renaissance building now serves as offices for the City of New York. Visit the CLOCKTOWER which houses an art gallery and stages free shows under the auspices of the Institute for Art and Urban Resources. You can enjoy a superb view of the Woolworth Building ▲ *180*, and Foley Square ▲ *182* from its terrace.

JAMES BOGARDUS WAREHOUSE. 85 LEONARD ST. (1861). This cast-iron building was built to house the grocery store KITCHEN, MONTROSS & WILCOX. It is one of the few remaining structures designed by the architect James Bogardus, who did pioneering work with this material.

DAVID BROWN STORE. 8 THOMAS ST. (1875–6, arch. J. Morgan Slade). This building, commissioned by a soap and eau de toilette manufacturer, is an exceptional example of High Victorian Gothic as applied to a commercial building ● *86*.

This building, at 55 White St., built by John Kellum & Son in 1861, sports a cast-iron version of the stone "Sperm candle" façade built by the same architect for 502 Broadway.

1 JEFFERSON MARKET COURTHOUSE LIBRARY
2 WASHINGTON COURT
3 NORTHERN DISPENSARY
4 CHRISTOPHER PARK
5 SHERIDAN SQUARE
6 GREENWICH HOUSE
7 175–179 W. 4TH ST.

GREENWICH VILLAGE

GANSEVOORT MEAT MARKET

GREENWICH AVE.

7TH AVE.

W. 4TH ST.

GANSEVOORT ST.

HORATIO ST.

GREENWICH ST.

WASHINGTON ST.

WEST VILLAGE

BANK ST.

PERRY ST.

CHARLES ST.

W. 10TH ST.

🏃 Five hours

19

18

17

"Céline said New York was a 'standing city'. True; but it seemed to me from the very first a lengthwise city. All priorities are given to length. Traffic stands still in the side streets but rolls tirelessly on the avenues. How often do cab drivers, who willingly take passengers north and south, refuse flatly to drive them east and west! The side streets are hardly more than the outlines of the buildings between the avenues. The avenues pierce them, tear them apart, and speed toward the north."

Jean-Paul Sartre,
Manhattan: the Great American Desert

JEFFERSON MARKET
View of Jefferson Market with its Fire Tower, in 1830.

GREENWICH VILLAGE

A "VILLAGE" WITHIN A CITY. With its low buildings and crooked streets, this neighborhood has, visually, something of the character of a small provincial town, deliberately rejecting the grid system typical of most of Manhattan. Nevertheless, its heterogeneous population perfectly accords with New York's cosmopolitan character. Earlier inhabitants of Manhattan, the CANARSIE INDIANS, called this swampy, wooded area *Sapohanikan*. They set up a trading post – dealing in goods between Hoboken and Manhattan – on the shore, near what is now Gansevoort Street. Tobacco farming was very important during the Dutch period (1613–64) and Governor Wouter Van Twiller appropriated 222 acres of "Northwyck" (as the Dutch called this area) for a private plantation. In 1696, Van Twiller's *Bossen Bouwerie* "wooded farm", was renamed Greenwich Village by the English. Over the next century or so, houses in various styles – Georgian, Federal and Greek Revival ● *82, 84* – were built bordering the huge estates. Greenwich became a thriving, prosperous village, whose activity was centered around the shipping industry. In the 1820's, as a result of an influx of New Yorkers from lower Manhattan, fleeing the cholera and yellow fever epidemics, Greenwich experienced rapid urbanization. In 1829 the male population of Newgate Prison, in the heart of the Village, was transferred to Ossining, along the Hudson River. Today Greenwich Village is a multifarious neighborhood offering an overview of three centuries of architecture.

"BOHEMIA". In the early 20th century, various social reformers interested in art joined the "Bohemians" living in the Village. These included the anarchist Emma Goldman and the "vagabond poet", Harry Kemp, who, around 1910, used to publish his writings in *The Masses*, a daily newspaper edited by Max Eastman, and in *Seven Arts*, a magazine that published such

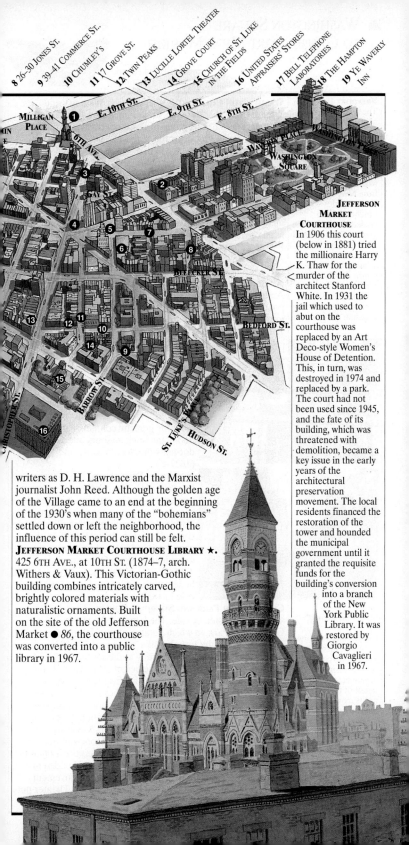

8 26–30 JONES ST.
9 39–41 COMMERCE ST.
10 CHUMLEY'S
11 17 GROVE ST.
12 TWIN PEAKS
13 LUCILLE LORTEL THEATER
14 GROVE COURT
15 CHURCH OF ST. LUKE IN THE FIELDS
16 UNITED STATES APPRAISERS' STORES
17 BELL TELEPHONE LABORATORIES
18 THE HAMPTON INN
19 YE WAVERLY INN

MILLIGAN PLACE

E. 10TH ST.
E. 9TH ST.
E. 8TH ST.

6TH AVE.

WAVERLY PLACE
WASHINGTON PL.
WASHINGTON SQUARE

GAY ST.

BLEECKER ST.

BEDFORD ST.

BARROW ST.

ST. LUKE'S PLACE
HUDSON ST.

CHRISTOPHER ST.

JEFFERSON MARKET COURTHOUSE
In 1906 this court (below in 1881) tried the millionaire Harry K. Thaw for the murder of the architect Stanford White. In 1931 the jail which used to abut on the courthouse was replaced by an Art Deco-style Women's House of Detention. This, in turn, was destroyed in 1974 and replaced by a park. The court had not been used since 1945, and the fate of its building, which was threatened with demolition, became a key issue in the early years of the architectural preservation movement. The local residents financed the restoration of the tower and hounded the municipal government until it granted the requisite funds for the building's conversion into a branch of the New York Public Library. It was restored by Giorgio Cavaglieri in 1967.

writers as D. H. Lawrence and the Marxist journalist John Reed. Although the golden age of the Village came to an end at the beginning of the 1930's when many of the "bohemians" settled down or left the neighborhood, the influence of this period can still be felt.

JEFFERSON MARKET COURTHOUSE LIBRARY ★.
425 6TH AVE., at 10TH ST. (1874–7, arch. Withers & Vaux). This Victorian-Gothic building combines intricately carved, brightly colored materials with naturalistic ornaments. Built on the site of the old Jefferson Market ● 86, the courthouse was converted into a public library in 1967.

▲ WASHINGTON SQUARE TO GANSEVOORT MEAT MARKET

Detail of the façade
of Bigelow's Pharmacy

WASHINGTON COURT. 6TH AVE., between WAVERLY and
WASHINGTON PLACES (1986, arch. James Stewart Polshek &
Partners) ● *102*. This group of Postmodern-style apartments
blends in well with the profile of the Village.

BIGELOW CO. PHARMACY. 414 6TH AVE., at 9TH ST. (1902,
arch. John E. Nitchie). This pharmacy, founded in 1838, is a
fine example of commercial architecture at the turn of the
century, with its three striking Beaux Arts-style double bays.
The interior, recently restored, still boasts its apothecary jars
and all the prescriptions made up since the pharmacy opened,
including one they had prepared for Mark Twain, who
lived nearby.

PATCHIN PLACE (W. 10TH ST.) **AND MILLIGAN PLACE** (6TH
AVE.) (1848–52). These two cul-de-sacs, enclosed by iron
gates, are lined with redbrick houses which once served as
accommodation for staff at the nearby Brevoort House.
Among the most famous residents of Patchin Place are the
poet e. e. cummings and John Reed, the committed left-wing
journalist who covered the Russian Revolution and wrote
Ten Days that Shook the World (1919).

GAY STREET. This narrow lane, which
epitomizes the neighborhood's charm,
served as a mews in colonial times.
The stables were later replaced by a
harmonious group of late Federal-style
houses (1827–31) and later by some
Greek Revival houses (1844–60).
Note the graceful columns flanking the
doors, the brick masonry and the wide
dormer windows of nos. 12 and 14
(1827–8).

NORTHERN DISPENSARY. 165 WAVERLY
PLACE (1831). The Northern Dispensary
was established by a group of citizens to
care for the poor and is one of New
York's oldest public hospitals. The
triangular Greek Revival building was
completed in 1831 and an extra story
was added in 1854. The writer Edgar
Allan Poe, one of the hospital's
benefactors, was treated here for a head
cold in 1837.

CHRISTOPHER PARK AND SHERIDAN SQUARE. These two
squares stand side by side. The larger of the two is
Christopher Park, in which a statue of the Union general
Philip Sheridan, by Joseph Pollia, was erected in 1936.
Sheridan Square is a small garden at the southeast end of
Christopher Park. In July, at the height of the Civil War,
Christopher Park was the site of the draft riots. Poverty-
stricken Irishmen, who feared that if they had to go to war
their jobs would be taken by Blacks, went on the rampage.
Despite the forceful intervention of the National Guard,
eighteen Blacks were lynched by the Irish. A century later,
Christopher Park was also the site of the Stonewall Inn Riot;
on the night of June 28 1969, the police raided the Stonewall
Inn, a gay bar at 51 Christopher Street. The raid ended in a
riot, which marked the start of the Gay Rights Movement
● 53. At 1 Sheridan Square, the Charles Ludlam Theater puts
on brilliant and farcical plays in drag.

175–179 W. 4TH STREET (1833–4). These houses feature the original door frames as well as Flemish bonding, overhanging roofs pierced by dormers at nos. 177 and 179 and the dimensions characteristic of the Federal style.

26–30 JONES STREET (c. 1830). The distinctive features of these three Greek Revival houses are their dentiled cornices, their wrought-iron stoop railings (nos. 28 and 30), their lantern-embellished doors (nos. 26 and 28) and their small-paned windows.

GREENWICH HOUSE. 29 BARROW ST. (1917, arch. Delano & Aldrich). This neo-Georgian building, built to serve as a social center for immigrants, is still used for socio-cultural activities.

AROUND ST. LUKE'S IN THE FIELD

With its array of well-preserved brick- and brownstone-Italianate houses built 1852–3 (nos. 5–16), St. Luke's Place is one of the most attractive streets in Greenwich Village.

39 AND 41 COMMERCE STREET (1831–2). Contrary to popular

legend, these two houses, nicknamed the "Twin Sisters", were not built by a naval officer for his two daughters, but by a milkman, Peter Huyler. They have a somewhat old-fashioned air, with their leafy courtyard and their mansard roofs, which were added after 1870, and give the Greek Revival architecture a top-heavy appearance.

CHUMLEY'S. 86 BEDFORD ST. (1831). During Prohibition, this innocuous-looking building housed one of the best-known speakeasies in New York. Its clientele included Edna St. Vincent Millay, Upton Sinclair, John Dos Passos and Theodore Dreiser. The owner disguised the façade with a garage front in order to put the police off the scent and his

Ruth McKenney, who lived at 14 Gay St. in the 1920's, published a group of stories in *The New Yorker* set against the bohemian backdrop of the Village. It described the ups and downs of life there with her younger sister, an actress finding it difficult to break into the big time. The stories were used as material for a Broadway hit musical called *Wonderful Town*.

ST. LUKE'S PLACE
In 1922 the writer Theodore Dreiser moved into 16 St. Luke's Place and began work on his novel *An American Tragedy*. The gas lamps that stand in front of No. 6 mark the residence of Mayor James J. Walker, who was notorious in the 1920's for his dissolute lifestyle. The playground on the other side of the road is a former graveyard in which Edgar Allan Poe once liked to stroll.

GANSEVOORT MEAT MARKET
General Gansevoort was the grandfather of Herman Melville. After years of adventure on the high seas and disillusioned by a career that did not pay him enough, the writer returned, in 1863, to his native neighborhood, where he became a district inspector of customs.

customers used to enter discreetly through the old stables at the back, at 58 Barrow Street. Two traditions that persist to this day are the absence of an inn sign and a display of the dust jackets from books by regulars. Take a look at 95 BEDFORD STREET, where another old stable, built in 1894, was converted into apartments in 1927. The brick and stone façade is embellished with a fancy ornamental cornice and the building still has its wide original doors.

17 GROVE STREET (1822). This frame house is one of the few vestiges of the period before laws were passed banning this type of structure in Manhattan for reasons of safety. The beautiful Greek Revival entrance is original, whereas the cornice and decorative wooden panels date from 1870, when another story was added.

TWIN PEAKS. 102 BEDFORD ST. (c. 1830). This "neo-Alpine style" half-timbered building was created by the artist Clifford Reed Daily. He converted this residence in 1925, aiming for a startling effect in defiance of the homogeneous Federal style of the other houses on this peaceful street. He even managed to persuade Otto Kahn, his wealthy patron, to finance the project.

LUCILLE LORTEL THEATER. 121 CHRISTOPHER ST. In the 1950's the former Hudson Cinema was converted into a theater specializing in experimental productions ▲ *258*.

Grove St. at the corner of Bedford St. (above).

"Rich, hemm'd thick all around with sailships and steamships, an island sixteen miles long, solid-founded, Numberless crowded streets, high growths of iron, slender, strong, light, splendidly uprising toward clear skies."
Sinclair Lewis,
The Empire City

U.S. Appraisers' Stores.

GROVE COURT ★. Through the gate between 10–12 GROVE ST. (1853–4). This address marks the entrance to six small houses, built by Samuel Cocks, a local grocer, to rent to workers. The courtyard once bore the name "Mixed Ale Alley", probably because of the inhabitants' propensity to drink. The houses were restored around 1920 and given their current name.

CHURCH OF ST. LUKE IN THE FIELDS. 485 HUDSON ST. (1822, arch. James N. Wells). Built by local residents with funds supplied by Trinity Parish, this was originally a village church adjoining several farms along the riverbank. Some parishioners used to come to church by boat – easier than traveling by road at that time. The brick exterior, whose simplicity verges on the severe, gives the church a distinctively rural look even today. The row of Federal-style houses bordering the old churchyard – especially the numbers 473 to 477 and 487 to 491 Hudson Street – creates an attractive setting for the church and its garden. The writer Bret Harte spent his boyhood at no. 487.

FORMER UNITED STATES APPRAISERS' STORES. 666–668 GREENWICH ST. (1892–9, arch. Willoughby J. Edbrooke). This massive Romanesque Revival structure, with its sturdy brick arcading, was used as a bonded warehouse when port activity was at its peak. The building was later used to house archives before being converted, in 1988, into apartments. Only the name of the MELVILLE BAR, on the corner of Barrow and Washington streets, evokes the ghost of the writer Herman Melville, who once worked as a customs inspector.

West Village

Formerly Bell Laboratories. 463 West St. and 155 Bank St. (1880–1900, arch. Cyrus W. Eidlitz). The first transcontinental telephone call was made from here on January 25, 1915, when Alexander Graham Bell spoke to Thomas Watson in San Francisco; the first experimental radio set, the 2XS, was invented here, as was the sound projector, in 1925, which paved the way for the talkies. It was also here, on April 7, 1927, that journalists attended the first television broadcast, during which the Secretary of Commerce and future President, Herbert Hoover, made a speech from the Capitol, Washington, D.C. ● *54.* The building now forms part of a complex of lofts and studios for artists.

The Hampton. 80–82 Perry St. (1887, arch. Thom & Wilson). The distinctive features of this apartment building, which blends in well with its surroundings, are its Moorish arches, its intricate brick decoration and its brownstone reliefs.

Pierre Deux. 369 Bleecker St. (1867). This attractive home decoration store, owned by two antique dealers both answering to the name of Pierre, occupies a complex designed to be divided into apartments, with commercial space on the ground floor. It was one of the first apartment buildings in New York.

301–319 W. 4th Street (1836–7). Out of these ten Greek Revival houses, nos. 311 and 313 still have their original proportions, while the others have been heightened with Italianate cornices ● *88.* The original wrought-iron railings still adorn the front steps.

Ye Waverly Inn. 16 Bank St. (1844–5). This inn is part of a group of buildings that combine elements of late Greek Revival style with typical Gothic Revival decoration, such as the motifs on the carved lintels. The inn has low beamed ceilings and wooden alcoves.

Gansevoort Meat Market. This covered wholesale meat market can be found east of 9th Avenue, between Gansevoort and 14th streets. Visit the market at dawn, when the auctioneering begins, or in the evening when the Florent restaurant is open.

Gansevoort Meat Market, in 1885.

1 THE ROW
2 WASHINGTON MEWS
3 ONE 5TH AVE.
4 MACDOUGAL ALLEY
5 N.Y. STUDIO SCHOOL
6 CHURCH OF THE ASCENSION
7 LOCKWOOD DE FOREST RESIDENCE
8 TILE CLUB
9 SALMAGUNDI CLUB
10 MARSHALL CHESS CLUB
11 SECOND SHEARITH ISRAEL CEMETERY
12 FORBES BLDG.
13 NEW SCHOOL FOR SOCIAL RESEARCH

✹ Four hours

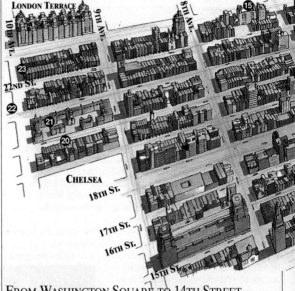

LONDON TERRACE
10TH AVE.
9TH AVE.
8TH AVE.
22ND ST.
CHELSEA
18TH ST.
17TH ST.
16TH ST.
15TH ST.

CONSTRAINTS ON PROPERTY DEVELOPERS
Rows of identical townhouses were built in response to the conditions laid down by landowners in their tenants' leases. How the land was used, the size of the residences (in case of construction), materials, even their decoration, were all strictly regulated. These constraints meant that homeowners often had to build their stables at some distance from their dwellings.

FROM WASHINGTON SQUARE TO 14TH STREET

THE ROW. 1–13 WASHINGTON SQUARE NORTH (1832–3). Some elegant residences were built around the square after the parade ground was constructed. This group is the most important row of early 19th-century houses in the city, and in their time they served as a model for adapting the Greek Revival style to private accommodation in New York. They are handsome redbrick residences, with porches, stairs and balustrades of white marble and railings embellished with acanthus finials and other classical motifs.
No. 3 was occupied, among others, by certain members of the Eight ● *109* and, later, by the painter Edward Hopper ● *111*. The houses at nos. 19–26 (1828–39) are in the same style but offer greater diversity, with their balconies and French doors, their varying shades of brick and their rich decoration.
WASHINGTON MEWS ★. Between UNIVERSITY PLACE and 5TH AVE. This charming cobblestone alley behind The

Row is lined on the north side by its former stables, now converted into houses. The south side was built in 1939.
ONE 5TH AVENUE. (1929, arch. Helmle, Corbett & Harrison; Sugarman & Berger).

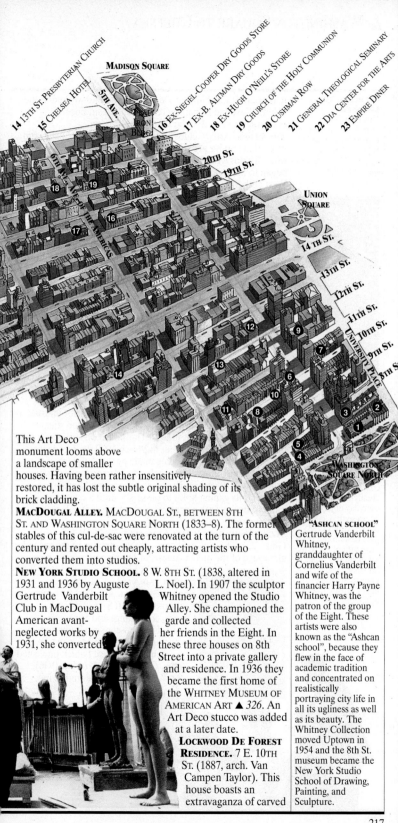

MADISON SQUARE

14 13TH ST. PRESBYTERIAN CHURCH
15 CHELSEA HOTEL
5TH AVE.
16 EX-SIEGEL-COOPER DRY GOODS STORE
17 EX-B. ALTMAN DRY GOODS
18 EX-HUGH O'NEILL'S STORE
19 CHURCH OF THE HOLY COMMUNION
20 CUSHMAN ROW
21 GENERAL THEOLOGICAL SEMINARY
22 DIA CENTER FOR THE ARTS
23 EMPIRE DINER

6TH AVE. AVE. OF THE AMERICAS

20TH ST.

19TH ST.

UNION SQUARE

14TH ST.

13TH ST.

12TH ST.

11TH ST.

10TH ST.

9TH ST.

8TH ST.

UNIVERSITY PLACE

WASHINGTON SQUARE NORTH

This Art Deco monument looms above a landscape of smaller houses. Having been rather insensitively restored, it has lost the subtle original shading of its brick cladding.

MACDOUGAL ALLEY. MACDOUGAL ST., BETWEEN 8TH ST. AND WASHINGTON SQUARE NORTH (1833–8). The former stables of this cul-de-sac were renovated at the turn of the century and rented out cheaply, attracting artists who converted them into studios.

NEW YORK STUDIO SCHOOL. 8 W. 8TH ST. (1838, altered in 1931 and 1936 by Auguste L. Noel). In 1907 the sculptor Gertrude Vanderbilt Whitney opened the Studio Club in MacDougal Alley. She championed the American avant-garde and collected neglected works by her friends in the Eight. In 1931, she converted these three houses on 8th Street into a private gallery and residence. In 1936 they became the first home of the WHITNEY MUSEUM OF AMERICAN ART ▲ 326. An Art Deco stucco was added at a later date.

LOCKWOOD DE FOREST RESIDENCE. 7 E. 10TH ST. (1887, arch. Van Campen Taylor). This house boasts an extravaganza of carved

"ASHCAN SCHOOL" Gertrude Vanderbilt Whitney, granddaughter of Cornelius Vanderbilt and wife of the financier Harry Payne Whitney, was the patron of the group of the Eight. These artists were also known as the "Ashcan school", because they flew in the face of academic tradition and concentrated on realistically portraying city life in all its ugliness as well as its beauty. The Whitney Collection moved Uptown in 1954 and the 8th St. museum became the New York Studio School of Drawing, Painting, and Sculpture.

217

CHURCH OF THE ASCENSION
This Episcopal church, on 5th Ave. at 10th St., was built in 1841 by Richard Upjohn. The interior was remodeled 1885–9.

MARCEL DUCHAMP (1887–1968). When he settled in New York in 1915, Duchamp abandoned painting to concentrate on his "ready-mades", everyday objects that he presented as works of art. Around 1935 the artist turned from the world of art to the art of chess. His anti-art stance had a great impact on all the major artistic trends of the day.

teakwood. It was built for De Forest, who had worked in the Middle East and India, where he founded studios to encourage a revival in the art of woodcarving.

THE CLUBS. Artists' clubs once abounded in the Village, and those that survive are open to the public. They were formed when friends with the same taste in art and conversation began to meet regularly. Among them are the TILE CLUB (58 West 10th Street) founded in 1877, and the SALMAGUNDI CLUB ● 88, formed in 1870 and located at 47 5th Avenue since 1917. This club owes its name to the journal run by Washington Irving, *Salmagundi*, an essentially mysterious name possibly from the French for a kind of "mixed salad". Women painters, who were barred from these clubs, founded the PEN & BRUSH (16 East 10th Street) in 1893; its beautifully appointed Victorian rooms are regularly used for exhibitions, concerts and receptions. The MARSHALL CHESS CLUB, at 23 West 10th Street, was founded in 1915 by Frank J. Marshall, United States champion between 1909 and 1936. Businessmen such as Edward Cornell and Gilbert Colgate rubbed shoulders here with the likes of Sinclair Lewis and Marcel Duchamp. Bobby Fischer, world chess champion in 1972, played his first competitive matches here. It is not unusual to see people playing it in Washington and Abingdon squares.

18 WEST 11TH STREET. (1845). This house was originally part of a group of rowhouses, but in March 1970 the façade was blasted away by a bomb being made by the daughter of the owner of the house and her cohorts, a terrorist organization called the *Weathermen*. For years, the maimed house proffered its gaping holes to passersby until a controversial modern design with a projecting rough brick façade was implemented.

SECOND SHEARITH ISRAEL CEMETERY. 72–76 W. 11TH ST. (1805–25). This tiny enclave is all that remains of the second graveyard of the oldest American Jewish community, most of whose tombs have been moved to another graveyard on 21st Street.

FORBES BUILDING ★. 60–62 5TH AVE. N. W. CORNER 12TH ST. (1925, arch. Carrère & Hastings and Shreve & Lamb). This neo-classical building was the headquarters of the MACMILLAN publishing house (which published *Gone with the Wind* in 1936), then the *Forbes* magazine headquarters.

NEW SCHOOL FOR SOCIAL RESEARCH. 66 W. 12TH ST. (1930, arch. Joseph Urban). This innovative institution, founded in 1919 by two lecturers from Columbia University, moved, in 1930, into this Bauhaus-inspired building ● *98*. Three years later the New School developed a curriculum for scholars and academics fleeing Nazi Germany; it became a veritable "university in exile" for the social sciences.

VILLAGE COMMUNITY CHURCH. 143 W. 13TH ST. (1847, attrib. Samuel Thompson) ● *84*. This former Presbyterian church, inspired by the Theseum in Athens, is one of the finest examples of Greek Revival style. It was converted into apartments in 1982.

CHELSEA

This neighborhood, which lies between 14th and 34th streets from 6th Avenue to the Hudson River, is named after Captain Thomas Clarke, a retired English naval officer who, in 1750, bought a large plot of land along the river here for a country estate. He named it Chelsea in honor of the Chelsea Royal Hospital in London. His grandson, the scholar Clement Clarke Moore (author of "A Visit from St. Nicholas"), parceled out the estate with the aim of creating a middle-class neighborhood. Although Chelsea was never to become the residential haven that Clarke had imagined, this area and the neighboring blocks did attract wealthy families. However, by the end of the 19th century, Chelsea had lost some of its residential character due to the arrival of the department stores that

Coats of arms of the American nations hang above 6th Ave., renamed the Avenue of the Americas in honor of the founding of the Organization of American States, 1948.

NEW SCHOOL FOR SOCIAL RESEARCH
This school's famous lecturers have included the photographer Berenice Abbott, the composer John Cage, the anthropologist Claude Lévi-Strauss and the writers William Styron and Tom Wolfe.

FORBES GALLERIES
The ground floor of the Forbes Bldg. houses an exhibition of Malcolm Forbes' superb collections: 12 Fabergé eggs and more than 500 scale models of boats, made between 1870 and 1950.

TILE CLUB
This club was founded in 1877 by twelve artists who painted on glazed tiles. They were later joined by members active in different creative professions such as Pearl Buck, Stanford White, Eleanor Roosevelt and the journalist Ida Tarbell.

Siegel Building.

drove away the wealthy residents. Warehouses and piers sprang up in the west of the neighborhood, attracting poor immigrants in search of work, and tenements were built to house them. The neighborhood is now in two distinct parts: west of 7th Avenue, where attractively restored rowhouses abound, and the more commercial area along 6th Avenue toward Broadway.

FORMER SIEGEL-COOPER DRY GOODS STORE ★. 616–632 6TH AVE., between 18TH and 19TH STS. (1895–7, arch. DeLemos & Cordes). On September 12, 1896, 150,000 spectators jostled at the inauguration of this department store (above), which the advertising campaign boasted was "a city in itself". The man behind the idea, Henry Siegel, revolutionized commerce by using every form of advertising available and by handing out samples to customers. This building was also famous for the fountain in its entrance hall, which boasted a statue by Daniel Chester French.

"The most famous apartment house [located at 222 W. 23rd St.] inaugurated in 1884, still exists. The Chelsea Hotel, whose semi-Victorian, semi-Gothic architecture still stirs passersby. These early buildings were striking because of their extremely flexible approach to composition.**"**
Anka Muhlstein, *Manhattan*

FORMER B. ALTMAN DRY GOODS STORE. 621 6TH AVE., between 18TH and 19TH STS. (1877, arch. D. & J. Jardine). The oldest cast-iron department store on 6th Avenue and famous for its sophisticated clothing, its silks, velvets and satins. In 1913, ALTMAN gave his collection of Italian Renaissance and Baroque paintings to the Metropolitan Museum of Art.

Hippest Digs in N.Y.: Still a Chelsea Morning

From Dylan Thomas to Sid Vicious

THE DINERS
Long before the arrival of fast food chains, the American "diner" – originally shaped like a railroad dining car – served inexpensive food at all hours of the day and night. The Empire Diner (below), founded in 1943, is located at 210 10th Ave.

FORMER HUGH O'NEILL'S STORE. 655–671 6TH AVE. between 20TH AND 21ST STS. (1875, arch. Mortimer C. Merritt, additions 1890–5). Hugh O'Neill's low prices were aimed at the working classes rather than a wealthy clientele. In 1902, at O'Neill's death, no one wanted to take over from the "Fighting Irishman of 6th Avenue". The establishment closed in 1915. The cast-iron building was later made into offices and the two cupolas that used to crown the building's corners disappeared.

CHURCH OF THE HOLY COMMUNION ★. 49 W. 20TH ST. (1846, arch. Richard Upjohn) ● 86. This was the first asymmetrical Gothic Revival church in the United States. Despite its conversion into a discothèque, The Limelight, it still retains most of its interior decorations. (You can enjoy an excellent view of the Empire State Building from the corner of 6th Avenue and 23rd Street.)

CUSHMAN ROW. 406–418 W. 20TH ST. (1839) ● 84. These Greek Revival rowhouses, built by Don Alonzo Cushman, are in mint condition.

GENERAL THEOLOGICAL SEMINARY ★. (mainly 1883–1902, arch. Charles C. Haight). Clement Clarke Moore gave the land in 1818 for the seminary. An exhibition on the history of Chelsea is now housed in the building.

DIA CENTER FOR THE ARTS. 548 W. 22ND ST. This modern art center is housed in a former warehouse. The terrace affords a view over the "sea of warehouses" lining the Hudson.

AROUND
UNION SQUARE

FROM UNION SQUARE TO
THE EAST VILLAGE, *222*
FROM UNION SQUARE
TO GRAMERCY PARK, *228*
FROM UNION SQUARE TO
MADISON SQUARE, *232*

▲ From Union Square to the East Village

GRACE CHURCH
2 St. Mark's in the Bowery
3 Cooper Union Bldg.
4 Astor Library

✶ **Five hours**

On April 10, 1927, *The New York Times* led with the story of Sacco's death sentence. The

The New York Times.

"All the News That's Fit to Print."

**SACCO AND VANZETTI GUILTY, SAYS FULLER, AND MUST DIE;
BAY STATE GOVERNOR UPHOLDS JURY, CALLS TRIAL FAIR;
HIS BOARD UNANIMOUS, EXECUTION OF PAIR SET FOR AUG. 10**

execution was deferred until August 23. A strike was called and on the 22nd some 5,000 workers converged on Union Square, where they kept vigil until the time of the execution.

Located at the intersection of Broadway and 4th Avenue (which in colonial times led to Albany and Boston), Union Square was laid out in 1831 and opened in 1839. In the 1840's this was a wealthy residential area; after the Civil War, it became New York's theater district, with the presence of the Academy of Music on 14th Street (the site now occupied by the Con Edison building), and several other theaters. In the 1880's, with the development of the Ladies' Mile, commercial establishments moved to the neighborhood and a few early examples of skyscrapers were erected to the west of Union Square. After 1910, as commercial and artistic establishments moved uptown, it became a favorite site for labor-union gatherings and political demonstrations, particularly during the inter-war years. These have included such unforgettable gatherings as the demonstration on August 22, 1927 against the execution of Sacco and Vanzetti,

and the protest march of 35,000 unemployed workers in March 1930, during the Great Depression. A fruit and vegetable market now occupies Union Square four days a week. The best day to go is Saturday, especially at the end of summer and in the fall, at harvest time.

Around Union Square

The few remaining commercial buildings around the square are fine examples of early skyscrapers ● *94*. At 1 Union Square West, there is the Romanesque Revival Lincoln Building (1889–90, arch. R. H. Robertson); farther north, at no. 31, stands the former Bank of the Metropolis Building (1902–3, arch. Bruce Price), an interesting

222

UNION SQUARE

5 ASTOR PLACE SUBWAY STATION **6** COLONNADE ROW **7** DE VINNE PRESS BLDG. **8** THE OLD MERCHANT'S HOUSE **9** BAYARD-CONDICT BLDG. **10** CABLE BLDG. **11** PUCK BLDG. **12** THE PALLADIUM **13** STUYVESANT-FISH HOUSE **14** ST. GEORGE UKRANIAN CATHOLIC CHURCH

3RD AVE.

E. 10TH ST.

STUYVESANT ST.

TOMPKINS SQUARE PARK

EAST VILLAGE

E. 4TH ST.

N. Y. MARBLE CEMETERY

1ST AVE.

2ND AVE.

E. HOUSTON ST.

---

example of neo-Renaissance tripartite architecture as applied to the skyscraper; and, close by, at no. 33, the Moorish-style DECKER BUILDING ★ (1892–3, arch. John Edelman), which for a time housed the Decker Piano Company. The finest building on Union Square is arguably the CENTURY (1880–1, arch. William Schickel) ★, at 33 East 17th Street, in Queen Anne style, with its abundance of highly fanciful ornaments. It was once the headquarters of the Century Publishing Company, which in the late 1800's, published various magazines including the *Century* and, for children, *St. Nicholas*. On the east side of the square, at no. 20, stands the former UNION SQUARE SAVINGS BANK.

This severely neo-classical granite building (1924, arch. Henry Bacon) was designed by the architect of the Lincoln Memorial in Washington, D. C.

ENLIST NOW!
In May 1917, two months after the U.S. entered World War One, John Mitchell, Mayor of New York, had a model of a warship *The Recruit* constructed in Union Square. In this building naval officers recruited marines to fight in the war.

A demonstration in Union Square (opposite) in the 1880's.

223

Cooper Square (opposite)
at the turn of the century.

This mural outside a Ukrainian café at 2nd Ave. and E. 9th St. is a reminder of the many Eastern Europeans who have settled in the East Village.

East Village

Formerly part of the Lower East Side ▲ 189, the East Village lies east of the Bowery and north of Houston Street. At the end of the last century, many immigrants – mainly Germans at first – moved into the neighborhood, where they settled in the many tenements, especially around Tompkins Square. A couple of wealthy German benefactors, Oswald and Anna Ottendorfer, founded the GERMAN POLIKLINIK (Dispensary) and the FREIE BIBLIOTHEK UND LESEHALLE on 2nd Avenue to help the poorest inhabitants. **THE NEW BOHEMIA.** After World War Two a new generation of artists moved into this neighborhood, where rents were lower than in Greenwich Village ▲ 210. They created a new Bohemia and gave the area its present name. The 1950's saw the arrival of the founders of the beat generation: the writers Allen Ginsberg, Jack Kerouac, William Burroughs and poet Gregory Corso; also the novelist Norman Mailer, the painter Andy Warhol, the jazz musicians Thelonius Monk, Charles Mingus and Ornette Coleman who created the underground movement. **GRACE CHURCH.** 800–804 BROADWAY AT E. 10TH ST. (1845–6, arch. James Renwick, Jr) ● 86. This Gothic Revival church with its delicate octagonal spire, was built where Broadway

The entrance of the CBGB (below right), on the Bowery.

PETER STUYVESANT (1592–1672)
This stern, rigidly moralistic man, always dressed in black, was the last governor of New Amsterdam (1647–64). He established a bouwerie (farm) on Indian territory, between Broadway and the East River and what are now 3rd and 23rd streets, from which the present-day Bowery takes its name. The Federal-style house at 21 Stuyvesant St. was given by his great-

grandson to his daughter as a wedding present in 1804. Since 1861 the site has been occupied by a group of Italianate brick and brownstone houses, known as the Renwick Triangle.

veers to the west, a location that makes it visible, even today, many miles to the south. The interior boasts a fine mosaic floor and some magnificent stained glass windows, such as the "Te Deum" in the choir (1879).

St. Mark's Historic District

The neighborhood to the northeast of Stuyvesant Street belonged to Peter Stuyvesant's bouwerie, in the 17th century, and the street that now bears his name was once a private alley between Bowery Road and his mansion. His great-grandson, Petrus, divided up the estate for development at the end of the 18th century. The church of St. Mark's-in-the-Bowery, the Stuyvesant-Fish House and the Nicholas William Stuyvesant House date from this period. Today, St. Mark's Place, which runs between 3rd Avenue and Tompkins Square, is a lively street lined with bars and restaurants.
ST. MARK'S-IN-THE-BOWERY ★ 2ND AVE. AT E. 10TH ST. (1799). The land on which the private chapel of Stuyvesant's

bouwerie is believed to have stood was sold to the Episcopal Church in the late 18th century for a token dollar. The small Georgian-style church built in 1799 was enhanced by a Greek Revival steeple in 1828 and an Italianate cast-iron porch in 1854.

LAFAYETTE STREET HISTORIC DISTRICT

In its heyday, the second quarter of the 19th century, this area, lying east of Broadway and running the length of Lafayette and Bond streets, was an elegant residential neighborhood, rivaling Washington Square as a Manhattan's smartest address. Two of the most influential businessmen of the 19th century, Peter Cooper and John Jacob Astor, contributed to its growth by building the Cooper Union and the Astor Library. After the Civil War, as the city continued to spread northward, this neighborhood became a commercial district.

COOPER UNION BUILDING. COOPER SQUARE (1859, arch. Frederick A. Peterson). This Italianate brownstone building ● *88*, was built to house the college founded by Peter Cooper in 1859. It incorporated various structural innovations such as an iron-frame elevator. The top-floor studios added in the 1890's, were lit by glass roofs and contained an exhibition of decorative arts which became

COOPER UNION
This school of art and engineering was founded in 1859 by Peter Cooper (1791–1883), an industrialist, philanthropist and inventor who wanted to provide free education in the arts and sciences for working-class people. The owner of an ironworks and glue factory, Cooper designed the first American steam locomotive, called "Tom Thumb", produced the first steel train rails and started his own telegraph company.

The first Wanamaker's department store (below).

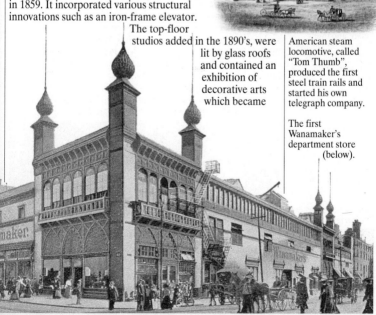

225

ASTOR PLACE RIOT
When the curtain of the Astor Place Opera House rose on the English actor William Macready in the title role of *Macbeth* on May 10, 1849, the audience, giving vent to anti-British feelings, booed and hissed. Meanwhile, a crowd numbering ten to twenty thousand gathered in the square and threw stones at the theater's entrance. The 7th Regiment of the Tompkins Market Armory quelled the riot by firing into the crowd, killing thirty-one people and wounding one hundred fifty others. The former Mercantile Library at 13 Astor Place now stands on the site of the opera house.

Astor Place Subway Station (right).

the nucleus of the future Cooper-Hewitt Museum ▲ *320* and which were used by the students as models. The building's Great Hall became a forum for lectures by such celebrities as Mark Twain, Andrew Carnegie, Fiorello La Guardia and Orson Welles. Above all, the hall is famous as the scene of Abraham Lincoln's first speech on slavery, "Right Makes Might", in 1860, which was a decisive factor in his election as President of the United States.

PUBLIC THEATER, FORMERLY ASTOR LIBRARY. 425 LAFAYETTE ST. (south wing 1849–53, arch. Alexander Saeltzer; center wing 1856–9, arch. Griffith Thomas; north wing 1879–81, arch. Thomas Stent). JOHN JACOB ASTOR founded the first public library in New York. Constructed in three stages, the building reflects the German influence on commercial architecture in mid-19th-century New York. In 1965, the theatrical director and producer JOSEPH PAPP persuaded the city to buy the building which, one year later, became the home of the SHAKESPEARE FESTIVAL.

ASTOR PLACE SUBWAY STATION (1904, arch. Heins & La Farge). This is one of the few subway stations that still have their original decoration. Among them are plaques

representing a beaver, symbol of the Astor fortune, which originated in the fur trade.
A black steel cube, entitled "Alamo" (1966), by Bernard T. Rosenthal, stands in the center of this square.

COLONNADE ROW. 428–34 LAFAYETTE ST. (1832–3, attributed to Seth Geer) ● *84*. These Greek Revival houses, with their marble façades, once ranked among the most magnificent residences in New York – home to such families as the Vanderbilts and the Astors. The series of Corinthian columns imposes a stylistic unity on the houses, which have suffered from lack of maintenance and infelicitous alteration. Only four of the nine original houses – formerly called LaGrange Terrace after Lafayette's estate in France – are still standing.

DE VINNE PRESS BUILDING. 393–9 LAFAYETTE ST. AT E. 4TH ST. (1885–6, arch. Babb, Cook & Willard) ● *91*. This printing works was one of several press buildings on Lafayette Street. The printer Theodore De Vinne (1828–1914) published books and magazines such as *Century*.

THE OLD MERCHANT'S HOUSE ★. 29 E. 4TH ST. (1831–2, attributed to Minard Lafever) ● *82*. This building (left), originally one of a group of six, was built by the property developer JOSEPH BREWSTER, and sold in 1835 to a wealthy hardware dealer, SEABURY TREDWELL. In 1936 it was converted into a museum evoking the life of a prosperous New York family in the 19th century.

BAYARD-CONDICT BUILDING ★. 65–69 BLEECKER ST. (1897–9, arch. Louis Sullivan and Lyndon P. Smith) ● *94*. This is the only work in New York by LOUIS SULLIVAN, one of the foremost architects of the Chicago school of architecture and Frank Lloyd Wright's revered "Master".

CABLE BUILDING. 621 BROADWAY (1894, arch. McKim, Mead & White). This building was once the head offices and power station for Manhattan's streetcars. Its arcaded bays, classically inspired stone carvings and prominent cornice, with its acanthus-motif ridgepole, make it one of the finest commercial buildings by the firm of McKim, Mead & White.

PUCK BUILDING. 295–309 LAFAYETTE ST. (1885–6 and 1892–3, arch. Albert Wagner, John Wagner). The originality of this 19th-century Romanesque Revival building lies in its wide arched windows and highly elaborate brickwork. It was built to house the satirical magazine *Puck*. The building was constructed in three stages, the last of which was when Lafayette Street was widened.

A statue of Puck, a character from Shakespeare's *A Midsummer's Night's Dream*, with the legend "What fools these mortals be", keeps watch over both entrances to the Puck Building. The statue at the former main entrance on Houston St. is the work of Caspar Buberl; the one on Lafayette St. is by Henry Baerer.

The cover of *Puck* Magazine of September 13, 1899 (above), attacking corruption.

Tammany Hall decorated for the national convention of July 4, 1868. During this period, the Democrats were based on 14th St., next to the Academy of Music, on the site of the future Con Edison Building.

During the 1840's, the district between Union Square and Gramercy Park became New York's newest and most glamorous residential area. Large private mansions sprang up along parks and avenues, cheek by jowl with the humblest row houses in adjacent streets. In the following decades, while the area west of 4th Avenue (now Park Avenue South) developed commercially around the "Ladies' Mile" of shops and stores, the area to the east remained staunchly residential. Around the turn of the 20th century, Gramercy Park became the chosen neighborhood of wealthy New Yorkers who preferred its artistic, liberal flavor to the more staid luxury of Uptown.

Around Irving Place

Tammany Hall. E. 17th St N. E. corner of Union Square E. (1928, arch. Thompson, Holmes & Converse). The Tammany Society – whose name was derived from Tammanend, a Delaware chief famed for his wisdom – was initially a patriotic organization, founded in 1789 as a response to the aristocratic Federalist party. Ten years after it was formed, the society began to take an interest in politics. Eventually it became the powerful New York Democratic Party machine, notorious for its corruption – especially under "Boss" Tweed ● *40*. Between 1866 and 1871 the Tweed Ring, which controlled key posts in the city government, pocketed several million dollars ▲ *185* of city funds. In 1928 the Tammany Society which, even after the death of "Boss" Tweed, still had a stranglehold on local politics, commissioned this Colonial-style building, inspired by Federal Hall (on Wall Street). In 1943 the International Ladies Garment Workers Union bought the building and turned it into their union headquarters. It now houses the Union Theater.

So-called Washington Irving House. S. W. corner of Irving Pl. and 17th St. This house was designed in 1845 and

Boss Tweed
Caricature of "Boss" Tweed, the notorious leader of the ring of the same name, who embezzled a huge amount of money from the city between 1866 and 1871.

its cast-iron verandah, wrought-iron balconies and wooden hood molding set it apart from the other 19th-century townhouses on the street. Elsie de Wolfe, the first professional interior designer in the United States, lived here with her companion, the playwright Elisabeth Marbury, from 1894 to 1911.

WASHINGTON IRVING HIGH SCHOOL. 40 IRVING PLACE (1908–13, arch. C. B. J. Snyder). This school, which was originally a women's college until 1986, takes its name from the writer WASHINGTON IRVING, author of *A History of New York from the Beginning of the World to the End of the Dutch Dynasty* (1809), a comic version of

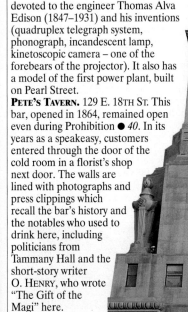

the city's history written under the name of Dietrich Knickerbocker. The neo-Gothic entrance hall is decorated with very fine murals by BARRY FAULKNER depicting scenes from Irving's work.

CON EDISON BUILDING. CORNER OF 14TH ST. AND IRVING PLACE (1915–29, arch. Henry Hardenbergh). This is the headquarters of the Consolidated Edison Company, which provides New York's gas and electricity supply. Its tower (1926–9, arch. Warren & Wetmore) which is brightly illuminated at night and called the "Tower of Light", was erected in memory of company employees who died in World War One. The building stands partially on the site of the Academy of Music, a huge concert hall, opened in 1854, which hosted performers such as Jenny Lind, Adelina Patti and Edwin Booth until it was superseded in 1883 by the Metropolitan Opera House, on Broadway. The CON EDISON ENERGY MUSEUM, at 145 East 14th Street, is devoted to the engineer Thomas Alva Edison (1847–1931) and his inventions (quadruplex telegraph system, phonograph, incandescent lamp, kinetoscopic camera – one of the forebears of the projector). It also has a model of the first power plant, built on Pearl Street.

PETE'S TAVERN. 129 E. 18TH ST. This bar, opened in 1864, remained open even during Prohibition ● *40*. In its years as a speakeasy, customers entered through the door of the cold room in a florist's shop next door. The walls are lined with photographs and press clippings which recall the bar's history and the notables who used to drink here, including politicians from Tammany Hall and the short-story writer O. HENRY, who wrote "The Gift of the Magi" here.

THE "BLOCK BEAUTIFUL"
The townhouses on 19th St. were remodeled in the 1920's and many were given stucco façades adorned with painted, glazed tiles, wrought iron and sculptures, such as these jockeys (left). The faces of these characters were originally black but were later repainted, as they were regarded as racist stereotypes.

The Con Edison Building.

SAMUEL B. RUGGLES
Born in 1800 in New Milford, Connecticut,

Samuel Ruggles attended Yale University, then studied law under his father, an influential lawyer twice elected to the Connecticut legislature. In 1820 Ruggles moved with his wife, Mary R. Rathbone, to New York, where he established his own practice.

Behind the railings of Gramercy Park stands the statue of Edwin Booth, a bronze commissioned by the Players Club from Edmond T. Quinn,

who has captured the actor in the role of Hamlet. It was erected in 1918.

Carved faces of Franklin, Milton, Goethe and Dante adorn the façade of the National Arts Club in true Italianate style, as was the fashion at the time of the building's restoration. The façade has been listed as a landmark since 1966. Woody Allen used this building for one of the scenes in his film *Manhattan Murder Mystery*.

GRAMERCY PARK ★

The name "Gramercy" is an anglicization of the Dutch names *Krom Moerasje*, "crooked little swamp", which described a meandering brook that used to run through here. In the early 1830's, Samuel B. Ruggles, who owned the land and who advocated planning towns around green spaces, designed the park and sold sixty-six building lots around it, stipulating that their owners would maintain the park and have exclusive access to it. To this day, Gramercy Park remains the only private square in New York.

EARLY HOUSES. Of the houses and other buildings designed in Ruggles' time, a few remain along the west and south sides of the park – among them nos. 3 and 4 GRAMERCY PARK WEST and the Friends' Meeting House, at 28 Gramercy Park South. Designed by King & Kellum for the Quakers between 1857 and 1859, this Italianate building was renovated in 1975 and sold to its current owners, the BROTHERHOOD SYNAGOGUE. At 34 Gramercy Park East, the GRAMERCY, built in 1883 by the architect George da Cunha, was one of Manhattan's first cooperative apartment buildings. It is also a fine example of New York Queen Anne style ● *90*, with its use of contrasting materials: brick, terracotta, wrought iron and stone. The sumptuous lobby boasts a mosaic floor and stained glass ceiling. Close by, at 36 GRAMERCY PARK EAST, stands the residence built between 1908 and 1910 by the architect James Riley Gordon. This building is almost entirely clad in terracotta with motifs of medieval inspiration.

THE PLAYERS. 16 GRAMERCY PARK SOUTH (1845; remodeled 1888–9, arch. Stanford White). In 1888, in founding The Players Club, the actor Edwin Booth realized a long-cherished dream – expressed in these words from 1886: "An actors club has been a dream of mine for many years. Having quite a number of theatrical books, pictures, etc., etc., I have dreamed of furnishing such an establishment with them someday. When I step aside and before I go, I hope to accomplish something of this kind." The only condition stipulated by Booth was that he should have an apartment at the club. The chosen premises, a townhouse in Gothic Revival style, were remodeled by Stanford White (free of charge) who added the porch, the impressive iron railings and the cornice graced with theatrical masks. The Players soon became the haunt of actors and their friends, including Stanford White and Mark Twain.

NATIONAL ARTS CLUB. 15 GRAMERCY PARK SOUTH (1845). The two original townhouses here were combined and remodeled between 1881 and 1884 by Calvert Vaux for the lawyer SAMUEL J. TILDEN, who had been governor of New York between 1874 and 1876. The elegant Victorian Gothic façade, with brick cladding in contrasting shades, is in typical

The stained glass roof (above) of the National Arts Club, executed by MacDonald.

3 AND 4 GRAMERCY PARK WEST

These two residences boast the finest cast-iron porches in New York. The two lamps that stand in front of no. 4 are a reminder that the house was the home of James Harper, Mayor of New York between 1844 and 1845 (and one of the founders of the publishers J. & J. Harper). Following a tradition dating back to Dutch times, the entrance to the mayor's house was flanked by two lamps which were lit when he was at home.

Ruskinian style; note the carved medallions of birds and plants over the windows and the busts on the first floor. The panels to the right of the porch are engraved with plants, animals and insects indigenous to New York. Three rooms were knocked together to house Tilden's library. This became the property of the New York Public Library in 1886 after the politician's death. In 1906 the residence was bought by the National Arts Club. This club, founded in 1898, was one of the first in New York to welcome a mixed membership. The residence was refurbished for its new owners, but the original decoration was preserved. A temporary exhibition hall provides a taste of the sumptuous interiors.

▲ From Union Square to Madison Square

1 Tammany Hall 2 49 Irving Place 3 W. Irving High School 4 Con Edison Bldg. 5 Pete's Tavern 6 Gramercy Park 7 The Players and National Arts Club

Between the 1860's and 1910, "Ladies' Mile", the stretch of Broadway and 5th and 6th avenues (left) running from 8th to 23rd Street, was the most fashionable area in New York. The most elegant shops and department stores of the "Ladies' Mile" were clustered along Broadway between Union Square and Madison Square. There was a constant stream of fashionable ladies in pursuit of luxury goods. Most of the shops that catered for this trade have long since closed down or moved Uptown.

BROADWAY

13

11

10

8   9

VESTIGES OF THE COMMERCIAL ERA

FORMER ARNOLD CONSTABLE & CO. 881–7 BROADWAY, S. W. CORNER OF 19TH ST. (1868–9, arch. Griffith Thomas). In 1825 Aaron Arnold, an English immigrant from the Isle of Wight, opened a little dry-goods store on Pine Street, in Lower Manhattan. Business thrived, and in 1853 his son-in-law, James Constable, became his partner. Subsequently, the store moved farther north several times, before opening on the "Ladies' Mile" in 1869. The new store was such a success that it had to be extended on 19th Street up to 5th Avenue. The extension is a cast-iron building with a mansard roof, the most striking in New York.

UNION SQUARE

FORMER W. & J. SLOANE. 884 BROADWAY, S. E. CORNER OF 19TH ST. (1881–2, arch. W. Wheeler Smith). For more than a century, Sloane's has been a renowned dealer of luxury furniture and carpets (the store supplied furnishings for the coronation of Tsar Nicholas II). The superb cast-iron store fronts can still be seen. Note also the plants carved around the columns inside.

FORMER GORHAM MANUFACTURING COMPANY. 889–91 BROADWAY, N. W. CORNER OF 19TH ST. (1883–4, arch. Edward Kendall). This impressive Queen Anne-style ● 90 building housed the main New York outlet of the GORHAM SILVER COMPANY.

FORMER LORD & TAYLOR DRY GOODS STORE. 901 BROADWAY, S. W. CORNER OF 20TH ST. (1867, arch. James H. Giles). This cast-iron building has a corner turret which was designed to attract customers. The store, founded around 1830 by two Englishmen, Samuel Lord and George W. Taylor, was originally a small shop in Lower

Cortez Cigars FOR MEN OF BRAINS —MADE AT KEY WEST—

TEDDY BEAR
A Brooklyn manufacturer decided to make a plush bear after he learned that president Theodore Roosevelt (shown below as a child) had spared a small bear while hunting. The president agreed to let it be called Teddy's Bear, in memory of his generous gesture.

8 Ex-Arnold Constable **9** Ex-W. & J. Sloane **10** Ex-Gorham M. C. **11** Ex-Lord & Taylor **12** Theodore Roosevelt's Birthplace **13** Flatiron Bldg. **14** Madison Square Park **15** Metropolitan Life Tower **16** Appellate Division Courthouse **17** N. Y. C. Life Insurance **18** Gilsey House

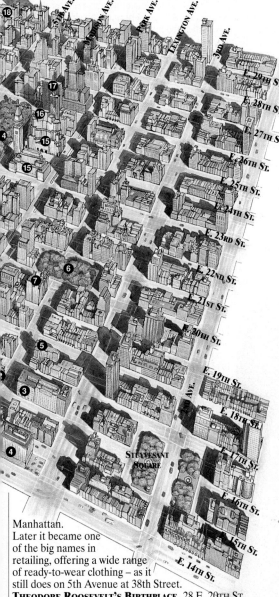

Four hours

The Broadway Central Hotel c. 1900

LADIES' MILE
"Looking out from Union Square, as this oasis in the desert of buildings is called, we get an idea of how interminable a Broadway crowd is. About a quarter of a mile farther north, Madison Square relieves the confine-ment of the street with fountains, grass, shrubs and trees, and between the two such a parade may be seen on fine afternoons, especially Saturdays, as no other city in America and few other cities in the world, can show. The great retail houses of the Stewarts, the Tiffanys, the Arnold Constables, and the Lords and Taylors, are concentrated within these limits . . . and women in their most elegant attire appear in quest of new addition to their already voluminous apparel."
Harper's New Monthly Magazine, 1878.

Manhattan.
Later it became one of the big names in retailing, offering a wide range of ready-to-wear clothing – as it still does on 5th Avenue at 38th Street.

THEODORE ROOSEVELT'S BIRTHPLACE. 28 E. 20TH ST. President Theodore Roosevelt was born here in 1858. The present building is a reconstruction dating from 1923, undertaken by his sisters, who engaged one of the first women architects, Theodate Pope Ridde, for the work. Inside, High Victorian Gothic rooms contain a MUSEUM devoted to Roosevelt's achievements as explorer, naturalist and politician.

FLATIRON BUILDING ★. BROADWAY AND 5TH AVE. AT 23RD ST. (1902, arch. D. H. Burnham & Co.) ● 96. This slender

Madison Square Garden in 1910. It was on the roof of Madison Square Garden (above, 1910) on June 25, 1906, that Stanford White was killed by the husband of a former mistress.

FLATIRON BUILDING
Much later, this name was given to other buildings on triangular sites, which occurred because of Broadway's irregular shape within the checkerboard town plan.

building, originally called the FULLER BUILDING after its developer, soon acquired its present name by virtue of its triangular shape – dictated by the awkward site. Its dramatic silhouette made it a familiar symbol of New York as well as a favorite subject for photographers and artists at the beginning of the 20th century ● *109*. This corner of 23rd Street and 5th Avenue was a popular haunt for "voyeurs", who took advantage of the air currents that swirled around the building, lifting women's skirts, to catch a glimpse of their ankles.

MADISON SQUARE

This square, which was named in memory of JAMES MADISON (1751–1836), president of the United States from 1809 to 1817, was established as a park on this site in 1811. The commemorative statues in the square include one of ADMIRAL DAVID FARRAGUT, who was a hero of the Mobile Bay naval battle, during the Civil War. This is the work of Augustus Saint-Gaudens (1880): the base, in the form of a bench, was designed by Stanford White.

METROPOLITAN LIFE TOWER ★. 1 MADISON AVE. (1893, 1909, arch. Napoleon LeBrun & Sons) ● *96*. The tower at the corner of 24th Street (modeled on Saint Mark's Campanile in Venice) is the company's symbol and was erected in order to make the building the tallest in the world (it was deposed by the Woolworth Building ▲ *180* in 1913). In 1932 Met Life enlarged its premises with another building on the opposite side of 24th Street, whose Italian marble lobby is particularly worth a visit. The existing building is a partial version of the project (above) which provided for a tower nearly 100 stories high; it was left incomplete because of the Depression.

APPELLATE DIVISION COURTHOUSE ★. 35 E. 25TH ST. (1900, arch. James Brown Lord) ● *92*. This small building, a Beaux Arts masterpiece, houses the Appellate Division of the New York State Supreme Court. The classical façade is adorned with sculptures depicting key figures from the history of law and various allegories evoking different aspects of Law and Justice. The lobby and the courtroom, which are richly decorated with murals and magnificent stained glass windows, are open to the public.

NEW YORK LIFE INSURANCE COMPANY. 51 MADISON AVE. (1928, arch. Cass Gilbert). This neo-Gothic skyscraper stands on the site of the first two Madison Square Gardens.

GILSEY HOUSE. 1200 BROADWAY (1869–71, arch. Stephen D. Hatch) ● *89*. This building, with its enormous mansard roof, now a private residence, was originally one of the city's most luxurious hotels.

AROUND
GRAND CENTRAL
TERMINAL

GRAND CENTRAL TERMINAL, 236
ISABELLE GOURNAY
GRAND CENTRAL TERMINAL
TO MADISON SQUARE GARDEN, 238
SETH KAMIL
EMPIRE STATE BUILDING, 242
ISABELLE GOURNAY
GRAND CENTRAL TERMINAL
TO THE THEATER DISTRICT, 250
SETH KAMIL
NEW YORK PUBLIC LIBRARY, 252
ISABELLE GOURNAY
GRAND CENTRAL TERMINAL
TO CHRYSLER BUILDING, 260
SETH KAMIL
UNITED NATIONS, 263
MICHELLE DE ROSSET
THE CHRYSLER BUILDING, 266
ISABELLE GOURNAY

▲ GRAND CENTRAL TERMINAL
TO MADISON SQUARE GARDEN

1 GRAND CENTRAL TERMINAL
2 PHILIP MORRIS INC. BLDG.
3 POLISH CONSULATE
4 UNION LEAGUE CLUB
5 PIERPONT MORGAN LIBRARY

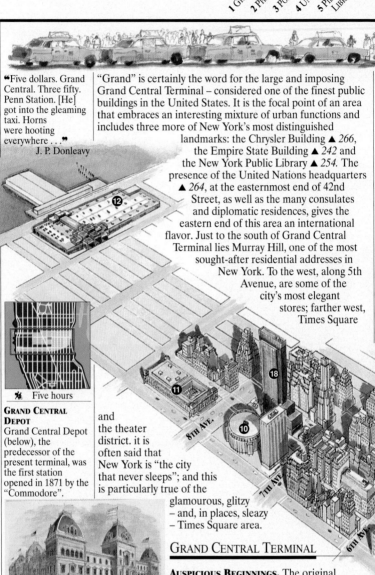

> "Five dollars. Grand Central. Three fifty. Penn Station. [He] got into the gleaming taxi. Horns were hooting everywhere . . ."
> J. P. Donleavy

"Grand" is certainly the word for the large and imposing Grand Central Terminal – considered one of the finest public buildings in the United States. It is the focal point of an area that embraces an interesting mixture of urban functions and includes three more of New York's most distinguished landmarks: the Chrysler Building ▲ 266, the Empire State Building ▲ 242 and the New York Public Library ▲ 254. The presence of the United Nations headquarters ▲ 264, at the easternmost end of 42nd Street, as well as the many consulates and diplomatic residences, gives the eastern end of this area an international flavor. Just to the south of Grand Central Terminal lies Murray Hill, one of the most sought-after residential addresses in New York. To the west, along 5th Avenue, are some of the city's most elegant stores; farther west, Times Square and the theater district. it is often said that New York is "the city that never sleeps"; and this is particularly true of the glamourous, glitzy – and, in places, sleazy – Times Square area.

🎫 Five hours

GRAND CENTRAL DEPOT
Grand Central Depot (below), the predecessor of the present terminal, was the first station opened in 1871 by the "Commodore".

GRAND CENTRAL TERMINAL

AUSPICIOUS BEGINNINGS. The original terminal (commonly called Grand Central Station) was built in 1871 by "Commodore" Cornelius Vanderbilt. The present building dates from the time of his grandson, William K. Vanderbilt, chairman of the New York Central Railroad, which included three major rail networks operating out of Manhattan. In 1903 a closed competition was launched for the reconstruction of the station. The winning firm, Reed & Stem, planned the layout of the station; later, Warren & Wetmore were asked to aid in the revision of the original design. The new station was opened in 1913. It was

the proverbial tip of the iceberg, with tracks running on two levels under Park Avenue. The terminal was central to an ambitious town-planning project devised by William Wilgus, the chief engineer of the New York Central Corporation. This program included electrifying the network and laying down and organizing the underground tracks. Concerned with obtaining a good return for its investment, the railroad company rented out the building rights of the land above the tracks. Hotels, offices and luxury apartments were built along Park Avenue, which became one of the most prestigious addresses in Manhattan. The view down the avenue toward the station, crowned by the New York Central Building (now the Helmsley Building) was one of New York's finest. When, in the early 1960's, the huge Pan Am (now MetLife) Building

"I must admit, however, that I am starting to become reconciled with the Pan Am Building, which juts out of Grand Central Station like the shoulder piece of a bayonet sticking out of a fine animal that has been stabbed in the back."

Donald Westlake,
Strange Brothers

▲ GRAND CENTRAL TERMINAL TO MADISON SQUARE GARDEN

PEDIMENT OF GRAND CENTRAL TERMINAL The central sculptural group on the station's pediment represents, Mercury (shown right), flanked by Hercules and Minerva. According to Warren, they embody, respectively "the glory of commerce", "moral energy" and "mental energy". The work was commissioned from Jules Coutan.

The Main Concourse of Grand Central Terminal.

was imposed on the station, thus spoiling this view, it raised a storm of public protest.

A CLASSICAL FAÇADE. The 42nd-Street façade, by the Beaux Arts-trained Whitney Warren, who was responsible for the station's exterior decoration, is a piece of architectural bravura. The architect saw the terminal as a triumphal gateway to the city and the façade, a stone facing on a metal frame, is remarkable for its use of a limited number of unusually large, boldly defined elements.

THE INTERIOR. The layout of Grand Central Terminal was revolutionary for its time. A system of ramps, which can be reached via the subway or from outside the station, helps prevent disorderly crowds, a common problem in other stations. The MAIN CONCOURSE was originally used exclusively for long-distance trains. Its VAULTED CEILING is decorated with the constellations: electric bulbs representing 2,500 stars joined by a gilt border "to form the celestial figures". The ARRIVAL HALL which is much smaller, formed part of the former Biltmore Hotel, now replaced by an office building. The original hall for suburban trains is on the lower level, along with the Oyster Bar, a restaurant known for its décor and seafood specialties.

GRAND CENTRAL TERMIN
Sectional View from Biltmore Hotel Looking East Toward Lexington
SHOWING PASSAGEWAYS TO HOTELS, OFFICE BUILD

1 – Hotel Commodore
2 – Biltmore Hotel
3 – Hotel Roosevelt
4 – New York Central Bldg. 230 Park Ave.
5 – Graybar Building
6 – Grand Central Terminal Office Building

A – Cab Baggage Service
B – Travel Information Bureau
C – Newsreel Theatre
D – Lower Level
E – Stairways from Vanderbilt Ave. to Upper & Lower Levels
F – Ticket Offices

G – Gr
H – Of
J – M
K – Re
L – 42
M – Pa

THE "PALACE OF DEPARTURE". This is how the French writer and diplomat Paul Morand labelled the terminal, whose monumentality, comfort and cleanliness are a source of admiration for European visitors. Movie-makers have filmed some unforgettable farewell scenes and chases here. For example, Alfred Hitchcock used it for some sequences for *North by Northwest*, starring Cary Grant. Grand Central Terminal's passenger figures reached a peak, in 1947, of 65 million – in other words more than 40 percent of the U.S. population at that time. Now that the era of transcontinental trips in Pullman cars is over, the concourse has lost some of its air of excitement, though its serenity is periodically shattered by hordes of scurrying commuters. In recent years the terminal almost suffered the fate of Pennsylvania Station ▲ *249*, which was demolished in 1963 to make way for the new Madison Square Garden ▲ *249*. In 1968, the Penn Central Corporation, the railroad's new owners, planned to demolish Grand Central's 42nd-Street façade and the waiting rooms to construct a 55-story tower designed by Marcel Breuer. The terminal was saved by a high-profile campaign led by Jacqueline Kennedy Onassis and the architect Philip Johnson, and the station was listed on the National Register of Historic Places in 1983. A vast rehabilitation program also includes the renovation of the entire station.

The building site in 1911.

"The evening she arrived at Grand Central Station was the turning point of her life. Disoriented, scared, she had crossed the huge concourse of the station, carrying her one and only suitcase; she had looked up and had stopped dead. She was probably one of the few people to have immediately realized that the heaven of the great vaulted ceiling had been painted back to front. The Eastern stars were in the West."
Marry Higgins Clark, *The Night of the Fox*

A PATRIOTIC WOMAN
According to a Revolutionary War legend, Mrs Murray (whose family name survives in Murray Hill (right, during the 1860's) played a trick on the British. By inviting General Howe and his officers – who had just landed with their troops – to tea, she enabled George Washington and his men to retreat to northwest Manhattan.

Façade, 149 E. 38th St.

POLISH CONSULATE
233 Madison Ave. This mansion, built in Second Empire style by C. P. H. Gilbert, was formerly the headquarters of the National Democratic Club. Its interior (below) is as opulent as its exterior.

MURRAY HILL

This neighborhood, lying between 34th and 42nd streets and between 5th and 3rd avenues, takes its name from Robert Murray, who, during the British colonial period, owned a country house in the center of this area. At the end of the 19th century, Murray Hill consisted of a collection of stables and outbuildings belonging to the private mansions on 5th Avenue owned by the "Upper Four Hundred". This expression referred to the four hundred people from the top families in New York, who were invited to Mrs Astor's annual ball (her ballroom being able to accommodate that number). When the mansions on 5th Avenue were demolished at the beginning of the 20th century to make way for department stores, a number of these outbuildings were refurbished. They now rank among the most sought-after addresses in the city. **PHILIP MORRIS INC. BUILDING.** 120 PARK AVE. (1982, arch. Ulrich Franzen and Associates) ● *103*. The ground floor of the New York headquarters of this well-known cigarette manufacturer (open to the public) houses an enclosed garden, a café and an annex of the Whitney Museum of Modern Art ▲ *326*, which mounts temporary exhibitions.
38TH STREET. With its varied styles of houses, the part of 38th Street between Park and 3rd avenues epitomizes the charm of the neighborhood. At no. 108, a small Art Deco building, built in 1930, proffers a "Cubist" façade, its redbrick bonding enhanced with polychromatic stringcourses made of glazed terracotta. At the corner of Lexington Avenue two PRIVATE MANSIONS stand opposite each other: no. 136, in Victorian style with little windowpanes made of blown glass, and no. 125, a well-preserved example of Old Charleston style. Farther east, at no. 149, is a Flemish Renaissance-style carriage house (above, left) decorated with the heads of bulldogs and horses. At no. 150–152, there is a Federal-style residence from 1858 (remodeled in 1935), dating from the time when Murray Hill was still a suburb of New York. This was the home of a member of the family of Martin Van Buren, the eighth President of the United States (1837–41).

"WHEN I WALKED DOWN MADISON AVENUE, PARK AVENUE, I
KNEW I WAS WALKING THROUGH THE VIOLENT CORRIDORS OF A
MUSEUM IN WHICH THE WOMEN WERE INTOXICATING FIGURES,
THAT THE WHOLE OF NEW YORK WAS A BOOK OF THE NEW ART."

P. BOURGEADE

MORGAN, FATHER AND SON
John Pierpont Morgan, Sr (1837–1913) and his son, John Pierpont, Jr (1867–1943), built up the most influential financial trust in America before the 1929 crash. Their bank served the most important families in New York, such as the Astors, Vanderbilts and Guggenheims, and it saved the city from bankruptcy on three occasions. Until 1933 a letter of credit from the Morgan bank was regarded as an impeccable testimonial.
J. Pierpont Morgan, Sr (above) was not only the greatest financier of his time but also an unrivaled collector of rare books and manuscripts, for which he built his private library (left). It was opened to the public in 1924, in accordance with his wishes.

SNIFFEN COURT HISTORIC DISTRICT ★. 150–158 E. 36TH ST. (1850–60). Grouped around a small court, these ten Romanesque Revival brick houses once served as stables for some wealthy 5th Avenue residents. In the 1920's they were converted into homes, studios and offices.

UNION LEAGUE CLUB. S. W. CORNER OF PARK AVE. AND E. 37TH ST. (1931, arch. Morris and O'Connor). This imposing building in neo-Georgian style is the headquarters of a club founded in 1863 by some Republican former members of the Union Club. A conflict had arisen between them and some other members over the Club's admission of some Confederate sympathizers. To express their staunch support for the Northern cause and President Lincoln, these Republicans formed their own club, which they called the Union League.

PIERPONT MORGAN LIBRARY ● 93 ★. 29 AND 33 E. 36TH ST. AND 231 MADISON AVE. The Pierpont Morgan Library comprises three buildings. At 29 East 36th Street, the former library of J. P. Morgan, Sr ● 93 (designed by Benjamin W. Morris) contains his collection of works of art and antique manuscripts and books, including a Gutenberg Bible. The main entrance to the library is through the annex at 29 East 36th Street, a museum that mounts temporary exhibitions. A pleasant covered garden leads to 231 Madison Avenue, a brownstone ● 88 that was once the home of J. P. Morgan, Jr. It was bought in 1990 by the museum to house a bookshop and a conference hall.

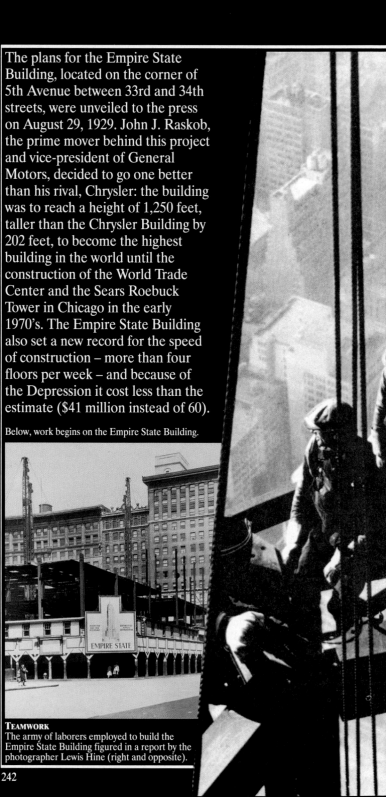

The plans for the Empire State Building, located on the corner of 5th Avenue between 33rd and 34th streets, were unveiled to the press on August 29, 1929. John J. Raskob, the prime mover behind this project and vice-president of General Motors, decided to go one better than his rival, Chrysler: the building was to reach a height of 1,250 feet, taller than the Chrysler Building by 202 feet, to become the highest building in the world until the construction of the World Trade Center and the Sears Roebuck Tower in Chicago in the early 1970's. The Empire State Building also set a new record for the speed of construction – more than four floors per week – and because of the Depression it cost less than the estimate ($41 million instead of 60).

Below, work begins on the Empire State Building.

TEAMWORK
The army of laborers employed to build the Empire State Building figured in a report by the photographer Lewis Hine (right and opposite).

The Waldorf-Astoria (left), demolished in 1929 and replaced by the Empire State Building.

AN ENORMOUS PROJECT
The photomontage on the right shows an early design for the Empire State Building superimposed onto the background of the city. This design was not finally used.

"THE HAPPY WARRIOR"
Alfred E. Smith (right), a former governor of the State of New York and president of the corporation that managed the building, announced the project in 1929.

A FAILURE
When it was opened on May 1, 1931, the "Empty State Building" had rented out only 46 percent of its office space, despite an extensive publicity campa

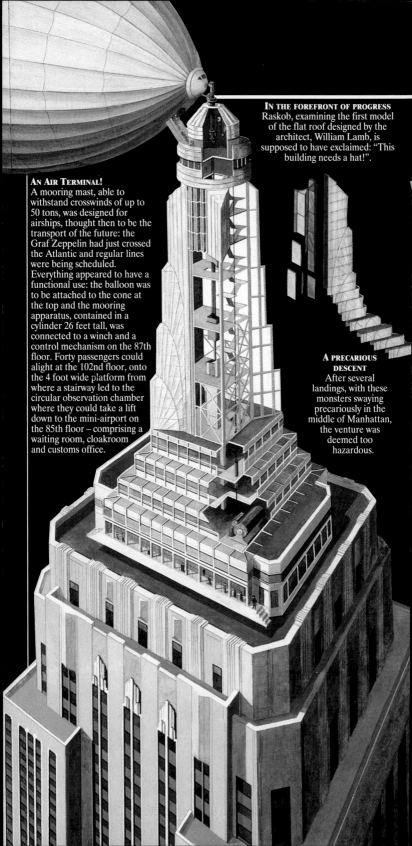

IN THE FOREFRONT OF PROGRESS
Raskob, examining the first model of the flat roof designed by the architect, William Lamb, is supposed to have exclaimed: "This building needs a hat!".

AN AIR TERMINAL!
A mooring mast, able to withstand crosswinds of up to 50 tons, was designed for airships, thought then to be the transport of the future: the Graf Zeppelin had just crossed the Atlantic and regular lines were being scheduled. Everything appeared to have a functional use: the balloon was to be attached to the cone at the top and the mooring apparatus, contained in a cylinder 26 feet tall, was connected to a winch and a control mechanism on the 87th floor. Forty passengers could alight at the 102nd floor, onto the 4 foot wide platform from where a stairway led to the circular observation chamber where they could take a lift down to the mini-airport on the 85th floor – comprising a waiting room, cloakroom and customs office.

A PRECARIOUS DESCENT
After several landings, with these monsters swaying precariously in the middle of Manhattan, the venture was deemed too hazardous.

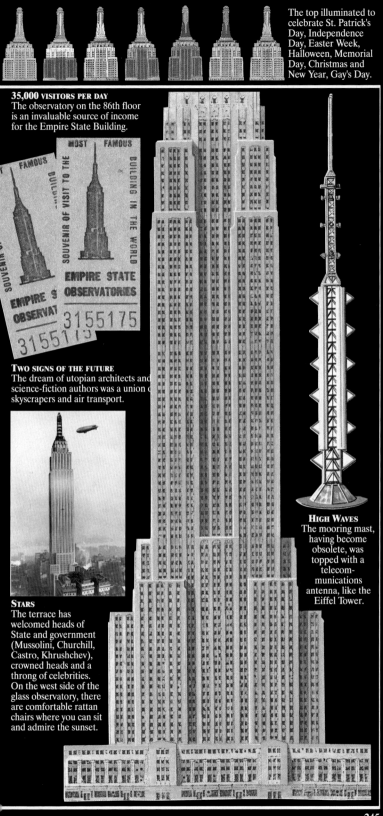

The top illuminated to celebrate St. Patrick's Day, Independence Day, Easter Week, Halloween, Memorial Day, Christmas and New Year, Gay's Day.

35,000 VISITORS PER DAY
The observatory on the 86th floor is an invaluable source of income for the Empire State Building.

MOST FAMOUS

FAMOUS

SOUVENIR OF VISIT TO THE

BUILDING IN THE WORLD

EMPIRE STATE OBSERVATORIES

EMPIRE S OBSERVAT

3155175

3155175

TWO SIGNS OF THE FUTURE
The dream of utopian architects and science-fiction authors was a union of skyscrapers and air transport.

STARS
The terrace has welcomed heads of State and government (Mussolini, Churchill, Castro, Khrushchev), crowned heads and a throng of celebrities. On the west side of the glass observatory, there are comfortable rattan chairs where you can sit and admire the sunset.

HIGH WAVES
The mooring mast, having become obsolete, was topped with a telecommunications antenna, like the Eiffel Tower.

245

REAL CATASTROPHES
The Empire State Building has been the scene of many spectacular disasters, at least as dramatic as the one in the legendary film, *King Kong*.

THE BIG JUMP
Sixteen people have committed suicide by jumping off the top of the platform on the 86th floor. A railing was erected to stop suicide attempts, but has done nothing to discourage the truly desperate. This figure is actually fairly low given that 70 million visitors have come up to admire the view; the Eiffel Tower has recorded 400 suicides.

FACT IS STRANGER THAN FICTION
On July 28, 1945, a B-25 bomber, piloted by William Smith, flew over Manhattan at more than 186 mph and at an altitude of 1148 feet, less than half the minimum authorized altitude. It is not known why he was weaving between the skyscrapers of Midtown but at 9.52am, having just missed the Helmsley Building, he crashed into the Empire State Building, devastating the north façade of the 79th floor. One of the engines went straight through the tower and crashed down on the other side of 33rd St. The outcome of this catastrophe was fourteen dead and twenty-six wounded. Luckily, as it was a Saturday, the offices were all virtually deserted.

MIRACLE ON 34

Gust of wind saves woman who leaped from 86th floor of Empire State Building

Left, lightning striking the spire.

AROUND THE EMPIRE STATE BUILDING

FORMER B. ALTMAN BUILDING ▲ *361.* 5TH AVE. BETWEEN 34TH AND 35TH STS. (1906, arch. Trowbridge & Livingston). Benjamin Altman was the first to open a department store in this previously residential neighborhood. He built it in the style of a grand Italianate palace to blend in with the surrounding mansions. The store closed in 1990, but the building is being redesigned to house the New York Public Library's Science and Industry collection.

HERALD AND GREELEY SQUARES. INTERSECTION OF 6TH AVE., BROADWAY AND 34TH ST. These two triangular squares face each other. Herald Square commemorates the New York Herald Building (founded in 1835 by James Gordon Bennett), whose headquarters, built in 1893, stood just north of here. The clock that used to crown the building, which was demolished in 1921, now lords it over the square. Two bronze figures, nicknamed Stuff and Guff, chime the hours. The statue of Horace Greeley, founder of the *New York Tribune* (1841) and a crusading journalist, particularly in the cause of the abolition of slavery, seems to watch them from Greeley Square, just to the south. The statue was erected in 1890.

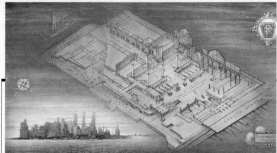

Pennsylvania Station before its demolition in 1963.

AN INSTITUTION
Every year Macy's organizes the Thanksgiving Day Parade ● *53*. Early in the morning, the parade leaves the Museum of Natural History, on Central Park West, and heads for the store.

Macy's logo, a red star, was once the emblem of Macy the whaler captain.

MACY'S. BROADWAY AND 7TH AVE., BETWEEN 34TH AND 35TH STS. (1901, arch. De Lemos & Cordes, additions 1924–31, arch. Robert D. Kohn). R. H. Macy, the former captain of a whaler, founded what was to become "the world's largest store" (as trumpeted by the huge billboard on the Broadway façade) in 1858. After occupying premises in the vicinity of 14th Street, Macy's moved to Broadway and 34th Street in 1902. Over the years the store was extended successively farther west to 7th Avenue. The 34th Street entrance still possesses its superb original decorations: four caryatids hold the emblems of commerce and abundance in their hands.

MADISON SQUARE GARDEN CENTER. BETWEEN 31ST AND 33RD STS., 7TH AND 8TH AVES. (1968, arch. Charles Luckman Assocs.). A masterpiece, Penn Station was destroyed in 1963 to make way for this vast leisure and office complex. By the 1960's Pennsylvania Station was one of the few "grand horizontals" left in an increasingly "vertical" New York. Built in 1910 and only four stories high, it covered 12 acres of land. Its architects, McKim, Mead & White, drew their inspiration directly from the great buildings of the Roman Empire. The general waiting room, which was modeled on the Baths of Caracalla, and the steel and glass roof over the train concourse, were particularly fine features. The demolition of the station gave rise to the first major public outcry in support of preserving landmarks. By contrast, the present Penn Station is unobtrusively hidden underground, below Madison Square Garden. This massive complex, which offers cultural and sporting events all year round, is the third with this name; the first was located at Madison Square and the second on 9th Avenue at 49th Street. All of them fell victim to fire.

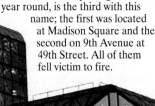

GENERAL POST OFFICE OF NEW YORK
Between 8th and 9th aves., 31st and 33rd sts. Impressed by McKim, Mead & White's Penn Station, the government commissioned this firm to design the General Post Office, which was completed in 1913. Forty percent of its mail used to come via the station, which it faced across 8th Ave. It is, however, merely a pale reflection, aesthetically, of its former neighbor. The width of the façade bears a quotation, loosely adapted from Herodotus: "Neither snow nor rain nor heat nor gloom of night stays these couriers from the swift completion of their appointed rounds."

1 GRAND CENTRAL TERMINAL
2 LINCOLN BLDG.
3 GEN. SOCIETY OF MECHANICS AND TRADESMEN
4 CENTURY ASSOCIATION
5 N. Y. PUBLIC LIBRARY
6 BRYANT PARK
7 N. Y. YACHT CLUB
8 ROYALTON HOTEL
9 ALGONQUIN HOTEL

TOWARD THE NEW YORK PUBLIC LIBRARY

LINCOLN BUILDING. 60 E. 42ND ST. (1929–30, arch. J. E. R. Carpenter). This neo-Gothic tower, designed at the end of the 1920's when skyscraper architecture was booming, rigorously applied the regulations laid

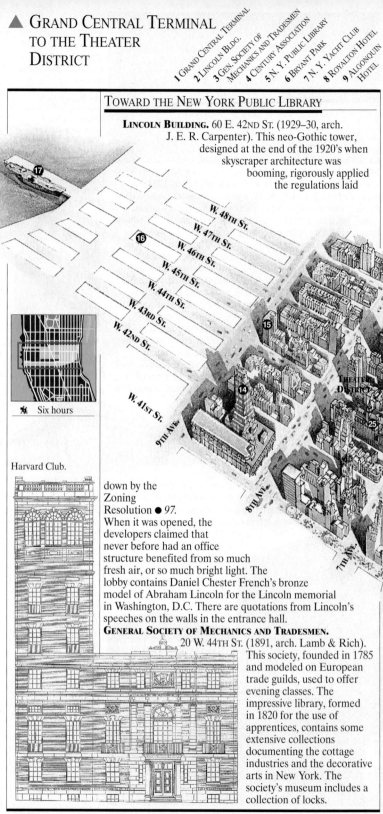

W. 48TH ST.
W. 47TH ST.
W. 46TH ST.
W. 45TH ST.
W. 44TH ST.
W. 43RD ST.
W. 42ND ST.
W. 41ST ST.

🕴 Six hours

9TH AVE.
8TH AVE.
7TH AVE.

THE THEATER DISTRICT

Harvard Club.

down by the Zoning Resolution ● 97. When it was opened, the developers claimed that never before had an office structure benefited from so much fresh air, or so much bright light. The lobby contains Daniel Chester French's bronze model of Abraham Lincoln for the Lincoln memorial in Washington, D.C. There are quotations from Lincoln's speeches on the walls in the entrance hall.

GENERAL SOCIETY OF MECHANICS AND TRADESMEN. 20 W. 44TH ST. (1891, arch. Lamb & Rich). This society, founded in 1785 and modeled on European trade guilds, used to offer evening classes. The impressive library, formed in 1820 for the use of apprentices, contains some extensive collections documenting the cottage industries and the decorative arts in New York. The society's museum includes a collection of locks.

10 BUSH TOWER **11** EX-KNICKERBOCKER HOTEL **12** TIMES SQUARE **13** EX-PARAMOUNT BLDG. AND THEATER **14** EX-MCGRAW-HILL BLDG. **15** FILM CENTER **16** LANDMARK TAVERN **17** INTREPID SEA-AIR-SPACE MUSEUM **18** MARRIOTT MARQUIS HOTEL **19** FATHER DUFFY SQUARE **20** MCGRAW-HILL BLDG. **21** ROCKEFELLER CENTER **22** HELMSLEY BLDG. **23** METLIFE BLDG. **24** GRACE BLDG. **25** THE N. Y. TIMES BLDG.

THE CLUBS. This neighborhood is the home of some of the city's most venerable clubs. Leading universities such as Yale, Princeton and Harvard have established their clubs here, and admission is reserved exclusively for former students. The lobby of the Yale Club, at the corner of Vanderbilt Avenue and 44th Street, contains a commemorative plaque for one of the university's former students, Captain Nathan Hale, ▲ 168, a hero of the American Revolution.

CENTURY ASSOCIATION
7 W. 43rd St. This Italianate-style club, founded in 1891 to provide a forum for artists and intellectuals, takes its name from its original number of members – one hundred.

NEW YORK YACHT CLUB ★. 37 W. 44TH ST. ● *93* (1901, arch. Warren & Wetmore). The extraordinary windows which suggest the stern of an 18th-century ship and the waves, shells, and seaweed which are carved into the façade ● *93*, indicate this club's sphere of activity. Founded in 1844, the New York Yacht Club is the patriarch of American yacht clubs. Until 1983 it organized the celebrated America's Cup ● *65*, which has taken place every four years since 1851.

THE AMERICA'S CUP
In 1851, when Queen Victoria asked who had come second in the race, she received the answer "But, Ma'am, there is no second place".

251

The lobby (right) of the Royalton Hotel.

ALGONQUIN HOTEL
Harold Ross, who founded the witty, intellectual magazine *The New Yorker*, regularly attended meetings of the Algonquin's Round Table, whose sparkling conversation enlivened lunchtime in the hotel's Oak Room. One of its members, the cartoonist James Thurber, became a contributor to the magazine.

N.Y. PUBLIC LIBRARY
The main façade, which is set back from 5th Ave., is dominated by a triumphal arch crowned by allegorical figures by Paul Wayland Bartlett, representing, from left to right, History, Drama, Poetry, Religion, Romance, and Philosophy. The statues above the fountains on the terrace are the work of Frederick MacMonnies, while the two white marble lions guarding the steps (dubbed Patience and Fortitude) are by Edward Clark Potter. In fine weather the terrace is an ideal spot from which to watch the world go by – perhaps while having a drink in one of its two cafés.

ROYALTON HOTEL. 44 W. 44TH ST. The ultra-modern lobby of this hotel, designed by Philip Starck, is worth a visit. The writer William Saroyan used to stay here for long periods of time; this is where he was living when he was awarded the Pulitzer Prize for his play *The Time of Your Life* in 1940.

ALGONQUIN HOTEL. 59 W. 44TH ST. (1902, arch. Goldwyn Starrett). In the 1920's, this hotel served as a meeting place for leading figures in theatrical and literary circles. Its oak-paneled dining room has been immortalized for the lovely lunches held here by the Round Table, a group of wits, mainly from *The New Yorker*, including Robert Benchley, Edna Ferber, Ring Lardner, George S. Kaufman and Dorothy Parker. The place to be seen in now is the Blue Bar in the lobby.

FRED F. FRENCH BUILDING ★. 551 5TH AVE. AT N. E. CORNER OF 45TH ST. (1927, arch. H. Douglas Ives and Sloan & Robertson). The faience mosaics decorating the upper setbacks of this building were sharply criticized when it was completed. They are now praised for their originality. The lobby is typical of those found in skyscrapers of this period.

NEW YORK PUBLIC LIBRARY

HISTORY. With its valuable collections and majestic, lavishly decorated architecture, the Main Branch of the New York Public Library ranks among the great libraries of the world.

Its research collection was founded on May 23, 1895, with a
bequest from Samuel J. Tilden which enabled the collections
of the Astor and Lenox libraries to be consolidated. New
York's municipal government agreed to contribute a plot of
land on the condition that the library be open to the public in
the evenings and on Sundays and public holidays. The library
site, on 5th Avenue between 40th and 42nd streets, had
formerly been occupied by the Croton Reservoir, which was
erected in 1842 to supply the city with drinking water. The
new library, designed by the Beaux Arts architects John M.
Carrère and Thomas Hastings, was opened in 1911. Built of
white marble, it sits grandly back from the street on a terrace,
approached by wide steps flanked by two haughty-looking
stone lions.

THE INTERIOR. On the first floor, the Gottesman Exhibition
Hall mounts some extremely interesting temporary
exhibitions. Since 1983 the murals by Richard Haas, depicting
the headquarters of New York's leading newspapers and
publishing houses, have graced the De Witt Wallace
Periodical Room. This room owes its name to the founder of
the *Reader's Digest*, who recopied the
first texts he was to publish here. The
main Reading Room, on the top floor,
which is divided by the delivery desk,
runs the length of the building and can
accommodate seven hundred readers.
There is a guided tour which includes all
the rooms.

THE COLLECTIONS. The library holds
about 36 million objects, including 11.3
million books. Its specialist departments
include the Jewish, Slavic and Oriental
divisions; the History and Genealogy
department, which boasts a collection of
100,000 views of New York; the Scientific
department, in which Edwin Land,
inventor of the Polaroid camera and
Chester Carlson, inventor of xerography,
did research; and the Economics
department, which houses 1.5 million
books and 11,000 periodicals. The library
is also the proud owner of some rarities
such as a Gutenberg Bible and a globe
dating from 1519, the first one to show
America.

In 1970 the small shops lining the Avenue of the Americas, or 6th Ave. (above) between 43rd and 44th sts. were knocked down and 1133 (below) was built in their place, continuing the transformation of the avenue.

AMERICAN STANDARD BUILDING
The carved allegories on the façade of this building, first owned by the American Radiator Company, symbolize the transformation of matter into energy. This figure (right) embodies hydraulic energy.

1133 Ave. of the Americas.

FROM THE NEW YORK PUBLIC LIBRARY TO TIMES SQUARE

REPUBLIC NATIONAL BANK TOWER, FORMER KNOX HAT BUILDING. 452 5TH AVE., S. W. CORNER 5TH AVE. AND 40TH ST. (1902, arch. John H. Duncan). This Beaux Arts-style building originally housed an enormous hat store owned by Colonel Edward M. Knox, the "hatter of presidents".

BRYANT PARK. The site of Bryant Park – and of the New York Public Library ▲ 252 – was a potter's field in 1823. In 1853 the Crystal Palace ● 39 (a replica of the one in London) was built on this site to host the first American world's fair; it was destroyed by fire five years later. The park was named after the poet and journalist William Cullen Bryant in 1894 and redesigned in its present form in 1934. During lunch hour people working in the neighborhood come to unwind in this green oasis, the only one in Midtown. It affords a splendid view of the surrounding buildings.

AMERICAN STANDARD BUILDING, FORMER AMERICAN RADIATOR BUILDING ★. 40 W. 40TH ST. (1924, arch. Hood & Foulhoux). This was the first Art Deco building constructed in New York by Hood, who subsequently designed the *Daily News* Building and much of Rockefeller Center ▲ 274. The characteristic features of this building are the top's black brickwork with gold terracotta trimmings (designed by Hood) and the bronze and black granite façade of the ground floor. Its black marble lobby gleams with mirrors.

BUSH TOWER. 132 W. 42ND ST. (arch. Helmle & Corbett). "We wanted to make the structure a model for the tall, narrow building in the center of a city block", the architects remarked about this slender skyscraper, regarded as a prototype for the next ten years. It was built to house the headquarters of the Bush Terminal Company, a shipping firm. Note the allegories carved above the façade and the trompe l'oeil brickwork on the side walls which enhance the effect of verticality.

FORMER KNICKERBOCKER HOTEL. 1466 BROADWAY, AT S. E. CORNER OF 42ND ST. (1902, arch. Marvin & Vavis). This hotel was built by Colonel John Jacob Astor IV. One of its famous residents, Enrico Caruso, lived here in a fourteen-room apartment between 1908 and 1920. Mary Pickford, the silent movie star, also stayed here.

TIMES SQUARE

Times Square owes its name to *The New York Times*, which in 1904 moved into the Times Tower, at the south end of the square. This intersection of Broadway and 7th Avenue was, from the turn of the century until the 1960's, the center of the performing arts in New York.

Times Square has lost most of its glamour in recent years and looks distinctly seedy. However, one popular tradition from its heyday persists: people still come in their thousands to welcome in the New Year. The illuminated ball that used to descend along the façade at the stroke of midnight has been replaced by a big apple.

1 TIMES SQUARE, FORMER TIMES TOWER. (1904, arch. Eidlitz & MacKenzie). *The New York Times* occupied Times Tower for only about ten years before moving most of its operations into its present premises at 229 West 43rd Street. In 1966 the tower was converted (and renamed the Allied Chemical

> **"The age of the huge advertising billboards dawned in 1916. The whole district was electrified. Times Square . . . was a new wonderland, an electric city, the Great White Way of Broadway."**
>
> Jerome Charyn,
> *Metropolis*

Tower) and its original granite and terracotta facing was replaced by a marble one. Today the moving electric sign that wraps around the tower is operational again after several years of darkness. When first switched on in 1928, it announced the result of the presidential elections with Herbert Hoover's victory.

FORMER PARAMOUNT BUILDING. 1501 BROADWAY (1927, arch. Rapp & Rapp). The most eye-catching building on Times Square used to house the offices for Paramount Pictures, as well as the Paramount Theater which no longer exists. The day after its opening, in 1926, the *New York Times* ran this advertisement: "30,222 spectators in two days! Into the paradise of luxury, color and enchantment they came." The grandiose "movie palace" seating 3,664 people, had a huge lobby, the Grand Hall, larger than that of the Paris Opera House, as well as various lounges and promenades. The movie theater had to close in 1965, as it was not making a profit, and the building was converted into offices. Dolly Down, a singer who once performed there, said of its new occupants: "These kids have no idea what it was and they'll never know because there will not be anything like those theaters again." This building has fourteen symmetrical setbacks, rising to a sphere, formerly illuminated, at the top.

PARAMOUNT THEATER
Before the 1929 crash, an evening's program here comprised sketches, a play and a movie from Paramount Pictures.

The Paramount subsequently billed big bands and singers. Frank Sinatra gave some of his most famous performances here, singing with the Tommy Dorsey Orchestra.

LOBBY OF THE FILM CENTER BUILDING
Although the exterior of the Film Center Building is ordinary, its lobby is stunning. The architect, Albert Kahn, was influenced by the Decorative Arts exhibition in Paris (1925) and this building marked the start of his polychromatic phase. For the floor he created a composition combining pinkish marble circles with white and black marble strips; for the walls (above right) a mosaic of blue and orange tiles.

Façade of the Actors Studio.

MURAL PAINTING
The façade of this bicycle store at the corner of 9th Ave. and 47th St. is decorated with a reproduction of a drawing by Sempé, whose *New Yorker* illustrations had caught the eye of the store's owner.

DETOUR TO THE HUDSON RIVER

Rather than continuing toward the Theater District, leave Broadway and head for the Hudson River.

FORMER MCGRAW-HILL BUILDING. 330 W. 42ND ST. (1931, arch. Hood, Godley & Fouilhoux). This New York landmark ● 99, a fusion of Art Deco and International Style, has a beautifully decorated lobby, whose opaque Carrera glass and stainless steel benefit from a sophisticated lighting system.

FILM CENTER BUILDING ★. 630 9TH AVE. (1929, arch. Ely Jacques). This building is a typical example of 1920's Art Deco ● 99 architecture. Its extraordinary polychromatic lobby is well worth the walk from Broadway.

ACTORS STUDIO. 432 W. 44TH ST. (1858). The famous drama school, founded by Elia Kazan in 1947, moved into this former Presbyterian church in 1955. The Actors Studio became internationally famous through the work of its director, Lee Strasberg, and radically influenced the New York theater scene. The "Strasberg Method", inspired by Stanislavsky and his Art Theater in Moscow, advocated an intensive course of mental exercises to improve actors' self-awareness and their empathy with the character. Marlon Brando attended classes here.

"HELL'S KITCHEN". The area lying to the west of 6th Avenue, between 30th and 57th streets was long known as "Hell's Kitchen". This nickname allegedly emerged from a conversation between two policemen who had been called out to deal with a street brawl at the height of summer. One of them apparently exclaimed, "It's as hot as Hell here." The other corrected him, saying "It's cool in Hell. This is Hell's kitchen." Until 1945 the nickname was fairly apt, for the area was then controlled by the underworld. Over the past few decades, however, the inhabitants and real estate developers have done their utmost to revamp its image, including renaming it Clinton, after the current President.

LANDMARK TAVERN. S. E. CORNER 11TH AVE. AND 46TH ST. (1868). This establishment has remained more or less unchanged for

Bicycles

years. Inside, the dark wood paneling, the old mirrors, the paved floor and the wood-burning stoves give visitors the impression of having stepped back in time.

INTREPID SEA-AIR-SPACE MUSEUM. PIER 86, W. 46TH ST. The *Intrepid* is an aircraft carrier from World War Two which has been converted into a floating museum. Two blocks farther north is the N.Y.C. Passenger Ship Terminal, which belongs to the Port Authority of New York and New Jersey. This was built by the city in 1974 to accommodate the huge luxury cruisers, but with the exception of the *Queen Elizabeth II*, few liners have actually opted to use it.

TOWARD THE THEATER DISTRICT

MARRIOTT MARQUIS HOTEL.
1531–49 BROADWAY (1985, arch. John C. Portman & Assocs.). Three theaters were demolished to make way for the Marriott, one of Manhattan's largest hotels. Like many hotels of this period, it is built around a spectacular atrium. Take a dizzying ride in one of the hotel's transparent elevators.

I. MILLER BUILDING. N. E. CORNER OF 46TH ST. AND 7TH AVE.

The south façade here is decorated with an impresssive array of sculptures by A. Stirling Calder (1929), depicting actresses and singers in their most famous roles: Mary Pickford as Little Lord Fauntleroy, Ethel Barrymore as Ophelia, Rosa Ponselle as Norma and Marilyn Miller as Sunny.

FATHER DUFFY SQUARE. The north triangle of Times Square was named after Father Duffy, the "Fighting Chaplain of the 69th regiment". This New York unit served in France during World War One. Later, in his parish church, Holy Cross Roman Catholic Church (42nd Street), Father Duffy became friendly with many actors and comedians. His statue (1937, Charles Keck) is decorated with a Celtic cross. Father Duffy Square is also the site of the TKTS booth, where one can buy half-price tickets for Broadway shows.

1580 BROADWAY. BETWEEN 47TH AND 48TH STS. (1989, arch. Mayers & Schiff). This building's enormous advertising billboards are reminiscent of Times Square during the 1940's, when it used to sparkle with a constellation of lights. This building boasts a bold glass spire and, along with 750 7th Avenue (1989, arch. Roche, Dinkeloo & Assocs), is one of the new office towers that, during the 1980's transformed the skyline north of Times Square.

For over a century, Broadway has been almost synonymous with American theater. There is no better yardstick of talent than acting or directing on Broadway. Originally New York's theater district was centered around City Hall ▲ 168, but by the end of the 19th century it had moved to Broadway, around 42nd Street, and it has stayed there ever since. In the 1920's, the movie companies moved here and built huge movie palaces in the vicinity of Times Square. The recession in the movie industry during the 1950's and 1960's led to the closing of several movie theaters. Today the Theater District includes some forty legitimate theaters located between 40th and 57th streets, 6th and 8th avenues. A subtle hierarchy distinguishes between "Broadway" shows (large-scale productions staged in the Theater District), "Off Broadway" shows (more modest-sized productions) and "Off-off Broadway" productions (avant-garde and fringe theater).

"SIN STREET". At the beginning of the century, the first theaters in the district, some twelve in all, were clustered along a small stretch of 42nd Street, between Broadway and 8th Avenue. Most of them are now sex shops and cinemas showing "adult" movies, hence the name "Sin Street". The NEW AMSTERDAM THEATER (1903), at 214 West 42nd Street, closed since 1983 and currently being restored, is the most interesting of the theaters on 42nd Street. The producer Florenz Ziegfeld was a partial owner and he converted the roof into another theater, AERIAL GARDENS. Ziegfeld's famous revue – the annual Ziegfeld Follies, was performed at the New Amsterdam from 1913 until 1927, when he had his own

WINTER GARDEN THEATER, 1634 Broadway at 50th St. (1911). This theater's opening starred Al Jolson. Below, Chanin's Theater and Biltmore Theater (above right), built by the Chanin brothers.

BOOTH THEATER 222 W. 45th St. (1913) The theater (below, center) owes its name to the actor Edwin Booth ▲ 230. Flanking it are the Shubert and Majestic Theaters.

theater built on the corner of 54th Street and 6th Avenue. THE LYRIC (1903), at 213 West 42nd Street, was the New Amsterdam's main rival and engaged prestigious stars such as Douglas Fairbanks and Fred Astaire and his sister Adele; the Astaires were wooed by both theaters. In 1925 the Lyric staged the first performance by the Marx Brothers of George S. Kaufman's play *The Cocoanuts*, with music by Irving Berlin.

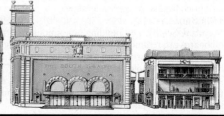

THE "GREAT WHITE WAY".

The stretch of 44th Street between 7th and 8th avenues includes five Broadway theaters. The MAJESTIC (1927) at no. 245, the HELEN HAYES (1912) at no. 238 and the BROADHURST (1917) at no. 235 were all the work of Herbert J. Krapp. Krapp was a prolific and talented architect who designed some twenty theaters; all are highly regarded for the quality of their acoustics, their unimpeded sightlines and their decoration. The SHUBERT THEATER (1913) at 225 West 44th Street, was built at the same time as the Booth Theater for

Rodger's Theater, 1924, the former Chanin's Theater.

BARRYMORE THEATER
243 W. 47th St. (1928). This theater was built in honor of the actress Ethel Barrymore. Fred Astaire appeared in Cole Porter's *The Gay Divorce* (1932). In 1947, Marlon Brando made his debut, alongside Jessica Tandy, in *A Streetcar Named Desire*.

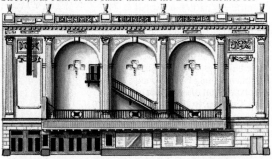

the Shubert brothers. It runs along the east side of Shubert Alley, a famous passageway formerly frequented by actors who would meet outside the offices of Sam J. J. and Lee Shubert when new productions were being cast. The LAMB'S THEATER (1904) situated at 130 West 44th Street, shares the former premises of the Lambs Club with the Manhattan Church of the Nazarene. Many personalities , such as Al Jolson, W. C. Fields, Spencer Tracy and John Barrymore used to meet and stay at the Lambs Club. One block away, at 149 West 45th Street, is the LYCEUM THEATER, the first of the Times Square theaters to be built north of 42nd Street. Completed in 1903, it was considered the height of

modernity, for its auditorium had no balcony and there were gift shops inside. The most famous venue for musicals is the IMPERIAL THEATER (1923), 249 West 45th Street; shows by such greats as George and Ira Gershwin, Cole Porter, Irving Berlin and Leonard Bernstein have been staged here. The LONGACRE THEATER (1913), at 220 West 48th Street, had its heyday in the 1930's when the Group Theater staged plays directed by Lee Strasberg.

LYCEUM THEATER
A window in the apartment of producer Daniel Frohman, for whom this theater was built (1903), looked out over the stage, apparently so he could watch his wife Margaret Illington in plays.

From left to right, the Longacre, Simon and Imperial theaters.

CORNELIUS VANDERBILT (1794–1877) Vanderbilt's statue used to grace the pediment of his Hudson River Railroad Freight Depot, built in 1869. When the depot became obsolete in 1927, the statue was moved to Grand Central Terminal.

The building site of Grand Central Terminal ▲ 239, in 1910, seen from the north.

THE HELMSLEY EMPIRE
Harry and Leona Helmsley have taken their place among New York's legendary entrepreneurs. He possesses a huge property empire and a fortune estimated at $5 billion. Among the jewels in their crown are the Helmsley Building (right), the Empire State Building and the Helmsley Palace Hotel ▲ 284.

PARK AVENUE TO SUTTON PLACE

PARK AVENUE. In 1888 the city of New York renamed the section of 4th Avenue between 43rd and 96th streets. Although enjoying the new name of Park Avenue, it remained a mass of railroad tracks until the rails were electrified in 1904 and then completely covered. This incentive was part of an overall planning program which included the reconstruction of Grand Central Terminal (1903–13) ▲ 236, as well as the construction of office buildings, hotels and luxury apartments along Park Avenue.

HELMSLEY BUILDING, FORMERLY NEW YORK CENTRAL BUILDING. 230 PARK AVE., BETWEEN 45TH AND 46TH STS. (1929, arch. Warren & Wetmore). This was built to house the headquarters of the railroad company founded by Cornelius Vanderbilt. "Commodore" Vanderbilt was, by the time he died in 1877, the most famous millionaire in the United States. By 1810, at the age of sixteen, he had bought a sailing ship and started a ferryboat service between Staten Island and Manhattan. He then assembled a fleet of transatlantic liners and coasting vessels. At the age of seventy he embarked on a career as railroad magnate, eventually creating the New York Central Railroad Company. The former New York Central Building, which is now part of the Helmsley real estate empire, has the disctinction of being the only building in New York to straddle an avenue. Two giant portals provide vehicles with access, in the south, to the Pershing Viaduct, built in 1919, and to Park Avenue South. The building's elegant white marble lobby is well worth a visit.

METLIFE BUILDING, FORMERLY PAN AM BUILDING. 200 PARK AVE. (1963, arch. Emery Roth & Sons, Pietro Belluschi and Walter Gropius). Built for Pan Am and bought in 1981 by the Metropolitan Life Insurance Company, this fifty-eight-story skyscraper is disliked by almost all New Yorkers. It looms over the Helmsley Building and Grand Central Terminal ▲ 236, spoiling the view down Park Avenue. In 1977 its roof was the scene of a helicopter crash. Trying to land

1 GRAND CENTRAL TERMINAL. 2 MetLife BLDG. 3 HELMSLEY BLDG. 4 CHEMICAL BANK BLDG. 5 EX-SHELTON TOWERS HOTEL. 6 TURTLE BAY GARDENS AND EX-LESCAZE HOUSE. 7 RIVER HOUSE. 8 BEEKMAN PLACE. 9 U.N. PLAZA. 10 FORD FOUNDATION BLDG. 11 TUDOR CITY. 12 N.Y. DAILY NEWS BLDG. 13 CHANIN BLDG. AND EX-BOWERY SAVINGS BANK. 14 MOBIL BLDG. 15 GRAYBAR BLDG. 16 GRAND HYATT BLDG. 17 CHRYSLER BLDG.

E. 49TH ST. E. 50TH ST. E. 51ST ST. E. 52ND ST. E. 53RD ST.
E. 48TH ST. 7TH ST.
1ST AVE.

U.N. PLAZA

🍴 Five hours

on the rooftop heliport, the helicopter lost its undercarriage. The debris rained down on the streets below, killing five people and wounding seven others.

CHEMICAL BANK BUILDING. 277 PARK AVE. (1962, arch. Emery Roth and Sons). In 1982 the owners of this building added the three-story Chemcourt Atrium, a lush open space with a fountain. The writer George Chesbro, described this in *Bone*: the "wall of glass panels which surrounded the Chemical Bank's terrarium . . . , a bright, airy parallelepiped which faced Park Avenue and contained a wonderful miniature jungle of trees, ferns and plants, [provided] a striking counterbalance to the bushes on the pedestrian islands which bisected the elegant thoroughfare."

MARRIOTT EAST SIDE HOTEL, FORMER SHELTON TOWERS HOTEL. 525 LEXINGTON AVE. (1924, arch. Arthur Loomis Harmon). This hotel was the tallest in the world when it was built. The building's three-tiered composition and the delicate Romanesque Revival ● *90* detailing at its base are an attractive application of the Zoning Resolution ● *97*. The painter Georgia O'Keeffe ● *107* and her husband the photographer, Alfred Stieglitz lived here, when it was built; they occupied Suite 3003, which O'Keeffe also used as a studio until 1934. This suite affords a magnificent view over the tops of the Chrysler Building ▲ *266* to the south and the RCA Building ▲ *275* to the west.

"TAXI"
At the northwest corner of the Chemical Bank is a bronze statue of a man hailing a taxi. It was designed by J. Seward Johnson Jr. and built in 1983 to illustrate life on the streets of New York. Similar statues can be found elsewhere in Manhattan – *Out to Lunch* (Exxon Building), *The Commuters* (south wing of the Port Authority Bus Terminal), *The Garment Worker* (opposite 555 7th Ave.).

261

TURTLE BAY GARDENS HISTORIC DISTRICT. 227–247 E. 48TH AND 226–246 E. 49TH STS. (1820, restored in 1920, arch. Dean and Bottomley). In the mid-19th century, Turtle Bay, the site on which the Dutch governor William Kieft had built his farm in 1639, was overrun by factories and slaughterhouses. However, some attractive Italianate rowhouses were also built in this period, and in 1920 an enlightened developer bought a group of them and combined all their back gardens into one common garden. The houses were remodeled so that the living rooms face the garden, thus turning their backs on the surrounding commercial activity.

FORMER LESCAZE HOUSE. 211 E. 48TH ST. (1934, arch. William Lescaze). The style and size of this white house form a contrast with the brownstones of Turtle Bay Gardens. Lescaze designed this International Style ● *100* residence-cum-studio to advertise his own firm. The influence of Le Corbusier is apparent in the judicious use of materials: the glass block panels used in the façade overlooking the street create a bulwark against the city, and the glazed bays at the rear overlook a terrace. This structure fascinated neighbors to such an extent that for a time Lescaze opened his home to visitors.

BEEKMAN PLACE. BETWEEN 49TH AND 51ST STS. This pleasant site overlooking the East River is named after a local resident, James Beekman, whose mansion, Mount Pleasant, built in 1765, was used by the British as headquarters during the War of Independence ● *27*. Nathan Hale ▲ *168* was sentenced to death here for spying and hanged on September 22, 1776. The house was destroyed in 1874 when, due to the proliferation of harbor industries, the area became rundown and overcrowded.

RIVER HOUSE. 435 E. 52ND ST. (1931, arch. Bottomley, Wagner & White). Originally, yacht-owning tenants could reach this luxury apartment block from a landing stage on the East River. The residence was cut off from the river in the 1940's when the Franklin D. Roosevelt Drive (also called F.D.R. or East River Drive) was built. The landfill consisted partially of debris from bombing raids on London during World War Two, which had been used as ballast for ships carrying American troops back to the United States.

TURTLE BAY
The name of this neighborhood refers to a marshy cove in the East River where turtles once abounded. They – and other creatures – figure as decorative motifs on the walls and the newel posts of the railings of some of the houses in the Turtle Bay Historic District. The area's distinguished residents have included E. B. White, Leopold Stokowski, Tyrone Power and Katharine Hepburn. The U.N. Headquarters ▲ *264* is also located in this neighborhood.

Turtle Bay in 1852.

A Detour North: Sutton Place.

BETWEEN 57TH AND 58TH STS. This little enclave, lined with townhouses, owes its name to Effingham B. Sutton, who made his fortune during the California Gold Rush of 1849 and launched the first shipping line operating between New York and San Francisco. He invested some of his profits to develop this neighborhood, but it did not become fashionable until the 1920's. Nearby Riverview Terrace consists of five townhouses, with terrace gardens, overlooking the East River, Queensboro Bridge and Roosevelt Island.

Construction of F.D.R. Drive along the East River, viewed from the Queensboro Bridge.

THE UNITED NATIONS

Located along the bank of the East River, between 42nd and 48th streets, the headquarters of the U.N.O. (United Nations Organization) covers more than 15 acres .

THE WORLD'S PARLIAMENT. The U.N.O., created in the aftermath of World War Two, succeeded the League of Nations, its fundamental task being to "save succeeding generations from the scourge of war". The General Assembly, which is a true international parliament, is presently made up of delegations from 180 states. It meets every year from September to December, dealing with some 150 cases relating to issues as diverse as disarmament, economic aid and women's rights.

THE ROLE OF NELSON A. ROCKEFELLER.
The fifty founding states of the U.N.O. agreed, at the first General Assembly in London, in 1946, that the headquarters should be located in the United States. Several sites were considered: New York, Connecticut, Boston, Philadelphia and San Francisco. Once New York had been chosen, a committee of prominent figures, including Nelson Rockefeller, tried to promote Flushing Meadow, the site of the Universal Exhibition of 1939, as a suitable base. The U.N.O. rejected this proposal (although the General Assembly did meet there between 1946 and 1949).

U.N. SECRETARIAT BUILDING

Along 1st Ave., the multicolored flags of the member nations mark the boundary between the territory of New York and the international enclave of the United Nations. The grayish-blue glass skin of this skyscraper's east and west façades was chosen to minimize the effects of the sun; its north and south façades are clad in Vermont marble. The thirty-eighth floor houses the Secretary General's offices.

AN ARCHITECTURAL COMPLEX
A team of ten architects, including Le Corbusier and Oscar Niemeyer, began work on the U.N. headquarters in January 1947. They opted for three self-contained buildings: the Secretariat, the General Assembly and the Conference Building. The first cornerstone was laid on October 24, 1949 (above) and at the end of August 1950 the first civil servants moved into their offices. The library – south of the General Assembly – was added in 1963.

U.N. coat of arms.

THE CONFERENCE BUILDING
This building houses the Security Council Chamber, the Trusteeship Council Chamber, the Economic and Social Council Chamber and a number of smaller rooms. There are daily tours around the U.N. and it is possible to attend public meetings of the General Assembly and the Security Council, here shown (right) in a meeting on January 31, 1992.

As the United Nations was on the point of opting for a headquarters in Philadelphia, Nelson Rockefeller persuaded his father, John D. Rockefeller, Jr, to donate the $8.5 million needed to buy some land along the East River.

TUDOR CITY

SHCHARANSKY STEPS. These steps leading to Tudor City were named in homage to the Soviet Jewish dissident Anatoly Shcharansky. The best view of the United Nations headquarters can be obtained from the top of these steps.

GENERAL ASSEMBLY BUILDING
The curved roof of this building is crowned with a dome, which is considered a symbol of governmental authority.

A "SELF-CONTAINED CITY". (1925–8, arch. Fred F. French Co.). Tudor City occupies the entire area between E. 40th and E. 43rd streets, 1st and 2nd avenues. Exclusively financed by private funds, and built in a quasi-Tudor style which inspired its name, it was a bold attempt at urban renewal. The aim was to create "a self-contained city" in a then insalubrious neighborhood. There are twelve apartment buildings containing three thousand apartments, a hotel with six hundred

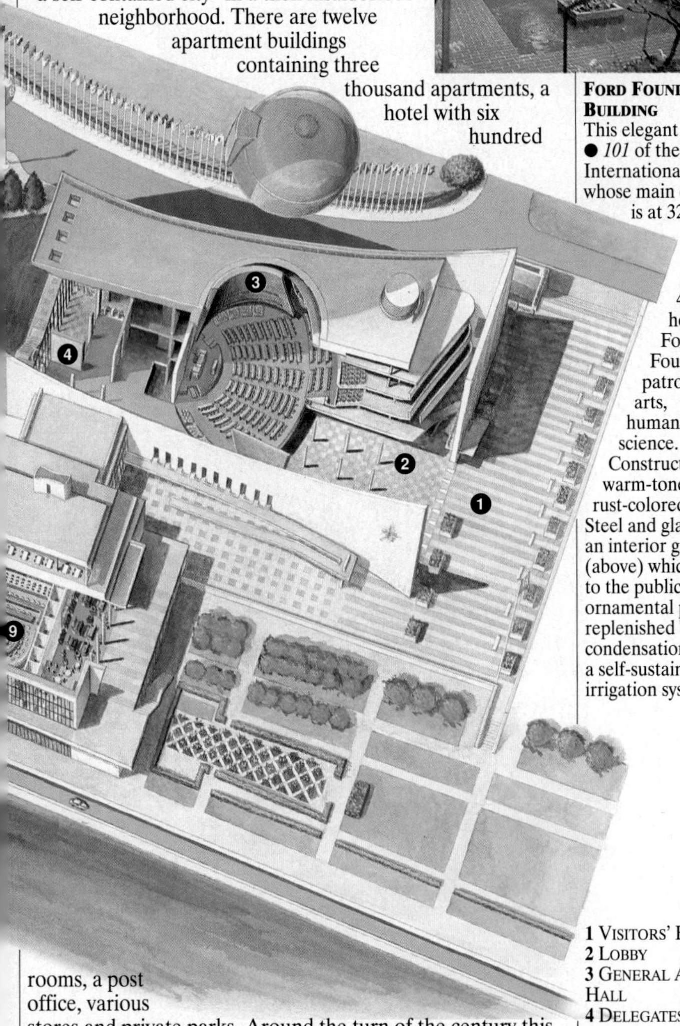

FORD FOUNDATION BUILDING
This elegant example ● *101* of the International Style, whose main entrance is at 321 E. 42nd St., houses the Ford Foundation, patrons of the arts, humanities and science. Constructed of warm-toned brick, rust-colored Cor-Ten Steel and glass, it has an interior garden (above) which is open to the public. An ornamental pond, replenished by condensation, acts as a self-sustaining irrigation system.

rooms, a post office, various stores and private parks. Around the turn of the century this area was frequented by criminals and gangsters. At one time, it was dubbed "Corcoran's Roost", after the notorious band it Paddy Corcoran and his "Rag Gang". The neighborhood was also heavily industrialized, filled with factories, breweries and slaughterhouses. Consequently the architects designed its buildings so they faced inward, placing very few windows in the walls bordering the surrounding squalor. Today its residents regret being deprived of some stunning views.

1 VISITORS' ENTRANCE
2 LOBBY
3 GENERAL ASSEMBLY HALL
4 DELEGATES' LOUNGE
5 SECRETARIAT BUILDING
6 CONFERENCE BUILDING
7 SECURITY COUNCIL
8 TRUSTEESHIP COUNCIL
9 ECONOMIC AND SOCIAL COUNCIL

265

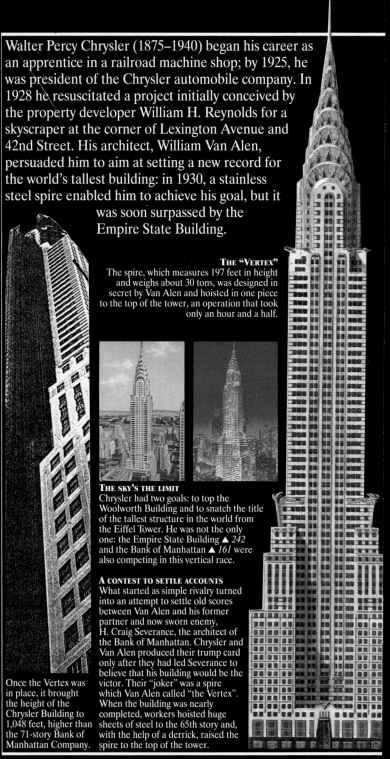

Walter Percy Chrysler (1875–1940) began his career as an apprentice in a railroad machine shop; by 1925, he was president of the Chrysler automobile company. In 1928 he resuscitated a project initially conceived by the property developer William H. Reynolds for a skyscraper at the corner of Lexington Avenue and 42nd Street. His architect, William Van Alen, persuaded him to aim at setting a new record for the world's tallest building: in 1930, a stainless steel spire enabled him to achieve his goal, but it was soon surpassed by the Empire State Building.

THE "VERTEX"

The spire, which measures 197 feet in height and weighs about 30 tons, was designed in secret by Van Alen and hoisted in one piece to the top of the tower, an operation that took only an hour and a half.

THE SKY'S THE LIMIT

Chrysler had two goals: to top the Woolworth Building and to snatch the title of the tallest structure in the world from the Eiffel Tower. He was not the only one: the Empire State Building ▲ *242* and the Bank of Manhattan ▲ *161* were also competing in this vertical race.

A CONTEST TO SETTLE ACCOUNTS

What started as simple rivalry turned into an attempt to settle old scores between Van Alen and his former partner and now sworn enemy, H. Craig Severance, the architect of the Bank of Manhattan. Chrysler and Van Alen produced their trump card only after they had led Severance to believe that his building would be the victor. Their "joker" was a spire which Van Alen called "the Vertex". When the building was nearly completed, workers hoisted huge sheets of steel to the 65th story and, with the help of a derrick, raised the spire to the top of the tower.

Once the Vertex was in place, it brought the height of the Chrysler Building to 1,048 feet, higher than the 71-story Bank of Manhattan Company.

"HE KNEW [THE CHRYSLER BUILDING] WAS REALLY THE INCARNATION OF GOD WITH ITS GARISHLY ILLUMINATED, MULTI-FACETED ROOF SHAPED LIKE A STEEPLE. . . ."

GEORGE CHESBRO

THE "HIGHEST MAN IN THE WORLD"
A luxurious duplex apartment (left) was built for Walter Chrysler in the building's spire. The triangular windows of the apartment looked out over the vast panorama of Manhattan. The Cloud Club (bottom) was a meeting room for American industrial magnates and is also decorated in the purest Art Deco style. The view is complemented by a painted mural of the city.

"WALKING BUILDING"
The anthropomorphic character of the Chrysler Building is due to the spire, which has been compared to a wildly exaggerated hairstyle. Van Alen himself wore a replica of it to the Beaux Arts Ball.

▲ CHRYSLER BUILDING

On the sixteenth story, you can see classical urns reworked to reflect an Art Deco vision.

A VIRTUOSO DESIGNER

Van Alen, who had been an outstanding student at the École des Beaux Arts, was nicknamed "the Ziegfeld of his profession" by one of his colleagues in *The American Architect*. This architect, with his wearing of the replica of the Chrysler building spire, created rather a spectacle worthy of the best shows of Busby Berkeley.

IN HONOR OF THE AUTOMOBILE

The corners of the main setbacks, designed in compliance with the 1916 Zoning Resolution, are set off by ornamental sculptures made of reflective sheets of steel. The skyscraper's "neck" is adorned by eight stylized eagle heads, modern style gargoyles (below). The thirtieth story, which houses the mechanical equipment and is therefore blind, sports a frieze of two-colored brick representing car wheels with their metal hubcaps and fenders. The corners are decorated with giant Chrysler radiator caps, inspired by Mercury's winged helmet (above).

A BEACON ON THE NEW YORK SKYLINE

The building's visual impact is due partly to the richness of form and partly to the clever use of materials, in particular the plates of stainless steel – evocative of car ornaments – which glitter in the sunshine.

AN EXPRESSIONIST SPIKE

The spire, with its dovetailed arches fitting inside each other like Russian dolls (right), differs markedly from other skyscraper tops of the period, which were inspired mainly by the 1925 Exhibition of Decorative Arts in Paris. The Chrysler Building's spire has more in common with German Expressionism, the utopian drawings of Bruno Taut and movie sets, such as those in Robert Wiene's *The Cabinet of Dr Caligari* (1919).

A SUBTLE BALANCE

Adding the spire of the building – which has been compared to Nijinsky's headdress in a ballet produced by Sergei Diaghilev, or a Balinese dancer's headdress or the crown worn by some exotic monarch – to the main part of the building entailed a subtle arrangement of façades, in which the curved, vertically thrusting shapes rhythmically echo the outline of the three central bays, in turn stabilized by horizontal bands of decoration. The result is as exuberant as New York itself. The complete elevation ▲ *266*, clearly illustrates the use of different motifs.

A door (right) in the main entrance.

‘We certainly do lead the world in architecture,’ said Professor Timson. ‘Architecture, I take it, is the natural artistic expression of a young nation. Youth wants to build, and Manhattan Island kind of looks as though we’ve done what we wanted.’…
Erik Linklater,
Juan in America

THE LOBBY

The Chrysler Building's décor is eye-catching from top to bottom. The truncated shape of the deeply recessed entrance, which some critics have compared to that of a coffin, and which rises over three stories, sets the tone for the angular interior polished design. For example, metal triangles are superimposed on the notched strip dividing the doors of a huge stained-glass window. The extraordinary triangular lobby narrows as it rises. Glowing red in the semi-darkness, it is probably the most spectacular interior to be found in any office building built during the inter-war years. Red Moroccan marble walls, sienna-colored floor, moldings made of amber-colored onyx and bluish marble are orchestrated in a vivid symphony which builds to a climax: the ceiling, painted by Edward Trumbull, symbolizing Energy, Result, Workmanship and Transportation. . . .

ZIGZAG MOTIFS

The lavishness of the décor – even the veins in the huge marble slabs of the walls form zigzag motifs – is breathtaking. The fountain motifs (top left), the palm leaves and the vividly portrayed eagles on the mailboxes (left) add to the profusion of images. Taken as a whole, the decoration of the Chrysler Building represents an apex in Art Deco design, a style which, though created in Europe, became immensely popular in the United States.

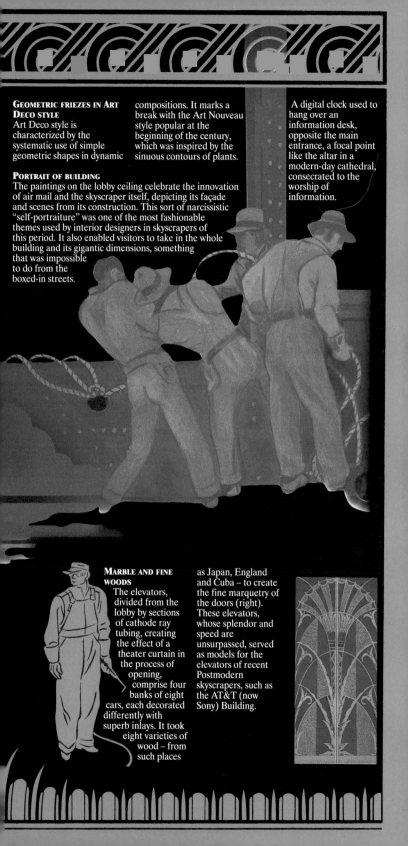

GEOMETRIC FRIEZES IN ART DECO STYLE

Art Deco style is characterized by the systematic use of simple geometric shapes in dynamic compositions. It marks a break with the Art Nouveau style popular at the beginning of the century, which was inspired by the sinuous contours of plants.

PORTRAIT OF BUILDING

The paintings on the lobby ceiling celebrate the innovation of air mail and the skyscraper itself, depicting its façade and scenes from its construction. This sort of narcissistic "self-portraiture" was one of the most fashionable themes used by interior designers in skyscrapers of this period. It also enabled visitors to take in the whole building and its gigantic dimensions, something that was impossible to do from the boxed-in streets.

A digital clock used to hang over an information desk, opposite the main entrance, a focal point like the altar in a modern-day cathedral, consecrated to the worship of information.

MARBLE AND FINE WOODS

The elevators, divided from the lobby by sections of cathode ray tubing, creating the effect of a theater curtain in the process of opening, comprise four banks of eight cars, each decorated differently with superb inlays. It took eight varieties of wood – from such places as Japan, England and Cuba – to create the fine marquetry of the doors (right). These elevators, whose splendor and speed are unsurpassed, served as models for the elevators of recent Postmodern skyscrapers, such as the AT&T (now Sony) Building.

▲ GRAND CENTRAL TERMINAL TO THE CHRYSLER BUILDING

Details of the elaborate radiator grills from the Chanin Building, designed by René Chambellan.

LOBBY OF THE CHANIN BUILDING

This was designed by Jacques Delamarre to celebrate the success of Irwin Chanin in New York and to illustrate "the story of a city in which it is possible for a man to rise from a humble place to wealth and influence by the sheer power of his mind and hands".
New York, 1930

THE NEWS BUILDING. 220 E. 42ND ST. (1930, arch. Howells & Hood). This is the headquarters of one of New York's few remaining daily newspapers, which still boasts a wide circulation. It was founded in 1919 as the *Illustrated Daily News* by two army officers, Captain Patterson and Colonel ("Bertie") McCormick. The first issue, on June 26, 1919, proclaimed: "See New York's most beautiful girls every morning in the *Illustrated Daily News.* . . ." The paper was renamed the *Daily News* two years later. When the building was opened, the large GLOBE in the lobby was found to be revolving in the wrong direction. This mistake was hastily rectified. The details on the globe are regularly updated as the names and borders of the countries around the world are changed.

AROUND THE CHRYSLER BUILDING

CHANIN BUILDING. 122 E. 42ND ST. (1929, arch. Sloan & Robertson, lobby designed by Jacques Delamarre). Magnificent bas-reliefs, composed of animal motifs, run the length of the façade on the lower part of this 56-story building. The breathtaking Art Deco lobby, with its bronze screens and richly decorated elevator doors and mailboxes, is a "must". The building originally had a scenic roof and a theater on the 50th floor; unfortunately neither is now accessible. You can see the top of the Chanin Building by walking several blocks down Lexington Avenue.

The bronze flooring in the lobby of the Chanin Building uses typical Art Deco motifs: boats, planes, trains and cars.

GRAYBAR BUILDING. 420 LEXINGTON AVE. (1927, arch. Sloan & Robertson). When this was built, it was the largest office building in the world, capable of accommodating twelve thousand employees. Lines for Grand Central Terminal ▲ *236* used to run through the basement, and one of the three entrances located on Lexington Avenue still serves as an entrance to the station. One of the arches along this corridor is decorated with frescoes depicting trains, planes and building sites.

BESTIARY

The carved animal forms that appear on the capitals, cornices and other places in the former Bowery Savings Bank include squirrels, lions, and bulls and bears which symbolize respectively thrift, power and the world of finance.

HOME SAVINGS BANK, FORMER BOWERY SAVINGS BANK. 110 E. 42ND ST. (1923, arch. York & Sawyer). Constructed in the style of a Roman basilica, this imposing bank has a distinctive arched entrance as well as a huge 65-foot-high banking hall with a coffered ceiling, which should not be missed. The counters are still positioned in the center of the hall, leaving exposed large areas of the richly patterned mosaic floor. The huge original solid bronze doors now adorn the east and west walls of this splendid room.

PERSHING SQUARE BUILDING. 100 E. 42ND ST. (1914–23, arch. York & Sawyer). Although the word "square" figures in the building's name, the "square" is actually just an intersection of 42nd Street and Park Avenue South, named in homage to General John J. Pershing, who commanded the American Expeditionary Forces in France in 1917–18. It was the last skyscraper in New York to be built without setbacks, its plans having predated the Zoning Resolution of 1916 ● *97*.

AROUND
ROCKEFELLER CENTER

ROCKEFELLER CENTER, *274*
ISABELLE GOURNAY
FROM ROCKEFELLER CENTER
TO THE EAST SIDE, *282*
EDWARD O'DONNELL
MOMA, *290*
RICHARD OLDENBURG
FROM ROCKEFELLER CENTER
TO THE WEST SIDE, *298*
EDWARD O'DONNELL

SUNSHINE AND ICE
Since 1936, the lower Plaza has been a sunny terrace in summer but is transformed from October through April into a 957-square yard open-air skating rink.

ATLAS
The bronze Atlas by Lee Lawrie, placed at the entrance of the International Building in 1937, faces St. Patrick's Cathedral on 5th Ave. He holds an armillary sphere, decorated with the signs of the zodiac, whose axis points toward the North Star.

THE MODERN AGE. "This Titanesque composition of stone, concrete, glass and steel is symbolic of New York – it embodies its essence, trumpets its pride in the same way as the solemn splendor of cathedrals symbolized the very essence of urban communities in the Middle Ages, handing it down to future generations" (Klaus Mann, 1936). The image of the cathedral seems appropriate for Rockefeller Center, just as it was for the Woolworth Building, since it evokes time-honored tradition, though it fails to take account of the innovative nature of the project. The driving force behind the project, John D. Rockefeller Jr, was not attempting, like Chrysler or John Jakob Raskob – two patrons of the motor car, another symbol of modernity – to feed his ego by building a larger and more magnificent monument than that of his precursors. On the contrary, as Klaus Mann pointed out, his project was the very embodiment of quintessential New York and, more generally, of a type of modernity which was, by definition, American.

A CLASSICAL MODEL. Rockefeller Center is made up of a whole complex of fourteen buildings, built in the 1930's, plus another five buildings completed after 1945, on the other side of

> "THE BUILDINGS ARE A SHIMMERING VERTICALITY, A GOSSAMER VEIL, A FESTIVE SCENE-DROP HANGING THERE AGAINST THE BLACK SKY TO DAZZLE, ENTERTAIN, AMAZE"
>
> FRANK LLOYD WRIGHT

A City within a City
The nineteen buildings that make up Rockefeller Center are arranged in a gridiron pattern. The main axis is composed of Rockefeller Plaza (1), then the Lower Plaza (2), and finally Channel Gardens (3), flanked by La Maison Française (4) and the British Empire Building (5); among other stores, this latter houses a Metropolitan Museum of Art shop. From its height of 850 feet (70 stories), the General Electric Building (6) towers above the complex which boasts altogether 557 stories, 67 elevators, 48,000 windows cleaned by 893 employees and 100,000 telephones. Sixty thousand people work there and every day Rockefeller Center welcomes 175,000 visitors.

6th Avenue. It is currently home to a number of diverse businesses (Radio City Music Hall, General Electric – the former RCA Building), and links older nations (Maison Française and the British Empire Building) which were there from its inception. Its careful layout provides the population of the city with an open space, dotted with fountains and statues whose transparent symbolism reiterates American values by dint of a great many mythological allusions (*Prometheus* lording it over the Lower Plaza, for example). It is a strange mixture of idealism and pragmatism, inspired by functionalist theories similar to those of Le Corbusier but which yield to the constraints of New York's urban fabric. It is also a democratic, liberal American counterweight to the Imperial giganticism of Fascist and Communist totalitarian regimes, as well as an answer to the equally harsh challenge of the Great Depression.

275

▲ Rockefeller Center

Photograph of John D.
Rockefeller, taken in 1933.

Manhattan's largest-scale building project was financed by John Davison Rockefeller Jr (1874–1960). He set his heart on three large blocks between 48th and 51st streets, 5th and 6th avenues and, in December 1929, he signed an eighty-year lease with their owner, Columbia University. The lease has since been extended until 2069, much to Mitsubishi's satisfaction, as this company is currently the majority shareholder of Rockefeller Center. The center owes the purity of its design to Nelson Aldrich Rockefeller (1908–79), the financier's second son, who was a collector of modern art, future governor of the State of New York and vice president of the United States.

A COLOSSAL BUILDING SITE
The board of architects, headed by Raymond Hood and Wallace K. Harrison, who were to be the chief designers for the United Nations building, made the best of continual changes to the plans: the Rockefeller family fortune went through a very rough time which lasted until the end of the 1930's.

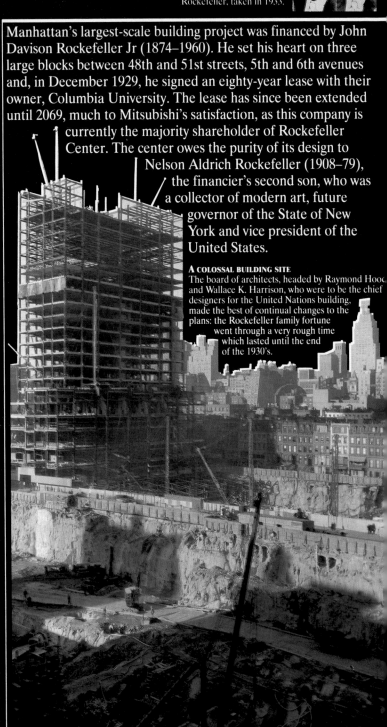

A Depth of 85 feet
The parking lots, underground passages and shopping center, around Lower Plaza, were built below ground level, creating space for vast terraces at street level.

RCA Building
(since 1988, General Electric). Opened in 1933, this building took only sixteen months to build. Above, an RCA advertisement.

After the crash
The collapse of the stock market in 1929 made the realization of the original plans for an opera house impossible and, while demolition work was being completed, in July 1931, the Rockefellers developed the plans for a commercial center. The extension, west of 6th Ave., was completed in 1973.

Historic monuments
The smoking rooms (above) and powder rooms (opposite) of Radio City Music Hall still contain the original furniture.

Radio City Music Hall
The auditorium, an homage to American Art Deco decoration, was opened on December 27, 1932. The décor was coordinated by Donald Deskey, and many painters contributed to the murals in the lobbies, lounges and stairways (above). These design features are designated as historic landmarks.

In the clouds
The recently restored Rainbow Room, on the sixty-fifth floor of the RCA buildings, affords a spectacular view of the entire Manhattan skyline. Opposite, a poster from the 1930's, advertising this exceptional view. Today, Rockefeller Center has nearly forty restaurants and several theaters.

A NEW CONCEPT IN TOWN PLANNING

The decoration is mainly restricted to the lower stories because the architects of Rockefeller Center felt it was less important to apply motifs to an architectural mass – which was, in this case, inordinately tall – than to create a landscaped environment whose variety would attract new tenants as well as sightseers. This was a revolutionary attitude for an urban complex composed mainly of office buildings. The Promenade overlooking 5th Ave. was nicknamed "Channel Gardens" because it separates the Maison Française from the British Empire Building. The gardens, which are re-planted several times a year, provide a setting for fountains that have tritons and nereids riding dolphins. The regular gridiron pattern of Manhattan is broken here by other axes, creating a geometrical effect that highlights the feeling of being in a "city within a city".

THE MAJOR ART DECO COMPLEX IN NEW YORK. At the center of Lower Plaza, a gilded bronze *Prometheus* by Paul Manship rises from the waves (opposite). The main entrance of the General Electric Building is crowned by *Genius* by Lee Lawrie which pays homage to the miracle of radio broadcasting. Everything in Lower Plaza – fountains, flags snapping in the wind, sunshades or a huge Christmas tree – combines to create a continual mood of festivity, an atmosphere more in keeping with world fairs than a traditional financial district.

The cladding of Rockefeller Center is white limestone, quarried in Indiana. It contains numerous fossils of tiny animals (left) which lived in the sea 300 million years ago.

LOWER PLAZA
The former RCA Building is reached via the Lower Plaza, originally designed as the entrance to the underground shopping center.

At the height of the Depression, one by one the luxury stores around the plaza folded but, in 1936, an incredible publicity stunt diverted attention away from this commercial failure: the Lower Plaza was transformed into a skating rink or an elegant café depending on the time of year. This was one of the attractions which made Rockefeller Center so popular with all New Yorkers. It was the hub of this cosmopolitan quarter with its travel agencies, shipping companies, consulates, luxury stores and press offices. The New York Bound Bookshop, which specializes in books on the city's history, is situated on the ground floor of the Associated Press Building.

A SLENDER SILHOUETTE
"A colossal structure, brazen in its height . . . graceful and monumental, sober and fantastic." (Klaus Mann). The squares and thoroughfares which lead to the General Electric Building provide the perfect vantage point to appreciate the tower's silhouette (above, illuminated at night). The tower's slenderness was dictated by the architect's aim of providing every work station with direct lighting. Each horizontal setback also corresponds to a reduction in the size of the elevator shafts.

A MODERN FORUM

Rockefeller Center marks a return to classical tradition, to a collective style of architecture for use by the whole city, not just an individual (the Prince), a religious order (the Church) or the commercial sector. Its style of decoration also reflects a return to mythology, with its allegorical evocation of the key principles which govern the world it depicts. Inside as well as outside the building, clocks remind passers-by that "Time Is Money"

A FANTASTIC BESTIARY

The treatment of the American eagle (below) irresistibly calls to mind the winged bulls found in Assyrian art, while Hermès, the god of commerce (right), is more in line with Greco-Roman tradition.

THE AMERICAN IDEAL AS SEEN BY A SPANIARD

Even the name of the works that decorate the buildings' interiors show a desire to return to the world of myth; for example, the grandiloquent mural, *Triumph of Man's Accomplishments through Physical and Mental Labor*, by José Maria Sert in the General Electric Building.

FROM EGYPT TO ASSYRIA VIA CLASSICISM

The mural with its shallow-carved characters (right) calls to mind bas-reliefs from Ancient Egypt, while the classical goddess in the allegory (opposite), who is a successful blend of the American eagle and an olive branch, bears an undeniable likeness to *La Marseillaise* by Rude which adorns the Arc de Triomphe in Paris.

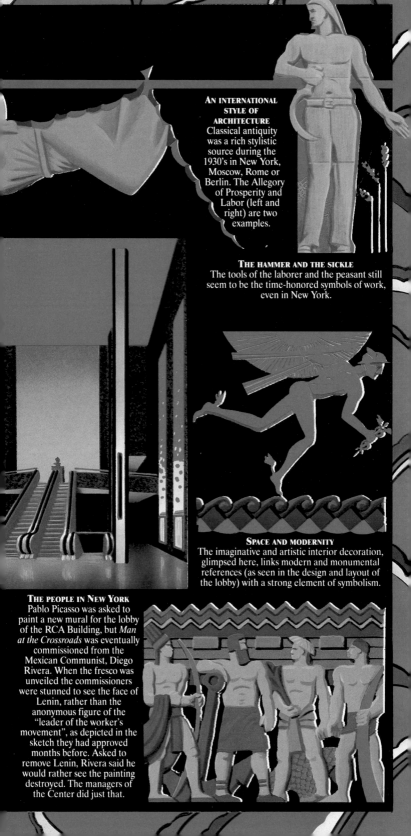

AN INTERNATIONAL STYLE OF ARCHITECTURE
Classical antiquity was a rich stylistic source during the 1930's in New York, Moscow, Rome or Berlin. The Allegory of Prosperity and Labor (left and right) are two examples.

THE HAMMER AND THE SICKLE
The tools of the laborer and the peasant still seem to be the time-honored symbols of work, even in New York.

SPACE AND MODERNITY
The imaginative and artistic interior decoration, glimpsed here, links modern and monumental references (as seen in the design and layout of the lobby) with a strong element of symbolism.

THE PEOPLE IN NEW YORK
Pablo Picasso was asked to paint a new mural for the lobby of the RCA Building, but *Man at the Crossroads* was eventually commissioned from the Mexican Communist, Diego Rivera. When the fresco was unveiled the commissioners were stunned to see the face of Lenin, rather than the anonymous figure of the "leader of the worker's movement", as depicted in the sketch they had approved months before. Asked to remove Lenin, Rivera said he would rather see the painting destroyed. The managers of the Center did just that.

▲ FROM ROCKEFELLER
CENTER THROUGH
THE EAST SIDE

1 ROCKEFELLER CENTER
2 SWISS CENTER
3 BRENTANO'S
4 SAKS FIFTH AVE.
5 ST. PATRICK'S CATHEDRAL
6 OLYMPIC TOWERS
7 NEW YORK PALACE HOTEL
8 WALDORF-ASTORIA HOTEL
9 ST. BARTHOLOMEW'S CHURCH
10 GENERAL ELECTRIC BLDG.

✖ Six hours

❝When I am in New York, I never miss a visit to the basement of Brentano's, which contains catacombs of information. Here, you will find all the American periodicals, most of them published in New York. Their brightly colored covers resemble a flower display.❞
Paul Morand
New York

Midtown began to develop after the Civil War when new millionaires built luxurious mansions along that stretch of 5th Avenue. In the 1880's, the Vanderbilts, Whitneys, Goulds, Astors and other top families settled here. At the beginning of the 20th century the neighborhood began to change drastically, with many businesses moving into the area, and to escape this invasion the wealthier residents began to migrate northward. Today, Midtown is the second-largest business center in the city after Downtown, with some 750,000 employees flocking into its offices every day. The area has been shaped by magnates such as Trump and Helmsley.

AROUND ST. PATRICK'S CATHEDRAL

BRENTANO'S. 597 5TH AVE. (1913, arch. Ernest Flagg). For more than seventy years this building was the home of Charles Scribner's Sons bookshop – as the sign above its huge glass and iron storefront reminds one. The interior, which is listed as a landmark, has a vast single-story vaulted space, covered in fine wood paneling. Scribners, founded in 1846, published such authors as F. Scott Fitzgerald and Ernest Hemingway. The company was bought out by another publishing house and in 1989 the store was sold to the Brentano's chain of bookstores.

SWISS CENTER, FORMER GOELET BUILDING. 5TH AVE. AT 49TH ST. (1932, arch. E. H. Faile & Co.). This building occupies the site formerly occupied by the house of the Goelet family, who built up a fortune in real estate. It is a striking example of Art Deco with a façade juxtaposing green and white marble and aluminum. The lobby is worth a visit, especially for its elevator doors. The Swiss Center houses the Swissair offices and the Swiss National Tourist Board.

LOBBY OF THE SWISS CENTER
The gold and silver Art Deco ● 98 elevator doors in the Swiss Center are decorated with floral motifs and nymphs.

SAKS FIFTH AVENUE. 611 5TH AVE. BETWEEN 49TH AND 50TH STS. (1924, arch. Starrett & Van Vleck). The first Saks store opened in 1902 on 34th Street. The son of the founder,

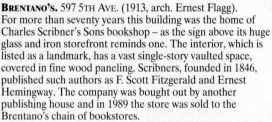

282

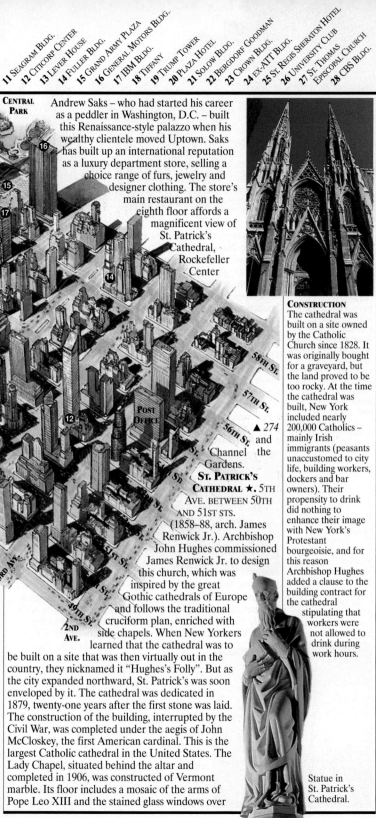

CENTRAL PARK

Andrew Saks – who had started his career as a peddler in Washington, D.C. – built this Renaissance-style palazzo when his wealthy clientele moved Uptown. Saks has built up an international reputation as a luxury department store, selling a choice range of furs, jewelry and designer clothing. The store's main restaurant on the eighth floor affords a magnificent view of St. Patrick's Cathedral, Rockefeller Center

CONSTRUCTION

The cathedral was built on a site owned by the Catholic Church since 1828. It was originally bought for a graveyard, but the land proved to be too rocky. At the time the cathedral was built, New York included nearly 200,000 Catholics – mainly Irish immigrants (peasants unaccustomed to city life, building workers, dockers and bar owners). Their propensity to drink did nothing to enhance their image with New York's Protestant bourgeoisie, and for this reason Archbishop Hughes added a clause to the building contract for the cathedral stipulating that workers were not allowed to drink during work hours.

▲ 274 and Channel the Gardens. **ST. PATRICK'S CATHEDRAL ★.** 5TH AVE. BETWEEN 50TH AND 51ST STS. (1858–88, arch. James Renwick Jr.). Archbishop John Hughes commissioned James Renwick Jr. to design this church, which was inspired by the great Gothic cathedrals of Europe and follows the traditional cruciform plan, enriched with side chapels. When New Yorkers learned that the cathedral was to be built on a site that was then virtually out in the country, they nicknamed it "Hughes's Folly". But as the city expanded northward, St. Patrick's was soon enveloped by it. The cathedral was dedicated in 1879, twenty-one years after the first stone was laid. The construction of the building, interrupted by the Civil War, was completed under the aegis of John McCloskey, the first American cardinal. This is the largest Catholic cathedral in the United States. The Lady Chapel, situated behind the altar and completed in 1906, was constructed of Vermont marble. Its floor includes a mosaic of the arms of Pope Leo XIII and the stained glass windows over

Statue in St. Patrick's Cathedral.

5TH AVENUE IN 1900
"Sunday afternoon Fifth Avenue filed by rosily dustily jerkily. On the shady side there was an occasional man in top hat and frock coat. Sunshades, summer dresses, straw hats were bright in the sun that glinted in squares on the upper windows of the houses, lay in bright slivers on the hard paint of limousines and taxicabs."

John Dos Passos, *Manhattan Transfer*

THE "VANDERBILT COLONY"
The owner of one "Vanderbilt Colony" mansion, William H. Vanderbilt (a son of the "Commodore"), created an art gallery in his home (right and below) to which the public was admitted on Thursdays.

the altar depict the mysteries of the rosary.

OLYMPIC TOWER. 645 5TH AVE., N. E. CORNER OF 51ST ST. (1976, arch. Skidmore, Owings & Merrill). This is one of the last of the "glass boxes" – as they are dismissively called these days – which typifies the International Style ● *100*. This skyscraper, built at the instigation of Aristotle Onassis, houses boutiques, offices and luxury apartments. One can visit the Olympic Place Gallery, which, despite its unremarkable décor, is a pleasant setting with its waterfall, trees and pianist.

FORMER VANDERBILT RESIDENCE. 647 5TH AVE. (1905, arch. Hunt & Hunt). In the late 1800's several private mansions belonging to the Vanderbilts clustered along 5th Avenue north of 51st Street and were nicknamed "the Vanderbilt Colony". The only house to survive is no. 647, George W. Vanderbilt's former residence. Around 1915, when the neighborhood was taken over by businesses, the Vanderbilts moved to the Upper East Side.

VILLARD HOUSES/NEW YORK PALACE HOTEL ● *92*. 451–457

MADISON AVE. BETWEEN 50TH AND 51ST STS. (1883–6, arch. McKim, Mead & White). This brownstone structure, which suggests a great Renaissance palazzo, actually consists of six private mansions. They were built, beginning in 1883, for Henry Villard, the president of the Northern Pacific Railroad and owner of the *New York Evening Post*.

When Villard went bankrupt, he sold the unfinished mansions to several individuals. In recent years they were owned by the archdiocese of New York, who sold them to the Helmsley Corporation, for inclusion in the former HELMSLEY PALACE HOTEL (1980), only after the corporation had agreed to preserve the courtyard as well as the interior of the north and south wings. Tea and cocktails are served at appropriate hours in the Gold Room; its décor, supervised by Stanford White, includes murals by John La Farge and a gilded, barrel-vaulted ceiling.

The adjacent hallway features a gilt and marble clock by Augustus Saint-Gaudens and Tiffany stained-glass windows. The north wing houses the Urban Center, a group of organizations dedicated primarily to historic preservation. For example they have saved Grand Central Terminal ▲ *236* and Radio City Music Hall ▲ *275* from demolition. Step inside to consult the varied range of literature (including suggested historic and architectural tours of the city).

ON PARK AND LEXINGTON AVENUES

WALDORF-ASTORIA HOTEL. 301 PARK AVE. BETWEEN 49TH AND 50TH STS. (1931, arch. Schultze & Weaver). Although it was constructed during the Great Depression, this Art Deco brick- and limestone-faced hotel, with its granite base, is a monument to luxury. It succeeded the first Waldorf-Astoria (5th Avenue and 33rd Street), owned by the Astor family, which had been demolished in 1929 to make way for the Empire State Building ▲ *242*. Rising above the hotel (below right) are the forty-two-story WALDORF TOWERS – which can be seen from several blocks to the north. These private apartments have had some famous tenants, including the Duke of Windsor, President Herbert Hoover, General MacArthur and "Lucky" Luciano ● *40*, once head of the New York Mafia. The lobby of the hotel's Park Avenue entrance is richly decorated with murals and a mosaic by Louis Rigal, *The Wheel of Life*. The clock in the lobby – made by the Goldsmith's Company (London) for the Chicago World's Fair of 1893 – was bought by the Astor family and stood in the first hotel. It is embellished with portraits of heads of state including George Washington, Abraham Lincoln and Queen Victoria. The chimes, which sound every quarter of an hour, are copies of those in Westminster Cathedral. Among the public rooms, the Silver Room and GRAND BALLROOM, which have been restored to their original splendor, are especially worth visiting.

ST. BARTHOLOMEW'S CHURCH ★. PARK AVE. BETWEEN 50TH AND 51ST STS. (1919, arch. Bertram G. Goodhue). The portico (1912) that graces this Episcopal church came from the first St. Bartholomew's, on Madison Avenue, designed by Stanford White, who modeled it on that of St. Gilles in Provence. The figures were commissioned from Daniel Chester French and Philip Martiny, among others. Inside the STAINED GLASS WINDOWS, some

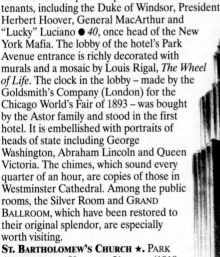

the vaulted ceiling of the Waldorf-Astoria's famous Starlight Roof. Less fortunate fans of the big band sound tuned in at home to the Starlight Roof's regular radio broadcasts.

ON PARK AVENUE
The Four Seasons, one of the best restaurants in New York, is on the ground floor of the Seagram Building (above, center). In the entrance to the restaurant hangs Picasso's stage backdrop for the ballet The Three-Cornered Hat (1919). Opposite the Seagram Building, at 370 Park Ave., is the Racquet and Tennis Club ● *93* (above), a sports club for affluent New Yorkers. The Florentine Renaissance-style palazzo houses one of the few courts in the United States for playing real (indoors) tennis – the precursor of lawn tennis.

of which also were taken from the older church, are worth seeing.

GENERAL ELECTRIC BUILDING, FORMER RCA VICTOR BUILDING ★. 570 LEXINGTON AVE. S. W. CORNER OF 51ST ST. (1931, arch. Cross & Cross) ● *98*, ▲ *275*. This building towers above ST. BARTHOLOMEW'S, its proximity creating a visual shock. It has little in common with the church except for its limestone and pinkish brick, materials chosen by its architects. The crown – part neo-Gothic, part Art Deco – is one of the most spectacular on the Manhattan skyline. Walk down Lexington Avenue for several blocks to see the figures, facing the four cardinal points, which seem to watch over the city. Visit the Art Deco lobby with its aluminum-plated ceiling, decorated with sunburst motifs. The building was donated to Columbia University in 1993.

LEVER HOUSE. 390 PARK AVE. BETWEEN 53RD AND 54TH STS. (1952, arch. Skidmore, Owings & Merrill). Now a designated landmark, this building belonging to the Lever Brothers Company (a major soap manufacturer) is regarded as an exemplar of the minimalist, International Style skyscraper ● *100*. When this ultramodern office block first appeared on Park Avenue – then lined almost entirely with sedate masonry apartment houses – it provoked a storm of protest, but it seems rather subdued now.

SEAGRAM BUILDING. 375 PARK AVE. (1958, arch. Ludwig Mies van der Rohe and Philip Johnson). The design of this building owes much to the architect daughter of Samuel Bronfman, Seagram's president, who persuaded her father to abandon the original undistinguished design in favor of an innovative one by an internationally renowned architect. Mies' dramatic bronze tower, set back on its open plaza, met with unanimous approval when it was completed and for years it served as a model for the skyscraper design.

CITICORP CENTER. LEXINGTON AVE. BETWEEN 53RD AND 54TH STS. (1978, arch. Hugh Stubbins & Assocs.)● *101*. This monumental white aluminum structure, with its top sliced off at an angle (originally designed to accommodate solar

panels) has become one of the most distinctive landmarks on the New York skyline.

5TH AVENUE, 52ND AND 53RD STREETS

CARTIER, INC. 651 5TH AVE. AND 4 E. 52ND ST. (1905, arch. Robert W. Gibson). This mansion was built for Morton F. Plant, a banker and "Commodore" of the New York Yacht Club. William K. Vanderbilt had sold him the land, stipulating that the site remain residential for twenty-five years. Eleven years later, however, Plant sold the house. Legend has it that Cartier, the Parisian jeweler, bought it at the price of a pearl necklace, reputed then to be worth one million dollars.

TISHMAN BUILDING. 666 5TH AVE. BETWEEN 52ND AND 53RD STS. (1957, Carson, Lundin & Shaw). The red limestone that lines the lobby was quarried in the south of France. On close examination the stone is seen to contain fossils (brachiopods, crinoidea, goniatites). The shopping arcade boasts a waterfall designed by Isamu Noguchi. The top-floor restaurant, The Top of the Sixes, affords a panoramic view of Midtown.

SWING STREET. 52ND ST. BETWEEN 5TH AND 6TH AVES. At the end of the 1930's and during the 1940's, this part of 52nd Street (above left and right) was a mecca for jazz ● 60. Audiences who wanted to hear Charlie Parker or Dizzie Gillespie flocked to such clubs as the Onyx, the Three Deuces, Kelly's Stables and the Famous Door. Performances often lasted all night and ended with jam sessions or occasionally with competitions between musicians.

21 CLUB ★. 21 W. 52ND ST. (1872, arch. Duggin & Crossman). During Prohibition this smart restaurant was a speakeasy called Jack and Charlie's Place. Of the many clandestine bars on this street, it was the only one to survive. The owners and their customers escaped police raids by disposing of their drinks into trapdoors under the tables and hiding behind concealed doors. The outside staircase and balcony

In the 1940's, at the *Three Deuces* (above, left and right) on 52nd St., Miles Davis (below) enjoyed top billing for several months.

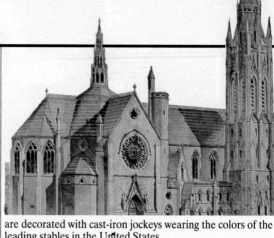

St. Thomas Church
1 W. 53rd St. (arch. Richard Upjohn). In 1895 this Episcopal church on 5th Ave. was the scene of a glittering wedding – that of a local girl, Consuelo Vanderbilt, to the ninth Duke of Marlborough. Ten years later the church burned down; it was replaced by the present St. Thomas Church (1914, Cram, Goodhue & Ferguson), a fine example of neo-Gothic style, with magnificent reredos and stained-glass windows.

University Club
A carved panel in the hall, inspired by classical Rome.

The University Club's library is decorated with murals reminiscent of the frescoes by Pinturicchio in the Borgia apartments in the Vatican.

are decorated with cast-iron jockeys wearing the colors of the leading stables in the United States.

CBS Building. 51 W. 52ND ST. AT 6TH AVE. (1965, arch. Eero Saarinen). This building, which was nicknamed "Black Rock" because it was built of dark gray granite, stands as a monument to the success and egocentricity of William S. Paley – founder (in 1929) of the Columbia Broadcasting System – who had a profound influence on media and entertainment in the United States ● *56*.

Paley Park. 5 E. 53RD ST. (1967, landscape arch. Zion & Breen). William S. Paley donated the park in 1965 on the site of the defunct Stork Club (a popular nightclub in the 1950's) and named it after his father, SAMUEL PALEY. This was the first public space to be created in Midtown after that of Rockefeller Center ▲ *274*. Although small, it is artfully designed, and the shade of its honey locust trees and the muffled roar of its waterfall, masking the noise of traffic, make it a haven of tranquility.

University Club. 1 W. 54TH ST. (1899, arch. McKim, Mead & White). The imposing façade of this Italianate palazzo appears to be three stories high but the building actually contains seven. The elegant interior is richly endowed with marble hallways, high ceilings and wood-paneled walls. Although the club is for members only, one can glimpse some of the rooms from the street, especially in the evenings, when they are illuminated.

Rizzoli Building and former Coty Building. 712 and 714 5th aves. (1908, arch. Adolf S. Gottlieb; 1909, arch. Woodruff Leeming). These office blocks were scheduled for demolition in the 1980's, but were saved when it was realized that some of the Coty Building's upper windows were the work of René Lalique, who created scent bottles for Coty, the French perfume company.

AROUND THE SONY BUILDING

St. Regis-Sheraton Hotel. 2 E. 55TH ST. (1904, arch. Trowbridge & Livingston). Encouraged by the success of his first hotel, the original Waldorf-Astoria ● *285*, John Jacob Astor IV decided to create a second deluxe establishment. This elegant Beaux Arts-style hotel represents the height of opulence. Of the hotel's once-famous restaurants, all are gone, except for the King Cole Room. The name of this restaurant was derived from the mural painting, *King Cole*, previously commissioned from Maxfield Parrish to decorate the Knickerbocker, an Astor hotel on Times Square.

SONY BUILDING, FORMER AT&T BUILDING. 550 MADISON AVE. BETWEEN 55TH AND 56TH STS. (1984, arch. Philip Johnson & John Burgee). The grayish-pink granite, used here instead of glass as the facing, is one of the elements that mark the advent of Postmodernism ● *102*. At street level a Renaissance-style colonnade surrounds a pedestrian space, which adjoins the Sony Wonder, a store-cum-gallery, which displays and sells a range of the company's electronic products (such as camcorders, laser disks and computers).

IBM BUILDING. 590 MADISON AVE. BETWEEN 57TH AND 58TH STS. (1983, arch. Edward Larrabee Barnes Assocs.). The best view of this five-sided prism, faced with greenish-black polished granite, can be obtained from the intersection of 5th Avenue and 57th Street. On the southern side of the building is a large ATRIUM, planted with a forest of bamboo trees, open

The lobby of the St. Regis-Sheraton (top), where Dali stayed on his visits to New York, and (above) the atrium of the IBM Building.

THE SONY BUILDING
The construction of the former AT&T Building aroused a great deal of public debate. Certain architecture critics, referring to its unusual pediment, which can be seen from the southwest corner of 5th Ave., and 55th St., nicknamed the building "the Chippendale skyscraper". Not only did the AT&T Building open up new vistas for architects; it also served as a source of inspiration for some American painters. In 1987 Richard Haas ▲ *112* depicted the building with Trump Tower in the foreground (left).

When the Museum of Modern Art (MOMA) was founded in 1929, the intention was to make it the largest museum of modern art in the world. Its collections now form one of the most wide-ranging panoramas of modern art: paintings, sculpture, drawings, engravings and photographs, as well as films, architectural models and highstyle functional objects in eye-catching designs.

PABLO PICASSO, *Les Demoiselles d'Avignon* (1907). The rough, almost violent, brushstrokes, the heads turned to the right, their hypnotically staring eyes, the fragmented faces refuting the laws of symmetry and the angular hangings, all contribute to this work's expressive intensity. Picasso initially intended to add two male figures.

PAUL CÉZANNE, *The Bather* (c. 1885) Despite or because of a certain freedom in his treatment of line and scale, this monumental, formal work is extraordinarily powerful.

AUGUSTE RODIN, *Balzac* (1897–8). This bronze statue's full cloak and huge head give it a revolutionary appearance. This colossal being symbolizes much more than the writer – it is the universal embodiment of genius.

VINCENT VAN GOGH, *The Starry Night* (1889) This canvas is simultaneously stormy and transcendent. The stable geometry of the village acts as a foil for the flamelike cypress trees, the roiling sky and the vortex of the planets, rendered with coarse, vigorous brushstrokes, loaded with vision and feeling never before expressed in painting.

HENRI MATISSE, *The Red Studio* (1911) Everything but the painter's works appears in outline.

HENRI ROUSSEAU, *The Sleeping Gypsy* (1897). The central figure sleeps near a lion, as she has nothing to fear. The supernatural atmosphere of this scene is typical of this painter's work.

MOMA, built in 1939, was designed by Philip Goodwin and Edward Durrell Stone, and later extended by Philip Johnson, who also created the Sculpture Garden (Abby Aldrich Rockefeller). In 1984, Cesar Pelli was responsible for the final extension work.

Orson Welles' movie *Citizen Kane* (1941), which was suggestive of William Randolph Hearst, caused such a scandal that members of Hearst's empire tried to squash its release. But the film made it to the theater and won popular and critical acclaim.

JOAN MIRÓ, *Hirondelle/Amour* (1933–4). In this painting, the fluid lines of the abstract shapes move against an ethereal blue background, which gives the work a dream-like serenity.

The aerodynamic lines of the Cisitalia "202" GT, body designed by Pininfarina (1946), create an impression that the car is moving, even when stationary.

"UNTIL THE SECOND WORLD WAR, WHICH CAUSED EUROPEAN PAINTERS TO TAKE REFUGE IN NEW YORK, ABSTRACT ARTISTS WERE LITTLE MORE THAN A SMALL EXPERIMENTAL GROUP."

BARBARA ROSE

CONSTANTIN BRANCUSI, *The Fish* (1930). The artist is not interested in representing one particular fish but rather has distilled the creature's very essence, reducing it to its natural condition.

PIET MONDRIAN
Broadway Boogie-Woogie (1942–3). This painting (above) embodies the artist's search for rhythm, apparent in his later works, and is a dazzling interpretation of New York, where he was living at the time he painted it.

MUSEUM GALLERY
The collection retraces the history of photography from its invention, around 1840. Besides works by artists, it shows photographs taken by journalists, scientists and amateurs.

JASPER JOHNS, *Flag* (1954–5). Flag or painting? The illusion is almost perfect. The artist has blurred the traditional concept of reality in painting by merging the pictorial form and space of his subject – here, as often, an everyday object – with those of his painting.

WILLEM DE KOONING, *Woman, I* (1950–2). The painter has given this figure, with its staring eyes and artificial grin, a sinister, ironic look. This figurative work was painted at a time when critics favored more abstract works.

JACKSON POLLOCK, *One (Number 31, 1950)*. Despite the illusion of complete spontaneity, Pollock never lost control of his line, thickening, thinning, spreading or layering its applications. The overall effect, although rhythmic and lyrical, is aggressive.

ROBERT RAUSCHENBERG, *Bed* (1955). This abstract expressionist work uses the components of a real bed, and is firmly rooted in "the gulf between art and life" – a phenomenon that Rauschenberg was exploring in his work.

ANDY WARHOL, *Gold Marilyn Monroe* (1962). The gold background of this portrait is reminiscent of Byzantine art, which surrounds its subject with an almost mystical aura. Andy Warhol, who painted the actress on many occasions, was clearly aware of the irony of this symbolism.

MERET OPPENHEIM, *Object, Fur Covered Cup* (1936). The Surrealists liked to invent bizarre, nightmarish objects. *Object*, a teacup, saucer and spoon covered in fur, is a good example of the surprise and unease they aimed to create by an unexpected juxtaposition of subject and material.

Trump Trips Up

to the public. Concerts are sometimes given here. The IBM Gallery of Science and Art mounts temporary exhibitions.

FULLER BUILDING. 41 E. 57TH ST. (1929, arch. Walker & Gillette). This black, gray and white building, a fine example of restrained Art Deco style, formerly housed the offices of the Fuller Company, a large building firm which previously occupied the Flatiron Building▲ *234*. The façade bears a sculpture by Elie Nadelman, depicting some idealized construction workers. The top of the building can be seen from the corner of 5th Avenue and 57th Street.

TRUMP TOWER. 725 5TH AVE. (1983, arch. Der Scutt). This tower, which houses six floors of shops and stores, including Galeries Lafayette, twenty floors of offices and forty of luxury apartments, is named after the real estate developer who built it, Donald J. Trump. Reactions to the building have been mixed, with some critics finding the ATRIUM's waterfall, its pink marble and sparkling brass trimmings too brash.

TOWARD GRAND ARMY PLAZA

TIFFANY & CO. 727 5TH AVE. AT S. E. CORNER OF 57TH ST. (1940, arch. Cross & Cross). This famous jewelry store was founded by Charles Tiffany in 1837. Above the main entrance there is a carving of Atlas on bronzed wood, commissioned for an earlier store. Charles' son, Louis Comfort Tiffany ● *66*, was renowned for his designs in jewelry, enamel and glass. The store's small windows, with their ingenious displays of jewels, acquired worldwide fame when Audrey Hepburn, as Holly Golightly (left), enjoyed "Breakfast at Tiffany's" in the film (1962) of that name.

CROWN BUILDING ★. 730 5TH AVE. (1921, arch. Warren & Wetmore). This was the first skyscraper to be built at the top of 5th Avenue and the first office block to be built after the 1916 ordinances. It housed the Museum of Modern Art when it opened in 1929, pending the construction of the museum at its current address (1939) ▲ *290*. The Crown Building was once owned by Ferdinand and Imelda Marcos.

AIR RIGHTS
In Manhattan, where a square foot of land can cost as much as several thousand dollars, each square inch is worth its weight in gold. Historic buildings, even functional buildings, have often been destroyed to make way for taller buildings simply because they were much lower than the permitted height for their surface area. A few years ago, an ingenious scheme was devised, enabling these buildings to be saved: their "air rights" can be transferred to a nearby building project. In other words, the available air space left unused by a low historic building legally can be used by a new building; the latter can therefore exceed current specifications, and the historic building need not be demolished. Thus, in recent years Tiffany sold its air rights to Trump Tower.

The gilded top of the Crown Building, which conceals a water tower, is an eye-catching feature of the Midtown skyline.

BERGDORF GOODMAN. 754 5TH AVE., AT S. W. CORNER OF 58TH ST. (1928, arch. Buchman & Kahn). Herman Bergdorf, a tailor of Alsatian extraction, founded a store in 1894 and sold his shares to his partner, Edwin Goodman, in 1901. The latter was responsible for assuring the store's reputation for a wide range of top-quality European clothing. In 1928 Bergdorf's moved to its present site.

SOLOW BUILDING. 9 W. 57TH ST. (1974, arch. Skidmore, Owings & Merrill). This is the twin of the Grace Building, opposite Bryant Park. The giant red 9 sculpture on the sidewalk was created by Ivan Chermayeff.

GENERAL MOTORS BUILDING. 767 5TH AVE. BETWEEN 58TH AND 59TH STS. (1968, arch. Edward Durell Stone, Emery Roth & Sons). The Savoy Plaza Hotel was demolished to make way for this tower, much to the chagrin of New Yorkers who loved the hotel both for its intrinsic merits and for its contribution to the architectural ensemble of Grand Army Plaza. General Motors cars are on display on the ground floor. The toyshop F.A.O. Schwarz, founded in 1862, moved here in 1986.

The Oak Room (above center) of the Plaza Hotel is named for its oak paneling. This watercolor (above, 1982) of the hotel is by the American artist A. Troubetzkoy.

PLAZA HOTEL. GRAND ARMY PLAZA, BETWEEN W. 58TH AND 59TH STS. (1907, arch. Henry J. Hardenbergh). Twenty years after the completion of his earlier masterpiece the Dakota Apartments, H. J. Hardenbergh designed this grand French Renaissance-style hotel. For nearly a century it has welcomed a succession of eminent guests, including Eleanor Roosevelt, Mark Twain, Groucho Marx, F. Scott Fitzgerald and Frank Lloyd Wright. Donald Trump bought the hotel in 1988.

GRAND ARMY PLAZA. Created in 1912, this plaza was the first European-style square in New York. It takes its name from the Northern army in the Civil War. The army is also commemorated by a statue of General William Tecumseh Sherman, famous for his victorious march through Georgia to the sea. This work, by Augustus Saint-Gaudens, is regarded as one of the finest equestrian statues in the United States. The PULITZER FOUNTAIN (1916), which is dominated by the statue of Pomona (goddess of Abundance) by Karl Bitter, was financed by the publisher Joseph Pulitzer. In 1919, on learning that his first book had been accepted for publication, F. Scott Fitzgerald joyfully leaped into this fountain.

Statue of William T. Sherman (1820–91), the famous Union general, which stands in Grand Army Plaza.

5 RUSSIAN TEA ROOM
6 CARNEGIE HALL
7 MANHATTAN LIFE INSURANCE BLDG.
8 HOTEL PARKER MERIDIEN
9 OSBORNE APARTMENTS AND ART STUDENT LEAGUE
10 ALWYN COURT
11 HEARST MAGAZINE BLDG.
12 N.Y. ATHLETIC CLUB

1 WORLDWIDE PLAZA
2 ST. MALACHY'S ROMAN CATHOLIC CHURCH
3 CITY CENTER OF MUSIC
4 OMNI PARK CENTRAL HOTEL

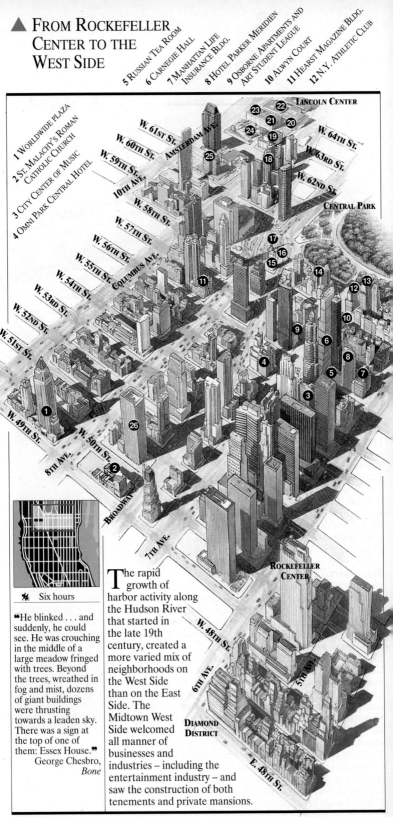

Six hours

"He blinked . . . and suddenly, he could see. He was crouching in the middle of a large meadow fringed with trees. Beyond the trees, wreathed in fog and mist, dozens of giant buildings were thrusting towards a leaden sky. There was a sign at the top of one of them: Essex House."
George Chesbro, *Bone*

The rapid growth of harbor activity along the Hudson River that started in the late 19th century, created a more varied mix of neighborhoods on the West Side than on the East Side. The Midtown West Side welcomed all manner of businesses and industries – including the entertainment industry – and saw the construction of both tenements and private mansions.

After World War Two, air transportation became more popular than sea travel, and the decline in harbor activity had a correspondingly adverse effect on this part of town. In the early 1980's the city of New York endeavored to rehabilitate the area west of Broadway and north of Times Square, as can be seen in the recent crop of skyscrapers. The entertainment and arts sectors, long concentrated on the West Side, have undergone a shift to the north. While the legitimate theaters remain clustered in the 40's, just north of Times Square, and Carnegie Hall still stands on West 57th Street, the Metropolitan Opera, New York City Ballet, New York Philharmonic and other companies have moved to Lincoln Center ▲ *305* at 65th Street.

THE DIAMOND DISTRICT

DIAMOND AND JEWELRY WAY. W. 47TH ST. BETWEEN 5TH AND 6TH AVES. Four hundred million dollars' worth of precious stones changes hands daily on this block. During the 1920's and 1930's, the diamond trade was concentrated among the Hassidim ▲ *194* on the Lower East Side; it moved to 47th Street around the outbreak of World War Two, when more Jewish gem traders and cutters arrived from Europe. The street is lined with stores; business transactions are carried out in rooms behind the stores and in clubs such as the Diamond Dealers Club. Until recently deals were also transacted on the sidewalk; the murder of two jewelers in the street in 1977 put an end to this informality.

GOTHAM BOOK MART ★. 41 W. 47TH ST. "Wise men fish here" is the motto of this bookshop, which was founded in 1920 by Frances Steloff. Her customers included T. S. Eliot, Henry

THE DIAMOND DISTRICT EARLY IN THIS CENTURY
At the beginning of the 1920's, about ten bookshops were gathered along this stretch of the street. Today only one remains: the Gotham Book Mart. "Gotham" was the nickname given to New York by Washington Irving around 1806 in his collection of essays and poems the *Salmagundi Papers*. According to a medieval legend, the people of the village of Gotham, in Nottinghamshire, pretended to be deranged in order to dissuade King John from collecting taxes there. In Irving's opinion New York, like Gotham, seemed inhabited by madmen.

Miller and Thornton Wilder, the novelist and playwright, whose most famous play is *Our Town*. Defying the censors, Frances Steloff stocked copies of *Lady Chatterley's Lover*, by D. H. Lawrence, a highly controversial work when published in 1928, which she secretly imported from England. She employed the poets Everett LeRoi Jones and Allen Ginsberg, as well as the playwright Tennessee Williams, as sales assistants when they were still struggling to make names for themselves. Woody Allen, Saul Bellow and the playwright John Guare, have been frequent visitors to the store. When Frances Steloff died in 1989, at the age of 101, letters and flowers poured in from all over the world. The shop supplies a wide range of books, antique and modern, and literary magazines, in particular those dealing with 20th-century poetry and prose. A gallery above the main floor displays a collection of art books and temporary exhibitions.

DIAMOND DISTRICT DISPLAYS
Firms selling precious stones and metals, antique and modern jewelry, now line both sides of 47th St. The lively trade being transacted in the diamond district brings a flavor of the Lower East Side to the otherwise cool commerce of Midtown.

ST. MALACHY'S – THE ACTORS' CHAPEL

ST. MALACHY'S CATHOLIC CHURCH
Built in 1903, this small neo-Gothic church, at 239–245 W. 49th St., has long been the parish church of Broadway's Catholic actors, since its proximity to the theater district enables them to attend services between performances. In 1926 Rudolph Valentino's funeral took place in this church, attended by thousands of women.

Window of the City Center of Music and Drama.

IN THE VICINITY OF ROCKEFELLER CENTER

Originally Rockefeller Center was intended to include a site between 47th and 52nd streets on the west side of 6th Avenue, but the El, which operated until 1938, checked its development. Work was not resumed until the 1960's, when a Modernist-style complex, including the new McGraw-Hill, Exxon and Time & Life buildings, was built.

WORLDWIDE PLAZA. 935 8TH AVE. BETWEEN 49TH AND 50TH STS. (1989, arch. Frank Williams). This commercial and residential complex, whose pyramidal top looms above the western side of 8th Avenue, is proof of the recent commercial recovery of this part of Midtown. It was built on the site of the second Madison Square Garden ▲ 249. The northwest corner of 49th Street and Broadway was named JACK DEMPSEY CORNER in memory of the world boxing champion who

JACK DEMPSEY CORNER

defended his title at Madison Square Garden. At the end of his boxing career, he opened a restaurant in this district called Jack Dempsey's.

ROSELAND BALLROOM. 239 W. 52ND ST. BETWEEN BROADWAY AND 8TH AVE. The original Roseland, a club that opened on December 31, 1919, became a mecca for ballroom dancers of all ages; thousands of people came here to learn the new dances: the lindy, shag and jitterbug or, later, the cha-cha and twist. Many top entertainers have performed here, including Ella Fitzgerald ● 61. The first Roseland was on 50th Street and moved in 1956 to the present location. Roseland boasts the largest dance floor in New York.

CITY CENTER OF MUSIC AND DRAMA ★. 135 W. 55TH ST. (1924, arch. Harry P. Knowles). This exotic-looking theater started life as the Mecca Temple of the *Ancient and Accepted Order of the Mystic Shrine* (a branch of Freemasonry). The institution foundered during the 1929 Wall Street crash. Fiorello La Guardia saved the building at the end of the 1930's by converting it into a theater. The City Center was the home of the New York City Ballet and the New York City Opera ● 62 until they moved to Lincoln Center in the 1960's. In recent years the City Center has offered performances by various companies including the Joffrey Ballet, the Paul Taylor Dance Company and the Dance Theater of Harlem.

PARK CENTRAL HOTEL. 870 7TH AVE. (1927, arch. Groneburg and Leuchtag). Throughout the Prohibition years this hotel was used by bootleggers ● 40 and small-time crooks. One of them, Arnold Rothstein, was thought to be the model for Meyer Wolfsheim in F. Scott Fitzgerald's novel *The Great Gatsby*.

TRISHA BROWN

The Russian Tea Room

He was shot in 1928, in room 349, for refusing to pay a poker debt. In 1957, the gangster Albert Anastasia was murdered in the hotel's barbershop. Both of these murders remain unsolved because, as they say in New York, "nobody saw anything."

TRATTORIA DELL'ARTE. 900 7TH AVE. One wall of this restaurant displays the sculpted noses of famous Italians and Italian-Americans, from Julius Caesar, Dante, and Verdi to Joe DiMaggio, the legendary baseball player and husband of Marilyn Monroe. Enormous sculptures representing different parts of the human body adorn the others.

57TH STREET

Before World War Two, this street became one of the most elegant in New York. A concert hall, art galleries, chic boutiques and restaurants abounded. New structures such as the SOLOW BUILDING (9 W. 57th St.) and the METROPOLITAN TOWER (140 W. 57th St.) have altered the street's appearance in recent decades, although many of its original attractions remain.

CARNEGIE HALL. 156 W. 57TH ST. AT THE CORNER OF 7TH AVE. (1891, arch. William B. Tuthill). This Italian Renaissance-style building was financed by the steel magnate, Andrew Carnegie, to house the Oratorio Society, a choir founded by Leopold Damrosch and presided by Carnegie. Tchaikovsky conducted the opening gala concert on May 9, 1891, and paid tribute to the concert hall's "magnificent" acoustics. A year later the New York Philharmonic Orchestra, also founded by Damrosch, took up residence here; it moved to Lincoln Center in 1962. A campaign led by the violinist Isaac Stern saved Carnegie Hall from demolition and it was restored in 1986.

Sign from the restaurant in Carnegie Hall and logo of the Russian Tea Room.

CARNEGIE HALL Carnegie Hall welcomes the leading performers of orchestral music, opera, pop and jazz. Its halls and corridors are decorated with scores and mementoes of the artists who have helped create its legend.

ANDREW CARNEGIE (1835–1919) He ended his days in the house now occupied by the Cooper-Hewitt Museum ▲ 320.

RUSSIAN TEA ROOM This charming restaurant (left), situated at 150 W. 57th St., began life in 1927 as a little store, which also served as a meeting place for Russian immigrants. The Christmas decorations, dating from 1910, commemorate the tradition of Christmas as celebrated before the Revolution. Its regular patrons have included George Balanchine, Rudolf Nureyev and Leonard Bernstein; Woody Allen shot scenes from *Manhattan* and *New York Stories* here in 1979 and 1989.

Sign from Planet Hollywood.

HARD ROCK CAFÉ
This New York establishment displays electric guitars that used to belong to Billy Joel and Brian Jones.

Steinway piano showroom.

Façade of the New York Delicatessen.

PLANET HOLLYWOOD. 140 W. 57TH ST. This bar-restaurant is in direct competition with the nearby HARD ROCK CAFÉ at no. 221 of the same street. It is regarded as the "Hollywood Studio" of New York. Its owners, Sylvester Stallone, Arnold Schwarzenegger and Bruce Willis used scenery from movies such as *Indiana Jones, Rambo, Star Wars* and *Terminator* to decorate the restaurant. The handprints of numerous stars adorn the establishment's façade.

HOTEL PARKER MERIDIEN. 118 W. 57TH ST. (1981, arch Philip Birnbaum). The main features of this Postmodern hotel are the breathtaking marble lobby-atrium and the view from the swimming pool terrace on the top floor.

MANHATTAN LIFE INSURANCE BUILDING. 111 W. 57TH ST. (1925, arch. Warren & Wetmore). This neo-classical building, not far from CARNEGIE HALL, used to belong to Steinway, the famous piano manufacturer. The company had to sell the building after the 1929 crash, although they retained the superb ground floor space as a showroom. At 211 West 58th Street, the MUSEUM OF THE AMERICAN PIANO exhibits 19th-century American musical instruments.

NEW YORK DELICATESSEN. 104 W. 57TH ST. (1938, arch. Ralph B. Bencker). The building originally housed an "automat". The Automatic Food Dispensing Systems, created in 1912 by Horn & Hardart, flourished from the 1930's to the 1950's. Customers inserted coins to open the glass flaps of pigeonholes containing dishes of food. Fast-food restaurants represented the kiss of death for the automat; the last one, on the corner of 42nd Street and 3rd Avenue, closed in 1991.

OSBORNE APARTMENTS ★. 205 W. 57TH ST. (1885, arch. James E. Ware). The plain brownstone façade of this building conceals an extravagant marble lobby. Leonard Bernstein, who composed the music for *West Side Story ● 305*, was one of the Osborne's illustrious residents. In 1978 the actor Gig Young, who was awarded an Oscar for his role in the film *They Shoot Horses, Don't They?*, with Jane Fonda, was found dead beside his wife in one of the apartments, a revolver in his hand.

ART STUDENTS LEAGUE. 215 W. 57TH ST. (1892, arch. Henry J. Hardenbergh). This French Renaissance-style building originally housed the AMERICAN FINE ART SOCIETY and was built by the Art Students League, founded in 1875. Among the eminent artists who have taught at this school are William Merritt Chase and Robert Henri ● *107*, who influenced an entire generation of students including Edward Hopper, George Bellows and John Sloane.

❝ I have often managed to dine for about ten francs in an Automat. . . . They are popular, these Automats with their change machines for nickels, people walking along with their trays, the jostling, the soup down the back of your neck, the smiling waitresses, blond nurses, all those ordinary people . . .❞
Paul Morand,
New York

Detail of the French Renaissance-style façade of Alwyn Court.

HEARST MAGAZINE BUILDING.

959 8TH AVE. (1928, Joseph Urban and George B. Post & Sons). This building was commissioned by William Randolph Hearst (1863–1951), the newspaper tycoon. At the height of his career, in 1935, Hearst – one of the pioneers of "yellow journalism"

The Hearst Magazine Building's classical sculptures symbolize music, comedy, tragedy, sport, industry, printing and the sciences.

● *54* – owned 28 newspapers and 18 magazines. He was immortalized on screen by Orson Welles in *Citizen Kane* (1941). This building, with its over-abundant decoration, including huge columns capped with urns, was intended to have seven more stories, but the 1929 crash forced Hearst to put a stop to the work. The building was never completed.

ALWYN COURT ★.

180 W. 58TH ST. (1909, arch. Harde & Short). This was designed as a luxury apartment building with no more than twenty-two apartments, each containing between fourteen and thirty-four rooms. In 1938 it was divided into seventy-five apartments of three to five rooms. The French Renaissance-style façade is covered with sculptures depicting dragons, crowns, leaves, flowers and crowned salamanders, the emblem of Francis I. A large interior courtyard, decorated with a mural by Richard Haas, is situated through the lobby and can be glimpsed through the glass front door.

CENTRAL PARK SOUTH

ESSEX HOUSE.

160 CENTRAL PARK SOUTH (1930, arch. Frank Grad). This Art Deco hotel enjoys an exceptional view over Central Park. Its residents have included such diverse artists as Betty Grable and Igor Stravinsky. Ingrid Bergman stayed here in 1946, when she was performing *Joan of Lorraine* on Broadway.

NEW YORK ATHLETIC CLUB.

180 CENTRAL PARK SOUTH (1929, arch. York & Sawyer). The sculptures decorating the main entrance of this club, founded in 1868, represent athletes in training or playing their sport.

THE GAINSBOROUGH STUDIOS.

222 CENTRAL PARK SOUTH (1908, arch. Charles W. Buckham). Originally this was a block of artists' studios; later converted into apartments. Only the frieze by Isidore Konti and the bust of Gainsborough on the façade point to the building's original purpose. The jazz clarinettist Artie Shaw lived here during the 1940's.

COLUMBUS CIRCLE

This traffic circle was given its present name in 1892 in celebration of the 400th anniversary of Europe's discovery of the New World. The marble column, topped by a statue of Christopher Columbus by Gaetano Russo, was a gift from America's Italian citizens.

MAINE MEMORIAL. S. W. CORNER OF CENTRAL PARK (1913, statue by Attilio Piccirilli and H. Van Bwen Magonigle). This monument commemorates the victims of the sinking of the *Maine* ▲ *174*, an American battleship which was blown up in Havana harbor in 1898, an event that helped to precipitate the Spanish-American War ● *28*.

NEW YORK CITY DEPARTMENT OF CULTURAL AFFAIRS. 2 COLUMBUS CIRCLE (1965, arch. Edward Durell Stone). The NEW YORK CONVENTION AND VISITORS BUREAU, a mine of information for tourists, can be found on the ground floor of this building.

LINCOLN CENTER CAMPUS OF FORDHAM UNIVERSITY. COLUMBUS AVE., BETWEEN 60TH AND 62ND STS. This houses the Fordham Law School, part of a Jesuit university based in the Bronx, founded in 1841.

MAINE MEMORIAL
The Maine Memorial was erected in 1913 at the behest of William Randolph Hearst, who covered the Spanish-American War extensively in the New York *Journal*.

Plan in perspective for Lincoln Center, displayed in the Avery Library at Columbia University.

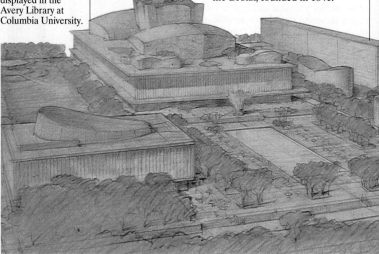

Some 1.5 million people attended the parade held on the day that the Columbus Circle monument was unveiled. It is situated an the southwest entrance to Central Park.

KENT GARAGE. 43 W. 61ST ST. (1930, arch. Jardine, Hill & Murdock). This garage, now converted into apartments, is considered an Art Deco gem. It was one of the first garages in New York with an elevator capable of transporting vehicles.

LINCOLN CENTER ★

The plans for the Lincoln Center for the Performing Arts date from the 1950's, when the Metropolitan Opera and the New York Philharmonic needed new premises more urgently than ever. The work was directed by John D. Rockefeller III and Robert Moses, the New York property developer and parks commissioner. President Eisenhower laid the first stone in 1959. Although most architectural critics have judged it to be conventional and flashy, it has become an important cultural center. It now employs seven thousand people and attracts more than five million patrons to some three thousand performances each year. The construction of Lincoln Center was postponed to allow the slums on 62nd Street to be used as a backdrop for scenes in *West Side Story*. The film's director, Robert Wise, employed some members of neighborhood gangs to play the parts of policemen.

NEW YORK STATE THEATER. (1964, arch. Philip Johnson and Richard Foster). This is the home of the New York City

Opera and the New York City Ballet ● *62*. The New York City Ballet was founded in 1948 by George Balanchine, who built it into a world-famous company. The two large statues dominating the Grand Promenade, *Two Nudes* and *Two Circus Women*, are huge replicas of original works by Elie Nadelman.

METROPOLITAN OPERA HOUSE. (1966, arch. Wallace K. Harrison). This is the centerpiece of Lincoln Center. The Metropolitan Opera House was founded in 1883 by wealthy New Yorkers, such as

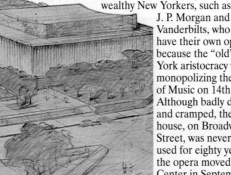

J. P. Morgan and the Vanderbilts, who wanted to have their own opera house because the "old" New York aristocracy were monopolizing the Academy of Music on 14th Street. Although badly designed and cramped, the old house, on Broadway at 39th Street, was nevertheless used for eighty years, until the opera moved to Lincoln Center in September 1966.

"AMERICA"
Lincoln Center was built on a large plot of West Side land marked for urban renewal. The developers were able to purchase this land due to a law of 1949 which allowed dwellings to be demolished so long as the site thereby cleared was allocated for artistic purposes. Before being bulldozed, the neighborhood (above) served as the backdrop for *West Side Story*. This musical was inspired by *Romeo and Juliet*. The action of Shakespeare's tragedy is moved to 20th-century New York, portraying the conflict existing there between two communities, gangs who roam the streets: the Jets (white Americans) and the Sharks (Puerto Rican immigrants). The tragic outcome of the love story between Maria and Tony (one connected with the Sharks, the other with the Jets) shows the enemies how absurd their rivalry is. *West Side Story*'s musical score, by Leonard Bernstein, is generally considered a milestone in the history of the Broadway musical.

The interior, with its red carpeting, gold leaf and marble is a modern version of traditional opera house design. The crystal chandelier was a gift from the Austrian government. The main staircase is flanked by two huge murals by Chagall, *The Triumph of Music* and *The Sources of Music*, which can best be seen from outside at night.

LINCOLN CENTER The name of the center was taken from the adjacent Lincoln Square, which marks the intersection of Broadway and Columbus Ave. The layout of Lincoln Center's three main

DAMROSCH PARK AND GUGGENHEIM BANDSHELL. (1969, arch. Eggers & Higgins). The park and its open-air theater are used for concerts in the summer. Every winter, in December, the BIG APPLE CIRCUS raises its tent here. The park takes its name from the conductor and composer Walter Damrosch, who conducted the NEW YORK SYMPHONY ORCHESTRA in the early part of the 20th century.

AVERY FISHER HALL. (1962, arch. Max Abramovitz). This is the home of the New York Philharmonic Orchestra.

Originally called Philharmonic Hall, it was renamed in 1973 after its principal patron, Avery Fisher. The acoustics in the hall were so poor that the interior was dismantled and reconstructed in 1976. The rebuilt hall was greeted warmly by performers and audiences alike. In the lobby areas are the *Tragic Mask of Beethoven* by Antoine Bourdelle and the bronze head of Mahler by Rodin.

buildings – the Metropolitan Opera, the New York State Theater and Avery Fisher Hall – is modeled on Michelangelo's Piazza del Campidoglio in Rome. Instead of a statue, as in the original, a fountain (above) adorns the center of this plaza. The fountain was financed by a special donation from the Charles Revson Foundation. The huge pool in the northeast plaza contains a sculpture by Henry Moore, *Reclining Figure*. Two other buildings of the center, the Vivian Beaumont Theater and the Juilliard School of Music, are even better examples of the aesthetic trends that dominated architecture in the 1960's.

VIVIAN BEAUMONT THEATER. 150 W. 65TH ST. (1965, arch. Eero Saarinen). This building is named after a philanthropist who made a large donation toward its construction. It has the largest stage of any legitimate theater in the city.

LIBRARY AND MUSEUM OF THE PERFORMING ARTS. 111 AMSTERDAM AVE. (1965, Skidmore, Owings & Merrill). The library and museum are part of the NEW YORK PUBLIC LIBRARY ▲ *252*. The museum's archives include recordings made at the Metropolitan Opera House since the beginning of the century, the Rodgers and Hammerstein sound archives and several thousand theater programs.

JUILLIARD SCHOOL OF MUSIC. 144 W. 56TH ST. (1969, arch. Pietro Belluschi with Eduardo Catalano and Westermann & Miller). This prestigious school of music, dance and drama, which can take its pick from the most brilliant students in the world, was founded in 1904 by Frank Damrosch and James Loeb and named after its patron, the millionaire Augustus D. Juilliard.

AROUND
CENTRAL PARK

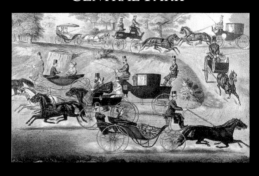

UPPER EAST SIDE, *308*
CENTRAL PARK, *314*
MUSEUM MILE, *320*
FRICK COLLECTION, *322*
EDGAR MUNHALL
WHITNEY MUSEUM, *326*
DAVID ROSS
METROPOLITAN MUSEUM, *328*
PHILIPPE DE MONTEBELLO
GUGGENHEIM MUSEUM, *338*
THOMAS KRENS
UPPER WEST SIDE, *342*
EDWARD O'DONNELL

1 HOTEL CARLYLE
2 COMMONWEALTH FUND
3 WHITNEY MUSEUM
4 FRENCH CONSULATE
5 LYCÉE FRANÇAIS
6 ST. JAMES EPISCOPAL CHURCH
7 FRICK COLLECTION
8 UNION CLUB OF NEW YORK
9 GEORGIAN GROUP
10 7TH REGIMENT ARMORY
11 45 E. 66TH ST.
12 TEMPLE EMANU-EL
13 ASIA HOUSE
14 BARBIZON HOTEL
15 KNICKERBOCKER CLUB
16 HOTEL PIERRE
17 METROPOLITAN CLUB
18 BLOOMINGDALE'S
19 ABIGAIL ADAMS SMITH MUSEUM
20 ROOSEVELT ISLAND TRAMWAY

View of the Upper East Side (1907) taken from the north, showing Roosevelt Island and the banks of the East River.

E. 77TH ST.
E. 76TH ST.
E. 75TH ST.
E. 74TH ST.
E. 73RD ST.
E. 72ND ST.
E. 71ST ST.
E. 70TH ST.
E. 69TH ST.
E. 65

The upper East Side has two natural boundaries – the East River and Central Park, and two urban limits, 60th and 96th streets – where the railroad tracks emerging from Park Avenue tunnel form an unmistakable border between the most elegant part of the city and Harlem. The first houses in the district were farms, built before 1860, to the east of Park Avenue, which was then named 4th Avenue and scored by above-ground railroad tracks. When the 3rd Avenue El was built in 1878, followed by the 2nd Avenue El ● 36, a crop of tenements sprang up and rural smells were obliterated by fumes. However, in 1880, to the west, the situation changed again with the completion, finally, of Central Park. The wealthy started to move northward once again and, for the first time in the city's history, they put down roots and stayed in one

✄ Five hours

AN ATTRACTIVE NEIGHBORHOOD
The sailing ships are long gone, the lawns no longer slope down to the river's edge, a highway runs along the banks, but the neighborhood is still one of the most desirable areas in New York. Its regular streets exude an air of financial ease and security. People still live the good life in this stylish, expensive neighborhood, with its aristocratic houses, luxury apartments, clubs, museums, galleries and churches, liberally interspersed with bars and cafés.

GRAND ARMY PLAZA

MADISON AVE.

neighborhood. They did not move again, particularly as, in 1907, Park Avenue – an attractive and uncluttered thoroughfare lined with sumptuous apartment buildings – was built over the 4th Avenue railroad tracks, which had been sunk beneath a planted center divider. Now the neighborhood runs along both sides of Lexington Avenue: to the west, residential and commercial prosperity; to the east, a more modest display of wealth dating from the 1950's. When the El was dismantled, the neighborhood regained its air of tranquility, attracting the middle classes. The side streets, with their carefully renovated workers' residences, are very attractive, while the many bars and movie houses at the foot of modern high-rises contribute to the vibrant bustle of 3rd, 2nd and 1st avenues, making them a favourite haunt for young people.

FROM 5TH AVENUE TO ROOSEVELT ISLAND

72ND STREET, A MARRIAGE OF OPPOSITES. CORNER MADISON AVE. The profusion of styles and professions represented by the elegant ROSARIO CANDELA BUILDING (N. W. CORNER, 1936), the Beaux Arts façades of the LYCÉE FRANÇAIS next door at nos. 7 and 9 (1899, arch. Flagg & Chambers; 1896, arch. Carrère and Hastings) and THE MANSION (S. W. CORNER, 1898, arch. Kimball & Thompson), which houses RALPH LAUREN, was formerly the OLIVETTI BUILDING, and originally the Gertrude Rhinelander WALDO RESIDENCE, are characteristic of this stretch of Madison Avenue.

ST. JAMES EPISCOPAL CHURCH. 861 MADISON AVE., N. E. CORNER 71ST ST. (1884, arch. Robert H. Robertson). Founded in 1810 as a parish church during the summer months, when people come here on vacation, a simple wooden church was replaced in 1869 by a

Victorian Gothic-style building which, in its turn, made way in 1884 for the present church. Note the TIFFANY stained-glass windows.

71ST AND 70TH STREETS. BETWEEN 5TH AND PARK AVES. The elegant streets that flank the Frick Collection ▲ 322, although a little stiff in appearance, still boast a number of neo-classical ashlar mansions dating from the neighborhood's early days: too large to be converted into apartments, they house private colleges, foundations or galleries. The streets to the east of Madison Avenue, which are less ostentatious and more eclectic, still possess some fine residences. The many garages were once stables belonging to the palazzos on 5th Avenue.

Since 1964, the children attending the Lycée Français, who come from 54 different countries, have studied here.

LUXURY ON MADISON
The Ralph Lauren boutique (the Mansion) has retained the appearance of a private residence, with its wood-paneled rooms and fireplaces.

LUXURY ON "FIFTH"
The doorman, who performs the role of caretaker, doorkeeper and porter, is essential to the Upper East Sider's sense of well-being. A superintendent and elevator man who act as plumbers, electricians and general repairmen, take care of the residents

continued comfort within the walls of these bastions of wealth.

THE 7TH REGIMENT ARMORY
The huge inner hall (187 feet by 270 feet), once used for military maneuvers, can be hired for private functions, exhibitions or shows. The interior is a museum, retracing the history of the unit, which defended Washington, D.C. during the Civil War. Tiffany was the interior designer for two rooms, which can be visited by appointment. On the fifth floor, the officers' mess – with its décor devoted to the sport of hunting – has been converted into a restaurant.

UNION CLUB OF NEW YORK. N. E. CORNER PARK AVE. AND 69TH ST. (1932, arch. Delano & Aldrich). This is the headquarters of the oldest club in the city, founded in 1836. Clubs have always played an important role in New York society, membership of specific clubs being taken as an accurate gauge of someone's social standing. The UNION CLUB is for affluent people of good family; the METROPOLITAN (1 E. 60th St., 1893, arch. McKim, Mead & White) places more importance on wealth, and the Knickerbocker (2 E. 62nd St., 1913, arch. Delano & Aldrich) insists on members having one ancestor dating directly back to colonial times. The CENTURY ASSOCIATION (7 W. 43rd St., 1891, arch. McKim, Mead & White) is more concerned with culture ▲ *251*. Walk down Park Avenue on the left-hand side, turning a blind eye to HUNTER COLLEGE's modern buildings, completed in 1940 – the old neo-Gothic style building (1913, arch. C. B. J. Snyder) is on Lexington – in order to concentrate on the avenue's only unspoiled block.

PARK AVENUE ★. WEST SIDE, BETWEEN 69TH AND 68TH STS. A cluster of Georgian houses provides a glimpse of how Park Avenue would have looked in the early 1900's. These are the CENTER FOR INTER-AMERICAN RELATIONS (1911, arch. McKim, Mead & White), the SPANISH INSTITUTE (1926, same arch.) the ITALIAN CULTURAL INSTITUTE (1919, arch. Delano & Aldrich) and the CONSULATE GENERAL OF ITALY (1916, arch. Walker & Gillette).

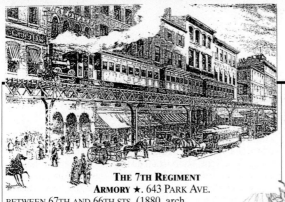

ELEVATED RAILWAYS
These were enthusiastically welcomed by New Yorkers.

THE 7TH REGIMENT ARMORY ★. 643 PARK AVE.
BETWEEN 67TH AND 66TH STS. (1880, arch. Charles W. Clinton). This impressive brick fortress used to be the rallying point for the 7th Regiment of the NATIONAL GUARD.

45 EAST 66TH STREET. (1908, arch. Harde & Short). The façade, a staggering array of double windows separated by terracotta ogives, swelling into a tower at the corner of the avenue, is a monument to the sumptuousness of the first buildings on Madison Avenue.

TEMPLE EMMANU-EL ★. 840 5TH AVE. N. E. CORNER 65TH ST. (1929, arch Robert D Kohn, Charles Butler and Clarence Stein). This SYNAGOGUE, with its Moorish and Romanesque-style decoration, is one of the city's largest places of worship.

ASIA HOUSE, RUSSELL SAGE FOUNDATION AND ROBERT STERLING CLARK FOUNDATION ★. 112 E. 64TH ST. (1959, arch. Philip Johnson). This is one of the architect's great successes, with its tinted glass façade crisscrossed with white steel. It was built to house John D. Rockefeller's collection of art from the Far East, currently at the ASIA SOCIETY (725 PARK AVE.).

LEXINGTON AVENUE. CORNER 64TH ST. The view to the north is obstructed by the footbridge straddling the avenue linking the buildings of Hunter College. Farther south, it loses its residential character and takes on a more commercial aspect.

BLOOMINGDALE'S. LEXINGTON AND 3RD AVES. BETWEEN 59TH AND 60TH STS. There is a constant throng of pedestrians around the most famous store in the city. Founded in 1870, in what was a working-class area, Bloomingdale's started out as a humble store. After the El was dismantled, a middle-class clientele moved into the area and Bloomingdale's supplied them with fashion, food and furniture.

ABIGAIL ADAMS SMITH MUSEUM. 421 E. 61ST ST. (1799). Among the neighborhood's many garages, stands the vestiges of one of the finest properties in 18th-century New York. This Federal-style building ● 82, which once belonged to the daughter of President John Adams, is now a nine-room museum of period furniture set in a tiny garden, an unlikely spot in the shadow of Queensboro Bridge ▲ 188.

ROOSEVELT ISLAND. For two centuries this small island was owned by a family of farmers: it was bought by the city in 1828 to serve as the site for a PENITENTIARY, a MADHOUSE and an ALMSHOUSE. Most of these buildings have now disappeared, and in 1973 mixed rent housing was built. It can be reached by aerial tramway from 2nd Avenue.

ROOSEVELT ISLAND TRAMWAY PLACE ★. S. W. CORNER 2ND AVE. AND 60TH ST. A four-minute ride in the Swiss-made cable car (1976, eng. Prentice & Chan), affords breathtaking views of the eastern part of the city.

Their comfort and speed soon made them indispensable. Furthermore, they afforded a breathtaking view of the city, a fleeting and intimate bird's-eye view of neighboring houses. At night, the spectacle was even more dazzling, due to the myriad sparkle of the lights. But these railways were incredibly noisy and devastated long stretches of the city.

45 EAST 66TH STREET
This eye-catching façade has a twin: Alwyn Court, 180 W. 58th St. ▲ 303.

YORKVILLE
In 1790 this was a
village; and the name
survived 19th-century
urbanization.

From 5th Avenue to Gracie Mansion

UKRAINIAN INSTITUTE. 2 E. 79TH ST. (1899, arch. C. P. H. Gilbert). This residence, encircled by a moat, was built for Isaac D. Fletcher, a reclusive industrialist who donated his collection of paintings to the Metropolitan Museum. There used to be a Renaissance château opposite, on the northeast corner of the street. The demolition of this building caused such a storm of protest that the Landmark Preservation Law was passed (1965).

HOTEL CARLYLE. 35 E. 76TH ST. (1929, arch. Bien & Prince). Crossing Madison Avenue, you can glimpse the Hotel Carlyle's green pyramid in the south. This hotel's suites have accommodated a vast number of stars and politicians. President Kennedy occupied the penthouse suite when he came to New York. There are some fine murals in the two bars, *Bemelmans Bar* and *Café Carlyle*.

80TH STREET, A REFUGE. BETWEEN PARK AND LEXINGTON AVES. On this street stand the last private residences dating from before the Depression. They have all been converted into apartments except for the largest, no. 130 (1928, arch. Mott B. Schmidt), sold in 1947 to the JUNIOR LEAGUE, a philanthropic and social organization for young women.

UNITARIAN CHURCH OF ALL SOULS. S. E. CORNER 80TH ST. AND LEXINGTON AVE. (1931, arch. Hobart Upjohn). Look up to see small children playing on the terrace. Space on the ground is so expensive that playgrounds are sometimes built on the rooftops. The church, which plays an important role in community life, houses a school, a theater and a soup kitchen.

YORKVILLE BRANCH, N. Y. PUBLIC LIBRARY. 222 E. 79TH ST. The beautiful Palladian façade belongs to the neighborhood's first library. In 1901, Andrew Carnegie founded sixty-five branch libraries.

1356–1368 3RD AVENUE, A REMINDER OF THE EL. BETWEEN 78TH AND 79TH STREETS (1938, eng. E. H. Faile). The windows of this building overlooking the avenue were glazed with triple-thick glass in an attempt to muffle the din from the El ● *36*. There is a terraced garden that can be reached via 78th Street.

78TH STREET, A MIXED STREET. BETWEEN 3RD AND 2ND AVES. This street's charm resides in the fact that houses built in the 1860's – nos. 208 to 218 are the most interesting – stand next to tenements built earlier, but so carefully maintained that the contrast is not displeasing. Beyond 2nd Avenue, leading down to the river, the neighborhood becomes more blue-collar. There are high-rises all along the avenues but the streets still have the five- and six-story worker's

Until the 1950's, E. 86th St. was the main street in a prosperous German neighborhood.

Over one hundred breweries were built in the surrounding district, including the one owned by Jacob Ruppert, which occupied three blocks between 2nd and 3rd aves. and 90th and 93rd sts.

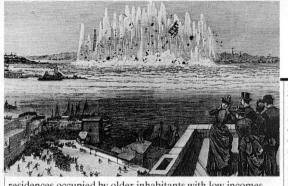

HELL GATE
The East River used to be more dangerous due to the tides, currents and violent eddies swirling around the rocks. In 1876, dynamite was used to clear these rocks away.

residences occupied by older inhabitants with low incomes, often from abroad, a reminder of the time when the neighborhood was nicknamed "little Europe", due to its many Czech, Hungarian, and German residents.

CHEROKEE APARTMENTS. 514 E. 78TH ST. AND 515 E. 77TH ST. (1910–11, arch. Henry Atterbury Smith). This bright, spacious six-story structure was built for families of patients suffering from tuberculosis. External staircases lead up to the apartments which are arranged around large courtyards, reached by paved passageways. .

HENDERSON PLACE. 86TH ST. BETWEEN YORK AND EAST END AVES. (1882, arch. Lamb & Rich). This group of Queen Anne-style buildings, with their many towers, turrets and gables ● *90*, was built on the site of a farm that once belonged to JOHN JACOB ASTOR.

CARL SCHURZ PARK ★. EAST END AVE. BETWEEN 84TH AND 90TH STS. (1876, reconstructed 1938, arch. Harvey Stevenson and Cameron Clarke). This park, which is small but has a variety of landscaping effects, affords a splendid view of the river.

GRACIE MANSION ★. (1799, arch. Ezra Weeks; modern wing, 1966, arch. Mott B. Schmidt). The mayor's private residence can be seen clearly from the park, especially in winter when trees are bare. Built for Archibald Gracie, a Scottish ship-owner whose guests included such famous figures as Louis-Philippe, the future king of France, and Lafayette, it is the only surviving 19th-century country home. The mayor has lived here since 1942. Note the wooden floor of the entrance, painted to look like marble and decorated with a compass – a reminder of the first occupant's maritime connections.

Above, and opposite page, E. 86th St. in 1939.

GRACIE MANSION
Before the construction of the F.D.R. Drive, the East River was an ideal place for bathing, fishing and mooring boats. Now only the promenade overlooking the river gives an idea of what the view used to be. However, the private and attractive park around Gracie Mansion remains unspoiled, as the F.D.R. Drive passes underneath Carl Schurz Park.

▲ CENTRAL PARK

Central Park in spring, its cherry trees and magnolias laden with blossoms.

"I reached Central Park, level with the street, and decided to walk across it to find Manhattan . . . The sky was pale green. Springtime was showering New York with flurries of damp blossom. . . . There was a river, boats, ducks . . . ."
Pierre Bourgeade, *New York Party*

HECKSCHER PLAYGROUND

It took twenty years and ten million cartloads of rock and soil to make this park in the middle of Manhattan. Its 844 acres comprise gently sloping meadows, winding paths and natural-looking lakes, created from the water which originally flooded the swampy site.

Central Park
in fall.

1 COLUMBUS CIRCLE **2** BIRD SANCTUARY **3** WOLLMAN RINK **4** THE DAIRY **5** THE LAKE

"They are walking up the Mall in Central Park . . . She is walking in her wide hat in her pale loose dress that the wind now and then presses against her legs and arms, silkily, swishily walking in the middle of the great rosy and purple and pistachiogreen bubbles of twilight that smell out of the grass and trees and ponds, bulge against the tall houses sharp gray as dead teeth round the southern end of the park, melt into the indigo zenith."

John Dos Passos, *Manhattan Transfer*

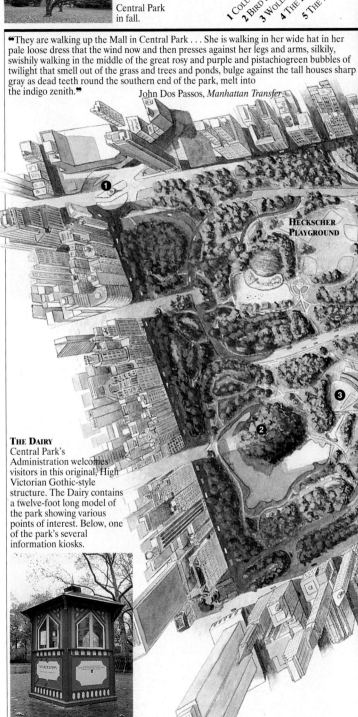

HECKSCHER PLAYGROUND

THE DAIRY
Central Park's Administration welcomes visitors in this original, High Victorian Gothic-style structure. The Dairy contains a twelve-foot long model of the park showing various points of interest. Below, one of the park's several information kiosks.

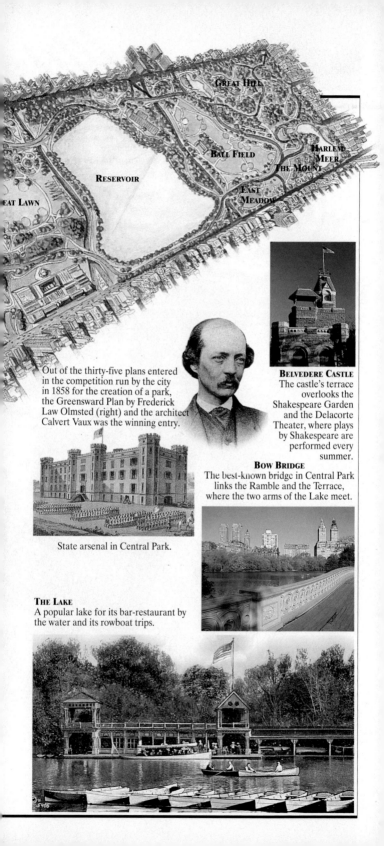

GREAT HILL

GREAT LAWN

RESERVOIR

BALL FIELD

EAST MEADOW

THE MOUNT

HARLEM MEER

Out of the thirty-five plans entered in the competition run by the city in 1858 for the creation of a park, the Greensward Plan by Frederick Law Olmsted (right) and the architect Calvert Vaux was the winning entry.

BELVEDERE CASTLE
The castle's terrace overlooks the Shakespeare Garden and the Delacorte Theater, where plays by Shakespeare are performed every summer.

BOW BRIDGE
The best-known bridge in Central Park links the Ramble and the Terrace, where the two arms of the Lake meet.

State arsenal in Central Park.

THE LAKE
A popular lake for its bar-restaurant by the water and its rowboat trips.

1 COLUMBUS CIRCLE
2 THE POND
3 THE ZOO
4 BETHESDA FOUNTAIN AND TERRACE
5 CONSERVATORY WATER
6 ALICE IN WONDERLAND
7 THE LAKE
8 BELVEDERE CASTLE
9 SHAKESPEARE GARDEN

STRAWBERRY FIELDS

7

THE RAMBLE

9
8

GI

CHERRY HILL

SHEEP MEADOW

BANDSHELL

4

6

5

EAST GREEN

Ornamental detail from the stone staircase of the Terrace, depicting nature and the seasons.

SHEEP MEADOW
Used for grazing until 1934, this "meadow" is a favorite haunt of New Yorkers in the summer.

THE ZOO
This boasts nearly one hundred species from three climatic regions - polar, temperate and tropical. In the 1880's, a pair of hippopotami bought for 5,000 dollars were the zoo's main attraction. Now people flock to see the polar bears.

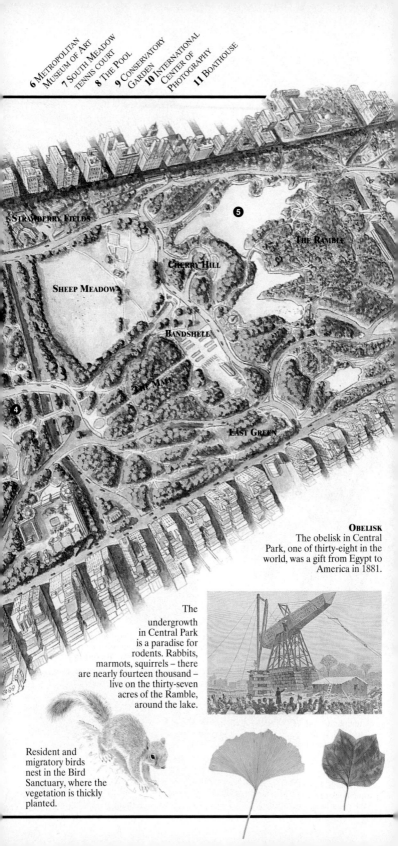

6 Metropolitan Museum of Art **7** South Meadow Tennis Court **8** The Pool **9** Conservatory Garden **10** International Center of Photography **11** Boathouse

5

Strawberry Fields

The Ramble

Cherry Hill

Sheep Meadow

Bandshell

The Mall

4

East Green

OBELISK
The obelisk in Central Park, one of thirty-eight in the world, was a gift from Egypt to America in 1881.

The undergrowth in Central Park is a paradise for rodents. Rabbits, marmots, squirrels – there are nearly fourteen thousand – live on the thirty-seven acres of the Ramble, around the lake.

Resident and migratory birds nest in the Bird Sanctuary, where the vegetation is thickly planted.

GREAT HILL

RESERVOIR

GREAT LAWN

BALL FIELD

HARLEM MEER

THE MOUNT

EAST MEADOW

GAPSTOW BRIDGE
This is one of the thirty-six bridges and arches which are an integral part of Central Park's traffic network. Take time out to watch the wild ducks that live on the Pond in winter.

DARKISH DUCK

RUDDY STIFF-TAILED DUCK

Female   Male
BUFFEL-HEADED DUCK

Female   Male
WHITE-FRONTED DUCK

WOLLMAN RINK
Renovated with assistance from the developer Donald Trump, the skating rink (right, in 1919) is a popular site.

In 1858, Ignaz Anton Pilat, an Austrian gardener, oversaw the planting of nearly four million trees and plants in the park. There are now some 25,000 trees.

▲ MUSEUM MILE

1 HOTEL CARLYLE **2** FRENCH EMBASSY CULTURAL SERVICES **3** GOETHE HOUSE **4** METROPOLITAN MUSEUM **5** GUGGENHEIM MUSEUM **6** NATIONAL ACADEMY OF DESIGN **7** COOPER-HEWITT MUSEUM **8** CONVENT OF THE SACRED HEART **9** JEWISH MUSEUM **10** INTERNATIONAL CENTER OF PHOTOGRAPHY **11** MT. SINAI HOSPITAL **12** MUSEUM OF THE CITY OF N.Y. **13** EL MUSEO DEL BARRIO

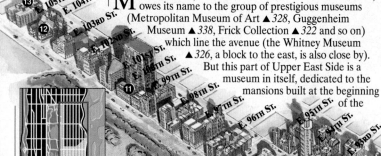

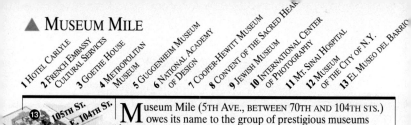

M useum Mile (5TH AVE., BETWEEN 70TH AND 104TH STS.) owes its name to the group of prestigious museums (Metropolitan Museum of Art ▲ *328*, Guggenheim Museum ▲ *338*, Frick Collection ▲ *322* and so on) which line the avenue (the Whitney Museum ▲ *326*, a block to the east, is also close by). But this part of Upper East Side is a museum in itself, dedicated to the mansions built at the beginning of the

✳ **Two days**

Although Washington is the political capital of the U.S., New York is its cultural capital. Recognizing this phenomenon, the French Embassy has restructured its departments accordingly. In 1952 the Republic bought this mansion, with its curved façade decorated with wave moldings, cherubs and lions' heads.

A little to one side, a plastic owl attached to the wall serves as a scarecrow to frighten off the pigeons.

Badge from the Metropolitan Museum.

century.
The Commonwealth Fund (1 E. 75TH ST., 1907, arch. Hale and Rogers), the N.Y.U. Institute of Fine Arts (1 E. 78TH ST., 1912, arch. Horâce Trumbauer) and the Duchesne Residence school facility, also known as the Convent of the Sacred Heart, originally the Kahn residence (1 E. 91ST ST., 1918, arch. J. Armstrong Stenhouse and C. P. H. Gilbert), formerly private residences, testify to past glory.
FRENCH EMBASSY CULTURAL SERVICES . 972 5TH AVE. BETWEEN 78TH AND 79TH STS. (1906, arch. McKim, Mead & White). When there is an exhibition in this building, you can see the circular entrance hall of Harry Whitney Payne's former mansion, with its border of pillars and marble floor.
GOETHE HOUSE. 1014 5TH AVE. BETWEEN 82ND AND 83RD STS. (1907, arch. Welch, Smith & Provot). This is the German cultural center. The libraries are open to the public.
NATIONAL ACADEMY OF DESIGN. 1083 5TH AVE. BETWEEN 89TH AND 90TH STS. (1914, arch. Ogden Codman). In 1825 some American artists got together to form an academy. Each member had to donate a work to the collection.
COOPER-HEWITT MUSEUM ★. 2 E. 91ST ST. (1901, arch. Babb, Cook & Willard). This is now the National Museum of Design, housed in the mansion built by Andrew Carnegie, the steel magnate. His wife lived here until 1946. The Carnegie Corporation gave the house to the Smithsonian Institution in 1972 and the Cooper-Hewitt moved here in 1977, the only branch of the Smithsonian located outside Washington. Taking its inspiration from the Musée des Arts Decoratifs in Paris and the Victoria and Albert Museum in London, the museum was founded in 1897 as the Cooper Union Museum for the Arts of Decoration, by the Hewitt sisters, who amassed an impressive collection of prints, textiles and furniture. The Smithsonian purchased the collection in 1967.

JEWISH MUSEUM. 1109 5TH AVE., N. CORNER 92ND ST. (1908, arch. C. P. H. Gilbert; 1962, arch. Samuel Glazer; 1993, arch. Kevin Roche). The building, which is reminiscent of the Cluny Museum in Paris, was built for the banker Felix Warburg. It has now become the largest American museum devoted to the history and art of the Jewish people: it contains a collection of coins and medals, antique books and valuable manuscripts, objects of worship, and a collection of prehistoric archeological artifacts.

INTERNATIONAL CENTER OF PHOTOGRAPHY ★. 1130 5TH AVE., N. CORNER 94TH ST. (1914, arch. Delano and Aldrich). Built for the financier Willard Straight, this Federal-style residence was not remodeled when the Museum of Photography moved into the premises, so it is worth visiting for those interested in architecture as well as photography.

MUSEUM OF THE CITY OF NEW YORK. 1220 5TH AVE. BETWEEN 103RD AND 104TH STS. (1932, arch. Joseph H. Freedlander). This museum, founded in 1923,

was first housed in Gracie Mansion ▲ 313. The city donated the present site in 1928 and 1,500 subscribers provided the two million dollars needed for the building. The museum, devoted to the city's history, with period rooms, dioramas, toys and dollshouses, not to mention a collection of old fire engines, is as fascinating for children as it is for adults.

EL MUSEO DEL BARRIO. 1230 5TH AVE. BETWEEN 104TH AND 105TH STS. (1934, arch. Frank N. Maynicke). Very popular with families living in this part of East Harlem, the museum is devoted to the art and culture of Puerto Ricans and other Latin Americans.

Badges from the Jewish Museum, the Yivo Institute, El Museo del Barrio, Museum of the City of New York and the International Center of Photography.

MUSEUM OF THE CITY OF NEW YORK Mrs John King van Rensselaer, a socialite who was shocked by how little New Yorkers knew about the history of their own city, was the driving force behind the foundation of this museum. The collection is highly instructive about past customs.

Museum Mile meets East Harlem at the Museo del Barrio, which is dedicated to the culture of Latin Americans.

321

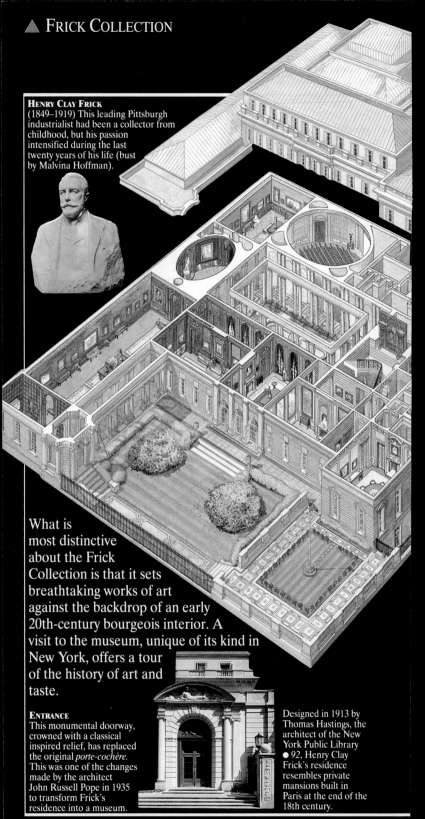

HENRY CLAY FRICK
(1849–1919) This leading Pittsburgh industrialist had been a collector from childhood, but his passion intensified during the last twenty years of his life (bust by Malvina Hoffman).

What is most distinctive about the Frick Collection is that it sets breathtaking works of art against the backdrop of an early 20th-century bourgeois interior. A visit to the museum, unique of its kind in New York, offers a tour of the history of art and taste.

ENTRANCE
This monumental doorway, crowned with a classical inspired relief, has replaced the original *porte-cochère*. This was one of the changes made by the architect John Russell Pope in 1935 to transform Frick's residence into a museum.

Designed in 1913 by Thomas Hastings, the architect of the New York Public Library ● *92*, Henry Clay Frick's residence resembles private mansions built in Paris at the end of the 18th century.

VERMEER, OFFICER AND LAUGHING GIRL (1655–60). There are only thirty-five authenticated paintings by the "Delft Sphinx". The Frick collection has three of them, including this radiant interior with its ambiguous subject/

JEAN-HONORÉ FRAGONARD (1771–3), *The Meeting* One of the four panels that make up "The Progress of Love", painted by Fragonard for Mme du Barry's residence in Louveciennes.

GIOVANNI BELLINI (1480), *Saint Francis in the Desert* This masterpiece by the *cinquecento* Venetian artist, long considered one of the finest paintings in America. It depicts Saint Francis of Assisi receiving Christ's stigmata in a lyrically rendered landscape in which the details (animals, plants, rocks) reflect the saint's emotions.

JEAN-ANTOINE HOUDON (1741–1828), *Diana the Huntress* A lifesize terracotta figure whose graceful appearance belies its technical virtuosity.

FRICK COLLECTION

Wandering through the rooms of Mr Frick's residence, one finds works by Boucher, Bruegel, Chardin, Claude Lorrain, Constable, Drouais, Gainsborough, Goya, Greuze, Ingres, De La Tour, Memling, Monet, Rembrandt, Reynolds, Ruysdael and Watteau.

REMBRANDT, *Self-Portrait* (1658), as an Oriental potentate.

JOHN CONSTABLE, *The White Horse* (1819) "One of my best efforts" said the artist, referring to this tranquil Suffolk landscape.

MAIN STAIRCASE
In response to Mr Frick's desire for a home that would be "simple, comfortable and unostentatious", his architect, Thomas Hastings, and the two interior designers Sir Charles Allom and Elsie de Wolfe, applied themselves to designing a discreetly luxurious house. The predominantly classical style of decoration contains references to 17th- and 18th-century English decoration, Renaissance and 18th-century French decoration, while incorporating some modern touches, typical of the turn of the century. This residence was designed primarily as a setting for the various works of art collected by its owner. This pink marble staircase acts as for the largest organ ever built for a New York residence, a neo-classical calendar clock (left) and a large sun-drenched painting by Renoir.

LIVING HALL
Houses English, French, Italian, Spanish, Chinese and Japanese works.

HANS HOLBEIN THE YOUNGER. *Portrait of Sir Thomas More* (1527), the great English humanist.

FURNISHINGS
There is a fine collection of tables, armchairs (above, 16th-century French chair), cassoni and carved cabinets from the Italian and French Renaissance, as well as furniture signed by great 18th-century French masters, including a chest of drawers and a secretaire made by Riesener for Marie-Antoinette.

DUCCIO DI BUONINSEGNA, *The Temptation of Christ on the Mountain* (c. 1308). This section of the famous reredos from the Maestà in Siena was one of the first pieces acquired by the museum after Frick's death. The beauty and historic importance of this panel makes it a worthy addition to the founder's collection, especially given his unflagging quest for excellence. His daughter, who took over from him as the museum's influential trustee, encouraged the purchase of works by Bastiani, Castagno, Gentile da Fabriano, Fra Filippo Lippi, Piero della Francesca and Paolo and Giovanni Veneziano.

In 1966 the Whitney Museum moved to its permanent address on the corner of Madison Ave., and 75th St., a building designed by Marcel Breuer, one of great masters of

the Bauhaus. Practically all the leading figures in American art in the last fifty years are represented here. They bear witness to Gertrude Whitney's unremittingly non-conformist stance.

STUART DAVIS, *The Paris Bit* (1959) This is a pastiche made up of remembered fragments of architecture and Parisian life and, according to Stuart, "There was simultaneously so much past and present there, in the same sphere, that you couldn't want for anything more."

The Whitney Museum of American Art, founded in 1931 by Gertrude Vanderbilt Whitney, a sculptor and an enlightened patron of the arts, now houses the largest collection of works by modern American artists in the world.

"Neither symbolism nor calligraphy" is how Franz Kline described his own mature abstract works, exclusively in black and white. In *Mahoning* (1956), as in Kline's later works, the black motifs touch at least two sides of the painting, giving the overall composition an architectural quality.

ANDY WARHOL, *Green Coca-Cola Bottles* (1962) Warhol was the first artist to use silk-screen techniques, hitherto reserved for advertising, in order to reproduce images of modern society for artistic purposes.

The idea for the Metropolitan Museum of Art was conceived in Paris on July 4, 1866, Independence Day. John Jay's proposal took shape in 1880 when the first building was opened on 5th Avenue and 82nd Street. Completed in 1902, the lavish Beaux Arts-style façade incorporated the original Renaissance Revival façade to give the building the appearance of a true civic institution.

OFFERING BEARER
(c. 2010 BC).
Wooden statuette from the tomb of Meket-Re.

GREAT HALL
Richard Morris Hunt, who designed the Great Hall, worked with monumental proportions and a wealth of Beaux Arts styling to create an effect of imposing grandeur. On his death, his son, Richard Howland Hunt, took over and completed the original project. There are extraordinary floral arrangements decorating the four symmetrical side niches and the central island, which are changed very regularly.

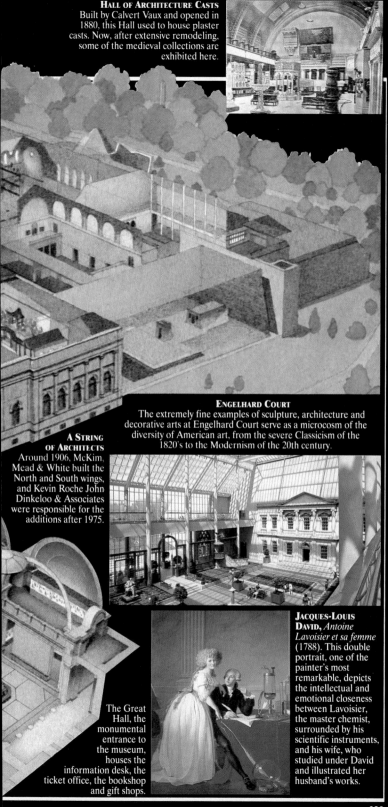

HALL OF ARCHITECTURE CASTS
Built by Calvert Vaux and opened in 1880, this Hall used to house plaster casts. Now, after extensive remodeling, some of the medieval collections are exhibited here.

ENGELHARD COURT
The extremely fine examples of sculpture, architecture and decorative arts at Engelhard Court serve as a microcosm of the diversity of American art, from the severe Classicism of the 1820's to the Modernism of the 20th century.

A STRING OF ARCHITECTS
Around 1906, McKim, Mead & White built the North and South wings, and Kevin Roche John Dinkeloo & Associates were responsible for the additions after 1975.

JACQUES-LOUIS DAVID, *Antoine Lavoisier et sa femme* (1788). This double portrait, one of the painter's most remarkable, depicts the intellectual and emotional closeness between Lavoisier, the master chemist, surrounded by his scientific instruments, and his wife, who studied under David and illustrated her husband's works.

The Great Hall, the monumental entrance to the museum, houses the information desk, the ticket office, the bookshop and gift shops.

PENDANT MASK
(early 16th century)
This extraordinary ivory and metal object is a typical example of the highly elaborate works of art which came out of the kingdom of Benin in Nigeria, usually from the royal court, and which astounded European travelers. The king probably wore this mask on his belt for ceremonies honoring the dead Queen Mother, of whom this may be a portrait.

HEADDRESS
(Nigeria)
Carved out of a single block of wood, this was worn by the Yorubas during masked invocations of the water spirits.

YAISUHASHI SCREEN
(Edo period, 1603–1867)
This screen is the work of the Japanese artist, Ogata Korin. Its design – a composition of irises, massed against a bridge made of eight planks of wood, and set against a gold background – unfolds across six sections.

ASTOR COURT

The court of the famous Garden of the Master of the Fishing Nets at Suzhou, was reproduced by Chinese craftsmen who used ancient techniques and aboriginal materials to recreate this perfect microcosm of the natural world: water, rocks and plants, where the contrast of light and shade, softness and hardness, creates a feeling of serenity.

RECEPTION ROOM FROM THE NUR AD-DIN HOUSE (1707)

This room comes from a residence in Damascus built during the reign of the Ottoman empire and its magnificent marble inlays, gilded and painted wood paneling, stained-glass windows and ceramic tiles encapsulate that period's harmonious luxury.

MICHAEL C. ROCKEFELLER WING

This wing was inaugurated in 1982 and houses collections of African, Pacific and American art. Nelson Rockefeller donated this wing to the museum, in memory of his son, an explorer who died during a trip to New Guinea.

MBIS TOTEM

(20th century) The Asmat tribe in New Guinea produces wood carvings, especially totem poles, which are reserved for ritual ceremonies associated with death.

▲ METROPOLITAN MUSEUM

TEMPLE OF DENDUR
A gift to the United States from the Egyptian government in recognition of American assistance in saving the monuments of Nubia, this small temple dedicated to Isis, built by Augustus around 15 BC, was reconstructed to look as it did on the banks of the Nile, with a pool in the foreground. It can be seen from the park and is illuminated at night.

FUNERARY STELE
(6th century BC)
This Attic sculpture shows a female sphinx watching over the tomb of two hieratic young men.

"PORTRAIT OF A MAN"
(Fayum, 2nd century BC) Funerary portrait in the Egyptian tradition influenced by Greco-Roman art.

"SEATED HARP PLAYER"
(3rd millennium BC) This Cycladic marble statue is beautifully simple and represents a male musician – a highly unusual subject.

BOSCOREALE
This town, which was buried by the eruption of Vesuvius in AD 79, left, like Pompeii, a superb legacy, including these trompe l'oeil paintings.

"KING'S HEAD"
(4th century AD). This engraved and embossed silver head shows the talent of Sassanian artists.

"QUEEN'S HEAD"
(c. 1400 BC)
This fragment of jasper
is a perfect illustration
of art during the reign
of Amenophis III.

**CHAIR BELONGING TO
THE SCRIBE RENYSENEB**
(c. 1450 BC)
This attractive chair,
skillfully worked in
wood and ivory, was
used during the
pharaoh's lifetime
and probably engraved
for his tomb after his
death.

KNEELING MAN
(6th century)
This Mayan wooden statue, from
the border between Mexico and
Guatemala, has miraculously
survived the tropical climate.

"PERSEUS WITH THE HEAD OF MEDUSA"
(1808) Inspired by the *Apollo of the
Belvedere* in the Vatican, this marble
statue displays Antonio
Canova's perfect mastery of
the neo-classical style.

JACKSON POLLOCK,
Autumn Rhythm
(1950)
This painting was the last in a series of large "drip" paintings, an innovative technique which contributed to the development of Abstract Expressionism.

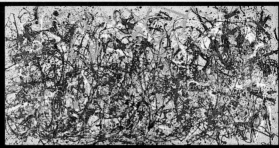

LIVING ROOM FROM THE LITTLE HOUSE
In 1914 Frank Lloyd Wright (1867–1959) designed a summer house for Francis W. Little in Wayzata, a suburb of Minneapolis. The ocher-colored walls, natural oak floor and brick fireplace contribute to the harmonious feeling of this room. The oak furniture, and even the way it is arranged, form an integral part of the overall architectural composition.

CHARLES DEMUTH,
I Saw the Figure 5 in Gold (1928)
This abstract impression of urban life is typical of the modernist American painter.

ROOM FROM THE HEWLETT HOUSE
(c. 1739)
The furniture and paneling of this room came from a farmhouse on Long Island at a time when English and European styles were being mixed. The large cupboard painted in grisaille, is typical of the Dutch colonial period.

Hartley's treatment of the military themes shows the influence of German Expressionism, as well as Cubism. This painting of an officer with its dense mass of symbols, insignias, medals and flags, enhanced by more personal references – letters and numbers – to a friend who had just been killed at the front, is intended to be a collective physical and psychological portrait.

MARSDEN HARTLEY,
Portrait of a German Officer
This powerful canvas was painted in November 1914, during a visit to Berlin.

THOMAS EAKINS,
Max Schmitt in a Single Scull (1871)
Between 1870 and 1874 Eakins painted a
series of canvases devoted to rowing – clear
evidence of his passion for sport. Note his
treatment of light and space, as well as his
great technical virtuosity and his immediate,
analytical approach to the subject matter.

WINSLOW HOMER,
The Gulf Stream
Homer painted this
canvas from sketches
done during a trip to
the Bahamas. It is a
fine example of one
of his favorite
subjects, the
reciprocal
relationship between
man and nature, a
subject that is most
powerfully expressed
in his seascapes.

SPANISH PATIO
(1506–15)
This inner courtyard
came from a castle
near Almería (Spain).
It is lavishly sculpted
and is a gem of
Renaissance-style,
Italo-Hispanic
architecture.

JAN VAN EYCK,
The Last Judgment
(c. 1425)
This painting, one of
the earliest by the
Flemish painter and a
masterpiece of the
new technique of oil
painting, foreshadows
Northern Realism.

EL GRECO,
View of Toledo (c. 1595)
This is one of the few surviving
landscapes by El Greco; he
limited himself to the use of
greens, grays and a dazzling
white, which gives the
painting an inner luminosity
and a mystical aura.

PARADE ARMOR
(c. 1550). Decorated
by the engraver
Étienne Delaune,
for Henry II, of
France, its superb
engravings depict
the themes of
Victory and Fame.

GEORGES DE LA TOUR, *The Fortune*
(1616–39). This is one of the painter's rare
daylight scenes, depicting betrayed innocence.

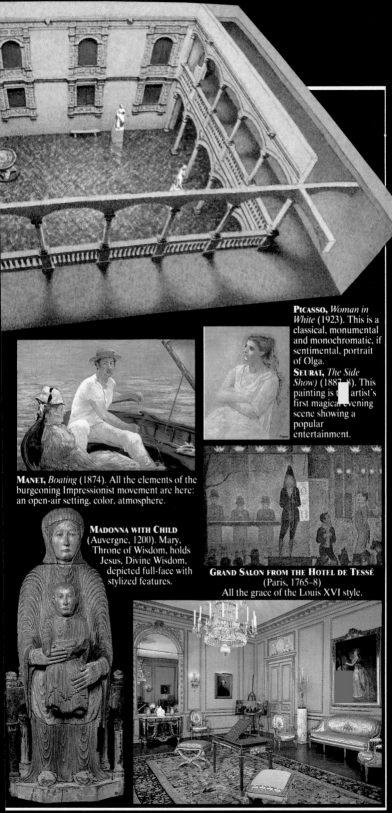

PICASSO, *Woman in White* (1923). This is a classical, monumental and monochromatic, if sentimental, portrait of Olga.

SEURAT, *The Side Show)* (1887–8). This painting is the artist's first magical evening scene showing a popular entertainment.

MANET, *Boating* (1874). All the elements of the burgeoning Impressionist movement are here: an open-air setting, color, atmosphere.

MADONNA WITH CHILD (Auvergne, 1200). Mary, Throne of Wisdom, holds Jesus, Divine Wisdom, depicted full-face with stylized features.

GRAND SALON FROM THE HOTEL DE TESSÉ (Paris, 1765–8) All the grace of the Louis XVI style.

Fernande with Black Mantilla (1905) by Pablo Picasso.

The baroness Hilla Rebay von Ehrenwiesen, who inspired Solomon Guggenheim's collection and was its director, commissioned the architect Frank Lloyd Wright to build a museum to house it, with the instruction: "I want a temple of spirit." Solomon Guggenheim, a copper magnate and enlightened patron of the arts, was already the proud owner of a collection of Old Masters and had been introduced to modern art twenty years before when he met the baroness, who had opened his eyes to the work of

Mountains at Saint-Rémy (1889) by Vincent van Gogh, left to the museum in 1976 by Justin K. Thannhauser.

King of Kings (c. 1930), oak carving by Constantin Brancusi, and *Femme cuiller* (*Spoon in the form of a woman*), (1926), a bronze by Giacometti.

Delaunay, Gleizes, Chagall, Kandinsky and Bauer. He set up an award for modern artists and founded the Solomon Guggenheim Foundation, whose aim was "the promotion and encouragement of education in art". "I do not want to found another museum such as now exists in New York . . . No such building as is now customary for museums could be appropriate for this one."

A MUSEUM ILLUMINATED BY NATURAL LIGHT.
The architect drew up plans which focused on the importance of natural light. As well as the glass dome over a central court – which figured in all the early proposals – Wright recommended a strip running along the walls, providing a constant source of daylight, modeled on his own studio in Wisconsin. Another concept which figured prominently in Wright's plans was that of an open space, without partitions, which a wheelchair could traverse from one end to another. In his original plans, Wright wrote the words "constant ramp" – the idea of a building with a spiral ramp was born.

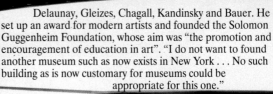

View of the dome from inside the museum.

Preparedness (1968), triptych by Roy Lichtenstein.

❝Abstract painting is stronger than figurative art because it creates beauty instead of reproducing what already exists in the natural world.**❞**
Jean Cocteau

Painting with White Border (May 1913), oil on canvas by the Russian artist Wassily Kandinsky, painted in Munich.

A CONTROVERSIAL PROJECT. It took sixteen years from the first plans to the final building. This was due to clashes with the building authorities and with the director of the Foundation, James Johnson Sweeney, who succeeded Baroness Rebay in 1952 and who felt that Wright's proposals might cause grave problems in terms of conserving and hanging the collections. Not only was Wright keen on having the paintings illuminated by natural light, which would change with the movement of the sun and the seasons, but he also wanted them to be displayed at an angle, as if on an easel. The following scheme was finally adopted: a spiral ramp, 1416 feet long, gently climbing up to a glass dome, about 92 feet higher, showering the whole building with light. Along the ramp, artificial lighting was used. In keeping with Wright's intentions, the paintings are exhibited without frames or with very simple frames, and are hung, "as if in an artist's studio", on the curved walls and partitions.

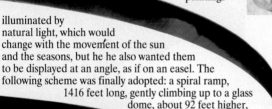

MUSEUM

A Main entrance to the Solomon R. Guggenheim Museum, 1071 5th Ave.

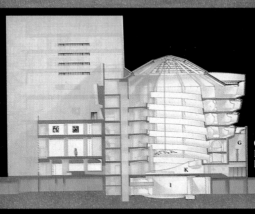

B Entrance to the café
C Gift shops
D Thannhauser Collection
E Thannhauser Galleries
F Sculpture Terrace

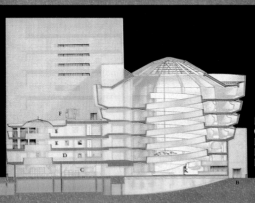

G High Gallery
I Auditorium
K Rotunda

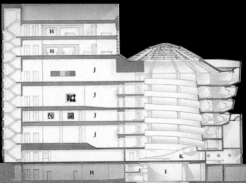

H Offices
I Auditorium
J Tower Gallery
K Rotunda

"A Ship within the City". Work started in August 1956. Wright visited his building site for the last time in January 1959 and died three months later,

Composition I A (1930), oil painting by Piet Mondrian.

without seeing his work completed. The museum opened in October of the same year and caused a storm of protest: people were considerably taken aback, not only by the concrete used for the façade (instead of marble as Wright had wanted) and the upended spiral defying the laws of balance, but also by the abstract works on display inside. Wright had already answered those who, well before it was completed, had called the museum a "washing machine" or a "monstrous mushroom" by saying: "One should no more judge a building from the outside than a car by its color."

Terremoto (1981) Installation by Joseph Beuys composed of eighteen objects: a

The Collection. The Guggenheim Museum is essentially made up of five major private collections: Solomon

Guggenheim's collection of non-objective paintings – Kandinsky, Bauer, Moholy-Nagy, Léger, Delaunay, Chagall, Modigliani; Justin K. Thannhauser's collection of Impressionist and modern art – including a large number of Picasso's early works; Karl Nierendorf's German Expressionist paintings (including over 100 works by Paul Klee); Katherine S. Dreier's historic avant-garde paintings and sculptures (Brancusi, Mondrian); Count Giuseppe Panzadi Biumo's collection

typewriter, a flag, some felt, nine paintings covered in chalk drawings and diagrams, a cask, a tape-recorder, a cassette and some brochures.

Morning in the Village after a Snowstorm (1912) oil painting by Kazimir Malevich.

of American "minimal art" from the 1960's and 1970's (Robert Ryman, Dan Flavin); as well as successive acquisitions by the museum's directors and curators – including works by Roy Lichtenstein and Joseph Beuys. Currently the Museum owns more than 5,000 paintings, sculptures and sketches ranging from the Impressionists to the present day. Many works have never been shown due to lack of space. An annex designed by Gwathmey Siegel and Associates was opened in 1992, inspired by the plans drawn up by Wright for artists' studios, intended to occupy the same site. At the same time, the museum opened a new exhibition space in SoHo ▲ 204.

Luminous Object by Dan Flavin, exhibited from June 28, to August 27, 1992.

1 JOAN OF ARC STATUE
2 SOLDIERS' AND SAILORS' MONUMENT
3 YESHIVA CHOFETZ CHAIM
4 RIVERSIDE DRIVE
5 APTHORP APARTMENTS
6 COLLEGIATE CHURCH AND SCHOOL
7 ANSONIA HOTEL
8 EX-PYTHIAN TEMPLE
9 LINCOLN CENTER

🏃 Six hours

The Upper West Side did not actually become a popular residential area until 1879, when the El was built on 9th Avenue (Columbus Avenue). The section of 8th Avenue between 59th and 110th streets was called Central Park West to encourage property developers to build quality residences there. It is now the most prestigious area in the district, its arresting skyline forming a contrast with that of 5th Avenue when seen from the east side of Central Park. The population of the Upper West Side is, like its architecture, eclectic and non-

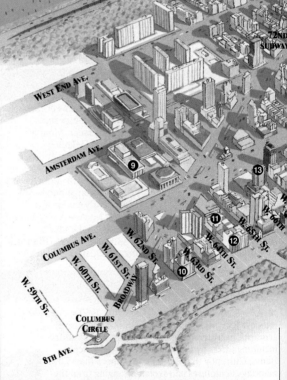

THE SOCIETY FOR ETHICAL CULTURE FOUNDED IN THE CITY OF NEW YORK MAY 1876

N.Y. SOCIETY FOR ETHICAL CULTURE
This society, founded by Felix Adler, made a name for itself primarily for its highly progressive teaching methods. It has established several schools (Ethical Culture Schools), one of which is nearby, at 33 Central Park West, on the corner of 63rd St. The N.Y. Society for Ethical Culture founded New York's first free kindergarten in 1878 and the first social work center in the United States.

conformist. Since the beginning of the 20th century, the district has acted as a magnet for intellectuals and artists, a trend which became even more marked when Lincoln Center was built in the 1960's ▲ *305*. The Upper West Side is now a lively, fashionable neighborhood with stores and restaurants. It is also the home of another stylish enclave lining the Hudson from 72nd to 153rd streets – Riverside Drive and Riverside Park, both designed at the end of the 19th century as part of an ambitious development program for the Upper West Side. Some of the city's finest examples of "residential

10 Century Apartments
11 Liberty Warehouse
12 N.Y. Society for Ethical Culture
13 American Broadcasting Company Television Studios
14 Café des Artistes
15 Tavern on the Green
16 Congregation Shearith Israel
17 Majestic Apartments
18 Dakota Apartments
19 San Remo Apartments
20 N.Y. Historical Society
21 American Museum of Natural History
22 The Beresford

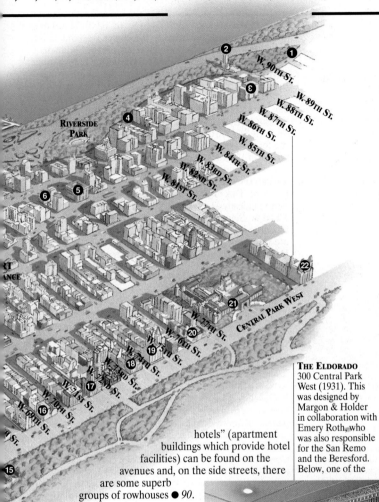

Riverside Park

W. 90th St.
W. 89th St.
W. 88th St.
W. 87th St.
W. 86th St.
W. 85th St.
W. 84th St.
W. 83rd St.
W. 82nd St.
W. 81st St.
W. 77th St.
W. 76th St.
W. 75th St.
W. 73rd St.
W. 72nd St.
W. 71st St.
W. 70th St.
W. 69th St.

CENTRAL PARK WEST

THE ELDORADO
300 Central Park West (1931). This was designed by Margon & Holder in collaboration with Emery Roth, who was also responsible for the San Remo and the Beresford. Below, one of the

hotels" (apartment buildings which provide hotel facilities) can be found on the avenues and, on the side streets, there are some superb groups of rowhouses ● *90*.

AROUND CENTRAL PARK WEST

CENTURY APARTMENTS. 25 CENTRAL PARK WEST (1931, arch. Irwin Chanin). This is the southernmost apartment building with twin towers of the five lining Central Park West. Heading northward, the others are, respectively, the *Majestic*, the *San Remo*, the *Beresford* (which actually has three towers) and the *Eldorado*. The group gives Central Park West its original and impressive skyline.

NEW YORK SOCIETY FOR ETHICAL CULTURE. 2 W. 64TH ST. (1910, arch. Robert D. Kohn). Founded in 1876, the aim of this humanist society was to encourage morality irrespective of religious principles and dogma. It now has twenty-three branches throughout the United States and three thousand members.

three murals from the lobby.

343

When it was opened the Hôtel des Artistes offered a communal kitchen, a squash court, a swimming pool, a ballroom and . . . the Café des Artistes.

TAVERN ON THE GREEN
Every year since 1970 the illuminated trees of the Tavern on the Green have marked the finishing line of the New York marathon. This 26.2 mile long race starts from Staten Island, at the entrance to the Verrazano Bridge, and takes in the city's five boroughs.

"CAFÉ DES ARTISTES"
The murals by Howard Chandler Christy, a long-time resident at the Hôtel des Artistes, depict thirty-six willowy, naked beauties in a woodland setting. Most of the artist's models were well-known by the hotel's other residents. Christy, nicknamed the "pin-up artist", was renowned for this type of painting and his pin-ups were often used as magazine illustrations. This was why he was asked to be one of the judges for the first Miss America beauty contest.

LIBERTY WAREHOUSE. 43 W. 64TH ST. (c. 1900). This is one of the most eccentric buildings on the Upper West Side. The owner built a fifty-five-foot-high replica of the Statue of Liberty on top of the warehouse roof. It used to be a prime attraction for visitors who would climb the mini-staircase inside to marvel at the view of the district. The site was closed in 1912, because the visits disturbed the workers. The statue can be seen clearly from the Lincoln Center plaza.

AMERICAN BROADCASTING COMPANY TELEVISION STUDIOS. 56 W. 66TH ST. (1901, arch. Horgan & Slattery). ABC restored the former First Battery Armory of the New York National Guard in 1978. Its television studios now occupy the building and many features have been filmed here.

TAVERN ON THE GREEN. CENTRAL PARK WEST AND 67TH ST. (c. 1870). This restaurant is in Central Park. It started life more modestly as a fold for the sheep grazing nearby in Sheep Meadow. Since first opening, in 1934, it has become a favourite haunt of celebrities. At night the surrounding trees are spectacularly festooned with lights.

HÔTEL DES ARTISTES, CAFÉ DES ARTISTES. 1 W. 67TH ST. (1918, arch. George Mort Pollard). This was one of a number of residences built along this street at the beginning of the 20th century by groups of artists who had pooled their finances. The buildings contained studios as well as apartments which could be rented out. The revenues from rents helped the artists to eke out a living and to pay back the money they had borrowed for the construction work. Isadora Duncan, Noel Coward, Norman Rockwell and John Lindsay, one of New York's former mayors, were among the many celebrities who lived here. The painter, Howard Chandler Christy, one of the first residents, painted the murals in the charming Café des Artistes which can be reached via the hotel lobby.

CONGREGATION SHEARITH ISRAEL. 99 CENTRAL PARK WEST (1897, arch. Brunner & Tryon). The oldest Jewish congregation in New York, whose name means "remnant of Israel", was formed in 1655 by refugees from Brazil who were fleeing persecution. The Dutch governor, Peter Stuyvesant, wanted to prevent them from settling here, but was informed by his employer, the Dutch West India Company, that the

company's Jewish shareholders would not tolerate such an attitude. The group was therefore allowed to stay and build its first synagogue in 1730 on Mill Street, in Lower Manhattan. That small Georgian-style synagogue has been recreated within the present building. It contains two millstones from a Dutch windmill that used to stand on Mill Street.

THE PYTHIAN CONDOMINIUM, FORMER PYTHIAN TEMPLE. 135 W. 70TH STREET (1927, arch. Thomas W. Lamb). This eye-catching building, west of Columbus Avenue, is worth making a detour to visit. It was created by Thomas Lamb, the theater designer, to house the headquarters of the brotherhood, the *Knights of Pythias*. In 1986 the building, whose décor evokes Hollywood epics of the 1920's, was remodeled and converted into apartments. Note the inscription above the front door: "If fraternal love held all men bound how beautiful this would be."

WEST 71ST STREET. BETWEEN CENTRAL PARK WEST AND COLUMBUS AVENUE (1890's). The rowhouses that line this stretch of 71st Street date from the time when the Upper West Side was just becoming established. Most of them were private houses.

MAJESTIC APARTMENTS. 115 CENTRAL PARK WEST (1930, arch. Jacques Delamarre). This apartment building was the successor to the sumptuous Majestic Hotel, built in 1893 and renowned for its *Roof Garden*. These hanging gardens, resplendent with fountains and waterfalls, were one of the fashionable haunts of New York's high society at the turn of the century. Fred Astaire stayed at the *Majestic Hotel* in 1919. Its successor, the Majestic

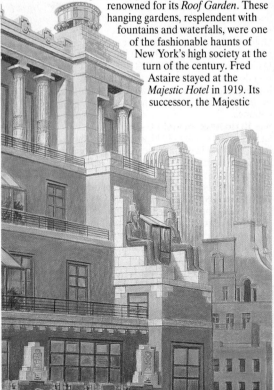

WEST 71ST STREET
The façade and main entrance of the houses lining the two sides of this street are decorated with carved ornamental motifs, including lions' heads, cupids and shells. The carved bas-relief of the first bay window of the house at no. 33 shows a fox holding a rabbit in its jaws, among other motifs.

"Once again, Stillman retreated to Riverside Park, this time to the edge of it, coming to rest on a knobby outcrop at 84th Street known as Mount Tom. On this same spot, in the summers of 1843 and 1844, Edgar Allan Poe had spent many long hours gazing out at the Hudson."
Paul Auster,
City of Glass

THE FORMER PYTHIAN TEMPLE
This building is one of the area's most interesting sights. Its façade offers a carefree mixture of ancient decorative styles (Sumerian, Assyrian, Egyptian) and has an unusual top, dominated by two colorful pharaohs.

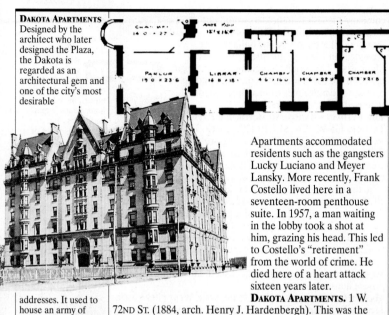

DAKOTA APARTMENTS Designed by the architect who later designed the Plaza, the Dakota is regarded as an architectural gem and one of the city's most desirable

addresses. It used to house an army of servants and provide a huge range of services to its rich residents. Roberta Flack, Leonard Bernstein and Judy Garland all lived here. Roman Polanski used it as the setting for his film *Rosemary's Baby* (1968). The Dakota was John Lennon's last address. In 1980 he was shot dead by a misfit as he stood under the hotel awning. His wife, Yoko Ono, still lives at the Dakota. The section of Central Park just opposite the hotel was landscaped at her request, including this mosaic (right) and is called Strawberry Fields, after the title of a Beatles song written by Lennon.

Apartments accommodated residents such as the gangsters Lucky Luciano and Meyer Lansky. More recently, Frank Costello lived here in a seventeen-room penthouse suite. In 1957, a man waiting in the lobby took a shot at him, grazing his head. This led to Costello's "retirement" from the world of crime. He died here of a heart attack sixteen years later.

DAKOTA APARTMENTS. 1 W. 72ND ST. (1884, arch. Henry J. Hardenbergh). This was the first residential luxury apartment house in New York, built by Edward Clark, president of the Singer Sewing Machine company. When people found out that he had decided on an Uptown site, many nicknamed the project, "Clark's folly". Why not in Dakota, in the Far West? asked one of his friends. Clark kept the name and had the building decorated with arrowheads, ears of corn and an Indian head over the main entrance.

SAN REMO APARTMENTS. 145–146 CENTRAL PARK WEST (1930, arch. Emery Roth). The actress Rita Hayworth lived until she died in 1987 in this luxury apartment building. A boat trip on Central Park lake probably affords the best view of the *San Remo* and its spectacular towers, each topped with a cupola (opposite).

NEW-YORK HISTORICAL SOCIETY. 170 CENTRAL PARK WEST (1908, arch. York & Sawyer). Founded in 1804 by New Yorkers keen to preserve the history of their city, the New-York Historical Society is a museum and reference library. Its permanent collections include three hundred watercolors by

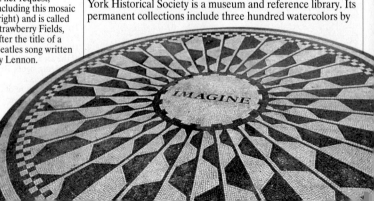

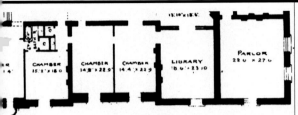

"HUDDLED TOGETHER ON THE NARROW ISLAND, THE BUILDINGS WITH THEIR THOUSAND WINDOWS WILL SOAR, SPARKLING . . . TOPS SURROUNDED BY WHITE CLOUDS, RISING ABOVE THE STORMS. . . ."

JOHN DOS PASSOS

Plans of the Dakota.

THE MUSEUM OF NATURAL HISTORY
This vast museum includes collections ranging from butterflies to dinosaurs, which are also shown in murals.

John James Audubon ▲ *361*, works by Thomas Cole and other members of the Hudson River School as well as a large collection of Tiffany glass and lamps ▲ *296*. Serious financial difficulties forced the museum to close temporarily in 1993.

AMERICAN MUSEUM OF NATURAL HISTORY. CENTRAL PARK WEST, BETWEEN 77TH AND 81 STS. (original wing 1872–7, arch. Calvert Vaux and J. Wrey Mould). Opened by President Ulysses S. Grant, the museum's original wing is now lost among an array of twenty-one later buildings. THE THEODORE ROOSEVELT MEMORIAL (1936, arch. John Russell Pope) now forms the main entrance of the museum, on Central Park West. The interior is decorated by murals depicting scenes

from the life of the former president, a great explorer who campaigned for the preservation of natural sites in the United States (such as the Grand Canyon). An equestrian statue standing outside (1940, James Earle Fraser) shows Roosevelt flanked by an Indian and an African to symbolize his "friendship for all races". This is one of the most visited museums in New York. The collections documenting Indian, African and Pacific civilizations, the dioramas of animal habitats, the lifesize reproduction of a blue whale and the Dinosaur Hall are particularly popular. THE HAYDEN PLANETARIUM (1935, arch. Trowbridge & Livingston) occupies the north wing of the museum, on 81st Street.

THE BERESFORD. 211 CENTRAL PARK WEST (1929, arch. Emery Roth). This huge luxury apartment building, designed by the architect who was responsible for the *San Remo* replaced a hotel of the same name on this site. Its main distinguishing characteristics are its three Baroque-style towers, which loom above Central Park.

FROM BROADWAY TO RIVERSIDE PARK

ANSONIA HOTEL. 2109 BROADWAY (1904, arch. Graves and Duboy). This Beaux Arts building has a sophisticated exterior, designed primarily by the French architect and sculptor Paul E. Duboy. Note the corner towers topped with domes and the many balconies. As a luxury hotel, it represented the height of modernity and was the first air-conditioned building in New York. Its excellent sound-proofing has attracted many musicians, including Stravinsky, Toscanini, Caruso, Chaliapin and Menuhin. Step into the lobby to see the display of photos retracing the Ansonia's glamorous history. These show that it once had two swimming pools, several shops, a fountain in the lobby with seals swimming in its basin and a roof garden

THE ANSONIA HOTEL
"It looks like a baroque palace from Prague or Munich enlarged a hundred times, with towers, domes, huge swells and bubbles . . . Under the changes of weather it may look like marble or like sea water, black as slate in the fog, white as tufa in sunlight.**"**
Saul Bellow,
Seize the Day

RIVERSIDE PARK
Riverside Drive, first
developed in the
1880's, has never
seriously rivaled 5th
Ave. as a fashionable
address, but the
proximity of
Riverside Park (right,
at the beginning of
the century) and its
magnificent views of
the Hudson River,
have ensured its
appeal for many New
Yorkers.

ALL THAT IS
NECESSARY FOR
THE TRIUMPH
OF EVIL IS FOR
GOOD PERSONS
TO DO NOTHING

EDMUND BURKE

**STATUE OF JOAN
OF ARC**
Riverside Drive and
W. 93rd St. This
statue, designed in
1915 by Anna Vaughn
Hyatt Huntington,
stands at the center of
Joan of Arc Park.
Some of the stones of
its pedestal come
from Rheims
Cathedral and others
from the tower in
Rouen where Joan of
Arc was imprisoned.

with a henhouse built by the owner who provided his guests
with fresh eggs.

COLLEGIATE CHURCH AND COLLEGIATE SCHOOL. 241 W. 77TH
ST. (1893, arch. Robert W. Gibson). The Collegiate Church's
gables, steeples and intricately worked dormer windows are a
reminder that it used to belong to the Dutch Reformed
Church, established in the United States in 1628. The
Collegiate School is no longer directly connected with the
church. This prestigious private boys' school is one of the
oldest schools in the United States.

APTHORP APARTMENTS. 2211
BROADWAY (1908, arch.
Clinton & Russell). Built by
William Waldorf Astor, this
Italian Renaissance-style
residential hotel, which covers
an entire block, attracted
wealthy boarders who wanted
to live on the Upper West Side. Its two large arched gateways
lead into a vast inner court with a decorative central fountain.

**RIVERSIDE DRIVE WEST 80TH–81ST STREETS HISTORIC
DISTRICT** (c. 1890). The thirty-two rowhouses that make up
this historic district were built by developers who were
reluctant to emulate the prevailing trend for residential
hotels. Note the embellishment of the ridgepoles and the
varied array of bow windows.

RIVERSIDE PARK. RIVERSIDE DRIVE, FROM 72ND TO 153RD
STS. (1873–1910, Frederick Law Olmsted). This is
Manhattan's other major park, after Central Park, designed
by the same landscape gardener. It covered the disused
tracks of the New York Central Railroad for a stretch
of seventy blocks. The riverside promenade, with its
small marina at 79th Street, running along the Hudson
between 72nd and 86th streets, is a worth a visit.

YESHIVA CHOFETZ CHAIM/FORMER VILLA JULIA. 346 W.
89TH ST. (1901, arch. Herts & Tallant). The former
home of Isaac L. Rice, who called it Villa
Julia after his wife, is one of the few
private mansions still standing on
Riverside Drive. Rice made his
fortune selling electric
batteries and made a name for
himself, in his later years, as
an outstanding chess player. His
house is now occupied by a Jewish
seminary (*Yeshiva* in Hebrew).

OFF THE BEATEN TRACK

MORNINGSIDE HEIGHTS AND
HARLEM, *350*
SETH KAMIL
THE CLOISTERS, *362*
MARY SHEPARD
BROOKLYN HEIGHTS, *366*
EDWARD O'DONNELL

🕱 Four hours

"I remember ... when you had to change trains at Washington and had to travel in a car for Blacks only – when you could not go to the dining car until all the Whites had finished. ... I don't mean that I want to eat with the Whites. It just makes life a

little easier – it may make my children's life a little easier. Perhaps that is all I want."

James Baldwin, *Harlem*

This itinerary includes Morningside Heights and Harlem – two adjacent neighborhoods which lie north of 110th Street and together run the width of Manhattan. The two areas present a dramatic contrast. Morningside Heights has various educational and religious establishments, notably Columbia University, Barnard College, Riverside Church and the huge and splendid Cathedral of St. John the Divine, reflecting the movement, that began in the 1890's, to make this part of town a spiritual and intellectual center.

Harlem's history is more checkered; it has a rich and varied past which dates back to the 17th century.

HISTORY. In 1658 Dutch farmers, attracted by the fertile soil, built the village of Nieuw Haarlem – named after a town in Holland – about 10 miles north of the main settlement, New Amsterdam. In the next century wealthy New Yorkers built country residences here. In 1837 the New York and Harlem railroad opened on 4th Avenue. This link, which ran from City Hall to the Harlem River transformed the village into a thriving suburb, whose western area acquired some fine

1 GENERAL GRANT NATIONAL MEMORIAL
2 RIVERSIDE CHURCH
3 UNION THEOLOGICAL SEMINARY
4 JEWISH THEOLOGICAL SEMINARY
5 BARNARD COLLEGE
6 AVERY HALL
7 LOW MEMORIAL LIBRARY
8 ST. PAUL'S EPISCOPAL CHAPEL
9 BUTLER LIBRARY
10 ST. JOHN THE DIVINE

116TH ST.

MORNINGSIDE AVE.

MORNINGSIDE PARK

MANHATTAN AVE.

110TH ST.

COLUMBUS AVE.

AMSTERDAM AVE.

CATHEDRAL PARKWAY

The trompe l'oeil façade of this Harlem house is a remnant of the elegance that prevailed here at the beginning of the 19th century.

❝Harlem, in New York, soon became the largest black community in the world; it became the symbol and the model of the city lifestyle that the Blacks, victims of segregation, were creating within their new group. Harlem ... formed a sort of urban frontier zone.❞

D. Boorstin

rowhouses. The building of the 3rd- and 2nd-Avenue elevated railways in 1879 led to the development of its eastern area with blocks of tenements inhabited by immigrants. The opening of the Lenox Avenue IRT subway in 1901 gave another boost to Harlem's growth.

THE BLACK COLONIZATION OF HARLEM.
Toward the end of the 1880's plummeting prices in this new district, caused by overly optimistic speculation by real estate developers, attracted an influx of poor Blacks. By 1920 200,000 Blacks were living in Harlem. This decade was the neighborhood's golden age, known to many as the "Harlem Renaissance"; Black musicians, intellectuals and writers came here in droves. However, the 1929 crash put an end to this revival.

THE 1960's. During this period Harlem became a center of political and social activism. The Black Muslims, led by Elijah Mohammed, founded the Temple of Islam on Lenox Avenue at 116th Street. Malcolm X worked there until 1964 before setting up his own organization. He was assassinated in February 1965 at the Audubon Ballroom on 165th Street. In 1968 Harlem was the scene of rioting by the Black residents, who were seeking social and economic justice.

COLUMBIA UNIVERSITY

STATUE OF THE ALMA MATER
Daniel Chester French's statue, completed in 1903, presides over the majestic staircase outside the Low Memorial Library. It personifies learning and knowledge.

SETH LOW
(1850–1916)
He was the Mayor of Brooklyn and, from 1890, President of Columbia University. He built the Low Memorial Library. In 1901, he was elected Mayor of New York.

Columbia University at the beginning of the century.

HISTORY. Founded in 1754 as King's College and renamed Columbia College after the War of Independence, Columbia University is now one of the oldest and largest universities in the country and one of the largest private landowners in New York, after the Catholic Church. Even in its infancy the college produced some distinguished citizens. Alexander Hamilton, the first secretary of the treasury; John Jay, the first chief justice of the Supreme Court, and Robert Livingston, the first secretary of foreign affairs, all graduated from King's College. More recently, both Theodore and Franklin D. Roosevelt attended the university's Law School. Dwight D. Eisenhower was president of the university from 1948 to 1953, before becoming President of the United States. Columbia University now has nearly 18,000 students and a faculty of 5,000. The campus is open to the public and guided tours can be arranged.

SEVERAL SITES. The first site of King's College was near Trinity Church ▲ *154* in Lower Manhattan. In 1857, it moved to Madison Avenue between 49th and 50th streets. It moved to its present site, bounded by 114th and 121st streets, Broadway and Amsterdam Avenue, in 1897. The plan and most of the original buildings on the campus were designed by McKim, Mead & White.

LOW MEMORIAL LIBRARY. (1897, arch. McKim, Mead & White). Low Memorial Library, standing in the middle of the campus and built in the

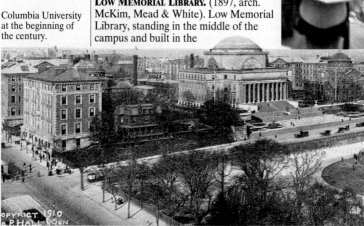

> "IT WAS REALLY HARLEM, AND ALL THE STORIES I HAD HEARD
> ABOUT THE CITY WITHIN THE CITY FLASHED INTO MY MIND."
> RALPH ELLISON

shape of a Greek cross, was the first building to be constructed on the campus. It has an exquisite Beaux Arts interior, featuring a vast rotunda capped with a dome, reminiscent of the Pantheon in Rome. The library was superseded by the Butler Library in 1934, and the building now houses the university's central administrative offices, as well as the COLUMBIANA LIBRARY COLLECTION, an assortment of documents, books and portraits relating to the university's history.

BUTLER LIBRARY. (1934, arch. James Gamble Rogers). Columbia University's main library is opposite the Low Memorial Library, on the southern side of the campus. Butler Library owes its name to Nicholas Murray Butler, president of the university from 1902 to 1945. With more than six million volumes, it is one of the largest libraries in the United States. Rogers was inspired by the Bibliothèque Sainte-Geneviève in Paris, designed by Henri Labrouste.

ST. PAUL'S EPISCOPAL CHAPEL. (1907, arch. Howells & Stokes). This nondenominational (formerly Episcopal) chapel, in the shape of a Greek cross, is situated east of Low Memorial Library. Its construction was financed by the family of Anson Phelps Stokes, a wealthy financier and philanthropist. Below the chapel, there is the Postcrypt, a small café-concert hall where students in the 1960's discovered the *Beat Generation* poet Jack Kerouac and the songs of the young Robert Zimmerman (Bob Dylan).

EAST HALL. BETWEEN LOW LIBRARY AND ST. PAUL'S EPISCOPAL CHAPEL (1878). This building, part of a former insane asylum, now houses the TEMPLE HOYNE BUELL CENTER FOR THE STUDY OF AMERICAN ARCHITECTURE as well as the MAISON FRANÇAISE OF COLUMBIA. On the lawn between East Hall and the Philosophy Department stands a replica of Rodin's *Thinker*, executed in 1930. Opposite stands Avery Hall and AVERY LIBRARY, the largest architecture library in the country. Although the campus as a whole is open to the public, you must have a Columbia University student card to get into the Butler and Avery libraries.

▲ MORNINGSIDE HEIGHTS AND HARLEM

1 GREEK AMPHITHEATER
2 GRAPHIC ARTS STUDIO
3 OMEGA LITURGICAL DANCE COMPANY
4 ENSEMBLE FOR EARLY MUSIC
5 HORIZON CONCERTS
6 SCULPTURE STUDIO
7 BIBLICAL GARDEN

At the beginning of the century, people were already impressed by the size of the cathedral, shown (below) under construction. When finished, Saint John the Divine will be the largest Gothic cathedral in the world, 601 feet long and 177 feet high under the nave.

ST. JOHN THE DIVINE ★

THE EPISCOPAL CATHEDRAL OF NEW YORK. This majestic cathedral stands on Amsterdam Avenue at 112th Street in Morningside Heights. Near this spot, on September 16, 1776, the patriot forces, under George Washington, defeated the British in the Battle of Harlem Heights, which took place during the War of Independence. In 1887, wishing to build a cathedral on a par with the finest in Europe, the Episcopal Diocese of New York paid an exorbitant sum of money for 15 acres of land and launched a competition for its design. Of the sixty entries, the winning plan was one for a Romanesque-style building submitted by the firm of Heins & La Farge.

A LONG AND DIFFICULT TASK. Work began on the cathedral in 1892, under the guidance of Bishop Henry Codman Potter; today, a century later, it still remains unfinished. The first phase, constructing the choir and the four arches of the great dome, took nearly twenty years. In 1916 the plans underwent radical changes; following the death of the two architects and Bishop Potter, it was decided to adopt plans by Cram & Ferguson for a Gothic-style cathedral. The construction of the nave did not start until 1925 after an appeal for contributions from the public, which

8 South Transept
10 Cathedral Works Exhibition
11 North Transept
9-12-13 Youth Program
14 School and Gymnasium
15 Soup Kitchen
3 Shops
17 Main Entrance
18 Poets' Corner
19 Piled Stone Area
20 Stone Court

The stonecutters have continued the Gothic tradition of depicting the world in which the cathedral exists by carving buildings on the pedestal of one of the central portal's statues.

raised $15 million. The first service was held in 1939. The work, disrupted by the war in 1941, was not resumed until 1979, under the guidance of Reverend Dean Morton. Today, the north and south transepts, the two west towers, the crossing, the roof of the choir and the sculptures for the central and south portals are still under construction. Young apprentices, many from the surrounding neighborhood, cut and carve the stone using techniques employed in the Middle Ages for building European cathedrals. One apprentice has carved the Manhattan skyline at the feet of one of the central portal's statues.

THE INTERIOR. The nave's fourteen bays symbolize the various spiritual and terrestrial vocations of mankind, while the seven chapels of the ambulatory, behind the choir, are each dedicated to a different ethnic group. The cathedral contains many works of art, including two 17th-century Gobelin tapestries. Before leaving the cathedral, be sure to visit the stoneyard, where you can watch the work in progress, the Biblical Garden and the Peace Fountain, which was created in 1985 by Greg Wyatt.

PEACE FOUNTAIN
This work illustrates the struggle between good and evil, embodied in the Archangel Michael and Satan. The giant crab symbolizes the sea and the origins of life, while the pedestal's double helix represents DNA, the genetic chain. The fountain is decorated with sixty small bronze animals, cast from children's works selected by competition.

▲ Morningside Heights and Harlem

"But when I opened my eyes we were turning into Riverside Drive. . . . To my right and ahead the church spire towered high, crowned with a red light of warning. And now we were passing the hero's tomb (Grant's Tomb) and I recalled a visit there. You went up the steps and inside and you looked far below to find him, at rest, draped flags . . .**"**

Ralph Ellison,
Invisible Man

BARNARD COLLEGE.

BETWEEN BROADWAY AND CLAREMONT AVE., 116TH AND 120TH STS. The campus of Barnard College, located west of the Columbia University campus, consists of nine buildings built between 1896 and 1988. The oldest wing is at 606 West 120th Street. The establishment was founded in 1889 as a women's college, affiliated with Columbia, which was at that point exclusively male (the first female students were admitted in 1983). Although Columbia now welcomes members of both sexes, Barnard College has proudly preserved its status as a women's college. It owes its name to Frederick A. P. Barnard, one of the first champions of equal rights for women in higher education.

NORTHERN MORNINGSIDE HEIGHTS

UNION THEOLOGICAL SEMINARY. BROADWAY, BETWEEN 120TH AND 122ND STS. (1910, arch. Allen & Collens). Some of the most eminent Protestant pastors in the United States – including Reinhold Niebuhr, who was professor of Christian ethics here between 1928 and 1960 – have been associated with this seminary, which was founded in 1836. Ask to visit the small garden within the cloisters and see the magnificent staircase.

JEWISH THEOLOGICAL SEMINARY. 3080 BROADWAY (1930, arch. Gehron, Ross, Alley). This seminary, founded in 1886 to train rabbis and theologians, has become the central institution of the American Jewish conservative movement. It boasts an immense Hebrew and Jewish library, a collection of rare books and documents relating to the Jewish community during the colonial period.

RIVERSIDE CHURCH ★. 490 RIVERSIDE DRIVE AND W. 120TH ST. (1930, arch. Allen & Collens, Henry C. Pelton). This neo-Gothic ● *86* church was founded by a Baptist congregation. It is now interdenominational and renowned for its liberalism and active involvement in community affairs. It was here, in 1967, that the Rev. Martin Luther King, Jr, gave his famous sermon, "It is time to break the silence", protesting against American intervention in Vietnam. Nelson Mandela was

UNION THEOLOGICAL SEMINARY. This building, designed by the architect of Riverside Church and Teachers College (on 120th St.), is based on the same theme with neo-Gothic ● *86* variations. It is one of the finest examples of the English Gothic style in New York.

> **"THE BEAUTY OF RIVERSIDE DRIVE, OVERLOOKING THE HUDSON, MAKES YOU WISH THAT NEW YORK COULD ONCE AGAIN BE WHAT IT WAS DURING DUTCH OCCUPATION, A SITE SURROUNDED BY WATER, WHOSE FINEST RESIDENCES STOOD ON THE RIVERSIDE".** P. MORAND

The Baptist Church, introduced in North America in the 17th century, became very popular, especially among Blacks. Here (left) a baptism in 1834 in the waters of the Hudson River.

CARILLON OF RIVERSIDE CHURCH
At the top of the church's bell tower is the Laura Spelman Rockefeller Memorial Carillon.

honored here in 1990, for his work in bringing an end to apartheid in South Africa. The interior of the church contains many remarkable works of art including some fine stained glass and a huge sculpture, *Christ in Majesty* by Jacob Epstein.

GENERAL GRANT NATIONAL MEMORIAL. RIVERSIDE DRIVE, NEAR W. 122ND ST. (1891–7, arch. John H. Duncan). Erected with funds raised by subscription, this tomb is the final resting place of Ulysses S. Grant (1822–85), commander-in-chief of the Union Armies during the Civil War and President of the United States from 1869 to 1877, and of his wife Julia. This shrine is a reconstruction of the tomb of King Mausolus in Halicarnassus (in modern-day Turkey), one of the seven wonders of the ancient world. The words spoken by Grant when he was nominated for President ("Let us have peace") are engraved above the entrance, flanked by allegories of Victory and Peace. The design of the tomb itself, clad in red marble, was modeled on Napoleon's tomb at the Hôtel des Invalides in Paris. The five busts on the colonnade, carved in 1938, portray the generals who served under Grant during the Civil War: Sherman, Thomas, McPherson, Ord and Sheridan. Three mosaics (1966, Allyn Cox) represent the Battle of Vicksburg, his first great victory; the Battle of Chattanooga, his first as commander of all the armies in the West and, between them, Grant and Lee shaking hands to seal the surrender of the Confederacy at Appomattox. More than one million people followed Grant's funeral procession on August 8, 1885. He has gone down in history as the man who saved the nation and restored peace; but he was more successful as a general than as President, as he failed in his attempts to rebuild the South and integrate Blacks into American society. His term of office was tainted by corruption.

Its 20-ton great bell, the largest in the world, and its 74 other bells cover a range of more than five octaves.

BLACK LEADERS
The clergy has often provided political leaders for the Black community, such as, in New York, Adoui Clayton Powell Jr. of the Abyssinian Baptist Church in Harlem and, more recently, Reverends Calvin O. Butts, Al Sharpton and Herbert Daughtry (below).

357

Tom-toms in the African Market, along 125th St., between Adam Clayton Powell Jr. Blvd. and 5th Ave.

THE HEART OF HARLEM

APOLLO THEATER. 253 W. 125TH ST. (1914, arch. George Keister). When this theater first opened it was a burlesque house for Whites only. In 1934, when its new owners, Leo Brecher and Frank Schiffman, opened it to Blacks, it became extremely popular, offering top-flight entertainment. Bessie Smith, "the Empress of the Blues", and Billie Holiday performed here in the 1930's. Duke Ellington and Count Basie played here in the 1940's as did Charlie Parker and Dizzie Gillespie, the fathers of bebop ● *60*. Many other artists, including Aretha Franklin and the Jackson Five, have since appeared on the bill. The Apollo Theater closed in 1976 for financial reasons, but reopened ten years later.

The African Market, which sells a wide variety of Afro-American products.

THERESA TOWERS, FORMER THERESA HOTEL. 2090 ADAM CLAYTON POWELL JR. BD. (1910, arch. George and Edward Blum). Built at a time when racial segregation was still widely practiced in New York, this establishment was reserved for Black customers, since Blacks, however wealthy, could not stay at most other New York hotels. It soon became one of the most popular haunts in Harlem. Years later it welcomed Fidel Castro, who stayed here in 1960, when he came to New York to speak before the United Nations General Assembly, and also Nikita Khrushchev. Malcolm X moved his offices into the hotel shortly before he was assassinated in 1965. The hotel was converted into offices in 1971.

MARCUS GARVEY MEMORIAL PARK. BETWEEN MOUNT MORRIS PARK W. AND MADISON AVE., 120TH AND 124TH STS. This was called Mount Morris Park when it was opened in 1839, and renamed in 1973 in homage to Marcus Garvey, the West Indian leader of the *Back to Africa* movement in the early 20th century. This park was built when it proved impossible to move the enormous central rock obstructing 5th Avenue. A fire watchtower, then visible from Madison Avenue, was built in 1855 on top of this promontory. This is the last of the city's many fire towers.

"We have not lost the habit of jostling in the market place, buying and selling, selling and buying. We like trading. We are born with the gift. We love it. The city is itself a huge market. You can't go more than a few steps without finding a store of some sort. We are all potential entrepreneurs, looking to make a deal in this country of commerce.**"**

Jerome Charyn,
Metropolis

SYLVIA'S RESTAURANT. 328 LENOX AVE. This Harlem institution has been serving Afro-American cooking for thirty years now. Its walls are covered with photos of famous Black Americans and with murals. The riot of August 1, 1943 broke out in this area when a White policeman shot a Black soldier. Thousands of Blacks poured into the streets, overturning cars, ransacking stores belonging to Whites and starting a number of fires.

SCHOMBURG CENTER FOR RESEARCH IN BLACK CULTURE. 515 LENOX AVE. (1978, arch. Bond Ryder Assocs.). This is one of the largest branches of the New York Public Library ▲ 252. It owes its name to Arthur A. Schomburg (1874–1938), a Black Puerto Rican who collected documents on Afro-American culture after being told at school that the Blacks had no history. THE CARNEGIE CORPORATION OF NEW YORK bought his collection in 1926 and employed him as the curator. The Schomburg Center is now – with some 75,000 books, 300,000 photographs and a collection of musical recordings – the largest historical collection devoted to all peoples of African descent in the world.

ABYSSINIAN BAPTIST CHURCH. 132 W. 138TH ST. (1923, arch. Charles W. Bolton). The church, whose name is a constant reminder to parishioners of their African heritage, was founded in 1808 on Worth Street, and was moved when the congregation migrated northward. Its main claim to fame is its former preacher, Adam Clayton Powell Jr (1908–72), elected to the House of Representations in 1945. He presented bills in favor of education and civil rights, campaigning in particular for a minimum wage and the abolition of racial segregation in the army. This church boasts one of the finest gospel choirs in Harlem.

ST. NICHOLAS HISTORIC DISTRICT. 138TH AND 139TH STS., BETWEEN ADAM CLAYTON POWELL, JR, AND FREDERICK DOUGLASS BLVDS. These rowhouses from 1891, grouped around a communal backyard, were built for middle-class Whites, but began to be occupied by Black middle-class families from 1919. As a result the district was nicknamed "Striver's Row". W. C. Handy, Noble Sissle and Eubie Blake – all famous jazz musicians – lived here.

THE AMERICAN NEGRO THEATRE
PRESENTS

"ANGEL STREET"
by Patrick Hamilton
Staged and Directed by Stanley Greene

"ANGEL STREET"
In 1943, at the same time as rioting broke out in the Black ghettos, a new style of music was born. It spread throughout the country and all over the world. Below, from left to right: Coleman Hawkins, Benny Harris, Don Byas, Thelonius Monk, Denzil Best, Eddie Robinson, photographed in 1944.

▲ HAMILTON AND WASHINGTON HEIGHTS

1 ST. JOHN THE DIVINE
2 LOW MEMORIAL LIBRARY
3 BARNARD COLLEGE
4 RIVERSIDE CHURCH
5 GENERAL GRANT NATIONAL MEMORIAL
6 THERESA TOWERS
7 APOLLO THEATER
8 HAMILTON GRANGE
9 THE CLOISTERS
10 DYCKMAN HOUSE
11 MORRIS-JUMEL MANSION
12 ABYSSINIAN BAPTIST CHURCH
13 SCHOMBURG CENTER
14 HARLEM STATE OFFICE BLDG.

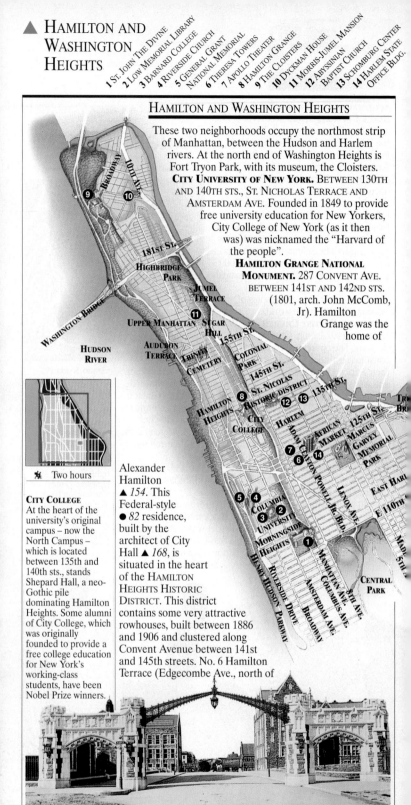

HAMILTON AND WASHINGTON HEIGHTS

These two neighborhoods occupy the northmost strip of Manhattan, between the Hudson and Harlem rivers. At the north end of Washington Heights is Fort Tryon Park, with its museum, the Cloisters.

CITY UNIVERSITY OF NEW YORK. BETWEEN 130TH AND 140TH STS., ST. NICHOLAS TERRACE AND AMSTERDAM AVE. Founded in 1849 to provide free university education for New Yorkers, City College of New York (as it then was) was nicknamed the "Harvard of the people".

HAMILTON GRANGE NATIONAL MONUMENT. 287 CONVENT AVE. BETWEEN 141ST AND 142ND STS. (1801, arch. John McComb, Jr). Hamilton Grange was the home of Alexander Hamilton ▲ 154. This Federal-style ● 82 residence, built by the architect of City Hall ▲ 168, is situated in the heart of the HAMILTON HEIGHTS HISTORIC DISTRICT. This district contains some very attractive rowhouses, built between 1886 and 1906 and clustered along Convent Avenue between 141st and 145th streets. No. 6 Hamilton Terrace (Edgecombe Ave., north of

🏃 Two hours

CITY COLLEGE
At the heart of the university's original campus – now the North Campus – which is located between 135th and 140th sts., stands Shepard Hall, a neo-Gothic pile dominating Hamilton Heights. Some alumni of City College, which was originally founded to provide a free college education for New York's working-class students, have been Nobel Prize winners.

360

> **"I** WILL BUY YOU THE FINEST HOUSE
> AT THE TOP OF THE FIFTH
> AND WE WILL GET MERRY
> THROUGH THE STREETS OF HARLEM.**"** G. GERSHWIN

145th Street) is occupied by Aunt Len's Doll and Toy Museum (temporarily closed).

SUGAR HILL. SUGAR HILL BETWEEN ST. NICHOLAS AND EDGECOMBE AVES., 143RD TO 155TH STS. This district used to be called Sugar Hill because its affluent Black residents had finally earned their place in the sun and the right to a "sweet life in Harlem". Duke Ellington and Cab Calloway, the Black leader W. E. B. DuBois and the writer Langston Hughes all lived along Edgecombe Avenue.

FROM AUDUBON TERRACE TO THE CLOISTERS

TRINITY CEMETERY. BETWEEN AMSTERDAM AVE. AND RIVERSIDE DRIVE, 153RD AND 155TH STS. This cemetery ▲ *154*, straddles Broadway. The entrance, on Riverside Drive, leads into the western part, which affords a magnificent view of the Hudson River and the George Washington Bridge. Clement Clarke Moore, author of "A Visit from Saint Nicholas", is buried in the eastern part of the cemetery and every Christmas eve a children's choir sings carols around his tomb.

AUDUBON TERRACE HISTORIC DISTRICT. BROADWAY, BETWEEN 155TH AND 156TH STS. (1908–30, arch. Charles Pratt Huntington and others). This is a group of museums clustered around a central courtyard in which stands a statue of El Cid (1927, Anna Hyatt Huntington). The AMERICAN ACADEMY OF ARTS AND LETTERS houses manuscripts, paintings, sculpture, and musical scores by its members, who are some of America's most respected artists. The HISPANIC SOCIETY OF AMERICA, devoted to the art, culture and history of Spain and Latin America, contains works by El Greco, Velázquez, Goya and Picasso. The AMERICAN NUMISMATIC SOCIETY is a museum of coins and civil and military decorations. Audubon Terrace was once the site of the MUSEUM OF THE AMERICAN INDIAN, founded in 1916, which possesses a magnificent collection of art and crafts made by America's Indian cultures. This is moving to the former U. S. Custom House ▲ *157* at Bowling Green.

MORRIS-JUMEL MANSION ● *82* ★. N. W. CORNER OF 160TH ST. AND EDGECOMBE AVE. (1765, remodeled in 1810). This superb residence gives an impression of the way rich New Yorkers lived two centuries ago. It was built in the Georgian style ● *82* by a British colonel, Roger Morris. During the War of Independence Washington used it briefly as his headquarters before it fell into British hands.

DYCKMAN HOUSE. ● *82* ★. 4881 BROADWAY AT N. W. CORNER OF 204TH ST. (1784). East of the Cloisters stands the last colonial farmhouse in Manhattan. It once belonged to a family of Dutch settlers, the Dyckmans, who settled here in 1661. After the War of Independence, during which the British burned down the original farmhouse, the Dyckmans built the house that stands today. Saved from demolition in 1916, it is now a museum, evoking rural life during the colonial period.

TRINITY CEMETERY
This covers a section of the land that once belonged to the naturalist and artist John James Audubon (1785–1851), who is buried in the eastern part, behind the Church of the Intercession.

MORRIS-JUMEL MANSION
This house has one of the finest Georgian interiors in New York. In 1810 Stephen Jumel, a wealthy merchant of French origin, related to Bonaparte's family, bought the house and remodeled it. In particular, he added the Federal-style entrance. After his death, his widow, Eliza Jumel, married Aaron Burr. She lived here until her death in 1865.

361

A part of the Metropolitan Museum of Art, the Cloisters was established in 1938 and is devoted exclusively to European art of the Middle Ages. On entering this building, with its powerful medieval style of architecture, the visitor is immediately immersed in the past. Here, medieval treasures, notably the architectural fragments, are sympathetically installed.

The flexible plan enabled the architects to incorporate the Romanesque apse from the escheated church of Fuentadueña in Spain. Composed of nearly three thousand slabs of pale limestone, it was dismantled stone by stone, brought back to New York and carefully reassembled.

This 14th-century Italian diptych, entitled *Crucifixion and Lamentation*, is one of the many works of medieval painting in the Cloisters.

The museum has many precious works of art such as *Saint John the Evangelist*, a Carolingian ivory (c. 800).

This silver ewer is a gem of medieval decorative art. (German, c. 1500).

COLLECTOR AND PATRON OF THE ARTS John D. Rockefeller, Jr, financed this building, which stands on top of a hill in Fort Tryon Park, (above), in Upper Manhattan. His own gifts and the acquisition, in 1925, of the collection owned by George Grey Barnard, an American sculptor living in France, formed the nucleus of the museum's collection, which has grown considerably since then.

Another masterpiece of European art, a *Virgin and Child* from 12th-century Burgundy.

The museum is so called because fragments of four medieval cloisters have been incorporated into the modern structure. The floral gardens in the cloisters of Cuxa, Bonnefont and Trie often include the same plants as those listed in inventories compiled in the Middle Ages. The cloister of Saint-Guilhem-le-Désert encloses a winter garden.

THE CLOISTERS

THE ANNUNCIATION
The Annunciation, a triptych by Robert Campin (c. 1425), clearly illustrates the convergence of religious and secular themes.

Although the symbolism of the *Annunciation* is still medieval, the treatment anticipates the Renaissance.

Manuscript from the end of the 15th century (below).

The 12th-century cloister from Saint-Michel-de-Cuxa (left), in the Pyrenees, is completely made of marble.

The rosary bead above, made of boxwood, dates back to the early 16th century.

J. P. Morgan's generosity was not limited to financing the construction of the Cloisters; he also endowed the museum with more than forty pieces from his own collection. Among the most important of these are the Unicorn Tapestries (right).

The famous Unicorn Tapestries, seven hangings (above, the *Unicorn at the Fountain*) probably designed in Paris and woven in Brussels c. 1500, represent the symbolic quest for this mythical animal.

One of the capitals from the cloister of Saint-Michel-de-Cuxa.

LIGHT AND COLOR
The nucleus of the building is made up of fragments of cloister arcading from Barnard's collection. The Cloisters' many windows are glazed with stained glass, resplendent when bathed in natural light, like the panels from Saint Leonhard, in Austria, created c. 1340–50, or these Rhenish stained-glass windows (left) dating from 1440–7.

George Grey Barnard bought medieval architectural elements from farmers and magistrates who had salvaged them in monasteries and churches damaged during the 16th-century wars of religion, then abandoned during the French Revolution. Although Barnard sold some of his acquisitions to subsidize his work as a sculptor, he exhibited the others in New York to introduce Americans to the mastery of what he called the "patient Gothic chisel".

"If those who come under the influence of this place go out to face life with a new courage and restored faith because of the peace, the calm, the loveliness they have found here . . . those who have built here will not have builded [sic] in vain.**"**

John D. Rockefeller

365

▲ Brooklyn Heights

View of the Fulton
Ferry Building in
Brooklyn, in June
1857.

**WILLIAMSBURG
SAVINGS BANK TOWER**
This skyscraper,
which was erected
during the 1929 crisis
and is the tallest
building in Brooklyn,
is reminiscent of a
Byzantine church,
with its mosaics,
carved capitals and its
vault (below) three
stories high. The
counters on the
ground floor are
small votive chapels.
Where the altar
would be a large
mosaic depicts an
aerial view of the city
of New York with
Brooklyn and the
Williamsburg Savings
Bank Tower in the
center.

Founded in 1657 by Dutch settlers, Brooklyn (after Breuckelen, a small town in the Utrecht region) is now the most densely populated borough of New York after Manhattan. The district of Brooklyn Heights, a headland that overlooks the East River, grew considerably after 1814, when Robert Fulton established a steam ferry service, which allowed people to cross the river more quickly than via the existing boats. The wealthy inhabitants moved out of Brooklyn Heights after the Brooklyn Bridge ▲ 186 was opened in 1883; Brooklyn was joined with Manhattan in 1898 and the first subway line was created in 1908. The elegant mansions were converted into apartments and the area lost some of its former charm. Today, about half of the houses date from before 1860 and most were restored some fifteen years ago.

BROOKLYN BOROUGH HALL, FORMER BROOKLYN CITY HALL 209 JORALEMON ST. AND CADMAN PLAZA (1846–51, Gamaliel King). Brooklyn's former city hall was designed by a carpenter; at the time, few public buildings were designed by architects. When Brooklyn became part of New York in 1898, the city hall was renamed Borough Hall and given a cupola, after the fashion of City Hall ▲ 168.

MONTAGUE STREET ★. With its many restaurants, stores, office buildings, small houses, and its church – ST. ANN'S AND THE HOLY TRINITY at no. 157 – Montague Street has an almost European-style charm. It was once nicknamed "Bank Avenue" because of the predominance of financial establishments. Note in particular, at no. 185, the FORMER NATIONAL TILE GUARANTY BUILDING, in Art Deco style (1930, arch. Corbett, Harrison and MacMurray). By the early 1920's, at the intersection of Flatbush and Atlantic avenues, there were so many trolley lines that all Brooklynites were called "trolley dodgers", thus the name of the legendary baseball team, the Dodgers (now in Los Angeles).

BROOKLYN HISTORICAL SOCIETY 128 PIERREPONT ST. AT S. W. CORNER OF CLINTON ST. (1878, arch. George B. Post). This society was founded in 1863 and opened to the public in 1880. It contains a remarkable collection documenting the history of Brooklyn, the city and the State of New York, and has one of the best genealogical research libraries in the country. Busts of Christopher Columbus and Benjamin Franklin decorate the façade.

**BROOKLYN HEIGHTS
ESPLANADE.** (1951)
Built to cover the
Brooklyn-Queens
expressway and lined
with houses and
gardens, this
promenade affords a
magnificent view of
Manhattan, the bay of
New York and the
Brooklyn Bridge.

TOWARD PROSPECT PARK

BROOKLYN MUSEUM. EASTERN PARKWAY AND WASHINGTON AVE. (1897, arch. McKim, Mead & White). This museum possesses a large collection of documents and various objects relating to the American Indians, as well as a magnificent collection of Egyptian art, which is considered one of the best collections in the States. The entrance to this neo-classical building is through a superb porch that is embellished with statues (depicting Manhattan and Brooklyn) designed by Daniel Chester French (1916).

PRACTICAL INFORMATION

Big apple

USEFUL INFORMATION, *368*
TRAVELING TO NEW YORK, *370*
FROM NORTH TO SOUTH, *372*
POINTS OF INTEREST, *374*
BUSES, TAXIS, LIMOUSINES, *375*
THE SUBWAY, *376*
MONEY, *378*
LIVING IN NEW YORK, *380*
TELEPHONE AND
POSTAL SYSTEMS, *381*
EXCURSIONS, *382*
PARKS AND GARDENS, *384*
IMAGES OF THE CITY, *386*
"TIME IS MONEY", *390*
LISTINGS, *391*
USEFUL ADDRESSES, *402*
NOTES, *428*

Even though for most visitors, New York City is synonymous with Manhattan, the city has, since 1898, been made up of five boroughs: Manhattan, Brooklyn, the Bronx, Queens and Staten Island. (A poll carried out on November 2, 1993, however, showed that Staten Islanders have begun to question whether their borough should be part of New York City at all.) Although the 13-mile-long island of Manhattan is the geographical heart of New York City, its 1.5 million inhabitants account for less than 20 percent of New York's total population.

CONSULATES

◆ CANADA
1251 Ave. of the Americas
Tel. 596-1700

◆ CHINA
520 12th Ave.
Tel. 868-7752

◆ FRANCE
934 5th Ave.
Tel. 606-3600

◆ GERMANY
460 Park Ave.
Tel. 308-8700

◆ ITALY
690 Park Ave.
Tel. 737-9100

◆ JAPAN
299 Park Ave.
Tel. 371-8222

◆ SPAIN
150 East 58th St.
Tel. 355-4090

◆ U.K.
845 3rd Ave.
Tel. 745-0202

FORMALITIES

United Kingdom citizens do not need a visa for holidays and business trips under 90 days. They must hold a valid passport and a return ticket (not essential for anyone entering the city overland), as well as adequate financial resources for their proposed stay in the United States. No vaccinations are needed for entry. You must have a visa for visits over 90 days, whether for study or business.

INTERNATIONAL STUDENT CARDS

An international student membership card enables students to obtain reductions on the price of airline tickets and admission to museums and various cultural events. It also ensures reimbursement for some kinds of medical treatment. Available from S.T.A Travel, Priory House, 6 Wrights Lane, London W8. Tel: 071 937 9971

MEDICAL INSURANCE

It is advisable to take out a personal medical insurance policy before your departure. Medical treatment is prohibitively expensive in the United States, many hospitals will not treat uninsured patients and no agreement exists with the Social Security office. Cover may be provided as an extra by your Visa or MasterCard accounts. Banks and travel agencies also have their own policies.

NEW YORK CITY MARATHON

This takes place in early November. New Yorkers line the race course to cheer on the 26,000 competitors, who run from Staten Island to the Tavern on the Green in Central Park, crossing the Verrazano Bridge, parts of Brooklyn, Queens and the Bronx. Domestic applicants should send a check for $6 payable to 'New York Road Runners Club', along with a self-addressed envelope to: Marathon Entries, P.O. Box 1388 GPO, New York, NY 10116. Foreign applicants should send a self-addressed envelope to Int'l Entries, P.O. Box 1766 GPO, New York, NY 10116. Some travel agencies are authorized to sell "competitor's number included" deals: more pricy, but a safer bet.

SPRING — March to May

The city is flooded with light, its inhabitants are invigorated by the sea air. The season of street fairs and parades begins.

MARCH 17	ST PATRICK'S DAY PARADE, 5th Ave. and Saint Patrick's Cathedral
EASTER SUNDAY	EASTER PARADE, 5th Ave.,44th-59th sts.
LAST MON. MAY, public holiday	MEMORIAL DAY

★ Have breakfast in the South St. Seaport.

MARCH 30°///46°
APRIL 43°☁61°
MAY 54°☀70°

SUMMER — June to August

The weather is hot and humid, New Yorkers escape to Long Island, the streets are packed with tourists and musicians perform in the parks.

2ND TUES., JUNE (6-9PM)	MUSEUM MILE FESTIVAL, FREE ADMISSION TO MUSEUMS, 5th Ave. (82nd-105th sts.)
JUNE, JULY AND AUGUST	FREE CONCERTS BY THE METROPOLITAN OPERA AND THE NEW YORK PHILHARMONIC, Parks and Great Lawn of Central Park
JUNE, JULY AND AUGUST	SHAKESPEARE IN THE PARK Delacorte Theater, Central Park (free)
END JUNE, BEGINNING JULY	JAZZ FESTIVAL
JULY 4, public holiday	INDEPENDENCE DAY, Firework display on the East River Best view from FDR Drive (14th-51st sts.)

★ Visit the Cloisters or the Botanical Garden.

JUNE 63°/81° ☁
JULY 70°/82° ☀
AUGUST 66°/79° ☀

FALL — September to November

An incredible wave of energy is unleashed by the mild fall weather in New York. There is no better time of year to fall under New York's spell.

SEPTEMBER	US OPEN TENNIS TOURNAMENT, Flushing Meadows
1ST MON., SEPTEMBER, public holiday	LABOR DAY WEST INDIAN AMERICAN DAY CARNIVAL, Departs from the Brooklyn Museum
2ND MON., OCTOBER, public holiday	COLUMBUS DAY
OCTOBER 31	HALLOWEEN, Fancy dress parade in Greenwich Village. Free sweets for the children!
OCTOBER OR NOVEMBER	NEW YORK CITY MARATHON
NOVEMBER 11, public holiday	VETERANS' DAY
4TH THURS. NOVEMBER, public holiday	THANKSGIVING DAY, Parade along Central Park West and Broadway

★ The Thanksgiving turkey (4 lb) eaten at this family occasion.

SEPTEMBER 61°/73° ☁
OCTOBER 54°/63° ☁
NOVEMBER 43°/52° ☁

WINTER — December to February

The East Coast is besieged by cold weather and snow and legendary storms occasionally bring everything to a standstill. But this city never sleeps!

DECEMBER 25, public holiday	CHRISTMAS
JANUARY 1, public holiday	
END JANUARY, BEGINNING FEBRUARY	CHINESE NEW YEAR, Chinatown
3RD MON. JANUARY, public holiday	MARTIN LUTHER KING'S DAY
FEBRUARY12, public holiday	LINCOLN'S BIRTHDAY
3RD MON. FEBRUARY, public holiday	PRESIDENT'S DAY

★ An ideal time to visit the museums!

DECEMBER 30°/39° ❄
JANUARY 28°/39° ❄
FEBRUARY 28°/41° ❄

☀ warm and sunny   ☁ changeable to cloudy   ☁ rainy   ❄ cold, possible snow

The minimum and maximum temperatures for each month are given in degrees Fahrenheit.

AIR TRAVEL

In high season there are 28 direct flights a day to New York from London Heathrow and Gatwick. The main carriers are British Airways (including Concorde), Continental, United, Virgin Atlantic, American Airlines and Air India. Some of these also offer direct flights from other UK cities, such as Glasgow and Manchester. From Paris, Air France offer a good service; from Rome, try Alitalia; from Bonn, Lufthansa have competitive rates; Nippon offer flights from Tokyo to New York and Air Canada operate from all major Canadian cities.

◆ British Airways 156 Regent Street London W1R 5TA Tel. 081 897 4000 C'tral Booking Office: Tel. 0345 222111

◆ American Airlines 23-59 Staines Road, Hounslow, TW3. Tel:081 572 5555

◆ Virgin Atlantic Unit 8, Radius Park, Faggs Road, Feltham, TW14. Tel: 081 890 0090 or 081 890 4411

◆ United Airlines United House Building, 451 Southern Perimeter Road, Heathrow Airport, London TW6. Tel: 081 990 9900

BY SEA

The *Queen Elizabeth II*, last of the great liners, crosses the Atlantic five times a year, leaving from Cherbourg, Liverpool and Southampton. The journey takes five days (from £1245 return per person). The Cunard Line Ltd, 30 Pall Mall, London SW1. Tel: 071 839 1414 or 071 930 4321.

BY AIR

New York City has three main airports: John F. Kennedy International Airport, Newark International Airport and La Guardia Airport, which handles internal flights exclusively. Many London–New York flights leave London around lunchtime and land in New York in the early afternoon, local time, after a journey of eight hours. Return flights tend to leave New York in the evening and arrive in London in the early hours of the following morning. The price of a standard economy-class return ticket from London to New York is rarely under £430. Charter flights are cheaper (between £200 and £320). Economy-class or excursion return tickets to New York from other areas can generally be found at the following rates (given in dollars): Paris $1992; Rome $1242; Bonn $600; Tokyo $1350; Ottawa $250.

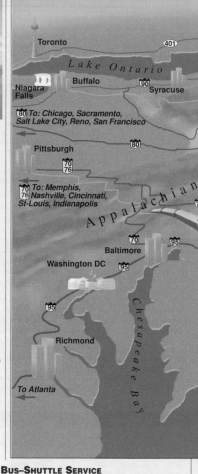

BY CONCORDE

This prestigious airplane leaves London's Heathrow airport daily (Terminal 4). The flight takes only four hours and a round-trip ticket costs $6319.
Tel: 0345 222100 for reservations. Air France's Concorde travels between Charles de Gaulle airport in Paris and J.F.K. airport daily. The least expensive one-way ticket costs $3106, while round trip costs $6213. Call 010 331 44-08-22-22 or 212-247-0100 for reservations.

BUS–SHUTTLE SERVICE

The three New York airports are all situated within a 16-mile radius of Manhattan and can all be reached by bus. The Carey Airport Express company provides a regular shuttle service (every 20–30 mins; no service between 1am and 5am) between Kennedy and La Guardia, and six drop-off points in Midtown Manhattan: opposite Grand Central Terminal (125 Park Avenue), the Hilton, Sheraton Manhattan, Holiday Inn Crown Plaza and Marriott Marquis hotels, and the Port Authority Bus Terminal. The Olympia Airport Express provides a similar service (every 20–30 mins; no service between 11pm and 5am) between Newark and Manhattan. Buses stop at Pennsylvania Station, Grand Central Terminal and the World Trade Center. The Gray Line Air Shuttle is slightly more expensive but provides a door-to-door service between these three airports and Manhattan, from 23rd Street to 63rd Street. Heading out to the airports from Manhattan it picks up passengers from sixty different hotels across Midtown.

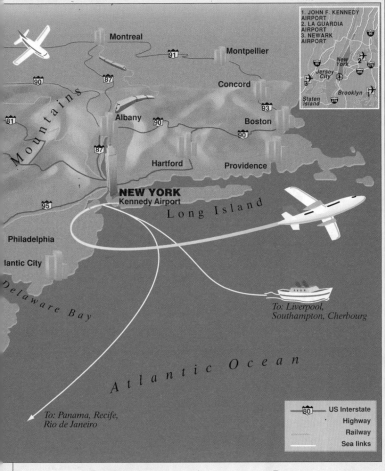

Montreal

Montpellier

Concord

91

87

90

Albany

90

Boston

81

87

90

Hartford   Providence

NEW YORK
Kennedy Airport

Long Island

95

Philadelphia

lantic City

Delaware Bay

Atlantic Ocean

To: Liverpool,
Southampton, Cherbourg

To: Panama, Recife,
Rio de Janeiro

1. JOHN F. KENNEDY
AIRPORT
2. LA GUARDIA
AIRPORT
3. NEWARK
AIRPORT

New York

Jersey City

Staten Island

Brooklyn

	US Interstate
80	Highway
	Railway
	Sea links

BY CAR

Access to Manhattan from the west and south is via the New Jersey Turnpike (I-95). From the east, take the Lincoln or the Holland Tunnels (into Midtown), and from the north, take the George Washington Bridge. The New England Thruway (I-95) connects the Triborough Bridge and the Cross Bronx Expressway. Highway I-87, from the north, also connects with the Triborough Bridge, the other bridges over the Harlem and the East River. Two expressways run the length of Manhattan: the West Side Highway along the Hudson and Franklin D. Roosevelt Drive, along the East River.

BY BUS

All "long distance" buses terminate at the Port Authority Bus Terminal (W. 41st St./8th Ave., Tel. 564-8484).

Greyhound Trailways (tel. 1-800-231-2222) is the best company to use for long bus journeys to Manhattan.

BY TRAIN

Manhattan has two stations:
Pennsylvania Station (7th Ave./W. 34th St.) and Grand Central Terminal (42nd St./Park Ave. South). Amtrak trains run between Pennsylvania Station and many cities in the United States and Canada. An express train, the Metroliner, links Washington to New York and Boston. A one-way (single) ticket from Chicago to New York costs about $130, from Washington or Montreal to New York about $70.
◆ Amtrak
Tel. 582-6875 or 1-800-USA-Rail (toll free 381). Trains from Grand Central Terminal run to all stations in Westchester County and Connecticut.

◆ POINTS OF INTEREST

At first glance visitors may find Manhattan overwhelmingly large and confusing, but most of its streets and avenues have numbers, not names, forming a straightforward, logical system. Above 14th Street the avenues, which run north to south, form a right angle with the streets, which run east to west. Only in the older part of Manhattan, below 14th Street, where the streets twist and turn as they do in European cities, will you need a map to find your way around.

AVENUES

Most avenues are numbered from east to west, although there are exceptions. On the East Side, Lexington, Park and Madison avenues are sandwiched, in that order, between 3rd and 5th avenues. In the East Village, four small avenues (A, B, C and D) lead to the neighborhood east of 1st Avenue. On the West Side, 6th Avenue is officially called the Avenue of the Americas, and on the Upper West Side, 8th, 9th, 10th and 11th avenues become, respectively, Central Park West, Columbus, Amsterdam and West End avenues. Building numbers increase from south to north, but because of the avenues' length, addresses will also give the relevant cross street.

THE SUN

On a sunny day it is easy to get your bearings in Manhattan (above 14th Street). In the morning, if the sun is to your right, you are facing uptown; in the afternoon, if it is to your right, you are facing downtown.

STREETS

Streets are numbered from south to north. 5th Avenue is the dividing line between the West Side and the East Side in Manhattan, so that a street with a given number is designated "West" or "East" to either side of it. It is easy to find a street address: apartment building numbers start on 5th Avenue, and increase by a hundred for every block, whatever the direction. 244 W. 38th Street, therefore, is between 7th and 8th avenues. Traffic generally travels eastward on even-numbered streets and westward on odd-numbered streets. On few, wider crosstown streets traffic moves in both directions. As a rule, even-numbered buildings line the south side of the street and odd-numbered buildings the north.

UPTOWN, MIDTOWN AND DOWNTOWN

When New Yorkers refer to Uptown, they are talking about neighborhoods north of 59th Street (the Upper East Side, Upper West Side and Central Park). Heading uptown means going north. Midtown is the part of the city between 14th and 59th streets. Downtown covers the south of the city from 14th Street (from Greenwich Village to the Financial District). Heading downtown means going south.

EAST SIDE/WEST SIDE

North of 59th Street and south of 110th, Central Park divides the Upper East Side from the Upper West Side. On the south side of 59th Street the dividing line between East Side and West Side is 5th Avenue.

BLOCKS

Distances are estimated in blocks (shorter north-south than east-west). There are about twenty blocks (north-south) to one mile.

STREET SIGNS

Most street names are given in white on a green background. Streets or squares named after famous figures or particular activities may appear on blue or brown signposts.

Although traffic can be a nightmare in Manhattan, particularly between 8am and 6pm, traveling by bus, taxi or perhaps limousine, is a fascinating way to see the city at close quarters. The buses (usually air-conditioned) are a welcome alternative to the subway. They are extremely handy for traveling from east to west (via the wide crosstown streets), which is not so easy by subway. The yellow taxis – there are nearly 12,000 licensed by the city – are easy to find and not overly expensive. People traveling in a group or wishing to cover fairly extensive distances can hire a chauffeur-driven limousine for an affordable price.

BUSES

Traveling by bus in Manhattan will take you close to your destination because buses travel both crosstown (east-west) and uptown and downtown (north-south), stopping every two or three blocks. Bus stops are indicated by a yellow mark on the curb, showing a stylized bus and line number, and occasionally by a bus shelter. Several lines may stop at one bus stop: check the number of the bus indicated on the front and back of the vehicle. Bus drivers are generally friendly and helpful.

FARES, TRANSFERS

The bus fare is the same as the subway fare and is paid by token or with the exact money in coin (no change is given).

If you need to change buses to reach your destination, the driver will give you a transfer paper on request.

LIMOUSINES

Taxi-limousines are also licensed by the New York City Taxi and Limousine Commission, but can only pick up passengers by prior arrangement. A private chauffeur-driven car can be hired by the hour or by contract for a tour around the city. You can even travel by limousine from the airport to the city center.

TAXI FARES

Medallion taxis have a meter fixed to the dashboard which indicates the exact cost of the ride. The minimum fare is $1.50, then 25c for every additional ⅕ mile. When the taxi is stationary, every 75-second waiting period costs 25c. You must also allow for an additional 50c for rides between 8pm and 6am. Check that the driver has re-set the meter to zero when you get in the cab. The vehicle's identity number (4 digits at the side of the meter) can be used to track down lost property or, if necessary, to file a complaint with the

Taxi and Limousine Commission, 220 W. 41st Street. Tel. 302-8294

HAILING A TAXI

In Manhattan finding a taxi is easy (except on rainy days). The yellow cabs are the only ones authorized to pick up passengers in the street and are hailed from the sidewalk (there are few taxi stands). They can carry up to a maximum of four passengers, unless they are the larger Checker cabs, which can carry five.

TRAVELING BY CAR

It is not a good idea to drive a car around Manhattan. Finding on-street parking is a lottery and garages are expensive. However, you may want to hire a car to visit the surrounding countryside. The main car-hire companies in Midtown are:
Avis:
1-800-331-1212
Hertz:
1-800-654-3131
National:
1-800-328-4567
Dollar:
1-800-421-6868
Budget:
1-212-807-8700

◆ THE SUBWAY

Green globe: ticket office open at all times.

Red globe: restricted opening times.

Graffiti have practically disappeared. The din remains, however…

With 710 miles of track, 469 stations and 5,950 trains, the New York subway is the largest urban transportation system in the world. It provides a reliable and efficient service, enabling you to travel quickly north or south. The network operates 24 hours a day, 7 days a week, but certain lines run only a part-time service (6am–12pm, at the very least). The authorities have made every effort to improve passenger safety and most subway cars are now clean and air-conditioned.

EXPRESS TRAINS AND LOCAL SLOW TRAINS

Lines are referred to by their original name (IRT, IND, BMT), by letters (A, B, C, etc.) or by numbers (1, 2, 3, 4, 5, 6, 9). Many lines have two tracks and operate a dual service: express or local. Local trains make all the stops, while express trains stop only at the larger stations, indicated by a rectangle on the maps. To change trains, just cross over the platform in the larger stations.

TAKING THE RIGHT TRAIN

To enter the subway system, deposit a token in the turnstile then follow the signs for the line you wish to take. Once on the platform, you will find other signs indicating the type of train (local or express) and its direction. The line and destination also appear on the train.

SAFETY

As in any large city, certain precautions should be taken when traveling on the subway, especially at night: beware of pickpockets and stand well back from the yellow line at the edge of the platform. It is not advisable to travel "after hours" (between 11pm and 7am). During this period, wait for your train in the areas indicated by a yellow sign (Off-Hour Waiting Areas), where the ticket clerks can see the passengers. Never get into an empty car.

STATIONS

Stations are generally named after streets. Subway entrances are indicated by green or red globes. The green globe signifies that the ticket office at that entrance is open 24 hours a day, but a red one means that this is not the case. All stations have at least one entrance and ticket office that is always open. Signs at the entrance indicate the lines running through that station, their direction and, if relevant, the type of train. Uptown and downtown trains often have separate entrances, one on either side of the street.

TOKENS

A token ($1.25) covers one journey, whatever its length or duration (but does not cover transfers by bus). Tokens, which can be bought in packets of ten for $12.50, are sold at ticket booths (notes larger than $20 are not accepted), by automatic ticket machines in some stations, at drugstores and at McDonalds, as well as in several major museums. Tokens can also be used on the bus (◆ 375) and as tips.

DISCOUNT FARES

Children shorter than 3½ feet travel free. To obtain reduced fares at certain times of the day, older people (over 65) should call 442-3000 and disabled people should call 878-7294. There is no season-ticket system, even for tourists.

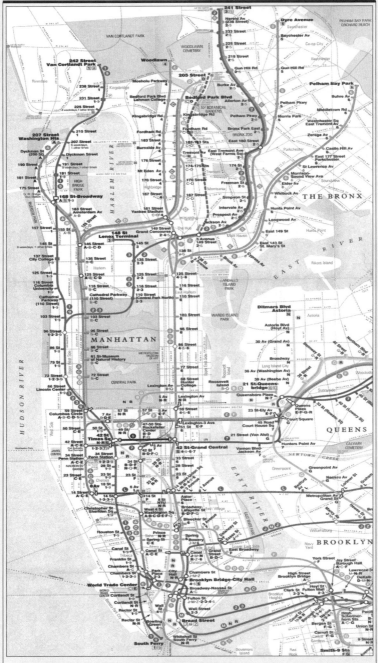

INFORMATION
Free subway maps are available from most ticket offices. A large-scale map of the system as well as information about how it operates are usually displayed nearby. The New York City Transit Authority can also be contacted 24 hours a day at 718-330-1234.

New York is the financial capital of the United States as well as its largest business center. The city is the home of two of the nation's major stock markets (the New York Stock Exchange and the American Stock Exchange), and also of many international institutions and some of the most prestigious banks in the world. Successful business deals and large amounts of money changing hands are daily features of a world which also offers free rock concerts and plays in Central Park yet has one of the most expensive hotel industries on earth. The consumer is king in this city if he or she does the "job" of comparing prices, asking questions and – in some cases – haggling before making a purchase.

CHANGING FOREIGN MONEY

Banks are generally open Monday to Friday, 9am to 3pm (some also open on Saturday mornings). Most large banks will change currency, as will many of the best hotels (but at a less competitive rate).

USEFUL ADDRESSES

AMERICAN EXPRESS
World Financial Center
Tel. 640-2000
374 Park Ave.
Tel 421-8240
Bloomingdale's
Corner of 59th St./Lexington Ave.
Tel. 705-3171
Macy's
Herald Square
Tel. 695-8075
BANK OF AMERICA INTERNATIONAL
355 Madison Ave.
Tel. 503 7000
CHECKPOINT
551 Madison Ave.
Tel. 980-6443
Open daily.
DEAK INTERNATIONAL
Kennedy Airport
Tel. 718-656-8444
630 5th Ave.
Tel. 757-6915
THOMAS COOK CURRENCY SERVICE
41 E. 42nd St.
Tel. 883-0400
29 Broadway
Tel. 363-6207

EXCHANGE RATE

The dollar exchange rate fluctuates depending on the policy of the Federal Reserve Bank. In 1994, it tends to be around UK £0.70, FF6, DM1.70 and Yen 104.

DOLLARS AND CENTS

The United States dollar is divided into 100 cents. The bills in circulation are $1, $5, $10, $20, $50, $100. You will occasionally come across $2 bills but these are rare. Coins in circulation are the penny (1c), the nickel (5c), the dime (10c), the quarter (25c), the half dollar (50c) and the $1 coin, although the last two are rarely used.

TRAVELERS' CHECKS

Dollar travelers' checks are extremely useful: they are accepted as hard currency in most hotels, restaurants and shops and can be replaced if lost or stolen.

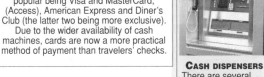

BANK CARDS

The United States leads the field in the use of plastic money as legal currency. Debit or credit cards are therefore widely accepted in hotels, restaurants and stores, the most popular being Visa and MasterCard, (Access), American Express and Diner's Club (the latter two being more exclusive). Due to the wider availability of cash machines, cards are now a more practical method of payment than travelers' checks.

CASH DISPENSERS

There are several networks of Automatic Teller Machines (ATM), the largest of which are Cirrus, affiliated to Visa, and Plus, affiliated to MasterCard. These cash dispensers are open 24 hours a day and can be found at branches of Citibank, Chemical Bank and Chase Manhattan as well as at other banks in Manhattan.
LISTING OF ATMs:
Cirrus:
1-800-424-7787.
Plus:
1-800-843-7587.

TIPPING

Tipping is obligatory, but a service charge is rarely added to the check (bill). Use the following scale to work out your tip:
Restaurants: 15–20 percent (double the local tax of 8.25 percent)
Bars: 15 percent
Taxis: 15 percent (minimum of 25c).

SALES TAX

Most goods bought in Manhattan are taxed at 8.5 percent. This tax is not generally included in the marked price. In hotels it can vary from 14.25 percent to 19.25 percent on top of the fixed hotel tax of $2. With the exception of confectionery and soft drinks, food bought at a grocery store is not taxed.

WHAT THINGS COST...

COFFEE: 75 CENTS

ALCOHOL: $3

BAGEL: $1.50

MUSEUM ADMISSION: $3 TO $6

CONCERT: $5 TO $30

CINEMA: $7.50

TOP-CLASS RESTAURANT: $35 TO $60

BUDGET HOTEL: $60 TO $75 PER NIGHT

CONVERSION TABLES FOR MEASUREMENTS

LIQUIDS

1 fluid ounce (fl. oz.)	= 0.03 l	*To convert liters into US gallons, multiply the number of liters by 0.26 (e.g.: 50 liters x 0.26 = 13 gal.). To convert gallons into liters, multiply the number of gallons by 3.79 (e.g.: 12 gal. x 3.79 = 45.48 liters)*
1 pint = 16 fl. oz.	= 0.47 l	
1 quart = 2 pints	= 0.94 l	
1 gallon (gal.) = 4 quarts	= 3.785 l	

LENGTHS AND DISTANCES

1 inch (in.)	= 2.54 cm	*To convert miles into kilometers, multiply the number of miles by 1.61 (e.g.: 50 miles x 1.61 = 80.5 km). To convert kilometers into miles, multiply the number of kilometers by 0.62 (e.g.: 25 km x 0.62 = 15.5 miles)*
1 foot (ft.) = 12 in.	= 30.48 cm	
1 yard (yd.) = 3 ft.	= 0.915 m	
1 mile (mi.)	= 1.609 km	

WEIGHTS

1 ounce (oz.)	= 2.54 cm	*To convert pounds into kilograms, multiply the number of pounds by 0.45 (e.g.: 90 lb. x 0.45 = 40.5 kg). To convert kilos to pounds, multiply the kilos by 2.2 (e.g.: 75 kg x 2.2 = 165 lb.)*
1 pound (lb.) = 16 oz.	= 30.48 cm	
1 ton = 2000 lb.	= 0.907 kg	

TEMPERATURES

-18°C	-10		0		10		20		30		40
0°F	10	20	32	40	50	60	70	80	90	100

To convert degrees Fahrenheit into degrees Celsius, subtract 32 from the degrees F, multiply by 5, then divide by 9 (example: 85°F − 32 = 53/53 x 5 = 265/265 ÷ 9 = 29.4°C)
To convert degrees Celsius into degrees Fahrenheit, multiply the degrees Celsius by 9, divide by 5 then add 32 (example: 20°C x 9 = 180/180 ÷ 5 = 36/36 + 32 = 68°F).

ELECTRICITY

The electric current is 110V and the sockets have two flat pins. You will need a transformer and an adaptor to use European appliances in the United States.

EQUIVALENT MEN'S SIZES

FRANCE	U.S. (U.K.)
JACKETS	
44	36
46	36/38
48	38
50	40
52	42
54	42/44
56	44
TROUSERS	
44	36
46	38
48	40
50	40/42
52	42
54	44
SHOES	
40½	8 (7½)
41	8½ (8)
42	9½ (9)
43	10½ (10)
44	11 (10½)
45	11½ (11)

EQUIVALENT WOMEN'S SIZES

FRANCE	U.S. (U.K.)
SKIRTS AND DRESSES	
34	4 (8)
36	8 (10)
38	10 (12)
40	12 (14)
42	14 (16)
44	16 (18)
46	18 (20)
JACKETS	
36	6 (8)
38	10 (12)
40	12 (14)
42	14 (16)
44	16 (18)
46	18
48	20
50	22
SHOES	
36½	5½ (4)
37	6 (4½)
37½	6½ (5)
38½	7 (5½)
39	7½ (6)
39½	8 (6½)
40	8½ (7)

THE TIME

In the United States, the 12-hour clock (as opposed to the 24-hour clock) is used: time in the afternoon is described as *post meridiem* or pm (eg. 2pm) and time in the morning is described as *ante meridiem*, or am (eg. 2am). Relative time zones: London: midnight New York: 7pm (of the previous day) Tokyo: 8am (of the following day).

TOBACCO

Smoking is strictly regulated in New York. It is illegal to smoke in any enclosed public area, on public transportation, in theaters, stores and office lobbies. Most restaurants have areas restricted for smokers, but the smoking of pipes and cigars is prohibited.

ALCOHOL

In New York, you cannot buy alcohol or be served in a bar before the age of twenty-one. Age is quite often checked. Restaurants that display a "No liquor license" sign are not allowed to serve alcohol, but you can generally bring your own wine or beer in with you, if this is the case. On the other hand, some bars generally operate a "happy hour" between 5 and 7pm on weekdays, when you can buy doubles for the price of a single or half-price cocktails.

All phone boxes have their own number, so you can be called back.

Letters to Europe cost 50c and postcards 40c.

PUBLIC TELEPHONES

A local call in New York City costs 25c. Public telephones accept 5, 10, and 25c cent pieces and do not give change. If you have not inserted the right amount, an electronic message will cut in, informing you how much more you need to insert; if you do not do this, the conversation will be cut off. Some telephones accept credit and debit cards.

THE POSTAL SYSTEM

"US Mail" appears on all American mailboxes. When sending a letter anywhere in the United States, you pay 29c for the first ounce, then 23c for every additional ounce. Sending a letter abroad costs 50c for the first half ounce and 45c for every additional half ounce; sending a postcard costs 40c. The General Post Office is open 24 hours a day. General Post Office: 8th Ave./33rd St., Tel: 967-8585.

LONG DISTANCE CALLS

To make a phone call from New York to anywhere else in the United States, dial 1 + the area code + the number you require (7 digits).
To make a call through the operator, dial 0. If making international calls, first dial 011, then the country + city code + rest of number. To call the U.S. from overseas, dial 0101 + area code + local number. To call Manhattan from the UK, for example, dial 0101 212 plus the 7 digit number. To call central London from New York, dial 011 44 71 plus the 7-digit number.

TELEGRAMS

In the United States, the telegram service is handled by private companies. Contact Western Union on 1-800-325-6000

NEW YORK AREA CODES

New York City is divided into three different codes, depending on whether you are calling Manhattan (212), the other boroughs (718), a radiophone or various services which carry special charges (900, 917, etc). When calling from Manhattan to another borough in the city, dial 1-718 and the 7 digits of the number you require. Unless otherwise indicated, the numbers mentioned in this book are all preceded by 212.

INFORMATION DIRECTORY INQUIRIES

Dial 411. The cost is 45c for every number required, unless you make the call from a public phone booth (when the service is free).

TOLL-FREE CALLS

Numbers preceded by 1-800 are free. Many hotels and companies have "toll-free" numbers. Unfortunately, you cannot dial these numbers from outside the United States. For further information, dial 1-800-555-1212, after you arrive in the United States.

THE COST OF A PHONE CALL (AT&T RATES)

NEW YORK — cost in $ for the first minute then every minute thereafter:

	7am	1pm	6pm	
FRANCE	1.71 / 1.08	1.39 / 82c	1.15 / 67c	
UK	1.44 / 96c	1.15 / 73c	98c / 62c	
GERMANY	1.77 / 1.09	1.42 / 87c	1.15 / 69c	
JAPAN	2.16 / 81c	3.05 / 1.24	2.55 / 99c	

Local call: 25c min

The Pierre Hotel (second from left) and its neighbors, seen from Central Park.

The Woolworth Building, seen from the top of the World Trade Center.

Manhattan's jagged skyscraper skyline is infinitely varied; depending on your location, the time of day or season, its buildings are transformed by a constantly shifting panoply of light and shadow. And although there is nothing to beat the view from the top of the city's highest buildings, there are many other places at street level that show the multifaceted building tops to good advantage.

SKY-HIGH VIEWS

INITIATION
The observation deck of the Empire State Building or of the World Trade Center is a "must" for the visitor to New York. The views they provide, however, are completely different: the Empire State Building, which is more central and not quite so tall, gives a better idea of the city's layout and the regular Midtown and Uptown grid pattern, whereas the World Trade Center affords a giddy view of the tangle of streets in Downtown Manhattan, as well as a wider view of the surrounding area.

CONTEMPLATION
Several other skyscrapers were built with observation decks. Although none of these are now accessible, there is a breathtaking view from some bars and restaurants, such as the *Rainbow Room* (65th floor of General Electricity Building), especially at night.

OBSERVATION
You can see the city from an unusual angle from the terrace of the Clocktower Gallery, the former skylobby of the Equitable Building in Broadway, or the terrace of the Dia Center in TriBeCa.

THE HEIGHT OF SOME STRUCTURES IN MANHATTAN
From left to right:
Dutch windmill
1664, 39 feet
Saint Paul's Chapel
1796, 220 feet
Federal Hall
1842, 59 feet
Pier of Brooklyn Bridge
1883, 436 feet
Flatiron Building
1902, 312 feet
Pulitzer Building
1903, 377 feet
Metropolitan Life Tower
1909, 699 feet
Woolworth Building
1913, 792 feet
Equitable Building
1915, 515 feet
Chrysler Building
1930, 1048 feet
Empire State Building
1931, 1250 feet
Seagram Building
1958, 476 feet
World Trade Center
1973–7, 1350 feet
Citicorp Building
1978, 915 feet
Sony Building former
ATT Building, 650 feet

VIEWS FROM OTHER PLACES

AROUND THE EDGES
The boat trip to Liberty Island or Staten Island is another form of initiation: as the ferry pulls out into the bay, the "prow" of Manhattan gradually takes shape. Likewise, a stroll across the Brooklyn Bridge's pedestrian walkway affords a splendid, ever-changing view, through the mesh of cables, of the island's eastern profile, with its most renowned skyscrapers thrusting skyward.

IN THE CENTER
One of Manhattan's most heart-stopping cityscapes can be seen from the reservoir in Central Park (90th Street). The buildings lining the two thoroughfares bordering the park – 5th Avenue and Central Park West (dominated by the twin peaks of the Eldorado) – come into view from this inland sea.

FROM AFAR
For an unusual perspective on Manhattan, take the short, breathtaking journey through the air above the roofs of Midtown, the Queensboro Bridge and then the East River, by aerial tramway to Roosevelt Island. The view from the top of the tower of Riverside Church, above the banks of the Hudson (120th Street), affords a good view of two of the city's hidden faces: Harlem and the Bronx.

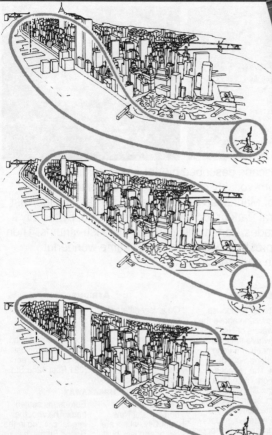

LIBERTY HELICOPTER TOURS
The highest building in New York . . . seen from above. A flight over Manhattan is a memory that will stay with you forever. It is a relatively affordable luxury (between $55 and $120) and most hotels will take care of reservations. All trips include a bird's-eye view of the Statue of Liberty, then a flight northward, often as far as Central Park. West 30th St., at Hudson River.
Tel. 967-6464 or 542-9933

CIRCLE LINE
This company offers excursions around the island up to eleven times a day. The trip lasts three hours and there is a commentary describing all the sites shown on the map. It is possible to organize a corporate mini-cruise or a social gathering on the company's boats! Pier 83, West 42nd St., Hudson River.
Tel. 563-3200

CIRCLE LINE
W. 42nd Street at the Hudson River,
New York, NY
Park on our pier.
By bus:
34th Street M16, 49/50th Street M50,
42nd Street M42
Westbound right to our pier.

South Pier,
Harborside Financial Center,
Jersey City, New Jersey, NJ
Park on our pier.
By train:
PATH to Exchange Place
Northbound right to our pier.

Enjoy the only sightseeing cruise that sails all the way around Manhattan.

The beautiful landscape described by Verrazano, with its thickly wooded hills, has irrevocably changed. However, nature has not been chased out of Manhattan entirely, as can be seen by the vast expanses of Central Park or, on a more modest scale, by the city's waterside promenades, community gardens and lush atriums. Then again, the other boroughs, which also boast some wonderful gardens, are within easy reach.

AT THE WATER'S EDGE

Surrounded by Midtown's towers, you could easily forget that Manhattan is an island. The riverside highways, too, with their heavy traffic, form a barrier between the city and its rivers. In a few spots, however, this barrier is breached by a park or a promenade running along the water's edge:
◆ Battery Park's esplanade and the peace of South Cove
◆ Riverside Park Marina (79th St. Boat Basin)
◆ The north tip of Roosevelt Island and its old lighthouse towering above the waters of Hell's Gate (where the East River meets the Long Island Sound).
◆ The terraces of Fort Tryon Park and the Cloisters museum, opposite the Hudson Palisades, sheer cliffs dramatically dropping away into the Hudson. Here, in the unexpected setting of medieval buildings brought over from France and Spain, green vistas and tranquillity reign supreme. It is hard to believe you are still in Manhattan.

MINIATURE GARDENS

"Community gardens" are small oases, wrested from the concrete and asphalt and lovingly tended by people living in the neighborhood who can be seen on weekends, digging and hoeing, dressed in their gardening clothes. These small gardens, which are well worth a visit, thrive in Manhattan and are particularly common in the East Village. They grow in vacant plots between the blind walls of two apartment blocks or rowhouses. The oldest (1973), Liz Christy Community Garden, at the corner of the Bowery and Houston Street is a wonderful refuge in summer.

ATRIUMS

On a very different scale, several office towers provide pedestrians with a cool, quiet sanctuary in vast atriums decked out with plants, trees and fountains. The most stunning of these is the one in the Ford Foundation Building, at the easternmost end of 42nd Street (321 East 42nd St.).

BREAKAWAY

The four other boroughs of New York City, which are larger and less built-up, offer numerous parks and gardens. The Bronx has two of the city's outstanding treasures: the New York Botanical Garden and the Bronx Zoo. The Botanical Garden's 40-acre forest, through which the Bronx River runs, is the only vestige of the forest that used to cover all of New York City before the Europeans settled here. The zoo, the largest city zoo in the United States, has re-created the natural habitats of animals from all over the world – among others an astonishing rain forest from southeast Asia. Although the Bronx has a bad reputation, these two parks, close to each other, can be easily and safely reached by bus or subway.

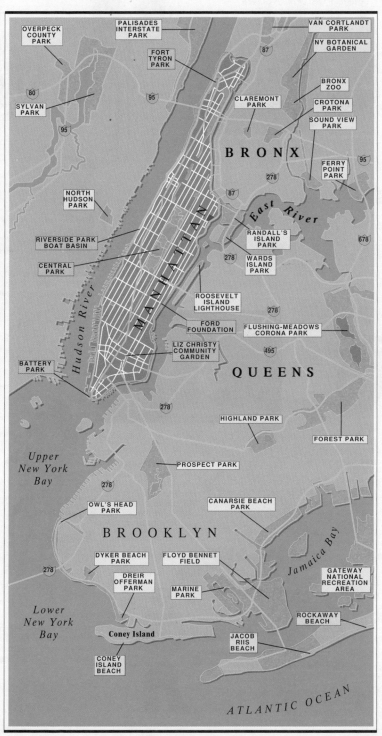

OVERPECK COUNTY PARK

PALISADES INTERSTATE PARK

VAN CORTLANDT PARK

NY BOTANICAL GARDEN

FORT TYRON PARK

BRONX ZOO

CLAREMONT PARK

CROTONA PARK

SOUND VIEW PARK

SYLVAN PARK

B R O N X

FERRY POINT PARK

NORTH HUDSON PARK

East River

RIVERSIDE PARK BOAT BASIN

RANDALL'S ISLAND PARK

WARDS ISLAND PARK

CENTRAL PARK

M A N H A T T A N

ROOSEVELT ISLAND LIGHTHOUSE

Hudson River

FORD FOUNDATION

FLUSHING-MEADOWS CORONA PARK

LIZ CHRISTY COMMUNITY GARDEN

BATTERY PARK

Q U E E N S

HIGHLAND PARK

FOREST PARK

Upper New York Bay

PROSPECT PARK

OWL'S HEAD PARK

CANARSIE BEACH PARK

B R O O K L Y N

Jamaica Bay

DYKER BEACH PARK

FLOYD BENNET FIELD

GATEWAY NATIONAL RECREATION AREA

DREIR OFFERMAN PARK

MARINE PARK

Lower New York Bay

Coney Island

ROCKAWAY BEACH

JACOB RIIS BEACH

CONEY ISLAND BEACH

ATLANTIC OCEAN

◆ IMAGES OF THE CITY

Café terrace east of Times Square.

Water tanks standing on three-legged metal stands can be seen all over the city.

Tennis at the top! Every square yard of Manhattan is used, including the roofs . . .

At apartment block entrances policemen with truncheons maintain a reassuring presence

"*Taxis . . . spent their time hooting or squealing to a halt, then nipping in and out of the traffic . . .***"**
Donald Westlake

Daily newspapers are now sold in automatic vending machines. Magazines, on the other hand, are still sold at newsstands

You have to be fit and athletic be a messenger in New York. Here, bicycles are used instead of motorcycles (as in London

The New York firemen, city guardians, are an integral part of daily life. The City Fire Museum is devoted to their work.

The positioning of the traffic lights in the middle of a junction or on the other side, may surprise more than one European driver.

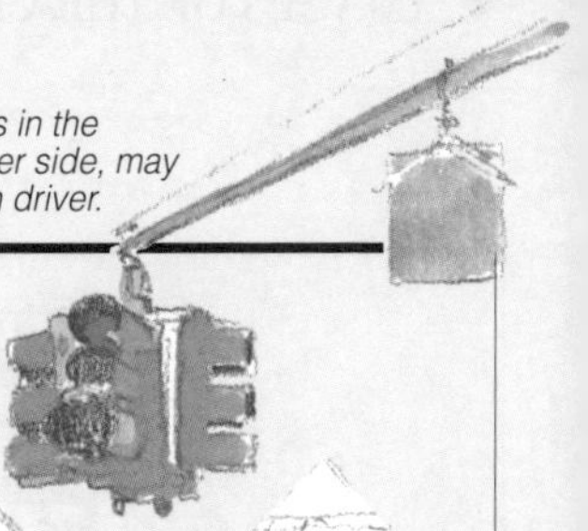

At rush hour, wave after wave of New Yorkers pour out of the elevators onto the subway platforms.

Fire escapes in SoHo.

For a long time, the New York "cop" carried a Python 357.

Playing with water in New Riverfront Park (Riverside Drive/138th St.)

"The square is also a small world: little old men, chess players, policemen on horseback watching the chess games from their high vantage point . . ."
Edgar Morin, New York

After taxis, limousines reign supreme in New York . . .

387

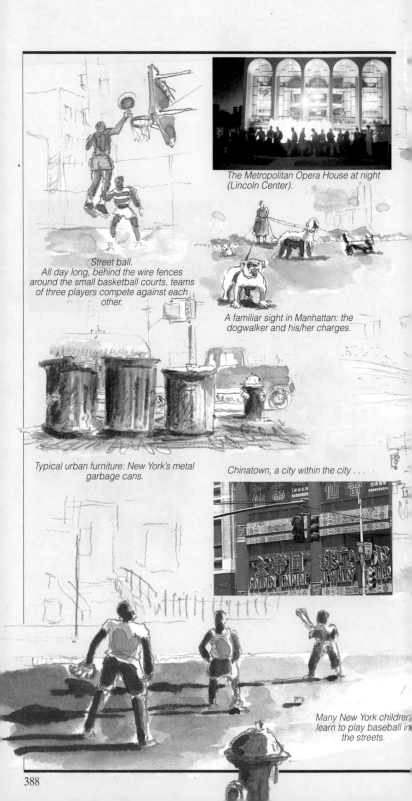

The Metropolitan Opera House at night (Lincoln Center).

Street ball.
All day long, behind the wire fences around the small basketball courts, teams of three players compete against each other.

A familiar sight in Manhattan: the dogwalker and his/her charges.

Typical urban furniture: New York's metal garbage cans.

Chinatown, a city within the city . . .

Many New York children learn to play baseball in the streets.

School buses are yellow.

A trompe l'oeil view of the Brooklyn Bridge from the South Street Seaport.

In summer, when the sidewalks sizzle, it's tempting to cool off by opening a fire hydrant.

Newsstands are traditionally found at street corners, near the "Walk/Don't Walk" signs.

In the garment district racks of "ready-to-wear" roll by.

The city is punctuated by the intermittent din of police and fire engine sirens.

You can get a quick snack anywhere in the city, at any time of day.

The horse-drawn carriages in Central Park are a relic of the 19th century.

389

RESTLESS

"New York was to become the restless city," wrote Jerome Charyn, "past, present and future seemed to merge into one single time zone, a different age altogether, nervy, jangling. . . .The Dutch merchants were never to put down firm roots here. The city has become a victim of incurable amnesia. It is the city of oblivion."

Although the writer of these words may have overstated his case, it is undeniable that New York is pre-eminently a city of the present. Time, as they say, is money; and a city that makes no apology for its dedication to the pursuit of money keeps its eye on the clock. Lots of clocks. They adorn buildings – inside and out – all over the town; some even stand commandingly on street corners, like temporal policemen, helping to organize one's time as efficiently as the grid street layout organizes the traffic. Many of them have a secondary purpose: advertising. Clocks vie for attention, outdoing each other in originality – a rivalry taken to extremes by Robert Venturi's 98-foot-diameter clock, which will crown the new Whitehall Ferry Terminal on the tip of Manhattan and will be visible from out in the harbor.

LISTINGS

MUSEUMS AND PLACES
TO VISIT, *392*
SHOPPING, *394*
CHOOSING A HOTEL, *398*
CHOOSING A RESTAURANT, *400*
USEFUL ADDRESSES, *402*
NOTES, *428*

◆ MUSEUMS AND PLACES TO VISIT

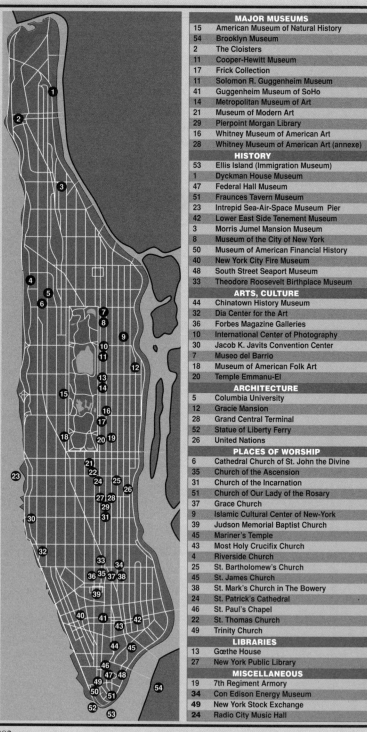

MAJOR MUSEUMS

15	American Museum of Natural History
54	Brooklyn Museum
2	The Cloisters
11	Cooper-Hewitt Museum
17	Frick Collection
11	Solomon R. Guggenheim Museum
41	Guggenheim Museum of SoHo
14	Metropolitan Museum of Art
21	Museum of Modern Art
29	Pierpoint Morgan Library
16	Whitney Museum of American Art
28	Whitney Museum of American Art (annexe)

HISTORY

53	Ellis Island (Immigration Museum)
1	Dyckman House Museum
47	Federal Hall Museum
51	Fraunces Tavern Museum
23	Intrepid Sea-Air-Space Museum Pier
42	Lower East Side Tenement Museum
3	Morris Jumel Mansion Museum
8	Museum of the City of New York
50	Museum of American Financial History
40	New York City Fire Museum
48	South Street Seaport Museum
33	Theodore Roosevelt Birthplace Museum

ARTS, CULTURE

44	Chinatown History Museum
32	Dia Center for the Art
36	Forbes Magazine Galleries
10	International Center of Photography
30	Jacob K. Javits Convention Center
7	Museo del Barrio
18	Museum of American Folk Art
20	Temple Emmanu-El

ARCHITECTURE

5	Columbia University
12	Gracie Mansion
28	Grand Central Terminal
52	Statue of Liberty Ferry
26	United Nations

PLACES OF WORSHIP

6	Cathedral Church of St. John the Divine
35	Church of the Ascension
31	Church of the Incarnation
51	Church of Our Lady of the Rosary
37	Grace Church
9	Islamic Cultural Center of New-York
39	Judson Memorial Baptist Church
45	Mariner's Temple
43	Most Holy Crucifix Church
4	Riverside Church
25	St. Bartholomew's Church
45	St. James Church
38	St. Mark's Church in The Bowery
24	St. Patrick's Cathedral
46	St. Paul's Chapel
22	St. Thomas Church
49	Trinity Church

LIBRARIES

13	Gœthe House
27	New York Public Library

MISCELLANEOUS

19	7th Regiment Armory
34	Con Edison Energy Museum
49	New York Stock Exchange
24	Radio City Music Hall

Address	Phone	Neighborhood
Central Park West, 79th Street	769-5100	Upper West Side
200 Eastern Parkway	718-638-5000 B	Brooklyn
Fort Tryon Park	923-3700	Harlem, Uptown
2 E 91st Street	860-6868	Upper East Side
1 E 70th Street	288-0700	Upper East Side
1071 5th Avenue	423-3500	Upper East Side
575 Broadway (Prince Street)	423-3500	Washington Square
5th Avenue and E 82nd Street	535-7710	Upper East Side
11 W 53rd Street	708-9480	Rockefeller Center
29 E 36th Street	685-0610	Grand Central
945 Madison Avenue (75th Street)	570-3676	Upper East Side
120 Park Avenue (42nd Street)	878-2550	Grand Central
New York Harbor	363-7620	World Trade Center
4881 Broadway (204th Street)	360-8123	Harlem, Uptown
26 Wall Street	264-8711	World Trade Center
54 Pearl Street	425-1778	World Trade Center
86, 12th Avenue and W 46th Street	245-2533	Grand Central
97 Orchard Street	431-0233	Lower East Side
W 160th Street and Edgecombe Avenue	923-8008	Harlem, Uptown
5th Avenue and 103rd Street	534-1672	Upper East Side
26 Broadway	908-4519	World Trade Center
278 Spring Street	691-1303	Washington Square
207 Front Street	669-9424	City Hall
28 E 20th Street	260-1616	Union Square
70 Mulberry St., 2nd floor	619-4785	Chinatown
548 W 22nd Street	989-5912	Washington Square
62 5th Avenue (12th Street)	206-5548	Washington Square
1130 5th Avenue	860-1777	Upper East Side
655 W 34th Street	216-2000	Grand Central
1230 5th Avenue	831-7272	Upper East Side
2 Lincoln Square (Columbus Avenue and 65th Street)	977-7298	Upper West Side
1 E 65th Street	744-1400	Upper East Side
114th and 120th sts, Broadway and Amsterdam avenues	854-2845	Harlem, Uptown
88th Street (in Carl Schurz Park)	570-4751	Upper East Side
42nd Street (Park and Lexington avenues)	532-4900	Grand Central
Liberty Island (New York Harbor)	269-5755	World Trade Center
1st Avenue (46th Street)	963-7713	Grand Central
Amsterdam Avenue (112th Street)	316-7540	Harlem, Uptown
5th Avenue (10th Street)	254-8620	Washington Square
209 Madison Avenue (35th Street)	689-6350	Grand Central
7-8 State Street	269-6865	World Trade Center
800–804 Broadway (10th Street)	254-2000	Union Square
1711 3rd Avenue (97th Street)	722-5234	Upper East Side
55 Washington Square South	447-0351	Washington Square
3 Henry Street and 12 Oliver Street	233-0423	Lower East Side
378 Broome Street	226-2556	Lower East Side
490 Riverside Drive	222-5900	Harlem, Uptown
109 E 50th Street	751-1616	Rockefeller Center
23 Oliver Street	233-0161	Lower East Side
131 E 10th Street	674-6377	Union Square
5th Avenue (50th Street)	753-2261	Rockefeller Center
Broadway (Fulton Street)	602-0874	City Hall
1 W 53rd Street	757-7013	Rockefeller Center
Broadway (Wall Street)	602-0872	World Trade Center
1014 5th Avenue (83rd Street)	439-8700	Upper East Side
5th Avenue (42nd Street)	930-0800	Grand Central
643 Park Avenue (67th Street)	439-0300	Upper East Side
145 E 14th Street	460-6244	Union Square
8 Broad Street	656-5167	World Trade Center
Rockefeller Center, Avenue of the Americas (50th Street)	632-4041	Rockefeller Center

◆ SHOPPING

ANTIQUES

LOST CITY ARTS	409	275 Lafayette Street / Washington Square
CHRISTIE'S	421	502 Park Avenue / Rockefeller Center
WILLIAM DOYLE GALLERIES	425	175 East 87th Street / Upper East Side
DARROW'S FUN ANTIQUES	424	1101 1st Avenue / Upper East Side
SOTHEBY'S	424	1334 York Avenue / Upper East Side

JEWELRY STORES

CARTIER	420	653 5th Avenue / Rockefeller Center
HARRY WINSTON	421	718 5th Avenue / Rockefeller Center
KENNETH JAY LANE	421	677 5th Avenue / Rockefeller Center
TIFFANY AND CO.	421	727 5th Avenue / Rockefeller Center

DEPARTMENT STORES

BARNEYS OF NEW YORK	409	106 7th Avenue / Washington Square
BERGDORF GOODMAN	420	754 5th Avenue (58th Street) / Rockefeller Center
BLOOMINGDALE'S	420	1000 3rd Avenue (59th and 60th streets) / Rockefeller Center
GALERIES LAFAYETTE	421	10 East 57th Street (Trump Tower) / Rockefeller Center
HENRI BENDEL	420	712 5th Avenue / Rockefeller Center
SAKS FIFTH AVENUE	421	611 5th Avenue (49th and 50th streets) / Rockefeller Center
A. & S.	414	899 Avenue of the Americas / Grand Central
LORD AND TAYLOR	415	424 5th Avenue (38th Street) / Grand Central
MACY'S HERALD SQUARE	415	151 West 34th Street (Broadway) / Grand Central
CENTURY 21 DEPARTMENT STORE	404	22 Cortland Street / City Hall
PIER 17 PAIRLION	404	89 South Street (South Street Port) / City Hall
BARNEYS	424	660 Madison Avenue (61st Street) / Upper East Side

BOOKSTORES

THE BIOGRAPHY BOOKSHOP	409	400 Bleecker Street / Washington Square
BARNES & NOBLE	426	2889 Broadway at 82nd Street / Upper West Side
STRAND BOOK STORE	411	828 Broadway (12th Street) / Union Square
FORBIDDEN PLANET	411	821 Broadway / Union Square
COLISEUM BOOKS	421	1771 Broadway (57th Street) / Rockefeller Center
BOOKS & CO.	424	939 Madison Avenue / Upper East Side
DRAMA BOOKSHOP	421	723 7th Avenue (48th and 49th streets) / Rockefeller Center
GOTHAM BOOK MART	421	41 West 47th Street / Rockefeller Center
LIBRAIRIE DE FRANCE / LIBRERIA HISPANICA	421	610 5th Avenue / Rockefeller Center
RIZZOLI	421	31 West 57th Street / Rockefeller Center
HAGSTROM MAP AND TRAVEL CENTER	414	57 West 43rd Street / Grand Central

MUSIC

MANNY'S MUSICAL INSTRUMENTS	415	156 West 48th Street / Grand Central
SAM GOODY	415	666 3rd Avenue (43rd Street) / Grand Central
J&R MUSIC WORLD	404	23 Park Row / City Hall
TOWER RECORDS	411	692 Broadway (4th Street) / Union Square
COLONY RECORD	421	1619 Broadway (49th Street) / Rockefeller Center

COMPUTERS, PHOTOGRAPHY, VIDEO

B. & H. PHOTO-VIDEO	411	119 West 17th Street / Union Square

HARVEY ELECTRONICS	415	2 West 45th Street / Grand Central
SPY STORE	409	164 Christopher Street / Washington Square
J&R COMPUTER WORLD	404	15 Park Row / City Hall
UNCLE STEVE'S	409	343 Canal Street / Washington Square
SHOES		
COLE-HAAN	424	667 Madison Avenue (61st Street) / Upper East Side
SUSAN BENNIS/WARREN EDWARDS	421	22 West 57th Street / Rockefeller Center
HARRY'S SHOES	426	2299 Broadway (83rd Street) / Upper West Side
STRIDE RITE	424	1241 Lexington Avenue / Upper East Side
BILLY MARTIN	424	812 Madison Avenue / Upper East Side
JOAN & DAVID	424	816 Madison Avenue / Upper East Side
TIMBERLAND	424	709 Madison Avenue (62nd Street) / Upper East Side
TOOTSIE PLOHOUND	409	413 West Broadway / Washington Square
MEN'S FASHIONS		
BANCROFT	414	363 Madison Avenue / Grand Central
BROOKS BROTHERS	414	346 Madison Avenue / Grand Central
J. PRESS	415	7 East 44th Street / Grand Central
NEW REPUBLIC	409	93 Spring Street / Washington Square
WOMEN'S FASHIONS		
COMPAGNIE INTERNATIONALE EXPRESS	414	452 5th Avenue at 38th Street / Grand Central
ANN TAYLOR	420	3 East 57th Street / Rockefeller Center
CHARIVARI	420	18 West 57th Street / Rockefeller Center
HENRI BENDEL	420	712 5th Avenue / Rockefeller Center
NORMA KAMALI	421	11 West 56th Street / Rockefeller Center
THE FORGOTTEN WOMAN	421	60 West 49th Street / Rockefeller Center
AGNÈS B	409	116 Prince Street / Washington Square
VICTORIA'S SECRET	421	34 East 57th Street / Rockefeller Center
UNISEX FASHIONS, CLASSIC SPORTSWEAR		
BANANA REPUBLIC	420	130 East 59th Street / Rockefeller Center
BURBERRY LIMITED	420	9 East 57th Street / Rockefeller Center
EDDIE BAUER	420	600 Madison Avenue / Rockefeller Center
ORIGINAL LEVI'S STORE	421	750 Lexington Avenue (59th / 60th streets) / Rockefeller Center
GAP	415	Broadway and 34th Street / Grand Central
BETSEY JOHNSON	409	130 Thompson Street / Washington Square
CANAL JEAN	409	504 Broadway / Washington Square
POP SHOP	409	292 Lafayette Street / Washington Square
REPLAY COUNTRY STORE	409	109 Prince Street / Washington Square
SCREAMING MIMI'S	409	382 Lafayette Street / Washington Square
POLO-RALPH LAUREN	424	867 Madison Avenue and 72nd Street / Upper East Side
TIMBERLAND	424	709 Madison Avenue (62nd Street) / Upper East Side
MISCELLANEOUS, ACCESSORIES		
J. J. HAT CENTER	415	Angle 310 5th Avenue and 32nd Street / Grand Central
PAUL STUART	415	Madison Avenue and 45th Street / Grand Central
WORTH AND WORTH	415	331 Madison Avenue (43rd Street) / Grand Central
SUSAN BENNIS / WARREN EDWARDS	421	22 West 57th Street / Rockefeller Center
COLE-HAAN	424	667 Madison Avenue (61st Street) / Upper East Side
TIMBERLAND	424	709 Madison Avenue (62nd Street) / Upper East Side

◆ SHOPPING

THE COACH STORE	424	710 Madison Avenue (63rd Street) / Upper East Side
SPORTS		
EDDIE BAUER	420	600 Madison Avenue / Rockefeller Center
YANKEE CLUBHOUSE SHOP	421	110 East 59th Street / Rockefeller Center
FOOT LOCKER	414	43–45 West 34th Street / Grand Central
POLO SPORT / POLO-RALPH LAUREN	424	888 Madison Avenue / Upper East Side
PARAGON	411	867 Broadway (18th Street) / Union Square
TOYS, USEFUL GADGETS, NOVELTIES		
THE COMPLETE STRATEGIST	415	11 East 33rd Street / Grand Central
F.A.O. SCHWARZ	421	767 5th Avenue (58th and 59th streets) / Rockefeller Center
HAMMACHER SCHLEMMER	421	147 East 57th Street / Rockefeller Center
THE SHARPER IMAGE	421	4 West 57th Street / Rockefeller Center
MAXILLA & MANDIBLE	426	451 9th Avenue / Upper West Side
SPY STORE	409	164 Christopher Street / Washington Square
THE ENCHANTED FOREST	409	85 Mercer Street / Washington Square
THINK BIG	409	390 West Broadway / Washington Square
VILLAGE CHESS SHOP	409	230 Thompson Street / Washington Square
DARROW'S FUN ANTIQUES	424	1101 1st Avenue / Upper East Side
LOVE SAVES THE DAY	411	Angle 119 2nd Avenue and 7th Street / Union Square
FOR CHILDREN		
BLADES EAST	424	160 East 86th Street / Upper East Side
BLADES-WEST	426	120 West 72nd Street / Upper West Side
WARNER BROS, STUDIO STORE	421	1 East 57th Street / Rockefeller Center
LOUIS TANNEN	415	24 West 25th Street (2nd Floor) / Grand Central
TOYS R US	415	1293 Broadway (34th Street) / Grand Central
FLEA MARKETS		
ANNEX ANTIQUES FAIR AND FLEA MARKET	411	6th Avenue and 25th Street / Union Square
CANAL STREET FLEA MARKET	409	335 Canal Street / Washington Square
IS 44 FLEA MARKET	426	9th Avenue (76th / 77th sts) / Upper West Side
GROCERY STORES		
BALDUCCI'S	409	424 6th Avenue / Washington Square
DEAN AND DELUCA	409	560 Broadway / Washington Square
ZABARS	426	2245 Broadway / Upper West Side
SHOPPING STREETS		
ELECTRONIC	404	Canal Street / Chinatown
SHOES	404	Canal Street / Chinatown
GENERAL GOODS	404	Mott, Pell, Bayard and Doers streets / Chinatown
	404	Grand Street / Little Italy
RELIGIOUS AND PICKLES	404	Essex Street / Lower East Side
CLOTHES AND LEATHER	404	Orchard Street / Lower East Side
GALLERIES		
65 THOMPSON STREET	407	65 Thompson Street / Washington Square
303 GALLERY	407	89 Greene Street (2nd floor) / Washington Square
A/D	405	560 Broadway / Washington Square
A.I.R.	405	63 Crosby Street / Washington Square
ARTISTS' SPACE	405	38 Greene Street (3rd floor) / Washington Square

Brooke Alexander Gallery	405	59 Wooster Street / Washington Square
Brooke Alexander Editions	405	476 Broome Street / Washington Square
American Fine Arts Co.	405	22 Wooster Street / Washington Square
Josh Baer Gallery	405	476 Broome Street (3rd floor) / Washington Square
Mary Boone Gallery	405	417 West Broadway / Washington Square
Janet Borden Inc.	405	560 Broadway (6th floor) / Washington Square
Leo Castelli Gallery	405	420 West Broadway (2nd floor) / Washington Square
Paula Cooper Gallery	406	155 Wooster Street / Washington Square
Crown Point Press	406	568 Broadway / Washington Square
James Danziger Gallery	406	130 Prince Street / Washington Square
The Drawing Center	406	35 Wooster Street / Washington Square
Exit Art/ The First World	406	548 Broadway (2nd floor) / Washington Square
Feature	406	76 Greene Street (2nd floor) / Washington Square
Ronald Feldman Fine Arts	406	31 Mercer Street / Washington Square
John Gibson	406	568 Broadway / Washington Square
Barbara Gladstone	406	99 Greene Street / Washington Square
John Good	406	532 Broadway (2nd floor) / Washington Square
Jay Gorney Modern Art	406	100 Greene Street / Washington Square
O.K. Harris Works of Art	406	383 West Broadway / Washington Square
Pat Hearn	406	39 Wooster Street / Washington Square
Lowinsky Gallery	406	573 Broadway / Washington Square
Luhring/ Augustine Gallery	406	130 Prince Street (2nd floor) / Washington Square
Curt Marcus Gallery	406	578 Broadway (Prince Street, 10th floor) / Washington Square
Pace Gallery	406	142 Greene Street / Washington Square
Metro Pictures	406	150 Greene Street Washington Square
P.P.O.W.	406	532 Broadway (4th floor) / Washington Square
Max Protetch	406	560 Broadway (3rd floor) / Washington Square
Tony Shafrazi Gallery	407	119 Wooster Street / Washington Square
Holly Solomon Gallery	407	172 Mercer Street / Washington Square
Sonnabend Gallery	407	420 West Broadway (3rd floor) / Washington Square
Sperone Westwater	407	142 Greene Street / Washington Square
Staley-Wise Gallery	407	560 Broadway (6th floor) / Washington Square
Thread Waxing Space	407	476 Broadway (2nd floor) / Washington Square
John Weber Gallery	407	142 Greene Street (3rd floor) / Washington Square
Blum-Helman Gallery	416	20 West 57th Street (2nd floor) / Rockefeller Center
Marian Goodman Gallery	416	24 West 57th Street (4th floor) / Rockefeller Center
Sidney Janis Gallery	416	110 West 57th Street (6th Floor) / Rockefeller Center
Robert Miller Gallery	416	41 East 57th Street (3rd floor) / Rockefeller Center
Pace Gallery	416	32 East 57th Street / Rockefeller Center
Pace/Mac Gill Gallery	416	32 East 57th Street (9th floor) / Rockefeller Center
Gagosian Gallery	422	980 Madison Avenue / Upper East Side
Hirschl & Adler Modern	422	21 East 70th Street (2nd Floor) / Upper East Side
Knoedler and Company	422	19 East 70th Street / Upper East Side
Matthew Marks Gallery	422	1018 Madison Avenue / Upper East Side
Michael Werner	422	21 East 67th Street / Upper East Side
Zabriskie Gallery	422	724 5th Avenue / Upper East Side

♦ under $100
♦♦ $100 to $150
♦♦♦ $150 to $200
♦♦♦♦ over $200

	PRICE	CHILDREN'S RATE	WEEKEND RATE	VIEW	QUIET	PARKING	HOTEL RESTAURANT	SPORTS	CONFERENCES	NO. OF ROOMS
WASHINGTON SQUARE										
CHELSEA HOTEL*	♦♦						●			400
WASHINGTON SQUARE HOTEL**	♦♦	●		●	●		●	●		160
UNION SQUARE										
ARLINGTON HOTEL**	♦				●		●			120
CARLTON ARMS HOTEL*	♦									32
GRAMERCY PARK HOTEL**	♦♦		●	●			●		●	509
GRAND CENTRAL, THEATER DISTRICT										
THE ABERDEEN**	♦	●					●			150
THE ALGONQUIN HOTEL***	♦♦♦		●				●		●	165
AMBASSADOR HOTEL	♦♦					●				80
THE CARLTON***	♦♦	●	●	●	●		●		●	280
COMFORT INN, MURRAY HILL**	♦♦	●	●							125
DORAL PARK AVENUE***	♦♦♦	●	●	●			●	●	●	188
GRAND HYATT***	♦♦♦♦		●	●			●	●	●	140
HERALD SQUARE HOTEL*	♦	●		●						114
HOLIDAY INN, CROWNE PLAZA**	♦♦♦♦	●	●			●	●	●	●	770
HOTEL INTER-CONTINENTAL	♦♦♦♦		●				●	●	●	693
HOTEL IROQUOIS*	♦	●					●			100
HOTEL MACKLOWE****	♦♦♦♦	●	●			●	●	●	●	638
HOTEL MANSFIELD*	♦					●	●			200
MARRIOTT EAST SIDE	♦♦♦♦	●	●			●	●	●	●	655
MARRIOTT MARQUIS***	♦♦♦♦	●	●	●			●	●	●	1877
MORGANS****	♦♦♦♦		●	●	●		●	●		154
NEW YORK'S HOTEL PENNSYLVANIA*	♦♦		●				●	●	●	1670
PARAMOUNT***	♦♦♦		●	●			●	●	●	610
RENNAISSANCE HOTEL***	♦♦♦♦		●	●		●	●		●	305
THE ROOSEVELT**	♦♦♦	●	●				●	●	●	995
ROYALTON****	♦♦♦♦		●	●			●	●		205
SHELBURNE MURRAY HILL***	♦♦♦♦		●	●			●	●	●	258
SOUTHGATE TOWER***	♦♦♦		●	●		●	●	●	●	523
TUDOR HOTEL***	♦♦♦♦		●			●	●	●	●	300
U.N. PLAZA PARK HYATT****	♦♦♦♦		●	●			●	●	●	428
ROCKEFELLER CENTER										
BEEKMAN TOWER***	♦♦♦♦	●	●	●			●	●	●	172
HOTEL BEVERLY***	♦♦	●	●	●			●		●	186
BOX TREE****	♦♦♦♦				●	●	●	●		12
HOTEL DORSET***	♦♦♦♦	●	●				●		●	400
HOTEL EDISON**	♦	●				●	●			890
EMBASSY SUITES HOTEL***	♦♦♦♦		●	●		●	●	●	●	463
THE ESSEX HOUSE (NIKKO)*****	♦♦♦♦		●	●	●	●	●	●	●	592
THE GORHAM***	♦♦♦♦	●	●		●		●			120
HELMSLEY MIDDLETOWNE***	♦♦♦	●	●		●		●			190
HELMSLEY WINDSOR***	♦♦♦	●			●		●			243
HOLIDAY INN, CROWNE PLAZA***	♦♦♦♦	●	●			●	●	●	●	770
HOTEL LEXINGTON***	♦♦♦♦	●	●		●		●		●	400
HOWARD JOHNSON PLAZA-HOTEL**	♦♦♦♦	●	●			●	●			300
LOEWS NEW YORK***	♦♦	●	●	●			●	●	●	728

	PRICE	CHILDREN'S RATE	WEEKEND RATE	VIEW	QUIET	PARKING	HOTEL RESTAURANT	SPORTS	CONFERENCES	NO. OF ROOMS
LYDEN HOUSE***	◆◆		●		●		●			81
NEW YORK HILTON & TOWERS***	◆◆◆		●			●	●		●	2041
THE NEW YORK PALACE****	◆◆◆◆		●	●	●		●		●	960
NOVOTEL NEW YORK***	◆◆	●	●	●		●	●		●	474
OMNI BERKSHIRE PLACE***	◆◆◆		●	●	●		●		●	415
OMNI PARK CENTRAL HOTEL***	◆◆◆◆		●			●	●		●	1269
PARK INN INTERNATIONAL HOTEL**	◆◆◆	●	●				●		●	596
THE PARK LANE (HELMSLEY)****	◆◆◆◆		●	●	●		●		●	640
PARKER MERIDIEN***	◆◆◆◆		●	●		●	●		●	700
THE PENINSULA*****	◆◆◆◆		●	●			●	●	●	250
PICKWICK ARMS HOTEL*	◆	●			●		●			400
THE PLAZA****	◆◆◆◆		●	●	●		●	●	●	820
PLAZA 50***	◆◆◆◆		●			●			●	
RIHGA ROYAL HOTEL****	◆◆◆◆		●	●	●		●		●	500
THE RITZ-CARLTON****	◆◆◆◆		●	●	●		●	●	●	214
THE ROGER SMITH***	◆◆◆		●	●	●		●		●	139
SAINT MORITZ ON THE PARK***	◆◆◆◆		●	●			●		●	680
ST. REGIS *****	◆◆◆◆		●	●			●		●	362
SALISBURY HOTEL**	◆◆		●				●		●	320
HOTEL SAN CARLOS***	◆◆◆	●	●	●	●		●		●	149
SHERATON HOTEL TOWER***	◆◆◆	●	●			●	●	●	●	2400
THE SHOREHAM**	◆◆		●		●		●		●	123
THE WALDORF ASTORIA & WALDORF TOWERS****	◆◆◆◆		●	●			●	●	●	1410
THE WARWICK***	◆◆◆◆		●	●			●		●	425
THE WESTPARK HOTEL*	◆	●	●		●		●			100
THE WYNDHAM***	◆◆		●	●	●		●			204
YMCA, VANDERBILT*	◆		●				●	●	●	430
YMCA, WEST SIDE*	◆		●				●	●	●	550
UPPER EAST SIDE										
THE BARBIZON***	◆◆◆		●	●	●		●	●		350
THE CARLYLE*****	◆◆◆◆			●	●		●	●	●	
THE LOWELL (LANDMARK)****	◆◆◆◆			●	●		●		●	60
LYDEN GARDENS***	◆◆◆		●	●	●					133
THE MARK****	◆◆◆◆	●	●	●	●		●	●	●	120
MAYFAIR HOTEL BAGLIONI****	◆◆◆◆		●	●			●		●	201
HOTEL PIERRE*****			●	●	●		●	●		206
HOTEL PLAZA ATHÉNÉE****	◆◆◆◆		●	●			●		●	160
THE REGENCY HOTEL****	◆◆◆◆		●	●			●	●	●	380
STANHOPE*****	◆◆◆◆		●	●			●		●	141
SURREY HOTEL***	◆◆◆◆		●	●	●		●		●	130
HOTEL WALES***	◆◆		●	●	●		●			100
HOTEL WESTBURY****	◆◆◆◆		●	●			●	●	●	179
UPPER WEST SIDE										
THE MAYFLOWER HOTEL***	◆◆◆		●	●	●		●		●	577
THE MILBURN HOTEL**	◆	●	●		●					80
OLCOTT HOTEL**	◆				●		●			100
THE RADISSON EMPIRE***	◆◆◆		●	●			●	●	●	375

◆ CHOOSING A RESTAURANT

♦ $10
♦♦ $20
♦♦♦ $30
♦♦♦♦ $40 and over

	PRICE	AMERICAN CUISINE	FRENCH CUISINE	ORIENTAL CUISINE	EASTERN EUROPEAN CUISINE	ITALIAN CUISINE	WINE CELLAR	GARDEN, TERRACE	SETTING	"INSTITUTION"
WORLD TRADE CENTER										
FRAUNCES TAVERN	♦♦♦♦	●							●	●
HUDSON RIVER CLUB	♦♦♦♦	●					●		●	
CITY HALL										
SLOPPY LOUIE'S	♦♦♦								●	●
LOWER EAST SIDE, LITTLE ITALY, CHINATOWN										
FERRARA	♦									
KATZ'S DELICATESSEN	♦				●					●
KWONG AND WONG	♦♦			●						
MANDARIN COURT	♦			●						
SAMMY'S	♦♦				●					
SILVER PALACE	♦♦			●						
WASHINGTON SQUARE										
ARQUÁ	♦♦♦					●			●	
AU TROQUET	♦♦♦	●					●		●	
BAROCCO	♦♦♦♦					●			●	
BENNY'S BURRITOS	♦									
BOULEY	♦♦♦♦	●					●		●	●
CAPSOUTO FRÈRES	♦♦♦♦						●		●	
CHANTERELLE	♦♦♦♦	●					●			
CHELSEA TRATTORIA	♦♦♦♦					●	●			
DA SILVANO	♦♦♦♦					●	●		●	
EMPIRE DINER	♦♦	●						●	●	
ENNIO & MICHAEL	♦♦♦♦					●				
FÉLIX	♦♦♦		●						●	
FLORENT, RESTAURANT	♦♦♦		●							
GOTHAM BAR & GRILL	♦♦♦♦						●		●	
HONMURA AN	♦♦♦♦			●					●	
JEAN-CLAUDE	♦♦♦		●					●		
JERRY'S	♦♦♦								●	
JOHN'S PIZZERIA	♦					●				
LA BOHÊME	♦♦♦		●					●		
LA LUNCHONETTE	♦♦♦		●			●				
LA METAIRIE	♦♦♦		●				●		●	
LE MADRI	♦♦♦♦					●	●	●	●	
LE PESCADOU	♦♦♦						●			
LE PROVENCE	♦♦♦		●						●	
MESA GRILL	♦♦♦	●					●		●	
MEZZOGIORNO	♦♦♦♦					●			●	
MONTRACHET	♦♦♦♦						●			
NOSMO KING	♦♦♦								●	
THE ODEON	♦♦♦♦	●	●				●		●	
OMEN	♦♦♦								●	
PERIYALI	♦♦♦									
SOHO KITCHEN AND BAR	♦♦♦	●					●			
TRIBECA GRILL	♦♦♦						●		●	
WEST BROADWAY	♦♦♦♦								●	
ZOÉ	♦♦♦						●		●	
UNION SQUARE										
AN AMERICAN PLACE	♦♦♦♦	●					●		●	
COFFEE SHOP	♦♦							●		
GREENMARKET CAFÉ	♦♦♦	●						●		
LA COLOMBE D'OR	♦♦♦♦		●				●			
LOLA	♦♦♦									
MITALI EAST	♦♦									
103	♦♦♦	●								
PARK BISTRO	♦♦♦♦		●				●			
UNION SQUARE CAFÉ	♦♦♦♦	●					●		●	●
GRAND CENTRAL, THEATER DISTRICT										
44	♦♦♦♦						●		●	
AMBASSADOR GRILL	♦♦♦						●		●	
BARBETTA	♦♦♦♦					●	●	●	●	
BECCO	♦♦♦					●	●		●	
BRASSERIE DES THÉÂTRES	♦♦♦		●						●	
CABAÑA CARIOCA	♦♦♦									
CHEZ JOSÉPHINE	♦♦♦		●						●	
JEZEBEL	♦♦	●							●	

400

	PRICE	AMERICAN CUISINE	FRENCH CUISINE	ORIENTAL CUISINE	EASTERN EUROPEAN CUISINE	ITALIAN CUISINE	WINE CELLAR	GARDEN, TERRACE	SETTING	"INSTITUTION"
JOE ALLEN	♦♦	●								
ORSO	♦♦♦♦					●			●	
OYSTER BAR AND RESTAURANT	♦♦♦♦									
THE PALM	♦♦♦♦	●					●			●
SPARKS STEAK HOUSE	♦♦♦♦	●					●			●
ROCKEFELLER CENTER										
AL BUSTAN	♦♦♦♦									
AQUAVIT	♦♦♦♦						●		●	
LE BERNARDIN	♦♦♦♦						●		●	
BICE	♦♦♦♦					●	●	●	●	
THE BRASSERIE	♦♦♦		●							
LA CARAVELLE	♦♦♦♦		●				●		●	
CARNEGIE DELI	♦				●					●
DAWAT	♦♦♦								●	
FELIDIA	♦♦♦♦					●	●		●	
THE FOUR SEASONS	♦♦♦♦	●					●		●	
HARD ROCK CAFÉ	♦♦	●							●	●
HARRY CIPRIANI	♦♦♦♦					●	●		●	
IL NIDO	♦♦♦♦					●			●	
LA GRENOUILLE	♦♦♦♦		●				●		●	
LUTÈCE	♦♦♦♦		●				●		●	
MICKEY MANTLE'S	♦♦♦	●						●	●	●
PETROSSIAN	♦♦♦♦						●		●	
P.J. CLARKE'S	♦♦	●							●	
PLANET HOLLYWOOD	♦♦	●							●	
RAINBOW ROOM	♦♦♦♦						●		●	
REMI	♦♦♦♦					●	●	●	●	●
ROYAL CANADIAN PANCAKE HOUSE	♦♦	●								
RUSSIAN TEA ROOM	♦♦♦♦				●		●		●	
SAN DOMENICO	♦♦♦♦					●	●	●	●	
SHUN LEE PALACE	♦♦♦♦			●			●			
SMITH & WOLLENSKY	♦♦♦♦	●					●		●	
TRATTORIA DELL'ARTE	♦♦♦♦					●			●	
"21" CLUB	♦♦♦♦	●					●		●	●
VONG	♦♦♦♦						●		●	
ZARELA	♦♦♦									
UPPER EAST SIDE										
ARCADIA	♦♦♦♦	●							●	
ARIZONA 206	♦♦♦♦	●					●		●	
BISTRO DU NORD	♦♦♦♦		●				●		●	
CAFÉ CROCODILE	♦♦♦						●			
COCO PAZZO	♦♦♦♦								●	
CONTRAPUNTO	♦♦♦					●				
DANIEL	♦♦♦♦		●		●		●		●	
JOJO	♦♦♦♦		●				●		●	
LE CIRQUE	♦♦♦♦		●				●		●	●
MEZZALUNA	♦♦♦				●			●	●	
MOCCA HUNGARIAN	♦♦♦				●					
MORTIMER'S	♦♦♦	●							●	●
PAPAYA KING	♦									●
PARK AVENUE CAFÉ	♦♦♦♦	●					●		●	
SETTE MEZZO	♦♦♦					●			●	
THE THREE GUYS	♦	●								
UPPER WEST SIDE										
CAFÉ DES ARTISTES	♦♦♦♦		●				●		●	
CAFÉ LUXEMBOURG	♦♦♦		●				●			
EJ'S LUNCHEONETTE	♦♦	●							●	
MEMPHIS	♦♦♦	●					●		●	
SARABETH'S KITCHEN	♦♦♦	●							●	
TAVERN ON THE GREEN	♦♦♦♦						●	●	●	●
VINCE & EDDIE'S	♦♦♦	●					●	●	●	
HARLEM, UPTOWN										
MIRAGE	♦♦♦									
SYLVIA'S	♦♦♦	●							●	●
THE TERRACE	♦♦♦♦		●				●	●	●	
BROOKLYN										
THE RIVER CAFÉ	♦♦♦♦						●	●	●	●

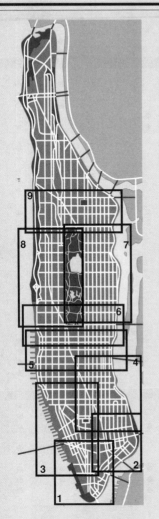

1. WORLD TRADE
   CENTER, CITY HALL
2. LOWER EAST SIDE,
   LITTLE ITALY,
   CHINATOWN
3. WASHINGTON
   SQUARE
4. UNION SQUARE

5. GRAND CENTRAL,
   THEATER DISTRICT
6. ROCKEFELLER
   CENTER
7. UPPER EAST SIDE
8. UPPER WEST SIDE
9. HARLEM,
   UPTOWN

GENERAL

INFORMATION SERVICES

CONSULATES
UK
845 3rd Avenue
Tel. 745-0202
GERMANY
460 Park Avenue
Tel. 308 8700
FRANCE
934 5th Avenue
Tel. 606-3600
CANADA
1251 Ave. of the
Americas
Tel. 596-1700
JAPAN
299 Park Avenue
Tel. 371-8222

NEW YORK CONVENTION AND VISITORS' BUREAU
2 Columbus Circle
New York, N Y 10019
Tel. 484-1200
Open Mon.–Fri. 9am–6pm. Open Sat., Sun. and holidays 10am–6pm
Multilingual reception desk.

TRAVELLERS' AID SOCIETY
1481 Broadway,
(2nd Floor)
Tel. 944-0013
Open Mon.–Fri.
9am–5pm
Emergency assistance for tourists. Same service and general information at JFK Airport, International Arrivals Building
Tel. (1) 718-656-4870

HOSPITALS
BETH ISRAEL MEDICAL CENTER
1st Ave. and 16th St.
Tel. 420-2840
(emergencies)
LENOX HILL HOSPITAL
100 E. 77th St.
Tel. 434-3030
(emergencies)
MOUNT SINAI MEDICAL CENTER
110th St. and 5th Ave.
Tel. 241-7171
(emergencies)

ROOSEVELT HOSPITAL CENTER
59th St. between 9th and 10th aves.
Tel. 523-4000
SAINT LUKE'S
114th St. and Amsterdam Ave.
Tel. 523-6800
SAINT VINCENT'S HOSPITAL
7th Ave. and 11th St.
Tel. 790-7000

PHARMACIES OPEN 24 HOURS A DAY
KAUFMAN PHARMACY
557 Lexington Ave.
(at 50th St.)
Tel. 755-2266

EMERGENCY NUMBERS
EMERGENCY Tel. 911
POLICE Tel. 374-5000

TOURISM

NEW YORK STATE DEPARTMENT OF ECONOMIC DEVELOPMENT (TOURIST DIVISION)
1515 Broadway
(near Times Square)
Open Mon.–Sat.
9am–5pm
Tel. 1-800-827-6255

NEW YORK DOUBLE DECKER TOURS
Empire State Building
350 5th Ave. Suite 6104
Tel. 967-6008
Bus tours around the city. Leave from the Empire State Building.

GRAY LINE NEW YORK TOURS
900 8th Ave.(between 53rd and 54th sts.) or 166 W. 46th St.
Tel. 397-2600
Guided tours of the city. Lasting from 2 hours to one day.

HARLEM SPIRITUALS
1697 Broadway
Suite 203
Tel. 757-0425
Tours of Harlem (including soul food, gospel and jazz).

THE LIMO TOUR
1636 3rd Ave.
Suite 420
Tel. 423-0101
Limousine hire.

CIRCLE LINE
W. 43rd St., Pier 83
Tel. 563-3200
Boat trip around Manhattan island (3 hrs).

1. HUDSON RIVER CLUB
2. VISTA INTERNATIONAL HOTEL
AMERICAN HARVEST
WINDOWS ON THE WORLD
AND CELLAR IN THE SKY
3. SLOPPY LOUIE'S
4. FRAUNCES TAVERN

LIBERTY HELICOPTERS
12th Ave. at W. 30th St.
(on the Hudson)
Tel. 967-6464
Open 9am–9pm 7 days
a week.

WORLD TRADE CENTER

CULTURAL LIFE

CHURCH OF OUR LADY OF THE ROSARY
Shrine of St. Elizabeth
Ann Seton

7 State St.
Tel. 269-6865
Open Mon.–Fri.
7am–5pm.
Open Sat.–Sun.
for Mass ▲ 157

ELLIS ISLAND
New York Harbor
Tel. 363-7620
Open daily
9.30am–5.30pm.
*Ferry every 30 mins
(9.30am–3.30pm) from
Battery Park for Ellis
Island and the Statue of
Liberty. Extraordinary
Museum of Immigration.
Ferry ride takes about
3 hours ▲148.*

FEDERAL HALL NATIONAL MEMORIAL
26 Wall St.
Tel. 264-8711
Open Mon.–Fri.
9am–5pm
*Museum of 18th-
century New York, and
history and founding of
the United States
▲162.*

FEDERAL RESERVE BANK OF NEW YORK
33 Liberty St.
Tel. 720-6130
Open Mon.–Fri. Tours
10.30am, 11.30am,
1.30pm, 2.30pm
*Guided tours: 45 mins
Limited number of
places. Reserve several
weeks in advance.
Contact the Public
Information Division.*

FRAUNCES TAVERN MUSEUM
54 Pearl St.
Tel. 425-1778
Open Mon.–Fri.
10am–4.45pm
Open Sat. 12am–4pm
Closed Sun., public
holidays.
*18th- and 19th-century
American history, with
reconstructions of
period interiors ▲166.*

HOBOKEN FERRY
Battery Park City
(at the foot of the World
Financial Center,
on the Hudson River).
Tel. 1-908-GO FERRY
*Leaves daily, virtually
every half hour on
weekends. Week day
schedule varies.
The journey (8 mins)
affords a fine view of
New York and the bay.*

MUSEUM OF AMERICAN FINANCIAL HISTORY
26 Broadway
Tel. 908-4519
Open Mon.–Fri.

11.30am–2.30pm
*Temporary exhibitions
on the financial history
of the United States
▲156.*

NEW YORK STOCK EXCHANGE (N.Y.S.E.)
20 Broad St.
Tel. 656-5167
Open Mon.–Fri.
9.15am–4pm
Closed Sat., Sun.,
public holidays.
*Free admission if there
is enough room; it is
advisable to get there
early (tickets available
beginning 9am).*

STATEN ISLAND FERRY
Battery Park,
South Ferry
Tel. 806-6940
*Leaves every 30 mins to
1 hr, 24 hours a day
Length of journey: ½ hr.
Superb view of lower
Manhattan, the Statue
of Liberty and the bay.*

STATUE OF LIBERTY
Liberty Island
New York Harbor
Tel. 363-3267
*Same times and place of
departure as for Ellis
Island.
Tickets can be bought
at Castle Clinton, in
Battery Park. The tour
lasts a total of 4 hours.
Very popular in summer
and at weekends
▲ 144.*

TRINITY CHURCH
Broadway and Wall St.
Tel. 602-0872
CHURCH
Tours Mon.–Fri. 2pm
MUSEUM
Open Mon.–Fri. 9–
11.45am and 1–3.45pm
Open Sat.
10am–3.45pm. Open
Sun. 1–3.45pm
▲ 154

JOHN STREET METHODIST CHURCH
44 John St.
Tel. 269-0014
*Museum open Mon.,
Wed., Fri. noon–4pm*

WORLD FINANCIAL CENTER
West St.
*Entry through the World
Trade Center via North
or South Bridge*
Tel. 945-0505
*Entertainment at the
Winter Garden.
Shopping mall.*

WORLD TRADE CENTER
Between Church, Vesey,
West and Liberty sts.
Tel. 435-7377
Open daily.
9.30am–9.30pm,
9.30am–11.30pm in
summer
*Breathtaking view from
the top of the
Observatory (Tower
Two, 107th floor)* ▲ 138.

RESTAURANTS

FRAUNCES TAVERN
54 Pearl St.
Tel. 269-0144
Closed Sat., Sun.
*A quintessentially
American restaurant.
Grills and seafood.
Breakfast* ▲ 166.

HUDSON RIVER CLUB
250 Vesey St. (4 World
Financial Center)
Tel. 786-1500
Closed Sat. noon,
Sun. evening
*In season, Hudson
River valley products.
Overlooking the mouth
of the Hudson.
Brunch.*

CITY HALL

CULTURAL LIFE

CITY HALL
City Hall Park (between

Broadway and Park
Row)
Tel. 788-2954
Open Mon.–Fri.
10am–2pm
*New York's City Hall
▲168.*

SOUTH STREET SEAPORT MUSEUM
207 Front St.
Tel. 669-9400
Open daily. 10am–5pm;
in summer 10am–6pm
*Tour of the fish market,
6am, first Thursday of
each month, Apr.–Oct.*
Tel. (reservations)
669-9416

1. KATZ'S DELICATESSEN
2. SAMMY'S
3. SILVER PALACE
4. FERRARA
5. MANDARIN COURT
6. KWONG AND WONG
1. CHELSEA HOTEL
2. EMPIRE DINER
3. PERIYALI
4. LA LUNCHONETTE
5. GASCOGNE
6. LE MADRI
7. MESA GRILL
8. CHELSEA TRATTORIA
9. BENNY'S BURRITOS
10. FLORENT
11. AU TROQUET
12. GOTHAM BAR & GRILL
13. LA METAIRIE

Maritime museums. Ships tours. Boat trips ▲172.

ST. PAUL'S CHAPEL
Broadway and Fulton St.
Tel. 602-0800
Open Mon.–Fri. 9am–3pm
Concerts and operas every Mon. and Thurs. at noon. Tel. 602-0768 for reservations.

RESTAURANTS

SLOPPY LOUIE'S
92 South St.
Tel. 509-9694
Open daily.
Charming surroundings, polite service. Wide range of freshly caught fish and shellfish. Closes early.

SHOPPING

CENTURY 21 DEPARTMENT STORE
22 Cortlandt St.
Tel. 227-9092
Three floors of "end of line" and marked-down goods: a popular store.

J&R COMPUTER/ MUSIC WORLD
15–33 Park Row
Tel. 238-9000
Photography, computers, records, videos. A wide choice, well-informed sales assistants.

PIER 17 PAVILION
89 South St.
(South Street Seaport)
Shopping center. 50 restaurants and cafés.

LOWER EAST SIDE LITTLE ITALY CHINATOWN

CULTURAL LIFE

CHINATOWN HISTORY MUSEUM
70 Mulberry St. (2nd Floor)
Tel. 619-4785
Open noon–5pm
Closed Sat.
Exhibition rooms and archives ▲191.

CATHOLIC CHURCH OF THE TRANSFIGURATION
29 Mott St.
Tel. 962-5157
Open only for services ▲192.

ST. JAMES CHURCH
23 Oliver St.
Tel. 233-0161
Refectory open Mon.–Sat. 10am–9pm ▲193.

LOWER EAST SIDE TENEMENT MUSEUM
97 Orchard St.
Tel. 431-0233
Open Tues.–Fri. 11am–5pm
Open Sun. 10am–6pm
Closed Sat., Mon.
Exhibitions on immigrant life on the Lower East Side. Guided walks and tour of a restored tenement building.

MARINERS' TEMPLE BAPTIST CHURCH
3 Henry St. and 12 Oliver St.
Tel. 233-0423
Open Sun. 10am
Service with gospel choir ▲193.

MOST HOLY CRUCIFIX CHURCH
378 Broome St.
Tel. 226-2556
Open for services ▲196.

ELDRIDGE ST. SYNAGOGUE
12 Eldridge St.
Tel. 219-0888
Open noon–5pm by appointment.
Closed Sat.

RESTAURANTS

FERRARA
195 Grand St.
Tel. 226-6150
Open daily.
The ice creams and a wide range of delicious pastries of Southern Italy. Variety of cordials.

KATZ'S DELICATESSEN
205 E. Houston St.
Tel. 254-2246
Open daily.
Entertaining and convivial. This is the place to go if you like real Jewish "delis". Brunch.

KWONG AND WONG
11 Division St.
Tel. 431-1040
Open daily.
Chinese fish restaurant (guaranteed fresh). The special dishes of the day are highly recommended.

MANDARIN COURT
61 Mott St.
Tel. 608-3838
Open daily.
Very popular dim sum restaurant, specializing in steamed dishes. Brunch. Chinese beer only.

SAMMY'S
157 Chrystie St.
Tel. 673-0330
Open daily.
Fairly stodgy Central European Jewish cuisine, huge helpings in a rather noisy setting.

SILVER PALACE
52 Bowery
Tel. 964-1204
Open daily.
Recommended for its steamed dumplings. Popular dim sum restaurant.

CAFÉS

CAFFÈ ROMA PASTRY
385 Broome St.
Tel. 226-8413
Traditional Italian café.

SHOPPING

CANAL ST. (CHINATOWN)
Electronic goods, clothes, perfume, and shoes.

ESSEX ST. (LOWER EAST SIDE)
Religious articles and pickles.

GRAND ST. (LITTLE ITALY)
An interesting array of small shops.

MATT, PELL, BAYARD AND DOYERS STS. (CHINATOWN)
South of Canal St. Lined with small shops and restaurants.

MULBERRY ST. (LITTLE ITALY)
A choice of restaurants.

ORCHARD ST. (LOWER EAST SIDE)
North of Delancey St. Clothes and leather goods.

14. WASHINGTON SQ. HOTEL
15. JOHN'S PIZZERIA
16. DA SILVANO
17. ENNIO & MICHAEL
18. NOSMO KING
19. WEST BROADWAY
20. JEAN-CLAUDE
LE PROVENCE
21. SOHO KITCHEN AND BAR
22. ZOÉ / JERRY'S
23. LE PESCADOU
24. MEZZOGIORNO
25. CAPSOUTO FRÈRES
26. MONTRACHET
27. TRIBECA GRILL
28. CHANTERELLE
29. ARQUÀ
30. BOULEY
31. THE ODEON

WASHINGTON SQUARE

CULTURAL LIFE

ALTERNATIVE MUSEUM
594 Broadway
(Houston St.)
Tel. 966-4444
Open Tues.–Sat.
11am–6pm
Exhibitions focus on social, political, and economic issues.

MUSEUM FOR AFRICAN ART
593 Broadway
Tel. 966-1313
Open Tues.–Fri.
10.30am–5.30pm
Open Sat. noon–6pm
Open Sun. noon–6pm
African art ▲ 203.

CHURCH OF THE ASCENSION
5th Ave. at 10th St.
Tel. 254-8620
Open Mon.–Sat.
noon–2pm and 5–7pm

CIRCLE IN THE SQUARE THEATRE
159 Bleecker St.
Tel. 254-6330
The birthplace of "Off-Broadway" productions.

CLOCKTOWER GALLERY
108 Leonard St.
(14th Floor)
Tel. 233-1096
Open Mon.–Thurs.
10am–6pm
Temporary exhibitions of contemporary artists. You can climb the clocktower ▲ 382.

DIA CENTER FOR THE ARTS
548 W. 22nd St.
Tel. 989-5912
Open Thurs.–Sun.
noon–6pm
Closed Jul.–Labor Day.
Modern art ▲ 220.

THE FORBES MAGAZINE GALLERIES
62 5th Ave. (12th St.)
Tel. 206-5548
Open Tues.–Wed. and Fri.–Sat. 10am–4pm
Malcolm Forbes' collections (Fabergé eggs, 12,000 toy soldiers, etc.) ▲ 219.

GENERAL THEOLOGICAL SEMINARY
175 9th Ave.
Tel. 243-5150
Open Mon.–Fri.
noon–3pm
Open Sat. 11am–2pm
Open Sun. 2–4pm
Exhibition in the lobby. Garden. The library is closed to the public.

GUGGENHEIM MUSEUM SOHO
575 Broadway
(Prince St.)
Tel. 423-3500
Open Sun., Mon. and Wed. 11am–6pm
Open Thurs.–Sat.
11am–8pm
Closed 5pm on public holidays.
Annex of the Guggenheim Museum ▲ 204.

JUDSON MEMORIAL CHURCH
55 Washington Square South
Tel. 477-0351
Open Mon.–Fri. 9am–5pm
Tours by arrangement ▲ 200.

NEW MUSEUM OF CONTEMPORARY ART
583 Broadway
(Prince and Houston sts.)
Tel. 219-1355
Open Wed.–Fri. and Sun. noon–6pm
Open Sat. noon–8pm
Contemporary artists ▲ 204.

NEW YORK CITY FIRE MUSEUM
278 Spring St.
Tel. 691-1303
Open Tues.–Sat.
10am–4pm

GALLERIES

A/D
560 Broadway
Tel. 966-5154
Open Tues.–Sat.
10am–6pm
A/D commissions limited editions of decorative everyday objects from various artists (Arman, Gerhard Richter, Donald Sultan, etc.)

A.I.R.
63 Crosby St.
Tel. 966-0799
Open Tues.–Sat.
11am–6pm
First women's cooperative, non-profit gallery founded in 1972.

ARTISTS' SPACE
38 Greene St.
(3rd Floor)
Tel. 226-3970

Open Tues.–Sat.
10am–6pm
Voluntary organization exhibiting avant-garde works. The curators also organize thematic exhibitions.

BROOKE ALEXANDER
59 Wooster St.
Tel. 925-4338
Open Tues.–Sat.
10am–6pm
Art gallery exhibiting contemporary European and American art.

BROOKE ALEXANDER EDITIONS
476 Broome St.
Tel. 925-2070
Open Tues.–Sat.
10am–6pm
A contemporary art gallery and a prestigious publishing house (limited edition prints, collections and high-quality illustrated books).

AMERICAN FINE ARTS CO.
22 Wooster St.
Tel. 941-0401
Open Tues.–Sat.
10am–6pm
A fascinating, unconventional gallery which mounts provocative exhibitions. A showcase for up-and-coming young artists.

JOSH BAER GALLERY
476 Broome St.
(3rd Floor)
Tel. 431-4774
Open Tues.–Sat.
10am–6pm
Conceptual artists focusing particuliarly on contemporary social issues.

MARY BOONE GALLERY
417 West Broadway
Tel. 431-1818
Open Tues.–Sat.
10am–6pm
Mary Boone launched the most outstanding artists of the 1980s.

JANET BORDEN INC.
560 Broadway
(6th Floor)
Tel. 431-0166
Open Tues.–Sat.
11am–5pm
Large-scale, color photographs.

LEO CASTELLI GALLERY
420 West Broadway
(2nd Floor)
Tel. 431-5160
Open Tues.–Sat.
10am–6pm
Leo Castelli was the man who introduced Johns, Rauschenberg, Lichtenstein, Warhol, Rosenquist, Stella, Judd and Nauman and he continues to exhibit their works. His influence has shaped the world of modern art for the past thirty years.

PAULA COOPER GALLERY
155 Wooster St.
Tel. 674-0766
Open Tues.–Sat.
10am–6pm
Exhibits works by contemporary artists. Women artists are given more consideration here than in other comparable galleries.

CROWN POINT PRESS
568 Broadway
Tel. 226-5476

Open Tues.–Fri.
9.30am–5.30pm
Open Sat. 11am–6pm
Founded in 1962. Artists learn to master traditional typographic techniques here. Crown Point Press takes care of the printing (limited editions).

JAMES DANZIGER GALLERY
130 Prince St.
Tel. 226-0056
Open Tues.–Sat.
11am–6pm
Represents some of the big contemporary names in fashion photography, and launches young unknowns.

THE DRAWING CENTER
35 Wooster St.
Tel. 219- 2166
Open Tues.–Fri.
10am–6pm
Open Sat. 11am–6pm
Four or five times a year, this center exhibits the work of artists who have yet to make a name for themselves. It also possesses an index of slides, covering recent works by nearly 5,000 artists, which is open to the public by appointment only.

EXIT ART THE FIRST WORLD
548 Broadway

(2nd Floor)
Tel. 966-7745
Open Tues.–Fri.
10am–6pm
Open Sat. 11am–6pm
One-man exhibitions as well as thematic exhibitions setting new faces alongside established names. The gallery also includes an "Apartment Store" (furniture and original objects) and the "Café Cultura" for a tasty bite to eat.

FEATURE
76 Greene St.
(2nd Floor)
Tel. 941-7077
Open Tues.–Sat.
11am–6pm
European atmosphere. A highly distinctive group of artists whose works run the gamut from conceptual installations to expressive drawing. A gallery where you are most likely to discover new artists.

RONALD FELDMAN FINE ARTS
31 Mercer St.
Tel. 226-3232
Open Tues.–Sat.
10am–6pm
American and contemporary Russian artists.

JOHN GIBSON
568 Broadway
Tel. 925-1192
Open Tues.–Sat.
10am–6pm
Unpretentious gallery which has faithfully reflected all the new artistic trends to appear over the past thirty years.

BARBARA GLADSTONE
99 Greene St.
Tel. 431-3334
Open Tues.–Sat.
10am–6pm
The most radical masterpieces of politicized conceptualism (Acconci, Faigenbaum, Holzer, Mullican, Trockel, etc.).

JOHN GOOD
532 Broadway
(2nd Floor)
Tel. 941-8066
Open Tues.–Sat.
10am–6pm
A group of painters who have turned their back

on the taste for irony and are concentrating on a more sensuous form of abstract art. This gallery focuses on new talents rather than established names.

JAY GORNEY MODERN ART
100 Greene St.
Tel. 966- 4480
Open Tues.–Sat.
10am–6pm
Contemporary artists with an awareness of social issues; also painters and sculptors who explore new dimensions in their medium.

O.K. HARRIS WORKS OF ART
383 West Broadway
Tel. 431-3600
Open Tues.–Sat.
10am–6pm
A gallery opened by Ivan C. Karp, the originator of the 1970's photo-realist movement.

PAT HEARN
39 Wooster St.
Tel. 941- 7055
Open Tues.–Sat.
10am–6pm
Pat Hearn was one of the first artists to settle in the East Village, before moving to SoHo. She exhibits emerging American and European contemporary artists.

LOWINSKY GALLERY
573 Broadway
Tel. 226-5440
Open Tues.–Sat.
11am–6pm
An array of 19th-century

works and contemporary photography.

LUHRING AUGUSTINE
130 Prince St.
(2nd Floor)
Tel. 219-9600
Open Tues.–Sat.
10am–6pm
Exhibits mainly

contemporary work by established German, American and Japanese artists.

CURT MARCUS GALLERY
578 Broadway
(Prince St., 10th Floor)
Tel. 226-3200
Open Tues.–Sat.
10am–6pm
The cream of up-and-coming artists as well as those who have already acquired some measure of renown.

METRO PICTURES
150 Greene St.
Tel. 925-8335

Open Tues.–Sat.
10am–6pm
In a vast gallery , artists tackle socio-cultural issues, pulling no punches with their playful and provocative stance.

PACE GALLERY
142 Greene St.
Tel. 431-9224
Open Tues.–Sat.
10am–6pm
A key player in the contemporary art world. After showing Picasso, Noguchi and Joseph Cornell, Pace made inroads into the contemporary art market with Martin, Richard Serra and Louise Nevelson. Another gallery at 32 E. 57th St ▲ 416.

P.P.O.W.
532 Broadway
(4th Floor)
Tel. 941-8642
Open Tues.–Sat.
10am–6pm
Photography, painting, and works of up-and-coming artists with a keen awareness of social issues and a sense of irony.

MAX PROTETCH
560 Broadway
(3rd Floor)
Tel. 966-5454
Open Tues.–Sat.
10am–6pm
This gallery contains

ancient and modern architectural drawings (Isozaki, Tschumi, Frank Lloyd Wright, etc.) and minutely detailed and architectonic works by artists.

TONY SHAFRAZI GALLERY
119 Wooster St.
Tel. 274-9300
Open Tues.–Sat.

10am–6pm, mid-June through Labor Day Mon.–Fri. 10am–6pm Tony Shafrazi achieved notoriety for defacing Picasso's "Guernica" with graffiti at the Museum of Modern Art. He now exhibits contemporary artists, some of whom (e.g. Basquiat, Keith Haring and Kenny Scharf) started out as graffitists.

65 THOMPSON STREET
65 Thompson St.
Tel. 219-2219
Open Tues.–Sat.
10am–6pm
Large-scale works hung in the vast uncluttered space of a former garage, shared by Leo Castelli and Larry Gagosian.

HOLLY SOLOMON GALLERY
172 Mercer St.
Tel. 941-5777
Open Tues.–Sat.
10am–6pm, summer hours Memorial Day–Labor Day Mon.–Fri. 10am–5pm. Holly Solomon has a flair for discovering important artists yet to make a name for themselves.

SONNABEND GALLERY
420 West Broadway
(3rd Floor)

Tel. 966-6160
Open Tues.–Sat.
10am–6pm
Monumental art often goes hand in hand with a quaint, almost kitsch sensibility in this gallery. Ileana Sonnabend knows artistic quality when she sees it and has a keen, ironic eye.

SPERONE WESTWATER
142 Greene St.
Tel. 431-3685
Open Tues.–Sat.
10am–6pm
Exhibits a group of young Italians, better-known artists and established names (Long, Richter, Rothenberg, etc.).

STALEY-WISE GALLERY
560 Broadway
(6th Floor)
Tel. 966-6223
Open Tues.–Sat.
11am–5pm
Commercial photographs used to create artistic effects. Striking and amusing.

303 GALLERY
89 Greene St.
(2nd Floor)
Tel. 966-5605
Open Tues.–Sat.
10am–6pm
Liz Larner and Thomas Ruff made a name for themselves here. The gallery continues to be on the lookout for young talent.

THREAD WAXING SPACE
476 Broadway
(2nd Floor)
Tel. 966-9520
Open Tues.–Sat.
10am–6pm
A former factory, now a cultural center. A multi-disciplinary visual arts and performing art space.

JOHN WEBER GALLERY
142 Greene St.
(3rd Floor)
Tel. 966-6115
Open Tues.–Sat.
10am–6pm
Primarily conceptual art. Artists interested in minimalism (Buren); others inspired by the soil (Fulton, Smithson), an entire group (Burgin, Haacke, Piper) with a

penchant for strident political comment.

RESTAURANTS

ARQUÁ
281 Church St.
Tel. 334-1888
Open noon and evening.
Closed Sat. noon, Sun. noon.
Stylish and convivial trattoria. Attractive menu.

AU TROQUET
328 W. 12th St.
Tel. 924-3413
Open every evening.
Romantic bistro with plenty of atmosphere.

BAROCCO
301 Church St.
Tel. 431-1445
Very lively, informal, cutting-edge art and fashion crowd.

BENNY'S BURRITOS
113 Greenwich Ave.
Tel. 727-0584
Open daily.
Mammoth tortillas with a huge variety of fillings, from cheese to guacamole. No credit cards.

LA BOHÈME
24 Minetta Lane
Tel. 473-6447
Open Tues.–Sun.
Excellent first courses (e.g. pizza with artichokes and snails). Brunch.

BOULEY
165 Duane St.
Tel. 608-3852

Open noon and evenings
Closed Sat. noon, Sun. Extremely inventive cuisine (sample the grilled prawns with wild

mushrooms). "The" place to eat in New York. Reservation essential, well in advance.

CAPSOUTO FRÈRES
451 Washington St.
Tel. 966-4900
Open noon and evenings.
Closed Mon. noon.
Contemporary French cuisine.

CHANTERELLE
2 Harrison St.
Tel. 966-6960
Open noon and evening.
Closed Sun., Mon.
Sophisticated dishes in peaceful surroundings: famous for seafood boudin and imaginative "nouvelle" cuisine.

CHELSEA TRATTORIA
108 8th Ave.
Tel. 924-7786
Closed Sat. noon, Sun.
Highly regarded, yet unpretentious (linguini with white clam sauce, risotto funghi and veal trastevere).

DA SILVANO
260 Ave.of the Americas
Tel. 982-2343
Closed Sat. noon and Sun noon.
A fresh approach to Northern Italian specialties.

EMPIRE DINER
210 10th Ave.
Tel. 243-2736
Open 7 days a week, 24 hours a day. Closed Tues. 4am–8am.
Magnificent restored Art Deco monument. Menu for eclectic tastes, ranging from chicken wings, nachos or Chinese wontons to bacon, lettuce and tomato sandwiches and ice cream sundaes seasoned with chili ▲ 220.

ENNIO & MICHAEL
539 LaGuardia Pl.
Tel. 677-8577
Open daily.
Nourishing and delicious dishes, such as fried zucchini, seafood salad, gnocchi in tomato sauce and gamberi à la diable.

FÉLIX
340 West Broadway
Tel. 431-0021
Open noon and
evening.
Closed Mon. noon.
*A lively, fashionable
bistro. American
Express only.*

GOTHAM BAR & GRILL
12 E. 12th St.
Tel. 620-4020
Open noon and
evening.
Closed Sat. noon,
Sun. noon.
*This is a "must". Sample
their ravioli à la
caponata, their morel
ravioli and their flour-
free chocolate cake.*

HONMURA AN
170 Mercer St.
Tel. 334-5253
*Original, very refined
Japanese cuisine
specializing in soba
dishes. Elegant,
modern space.*

JEAN-CLAUDE
137 Sullivan St.
Tel. 475-9232
Open every evening.
A good place to have a

*drink and savor
excellent, reasonably
priced bistro dishes. No
reservations. Brunch.*

JERRY'S
101 Prince St.
Tel. 966-9464
Open noon and
evenings.
Closed Sun. evenings.
*A former diner which
has come up in the
world. Delicious
sandwiches, whole
meals in themselves.
Brunch.*

JOHN'S PIZZERIA
278 Bleecker St.
Tel. 243-1680
Open daily.
*The best Neapolitan
pizza house in
Manhattan. Brunch. No
credit cards.*

LA LUNCHONETTE
130 10th Ave.

Tel. 675-0342
Open noon and
evening.
Closed Sun. dinner.
*Impressive menu: leek
and lentil salad, snails
in cognac, grilled lamb
sausages, brains in
brown butter and
cassoulet.*

LA METAIRIE
189 W. 10th St.
Tel. 989-0343
Open daily.
*Friendly atmosphere.
Cooking with a
Provençal touch.
Seafood sausage, quail
stuffed with foie gras
and spinach.*

LE MADRI
168 W. 18th St.
Tel. 727-8022
Open noon and
evening.
*The fashion and
publishing worlds flock
here to savor delicious
pizzas cooked in a
traditional wood-fired
oven and imaginative
pasta dishes.*

LE PESCADOU
18 King St.
Tel. 924-3434
Open daily.
*A combination of fish
and Provençal. You can
eat meals at the bar for
less.*

LE PROVENCE
38 MacDougal St.
Tel. 475-7500
Open daily.
*Authentic Provençal
cuisine in a lively bistro.*

MESA GRILL
102 5th Ave.
Tel. 807-7400
Open daily.
*Picturesque and
friendly. Specialties
from southwest
America. Ideal for family
meals, as well as for
brunch.*

MEZZOGIORNO
195 Spring St.
Tel. 334-2112
Open noon and
evenings.
*Fine, light Italian
cooking, if a little
expensive, in relaxed
surroundings. No credit
cards.*

MONTRACHET
239 West Broadway
Tel. 219-2777

Open in the evenings
and Fri. noon.
Closed Sun.
*Mouth-watering
creations by chef Debra
Ponzek: sautéed New
York foie gras, striped
bass with roasted*

*peppers and lemon,
pan-seared duckling
with salsify and sweet
potato flan.*

NOSMO KING
54 Varick St.
Tel. 966-1239
Closed Sat.–Sun. lunch.
*Contemporary
American cuisine: fresh
fish, local game and
vegetables.*

THE ODEON
145 West Broadway
Tel. 233-0507
Open daily.
*This Art Deco bistro was
a favorite haunt of Andy
Warhol's group. The
food is now rather
commonplace.
Brunch.*

OMEN
113 Thompson St.
Tel. 925-8923
Open in the evening.
Closed Mon.
*This restaurant has the
calm of the countryside.*

PERIYALI
35 W. 20th St.
Tel. 463-7890
Open noon and
evening. Closed Sat.
noon and Sun.
*The most original Greek
restaurant in New York.
Greek country salad,
grilled charcoal
octopus.*

RESTAURANT FLORENT
69 Gansevoort St.
Tel. 989-5779
Open 7 days a week, 24
hours a day.
*The food could be more
exciting, but the
restaurant has no lack
of customers (Madonna
is occasionally seen
here). Order a taxi to
get back. The
establishment does not
take credit cards.*

**SOHO KITCHEN AND
BAR**
103 Greene St.
Tel. 925-1866
Open daily.
*Superb wine bar with
more than 100 vintages
from all over the world,
served by the glass.
Pizzas, pasta and
grills.*

TRIBECA GRILL
375 Greenwich St.
Tel. 941-3900
Open noon and
evenings.
Closed Sat. noon.
*A large, lively basement
where you can sample
fine cooking and rub
shoulders with
celebrities.*

WEST BROADWAY
349 West Broadway
Tel. 226-5885
Open daily.
*The highly original
décor complements the
fish specialties
perfectly: sheared
yellowfin tuna with fried
ginger tips and tomato
coriander broth,
Moroccan shrimp
cocktail.*

ZOË
90 Prince St.
Tel. 966-6722
Open noon and
evening.
Closed Mon.
*Superb all-American
cuisine: crisp noodle
wrapped shrimp, grilled
salmon with Moroccan*

*and basil mash
potatoes, Mexican
pecan pie with caramel
icing. Reserve well in
advance for brunch on
weekends.*

ACCOMMODATION

CHELSEA HOTEL
222 W. 23rd St.
Tel./Fax. 243-3700
*Frequented by artists.
Relaxed service, simple,
fairly well-kept rooms.
Negotiate special rates
for long stays ▲ 220.*

**WASHINGTON SQUARE
HOTEL**
103 Waverly Pl.
Tel. 777-9515
or 1-800-222-0418
Fax. 979-8373
*Ideal for young people
who are not too fussy
about accommodation.
In the heart of
Greenwich Village.
Competitive prices
for children.*

SHOPPING

AGNÈS B
116 Prince St.
Tel. 925-4649
*Great basics and
separates with a
French flair.*

BALDUCCI'S
424 Ave. of the
Americas
Tel. 673-2600
*Italian grocery store
which moved to the
Village in 1948. Not just
excellent caterers: an
institution. Worth a visit
for the décor and the
people who shop there.*

BARNEYS NEW YORK
106 7th Ave.
Tel. 929-9000
*Department store. One
of the leading
menswear outlets. From
the most original
designs to classic cuts.
Also caters to women
and children. Chic and
expensive. Renowned
for its window displays,
especially at Christmas.*

BETSEY JOHNSON
130 Thompson St.
Tel. 420-0169
*Teenage fashions,
inspired by the 1960's.*

**THE BIOGRAPHY
BOOKSHOP**
400 Bleecker St.
Tel. 807-8655
*Specializes in
biographies, letters,
autobiographies, and
memoirs by both
famous and unknown
authors.*

CANAL JEAN
504 Broadway
Tel. 226-1130
*Four floors of jeans and
clothes for the young,
often at rock-bottom
prices. One whole floor
of secondhand clothes.*

**CANAL STREET FLEA
MARKET**
335 Canal St.
Open Sat.–Sun.
Closed Jan.–Feb.

DEAN AND DELUCA
560 Broadway
Tel. 431-1691
*SoHo's main quality
grocery store. Even if*

*you don't want to buy
anything, it is worth
visiting this store for its
décor. Espresso bar at
the entrance.*

**THE ENCHANTED
FOREST**
85 Mercer St.
Tel. 925-6677
*Wonderful plush toys in
delightful surroundings.*

LOST CITY ARTS
275 Lafayette St.
Tel. 941-8025
*Secondhand goods;
mainly used in
advertising and
architecture.*

NEW REPUBLIC
93 Spring St.
Tel. 219-3005
*Classic men's
sportswear and tailored
clothing.*

POP SHOP
292 Lafayette St.
Tel. 219-2784
*Designs by Keith Haring
and prints of his work
on T-shirts, books,
posters, etc.*

**REPLAY COUNTRY
STORE**
109 Prince St.
Tel. 673-6300
*Jeans and yet more
jeans, from Italy!*

SCREAMING MIMI'S
382 Lafayette St.
Tel. 677-6464
*Clothes for young
people, caters for all
tastes.*

SPY STORE
164 Christopher St.
Tel. 366-6466
*Everything for people
who are fascinated by
surveillance and
counter-surveillance
equipment.*

THINK BIG
390 West Broadway
Tel. 925-7300
*Gigantic objects. Goods
can be mailed abroad.*

TOOTSIE PLOHOUND
413 West Broadway
Tel. 925-8931
*Fashionable men's and
women's shoes.*

UNCLE STEVE'S
343 Canal St.
Tel. 226-4010
*Electronic goods at
discount prices.*

VILLAGE CHESS SHOP
230 Thompson St.
Tel. 475-9580
*Chess sets in all shapes
and sizes.*

NIGHT LIFE

THE BACK FENCE
155 Bleecker St.
Tel. 475-9221
*Simply a bar.
Open 4pm–4am
Live music every
evening: country, rock,
folk.*

THE BITTER END
147 Bleecker St.
Tel. 673-7030
*Music club.
Open 5.30pm–4am.
Bob Dylan, Joan Baez
and Neil Young started
out here, as did Woody
Allen. Shows at 8pm,
8.30pm, 9.30pm,
10.30pm, 11.30pm;
weekends 12.30am,
1.30am.*

BLUE NOTE
131 W. 3rd St.
Tel. 475-8592
*Bar-restaurant.
Open 7pm–3am
A jazz mecca.
The musical fare is of
a consistently high
standard, with great
classic performers such
as Ray Charles,*

*Dave Brubeck and
Lionel Hampton. You
can have brunch here
on Sat. and Sun.*

BOTTOM LINE
15 W. 4th St.
Tel. 228-6300
*This fast-food joint,
located in a student
quarter, is an excellent
place for rock music. All
the big names in pop
and country music play
here.*

BRADLEY'S
70 University Pl.
Tel. 473-9700
*Bar-restaurant.
Open 5.30pm–4am
One of the top jazz
clubs. Shows at 10pm,
midnight and 2am.*

EAR INN
326 Spring St.
Tel. 226-9060
*Music Mon.–Thurs.
11pm–3.30am
The house is allegedly
haunted. You can have
lunch or supper at this
bar, which is extremely
lively in the evenings.*

LIMELIGHT
47 W. 20th St.
Tel. 807-7850
*Disused church, now a
venue for the New York
smart set who enjoy
wild evenings here, with
masquerade parties
and shows.*

PECULIAR PUB
145 Bleecker St.
Tel. 353-1327
*Open from 5pm
Deservedly renowned
for its wide range of
beers from all over the
world.*

**S.O.B.'s
(SOUNDS OF BRAZIL)**
204 Varick St.
Tel. 243-4940
*Closed Sun. Bar-
restaurant.
Brazilian and Caribbean
cuisine. South American
and African music is
performed in the*

1. AN AMERICAN PLACE
2. PARK BISTRO
3. LA COLOMBE D'OR
4. ARLINGTON ARMS HOTEL
5. CARLTON ARMS HOTEL
6. LOLA
7. GREENMARKET CAFÉ
8. GRAMERCY PARK HOTEL
9. COFFEE SHOP
10. UNION SQUARE CAFÉ
11. "103 NYC"
12. MITALI EAST

evenings, 9pm and 11pm shows. Lunch only during the week.

SWEET BASIL
88 7th Ave.
Tel. 242-1785
Bar-restaurant.
Open daily, from noon
Brunch Sat.–Sun.
2–6pm.
Jazz sets at 9pm and 11pm.

TRAMPS
51 W. 21st St.
Tel. 727-7788
Only open on days of concerts.
Cajun restaurant. Blues, soul and music with a sunny beat.

VILLAGE VANGUARD
178 7th Ave.
Tel. 255-4037
Open 9.30pm–1am
The spirit of John Coltrane is still kept very much alive in this club frequented by the jazz old guard.

WETLANDS
161 Hudson St.
Tel. 966-4225
Open Mon.–Fri.
5pm–4am
Open Sat.–Sun.
9pm–4am
This venue comes alive with African rhythms, punk music, rock or jazz, depending on the evening.

CAFÉ-BARS

CAFÉ BORGIA
185 Bleecker St.
Tel. 674-9589

LE CAFÉ FIGARO
184 Bleecker St.

Tel. 677-1100
The original décor of this establishment, a meeting place for beatniks and café society during the 1950's, has been restored.

CAFFÈ DANTE
79 MacDougal St.
Tel. 982-5275

CAFFÈ REGGIO
119 MacDougal St.
Tel. 475-9557
The most famous café in the Village. It boasts the oldest coffee percolator in New York and still has the original Italian décor which dates from its opening in 1927.

CHUMLEY'S
86 Bedford St.
Tel. 675-4449
Bar-restaurant
Open Sun.–Thurs.
5–11pm
Open Fri., Sat.
5pm–1am ▲ 213.

WHITE HORSE TAVERN
567 Hudson St.
Tel. 243-9260
Bar-restaurant. Terrace in the summer ▲ 215.

UNION SQUARE

CULTURAL LIFE

APPELLATE DIVISION OF STATE SUPREME COURT
25th St. and Madison Ave.
Tel. 340-0477
Open Mon.–Fri.
9am–5pm
You can attend when the courts are in session: Tues.–Thurs., 2–6pm; Fri., 10am–1pm.

THE BROTHERHOOD SYNAGOGUE
28 Gramercy Park South
Tel. 674-5750
▲ 230.

CHURCH OF THE TRANSFIGURATION
1 E. 29th St.
Tel. 684-6770
Open 8am–6pm.

CON EDISON ENERGY MUSEUM
145 E.14th St.
Tel. 460-6244
Open Tues.–Sat.
9am–5pm
Reconstruction of New York's underground wiring system.

GRACE CHURCH
802 Broadway and 10th St.
Tel. 254-2000

Open Mon.–Fri.
10am–5.45pm
Open Sat. noon–4pm
▲ 224.

POLICE ACADEMY MUSEUM
235 E. 20th St.
Tel. 477-9753
Open 9am–2pm, by appointment only.
Closed Sat., Sun. and public holidays.

The history of the New York police force.

SAINT MARK'S CHURCH IN THE BOWERY
131 E. 10th St.
Tel. 674-6377
Visit by appointment.

THEODORE ROOSEVELT'S BIRTHPLACE
28 E. 20th St.
Tel. 260-1616
Open Wed.–Sun.
9am–4.30pm

UKRAINIAN MUSEUM
203 2nd Ave. and 12th St.
Tel. 228-0110.
Open Wed.–Sun.
1–5pm
Cultural heritage of Ukrainian people.

RESTAURANTS

AN AMERICAN PLACE
2 Park Ave.
Tel. 684-2122
Open noon and evening.
Closed Sat. noon, Sun.
American cuisine. All the inventiveness of a famous chef: Larry Forgione.

COFFEE SHOP
29 Union Square W.
Tel. 243-7969
Open 7 days a week, 24 hours a day
Pre-1940's style and fashionable clientele. At full swing around lunch–midnight. American cuisine with Brazilian flair.

LA COLOMBE D'OR
134 E. 26th St.
Tel. 689-0666
Open noon and in the evening.
Closed Sat.–Sun. noon.
Intimate and unpretentious.

GREENMARKET CAFÉ
Union Square Park
Outdoor restaurant. Classic American cuisine.

LOLA
30 W. 22nd St.
Tel. 675-6700
Open daily.
You can sample Cajun-style onion-rings or 100-spiced chicken against an increasingly noisy backdrop of conversation and live music. Brunch.

MITALI EAST
334 E. 6th St.
Tel. 533-2508
Open daily.

Nondescript décor, but fine cuisine from the north of India at unbeatable prices. Brunch on Sundays.

"103" NYC
103 2nd Ave.
Tel. 777-4120
Open daily.
Welcoming and relaxed.

PARK BISTRO
414 Park Ave. South
Tel. 689-1360
Open noon and in the evening.
Closed Sat. noon and Sun. noon.
Probably the best bistro in New York. Provençal-style dishes. Pétatou au chèvre, beef, cod-fish, lamb.

UNION SQUARE CAFÉ
21 E. 16th St.
Tel. 243-4020
Open noon and in the evenings.
Closed Sun. noon.
Reserve well in advance to sample the Union Square's oysters and chocolate marble brownies.

ACCOMMODATION

ARLINGTON HOTEL
18 W. 25th St.
Tel. 645-3990
Fax. 633-8952
Well-maintained hotel. Good value.

CARLTON ARMS HOTEL
160 E. 25th St.
Tel. 679-0680
Clientele mostly young Europeans. Unsophisticated rooms.

GRAMERCY PARK HOTEL
2 Lexington Ave.
Tel. 475-4320
or 1-800-221-4083
Fax. 505-0535

The small rooms would benefit from redecoration. But the neighborhood is attractive and you are right on Gramercy Park.

NIGHT LIFE

C.B.G.B.
315 Bowery
Tel. 982-4052
Open 7pm–3am
From the Ramones to the Talking Heads, many groups who have since shot to fame once played at this strange little elongated club.

CONTINENTAL
25 3rd Ave.
Tel. 529-6924
Open 4pm–3am
A rival of C.B.G.B. All the East Village's punk denizens come to listen or perform at this club.

THE GRAND
76 E. 13th St.
Tel. 777-0600
Classic rock, jazz-rock, reggae, hip-hop, dance music.

KNITTING FACTORY
47 E. Houston St.
Tel. 219-3055
A tiny place where you can hear musicians who were once household names as well as a new generation of rising stars. The emphasis is on New York musicians. An enthusiastic audience and a welcoming atmosphere.

CAFÉ-BARS

McSORLEY'S OLD ALE HOUSE
15 E. 7th St.
Tel. 473-9148
Open Mon.–Sat.
11am–1am. Open Sun.

1pm–1am
One of the oldest bars in New York, serving a wide range of fine beers.

PETE'S TAVERN
129 E. 18th St.
Tel. 473-7676
Open
11am–12.45am
O. Henry apparently wrote "The Gift of the Magi" sitting at the second booth on the left in this bar-restaurant, which is still a nice place to have a beer ▲ 229.

SHOPPING

ANNEX ANTIQUES FAIR AND FLEA MARKET
6th Ave.and 25th St.
Tel. 243-5343
Open Sat. and Sun.
9am–5pm
The largest flea market in the city.

B. & H. PHOTO-VIDEO
119 W. 17th St.
Tel. 807-7474
One of the biggest photography stores, selling photographic and video equipment, film. A favorite with professional photographers and enthusiasts.

FORBIDDEN PLANET
821 Broadway
Tel. 473-1576
Wide assortment of science fiction, fantasy and comic art books plus toys and videos.

LOVE SAVES THE DAY
119 2nd Ave. and 7th St.
Tel. 228-3802
Secondhand clothing and collectible toys.

PARAGON
867 Broadway and 18th St.
Tel. 255-8036
Three floors devoted to sporting goods.

STRAND BOOK STORE
828 Broadway and 12th St.
Tel. 473-1452
Secondhand books and rare editions.

TOWER RECORDS
692 Broadway and 4th St.
Tel. 505-1500
Music chain store. Two other outlets: Lincoln Center and the Upper East Side.

GRAND CENTRAL THEATER DISTRICT

CULTURAL LIFE

CIRCLE LINE
Pier 83, W. 42nd St.
Tel. 563-3200
Closed Jan., Feb.
A three-hour boat trip around Manhattan. Cruises throughout day 9am–5pm. During the summer, 9am–7pm.

EMPIRE STATE BUILDING
350 5th Ave. and 34th St.
Tel. 736-3100
Open daily
9am–11.30pm
Stupendous view over New York ▲ 242.

GENERAL SOCIETY OF MECHANICS AND TRADESMEN MUSEUM
20 W. 44th St.
Tel. 840-1840
Open Mon.–Fri.
10am–noon,
2–4pm

1. HOLIDAY INN CROWNE PLAZA
2. RENAISSANCE HOTEL
3. MARRIOTT EAST SIDE
4. U.N. PLAZA PARK-HYATT
5. BECCO
6. JOE ALLEN
7. ORSO
8. BARBETTA
9. BRASSERIE DES THÉÂTRES
10. PARAMOUNT
11. MARRIOTT MARQUIS
12. SPARKS STEAK HOUSE
13. JEZEBEL
14. AMBASSADOR GRILL
15. CABANA CARIOCA
16. AMBASSADOR HOTEL

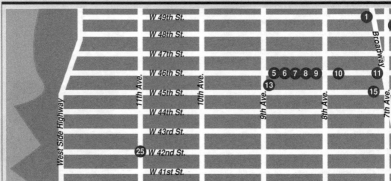

GRAND CENTRAL TERMINAL
42nd St. between Park and Lexington aves.
Tel. 935-3960
*Guided tour every Wed. at 12.30pm
Wait in front of the Chemical Bank, in the Main Concourse.*

INTREPID SEA-AIR-SPACE MUSEUM
Pier 86,12th Ave. and W. 46th St.
Tel. 245-2533
Open daily. 10am–5pm
Closed Mon.–Tues. out of season.
The chance to see one of the famous aircraft carriers of World War Two, a submarine, a lightship and a destroyer ▲ 257.

JACOB K. JAVITS CONVENTION CENTER
655 W. 34th St.
Tel. 216-2000
Opening times depend on the exhibitions ▲ 248.

MADISON SQUARE GARDEN
4 Pennsylvania Plaza.
Between W. 31st and W. 33rd sts and 7th and 8th aves.
Tel. 465-6741
Open daily.
Vast sports and entertainment complex. Home to the NHL's New York Penguins and NBA's New York Knicks. Also a forum for shows and concerts. Guided tours are available ▲ 249.

PIERPONT MORGAN LIBRARY
29 E. 36th St.
Tel. 685-0610
Open Tues.–Fri.

10.30am–5pm
Open Sat.
10.30am–6pm.
Open Sun. noon–6pm.
Closed Mon., public holidays.
Rare books (including 3 Gutenberg Bibles), manuscripts from the Middle Ages and the Renaissance, drawings, pictures, etc. Also mounts temporary exhibitions ▲ 241.

NEW YORK PUBLIC LIBRARY

5th Ave. and 42nd St.
Tel. 930-0831
Open Mon., Thurs., Sat.
10am–5.45pm
Open Tues. & Wed.11am–7.15pm
New York City's main reference library. Guided tours at 11am and 2pm ▲ 252.

UNITED NATIONS
1st Ave. and 46th St.
Tel. 963-7713
Open daily,
9.15am–4.45pm
Headquarters of the United Nations Organization. Guided tours in many languages. Cafeteria, gift shops, post office ▲ 264.

WHITNEY MIDTOWN
120 Park Ave.
(Philip Morris Building)
Tel. 878-2550

Open Mon.–Fri.
11am–6pm (Thurs. until 7.30pm)
Closed Sat., Sun.
Branch of the Whitney Museum of American Art.

RESTAURANTS

44
44 W. 44th St.
(Royalton Hotel)
Tel. 944-8844
Open daily.
Theatrical décor designed by Philip Stark for this branch of the Condé Nast publishing house. Reservation essential. Brunch.

AMBASSADOR GRILL
1 United Nations Plaza
(U.N. Plaza Park Hyatt Hotel)
Tel. 702-5014
Open daily.
American grill cuisine.

BARBETTA
321 W. 46th St.
Tel. 246-9171
Open Tues.–Sat.
The oldest family-owned and operated Italian restaurant in New York. A family concern renowned for its risotto and pasta dishes.

BECCO
355 W. 46th St.
Tel. 397-7597
Open daily.

A trattoria where the menu changes everyday.

BRASSERIE DES THÉÂTRES
243 W. 46th St.
(Paramount Hotel)
Tel. 719-5588
Open Mon.–Sat.
Its specialties: terrines, sauerkraut, beef ribsteak and profiteroles in chocolate sauce. Brunch.

CABAÑA CARIOCA
123 W. 45th St.
Tel. 581-8088
Open daily.
The best restaurant in New York for anyone who loves Brazilian food.

CHEZ JOSÉPHINE
414 W. 42nd St.
Tel. 594-1925
Open in the evening.
Closed Sun.
This is an entertaining place, enjoyed more for the décor (a collection of wonderful old posters), atmosphere and the music (pianist) than for the food.

JEZEBEL
630 9th Ave.
Tel. 582-1045
Open only in the evenings.
Closed Sun.
Friendly atmosphere and cheerful surroundings. Genuine food for the soul.

JOE ALLEN
326 W. 46th St.
Tel. 581-6464
Open daily.
For those who like a quick snack before or after the theater.

17. THE ROOSEVELT
18. THE PALM
19. THE ALGONQUIN HOTEL
20. HOTEL IROQUOIS
21. HOTEL MACKLOWE
22. ROYALTON
23. 44
24. HOTEL MANSFIELD
25. CHEZ JOSÉPHINE
26. OYSTER BAR AND RESTAURANT
27. TUDOR HOTEL
28. GRAND HYATT
29. HOTEL INTER-CONTINENTAL
30. DORAL PARK AVENUE HOTEL

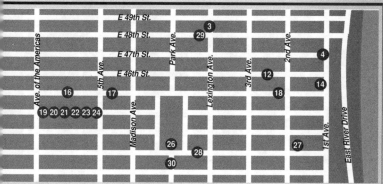

Hamburgers and spareribs, often served by young actors.

ORSO
322 W. 46th St.
Tel. 489-7212
Open daily.
The most popular restaurant in the theater district. Reservation essential.

OYSTER BAR AND RESTAURANT
Grand Central Terminal, Lower Level
Tel. 490-6650
Open 11.30am–9.30pm.
Closed Sat. and Sun.
Eye-catching surroundings, fresh fish and seafood.

THE PALM
837 2nd Ave.
Tel. 687-2953
Open noon and in the evenings.
Closed Sat. noon, Sun.
This quintessential steakhouse dates from the 1920's. Huge slabs of meat, lobster, fried onion rings and cheesecake. Reservations needed for parties of more than four.

SPARKS STEAK HOUSE
210 E. 46th St.
Tel. 687-4855
Closed Sat. noon, Sun.
A restaurant for connoisseurs and lovers of fine wines. New York-style cheesecake is a specialty.

ACCOMMODATION

THE ABERDEEN
17 W. 32nd St.
Tel. 736-1600
or 1-800-826-4667

Fax. 695-1813
Simply decorated rooms in a lively neighborhood packed with restaurants and Korean wholesalers.

THE ALGONQUIN HOTEL
59 W. 44th St.
Tel. 840-6800
Fax. 944-1419
A host of writers have stayed here, assuring its fame. The worlds of literature and publishing still use this hotel. Restored in 1990. Small rooms and Edwardian décor.

THE CARLTON
22 E. 29th St.
Tel. 532-4100
or 1-800-542-1502
Fax. 889-8683
A nice family hotel, with spacious rooms.

Recently redecorated. The lobby is an attractive meeting place.

AMBASSADOR HOTEL
132 W. 45th St.
Tel. 921-7600
or 1-800-242-8935
Fax. 719-0171
Neat and tidy. Sofa-beds for additional guests.

COMFORT INN, MURRAY HILL
42 W. 35th St.
Tel. 947-0200
or 1-800-228-5150
Ongoing renovations. Continental breakfast.

DORAL PARK AVE.
70 Park Ave.
Tel. 687-7050
or 1-800-22-DORAL
Fax. 949-5924

A chic hotel with an intimate, secluded atmosphere. Marble bathrooms and Scandinavian-style furniture.

GRAND HYATT
42nd St. between Park and Lexington aves. (Grand Central Terminal)
Tel. 883-1234
or 1-800-233-1234
Fax. 697-3772
Thirty-four stories sheathed in black glass in one of the busiest areas of Manhattan. Frequented by the business community.

HERALD SQUARE HOTEL
19 W. 31st St.
Tel. 279-4017 or 1-800-727-1888
Fax. 643-9208
Comfortable, with a friendly atmosphere. Cosmopolitan clientèle.

HOLIDAY INN, CROWNE PLAZA
1605 Broadway

Tel. 977-4000
or 1-800-243-NYNY
Traditional rooms, some with an unbeatable view of Times Square. Swimming pool.

HOTEL INTER-CONTINENTAL
111 E. 48th St.
Tel. 755-5900
Fax. 644-0079
Sumptuous lobby with

plush sofas and leather armchairs. Translation service and multilingual staff.

HOTEL IROQUOIS
49 W. 44th St.
Tel. 840-3080
or 1-800-332-7220
Fax. 398-1754
Plain and simple. Suites with kitchenettes.

HOTEL MACKLOWE
145 W. 44th St.
Tel. 768-4400
or 1-800-MACKLOWE
Fax. 768-0847
Small but stylish rooms. Jacuzzi in presidential suites.

HOTEL MANSFIELD
12 W. 44th St.
Tel. 944-6050
or 1-800-255-5167
Fax. 768-0847
W. B. Yeats lived in this building. Good for students.

MARRIOTT EAST SIDE
525 Lexington Ave.
Tel. 755-4000
Fax. 571-3440

31. MORGANS
32. SHELBURNE MURRAY HILL
33. COMFORT INN MURRAY HILL
34. NEW YORK'S HOTEL PENNSYLVANIA
35. THE ABERDEEN
36. HERALD SQUARE HOTEL
37. SOUTHGATE TOWER
38. THE CARLTON

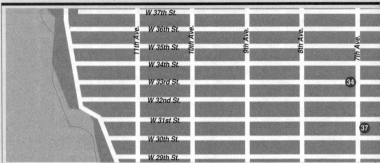

Sedate, functional rooms. Frequented by the business community.

MARRIOTT MARQUIS
1535 Broadway
Tel. 398-1900
or 1-800-228-9290
Fax. 704-8930
Spacious rooms. Always a hive of activity. The best hotel for conferences in the Times Square area.

MORGANS
237 Madison Ave.
Tel. 686-0300
or 1-800-334-3408
Fax. 779-8352
An elegant hotel with no signage. It can be recognized by the arched entrance flanked by impressive columns and a doorman standing on duty. A favorite with the world of show business.

NEW YORK'S HOTEL PENNSYLVANIA
7th Ave. and 33rd St.
Tel. 736-5000
or 1-800-223-8585
Fax. 502-8712
An old hotel, with an imposing, rather uninviting appearance, frequented by overseas tourists.

PARAMOUNT
235 W. 46 St.
Tel. 764-5500
or 1-800-225-7474
Fax. 354-5237
In the heart of the Theater District, an extraordinary mixture: a Renaissance-style building dating from the 1930's, redesigned by Philip Stark. Average-sized rooms.

RENAISSANCE HOTEL
714 7th Ave.

Tel. 765-7676
Fax. 765-1962
Unbeatable view of Times Square from the restaurant in this small, new tower of gleaming black glass. The huge bay windows gives you the impression of floating in space.

THE ROOSEVELT
Madison Ave. (45th St.)
Tel. 661-9600
or 1-800-223-1870
Fax. 687-5064
This hotel has a great deal of character, unlike many other budget hotels built more recently. Turn of the century European décor. Small rooms.

ROYALTON
44 W. 44th St.
Tel. 869-4400
or 1-800-635-9013
Fax. 869-8965
A fashionable hotel whose theatrical interior design is again the work of Philip Stark: cobalt blue carpeting, polished green granite, steel. Same management as the Morgan and Paramount hotels.

SHELBURNE MURRAY HILL
303 Lexington Ave.
Tel. 689-5200
or 1-800-ME-SUITE

Fax. 779-7068
Large comfortable rooms with kitchens. Hotel's rooftop garden open for reservations in summer. An affordable priced base for family holidays in an attractive and peaceful district.

SOUTHGATE TOWER
371 7th Ave.
Tel. 563-1800
or 1-800-ME-SUITE
Fax. 643-8028
Simply decorated suites, some with sofa-beds. Clientele primarily from the business community.

TUDOR HOTEL
304 E. 42nd St.
Tel. 986-8800
or 1-800-TRY-TUDOR
Fax. 986-1758
A bright, red-brick hotel surrounded by the bedlam of 42nd St. Fairly simple rooms, but comfortable. Traditional British interior and afternoon tea is served.

UNITED NATIONS PLAZA PARK HYATT HOTEL
1 United Nations Plaza
Tel. 355-3400
or 1-800-228-9000
Fax. 702-5051
Many diplomats stay here. Huge rooms, most enjoying a view of the New York skyline. Health and fitness center with indoor swimming pool, tennis, massage parlor.

SHOPPING

A. & S.
899 Ave. of the Americas
Tel. 594-8500
Department store. A little less chic and less expensive than the others.

BANCROFT
363 Madison Ave.
Tel. 678-8650
An institution for classic menswear, also catering to women.

BROOKS BROTHERS
346 Madison Ave.
Tel. 682-8800
Men's fashions. The place to go for shirts.

THE COMPLEAT STRATEGIST
11 E. 33rd St.
Tel. 685-3880
All kinds of games.

COMPAGNIE INTERNATIONALE EXPRESS
452 5th Ave. and 38th St.
Tel. 30-2769
Women's casual wear. Very popular chain which has outlets all over the city.

FOOT LOCKER
43–45 W. 34th St.
Tel. 971-9449
Sports goods.

GAP
Broadway and 34th St.
Tel. 643-8960
Classic sportswear for children and adults. Outlets of this chain can be found all over the city.

SAM GOODY
666 3rd Ave.
Tel. 986-8480
Wide range of records, CDs, cassettes. Specialist chain of stores.

HAGSTROM MAP AND TRAVEL CENTER
57 W. 43rd St.
Tel. 398-1222
Map and travel guide specialists.

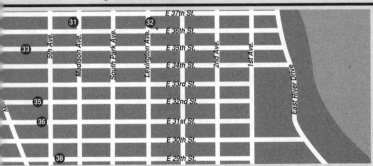

HARVEY ELECTRONICS
2 W. 45th St.
Tel. 575-5000
*Audio, video, home
entertainment
equipment. From the
inexpensive to top of
the line.*

J. J. HAT CENTER
310 5th Ave. and
32nd St.
Tel. 239-4368
*From stetsons to top
hats, every type of hat
for men and for women.*

J. PRESS
7 E. 44th St.
Tel. 687-7642
Men's fashions.

LORD AND TAYLOR
424 5th Ave.
Tel. 391-3344
*Department store
mainly for women's
fashions.*

MACY'S
151 W. 34th St.
Tel. 695-4400
*"The world's largest
store".*

**MANNY'S MUSICAL
INSTRUMENTS &
ACCESSORIES**
156 W. 48th St.
Tel. 819-0576
*A comprehensive range
of musical instruments.
The walls are lined with
photos of stars who
have bought their
instruments here.*

PAUL STUART
Madison Ave. and
45th St.
Tel. 682-0320
*Clothes and
accessories for men
and women.*

LOUIS TANNEN
24 W. 25th St.
(2nd Floor)
Tel. 929-4500

*For sixty-one years this
has been the largest
store for magicians'
supplies for children,
enthusiasts and
professionals.*

TOYS R US
1293 Broadway
and 34th St.
Tel. 594-8697
*Store selling a vast
assortment of
children's toys and
video games.*

WORTH AND WORTH
331 Madison Ave.
and 43rd St.
Tel. 867-6058
*The number-one men's
hat shop since 1918.*

ROCKEFELLER CENTER

CULTURAL LIFE

**AMERICAN CRAFT
MUSEUM**
40 W. 53rd St.
Tel. 956-6047
Open Wed.–Sun.
10am–5pm.
Open Tues. 10am–8pm.
Closed Mon.
*Arts and crafts from
1900 to the present
day: glassware, pottery,
metalwork, etc.*

CARNEGIE HALL
152 W. 57th St.
Tel. 247-7800
Guided tours (Mon.,
Tues., Thurs., Fri.) at
11.30am, 2pm and 3pm.

CENTRAL SYNAGOGUE
123 E. 55th St.
Tel. 838-5122
Open Mon.–Thurs.
noon–2pm.

**IBM GALLERY OF
SCIENCE AND ART**
590 Madison Ave.
and 56th St.
Tel. 745-6100
Open 11am–6pm
Closed Sun., Mon.
▲ 289.

LINCOLN CENTER
Broadway and 65th St.
Tel. 875-5400
Guided tours daily.
10am–5pm
(Tel. 875-5350)
*An enormous cultural
center which houses a
library and various
auditoria for
performances of dance,
opera, concerts and
drama.*
ALICE TULLY HALL
Tel. 875-5050
AVERY FISHER HALL
Tel. 875-5030
JUILLIARD THEATER
Tel. 799-5000
LIBRARY AND MUSEUM OF
THE PERFORMING ARTS
40 Lincoln Center Plaza
Tel. 870-1600
METROPOLITAN OPERA
HOUSE
Tel. 362-6000
Backstage tours,
Mon.–Fri. 3.45pm,
Sat. 10am.
Telephone reservations
(769-7020)

NEW YORK STATE
THEATER
Tel. 870-5570

**MUSEUM OF THE
AMERICAN PIANO**
211 W. 58th St.
Tel. 246-4646
*Open for temporary
exhibitions.*

**MUSEUM OF MODERN
ART (MOMA)**
11 W. 53rd St.
Tel. 708-9480
Open Sat.–Tues.
11am–6pm
Open Thurs.–Fri.
noon–8.30pm
Closed Wed.
*One of the largest
collection of modern art
in the world. Permanent
and temporary
exhibitions* ▲ 290.

**MUSEUM
OF TELEVISION
AND RADIO**
25 W. 52nd St.
Tel. 621-6600
Open Tues.–Sun.
noon–6pm. Open Thurs.
noon–8pm. Closed Mon.
*Extensive archives
containing recordings
of television and radio
broadcasts.*

**RADIO CITY MUSIC
HALL**
Ave. of the Americas
(50th St.)
Tel. 632-4041
*Tours of the auditorium
and backstage, daily
10am–5pm.*

ROCKEFELLER CENTER
5th and 6th aves.,
47th and 52nd sts.
NBC STUDIOS
Ave. of the Americas
(between 49th
and 50th sts.)
Tel. 664-4000
Closed public holidays.
Daily tours every 15
mins, from 9am–4pm.

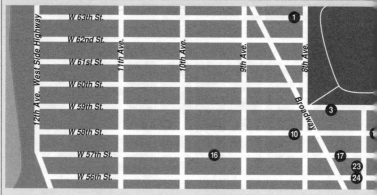
1. YMCA, WEST SIDE
2. HARRY CIPRIANI
3. SAN DOMENICO
4. THE ESSEX HOUSE HOTEL NIKKO NEW YORK
5. THE RITZ-CARLTON
6. SAINT MORITZ ON THE PARK
7. MICKEY MANTLE'S
8. THE PARK LANE (HELMSLEY)
9. THE PLAZA
10. THE WESTPARK HOTEL
11. PETROSSIAN
12. HELMSLEY WINDSOR
13. THE WYNDHAM
14. DAWAT
15. LE COLONIAL
16. PARKS INN INT'L NEW YORK
17. HARD RO...

ST. BARTHOLOMEW'S CHURCH
109 E. 50th St.
Tel. 751-1616
Open Mon.–Fri.
9am–6pm
Open Sat. 8am–3pm
▲ 285

ST. PATRICK'S CATHEDRAL
5th Ave. (50th St.)
Tel. 753-2261
Open daily
8.30am–8.45pm
New York's Roman Catholic cathedral
▲ 282.

ST. THOMAS EPISCOPAL CHURCH
1 W. 53rd St.

Tel. 757-7013
Open daily
7am–6.30pm
▲ 288.

SONY PLAZA
550 Madison Ave.
Tel. 833-8800
Open Mon.–Sat.
10am–8pm.
Atrium open
10am–10pm
Open Sun. noon–7pm
▲ 289.

URBAN CENTER
457 Madison and
50th St.
Tel. 935-3960
Organizes thematic tours of the city (history, architecture). Its bookstore stocks many works on architecture. (Tel. 935-3595).

GALLERIES

BLUM HELMAN GALLERY
20 W. 57th St.
(2nd Floor)
Tel. 245-2888
Open Tues.–Sat.
10am–6pm
Specialist in American and European contemporary art.

MARIAN GOODMAN GALLERY
24 W. 57th St.
(4th Floor)
Tel. 977-7160
All the key figures in the American and European conceptual movement.

SIDNEY JANIS GALLERY
110 W. 57th St.
(6th Floor)
Tel. 586-0110
Open Tues.–Sat.
10am–5.30pm
Founded in 1948. The gallery has exhibited Mondrian, Brancusi, Giacometti, Léger and Albers in the past. It was the first to show the Abstract Expressionists in the 1950's.

ROBERT MILLER GALLERY
41 E. 57th St.
(3rd Floor)
Tel. 980-5454
Open Tues.–Sat.
10am–6pm
A gallery with a
"Downtown" feel, despite its location. Contemporary painters, sculptors and photographers.*

PACE GALLERY
32 E. 57th St.
Tel. 421-3292
Open Tues.–Fri.
9.30am–5.30pm Open
Sat. 10am–6pm
Sections devoted to African art as well as to ancient and modern graphic art. The gallery also has a branch on Washington Square
▲ 406.

PACE/MACGILL GALLERY
32 E. 57th St.
(9th Floor)
Tel. 759-7999
Open Tues.–Fri.
9.30am–5.30pm
and Sat. 10am–6pm
in winter.
Open Mon.–Thurs.
9.30am–5.30pm and Fri.
9.30am–4pm in summer.
The gallery exhibits some of the leading contemporary photographers.

RESTAURANTS

AL BUSTAN
827 3rd Ave.
Tel. 759-5933
Open daily.
Excellent Lebanese cuisine.

AQUAVIT
13 W. 54th St.
Tel. 307-7311
Open noon and in the evenings.
Closed Sat. noon., Sun.
Scandinavian cuisine. Sample a
mouthwatering array of herring, salmon and venison dishes, downstairs near a waterfall.*

LE BERNARDIN
155 W. 51st St.
Tel. 489-1515
Closed Sat. noon, Sun.
Chinese-spiced red snapper with port sauce and capers, tuna carpaccio, halibut with vinaigrette, and roast monkfish with cabbage. Owned by the chef, Gilbert Le Coze.

BICE
7 E. 54th St.
Tel. 688-1999
Open daily.
Popular, lively trattoria, serving very varied cuisine.

THE BRASSERIE
100 E. 53rd St.
(Seagram Buiding)
Tel. 751-4840
Open 7 days a week,
24 hours a day
Cheerful surroundings in which to savor traditional brasserie dishes.

CARNEGIE DELI
854 7th Ave.
Tel. 757-2245
Open daily.
Ignore the offhand service, the noise and

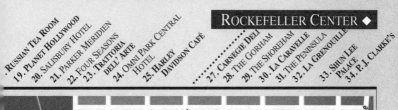

19. RUSSIAN TEA ROOM
19. PLANET HOLLYWOOD
20. SALISBURY HOTEL
21. PARKER MERIDIEN
22. FOUR SEASONS
23. TRATTORIA DELL'ARTE
24. OMNI PARK CENTRAL HOTEL
25. HARLEY DAVIDSON CAFÉ
27. CARNEGIE DELI
28. THE GORHAM
29. THE SHOREHAM
30. LA CARAVELLE
31. THE PENINSULA
32. LA GRENOUILLE
33. SHUN LEE PALACE
34. P.J. CLARKE'S

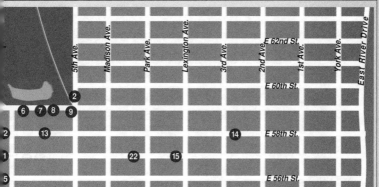

the crowds to feast on enormous sandwiches, frankfurters, hamburgers and french fries. No credit cards.

DAWAT
210 E. 58th St.
Tel. 355-7555
Closed Sun. noon
The best Indian restaurant in New York.

THE FOUR SEASONS
99 E. 52nd St.
(Seagram Building)
Tel. 754-9494
Closed Sat. noon, Sun.
The Grill Room is good for business lunches, the Pool Room is more romantic.

HARD ROCK CAFÉ
221 W. 57th St.
Tel. 459-9320
Open daily.
Packed with teenagers who come more for the boisterous atmosphere and the loud music than for the sandwiches and hamburgers, which are tasty nonetheless. No reservations.

HARLEY DAVIDSON CAFÉ
1370 Ave. of the Americas and 56th St.
Tel. 245-6000
Open daily.
Have a meal or a drink here merely to sample

the atmosphere and the décor: Harley Davidsons in photos. Gift shop.

HARRY CIPRIANI
781 5th Ave. (Sherry-Netherland Hotel)
Tel. 753-5566
Open daily.
Branch of Venice's legendary Harry's Bar. Simple dishes (risotto prima-vera) at exorbitant prices. Stick to set menu.

IL NIDO
251 E. 53rd St.
Tel. 753-8450
Closed Sun.
Cuisine from central and northern Italy: ravioli with truffles, chicken à la toscana with pine kernels and mint, game, zabaglione with raspberries.

LA CARAVELLE
33 W. 55th St.
Tel. 586-4252
Closed Sat. noon, Sun.
Romantic décor and gastronomic delights.

LA GRENOUILLE
3 E. 52nd St.
Tel. 752-0652
Closed Sun., Mon., Sat. noon, last week of July, 1st week after Labor Day in summer.
Famous for the fresh floral arrangements and French haute cuisine. Be sure to try the turbot poché aux deux céleris and soufflé with pistacchios.

LE COLONIAL
149 E. 57th St.
Tel. 752-0808

French-Vietnamese cuisine: ravioli pancakes, spicy beef salad, shrimp beansprout roll.

LUTÈCE
249 E. 50th St.
Tel. 752-2225
Closed Sat. noon, Sun., Mon. noon.
Bastion of the great tradition of French cuisine upheld by André Soltner. For gourmets – coquille Saint-Jacques, beignets (fritters), foie gras en brioche, caramelized rack of lamb and praline-coffee dessert.

MICKEY MANTLE'S
42 Central Park South
Tel. 688-7777
Open daily.
Children seem to like it here; you can devour enormous hamburgers, french fries and salads while watching a huge television screen.

PETROSSIAN
182 W. 58th St.
Tel. 245-2214
Open daily.
This restaurant's claim to fame is its caviar, foie gras and smoked salmon.

P. J. CLARKE'S
915 3rd Ave.
Tel. 759-1650
Open daily.

Saloon with a somewhat faded reputation. Brunch.

PLANET HOLLYWOOD
140 W. 57th St.
Tel. 333-7827
Open daily.
Mediocre fast-food style of menu; but teenagers love the atmosphere.

RAINBOW ROOM
30 Rockefeller Plaza (65th Floor)
Tel. 632-5000
Open in the evening. Closed Sun.
This sky-high restaurant serves classic dishes with a passing nod to "nouvelle cuisine".

REMI
145 W. 53rd St.
Tel. 581-4242
Closed Sat. noon, Sun. noon.
The cuisine and the décor of this restaurant re-create a piece of Venice in the middle of New York.

ROYAL CANADIAN PANCAKE HOUSE
1004 2nd Ave.
Tel. 980-4131
Open daily.
A hive of cheerful activity with more than sixty types of huge pancakes and waffles on the menu: children love it. Brunch. No alcohol.

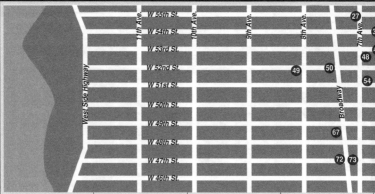

35. THE NEW YORK PALACE
36. RIHGA ROYAL HOTEL
37. THE WARWICK
38. HOTEL DORSET
39. AQUAVIT
40. BICE
41. VONG
42. THE NEW YORK HILTON & TOWERS
43. REMI
44. THE BRASSERIE
45. IL NIDO
46. ROYAL CANADIAN PANCAKE HOUSE
47. LYDEN HOUSE
48. SHERATON HOTEL TOWER
49. HOWARD JOHNSON PLAZA-HOTEL

RUSSIAN TEA ROOM
150 W. 57th St.
Tel. 265-0947
Open daily.
Sample the succulent appetizers, the delicious breads and the strawberries Romanov. Brunch
▲ 301.

SAN DOMENICO
240 Central Park South
Tel. 265-5959
Closed Sat. noon, Sun. noon.
Each dish is an astonishing combination of flavors.

SHUN LEE PALACE
155 E. 55th St.
Tel. 371-8844
Open daily.
The wonderful Cantonese, Mandarin and Szechwan dishes make you forget that you are being jostled on all sides as you eat. Brunch.

SMITH & WOLLENSKY
201 E. 49th St.
Tel. 753-1530
Closed Sat. noon, Sun. noon.
Typical New York fare (steaks, lobster). A wide selection of fine wines.

TRATTORIA DELL'ARTE
900 7th Ave.
Tel. 245-9800
Open daily.

Somewhere to go before and after a concert at Carnegie Hall. Its famous décor is more interesting than the cuisine. Brunch.

"21" CLUB
21 W. 52nd St.
Tel. 582-7200

Closed Sat. noon, Sun.
Formerly a speakeasy. Renowned, among other things, for its hamburgers.

VONG
200 E. 54th St.
Tel. 486-9592
Closed Sat. noon, Sun.
Very popular French-Thai restaurant.

ZARELA
953 2nd Ave.
Tel. 464-6740
Closed Sat. and Sun. noon
Adventurous Mexican cuisine in pleasant surroundings.

ACCOMMODATION

BEEKMAN TOWER
3 Mitchell Pl.
Tel. 355-7300
or 1-800-637-8483
Fax. 753-9366
Secretarial services, fax and other equipment are available for use by guests. Suites with self-catering facilities are available for families. Fixed monthly rates.

HOTEL BEVERLY
125 E. 50th St.
Tel. 753-2700
or 1-800-223-0945
Fax. 759-7300
Bright rooms, simple décor, with kitchenettes.

BOX TREE
250 E. 49th St.
Tel. 593-9810
Fax. 308-3899
Two brownstones dating from the 1840's and crammed to overflowing with antiques. Suites with individual styles of decoration – by turns, English, Egyptian, Japanese or Chinese. Guests may have the use of the hotel's chauffeur-driven Rolls-Royces and Bentleys. Credit of $100 for the restaurant included in the price of the room. American Express only.

HOTEL DORSET
30 W. 54th St.
Tel. 247-7300
or 1-800-227-2348
Fax. 581-0153
Often full, because some guests live there all year round. Large, bright rooms. Competitive special rates.

HOTEL EDISON
228 W. 47th St.
Tel. 840-5000
Fax. 596-6850
Art Deco-style building. Small rooms decorated in pastel colors.

EMBASSY SUITES HOTEL
1568 Broadway
Tel. 719-1600
or 1-800-EMBASSY
Fax. 921-5212

Well equipped for business people and practical for families with two-room suites fitted with self-catering facilities. Its "Kid's Club" organizes activities for children.

THE ESSEX HOUSE HOTEL NIKKO NEW YORK
160 Central Park South
Tel. 247-0300
or 1-800-NIKKO-US
Fax. 315-1839
Art Deco elements. Three restaurants, one

of which is French. Large rooms. Transportation to Wall St. provided.

THE FOUR SEASONS
57 E. 57th St.
Tel. 758-5700
or 1-800-332-3442
Fax. 758-5711
Designed by I. M. Pei and opened in June 1993, this is the tallest hotel in New York, with 52 floors, affording breathtaking views over the city.

50. NOVOTEL NEW YORK
51. "21" CLUB
52. OMNI BERKSHIRE PLACE
53. THE FOUR SEASONS
54. LE BERNARDIN
55. LOEWS NEW YORK
56. PICKWICK ARMS HOTEL
57. HOTEL BEVERLY
58. SAN CARLOS HOTEL
59. PLAZA 50
60. AL BUSTAN
61. LUTÈCE
62. ZARELA
63. THE WALDORF ASTORIA & WALDORF TOWERS
64. SMITH & WOLLENSKY
65. BOX TREE
66. BEEKMAN TOWER
67. HOLIDAY INN CROWNE PLAZA
68. RAINBOW ROOM

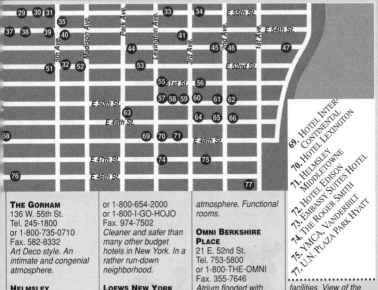

69. HOTEL INTER-CONTINENTAL
70. HOTEL LEXINGTON
71. HELMSLEY MIDDLETOWNE
72. HOTEL EDISON
73. EMBASSY SUITES HOTEL
74. THE ROGER SMITH
75. YMCA, VANDERBILT
77. U.N. PLAZA PARK HYATT

THE GORHAM

136 W. 55th St.
Tel. 245-1800
or 1-800-735-0710
Fax. 582-8332
Art Deco style. An intimate and congenial atmosphere.

HELMSLEY MIDDLETOWNE

148 E. 48th St.
Tel. 755-3000
or 1-800-221-4982
Fax. 832-0261
Quiet. Rooms are simple, fairly large, some with a terrace. A favorite among business travelers.

HELMSLEY WINDSOR

100 W. 58th St.
Tel. 265-2100
Fax. 315-0371
Business clientele: special rates for companies.

HOLIDAY INN, CROWNE PLAZA

1605 Broadway
Tel. 977-4000
or 1-800-243-NYNY
Gleaming public lounges with floor lighting. A superb view of Times Square from some of the rooms. Translation service. Large swimming pool.

HOTEL LEXINGTON

Lexington Ave. and 48th St.
Tel. 755-4400
or 1-800-228-5151
Fax. 751-4091
Very conveniently located. Stylish rooms.

HOWARD JOHNSON PLAZA HOTEL

851 8th Ave.
Tel. 581-4100
or 1-800-654-2000
or 1-800-I-GO-HOJO
Fax. 974-7502
Cleaner and safer than many other budget hotels in New York. In a rather run-down neighborhood.

LOEWS NEW YORK

569 Lexington Ave.
Tel. 752-7000
or 1-800-23-LOEWS
Fax. 758-6311
Famous for its bar/restaurant in the lobby.

LYDEN HOUSE

320 E. 53rd St.
Tel. 888-6070
Fax. 935-7690
Small hotel in a tree-lined street.

THE NEW YORK HILTON & TOWERS

1335 Ave. of the Americas
Tel. 586-7000
or 1-800-HILTONS
Fax. 315-1374
Unequaled for conferences and business meetings.

THE NEW YORK PALACE

445 Madison Ave.
Tel. 888-0161
or 1-800-NY-PALACE
Fax. 644-5750
Extremely plush. Ornate Italianate-style decoration. Spacious rooms.

NOVOTEL NEW YORK

226 W. 52nd St.
Tel. 315-0100
or 1-800-221-3185
Fax. 765-5369
Perfectly situated for theatergoers. European atmosphere. Functional rooms.

OMNI BERKSHIRE PLACE

21 E. 52nd St.
Tel. 753-5800
or 1-800-THE-OMNI
Fax. 355-7646
Atrium flooded with daylight, friendly atmosphere.

OMNI PARK CENTRAL HOTEL

870 7th Ave.
Tel. 247-8000
or 1-800-843-6664
Fax. 484-3374.
For the business community and groups. Multilingual staff. Limousine service provided to Wall St.

PARK INN INTERNATIONAL

440 W. 57th St.
Tel. 581-8100
or 1-800-231-0405
Fax. 581-0889
Very simple rooms in an industrial-style building, originally built to be a nursing home.

THE PARK LANE (HELMSLEY)

36 Central Park South
Tel. 371-4000
or 1-800-221-4982
Breathtaking view of Central Park from the upper floors of this 46-story hotel. Welcoming and obliging staff. Bright rooms.

PARKER MERIDIEN

118 W. 57th St.
Tel. 245-5000
Fax. 307-1776
Many rooms available with self-catering facilities. View of the New York skyline from the swimming pool on the top floor.

THE PENINSULA

700 5th Ave.
Tel. 247-2200
Fax. 903-3949
Justly proud of its "oriental-style" hospitality. Rooms decorated in Art Nouveau style. View of Midtown from the rooftop bar.

PICKWICK ARMS HOTEL

230 E. 51st St.
Tel. 355-0300
or 1-800-PICKWICK
Fax. 755-5029
Very competitive prices for people traveling alone. Small, rather gloomy rooms.

THE PLAZA

5th Ave. (Central Park South)
Tel. 759-3000
or 1-800-228-3000
Fax. 759-3167
A highly renowned hotel, the lobby of which is always thronged with people. Sumptuous rooms with marble bathrooms and European-style décor. The afternoon teas and morning brunches are superb. More formal meals are available in the Oak and Edwardian

rooms. Polynesian
lounge-bar: the Trader
Vic's.▲ 297.

PLAZA 50
155 E. 50th St.
Tel. 751-5710
or 1-800-ME-SUITE
Fax. 753-1468
*Suites available with
self-catering facilities,
reminiscent of New
York's luxury
apartments. For
business people or
families. Special fixed
monthly rates
negotiable. Part of the
East Suite Hotel chain.*

RIHGA ROYAL HOTEL
151 W. 54th St.
Tel. 307-5000
or 1-800-937-5454
Fax. 765-6530
*Brand new 54-story
building. Luxurious
suites (the "Grand"
suites have saunas and
jacuzzis). Panoramic
view of skyscrapers
from the restaurant and
many of the rooms.*

THE RITZ-CARLTON
112 Central Park South
Tel. 757-1900
Fax. 757-9620
*More understated than
many other luxury
hotels in New York.
Extremely friendly staff.
Shuttle service to
Wall St.*

THE ROGER SMITH
501 Lexington Ave.
Tel. 755-1400
or 1-800-445-0277
Fax. 319-9130
*Both more fashionable
and more comfortable
than its neighbors the
Waldorf, the Lexington
or the Intercontinental.
Piano-bar decorated
with comic strips.
Rooms have a
welcoming atmosphere.*

**ST. MORITZ ON
CENTRAL PARK**
50 Central Park South
Tel. 755-5800
Fax. 319-9458
*A lively hotel opened in
1932. European-style
décor. Lovely suites
with a view of Central
Park. Café on the
terrace.*

ST. REGIS
2 E. 55th St.
Tel. 753-4500
Fax. 787-3447

One of the city's most
sumptuous hotels, in a
building dating from
1904, built by John
Jacob Astor and
restored at great cost.
Financial information
service and secretarial
facilities available.
Major-domo attached to
each floor ▲ 288.

SALISBURY HOTEL
123 W. 57th St.
Tel. 246-1300
or 1-800-223-0680
Fax. 977-7752
*Sturdy furniture in old
English style. Rooms
available with
kitchenettes.*

SAN CARLOS HOTEL
150 E. 50th St.

Tel. 755-1800
or 1-800-722-2012
Fax. 688-9778
*Warm friendly welcome.
Rooms with fully fitted
kitchens. Special rates
for families are often
available.*

**SHERATON HOTEL
TOWER**
811 and 790 7th Ave.
Tel. 581-1000
or 1-800-325-3535
Fax. 262-4410
*The two hotels, located
opposite each other,
share the same
management.
Specialize in business
clientele, conferences.*

THE SHOREHAM
33 W. 55th St.
Tel. 247-6700
or 1-800-553-3347
Fax. 765-9741
*Simple. Ask to see your
room.*

**THE WALDORF-
ASTORIA & WALDORF
TOWERS**
301 Park Ave.
Tel. 355-3000
or 1-800-HILTONS
Fax. 872-7272

World-famous. The
building dating from
1931, has been
restored and now basks
in its original elegance.
Different décor in every
room ▲ 285.

THE WARWICK
65 W. 54th St.
Tel. 247-2700
Fax. 957-8915
*More comfortable than
the Hilton, its close
neighbor. But it can be
gloomy and a little
lackluster. It offers
particularly competitive
weekend rates and
promotions.*

**THE WESTPARK
HOTEL**
308 W. 58th St.
Tel. 246-6440
Fax. 246-3131
*Smallish, functional
rooms.*

THE WYNDHAM
42 W. 58th St.
Tel. 753-3500
or 1-800-257-1111
Fax. 754-5638
*Peaceful and attractive.
Much frequented by
the world of
entertainment.*

YMCA, VANDERBILT
224 E. 47th St.
Tel. 875-4253
or 1-800-FIT-YMCA
Fax. 308-3161
*Friendly, up-beat
atmosphere. Shared
bathroom facilities.*

YMCA, WEST SIDE
5 W. 63rd St.
Tel. 875-4253
or 1-800-FIT-YMCA
Fax. 308-3161
*The largest youth
hostel in the world.
Probably the best value
in New York. Reserve
in advance. Shared
bathroom facilities.
No credit cards.*

SHOPPING

ANN TAYLOR
3 E. 57th St.
Tel. 832-2010

Women's ready-to-wear
clothes.

BANANA REPUBLIC
130 E. 59th St.
Tel. 751-5570
*One of the casual wear
and fashion chains.*

EDDIE BAUER
600 Madison Ave.
Tel. 421-2450
*Sportswear for men and
women.*

HENRI BENDEL
712 5th Ave.
Tel. 247-1100
Chic women's boutique.

BERGDORF GOODMAN
754 5th Ave. and
58th St.
Tel. 753-7300
*Department store.
Luxury clothing for men
and women (the men's
store is opposite the
main building). A home
decoration department.*

BIG AND TALL
1301 Ave. of the
Americas and 52nd St.
Tel. 247-7500

BLOOMINGDALES'S
1000 3rd Ave.
(between 59th and
60th sts.)
Tel. 705-2000
*"Bloomie's" sells
everything: clothes,
furniture, perfume, fine
foods....*

BURBERRY LIMITED
9 E. 57th St.
Tel. 371-5010

CARTIER
725 5th Ave.
Tel. 308-0843
*The famous Parisian
jewelry store.*

CHARIVARI
18 W 57th St.
Tel. 333-4040
*Very chic and very
expensive.*

CHRISTIE'S
502 Park Ave.
Tel. 546-1000
One of the world's most famous auction rooms.

COLISEUM BOOKS
1771 Broadway
Tel. 757-8381
Wide range of books.

COLONY RECORDS
1619 Broadway
Tel. 265-2050
Records, CDs, cassettes and musical scores. Competent, helpful sales assistants.

DRAMA BOOKSHOP
723 7th Ave. (between 48th and 49th sts.)
Tel. 944-0595
Bookstore specializing in the theater.

F.A.O. SCHWARZ
767 5th Ave.
(between 58th and 59th sts.)
Tel. 644-9400
The most stylish toy shop in New York. Don't miss its animated clock.

THE FORGOTTEN WOMAN
60 W. 49th St.
Tel. 247-8888
Specializes in clothes for larger women.

GALERIES LAFAYETTE
10 E. 57th St. in Trump Tower
Tel. 355-0022
The New York branch of the Parisian department store caters only for women.

GOTHAM BOOK MART
41 W. 47th St.
Tel. 719-4448
Gallery and bookstore. New and antique books, especially literature.

HAMMACHER SCHLEMMER
147 E. 57th St.
Tel. 421-9000

Gadgets in weird and wonderful surroundings.

NORMA KAMALI
11 W. 56th St.
Tel. 957-9797
Ready-to-wear clothes for women.

LIBRAIRIE DE FRANCE LIBRERIA HISPANICA
610 5th Ave.
(Rockefeller Center Promenade Store)
Tel. 581-8810
French and Spanish books, cassettes, guides and posters.

KENNETH JAY LANE
677 5th Ave.
Tel. 750-2858
Jewelery store. Eye-catching reproductions of expensive pieces.

ORIGINAL LEVI'S STORE
750 Lexington Ave.
(between 59th and 60th sts.)
Tel. 826-5957
Jeans from floor to ceiling.

RIZZOLI
31 W. 57th St.
Tel. 759-2424
A store that stocks the books on art, fashion and photography published in the United States and in Europe.

SAKS FIFTH AVENUE
611 5th Ave.
Tel. 753-4000
Luxury department store.

THE SHARPER IMAGE
4 W. 57th St.
Tel. 265-2550
Gadgets.

SUSAN BENNIS WARREN EDWARDS
22 W. 57th St.
Tel. 755-4197
Shoes, boots, luggage made of exotic skins. Sometimes extravagant, often expensive.

TIFFANY AND CO.
727 5th Ave.
Tel. 755-8000
In a class of its own for jewelry. Also, a small souvenir department.

VICTORIA'S SECRET
34 E. 57th St.
Tel. 758-5592
Stylish lingerie.

WARNER BROS, STUDIO STORE
1 E. 57th St.
Tel. 754-0300
Three floors of T-shirts, toys, crockery, gadgets... and a unique theme: the Warner Studio's heros. It is worth a visit for the décor alone.

HARRY WINSTON
718 5th Ave.
Tel. 245-2000
The jewelery store that Marilyn Monroe sang about in "Diamonds are a Girl's Best Friend".

YANKEE CLUBHOUSE SHOP
110 E. 59th St.
Tel. 758-7844
Outlet for New York's famous baseball team. Also sells T-shirts and caps representing other teams.

NIGHT LIFE

THE BAR BAT
311 W. 57th St.
Tel. 307-7228
Open Mon.–Sat. 12–4am

A former chapel with funky décor. Several levels. Dancing, live music, Vietnamese and American cuisine.

ROSELAND BALLROOM
239 W. 52nd St.
Tel. 247-0200
Dance the hours away here between 2.30 and 11pm.
The age group is older on Thurs. and Sun. Chinese cafeteria.

UPPER EAST SIDE

CULTURAL LIFE

ABIGAIL ADAMS SMITH MUSEUM
421 E. 61st St.

Tel. 838-6878
Open Mon.–Fri. noon–4pm
Open Sun. 1–5pm
Closed Sat.
18th-century house
▲ 311.

THE ASIA SOCIETY
725 Park Ave.
Tel. 288-6400
Open Tues.–Wed. and Fri.–Sat. 11am–6pm
Open Thurs. 11am–8pm
Open Sun. noon–5pm
Closed Mon.
Shows, lectures, conferences and contemporary Oriental art exhibitions.

COOPER-HEWITT MUSEUM
2 E. 91st St.
Tel. 860-6868
Open Tues. 10am–9pm
Open Wed.–Sat. 10am–5pm
Open Sun. noon–5pm
Closed Mon.
Decorative arts and applied ornaments
▲ 320.

FRICK COLLECTION
1 E. 70th St.
Tel. 288-0700
Open Tues.–Sat. 10am–6pm
Open Sun. 1–6pm
Closed Mon. and
public holidays.
No admission for children under ten.
Henry Clay Frick's house and art collection
▲ 322.

GOETHE HOUSE
1014 5th Ave. and 83rd St.
Tel. 439-8700
German cultural center. Exhibitions, lectures, library.

GRACIE MANSION
88th St. and East End Ave. (in Carl Schurz Park)
Tel. 570-4751
Tours on Wed., Mar. 15–Nov. 15, by appointment.
The residence of the Mayor of New York.

INTERNATIONAL CENTER OF PHOTOGRAPHY
1130 5th Ave.

1. HOTEL WALES
2. PAPAYA KING
3. MOCCA HUNGARIAN
4. STANHOPE
5. THE MARK
6. DANIEL/SURREY HOTEL
7. THE CARLYLE
8. MORTIMER'S
9. THE THREE GUYS
10. MEZZALUNA
11. CAFÉ CROCODILE
12. SETTE MEZZO
13. HOTEL WESTBURY
14. LE CIRQUE
15. MAYFAIR HOTEL BAGLIONI

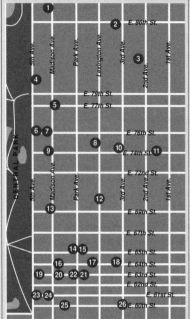

ROOSEVELT ISLAND TRAMWAY
2nd Ave. and 60th St.
Tel. 832-4543
Open daily, 6am–2am
Open Fri.–Sat.
6am–3.30am
Leaves every 15 mins.
Buy return tokens before departure, in Manhattan.

7TH REGIMENT ARMORY
643 Park Ave.
and 67th St.
Tel. 439-0300
Tour by appointment.
The mess doubles as a restaurant in the evenings.

SOLOMON R. GUGGENHEIM MUSEUM
1071 5th Ave.
and 88th St.
Tel. 423-3500
Open 10am–8pm
Closed Thurs.
One of the finest collections of modern art in the world on display ▲ 338.

TEMPLE EMANU-EL
1 E. 65th St.
Tel. 744-1400
Open Sun.–Fri.
10am–5pm
Closed to the public on Jewish holidays.
▲ 311

WHITNEY MUSEUM OF AMERICAN ART
945 Madison Ave.
and 75th St.
Tel. 570-3676
Open Wed., Fri., Sat.,
Sun. 11am–6pm
Open Thurs. 1–8pm
Closed Mon.–Tues.,
public holidays.
▲ 326.

GALLERIES

GAGOSIAN GALLERY
980 Madison Ave.
Tel. 744-2313
Open Tues.–Sat.
10am–6pm
Exhibits established contemporary artists as well as key works by

great 20th-century masters such as Beckman and Giacometti. A sculpture terrace has recently been added.

HIRSCHL & ADLER MODERN
21 E. 70th St.
(2nd Floor)
Tel. 535-8810
Open Tues.–Fri.
9.30am–5.15pm.
Open Sat.
9.30am–4.45pm.
This gallery offers a range of contemporary art. The main gallery contains works by 19th-century and early 20th-century American and European masters.

KNOEDLER AND COMPANY
19 E. 70th St.
Tel. 794-0550
Open Tues.–Fri.
9.30am–5.30pm Open
Sat. 10am–5.30pm
Many well-known American artists.

MATTHEW MARKS GALLERY
1018 Madison Ave.
Tel. 861-9455
Open Tues.–Sat.
10am–5.30pm
Matthew Marks has gained a sound reputation as an drawings expert.

MICHAEL WERNER
21 E. 67th St.
Tel. 988-1623
Open Tues.–Sat.
10am–6pm
Contemporary artists from Europe, especially from Germany (Michael Werner also has a gallery in Cologne), and older works by 20th-century masters.

ZABRISKIE GALLERY
724 5th Ave.
Tel. 307-7430
Open Mon.–Sat.
10am–5.30pm,
Sept.–May.
Open Mon.–Fri.

Tel. 860-1777
Open Tues. 11am–8pm
Open Wed. 11am–5pm
Open Thurs.–Sun.
11am–6pm
Closed Mon. and public holidays.

THE JEWISH MUSEUM
1109 5th Ave.
Tel. 423-3200
Open Sun.–Thurs.
11am–5.45pm
(Tues. until 8pm).
Closed Fri.–Sat.
and public holidays.
▲ 321.

ISLAMIC CULTURAL CENTER OF NEW YORK
1711 3rd Ave. and
97th St.
Tel. 722-5234
Open Sun.–Fri.
10am–noon and
2–4pm
Closed Sat.
New York's mosque.

METROPOLITAN MUSEUM OF ART
5th Ave. and 82nd St.
Tel. 535-7710
Open Tues.–Thurs.,
Sun. 9.30am–5.15pm
Open Fri., Sat.
9.30am–8.45pm
Closed Mon. and public holidays.
▲ 328.

EL MUSEO DEL BARRIO
1230 5th Ave.
and 104th St.
Tel. 831-7272
Recently re-opened
▲ 321.

MUSEUM OF THE CITY OF NEW YORK
1220 5th Ave.
at 103rd St.
Tel. 534-1672
Open Wed.–Sat.
10am–5pm
Open Sun. 1–5pm
Closed Mon., Tues.

NATIONAL ACADEMY OF DESIGN
1083 5th Ave.
(between 88th
and 89th sts.)
Tel. 369-4880
Open Wed.–Sun.
noon–5pm
Open Fri. noon–
8pm
Closed Mon., Tues.

16. HOTEL PLAZA ATHÉNÉE
17. JOJO
18. LYDEN GARDENS
19. THE LOWELL
20. PARK AVENUE CAFÉ
21. THE BARBIZON
22. THE REGENCY HOTEL
23. HOTEL PIERRE
24. COCO PAZZO
25. CONTRAPUNTO
26. ARIZONA, 206

10am–5.30pm,
June–Aug.
This gallery has made a name for itself primarily as a showcase for photography: old prints or works by artists such as Man Ray and Nicolas Nixon.

RESTAURANTS

ARCADIA
21 East 62nd St.
Tel. 223-2900
Exquisite intimate setting with chef/owner Anne Rosenzweig. Specializes in lobster club sandwiches and crab cakes.

ARIZONA 206
206 E. 60th St.
Tel. 838-0440
Closed Sun. noon
Spicy cuisine from southwest America, as colorful as the surroundings and the atmosphere.

BISTRO DU NORD
1312 Madison Ave.
Tel. 289-0997
Open daily.
Bustling and congenial atmosphere. Highly inventive brasserie dishes.

CAFÉ CROCODILE
354 E. 74th St.
Tel. 249-6619
*Open in the evenings only.
Closed Sun.
Cheerful atmosphere. American Express only.*

COCO PAZZO
23 E. 74th St.
Tel. 794-0205
Luxurious East-side décor with Tuscan cuisine. Specialties include grilled rib-eye steak florentine-style and fresh pasta with tomatoes and fresh herbs.

CONTRAPUNTO
200 E. 60th St.
Tel. 751-8616
Open daily.
Close to Bloomingdale's. Conveniently placed for delicious sandwiches, tasty pasta dishes and substantial grills when you are feeling hungry.

DANIEL
20 E. 76th St.
Tel. 288-0033
Closed Sat. noon, Sun.
Daniel Boulud, Le Cirque's former chef, has now gone into business for himself. Risotto with quail and crawfish, banana flan with caramelized apples.

JOJO
160 E. 64th St.
Tel. 223-5656

Closed Sat. noon, Sun.
The most fashionable bistro in New York.

LE CIRQUE
58 E. 65th St.
Tel. 794-9292
Closed Sun.
An institution. The French chef, Sylvain Portay, concocts some sophisticated creations for this restaurant: pappardelle au foie gras, veal kidneys, halibut curry. Desserts fit for the gods.

MEZZALUNA
1295 3rd Ave.
Tel. 535-9600
Open daily.
*Frequented by fashionable Europeans. Lively and convivial. Extremely simple dishes.
No credit cards.*

MOCCA HUNGARIAN
1588 2nd Ave.
Tel. 734-6470
Open daily.
Satisfying specialties in a restaurant that evokes bygone times: gulyas, chicken with paprika and sweet pancakes. No credit cards.

MORTIMER'S
1057 Lexington Ave.
Tel. 517-6400
Open daily.
Fairly exclusive club for New York's beautiful people, who come here to gossip over rather basic dishes.

PAPAYA KING
179 E. 86th St.
Tel. 369-0648
Open daily.
The bizarre combination of hot dogs and papaya juice, invented in the 1920's, has become a real New York tradition. No reservations. No alcohol. No credit cards.

PARK AVENUE CAFÉ
100 E. 63rd St.
Tel. 644-1900
Closed Sat. noon
Highly imaginative décor and menu. Brunch.

SETTE MEZZO
969 Lexington Ave.
Tel. 472-0400
Closed Sat., Sun. in summer.
Long waits before you can savor this fashionable restaurant's stuffed mozzarella and other house specialties. No credit cards.

THE THREE GUYS
960 Madison Ave.
Tel. 628-8108
Open daily, in the evenings.
A trendy place to grab a sandwich or a hamburger. Very popular with Madison Ave. gallery owners. No credit cards. No alcohol.

ACCOMMODATION

THE BARBIZON
140 E. 63rd St.
Tel. 838-5700
or 1-800-223-1020
Fax. 753-0360
One of the best hotels in New York in terms of value. In a stylish commercial neighborhood.

THE CARLYLE
Madison Ave. and
E. 76th St.
Tel. 744-1600
Fax. 717-4682
Perhaps the best hotel in New York.

Large rooms in exquisite taste. The bar boasts murals by Ludwig Bemelmans. Renowned for its afternoon teas and the equally famous Café Carlyle ▲ 312.

THE LOWELL
28 E. 63rd St.
Tel. 838-1400
or 1-800-221-4444
Fax. 319-4230
An extremely romantic hotel in a quiet residential neighborhood. All the huge rooms come with wine rack and books, and many have a fireplace.

LYDEN GARDENS
215 E. 64th St.
Tel. 355-1230
or 1-800-ME-SUITE
Fax. 758-7858
On an attractive tree-lined street. Rooms with extra sofa-beds and self-catering facilities. Ideal for families. Negotiable weekly rates.

THE MARK
Madison Ave.
and E. 77th St.
Tel. 744-4300
or 1-800-843-6275
Fax. 744-2749
Outside, Art Deco elements. Inside, antiques, paintings, architectural drawings. There are luxury suites with self-catering facilities, a collection of books and occasionally a terrace, on the three top floors.

MAYFAIR HOTEL BAGLIONI
Park Ave. and 65th St.
Tel. 288-0800
Fax. 737-0538
Famous for its restaurant, Le Cirque. Elegantly restored turn-of-the-century lobby. Large bright rooms.

HOTEL PIERRE
5th Ave. and E. 61st St.
Tel. 838-8000
or 1-800-332-3442
Fax. 940-8109
A tall tower with a mansard roof dating from 1929. Furniture made of inlaid wood, antiques and featherbeds in every room. A small number

of extremely expensive suites have a view over Central Park.

HOTEL PLAZA ATHÉNÉE
37 E. 64th St.
Tel. 734-9100
or 1-800-447-8800
Fax. 772-0958
Similar style to that of the Carlyle. French fin de siècle furniture and French gourmet cuisine. Duplex apartment with balcony.

THE REGENCY HOTEL
540 Park Ave.
Tel. 759-4100
Fax. 826-5674
This feels more like an elegant mansion than a hotel, since its rooms are furnished with 18th-century-style furniture and plush carpets.

STANHOPE
995 5th Ave.
Tel. 288-5800
or 1-800-828-1123
Fax. 517-0088
This building, which dates from 1926, has the atmosphere of an English club. Spacious, luxurious rooms, many of which have a view over Central Park.

SURREY HOTEL
20 E. 76th St.
Tel. 288-3700
or 1-800-ME-SUITE
Fax. 628-1549
Mainly suites with self-catering facilities. Secretarial services, fax and modems for use by guests on business. Sofa-beds for families. Negotiable weekly rates.

HOTEL WALES
1295 Madison Ave.
Tel. 876-6000
or 1-800-428-7252
Fax. 860-7000
This hotel has recently been restored to its original turn-of-the-century Edwardian style splendor. Relaxed,

friendly atmosphere. Tea tis served to the accompaniment of a harpist from 5 to 6pm.

HOTEL WESTBURY
Madison Ave. and E. 69th St.
Tel. 535-2000
or 1-800-321-1569
Fax. 535-5058
The effect is intentionally very British: walls decorated with hunting scenes, tapestries, floral bedspreads.

NIGHTLIFE

HOTEL CARLYLE
Madison Ave. and 76th St.
Tel. 744-1600
- BEMELMAN'S BAR
Open noon–1am
piano from 9.45pm
- CAFÉ CARLYLE
Open Tues.–Sat.
6pm–1am
Shows at 8.45pm and 10.45pm
Brunch on Sundays.

MANNY'S CAR WASH
1558 3rd Ave.
(between 87th and 88th sts.)
Tel. 369-2583
Open daily 5pm–2am
An excellent blues club with a different show every evening at 9.30pm. A limited number of tables are available.

SHOPPING

BARNEYS
660 Madison Ave. and 61st St.
Tel. 826-8900
The famous Chelsea store has set up shop on the Upper East Side. Clothes for men and women.

BILLY MARTIN
812 Madison Ave.
Tel. 861-3100
All kinds of cowboy boots, affordable prices to suit every pocket.

BLADES EAST
160 E. 86th St.
Tel. 996-1644
Roller skates to buy or rent (Central Park is quite close).

BOOKS & CO.
939 Madison Ave.
Tel. 737-1450
Strong in literature and fine arts. Celebrated author readings upstairs.

THE COACH STORE
710 Madison Ave. and 63rd St.
Tel. 319-1772
Fine leather bags at reasonable prices.

COLE-HAAN
667 Madison Ave. and 61st St.
Tel. 421-8440
Shoes, fancy leather goods.

DARROW'S FUN ANTIQUES
1101 1st Ave.
Tel. 838-0730
American toys, jukeboxes, slot machines, signs. Very entertaining and unusual.

JOAN AND DAVID
816 Madison Ave.
Tel. 772-3970
Shoes.

POLO-RALPH LAUREN
867 Madison Ave. and 72nd St.
Tel. 606-2100
Casual wear and stylish clothing in a splendid building.

POLO SPORT
888 Madison Ave.
Tel. 434-8000
Opposite the previously mentioned store. Specializes in sportswear.

SOTHEBY'S
1334 York Ave.
Tel. 606-7000
Antiques. Considered to be one of the most famous auction rooms in the world.

STRIDE RITE
1241 Lexington Ave.
Tel. 721-0900
A wide variety of shoes for children.

TIMBERLAND
709 Madison Ave. and 62nd St.
Tel. 754-0434
Shoes, clothes, accessories.

WILLIAM DOYLE GALLERIES
175 E. 87th St.
Tel. 427-2730
Antiques from 18th–20th century. Auction every other Wednesday.

CENTRAL PARK

CARRIAGES
5th Ave. and Central Park South
Trips around the park.

CENTRAL PARK ZOO
5th Ave. (E. 64th St.)
Tel. 861-6030
Open daily.

THE DAIRY
64th St.
Tel. 794-6564
Open Tues.– Sun. 11am–4pm (until 5pm in summer)
Park information center. Videos.

LOEB BOAT HOUSE
E. 74th St. (72nd St.)
Tel. 517-4723
Bar open all year round, Italian restaurant closed during the week in winter. Bicycle and boat rental, Mar–Nov. Gondola trips around the lake. Shuttle from 5th Ave. and Central Park West.

1. EJ'S LUNCHONETTE
SARABETH'S KITCHEN
2. THE MILBURN HOTEL
3. MEMPHIS
4. OLCOTT HOTEL
5. CAFÉ LUXEMBOURG
6. VINCE & EDDIE'S
7. CAFÉ DES ARTISTES
8. TAVERN ON THE GREEN
9. THE RADISSON EMPIRE
10. THE MAYFLOWER HOTEL

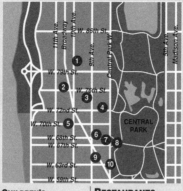

URBAN PARK RANGERS
Tel. 772-0210
Guided tours of the park.

WOLLMAN MEMORIAL RINK
59th St.
Tel. 517-4800
Ice skating rink (Nov.–Mar.). Roller-skating rink and miniature golf course (Apr.–Oct.). Rental of rollerskates and rollerblades for skating through the park.

UPPER WEST SIDE
CULTURAL LIFE

AMERICAN MUSEUM OF NATURAL HISTORY
Central Park West and 79th St.
Tel. 769-5100
Open Sun.–Thurs. 10am–5.45pm
Open Fri.–Sat. until 8.45pm
▲ 347.

BEACON THEATER
2124 Broadway (between 74th and 75th sts.)
Tel. 496-7070
Concert hall (rock, pop, jazz, etc.).

BUDDHIST TEMPLE OF NEW YORK
332 Riverside Drive
Tel. 678-0305
Open Sun. morning, only for services.

CHILDREN'S MUSEUM OF MANHATTAN
212 W. 83rd St.
Tel. 721-1234
Open Mon., Wed., Thurs. 1.30–5.30pm
Open Fri.–Sun. 10am–5pm
Exhibitions for children. They can touch everything, have a whale of a time and still learn.

HAYDEN PLANETARIUM
W. 81st St. and Central Park West
Tel. 769-5920
Open Mon.–Fri. 12.30am–4.45pm
Same opening hours, Sat.–Sun., in summer.
Open Sat. 10am–6.30pm and Sun. noon–4.45pm, in winter.

MUSEUM OF AMERICAN FOLK ART
2 Lincoln Square (between 9th Ave. and 65th St.)
Tel. 977-7298
Open Tues.–Sun. 11.30am–7.30pm
Museum of popular art.

NEW YORK HISTORICAL SOCIETY
170 Central Park West
Tel. 873-3400
Open Mon.–Fri. 10am–5pm
Museum temporarily closed. Library open to the public. Archives and photos of the city.

SYMPHONY SPACE
2537 Broadway (95th W. St.)
Tel. 864-5400
Auditorium.

RESTAURANTS

CAFÉ DES ARTISTES
1 W. 67th St.
Tel. 877-3500
Open daily.
Howard Chandler Christy's delightful

murals add to the enjoyment of the meal: gravlax (raw sea salmon), pot-au-feu, chicken flan, cassoulet and tarte Ilona. Brunch.

CAFÉ LUXEMBOURG
200 W. 70th St.
Tel. 873-7411
Closed Mon. noon
A marvelous place for dining late into the night.

EJ'S LUNCHONETTE
433 10th Ave.
Tel. 873-3444
Open daily.
This diner, with its pre-1940's appearance and simple but appetizing dishes, is ideal for family meals. There are branches of the same establishment at E. 73rd St. and 3rd Ave. Brunch. No credit cards.

MEMPHIS
329 9th Ave.
Tel. 496-1840
Open daily in the evenings.
Very popular for its Cajun cuisine: Cajun popcorn, crab pancake, Southern-style fried chicken, jambalaya (chicken and shellfish stew). The music might be too loud for some.

SARABETH'S KITCHEN
423 Amsterdam Ave.
Tel. 496-6280
Open daily.
This is a comfortable, family tearoom filled with the mouthwatering aroma of pastries, omelettes, pasta and hamburgers. Brunch. The East Side branch is at 1295 Madison Ave. at the Hotel Wales
▲ 424.

TAVERN ON THE GREEN
Central Park West and 67th St.
Tel. 873-3200
Open daily.
This caters mainly for tourists and is very kitsch. The dishes are nevertheless delicious. And there are some very reasonably priced set menus. Brunch.

VINCE & EDDIE'S
70 W. 68th St.
Tel. 721-0068
Open daily.
A taste of the countryside, substantial food, inexpensive menu: onion flan, fried oysters, knuckle of lamb with dried cherries, apple pie.

ACCOMMODATION

THE MAYFLOWER HOTEL
15 Central Park West
Tel. 265-0060 or 1-800-223-4164
Fax. 265-5098
Less expensive than the hotels near Central Park South. Splendid view from the rooms overlooking the park.

THE MILBURN HOTEL
242 W. 76th St.
Tel. 362-1006 or 1-800-833-9622
Fax. 721-5476
Small rooms, but with

microwaves and refrigerators. Washing machines and driers in the building.

OLCOTT HOTEL
27 W. 72nd St.
Tel. 877-4200
Fax. 580-0511
A simple hotel that will suit guests who wish, above all, to be right next to Central Park. Special reduced rates for long stays.

THE RADISSON EMPIRE
44 W. 63rd St.
Tel. 265-7400
or 1-800-333-3333
Fax. 765-6125
Good hotel near Lincoln Center and Broadway.

SHOPPING

BARNES AND NOBLE
2289 Broadway
Tel. 362-8835
The most extensive bookstore in New York. Several other outlets.

BLADES-WEST
120 W. 72nd St.
Tel. 787-3911
Roller skates for sale or for rent (Central Park is two minutes away).

HARRY'S SHOES
2299 Broadway
and 83rd St.
Tel. 874-2035
All the leading makes of shoe (Timberland, Sebago, etc.) for men, women and children.

I.S. 44 FLEA MARKET
162 West 72nd St.
Tel. 721-0900
Open Sun.

MAXILLA AND MANDIBLE
451 Columbus Ave.
Tel. 724-6173
Weird and wonderful or macabre: human skeletons, animal skulls, insects, fossils and minerals.

ZABAR'S
2245 Broadway
Tel. 787-2000
Started out as a "deli". Now it is a renowned food store, the least expensive of its kind. A "must", if only for the atmosphere and the wonderful aromas.

UPPER MANHATTAN INCLUDING HARLEM

CULTURAL LIFE

ABYSSINIAN BAPTIST CHURCH
132 W. 138th St.
Tel. 862-7474
Open Mon.–Fri.
10am–6pm
Open Sat.–Sun. by appointment.
Open Sun. 1–6pm
Service on Sundays at 11am with gospel choir. Memorial Room in memory of Adam Clayton Powell, Jr.

AMERICAN ACADEMY AND INSTITUTE OF ARTS AND LETTERS
633 W. 155th St.
(Audubon Terrace)
Tel. 368-5900
Opens only for the three annual exhibitions, or by appointment for the library.

AMERICAN NUMISMATIC SOCIETY
Broadway and 155th St.
Tel. 234-3130
Open Tues.–Sat.
9am–4.30pm
Open Sun. 1–6pm
Museum of coins and medals.

AUNT LEN'S DOLL AND TOY MUSEUM
6 Hamilton Terrace
(Saint Nicholas Ave. and 141st St.)
Tel. 281-4143
Temporarily closed. One of the largest collections of dolls in the world.

1 · SYLVIA'S
2 · THE TERRACE

BRONX

THE CLOISTERS
Fort Tryon Park
Tel. 923-3700
Open 9.30am–5.15pm
in summer.
Open 9.30am–4.45pm
in winter.
Closed Mon.
Free admission with the badge of the Metropolitan for the same day.
Museum of medieval art housed within old cloisters; part of the Metropolitan Museum. Easily reached by bus M4 on Madison Ave.
▲ *362.*

COLUMBIA UNIVERSITY
114th and 120th sts.
Broadway and 10th aves.
Daily guided tours. Inquiries at Dodge Hall, corner of 116th St. or by telephone on 854-2845.

DYCKMAN HOUSE MUSEUM
4881 Broadway
Tel. 360-8123 for information.
Temporarily closed. 17th-century house belonging to Dutch settlers. Free. ▲ *361.*

GENERAL GRANT NATIONAL MEMORIAL
Riverside Drive and 122nd St.
Tel. 666-1640
Open Wed.–Sun.
9am–5pm
Tomb of President Grant and his wife.

HAMILTON GRANGE NATIONAL MEMORIAL
287 Convent Ave. and W. 141st St.
Tel. 283-5154
Temporarily closed.

HISPANIC SOCIETY OF AMERICA
Broadway and 155th St.
Tel. 690-0743
Open Tues.–Sat.
10am–4.30pm
Open Sun. 1–4pm,
Closed Mon. and public holidays.
Spanish art, literature and culture. Free.

MORRIS-JUMEL MANSION
1765 Jumel Terrace, corner W. 160th St. and Edgecombe Ave.
Tel. 923-8008
Open Wed.–Sun.
10am–4pm
Closed Mon., Tues.
▲ *361.*

MUSEUM OF THE AMERICAN INDIAN
Broadway and W. 155th St.
Tel. 283-2420
Will move at the end of October 1994 to the Alexander Hamilton U.S. Custom House on Broadway and Bowling Green.

RIVERSIDE CHURCH
490 Riverside Drive
Tel. 222-5900
Open daily 8.30am–5pm
Tower Sun.
12.30am–3.30pm
Climb the tower to see the city from an unusual angle. Carillon recitals Sun. 12.30am and 3pm.

SCHOMBURG CENTER FOR RESEARCH IN BLACK CULTURE
515 Lenox Ave.
Tel. 491-2200
Open Mon.–Wed.
10am–8pm
Open Thurs., Fri.
10am–6pm
Closed Sun.

The hotels and restaurants in the address book were selected by Peter MELTZER, author of *Passport to New York restaurants*, Passport Press Ltd, New York 1994.

A branch of the New York Public Library specializing in the Black culture of the United States.

STUDIO MUSEUM IN HARLEM
144 W. 125th St.
Tel. 864-4500
Open Wed.–Fri.
10am–5pm
Open Sat., Sun. 1–4pm
Closed Mon.–Tues.

CATHEDRAL CHURCH OF SAINT JOHN THE DIVINE
Amsterdam Ave.
and 112nd St.
Tel. 316-7540
Open Mon.–Sat.
7am–5pm
Open Sun.
7am–7.30pm
New York's Episcopal Cathedral.

RESTAURANTS

MIRAGE
185 Dyckman St.
Tel. 567-9000
Open daily.
Cuisine from Santo Domingo in modern, attractive surroundings. Specialties include sancocho (which has a meat, vegetable and sweet-smelling root base).

SYLVIA'S
328 Lenox Ave.
Tel. 996-0660
Open daily.
People come here in droves to sample a cuisine combining barbecue with soul. An after-dinner stroll in the vicinity is dangerous ▲ 358.

THE TERRACE
400 W. 119th St.
Tel. 666-9490
Open noon and in the evening.

Closed Sat. noon and Sun.–Mon.
The delicious cuisine is as memorable as the view.

NIGHTLIFE

LAURITA'S BIRDLAND
2745 Broadway
Tel. 749-2228
Afro-American cuisine. Music (jazz, blues, etc.) from 9pm.

APOLLO THEATER
253 W. 125th St.
Tel. 749-5838
The mecca for rhythm-and-blues and soul music. Making a record, "Live at the Apollo", is considered the hallmark of success. Don't miss: the amateur nights, Wed. at 7.30pm. The shows also take place in the auditorium ▲ 358.

WEST END GATE
2911 Broadway
and W. 114th St.
Tel. 662-8830
Open until 4am
Bar, restaurant, and concert hall. Drama and great jazz concerts. An extremely popular haunt of Columbia University students.

BROOKLYN

CULTURAL LIFE

BROOKLYN ACADEMY OF MUSIC
30 Lafayette Ave.
*Tel. 718-636-4100
Organizes theatrical and musical shows as well as highly regarded dance events. Take the shuttle from Manhattan.*

BROOKLYN BOTANIC GARDEN
1000 Washington Ave.
Tel. 718-624-0890
Open Tues.–Fri.
8am–4.30pm (6pm in summer).
Open Sat.–Sun.
10am–4.30pm
(6pm in summer)
Botanical garden housed within a huge park. Greenhouses, cafeteria. Shuttle from Manhattan.

BROOKLYN HISTORICAL SOCIETY
128 Pierrepont St.
Tel. 718-624-0890

Open Tues.–Sat.
noon–5pm
Museum documenting the history of Brooklyn. Library.

BROOKLYN MUSEUM OF ART
200 Eastern Parkway
Tel. 718-638-5000
Open Wed.–Sun.

10am–5pm
Closed Mon.–Tues. and public holidays.
The second-largest museum in New York. Renowned for its department of Egyptian antiquities (recently renovated). Shuttle from Manhattan.

NEW YORK TRANSIT MUSEUM
Boerum Place and Schermerhorn St.
(Brooklyn Heights)
Tel. 718-330-3060
Open Tues.–Fri.
10am–4pm
Open Sat., Sun.
11am–4pm
History of public transportation in New York.

RESTAURANTS

THE RIVER CAFÉ
1 Water St.
Tel. 718-522-5200
Open daily.
Unbeatable view over Manhattan. Desserts are always delectable. Some of the dishes may hold unpleasant as well as pleasant surprises in store.
Brunch.

BRONX

NEW YORK BOTANICAL GARDEN
200th St. and Southern Blvd, Bronx
Tel. 718-817-8700
Open Tues.–Sun.
and public holidays,
10am–6pm, Apr.–Oct.
10am–4pm Nov.–Mar.

*Guided tours every 20 mins, Apr.–Oct.
Subway: line D, Bedford Park station. Train: Metro North at Grand Central Terminal, Botanical Garden station. Bus: BX12, BX19, BX41. Stop in front of the entrance.*

NEW YORK ZOOLOGICAL PARK (BRONX ZOO)
Bronx River Parkway
(Fordham Road)
Tel. 718-367-1010
Open daily, 10am–4.30pm, Nov.–Feb.
Open Mon.–Fri.
10am–5pm, and
Sat.–Sun.
10am–5.30pm,
Mar.–Oct.
*Free on Wed.
Subway: line 2, Pelham Parkway station.
Train: Metro North at Grand Central Terminal, Fordham University station, then bus BX9, Southern Blvd. entrance stop.*

APPENDICES

BIBLIOGRAPHY, *430*
LIST OF ILLUSTRATIONS, *431*

◆ BIBLIOGRAPHY

◆ **ESSENTIAL READING** ◆

◆ ALLEN (Oliver E.):*New York, New York*, Atheneum, NY, 1990
◆ CARO (Robert): *Power Broker, Colin Robert Moses and the Fall of New York*, Alfred A. Knopf, NY, 1974
◆ WHITE (E. B.): *This is New York*, Warner Books, NY, 1988
◆ WILLENSKY (Elliot) and WHITE (Norval) eds., *AIA Guide to New York City*, Harcourt Brace Jovanovich, Publishers, NY, 1988

◆ **GENERAL READING** ◆

◆ ALLEN (Irving Lewis): *The City in Slang: New York Life and Popular Speech*, Oxford University Press, NY, 1993
◆ BOORSTIN (Daniel):*The Americans*, 3 vols, Random House, NY, 1975
◆ CHARYN (Jerome): *Metropolis: New York as Myth, Marketplace, and Magical Land*, Avon, NY, 1987
◆ COHN (Nik): *Heart of the World*, Alfred A. Knopf, NY, 1992
◆ DIAMONSTEIN (Barbaralee): *Landmarks: Eighteen Wonders of the New York World*, Harry Abrams, NY, 1992
◆ FONER (NANCY): *New Immigrants in New York*, Columbia University Press, NY, 1987
◆ GOLD (Joyce): *From Windmills to the World Trade Center: A Walking Guide to Lower Manhattan History*, Old Warren Road Press, NY, 1988
◆ GLUECK (Grace) and GARDNER (Paul): *Brooklyn: People, Places, Past and Present*, Harry Abrams, NY, 1991
◆ GRAFTON (John): *New York in the Nineteenth Century*, Dover, NY, 1992
◆ HORNUNG (Clarence P.): *The Way It Was, New York, 1850–1890*, Schocken Books, NY, 1977
◆ JOHNSON (Harry) and LIGHTFOOT (Frederick S.): *Maritime New York in Nineteenth Century Photographs*, Dover, NY, 1980
◆ KINKEAD (Gwen.): *Chinatown: A Portrait of a Closed Society*, Harper Collins, NY, 1992
◆ KOUWENHOVEN (John A.): *The Columbia Historical Portrait of New York*, Harper & Row, NY, 1972
◆ MANGIONE (Jerre) and MORREALE (Ben): *La Storia: Five Centuries of the Italian American Experience*, Harper Collins, NY, 1992
◆ PLOTCH (Batia) ed. with MORSE (John) et al.: *New York walks*, Henry Holt, NY 1992
◆ SANTE (Luc): *Low Life: Lures and Snares of Old New York*, Random House, NY, 1992
◆ SALWEIN (Peter): *Upper West Side Story*, Abbeville Press, NY 1989
◆ SHEPARD (Richard F.): *Broadway from Battery to the Bronx*, Harry Abrams, NY, 1987
◆ STARR (Roger): *The Rise and Fall of New York City*, Basic Books, NY, 1985
◆ TRACHTENBERG (Alan): *Brooklyn Bridge: Fact and Symbol*, Univ. of Chicago Press, Chicago, 1979
◆ TRAGER (James): *Park Avenue: Street of Dreams*, Atheneum, NY, 1990
◆ WALLOCK (Leonard) ed.: *New York: Culture Capital of the World, 1940–1965*, Rizzoli, NY, 1988

◆ **ARCHITECTURE** ◆

◆ ALPERN (Andrew): *Luxury Apartment Houses of Manhattan*, Dover, NY, 1993
◆ BADGER (Daniel D.): *Badger's Illustrated Catalogue of Cast-Iron Architecture*, Dover, NY, 1982
◆ BOYER (M. Christine): *Manhattan Manners, Architecture and Style 1850–1900*, Rizzoli, NY, 1985
◆ BREEZE (Carla): *New York Deco*, Rizzoli, NY 1993
◆ CROMLEY (Elizabeth Collins): *Alone Together: A History of New York's Early Apartments*, Cornell Univ. Press, Ithaca, 1990
◆ DOLKART (Andrew S.): *A Guide to New York City Landmarks*, Preservation Press, NY, 1992
◆ DUNLAP (David W.): *On Broadway, A Journey Uptown over Time*, Rizzoli, NY, 1990
◆ FRIEDMAN (Joe) and BERENHOLTS (Richard): *Inside New York: Discovering New York's Classic Interiors*, Harper Collins, NY, 1992
◆ GILLON (Edmund V.), REED (Henry. H.): *Beaux-Arts Architecture in New York*, Dover, NY, 1988
◆ GOLDBERGER (Paul): *The Skyscraper*, Alfred A. Knopf, NY, 1983
◆ HAWES (Elizabeth) : *New York, New York*, Alfred A. Knopf, NY, 1993
◆ HOOD (Clifton): *722 Miles: The Building of the Subways and How They Transformed New York*, Simon & Schuster, NY, 1993
◆ IRACE (Fulvio): *Emerging Skylines: The New American Skyscrapers*, Whitney Library of Design, NY, 1990
◆ KLOTZ (Heinrich): *New York Architecture, 1970–1990*, Rizzoli, NY, 1989
◆ MACKAY (Donald A.): *The Building of Manhattan*, Harper Collins, NY, 1989
◆ ROSEN (Laura): *Top of the City*, Thames and Hudson, London, 1983
◆ ROTHSCHILD (Nan): *New York City Neighborhoods: The 18th Century*, Academic Press, NY,1990
◆ SHAPIRO (Mary J.): *A Picture History of the Brook-lyn Bridge*, Dover, NY, 1983
◆ SILVER (Nathan) : *Lost New York*, Schocken Books, NY, 1967
◆ STERN (Robert. A.),

GILMARTIN (G.), MELLINS (T.): *New York Nineteen Thirty*, Rizzoli, NY, 1987
◆ WHYTE (William H.): *City: Rediscovering the Center*, Doubleday, NY, 1990
◆ WOLFE (Gerard R.): *New York: A Guide to the Metropolis*, McGraw-Hill, NY, 1994

◆ **ARTS** ◆

◆ ABBOTT (Berenice): *New York in the Thirties*, Dover, NY, 1973
◆ AVEDON (Richard): *Autobiography*, Random House, NY, 1993
◆ CHWAST (Seymour) and HELLER (Steven) ed.: *The Art of New York*, Harry Abrams, NY, 1983
◆ COHEN (Barbara) CHWAST (Seymour) and HELLER (Steven) ed.: *New York Observed: Artists and Writers Look at the City*, Harry Abrams, NY, 1987
◆ FIELDS (Armond and Marc L.): *From the Bowery to Broadway: Lew Fields and the Roots of the American Popular Theatre*, Oxford University Press, NY, 1993
◆ HINE (Lewis): *Men at Work*, Dover, NY, 1977
◆ KIRSTEIN (Lincoln): *Mosaic*, Farrar, Straus & Giroux NY, 1994
◆ WILLIS-BRAITHWAITE (Deborah): *Van Der Zee, Photographer*, Harry Abrams, NY, 1993

◆ **LITERATURE** ◆

◆ AUSTER (Paul): *New York Trilogy: City of Glass, Ghosts, The Locked Room*, Viking Penguin, NY, 1990
◆ BELLOW (Saul): *Seize the Day*, Viking Penguin, NY, 1984
◆ CAPOTE (Truman): *Breakfast at Tiffany's*, Random House, NY, 1994
◆ CARR (Caleb): *The Alienist*, Random House, NY, 1994
◆ DOCTOROW (E. L.): *The Waterworks*, Random House, NY, 1994
◆ DONLEAVY (J. P.): *A Fairy Tale of New York*, Atlantic Monthly, NY, 1989
◆ DOS PASSOS (John): *Manhattan Transfer*, Houghton-Mifflin, NY, 1991
◆ EDMISTON (Susan) and CIRINO (Linda D.): *Literary New York*, Gibbs Smith Pubs., Indianapolis, 1991
◆ ELLISON (Ralph): *The Invisible Man*, Random House, NY, 1989
◆ FITZGERALD (F. Scott): *Tender is the Night*, Macmillan, NY, 1977
◆ GOOCH (Brad): *City Poet: The Life and Times of Frank O'Hara*, Alfred A. Knopf, NY, 1993
◆ HALEY (Alex): *The Autobiography of Malcolm X*, Ballantine, NY, 1992
◆ HIMES (Charles): *A Rage of Harlem*, Random House, NY, 1989
◆ JAMES (Henry) : *The American Scene*, St. Martin's Press, NY, 1987
◆ LORCA (Federico Garcia): *Poet in New York*, W. W. Norton, NY, 1940

◆ MITCHELL (Joseph):*Up in the Old Hotel*, Pantheon, NY, 1992
◆ WAKEFIELD (Dan): *New York in the '50s*, Houghton-Mifflin, NY, 1992
◆ WHARTON (Edith): *Age of Innocence*, Alfred A. Knopf NY, 1993
◆ WHITMAN (Walt): *Leaves of Grass*, Random House, NY, 1993
◆ WOLFE (Thomas): *Bonfire of the Vanities*, Farrar, Straus & Giroux, NY 1987

◆ **PAINTING** ◆

◆ COOPER (Martha), CHALFANT (Henry): *Subway Art*, Henry Holt and Co., NY, 1988
◆ GLUECK (Grace): *New York: The Painted City*, Gibbs Smith Pubs., Indianapolis, 1992
◆ MAJOR (Mike): *Drawings & Paintings of New York*, Main Graphics, 1990
◆ WALDMAN (Diane): *Roy Lichtenstein*, Guggenheim Museum, NY, 1993
◆ WATSON (Steven): *Strange Bedfellows*, Abbeville Press, NY, 1991

◆ **FILM** ◆

◆ *Annie Hall*, Woody Allen, 1977
◆ *Breakfast at Tiffany's*, Blake Edwards, 1961
◆ *A Bronx Tale*, Robert DeNiro, 1993
◆ *Carlito's Way*, Brian de Palma, 1993
◆ *Do the Right Thing*, Spike Lee, 1989
◆ *The French Connection*, William Friedkin, 1971
◆ *Ghostbusters*, Ivan Reitman, 1984
◆ *The Godfather Parts I–III*, Francis Ford Coppola, 1972–90
◆ *Manhattan*, Woody Allen, 1979
◆ *The Man in the Grey Flannel Suit*, Nunnally Johnson, 1956
◆ *Miracle on 34th Street*, George Seaton, 1947
◆ *On the Waterfront*, Elia Kazan, 1954
◆ *Raging Bull*, Martin Scorsese, 1980
◆ *Rear WIndow*, Alfred A. Hitchcock, 1954
◆ *Seven Year Itch*, Billy Wilder, 1955
◆ *Six Degrees of Separation*, Fred Schepisi, 1993
◆ *Taxi driver*, Martin Scorsese, 1976
◆ *West Side Story*, Robert Wise, 1961
◆ *The World of Henry Orient*, George Roy Hill, 1964
◆ *Year of the Dragon*, Michael Cimono, 1985

List of abbreviations used in the picture credits:
MCNY = Museum of The City of NY;
MMA = The Metropolitan Museum of Art;
MOMA = Museum of Modern Art;
MP = Magnum, Paris;
TO = United States Tourist Office in Paris;
RB = Richard Berenholtz;
Sch C = Schomberg Center for Research in Black Culture, The NY Public Library;
SC = Steven L. Cohen;
SD = Seymour Durst Old York Library;
TH = Ted Hardin.
Front Cover US/UK: New York taxi in the seventies. Photo TH. New York at Night, detail, oil painting by Stephen J. Card (30x20). Private coll. Skyline, drawing Ch. Broutin.
Spine US/UK: Chrysler Building, drawing by P.-M. Valat, all rights reserved. US only: window of the New York Yacht Club, drawing Ted Hardin © Gallimard.
Back Cover US: Logo of the Yankees, RR. Astor Place subway station (terracotta motif inside), photo Ted Hardin, RR. New York's Beers, photo P. Léger, RR. City of New York's coat of arms, engraving, Seymour Durst Old York Library.
Back Cover UK: Map of the neighborhood around Grand Central Terminal, all rights reserved. New York Cop. In Fortune, July 1939. "Big Apple" logo. Monarch butterfly, ill. F. Desbordes. United States stamp, depicting Duke Ellington, all rights reserved.
1 Skyscraper, at night, photo, all rights reserved.
2–3 "Theoline", Pier 11, East River, photo 1936. Berenice Abbott/Commerce Graphics.
4–5 Interior of the El station (Columbus Ave/72nd Street), photo 1936. Berenice Abbott/Commerce Graphics.
6–7 The Bowery, beneath the 3rd Ave El, photo c. 1940, Andreas Feininger.
9 Imaginary dinner at the top of the Waldorf-Astoria hotel under construction, photo. Keystone, Paris.
10 Ill. B. Duhem, all rights reserved. New York Cop. In Fortune, July 1939. The Paul Taylor Dance Company. AP/Wide World Photos. American Radiator Building. Drawing B. Lenormand, all rights reserved. Gilsey House. Drawing B. Lenormand, all rights reserved. View of Manhattan West from Philip Morris (Park Ave/41st St), painting by Richard Haas, 1982, private coll.
16 Snowstorm, 19th-century engraving, all rights reserved. Ill. P. Biard, all rights reserved.
16–17 Map, P. Coulbois, all rights reserved. Drawings T. Sarg. SD.
17 The Ice-bound Hudson, photo L. Freed. MP. Midtown Garment District, in the Rain,

photo T. Hoepker. MP. Dog Days in Manhattan, photo B. Keystone, Paris. Woolworth Building in the Fog, photo, all rights reserved. Upper West Side in the snow, photo, all rights reserved. Depression over the East Coast, satellite photo, NASA.
18 North bank of Manhattan, photo S. Horenstein.
18–19 Ill. J. Torton and G. Houbre, all rights reserved.
19 Marble outcrop in Isham Park, photo S. Horenstein.
20 Leaping sturgeon in Hudson Bay, 19th-century engraving. SD. Manhattan piers, photo, all rights reserved. Ill. F. Desbordes, all rights reserved.
22 Ill. F. Desbordes and P. Merienne, all rights reserved.
23 Red Cardinal, photo P. Dubois, all rights reserved.
24 Ill. J. Chevallier, B. Duhem, J. Wilkinson and F. Desbordes, all rights reserved.
25 Centennial of the evacuation of New York by the British, poster by Joseph Koehler, 1883. Coll. of the NY Historical Society.
26 Algonquin Natives, engraving, by Théodore de Bry, all rights reserved. Bernardo da Verrazano, engraving 1767, all rights reserved. Peter Minuit buys the island of Manhattan from the natives, engraving. Library of Congress.
27 City of New York's coat of arms, engraving. SD. Washington's arrival in New York, 1783, lithograph. Federal Hall Archives, NYC. Federal sugar refinery, engraving. Old Print Shop.
28 Leaving for the Civil War, engraving. New York Bound. "Wanted" notice for William Tweed, December 6,1875, all rights reserved. Flatiron Building, all rights reserved.
29 Panic in Wall Street, engraving. SD. Einstein and La Guardia in 1936, the Bettmann Archive/UPI, NY.
30 New Holland, engraving by Joost Hartgers, 1651. Coll. of the NY Historical Society. Barry Faulkner, detail from a mural (Fur Trade). Washington Irving High School, reproduced with kind permission of the NYC Art Commission. King's College, 1790, engraving. SD.
30–31 View of Fort George in New York, engraving, 1731–6. SD.
31 New Amsterdam, engraving, Nicholas Visscher, 1651–5. SD. Peter Stuyvesant's army arriving in New Amsterdam, oil painting by W. Mulready, in Valentine's Manual, 1859. SD. Trinity Church in 1737, engraving G. Hayward, in Valentine's Manual, 1859. SD.
32 Map showing the Dutch East India Company's allocation of original plots of land in New Amsterdam to its inhabitants, engraving, in

Valentine's Manual, 1857. SD.
32–33 Map of New York City, 19th century. SD. Commissioners' Map of New York City. SD.
33 Boulevard lining the Hudson River, all rights reserved. Plan of south Manhattan, all rights reserved. Plan of Central Park, 19th century. SD.
34 New York cop. In Fortune, July 1939. Croton Reservoir, 19th-century engraving, Mary Black, all rights reserved. Mounted metropolitan police officer, engraving, in Harper's Weekly, May 31, 1884. Lamp lighter, lithograph. SD.
34–35 Laying underground telephone cables and electric wiring. In Frank Leslie's Illustrated Newspaper, January 29, 1887.
35 Underground section of New York. In Fortune, July 1939. Interior of an ambulance, engraving in Harper's Weekly, May 24, 1884. Public School in New York, engraving, end 19th century, all rights reserved.
36 Disembarking from the ferry on the East River, at 26th St, lithograph. SD. The first yellow taxis in New York in the 1970's. Photo TH.
36–37 Lines of taxis seen from above in a New York street, all rights reserved.
37 Bend of the El over 110th St, all rights reserved. The Bowery and its El, all rights reserved. City Hall subway station, all rights reserved. Hackney Carriage, 19th-century engraving, advertisement, all rights reserved.
38 Detail from the façade of a New York fire house, all rights reserved. Triangle shirtwaist Company Fire, painting by Victor J. Gatto. MCNY. New York firemen, drawing by D. Grant, all rights reserved.
38–39 Fire Department fire engine, all rights reserved.
39 Fire at Crystal Palace, engraving. SD. Fire at the headquarters of the Equitable Insurance Company, on Broadway, in March 1908, all rights reserved. Fire Escapes. Photo R. Arroche, all rights reserved.
40 Lucky Luciano. NY City Municipal Archives. W 47th Street Police Station, by Robert Riggs. In Fortune, July 1939, all rights reserved. Poster for the movie "Mean Streets". Ciné plus. Arrest of "Boss Tweed", engraving. NY Bound. Destruction of 10,000 gallons of liquor and alcohol by the New York police, in 1937, photo. Coll. Roger Viollet, Paris.
40–41 The weapon of crime, photo by Weegee. Shirner Mosel, Munich.
41 Gotti's Trial, drawing. AP/Wide World Photos. Front Headline from the "Times" of July 25, 1977. Headline from the "Times" of December 1980. Police inquiry in the

Oriental community. Photo F. Dannen. Photofit of the "Son of Sam". AP/Wide World Photos.
42 Barges in Coenties Slip, engraving. In Harper's Weekly, February 16,1884.
42–43 The southern tip of Manhattan. In King's Views of New York. Passengers disembarking from a ship, engraving. In Harper's Weekly, July 14, 1877.
43 View of New York Harbor over the East River, and The construction of the Brooklyn Bridge, late 19th-century photo, all rights reserved. Satellite view of Manhattan. NASA Archives and photo. Cruiser in New York Harbor. SD. The "Normandie" after its fire in New York Harbor. C.G.M. Archives and photo.
44 Postcard of Saint Patrick's Day. Coll. Gallimard. Sweatshop in the Jewish Quarter, photograph by Jacob Riis, all rights reserved. SD. Street scene in Chinatown, all rights reserved.
45 German brasserie in the Bowery district, 19th-century engraving, by J. R. Brown. In The London Graphic, February 10, 1877. The Vesuvio Bakery, 160 Prince Street. Photo RB. Street scene in Harlem. Sch C.
46 Map of Blackwells Island, 1879. SD. Street News, the newspaper for the homeless. The McAuley Mission. McAuley Mission Archives. Homeless. Photo Mary Allen.
47 Makeshift shelters near the Brooklyn Bridge. Photo K. Hopper. The Potter's Field on Hart Island, photo J. A. Riis 1889, all rights reserved. Homeless. Photo Mary Allen. I am homeless, notice in the street, detail. AP/Wide World Photo. Fort Washington Armory. Photo Kim Hopper.
48 "We speak French, etc.", photo. SD. "Big Apple" logo. Street in Chinatown, all rights reserved.
49 Fashion ill., watercolor by Benegni, for Femina, Christmas 1928. Bibliothèque des Arts décoratifs, Charmet, Paris.
50 Saint Elizabeth Seton, 19th-century engraving, all rights reserved. Saint Patrick's Cathedral, photo. OT. Jehovah's Witness magazines, all rights reserved. Protestant anti-Catholic engraving, in Harper's Weekly, September 30, 1871, all rights reserved.
50 Two Chassidic Jews, diamond dealers on 47th St/5th Ave, photo R. Burri. MP.
51 Mosque in Manhattan. U.S. Kuwait Embassy Archives. Moonie Wedding, photo. AP/Wide World Photos. Statue of Shinran-Shonin, photo, all rights reserved. Gospel Choir in Harlem, photo Leonard Freed. MP.
52 Thanksgiving Greetings, all rights reserved. Marquis de Lafayette, engraving, all

431

rights reserved. *Hanging out the flags at the end of the Civil War*, detail from engraving. In *Harper's Weekly* of March 25, 1865.

52–53 *Ticker-tape Parade*, 1991. AP/Wide World Photos.

53 *Fourth of July celebrations in New York*, photo J. Lukas, taken from Brooklyn Heights. Explorer. *Macy's Thanksgiving Day*, photo by John F. Nugent. Kind permission of Macy's. *Chinese New Year*. AP/Wide World Photos. *Halloween celebrations in Greenwich Village*, 1990. AP/Wide World Photos.

54 *Newspaper seller*, Nicolino Calyo, watercolor c. 1840–44. MCNY. *Hamilton defends Zenger*, 18th-century engraving, all rights reserved. *The Yellow Dugan Kid*, watercolor, all rights reserved.

54–55 Headline from the "New York Times," December 8, 1941.

55 *Interiors from "Frank Leslie's Newspaper" publishing house*: editorial office, typesetting office, printing press, all rights reserved. Covers of *The New Yorker*, including one by Sempé, all rights reserved.

56 *Lee De Forest, inventor of the triode lamp*, photo. Roger Viollet. *David Sarnoff, champion of the Morse code*, photo. AP/Wide World Photos. *Broadcast with George Burns and Gracie Allen*. FPG International, Explorer. *Felix the Cat*, ill. P. Sullivan, all rights reserved. *Television Broadcaster, Walter Cronkite*. Library of Congress.

56–57 *Radio City Music Hall sign*, all rights reserved.

57 *Big Bird*, all rights reserved. *Televised Kennedy-Nixon debate*, the Bettmann Archive. *Jimmy Young's victory in San Juan, Puerto Rico, March 1977*, photo. AP/Wide World Photos. ABC, NBC, CBS, HBO Logos, all rights reserved. *Yasser Arafat, interviewed in Beirut by ABC*, in 1977, photo. AP/Wide World Photos. MTV Logo. The Bettmann Archive. *Orson Welles broadcasting his hoax about the Martians in 1938*, photo. AP/Wide World Photos.

58 From left to right *Ira and George Gershwin*, photo, all rights reserved. *Poster for "Les Misérables"*, all rights reserved. *Program from "Show Boat"*, all rights reserved. *Poster for "Kiss Me Kate"*, all rights reserved.

58–59 *Theaters on Broadway*. Photo RB. *Katharine Sergava and Marc Platt, in "Oklahoma!"*, Rodgers & Hammerstein Organization. *Les Misérables*. Photo J. Marcus.

59 *Poster for "Cats"*. The Really Useful Company Limited. *Bob Fosse, directing "Big Deal"*. AP/Wide World Photos.

60 *Poster for a performance of the Cotton Club Parade*, all

rights reserved. *Louis Armstrong with Fletcher Henderson's band*, photo 1925. MP. *United States stamp, depicting Duke Ellington*, all rights reserved.

60–61 From left to right: *Tommy Potter, Charlie Parker, Dizzy Gillespie, John Coltrane*, photo 1951. Frank Driggs Collection.

61 *Poster for a Cab Calloway show*, 1934. *Sarah Vaughan in New York*, photo 1946. MP. *Exterior of the Apollo Theater*. Sch C, NY. *Sun Ra*, photo R. Burri. MP.

62 *Martha Graham in New York in 1946*. Photo Philippe Halsman, MP. *George Balanchine, teaching at the American Ballet School in 1961*, photo N. Lassalle. Ballet Society.

62–63 *The Paul Taylor Dance Company*. AP/Wide World Photos. *Michael Cole and the Merce Cunningham Dance Company, dancing "Beach Birds"*, photo M. O'Neill.

63 *The Nutcracker*. Photo P. Kolnik. New York City Ballet. *Dance Theater of Harlem program*, March 1993. *Dance Studio on Broadway*. Photo TH. *André Tyson and Renée Robinson, in Alvin Ailey's creation "Revelations"*. Photo J. Mitchell. *Meredith Monk in concert at Town Hall, on December 10, 1988*, photo J. Mitchell. AP/Wide World Photos.

64 *Advertisements in Yankee Stadium*. Explorer, Paris. *Logo of the Yankees*, all rights reserved. Babe Ruth. Explorer, Paris. *The New York Rangers*, photo M. Digirolamo. *At any moment a great moment*, all rights reserved.

64–65 *Madison Square Garden*, detail. AP/Wide World Photos. *Madison Square Garden*, all rights reserved.

65 *Ticket for a basketball game at Madison Square Garden. Joe Namath*. Photo D. Boss. Kind permission of NFL Photos. *New York Yacht Club*, 1865 logo. SD. *John McEnroe*. AP/Wide World Photos.

66 *Tiffany Lamp*. Coll. of the NY Historical Society. *Interior of William H. Vanderbilt's residence*.

66–67 *"Skyscraper" bookcase*, drawing P. M. Valat, all rights reserved.

67 *Chair*, 19th century. MCNY. *Chair, designed by Alexander Jackson Davis c. 1855*. MCNY. *Card Table, 1765–80*, photo. MCNY. *Table by John Henry Belter, 1856–61*. MCNY.

68 *Façade of Lindy's Restaurant*. SD.

68–69 *Making a cheesecake step by step*. Photo E. Guillemot.

70 *Bagel and pretzel*. Photo P. Léger, all rights reserved. *Pretzel seller, in the 1940's*. SD. *Set of café-restaurant

table mats. Motif on a glass*, all rights reserved. *International Foods*, 9th Ave. Photo TH. *Doggie Bag*, all rights reserved. *"Waldorf Salad"*. Photo TH. *New York's Beers*. Photo P. Léger, all rights reserved. *Jigsaw Puzzle of New York*, all rights reserved. *Tie*, all rights reserved.

105 *The Bowery at Night*, watercolor by Louis Sonntag Jr, 1895. MCNY.

106–107 *New York in Winter*, oil painting by Robert Henri, 1902 (32.5 in/ 81.3 cm X 26.2 in/65.5 cm), Coll. Chester Dale. National Gallery, Washington D. C.

107 *The Radiator Building, by night*, oil painting by Georgia O'Keeffe, 1927. Fisk University, Nashville © ADAGP. *Idem*, detail © ADAGP.

108–109 *Central Park*, oil painting by Maurice Prendergast, 1908–10 (21.1 in/52.7 cm X 27.4 in/68.6 cm). George A. Hearn Fund, 1950. MMA. *East River*, watercolor and pencil on paper by Maurice Prendergast, 1901 (14 in/35 cm X 20.1 in/50.2 cm). Given by Abby Aldrich Rockefeller, 1954, MMA, NY.

109 *Grand Central Terminal*, watercolor by Richard Haas, 1987. Photo Peter Mauss/Esto. Private coll. *The Chrysler Building under construction*, ink and watercolor on paper, by Earle Horter, 1931, Mrs William A. Marsteller Fund, Whitney Museum of American Art, NY.

110–111 *Roofs of Washington Square*, oil painting by Edward Hopper, 1926. Mr & Mrs James H. Beal Est. Carnegie Museum, Pittsburgh. *The New York Subway*, oil painting by George Tooker, 1950. Whitney Museum of American Art, NY. *Idem*, detail.

111 *Self-Portrait in a Hat*, Edward Hopper, etching, 1918. Josephine Hopper Est. Coll. Whitney Museum of American Art, NY.

112 *View of Manhattan West from Philip Morris Bldg.* (Park Ave/41st St), painting by Richard Haas, 1982. Private coll. *Brooklyn Bridge: Variation on an Old Theme*, oil painting by Joseph Stella, 1939. Whitney Museum of American Art, NY.

113 *Utopian New York*. Ill. in *King's Views of New York*, all rights reserved.

114 *View of the Harbor*, 19th-century engraving. SD.

115 *View of the Harbor*, 18th-century engraving. SD.

116 *Skyline in the 40s*, all rights reserved. *On the Bridge of the "Normandie", laid up in New York*, watercolor by J. Simont, 1937.

117 *Skyline*, all rights reserved.

118–119 *Scaffolding and staircases*, all rights reserved.

120 *Shoe-shine boy*. SD.

121 *New York Cops*,

watercolor 1939. In *Fortune*, July 1939.

122 *French Line*, 1930's photo. Berenice Abbott/Commerce Graphics.

123 Drawing Mark Lacaze.

124 *52nd Street*, 1949. Coll. Frank Driggs.

125 *In the Subway*, watercolor by J. Simont, 1937. *Louis Armstrong*, all rights reserved.

126 *In the Jewish Quarter*. SD.

126–127 *Brooklyn Bridge*, photo. SD.

128 *Street scene in Manhattan*, all rights reserved.

129 *3rd Avenue, between 53rd and 54th sts*. Photo RB.

130 *The World Trade Center*. Photo RB.

130–131 *90 West Street in the foreground and World Trade Center*. Photo RB.

131 *Fuller Building*. Photo Reinhart Wolf.

132 *The Hotel Pierre*. Photo RB. *1 United Nations Plaza*. Photo R. Wolf.

133 *World Financial Center*. Photo RB. *American Standard Building, former American Radiator Building*. Photo Reinhart Wolf.

134 *3 Park Avenue*. Photo R. Wolf. *The Waldorf-Astoria*. Photo RB.

135 *Wall Street*, all rights reserved.

138 *End of Courtlandt Street, on the present site of the World Trade Center*, 19th-century engraving. SD. *Wharfs on the Hudson, present site of the World Trade Center* (between Fulton and Cortlandt sts). In *King's Views of New York*, all rights reserved.

139 *The World Trade Center seen from Brooklyn*. Photo RB. *"King Kong"*, still from the movie by John Guillermin, 1976. Ciné plus, Paris. *Lobby of the World Trade Center, at 5pm*. Photo TH.

140 *90 West Street*, all rights reserved. *Interior of the New York Telephone Building*, photo. Kind permission of American Architecture Archives. *Street signs*. Drawing Mark Lacaze. *Saint Nicholas Day Procession (Greek Orthodox Chapel), for the 1993 Epiphany*. Kind permission of Saint Nicholas Hellenic Orthodox Church. *West Street looking toward Liberty Street*, 1900, color photo. Library of Congress.

141 *View of the entire World Financial Center*. AP/Wide World Photos. *"On The Waterfront"*, movie by Elia Kazan: titles and scene with Marlon Brando. Cinémathèque, Paris.

142 *View of New York Harbor*, engraving. SD. *Shipwreck*, sculpture by Marisol on Pier A, 1991. Photo TH ©ADAGP.

142–143 *Global view of the Battery*. Ill. in *King's Views of New York*, all rights reserved.

143 *Jenny Lind's First Appearance at Castle*

Garden, 1850, engraving. Coll. Federal Hall National Memorial. *Interior of the Battery Park Aquarium, at the beginning of the century*, all rights reserved.

144 *The Statue of Liberty being constructed in Paris*, photo. Bartholdi Museum, Colmar, France. Photo Ch. Kempf. *Uncle Sam congratulates Miss Liberty*, engraving. In *World*, May 16, 1885. *Portrait of Frédéric-Auguste Bartholdi*, painting by J. Frappe. Bartholdi Museum, Colmar, France. Photo Ch. Kempf.

144–145 *Exploded view of the Statue of Liberty*, drawing D. Grant, all rights reserved.

145 *Face of the Statue of Liberty, suspended in a wooden frame*, photo, 1885–6. Coll. A. J. Spano. *Portrait of Charlotte Bartholdi*, painting by Ary Scheffer. Bartholdi Museum, Colmar, France. photo Ch. Kempf. *Inner view of the face of the Statue of Liberty, suspended in a wooden frame*, photo, 1885–6. Coll. A. J. Spano. NY Bay, photo, all rights reserved.

146 *Sketch showing the scaffolding system for the Statue of Liberty's frame*. In *Scientific American*, June 13, 1885. *Assembling the Statue of Liberty in Paris*, 1884, painting by Victor Dargaud. Musée Carnavalet. Photo. Musées de La Ville-de-Paris © SPADEM. *Modeling the Statue of Liberty's head in Monduit and Bechet's studios in Paris*, engraving, 1878. *Foundations for the Statue of Liberty's pedestal*, engraving. In *Harper's Weekly*, July 12, 1884.

146–147 *Product labels from the end of the 19th century*, all rights reserved. *Modeling the Statue's hand in Paris*, photo by P. Petit. Bartholdi Museum, Colmar, France. Photo Ch. Kempf.

147 *Unveiling of the Statue of Liberty*, October 28, 1886, painting by Edward Moran. Coll J. Clarence Davies, MCNY. *Internal framework*, all rights reserved. *Restoration of the Statue*. Photo René Burri, MP.

148 *Immigrants on Ellis Island*, c. 1900, photo. Coll. Roger Viollet, Paris. *New York Bay and Harbor*, painting by Samuel Waugh. MCNY.

149 *Exploded view of the Ellis Island Building*, drawing V. Stetten, all rights reserved.

150 *Main Entrance to Ellis Island*, all rights reserved. *Medical examination for immigrants*, photo, early 19th century, all rights reserved. *Immigrants arriving in the United States*, 1914, photo. Coll. Roger Viollet, Paris. *Luggage belonging to an immigrant*. Ellis Island Museum. Photo TH.

150–151 *Ellis Island buildings at the beginning of the century*, drawing

H. Goger, all rights reserved.

151 *Ellis Island sorting hall*, all rights reserved. *Albert Einstein on his arrival in New York, October 27, 1933*, photo. Keystone.

152 *Double Check*, sculpture by J. Seward Johnson, all rights reserved. *Singer Building*, all rights reserved.

153 *East River Savings Bank*, all rights reserved. *The "Sky Lobby" of the Equitable Building*. *Sculpture at 140 Broadway by Naguchi*. Photo SC. *Equitable Building*, 1914. Ill. in *King's Views of New York*, all rights reserved.

154 *Trinity Building*, cartoon. SD. *Interior of the Irving Trust Building*. Photo RB. *Trinity Church*, 1916, photo. Édimédia, Paris.

155 *View of earlier Trinity Church*, engraving. SD. *Street sign*. Drawing Mark Lacaze. *Ceiling of the Cunard Building*. Photo TH.

156 *Government House*, engraving, 1797. Old Print Shop. *Standard Oil Building*. SD. *The Bowling Green Bull*, sculpture by Arturo di Modica, 1989. Photo SC.

157 *Custom House sculptures, depicting America, Europe, Africa and Asia*, all rights reserved. *U.S. Custom House*, all rights reserved. *Portrait of Saint Elizabeth Seton*, painting by Joseph Dawley. Coll. *Chapel of Our Lady of the Rosary. Battery Maritime Building*, all rights reserved.

158 *Financial District*, 1908, ill. in *King's Views of New York*, all rights reserved. *Federal Reserve Bank, in the movie by S. Leone: "Once Upon a Time in America"*. Cinémathèque, Paris.

159 *Advertisement in Harper's Weekly. Liberty Tower*, early 20th century. SD. *Group of Four Trees*, sculpture by Jean Dubuffet. Photo SC ©ADAGP.

160 *Detail from the door at 20 Exchange Place*, all rights reserved. *Lobby of 60 Wall Street*, all rights reserved. *55 Wall Street*. Photo SC.

161 *Bank of Manhattan Building*, 1928, engraving Hugh Ferriss. MCNY. *Exchange place seen from Broadway*, photo. Berenice Abbott/Commerce Graphics.

162 *Federal Hall, former Sub-Treasury*, photo. Robert D. Rubic. *Former Sub-Treasury, President Harrison's speech in 1880*. SD. *Custom House*, engraving, 1834. SD.

163 *Façade of the New York Stock Exchange*, all rights reserved. *Portrait of Hetty Green*. Library of Congress. *Bankers' Trust Building*. Ill. in *King's Views of New York*, all rights reserved.

164 *Stock Market panic in the 19th century in Wall Street*, two engravings taken from *Frank Leslie's Illustrated Newspaper. Stockbrokers in 1899, at the New York Stock

Exchange*, all rights reserved. *"Curb Market" on Broad Street*, 1918, photo. Coll. Roger Viollet, Paris.

164–165 *At a stockbroker's office*, photo. Rapho, Paris.

165 *Battle of the Bears and the Bulls in Wall Street*, painting by William H. Beard, 1879. Coll. of The NY Historical Society. *Headlines from the "New York Times"*, October 25, 1929. *Stockbrokers in 1992, at the New York Stock Exchange*, photo. Rapho, Paris. *Michael Milken taking the oath, April 27, 1988, in Washington*. AP/Wide World Photos.

166 *Vietnam Memorial*. Photo SC. *Detail from the façade of 67 Broad Street*, all rights reserved. *Fraunces Tavern sign*, all rights reserved. *India House*, 1984, watercolor by A. Troubetzkoy, all rights reserved.

167 *Civic Center*, all rights reserved.

168 *City Hall*, engraving, 1826. SD. *Façade of City Hall*. Photo RB. *Interior of City Hall's cupola*, photo. Photo RB. *City Hall's cupola*, photo. Kind permission of American Architecture Archives.

170 *City Hall's fountain, on the site of the former Post Office, before 1875*. SD. *Construction of the former Post Office in front of City Hall*. SD. *Newspaper Row*, 1900, color photo. Library of Congress.

171 *Riot quelled by the police in front of the Tribune Building*, engraving in *Harper's Weekly*, August 1, 1863. *Park Row building under construction*, 19th-century photo. NY Bound. *Park Row building*, 1917, all rights reserved.

172 *Oyster seller*, engraving. SD. *Silhouettes of ships: the "Peking" 1911, the "Lettie G. Howard" 1893, the "Pioneer" 1885 and the "Wavertree" 1885*. South Street Seaport Museum.

172–173 *Drawing Donald Grant*, all rights reserved.

173 *South Street Seaport Boat Building Museum*, all rights reserved.

174 *South Street Seaport in 1900*, color photo. Library of Congress. *Smith & Dimon Shipyard*, oil painting by James Pringle, 1833. NY State Historical Association, Cooperstown. *Warship, the U.S.S. Maine*, engraving, all rights reserved. *Sea Battle between the Battleships, the "Monitor" (two cannons) and the "Virginia" ("Merrimac") (ten cannons)*, engraving, all rights reserved. *Handcart in the Port*, all rights reserved.

175 *Shop window on Fulton Street*, all rights reserved. *Sign of 11 Fulton Street*, all rights reserved. *Sign*, all rights reserved. *New York Central No. 13 Cabin*, all rights reserved. *Fish Market wall*, all rights reserved. *Models inside the Fish

Market*, all rights reserved. *Façade of the South Street Seaport Museum*, all rights reserved.

176 *195 Broadway*, detail, all rights reserved. *Lobby of 195 Broadway*, all rights reserved.

176–177 *Saint Paul's Chapel*, painting by Saul Berman, 1940. Coll. of The NY Historical Society. *Saint Paul's Chapel, interior*. Photo RB. *Cemetery of Saint Paul's Chapel*, all rights reserved.

178 *20 Vesey Street*, all rights reserved. *Federal Office Building*, all rights reserved.

179 *Postmark*, all rights reserved. *Eagles*. Photo SC, all rights reserved, all rights reserved, all rights reserved, SC, SC, all rights reserved, SC, all rights reserved, RB.

180 *Lobby of the Woolworth Building*. Photo RB. *Detail from a console in the lobby of the Woolworth Building*, photo by Ken Walmsley. Woolworth Corp. *Woolworth Building, watercolor*. SD.

180–181 *The Woolworth Building emerging from the Clouds*, photo. NY Bound. *The Top of the Woolworth Building*. Photo RB.

181 *Detail from the lobby of the Woolworth Building*. Photo RB.

182 *Five Points in 1859, at the intersection of Baxter, Park and Worth streets*, engraving. SD.

182–183 *Municipal Building*, all rights reserved.

183 *Reformatories and corrections*, engraving in *King's Handbook of New York*, 1893. *Policeman*. Drawing M. Lacaze. *Old prisons in the "Tombs", before 1899*, engraving. SD.

184 *Details from the façades of 4, 5, 6 Thomas Paine Street*, all rights reserved. *Engine Company, façade*, all rights reserved.

184–185 *Torch at the N.Y.C. Department of Health on Center Street*, all rights reserved.

185 *Detail from the façade of the Emigrant Savings Bank*, all rights reserved. *Tweed Courthouse*. Photo RB. *Hall of Records, Façade and Interior*, all rights reserved.

186 *Ticket for the 19th-century Union Ferry Company of Brooklyn*. Coll. Bella C. Landauer. Coll. of The NY Historical Society. *Sectional view of the caissons*, 1870, 19th-century engraving, all rights reserved.

186–187 *View of the Brooklyn Bridge*, engraving, 19th century. Old Print Shop. *Construction of the Brooklyn Bridge*, engraving, 19th century, all rights reserved.

187 *Advertising card*, engraving, 19th century. Coll. of The NY Historical Society. *Construction of the Brooklyn Bridge*, engraving, 19th century, all rights reserved. *Covering one of the Brooklyn

Bridge's cables, engraving, 19th century, all rights reserved. Manhattan seen from Brooklyn. Explorer, Paris.
188 The New Harlem Bridge, 1868, engraving. SD. Outlines of Brooklyn, Manhattan, Williamsburg, Queensboro, Verrazano and George Washington bridges. ill. in Spanning the 21st Century, NYC Dept. of Transportation, 1988. Comparative table (number of people per year) crossing Brooklyn, Manhattan, Williamsburg and Queensboro bridges. Idem. The Williamsburg Bridge, c. 1900. Coll. Charmet, Paris.
189 The Bowery Savings Bank, color photo 1900. Library of Congress.
190 On the Lower East Side, photo early 20th century. MCNY. In the Chinese Neighborhood, photo 1909–12. Édimédia, Paris.
192 Street in Chinatown, drawing by Tony Sarg. SD.
192–193 Greetings from Chinatown, detail from a postcard, all rights reserved.
193 Doyers Street, all rights reserved. Chinese barber on Doyers Street, all rights reserved. Sun Wui Association, all rights reserved.
194 Drawing M. Lacaze.
194–195 Fruit seller on the Bowery, photo c. 1900. Roger Viollet, Paris.
195 Drawing M. Lacaze. Outside Guss' Pickles, all rights reserved. Store selling religious objects on Essex Street, all rights reserved. Jewish Market. Photo Tito Barberis.
196 Laundry day on Monday in the "Tenements", 1900, color photo. Library of Congress. Italians selling bread, on Mulberry Street, photo early 20th century. Library of Congress. Rossi's sign, all rights reserved. Italians selling fruit, on Mulberry Street.
197 Washington Market, engraving, 19th century. Old Print Shop.
198 Inspection of the Seventh Regiment, 1851, engraving. MCNY, J. Clarence Davies Collection. Washington Square. OT.
199 Triumphal Arch in Washington Square in the snow, watercolor. SD.
200 Sign for the Provincetown Playhouse, all rights reserved. Portrait of Mathew Brady, daguerreotype, all rights reserved. Portrait of Samuel Morse, engraving. Illustration, Vol. 1, 1872, all rights reserved. Portrait of Samuel Colt, engraving, 19th century, all rights reserved. New York University Building, all rights reserved. Judson Memorial Church, all rights reserved.
200–201 Colt, pistol invented by Samuel Colt. Smithsonian Institution; Washington D.C.
201 Program cover for a

show in the Latin Quarter. SD. Playhouse owned by the Provincetown Players, ill. early 20th century. SD.
202 Cast-iron architectural elements, engraving, 1865. Page from Daniel D. Badger's catalogue. Ill. of Iron Architecture, all rights reserved. Market on Spring Street, photo by Paul Fusco. MP. Richmond Hill House or Theater, watercolor, 1832. MCNY, J. Clarence Davies Collection.
202–203 MacDougal Street, engraving by Carol Creutzburg. MCNY.
203 Façade overlooking Duane Park, all rights reserved. Street Signs. Drawing M. Lacaze.
204 Bemba figure sitting cross-legged (Republic of the Congo), carved wood. Museum for African Art, NY. Little Singer Building, all rights reserved. Roosevelt Building, Details of cast-iron architecture, all rights reserved. Roosevelt Building, fabric store, all rights reserved.
204–205 Guggenheim Museum of SoHo, before conversion, all rights reserved.
205 Portrait of Isaac Merritt Singer, inventor of the sewing machine. Coll. Singer Company. External decorations (Greene Street/6th Avenue) , all rights reserved.
206 Plans for the Holland Tunnel, sectional view, watercolor. Avery Library, Columbia University. House at 2 White Street, all rights reserved. New York Life Insurance Company. Ill. in King's Views of New York, all rights reserved.
207 New Hudson River Railroad Depot, engraving 1868. SD. The New Washington Market, engraving in Harper's Weekly, December 29, 1888, all rights reserved. 135 Hudson St. Warehouse, terracotta street name plates, all rights reserved. Broadway, at Canal Street. Photo Dister.
208 Wharves along the Hudson River (along West Street), watercolor, 1921. SD. Street Signs. Drawing M. Lacaze. The elevated railway ("El") in Franklin Square, engraving in Harper's Weekly, September 7, 1878, all rights reserved. Mounted police on West Broadway, SoHo. Photo Dister.
209 Cary Building. Photo RB. El Teddy's (former International Restaurant). Photo Eric Courtade. Condict Store, all rights reserved.
210 Jefferson Market and Fire Tower, engraving, 1830. In New York Illustrated, all rights reserved.
211 Jefferson Courthouse, watercolor by John B. Robinson, 1881. MCNY.
212 External detail from Bigelow's Pharmacy, all rights

reserved. Gateway to Milligan Place, all rights reserved. Gay Street, all rights reserved.
213 Detail from a poster for "Wonderful Town". Lincoln Center Library for the Performing Arts. Coll. Billy Rose Theater. Detail from a poster for "My Sister Eileen". Lincoln Center Library for the Performing Arts. Coll. Billy Rose Theater. Saint Luke's Place, all rights reserved.
214 17 Grove Street, corner of Bedford Street, all rights reserved. United States Appraiser's Store, all rights reserved.
214–215 Gansevoort Market, photo 1885, all rights reserved.
215 White Horse Tavern. Photo TH. Gansevoort Market, photo 1885, detail, all rights reserved.
216 Washington Mews. Photo RB.
216–217 The New York Studio School. NY Studio School Archives.
218 Church of the Ascension, kind permission of American Architecture Archives. Portrait of Marcel Duchamp. Marshall Chess Club Archives. Photo John C. Fletcher.
218–219 Interior of the Tile Club, 19th-century engraving. Library of Congress.
219 Coats of arms of the American nations (6th Ave), all rights reserved. Fresco by José Clemente Orozco in the former canteen of the New School for Social Research. Photo RB. Toy Boat, in the Forbes Magazine Collection. Photo Larry Stein.
220 The Siegel-Cooper Department Store. SD. Street Signs. Drawing M. Lacaze. Headline from the New York press. The Empire Diner, 510 10th Ave. Photo RB.
221 Madison Square in 1900, color photo early 20th century. Library of Congress.
222 Headline from the "New York Times", August 4, 1927. The New York Times.
222–223 Workers' demonstration in Union Square, on September 5, 1882, engraving, 1882. In Frank Leslie's Illustrated Newspaper, all rights reserved. Model of the "Recruit" on display in Union Square (First World War). Coll. Charmet, Paris.
224 Mural (2nd Ave/9th St), all rights reserved. Entrance to the CBGB, 315 the Bowery (near Saint Mark's Place). Photo Dister. Peter Stuyvesant, engraving, all rights reserved.
224–225 Wanamaker's first building (Broadway/10th Ave/11th Ave). SD.
225 Cooper Square at the beginning of the century, all rights reserved. Cooper Union Building, 1861, engraving. SD.
226 Riot in front of Astor Place Opera House on May 10, 1849, engraving. Currier

and Ives, all rights reserved. Astor Place subway station (terracotta motif inside). Photo TH. Astor Place subway station. Photo TH.
227 Scribner's Monthly, frontispiece, 1870, all rights reserved. Old Merchant's House, front parlor, Old Merchant's House Archives. Cover of the magazine, "Puck", September 13, 1899, all rights reserved.
228 Tammany Hall: Decorations for the National Convention of July 4, 1868, engraving. SD. Caricature of Boss Tweed, engraving in Harper's Weekly, November 25, 1871, all rights reserved.
229 Newspaper advertisements, all rights reserved. Decorations at 145 East 19th Street (Jockeys), all rights reserved. Consolidated Edison Company. Photo RB.
230 Portrait of Samuel B. Ruggles, painting by Henry Inman, kind permission of Stephen S. Garmey. Gramercy Park. Photo TH. Façade of the National Arts Club (carvings of Goethe and Dante), all rights reserved.
231 The bar at the National Arts Club. Photo RB. National Arts Club, glass roof by McDonald. Photo TH. 3 and 4, Gramercy Park West, photo 1935. Berenice Abbott/Commerce Graphics.
232 Ladies' Mile, Broadway, engraving in Harper's Weekly, February 15, 1868, all rights reserved. Advertisement for Cortez Cigars, all rights reserved. Theodore Roosevelt as a Child, 19th-century photo. Kind permission of the Theodore Roosevelt House.
233 The Broadway Central Hotel at the beginning of the century, since demolished (corner 19th St). SD.
234 Madison Square Garden, 1910, all rights reserved. Advertisement for Madison Square Garden, all rights reserved. Plans for the 80-story Metropolitan Life Insurance Company Building, 1929, drawing H. W. Corbett and D. Everett Waid. SD. Flatiron Building. Photo RB.
235 Grand Central Terminal, drawing T. Sarg. SD.
236 New Union Depot, engravings in Frank Leslie's Illustrated Newspaper, November 1870. SD.
236–237 Taxis, drawing by Mark Lacaze. Grand Central Terminal and Pan Am Building, Photo Éric Courtade.
238 Façade of Grand Central Terminal. Photo RB. Grand Central, Main Waiting Room, all rights reserved.
238–239 Grand Central, Sectional View, color drawing, in The Gateway to a Continent, 1939.
239 Grand Central, Sectional View, black and white drawing. MCNY. Different stages in the construction of Grand Central, photos 1911. MCNY.
240 Murray Hill

neighborhood (3rd Ave/34th St), engraving 1865. SD. *Façade of 149 East 38th Street*, all rights reserved. *Interior of the Polish Consulate*. Photo RB.

241 *Morgan Library: East Room*. Coll. The Pierpont Morgan Library. Photo David A. Loggie. *John Pierpont Morgan*, 1902. Coll. The Pierpont Morgan Library. Photo Pach Bros. Studio, N.Y. *Shoe-Shine Boy near the Empire State Building*, drawing by Mark Lacaze.

242 *Building at street level (Empire State Building)*, photo 1930. NY Bound.

242–243 *High altitude construction (Empire State Building)*, photo by Lewis Hine. Avery Library, Columbia University.

243 *External view of the former Waldorf-Astoria*, engraving, 1905. SD. *Early plans for the Empire State Building*, photomontage 1926. Roger Viollet, Paris. *Empire State Building observatory*. Drawing M. Lacaze. *Portrait of Alfred Emanuel Smith*, by E. H. Baker. In *Fortune*, September 1930. *High altitude construction (Empire State Building)*, photo L. Hine. Avery Library, Columbia University.

244 *The top of the Empire State Building*, drawing J.-M. Guillou, all rights reserved.

245 *Top of the Empire State Building, illuminated in different colors*, drawing by J.-M. Guillou, all rights reserved. *Tickets for admission to the Empire State Building*. *Empire State Building*, drawing by J.-M. Guillou, all rights reserved. *Antenna of the Empire State Building*, drawing by J.-M. Guillou, all rights reserved. *Airship about to draw alongside the Empire State Building*, photo 1930. MCNY.

246 *Façade of the Empire State Building after the bomber accident in 1945*. AP/Wide World Photos. "*King Kong*", movie by M. Cooper, 1933. BFI, London. *Headline in New York newspaper*, all rights reserved. *Lightning striking the Empire State Building*. Explorer, Paris.

247 *King Kong on the Empire State Building*, drawing by Jean-Philippe Chabot, all rights reserved.

248 *Andy Warhol in 1966 in his studio, the "Factory" (19 East 32nd St)*. Photo H. Gloaguen. Rapho, Paris.

248–249 *Javits Center*. Photo RB.

249 *Sectional view of Pennsylvania Station*, drawing by McKim, Mead & White. Coll. of The NY Historical Society. *Macy's Department Store*. Coll. Macy's. *Former U.S. Post Office, on 8th Ave (West 31st/West 33rd sts)*. Courtesy of American Architecture Archives.

250 *The Harvard Club*, architectural drawing by McKim, Mead & White, all rights reserved.

251 *Century Club*, engraving, all rights reserved.

252 *Interior of the Royalton Hotel*. Photo RB. *Algonquin Hotel*, all rights reserved. *New York Public Library*, all rights reserved.

253 *New York Public Library*. Photo RB. *Tower with traffic signals, built in 1922 to regulate traffic on 5th Ave/42nd St*. SD.

254 *Durst Tower*. SD. *Sculpture on the American Radiator Building*. Photo RB. Drawing M. Lacaze.

254–255 *Small shops along the Avenue of the Americas, on the site of the present Durst Tower*, photo by Todd Webb. SD.

255 *Times Square*, all rights reserved. *Theater program (the Paramount)*. SD.

256 *Art Deco detail from the interior of the Film Center*, drawing, all rights reserved. *Actors Studio*, all rights reserved. *Mural by Sempé (9th Ave/47th St)*, all rights reserved.

257 *Street signs*. Drawing M. Lacaze. *The Intrepid, Sea, Air and Space Museum*, all rights reserved. Drawing M. Lacaze. *Father Duffy*, statue by Charles Keck, 1936, all rights reserved.

258 *Ticket for the Winter Garden theater*.

258–259 *Theaters: Biltmore, Chanin's, Majestic, Schubert, Booth, Roger's (former Chanin's), Barrymore, Lyceum, Longacre, Simon (former Alvin), Imperial*, drawings D. Grant, all rights reserved.

260 *Statue of Cornelius Vanderbilt at Grand Central* by Ernst Plassmann, 1869, all rights reserved. *Grand Central Terminal, seen from the north*, 1910, drawing. MCNY. *Helmsley Building*, painting by Richard Haas. Photo Peter Mauss/Esto.

261 *Street signs*. Drawing M. Lacaze. "*Taxi!*", statue by J. Seward Johnson Jr, 1983, all rights reserved.

262 *Turtle Bay District, façade and details*, all rights reserved. *Former "Store House" in Turtle Bay*, engraving, 1852. SD.

263 *Construction of the riverside highway running along East River, taken from Queensboro Bridge*. Photo Keystone, Paris. *United Nations Headquarters*. U.N. Photos.

264 *Laying the first stone of the United Nations Headquarters, October 24, 1949*. Photo, United Nations (Department of Public Information). *United Nations coat of arms*, all rights reserved. *Meeting of the Security Council, January 31, 1992*. Official United Nations photo 179195/M. Grant.

264 *Exploded view of the United Nations buildings*, drawing B. Lenormand.

265 *Atrium at the Ford Foundation*, all rights reserved.

266 *Construction of the Chrysler Building*, photo. In *Fortune*, July 1930. *Chrysler Building*, all rights reserved. *Chrysler Building*, drawing by Claude Quiec, all rights reserved.

267 *The top floor of the Chrysler Building*. Photo RB. *The Cloud Club, at the top of the Chrysler Building*. Photo RB. *William Van Alen, at the Chrysler Building's opening celebrations*, photo. Avery Library, Columbia University.

268–269 *Details from the façade of the Chrysler Building*, drawings by Pierre-Marie Valat, all rights reserved.

270–271 *Details from the lobby of the Chrysler Building*, drawings by Pierre-Marie Valat, all rights reserved.

272 *Chanin Building, details from the grilles*, all rights reserved. *Chanin Building, elements of the lobby's bronze flooring*, all rights reserved. *Chanin Building, architectural drawing* by H. Ferriss, all rights reserved. *Bowery Savings Bank*. Kind permission of American Architecture Archives.

273 *View of the plaza of Rockefeller Center*, photo. OT.

274 *Aerial view of Rockefeller Center's central plaza*. Photo RB. *Skating rink in Rockefeller Center plaza*, photo. OT. *Saint Patrick's Cathedral, seen from Rockefeller Center*. Photo RB.

274–275 *Global view of Rockefeller Center*. Photo RB. *Plan of Rockefeller Center*, authorized by Rockefeller Center © Rockefeller Group.

276 *Construction of Rockefeller Center*, photo 1932. Berenice Abbott/Commerce Graphics.

276–277 *Moving portrait of John D. Rockefeller Sr*, photo 1933. Keystone, Paris.

277 *Construction of Rockefeller Center*, photo 1932. Berenice Abbott/Commerce Graphics. *Advertisement*. In *Fortune*. *Men's room, at Radio City*. Photo RB. *Women's room, at Radio City*. Photo RB. *Window of the "Rainbow Room", restaurant on the 65th floor of Rockefeller Center*, watercolor by J. Simont.

278 *Detail from bas-reliefs in Rockefeller Center, near the entrance of the RCA building, at 49 W. 49th St*. Photo RB.

278–279 *Details from the exterior decoration of Rockefeller Center*, drawings P.-M. Valat, all rights reserved.

279 *Fossils embedded in the stone walls of 30 Rockefeller Center*, photo Sidney Horenstein. *Rockefeller Center at night*, all rights reserved.

280–281 *Details from the decoration inside Rockefeller Center*, drawings P.-M. Valat, all rights reserved.

282 *Brentano's sign*, all rights reserved. *Swiss Center*, all rights reserved. *Door inside the Swiss Center*. Photo RB.

283 *Saint Patrick's Cathedral*. Photo Éric Courtade. *Statue inside Saint Patrick's Cathedral*, all rights reserved. Photo TH.

284 *5th Ave/51st St*, colored photo, 1900. Library of Congress. *Interiors of William Vanderbilt's house (5th Ave/51st St)*. Coll. Gordon McCollum.

285 *Interior of the Waldorf-Astoria*. Photo RB. *Waldorf-Astoria, architectural drawing*, all rights reserved.

286 *52nd St during the 40s*. Coll. Frank Driggs. *Seagram Building*. Photo RB. *Racquet and tennis Club*. Photo RB. *General Electric, detail*, all rights reserved.

287 *52nd St in 1949*, photo Charles B. Nadell. Coll. Frank Driggs. *Miles Davis, performing at the "Three Deuces", 52nd St*, photo 1947. Coll. Frank Driggs.

288 *Previous Saint Thomas Church*, engraving. Avery Library, Columbia University. *Carved panel from the ground floor hall of the University Club*, architectural drawing, McKim, Mead & White. *Interior of the University Club*. Photo RB.

289 *Lobby of the Saint Regis-Sheraton*. Photo RB. *Atrium in the IBM building*, all rights reserved. *Former AT&T Building (in the foreground, Trump Tower)*, painting by Richard Haas. Photo Peter Mauss/Esto Photographics Inc.

290 *Les Demoiselles d'Avignon*, oil painting by Pablo Picasso, 1907 (97.6 in/243.9 cm X 93.5 in/233.7 cm). Lillie P. Bliss Estate. 1992 MOMA © SPADEM. *Le Baigneur*, oil painting by Paul Cézanne, c. 1885, *idem*. *Balzac*, sculpture by Auguste Rodin, 1897–8. Photo RB. © SPADEM.

291 *The Starry Night*, oil painting by Vincent Van Gogh, 1889, *idem*. *The Red Studio*, oil painting by Henri Matisse, 1911, (72.4 in/181 cm X 87.6 in/219.1 cm). Simon Guggenheim Fund, *idem*. *The Dream*, oil painting by the Douanier Rousseau, 1897, *idem*.

292 MOMA, *architectural drawing*, 1974, Philip Johnson. NY Department of Architecture. *Orson Welles, still from the movie "Citizen Kane"*, 1941, *idem*. *Hirondelle*, *amour*, painting by Joan Miro, 1933–4. Given by Nelson A. Rockefeller, *idem* © ADAGP. *Cisitalia "202" GT car*, 1946, Pininfarina. Given by Pininfarina, *idem*.

292–293 *Broadway Boogie Woogie*, Piet Mondrian, 1942–3 (127 X 127), *idem* © SPADEM.

293 *The Fish*, sculpture by Constantin Brancusi, 1930, *idem* © ADAGP.

294 *Museum Gallery,* photo. *idem. Woman,* painting by Willem De Kooning, 1950–2, *idem.*
294–295 *Flag,* painting by Jasper Johns, 1954, *idem* © ADAGP.
295 *One,* oil painting by Jackson Pollock, 1950, *idem* © SPADEM. *Bed,* oiled and pencil on pillow, sheets and eiderdown, by Robert Rauschenberg, 1955. Given by Leo Castelli, *idem* © ADAGP. *Gold Marilyn Monroe,* by Andy Warhol, 1962. Given by P. Johnson, *idem* © ADAGP. *Object,* by Meret Oppenheim, 1936, *idem* © SPADEM.
296 *Trump Trips Up.* Newspaper headline. *Audrey Hepburn,* in *"Breakfast at Tiffany's",* still from the movie by Blake Edwards, 1961. Cinémathèque, Paris.
297 *The Crown Building.* Photo SC. *Wood paneling in the "Oak Room" of the Plaza Hotel.* Photo RB. *The Plaza,* 1982, watercolor by A. Troubetzkoy. Coll. artist. *Statue of General William T. Sherman,* by Augustus Saint-Gaudens (1892/1903), all rights reserved.
299 *Street scene in the diamond district,* all rights reserved. *Shop window in the diamond district,* all rights reserved.
300 *Saint Malachy's,* detail, all rights reserved. *Street sign,* all rights reserved. *Window, City Center of Music and Drama,* all rights reserved.
301 *Restaurant sign,* all rights reserved. *Logo of the Russian Tea Room.* Russian Tea Room. *Portrait of Andrew Carnegie.* SD. *Carnegie Hall,* all rights reserved. *Russian Tea Room,* all rights reserved.
302 *Planet Hollywood sign,* all rights reserved. *Façade of the Hard Rock Café.* Photo Éric Courtade. *Steinway piano showroom.* Photo RB. *Façade of the New York Delicatessen,* all rights reserved. *Horn & Hardart Automat.* SD.
303 *Façade of Alwyn Court,* detail. Photo RB. *Hearst Magazine Building,* detail. Photo RB.
304 *Columbus Circle and Central Park,* all rights reserved. *Detail from the "Maine" Memorial,* all rights reserved.
304–305 *Lincoln Center, plan in perspective.* Avery Library, Columbia University.
305 *Detail from the façade of 43 West 61st Street,* all rights reserved. *Plan of the area around the Lincoln Center before it was built,* all rights reserved. *Still from the movie "West Side Story".* BFI Stills, London.
306 *Lincoln Center.* Photo RB. *Lincoln Center fountain.* Photo René Burri, 1967. MP. *Lincoln Center* press office.
308 *Aerial view of Upper*

East Side, 1907. Ill. in *King's Views of New York,* all rights reserved.
309 *New York's Lycée Français,* all rights reserved. *Interior of the Polo-Ralph Lauren Building.* Document Polo-Ralph Lauren.
310 *View of 5th Ave. at 85th St.* Photo SC. *Street sign.* Drawing M. Lacaze. *Interior design by Tiffany at the Armory.* Photo John Hall.
311 *The 3rd Avenue elevated railway (El),* 19th-century engraving. Drawing M. Lacaze. *Building at 45 E. 66th St,* all rights reserved.
312 *Yorkville (at E. 86th St) on April 9, 1939,* detail. SD. *Brasserie on 86th St,* greeting card. SD.
312–313 *Gracie Mansion and Carl Shurz Park.* SD.
313 *Yorkville (at E. 86th St), on April 9, 1939,* detail. SD. *Destroying the rocks at Hell's Gate,* engraving. Coll. Roger Viollet, Paris. *Gracie Mansion,* photo. Gracie Mansion Conservancy.
314–316 *Aerial view of Central Park,* drawings by Claude Quiec, all rights reserved.
314 *Cherry tree and magnolia tree in Central Park,* photo S. C. Miller. Central Park Conservancy.
315 *Detail from the flight of steps on Bethesda Terrace,* all rights reserved. *Great Lawn in Central Park.* Photo É. Courtade. *Hippopotami in Central Park Zoo,* engraving 1888. In *Harper's Weekly,* September 29, 1888.
316 *Belvedere Castle,* photo by Sarah Cedar Miller. Central Park Conservancy. *Frederick Law Olmsted,* 19th-century photo. National Park Service. *State Arsenal in Central Park, at 57th St,* 19th-century engraving. SD. *Central Park West, seen from the park, around 74th St.* Photo RB. *Boat pond in Central Park,* all rights reserved.
317 *Tree,* all rights reserved. *Information booth,* all rights reserved.
318 *The Central Park obelisk being erected,* 19th-century engraving. New York Bound. *Squirrel,* drawing by Jean Chevallier, all rights reserved. *Leaves,* drawings by Gismond Curiace, all rights reserved.
319 *Ducks: Ruddy stiff-tailed duck (male 15.2 in/38 cm) and Darkish Duck (female 23.2 in/58 cm),* drawings F. Desbordes, all rights reserved. *Gapstow Bridge, spanning the pond at 59th St,* photo by Sarah Cedar Miller. Central Park Conservancy. *Winter in Central Park,* on the skating rink, engraving, 1919. SD.
320 *Lobby of the French Embassy.* Photo Henri Ebuna. *Badge from MMA,* all rights reserved.
320–321 *Badges: NY Historical Society, Jewish*

Museum, Yivo Institute, Museo del Barrio, Museum of the City of NY, International Center of Photography; entrance ticket to the Cooper Hewitt-Museum.
321 *Façade of the MCNY.* Photo MCNY.
322 *Henry Clay Frick,* photo from the Frick Collection. *Entrance to the Frick Collection,* idem.
322–323 *Drawing by Bruno Lenormand.*
323 *Detail from the entrance to the Frick Collection,* photo from the Frick Collection. *Officer and Laughing Girl,* oil painting by Vermeer. Frick Collection. *The Meeting,* oil painting by Fragonard, *idem. Saint Francis in Ecstasy,* oil painting by Giovanni Bellini, *idem. Diana the Huntress,* sculpture by Houdon, *idem.*
324 *Badge from the Frick Collection. The White Horse,* oil painting by Constable, *idem. Self-Portrait,* Rembrandt, *idem. Main Staircase,* photo from the Frick Collection.
325 *Detail from the entrance to the Frick Collection, idem. Living Hall,* idem. *Portrait of Sir Thomas Moore,* oil painting by Hans Holbein the Younger. Frick Collection. *The Temptation of Christ,* reredos by Duccio, idem. French 16th-century armchair, idem.
326 *Façade of the Whitney Museum of American Art.* Photo RB. Entrance ticket for the museum, all rights reserved. *The Paris Bit,* painting by Stuart Davis, 1959 (46.7 in/116.8 cm X 70 in/152.4 cm). Whitney Museum of American Art.
327 *Mahoning,* painting by Franz Kline, 1956 (81.3 in/203.2 cm X 101.6 in/254 cm), idem. *Green Coca-Cola Bottles,* painting by Andy Warhol, 1962 (83.8 in/209.6 cm X 57.9 in/144.8 cm), *idem* © ADAGP.
328 *Funerary statuette,* Egyptian art, c. 2009–1998 BC. Rogers Fund & Edward S. Harkness, 1920. MMA. Drawings P. Biard.
329 *Interior of the Metropolitan Museum of Art,* engraving, all rights reserved. *The Met's glass roofs.* Photo RB. *Antoine Laurent Lavoisier et sa femme,* oil painting by Jacques Louis David, 1788 (103.9 in/259.7 cm X 77.8 in/194.6 cm). Given by Mr and Mrs Charles Wrightsman, 1977. MMA.
330 Drawing P. Biard *Headdress,* Nigerian art, 19th/20th-century. Fletcher & Rogers Fund, 1976. MMA. *Pendant Mask,* ivory, brass, steel, Benin, 16th century (9.5 in/23.8 cm). Coll. Michael C. Rockefeller Memorial. Given by Nelson A. Rockefeller, 1972, idem. *Screen,* Japanese art, 18th century. Given by Louisa E. McBurney, 1953, idem.
331 *Nur al-Din Room,* Syrian art, Ottoman period, 1707 (ht.

21 ft/6.71 m, l. 26 ft/8.04 m, b.16 ft/5.09 m). Hagop Kevorkian Fund, 1970, idem. *Totem Mbis,* Oceanic art, 20th century. Coll. Michael C. Rockefeller Memorial, given by Nelson A. Rockefeller, 1965, idem. *View of the Rockefeller Wing,* idem.
332 *Funerary Stele,* Attic art, c. 540 BC (169.3 in/423.3 cm). Frederick C. Hewitt, Rogers & Munsey Funds, 1911, idem. *Funerary Portrait,* art from Fayoum, 2nd century BC. Rogers Fund, idem. *"Seated Harp Player",* marble, Cycladic art, 3rd millennium BC. (11.7 in/29.2 cm). Rogers Fund, idem. *King's head,* silver, Sassanian art, 4th century BC (15.4 in/38.4 cm). Fletcher Fund, idem. Drawing P. Biard.
333 *Queen's Head,* fragment of Egyptian sculpture, 18th dynasty, c.1417–1379 BC (5.6 in/14.1 cm). Given by Edward S. Harkness, 1926, idem. *Chair belonging to Renyseneb,* Egyptian art, 18th dynasty, c.1450 BC (34.5 in/86.2 cm). Given by Patricia B. Lassalle, 1968, idem. *Perseus with the Head of Medusa,* sculpture by Antonio Canova (88 in/220 cm), 1808. Fletcher Fund, idem. *Kneeling Man,* Mayan art, 6th century (14.2 in/35.5 cm). Coll. Michael C. Rockefeller Memorial, given by Nelson A. Rockefeller, 1979, idem.
334 *Autumn Rhythm,* painting by Jackson Pollock, 1950 (106.7 in/266.7 cm X 210.3 in/525.8 cm). George A. Hearn Fund, 1957, idem. © SPADEM. *I Saw the Figure 5 in Gold,* oil painting by Charles Demuth (36.1 in/90.2 cm X 30.5 in/76.2 cm). Coll. Alfred Stieglitz, 1949, idem. *Room from the Hewlett house, New York,* 1740–60 (ht. 8.90 ft/2.78 m, l. 17.1 ft/5.33 m, b. 13.7 ft/4.27 m). Given by Mrs Robert W. de Forest, 1910, idem. *Portrait of a German Officer,* oil painting by Marsden Hartley (69.4 in/173.4 cm X 42.4 in/106 cm). Coll. Alfred Stieglitz, 1949, idem. Drawing P. Biard.
335 *Max Schmitt in a Single Scull,* oil painting by Thomas Eakins (33.0 in/82.6 cm X 47 in/117.5 cm). Alfred N. Punnett Fund, given by George D. Pratt, 1934, MMA. *The Gulf Stream,* oil painting by Winslow Homer, 1899 (28.6 in/71.4 cm X 49.9 in/124.8 cm). Wolfe Fund, coll. Catherine Lorillard Wolfe, idem.
336 *The Last Judgment,* painting by Jan van Eyck (22.6 in/56.5 cm X 7.9 in/19.7 cm). Fletcher Fund, 1933, idem. *View of Toledo,* painting by El Greco (48.5 in/121.3 cm X 43.4 in/108.6 cm). Bequest from Mrs H. O. Havemeyer. Coll. H. O. Havemeyer, 1929, idem. *La diseuse de bonne aventure,* painting by Georges de La Tour (40.8 in/101.9 cm X 49.4 in/123.5

LIST OF ILLUSTRATIONS ◆

m). Rogers Fund, 1960, *idem. Armour*, France, 1550–9 70.1 in/175.3 cm, 53.6 /24.1 kg). Harris Brisbane Dick Fund, 1939, *idem.*

436–337 *View of the patio of Vélez Blanco*, Spanish art, 506–15. Drawing P. Biard, all rights reserved.

437 *Boating*, painting by Edouard Manet (38.9 in/97.2 cm X 52.1 in/130.2 cm). Bequest from Mrs H. O. Havemeyer. Coll. H. O. Havemeyer, 1929. MMA. *Woman in White*, painting by Pablo Picasso, 1923. Rogers Fund, 1951. Coll. Lizzie P. Bliss, *idem.* © SPADEM. *La Parade*, painting by Georges Seurat (39.9 in/99.7 cm X 60 in/149.9 cm). Stephen C. Clark Estate, 1960, *idem. Madonna with Child*, France (Auvergne), 2nd half of the 12th century (31.5 in/78.7 cm). Given by J. Pierpont Morgan, 1916, *idem. Grand Salon from the Hôtel de Tessé*, French art, 1768–72 (ht. 15.6 ft/4.88 m, l. 32.8 ft/10.25 m, b. 28.8 ft/9 m). Given by Mrs Herbert N. Strauss, 1942, *idem.*

338 *Fernande, à la mantille noire*, oil painting by Pablo Picasso, 1905–6 (40 in/100 cm X 32.4 in/81 cm). Hilde Thannhauser Bequest, 1991. Coll. Justin K. Thannhauser, The Solomon R. Guggenheim Museum. Photo David Heald © SPADEM. *Montagnes à Saint-Rémy*, oil painting by Vincent van Gogh, July 1889 (28.7 in/71.8 cm X 36.3 in/90.8 cm). Coll. Justin K. Thannhauser, 1978. *Idem.* Photo David Heald. *King of Kings*, oak carving by Constantin Brancusi, c. 1930 (120 in/300 cm high). *Idem.* Photo David Heald © ADAGP. *Femme cuiller*, bronze sculpture by Alberto Giacometti, 1926 (57.5 in/143.8 cm X 20.6 in/51.4 cm X 8.6 in/21.6 cm). *Idem.* Photo David Heald © ADAGP.
338–339 *External view of the Guggenheim Museum. Idem.*
339 *Interior view of the Guggenheim Museum*, all rights reserved. *Preparedness*, painting by Roy Lichtenstein, 1968 (triptych, total size 121.9 in/304.8 X 219.5 in/548.7 cm). *Idem.* Photo David Heald © ADAGP. *Painting with White Edge*, oil painting by Wassily Kandinsky, May 1913 (56.1 in/140.3 cm X 80.1 in/200.3 cm). *Idem.* Photo David Heald © ADAGP.
340 *Sectional views of the Guggenheim Museum*, drawings by M. Gabellini © 1992. The Solomon R. Guggenheim Foundation.
341 *Composition 1 A*, oil painting by Piet Mondrian, 1930 (30.1 in/75.2 cm X 30.1 in/75.2 cm). Coll. Hilla Rebay, 1971. *Idem.* Photo David Heald © SPADEM. *Terremoto*, installation by Joseph Beuys, 1981 (81.2 in/203 cm X 140

in/350 cm X 196 in/490 cm). *Idem.* Photo David Heald © ADAGP. *Matin au village après tempête de neige*, oil painting by Casimir Malevitch, 1912 (32.3 in/80.7 cm X 32.3 in/80.8 cm). *Idem.* Photo David Heald. Exhibition by Dan Flavin, *Luminous object at the center of the museum. Idem.* Photo David Heald.
342 *Lettering outside the New York Society for Ethical Culture*, all rights reserved.
343 *Lobby of the Eldorado.* Photo RB.
344 *Café des Artistes sign*, all rights reserved. *Tavern on the Green*, all rights reserved. *Interior of the Café des Artistes.* Photo RB.
345 *Street sign.* Drawing M. Lacaze. *On W. 71st St: detail from a house*, all rights reserved. *Pythian Temple*, painting by Richard Haas. Photo Peter Mauss/Esto Photographics Inc.
346 *The Dakota*, photo, all rights reserved. *San Remo Apartments.* OT. *Plaque in "Strawberry Fields"*, all rights reserved.
346–347 *Plans for the Dakota.* Drawing M. Lacaze.
347 *Museum of Natural History, façade and interior design*, all rights reserved. *Façade of the Ansonia.* Photo TH.
348 *Riverside Park*, engraving. SD. *Collegiate Church, detail*, all rights reserved. *"Zabars".* Photo TH. *Statue of Saint Joan of Arc.* Photo SC.
349 *Mr and Mrs William Cops Rogers' house, at 140th St, in 1870–1875*, watercolor. MCNY.
350 *Street scene in Harlem.* Photo René Burri. MP. *Street in Harlem.* MP. *Street scene in Harlem.* Photo René Burri. MP.
351 *Trompe l'oeil.* Photo Eve Arnold, MP. Detail from a photo by Bruce Davidson. MP.
352 *Alma Mater*, sculpture by Daniel Chester French, 1903, all rights reserved. *Columbia University students*, all rights reserved. *Seth Low*, photo. MCNY. *Columbia University*, engraving. Ill. in *King's Views of New York*, all rights reserved.
353 *Columbia University*, all rights reserved. *Columbia University Campus, seen from the north*, all rights reserved. *Hoyne Buell Centre and the Maison française at Columbia University*, all rights reserved.
354 *Saint John the Divine under construction with the elevated railway, the El*, colored photo, 1900. Library of Congress.
354–355 *Sectional view of Saint John the Divine Cathedral*, drawing by Burden, 1984, with the kind permission of the Cathedral Church of Saint John the Divine.
355 *Detail from the central porch of Saint John the Divine*, all rights reserved. *Fountain of Peace*, all rights

reserved. *Saint John the Divine under construction*, photo. New York Bound.
356 *Grant's Tomb*, photo 1897, all rights reserved. Union Theological Seminary, all rights reserved.
357 *Baptism in the Hudson River*, watercolor 1834. Coll. J. Clarence Davies. MCNY. Carillon of Riverside Church, all rights reserved. *The Reverend Herbert Daughtry, pastor.* Photo T. Hopker, MP.
358 *Tom-toms in the African market*, all rights reserved. Harlem Plaza, 125th St, all rights reserved. *African market (115th St/Lenox Ave).* Photo Eli Reed. MP.
359 *Apollo Theater*, all rights reserved. *Program for the American Negro Theater.* Sch C. *Jazz band (from left to right: Coleman Hawkins, Benny Harris, Dan Byas, Thelonious Monk, Denzil Best, Eddie Robinson)*, photo 1944. Coll. F. Driggs.
360 *City College Porch*, photo 1908. Coll. Byron. MCNY.
361 *John James Audubon's tomb, in Trinity Cemetery.* Photo John C. Fletcher. *Interior of the Morris-Jumel Mansion.* Photo *idem.*
362 *Diptych of Saint George*, 1310–40, Italy (15.9 in/39.7 cm X 10.8 in/27 cm). The Cloisters Collection.
362–363 *Exploded view of The Cloisters*, drawing P. Biard, all rights reserved.
363 *Saint John the Evangelist*, Carolingian ivory, beginning 9th century (7.3 in/18.3 cm X 3.8 in/9.5 cm). The Cloisters Collection. *Silver Ewer*, c.1500, Nuremberg (25 in/63.5 cm), *idem. The Cloisters*, all rights reserved. *Virgin and Child*, Bourgundy, first half of the 12th century, France (41.2 in/102.9 cm), *idem.*
364 *The Annunciation*, triptych by Robert Campin, 1425. *Rosary bead*, early 16th century, Scottish, *idem. The cloister of Saint Michel-de-Cuxa*, French 12th century, all rights reserved. *Book of Hours belonging to Jeanne d'Evreux, Jean Pucelle*, France, c.1320–50. The Cloisters Collection. *The Unicorn at the Fountain*, French tapestry c.1500 (147.3 in/368.3 cm X 151.4 in/378.5 cm). Given by John D. Rockefeller Jr, 1937, *idem.*
365 *Rhenish stained glass windows*, 1440–7 (150.9 in/377.2 cm X 28.7 in/71.8 cm). The Cloisters Collection. *Capital from the cloister of Saint Michel de Cuxa*, French, 12th century, all rights reserved. *The Cloister of Saint-Michel-de-Cuxa*, French, 12th century. The Cloisters Collection.
366 *View of the Fulton Ferry Building in Brooklyn*, engraving in *Ballou's Pictorial Drawing-Room Companion*, June 6, 1857. *Williamsburg Savings Bank.* Photo RB.

Brooklyn Heights Esplanade, all rights reserved.
368 *The New York Marathon.* Photo Andy Levin. Explorer.
370 *The "Queen Elizabeth II", laid up in New York.* C.G.M. archives and photo. *Shuttle ticket*, all rights reserved. *Concorde in flight*, photo. Marketing Division of Air France.
374 Drawings M. Lacaze.
375 *New York Taxi.* Photo TH. *Bus.* Photo TH. *Taxi meter.* Photo TH. *Bus ticket.* Photo, all rights reserved.
376 *Subway token.* Photo Patrick Léger. *Green globes and red globe*, all rights reserved. *The New York Subway.* Photo TH.
377 *Subway sign.* Photo TH.
378 *Bank notes.* Photo P. Léger. *Traveler's check.* Photo TH.
378–379 *Coins.* Photo P. Léger. *Credit cards*, all rights reserved. *Cash dispenser.* Photo TH.
381 *Emblem of the Postal System.* Photo TH. *Telephone signs.* Photo TH. *Phone Booth.* Photo TH. *Stamp*, all rights reserved.
382 *Skyscrapers seen from Central Park*, all rights reserved. *Woolworth Building, seen from the World Trade Center*, all rights reserved. *Silhouettes of structures, in chronological order*, all rights reserved.
386–389 Drawings M. Lacaze.
386 *"Au Café", near Times Square.* Photo TH. *Stacks of newspapers*, all rights reserved.
387 *Fire Escapes in SoHo*, photo. Dister. *Fountain in the New Riverfront Park (Riverside Drive/138th St).* Photo SC.
388 *Metropolitan Opera House*, photo. OT. *Golden Empire (Canal St-Centre St).* Photo SC.
389 *Mural at the South Street Seaport*, all rights reserved. *Police at night*, photo. Éric Courtade. *Little Italy*, photo. Dister.
390 *From left to right and from top to bottom, clocks: Grand Central Terminal.* Photo RB. *Con Edison Building.* Photo SC. *Metropolitan Life Insurance Company.* Photo RB. *Helmsley Building*, all rights reserved. *Nat Sherman*, all rights reserved. *F.A.O. Schwartz*, all rights reserved. *Old New York Insurance Company, 346 Broadway, with "clockmaster"*, all rights reserved. *Paramount Building*, all rights reserved. *New York Savings Bank*, all rights reserved. *Tiffany's.* 1 Photo. RB. *Standard Oil*, all rights reserved. *Warehouse on Riverside Drive.* Photo RB. *Clock in the ground (William Barthman, at 174 Broadway, corner Maiden Lane)*, all rights reserved. *Public clock at the S. W. corner of Fifth Ave/44th St*, all rights reserved.

◆ ACKNOWLEDGMENTS

We would like to thank the following for their assistance:

Seymour Durst, *Old New York Foundation*
Gordon MacCollum, *American Architecture Archives*
Luis Cancel, *former commissioner of the New York City Department of Cultural Affairs*
Deborah Bershad, Margaret Hammerle, *Art Commission of the City of New York*
Idilio Gracia-Peña, *commissioner of the New York City Department of Records and Information Services*
Kenneth Cobb, *NYC Municipal Archives*
Jane Harris, *Manhattan Sites*
Jane Hausen, *The NYC Landmarks Preservation Commission*, all rights reserved. Sherrill Wilson, Tuesday Brooks, *The Office of Public Education and Interpretation*
Cathy del Priori, Betsy Becker, *Madison Square Garden*
Robert M. Browning, *National Baseball Hall of Fame and Museum*
Anne Marie Gilmartin, *N. Y. Rangers*
Paul Spinelli, Lisa Shulman, Frank Ramos, *Jets NFL Properties*
Ro Lohin, *The New York Studio School*
Nancy Cricco, *New York University*
Kathleen Goncharov, *The New School for Social Research*
Janet Parks, *Avery Library, Columbia University*
Robert MacDonald, Leslie Nolan, Marguerite Lavin, Tony Piasani, Terry, Ariano, Peter Simmons, Billie Heller, Marty Jacobs, *Museum of the City of New York*
Alison Whiting, Mary Beth Betts, *The New York Historical Society*
Diana Pardue, Jeffrey S. Dosik, Geraldine Santoro, Kevin Daley, *Ellis Island Immigration Museum*
Amy Hines, Neil Calvanese, Sarah Cedar Miller, *Central Park Conservancy*
Tom Ching, *Parks Horticulture*
Barbara Treitel, *The Jewish Museum*
The Jewish Forward
Lori Duggan Gold, *Brooklyn Botanic Garden*
Karen L. Saber, *New York Botanical Garden*
Linda Corcoran, *NYZS The Wildlife Conservation Society*
Harry Hunter, *National Museum of American History, Smithsonian Institution*
Mary Ison, *Prints and Photographs Division, Library of Congress*
Michelle Saffir, *Asia Society*
Susan George, *Fraunces Tavern*
Charles Juno, *Empire State Building*
Patty Schickram, *Macy's*
James Reed, Celeste Torello,
Rockefeller Group
Joe Grabowski, Ken Walmsley, *The Woolworth Corporation*
Geraldine Barnett, *US Post Office Bowling Green Station*
Lisa Berlin, *US Post Office*
Steve Gilkenson, *McAuley Mission*
Mons. Anthony Dalla Villa, Thomas Young, *Saint Patrick's Cathedral*
The Very Rev. James P. Morton, William Logan, *The Cathedral Church of Saint John the Divine*
Rebecca Carlisle Blind, *Saint James Episcopal Church*
Joan Baachus-Patterson, *Riverside Church*
Eric Hilton, *First Presbyterian Church*
Sister Rita King
Sister Margarita Smith
Anthony Bellov, *Abigail Adams Smith Museum*
Paul Glassman, *Morris-Jumel Mansion*
Kathy Stocking, *New York State Historical Association*
Aldon James, Carol Lowrey, *The National Arts Club*
Tom Gilbert, *AP/Wide World Photos-Inc.*
Helaine Pardo, *Commerce Graphics*
Dan May, Karl Nemchek, *Met Life*
Barbara Cohen, Judith Stonehill, Francis Morrone, *New York Bound Bookshop*
Mike Regan, *World Trade Center*
Leon Haft, *Marshall Chelsa Club*
Ian Ginsberg, *Bigelow Pharmacy*
Major Waddington, *Salvation Army*
Melissa L. Burian, *US Dept. of Commerce*
Lloyd Morgan, *Morgan Press*
Don Luck, Ester Smith, *Institute of Jazz Studies*
Donna Walker Collins, *Dance Theater of Harlem*
Nancy Lassale, Steve Miller, *New York City Ballet*
James Johnson, *Martha Graham*
Yee Chan, *Alvin Ailey*
Ellen Jacobs, *Merce Cunningham*
Nicole Vestienne, *Paul Taylor Dance Company*
RCA Archives
Azita Corton, *CBS*
Scott Fain, Carol Brokaw, *ABC*
Betty Hudson, *NBC*
Lida Lauffer, *HBO*
Richard Betz, *La Verne*
J. Carter, Stacey Friedman, *MTV Networks*
Mark Magner, Kingson Chou, Richard Termini, *Children's Television Workshop*
William L. Noble
Walter Gasnick
Rev. Stephen S. Garney

We would like to thank the following for permission to reproduce the extracts on pages 114 to 128

◆ DONADIO & ASHWORTH, INC: Excerpt from *Good As Gold* by Joseph Heller, copyright © 1979 by Joseph Heller. Reprinted by permission of Donadio & Ashworth, Inc. (UK) Excerpt from *Good As Gold* by Joseph Heller, published by Jonathan Cape Ltd, reprinted by permission of Jonathan Cape Ltd, London.

◆ ELIZABETH H. DOS PASSOS: Excerpt from *Manhattan Transfer* by John Dos Passos (Harper and Brothers, 1925). Reprinted by permission of Elizabeth H. Dos Passos, Co-Executor, the Estate of John Dos Passos.

◆ THE DREISER TRUST: Excerpt from *The Color of a Great City* by Theodore Dreiser, copyright © 1923 by Boni & Liveright, Inc. copyright renewed 1951 by Mrs Theodore Dreiser, as widow of the author. Reprinted by permission of The Dreiser Trust, Harold J. Dies, Trustee.

◆ FABER AND FABER LIMITED: "Broadway" by Vladimir Mayakovsky, translated by Peter Jukes from *A Shout in the Street* by Peter Jukes (1990). Reprinted by permission of Faber and Faber Ltd. Also reprinted in the U.K. by permission of Faber and Faber Ltd.

◆ FARRAR, STRAUS & GIROUX, INC.: Excerpt from *I Thought of Daisy* by Edmund Wilson, copyright © 1953 by Edmund Wilson, copyright renewed 1981 by Helen Miranda Wilson. Reprinted by permission of Farrar, Straus & Giroux, Inc. Also reprinted in the U.K. by permission of Farrar, Straus & Giroux, Inc.
– Excerpt from "Harlem Literati" from *The Big Sea* by Langston Hughes. Copyright © 1940 by Langston Hughes. Copyright renewed 1968 by Arna Bontemps and George Houston Press. Reprinted by permission of Hill and Wang, a division of Farrar, Straus & Giroux, Inc.

◆ HARPERCOLLINS PUBLISHERS, INC.: Excerpt from 'Here is New York' from *Essays of E. B. White* by E. B. White, copyright © 1949 by E. B. White, copyright renewed 1977 by E. B. White. Reprinted by permission of HarperCollins Publishers, Inc.

◆ ALFRED A. KNOPF, INC: Excerpt from *Souvenir and Prophecies* by Holly Stevens, copyright © 1966, 1976 by Holly Stevens. Also reprinted in the U.K. by permission of Alfred A. Knopf, Inc.

– Excerpt from *Odd Jobs*, by John Updike, copyright © 1991 by John Updike. Reprinted by permission of Alfred A. Knopf, Inc. (UK) Excerpt from *Odd Jobs*, by John Updike (Penguin Books 1992, first published in the U.K. by André Deutsch) copyright © 1991 by John Updike. Reprinted by permission of Hamish Hamilton Ltd.

◆ LITTLE, BROWN AND COMPANY: "A Brief Guide to New York" from *Verses from 1929 On*, by Ogden Nash, copyright © 1940 by Ogden Nash. Reprinted by permission of Little, Brown and Company. (UK) "A Brief Guide to New York" poem published in *Many Long Years Ago*, Little, Brown 1945 © 1945 by Ogden Nash. Reprinted in the UK by permission of Curtis Brown Ltd.

◆ MACMILLAN PUBLISHING COMPANY: Excerpt from *The Diary of George Templeton Strong* by Allan Nevins and Milton Halsey Thomas, copyright © 1952 by Macmillan Publishing Company, copyright renewed 1980 by Milton Halsey Thomas. Reprinted by permission of Macmillan Publishing Company.

◆ NEW DIRECTIONS PUBLISHING CORP.: Excerpt from *The Crack-Up* by F. Scott Fitzgerald, copyright © 1945 by New Directions Publishing Corp. Reprinted by permission of New Directions Publishing Corp. (UK) Excerpt from *The Crack-Up* by F. Scott Fitzgerald, published by the Bodley Head, reprinted by permission of the Fitzgerald Estate and the Bodley Head, London.

◆ PANTHEON BOOKS: Excerpt from *Up in the Old Hotel* by Joseph Mitchell, copyright © 1992 by Joseph Mitchell. Reprinted by permission of Pantheon Books, a division of Random House, Inc.

◆ THE WALLACE LITERARY AGENCY, INC : Excerpt from *Great Jones Street* by Don DeLillo, copyright © 1973 by Don DeLillo (Penguin Books). Reprinted by permission of The Wallace Literary Agency, Inc. Also reprinted in the U.K. (published there by Picador Books) by permission of The Wallace Literary Agency, Inc.

◆ A. P. WATT LTD: Excerpt from *What I Saw in America* by G. K. Chesterton (Hodder & Stoughton, London, 1922). Reprinted by permission of A. P. Watt Ltd on behalf of the Royal Literary Fund.

INDEX

◆ A ◆

A. A. Low warehouse, 173
Abigail Adams Smith Museum, 311
Abyssinian Baptist Church, 51, 359
Academy of Music, 222
Actors Studio, 256
Adamic, Louis, 148
Adler, Felix, 342
Admiral George Dewey promenade, 143
Aerial Gardens, 258
African Market, 358
African Methodist Episcopal Zion Church, 51
Aldrin, Edwin, 29
Allen, Gracie, 56
Allen, Woody, 301
Allom, Charles, 324
Alvin Ailey American Dance Theater, the, 63
Alwyn Court, 303, 311
American Broadcasting Company Television Studios, 344
American Express, 141
American Fine Art Society, 302
American International Building, 159
American Merchant Mariners' Memorial, 142
American Museum of Natural History, 347
American Radiator Building, 99
American Standard Building, former American Radiator Building, 99, 254
American Tract Society Building, 170
Angel Street, 359
Apollo Theater, 61, 358
Appellate Division Courthouse, 234
Apthorp Apartments, 348
Armstrong, Louis, 60
Ashcan School, 199, 217
Asia House, 311
Astor, John J., 226, 285
Astor Court, 331
Astor Library, 226
Audubon, John J., 346
Audubon Terrace Historic District, 361
Aunt Len's Doll and Toy Museum, 359
Auster, Paul, 47
Ave. (3rd) 356–68, 312
Ave. (5th), 34, 50, 64, 86, 88, 92, 96, 162, 178, 284, 309
Ave. (6th), 102, 134, 135, 232
Avery Fisher Hall, 306
Avery Library, 20, 353

◆ B ◆

Badger, Daniel D. 94
Balanchine, George, 62
Baldwin, James, 350
Banca Stabile, 196
Bank of Manhattan, 266
Bank of New York Building, 154, 161
Bank of the Manhattan Co. Building, 161
Bankers Club,153
Bankers Trust, 97, 163
Bankruptcy Court, 157
Barclay-Vesey Building, 98, 140
Barnard College, 356
Barrymore Theater, 259
Bartholdi, Frédéric Auguste, 144
Battery Maritime Building, 157
Battery Park, 19, 138, 140, 142, 143
Battery Park Center, 29
Battery Park City, 29, 103, 138, 141, 142
Bayard-Condict Building, 95, 227
Beaver St., 166
Beekman Place, 262
Bell, Graham, 176
Bellini, Giovanni, 323
Bellow, Saul, 347
Bemelmans Bar, 312
Bennett, Michael, 59
Beresford, The, 347
Bergdorf Goodman, 297
Berkman, Alexandre, 195
Berman, Saul, 177
Bernstein, Leonard, 305
Bessemer, 94
Beuys, Joseph, 341
Bigelow Co. Pharmacy, 212
Biltmore Theater, 258
Birdland, the, 60
Bitter, Karl, 297
Blackwell's Island, 46
Bleecker St., 95
Bloomingdale's, 311
Bolton, William Jay, 367
Boorstin, 351
Booth, Edwin, 230
Booth Theater, 258
Borglum, Gutzon, 178
Bowery, 37, 45, 48, 194
Bowling Green, 152, 156, 157
Brancusi, Constantin, 293, 340
Brando, Marlon, 141
Brentano's, 282
Breuer, Marcel, 104, 239, 326
British Empire Building, 275
Broad St., 38, 163, 166
Broad St. (85), 166
Broadway, 34, 39, 47, 58, 59, 61, 86, 87, 89, 95, 97, 138, 152, 153, 155, 156, 176, 180, 232, 258
Broadway (1), 156
Broadway (9), 155
Broadway (165), 152
Broadway (1580), 257
Broadway Dance Center, 61
Bronx, The, 18, 26, 28, 45
Brooklyn, 26, 27, 28, 33, 43, 48, 50, 142, 157, 366
Brooklyn Borough Hall, 367
Brooklyn Botanic Garden, 368
Brooklyn Heights Esplanade, 368
Brotherhood Synagogue, 230
Brown, Trisha, 60
Brown Building, 200
Bry, Théodore de, 26
Bryant Park, 39, 254, 297
Buberl, Casper, 227
Buell Hall, 353
Buoninsegna, Duccio di, 325
Burns, George, 56
Burr, Aaron, 161, 228
Burroughs, William, 224
Bush, George, 29
Bush Tower, 254
Butler Library, 353

◆ C ◆

Cable Building, 227
Cafe Carlyle, 312
Café des Artistes, 344
Cage, John, 60
Calder, A. Stirling, 199, 257
Callahan's, 192
Calloway, Cab, 61
Carl Schurz Park, 313
Carnegie, Andrew, 226, 301, 312
Carnegie Hall, 299, 301, 305
Cartier Inc., 287
Cartwright, Alexander J., 64
Caruso, Enrico, 56
Cary Building, 88, 209
Castle Clinton, 142
Castle Garden,143
Catholic Church of the Transfiguration, 191
CBS Building, 288
Cedar St., 140
Céline, Louis-Ferdinand, 161
Central Park, 22, 28, 32, 33, 99, 314–9
Central Park South, 303
Centre St., 96
Centre St. (240), 196
Century Apartments, 343
Century Buildling, 90, 223, 310
Cézanne, Paul, 290
Chagall, Marc, 29
Chambellan, René, 98
Chambers St.,141, 142
Chanin Building, 98, 272
Chanin's Theater, 258
Channel Gardens, 275
Charles II, 26, 31
Charles Ludbon Theater, 213
Charlton-King-Vandam Historic District, 203
Charyn, Jérôme, 48, 358
Chase, William Merritt, 302
Chase Manhattan Bank, 159
Chase Manhattan Plaza, 159
Chatham Square, 193
Chelsea, 219
Chemical Bank Building, 261
Cherokee Apartments, 313
Chinatown, 48, 53, 190
Chinatown History Museum, 191
Christopher Park, 212
Christy, Howard Chandler, 344
Chrysler, Walter Percy, 266
Chrysler Building, 29, 98, 139, 161, 236, 266
Chumley's, 213
Church of St. Ann and The Holy Trinity, 367
Church of St. Luke in the
Fields, 214
Church of the Holy Communion, 86, 220
Church of the Unification, 51
Citibank, 160
Citicorp Center, 101, 286
City Center of Music and Drama, 300
City College, 360
City Hall, 37, 46, 162, 168, 258
City Hall Park, 168, 170
City of New York Office Building, 184
Civic Center, 182
Clark, Edward, 346
Clinton (Hell's Gate), 29
Cloisters, the, 362
Cocks, Samuel, 215
Cole, Thomas, 346
Collect Pond, 182
Collegiate Church and Collegiate School, 348
Colonnade Row, 84, 227
Colt, Samuel, 201
Coltrane, John, 60
Columbia University, 30, 93, 352–3
Columbia Library Collection, 353
Columbus, Christopher, 26, 29, 34
Columbus Park, 190
Commerce St. (39 and 41), 213
Community College, 209
Con Edison Building, 229
Con Edison Energy Museum, 229
Coney Island, 143
Constable, John, 324
Cooper, Merian, 139
Cooper, Peter, 225
Cooper Hewitt Museum, 132, 225, 320
Cooper Square, 224
Cooper Union Building, 225
Corner, Jack Dempsey, 300
Corso, Gregory, 224
Cortlandt St, 152
Cotton Club, The, 60
Croton Fountain, 170
Croton Reservoir, 34, 156, 170
Crown Building, 296
Cunard Building, 155
Cunningham, Merce, 62
Cushman Row, 85, 220

◆ D ◆

Dakota Apartments, 346
Damrosch Park, 306
Dance Theater of Harlem, 61
David, Jacques Louis, 329
Davis, Miles, 60, 287
Davis, Stuart, 326
Daylight Factories, 205
De Foust St., Lee, 56
De Mille, Agnes, 58
De Vinne Press Building, 91, 227
Decker Building, 223
Delmonico's, 166
Demuth, Charles, 334
Deskey, Donald, 277
Deutschlandle, 45
Di Modica, Arturo, 156
Dia Center for the Arts, 220

Diamond Dealers' Club, 299
Donleavy, J. P., 236
Dos Passos, John, 123, 177, 214, 284
Douanier Rousseau, 291
Doubleday, Abner, 64
Downtown Athletic Club, 142
Doyers St., 192, 193
Dreiser, Theodore, 116, 214
Duane Park, 209
Duane St. (165), 208
Dubuffet, Jean 159
Duchamp, Marcel, 218
Duncan, Isadora, 62
Dyckman House, 82, 361
Dylan, Bob, 201

◆ E ◆

Eakins, Thomas, 335
Ear Inn, 205
East Harlem, 48
East River, 264
East River Savings Bank Building, 152
East 66th St. (46), 310, 311
East Village, 48, 124
Eastern Parkway, 33
Eastman Kodak, 233
Edgecombe Ave., 360
Edison, Thomas, 34, 229
Edward Mooney House, 83
Ehrenwiesen, Hilla Rebay von, 338
Einstein, Albert, 29, 151
El Greco, 336
Ellington, Duke, 60
Ellis Island, 138, 143, 148–50
Ellison, Ralph, 353
Elmer Holmes Bobst Library, 200
Empire Diner, 220
Empire State Building, 29, 139, 161, 236, 242
Engelhard Court, 329
Engine Company no. 31, 184
Equitable Building, 39, 97, 153
Eriksson, Leif, 26
Essex House, 303
Exchange Place, 160

◆ F ◆

Farragut, David, 234
Father Duffy Square, 257
Faulkner, Barry, 229
Faure, Élie, 178
Federal Hall National Memorial, 27, 85, 157, 162, 163, 168
Federal Office Building, 178, 184
Federal Reserve Bank, 158
Film Center Building, 99
Financial District, 52, 138, 156–8
First Church of Zion, 192
Fitzgerald, Ella, 61
Fitzgerald, Francis Scott, 115
Five Points, 182, 191, 196
Flatiron Building, 28, 96, 233
Fleming Smith Warehouse, 208

Flushing Meadow, 65
Foley Square, 182
Forbes Building, 218–19
Ford Foundation Building, 101, 265
Fordham Law School, 304
Former Arnold Constable & Co., 232
Former Asch Building, 200
Former AT&T Building, 176
Former B. Altman Building, 249
Former B. Altman Dry Goods Store, 220
Former Bell Laboratories, 215
Former Bowery Savings Bank, 272
Former Bank of the Metropolis Building, 222–3
Former Gorham Manufacturing Company, 232
Former Coty Building, 288
Former Hugh O'Neill's Store, 220
Former James Brown Residence, 205
Former Knickerbocker Hotel, 254
Former Little Singer Building, 204
Former Lord & Taylor, 232
Former McGraw-Hill Building, 99, 256
Former New York Chamber of Commerce, 159
Former New York Mercantile Exchange, 207
Former Paramount Building, 255
Former Seamen's Bank for Savings, 160, 161
Former Siegel-Cooper Dry Goods Store, 220
Former Standard Oil Building, 56, 156, 159
Former United States Appraisers' Stores, 214
Former Vanderbilt Residence, 283
Former W. & J. Sloane, 232
Fort Washington Ave., 47
Forward Building, 195
Fragonard, J.-H., 323
Franklin, Benjamin, 170
Franklin St., 208
Fraunces, Samuel, 166
Fraunces Tavern, 166
Fraunces Tavern-Block Historic-District, 168
Fred F. French Building, 252
Frei Bibliothek und Lesehalle, 224
Frick, Henry Clay, 322
Frick Collection, 309, 320, 322–5
Friends' Meeting House, 230
Fuller Building, 296
Fulton, Robert, 27, 154, 174
Fulton Ferry Building, 366

Fulton Ferry Hotel, 172
Fulton Fish Market, 175

◆ G ◆

Gainsborough Studios, The, 303
Galland, Pierre Victor, 64
Gallatin, Albert, 155, 200
Gallery Olympic Place, 283
Gansevoort Meat Market, 214, 215
Gatto, Victor Joseph, 38
Gay St., 212
General Electric Building, Former RCA Victor Building, 98, 261, 277, 278, 286
General Motors Building, 297
General Post Office of New York, 170, 249
General Society of Mechanics and Tradesmen, 250
General Consulate of Italy, 310
General Theological Seminary, 220
German Poliklinik, 224
Gershwin, George, 58
Gershwin, Ira, 58
Giacometti, Alberto, 340
Gilbert Kiamie House, 91
Gillespie, Dizzy, 60
Gilsey House, 88, 89, 234
Goethe House, 320
Gotham Book Mart 299
Gotti, John ("Dapper Don"), 41
Gould, Joe, 203
Gould, John J., 164
Government House, 156
Governor's Island, 142, 157
Governor Tilden's House, 87, 230
Grace Church, 87, 224
Gracie Mansion, 313, 321
Graham, Martha, 62
Gramercy, The, 48, 230
Gramercy Park, 87, 89, 230
Gramercy Park W. (3–4), 230
Grand Army Plaza, 297
Grand Central Station, 29
Grand Central Terminal, 103, 236–8
Grant's Tomb, 357
Graybar Building, 272
Green, Hetty, 163
Greene St., 207
Greenwich House, 213
Greenwich St., 138
Greenwich Village, 26, 53, 102, 198, 201, 210, 224
Gropius, Walter, 260
Grove St., 214, 215
Guggenheim, Solomon, 338
Guggenheim Museum, 338–41
Guggenheim Museum of SoHo, 204, 205, 320

◆ H ◆

Haas, Richard, 289
Hale, Nathan, 251, 262
Hall of Architecture Casts, 329

Hall of Records, 185
Hamilton, Alexander, 154, 161, 178
Hamilton Grange National Monument, 360
Hamilton Heights, 360
The Hampton, 215
Hanover Square, 38, 166
Hard Rock Café, 302
Harlem, 26, 27, 29, 37, 40, 51, 60, 61, 88, 350
Harper, James, 231
Harrison Street Row, 209
Hart Island, 47
Hartley, Marsden, 334
Harvard Club, 250
Haughwout Building, 88, 94, 95, 204, 206
Hawkins, Coleman, 60
Hearst, William Randolph, 54, 303
Helen Hayes Theater, 259
Helleu, Paul, 239
Hell's Kitchen, 256
Helmsley Building, 260
Henderson, Fletcher, 60
Henderson Place, 313
Henri, Robert, 107, 302
Henry Villard Houses, 92, 284
Hepburn, Audrey, 296
Herald and Greeley squares, 249
Hewlett house, 334
Himes, Chester, 40
Hitchcock, Alfred, 239
Hitchcock, Henry-Russell, 100
Hoboken Ferry, 141
Hoffman, Malvina, 322
Holbein, Hans, 325
Homer, Winslow, 335
Hopper, Edward, 216
Houdon, Jean-Antoine, 323
House of Relief, New York Hospital, 209
Houston St., 33
Hudson, Henry, 26
Hudson Street Warehouse, 208
Hunter College, 310

◆ I ◆

IBM Building, 289
IBM Gallery of Science and Art, 289
India House, 166
Inter-American relations, Center for, 310
International Building, 281
International Center of Photography, 321
International Telephone Building, 163
Intrepid Sea-Air-Space Museum, 257
Irving, Washington, 154, 229
Irving Hall, 222
Irving Place (49), 229
Isham Park, 19
Islamic Center, 51
Italian Cultural Institute, 310

◆ J ◆

Jacob Javits Convention Center, 248

James, Henry, 198, 199
Jamestown, 26
Jarmulowsky Bank, 194
Jefferson, Thomas, 169
Jefferson Market
Courthouse, 211
Jewish Museum, 321
Jewish Theological
Seminary, 356
John Ericsson Memorial,
142
John St., 85, 158
John St. United
Methodist Church, 158
Johns, Jasper, 294
Jones St. (26–30), 213
Judson Memorial
Church, 200, 201
Juilliard School of Music,
306
Juilliard Theater, 306

◆ K ◆

Kandinsky, Wassily, 341
Kafka, Franz, 45
Kaoshen Club, 192
Kazan, Elia, 141, 256
Kennedy, John F., 29, 57
Kent Garage, 305
Kerouac, Jack, 224
King's College, 30
Kline, Franz, 327
Kooning, Willem de, 294
Kostolamy, André, 156

◆ L ◆

Lady Chapel, 283
La Farge, John, 284
LaFayette, 52, 143
Lafayette St., 84, 91
La Guardia, Fiorello, 29,
226
Lambs Theater, 259
Lancey, Étienne de, 166
Landmark Tavern, 256
La Tour, Georges de, 336
Langston Hughes House,
88
Lauren, Ralph, 309
Lawrence, James, 154
Lawrie, Lee, 274
Leisler, Jacob, 168
Lennon, John, 41
Leone, Sergio,158
Lescaze House, W., 100,
262
Lever House, 100, 286
Lewis, Sinclair, 343
Lexington Ave., 64, 101,
286, 311
Liberty Plaza, 152, 159
Liberty St.,140, 158, 159
Liberty Tower, 159
Liberty Warehouse, 343
Library and Museum of
the Performing Arts, 306
Lichtenstein, Roy, 341
Lincoln, Abraham, 27
Lincoln Building, 222, 250
Lincoln Center, 299, 304,
305–6
Lind, Jenny, 143
Lindsay, John, 29
Little Italy, 40, 53, 196
Lockwood De Forest
Residence, 218
Long Island, 28, 65
Louise Nevelson Plaza,
159
Low, Seth, 352

Low Memorial Library,
93, 353
Lower Bay, 42
Lower East Side, 45,
189–96, 224, 299
Lower Plaza, 274, 279
Luciano, Charles
("Lucky"), 40, 285
Lucille Lortel Theater, 214
Lycée Français, 309
Lyceum Theater, 259
Lyric, The, 258

◆ M ◆

MacDougal Alley, 217
MacDougal St., 201
MacDougal Sullivan
Gardens, 202
Macy's, 249
Madison, James, 234
Madison Ave., 102, 176,
289, 309
Madison Square, 234
Madison Square Garden,
51, 64, 239, 300
Maiden Lane, 48
Mailer, Norman, 224
Main Emigrant Landing
Depot, 143
Maine Memorial, 174, 304
Majestic Apartments, 345
Majestic Theater, 259
Malévitch, Casimir, 341
Manet, Edouard, 337
Manhattan Community
College, 207
Manhattan Life Insurance
Company, 302
Mann, Klaus, 279
Manship, Paul, 278
Marcus Garvey Park, 358
Marine Midland Bank, 153
Mariners' Temple Baptist
Church, 193
Maritime Exchange
Building, 166
Marshall Chess Club, 218
Matisse, Henri, 291
McEnroe, John, 65
McGraw-Hill Building, 99
McMonnies, Frederick, 252
McNeil, Herman A., 199
Melville, Herman, 143,
199, 215
Merman, Ethel, 58
Merrill Lynch, 141
Mersereau, William, 166
MetLife Building, former-
Pan Am Building, 237,
260
Metropolitan Life Tower,
234
Metropolitan Museum of
Art, 161, 217, 320,
328–37
Metropolitan Opera
House, 305
Metropolitan Tower, 301,
310
Milken, Michael,165
Milligan Place, 212
Mills House no. 1, 202
Minetta Brook, 198
Minetta St., 202
Mingus, Charles, 224
Minuit, Peter, 26, 30, 156
Miró, Joan, 292
Mitchell, John, 223
Mondrian, Piet, 29, 293,
341
Monitor, 142

Monk, Meredith, 61
Monk, Thelonious, 60, 224
Monroe, Marilyn, 65
Montague St., 367
Moore, Henry, 306
Morand, Paul, 153, 233,
282, 302, 357
Morgan, John Pierpont,
93, 162, 163, 241, 249
Morgan Guaranty Trust
Company, 162
Morris-Jumel Mansion,
82, 361
Morse, Samuel, 200
Morton St., 83
Most Holy Crucifix
Church, 196
Mulberry St., 190
Municipal Building, 96,
168, 182
Murray, David, 61
Murray Hill, 48, 241
Museum for African Art,
204, 205
Museum of American
Financial History, 156
Museum of the City of
New York, 321
Museum of Immigration,
148
Museum Mile, 320
Museum of Modern Art,
290–5
Musical Theater, 58

◆ N ◆

N. Y. City Fire Department
Museum, 207
Nadelman, Elie, 296
Naguchi, Isamu, 153, 159
Namath, Joe, 65
Nassau St., 159
National Academy of
Design, 320
National Arts Club, 87, 230
National Democratic
Club, 240
Netherlands Memorial
Monument, 142
New Amsterdam Theater,
258
New Museum of
Contemporary Art, 204
New School for Social
Research, 219
New York Athletic Club, 303
New York Central 13, 175
New York Central &
Hudson River Railroad
Freight Depot, 208
New York Central
Railroad Company, 260
New York City Criminal
Court Building, 183
New York City Opera, 300,
305
New York County
Courthouse, 183
New York Delicatessen,
302
New York Public Library,
92, 236, 253, 306, 312
New York State Theater,
305
New York Stock
Exchange, 27, 156, 163,
164–5
New York Studio School,
217
New York Telephone
Building, 140

New York University, 200,
216
New York Yacht Club, 65,
93, 251
News Building, The, 272
Newspaper Row, 170
North Cove, 141
Northern Dispensary, 212

◆ O ◆

O'Hara, Thomas, 141
O'Henry, 59, 229
Old Merchant's House,
The, 227
Old St. Patrick's
Cathedral, 196
Olmsted, Frederick Law,
32, 33, 317
O'Neill, Eugene, 199, 202
Olympic Towers, 283
Oppenheim, Meret, 295
Osborne Apartments, 302
Otis, Ellis, 95, 206
Oyster Bar, 175

◆ P ◆

Pace University, 170
Paley, William S., 288
Paley Park, 288
Paramount Theater, 255
Parish House, 288
Park Ave., 93, 98, 100,
101, 103, 260, 285, 310
Park Row, 28, 90, 168, 170
Park Row Building, 171
Parker, Charlie, 60
Parker, Dorothy, 55
Patchin Place, 212
Pearl St.,166
Peck Slip, 171
Pell St., 83, 192
Pennsylvania Station, 29
Perry St., 89
Pershing Square
Building, 272
Pete's Tavern, 229
Philip Morris Inc.
Building, 103, 241
Picasso, Pablo, 290, 337,
340
Pier A, 143
Pierpont Morgan Library,
93, 241
Pine St., 83, 91, 159
Pininfarina, 292
Pitt, William, 193
Players, The, 230
Poe, Edgar Allan, 199, 213
Pollock, Jackson, 295, 334
Porter, Cole, 58
Potter Building, 90, 170
Potter, Edward Clark, 252
Potter, Tommy, 60
Printing House Square, 170
Provincetown Playhouse,
202
Puck Building, 227
Pulitzer Fountain, 297
Pythian Condominium,
former Pythian Temple,
The, 345

◆ Q ◆

Queens, 28, 45, 65

◆ R ◆

Racquet & Tennis Club of
New York, 93, 286

dio City Music Hall, , 277, 285
skob, John Jakob, 242
uschenberg, Robert, 5
ealty Buildings, 154
ectory and Shrine of St. zabeth Ann Seton, 157
embrandt, 324
epublic National Bank, 4
chmond Hill House, 202
is, Jacob, 47
ver House, 262
vera, Diego, 281
iverside Church, 356
iverside Park, 348
izzoli Building, 288
ockefeller, David, 159
ockefeller, John D., 156, 01, 311, 365
ockefeller, Nelson A., 41, 263, 276
Rockefeller Center, 29, 74–81, 282, 299
Rockefeller Plaza, 275
Rodin, Auguste, 290
Roebling, John, 187
Rogers, Ginger, 58
Roman Catholic Orphan Asylum, 83
Roosevelt, Eleanor, 143
Roosevelt, Franklin D., 29
Roosevelt, Theodore, 55, 232
Roosevelt Building, 206
Roosevelt Island, 46, 311
Roseland Dance City, 300
Rosenfeld, Bernard T., 226
Ross, Herold, 252
The Row, 216
Rubinstein, Arthur, 29
Ruggles, Samuel B., 230
Rumbald Kohn, Estelle, 178
Rushmore National Monument, 178
Russo, Gaetano, 304

◆ S ◆

Sacco and Vanzetti, 222
St. Bartholomew's Church, 285
St. Denis, Ruth, 62
St. James Church, 193
St. James Episcopal Church, 309
St. John the Divine, 354
St. John's Park, 208
St. Luke's Place, 213
St. Malachy Roman Catholic Church, 300
St. Mark's in the Bowery 224
St. Nicholas Greek Orthodox Chapel, 140
St. Nicholas Historic District, 359
St. Patrick's Cathedral, 50, 282
St. Paul's Chapel, 176
St. Peter's Church, 178
St. Thomas Episcopal Church, 86, 87, 288
Saint-Gaudens, Augustus, 234, 284
Saks, Andrew, 282
Saks Fifth Avenue, 282
Salmagundi Club, 88, 218

Samuel Paley Plaza, 288
San Remo, 346
Scharansky, Anatoli, 264
Schepp, Leonard, 209
Schermerhorn Row, 172
Schomburg Center for Research and Black Culture, 359
Scorsese, Martin, 40
Seagram Bldg, 101, 286
Segalen, Victor, 182
Sert, José Maria, 280
Sesame Street, 57
Seton, Elizabeth, 50, 157
7th Regiment Armory, The, 310
Seurat, Georges, 337
Seward Park, 195
Shea Stadium, the, 64
Shearith Israel Graveyard (first), 193
Shearith Israel Cemetery (second), 218
Sheridan Square, 212
Shubert Theater, 259
Siegel, Henry, 220
Sinatra, Frank, 141
Sinclair, Upton, 214
Singer Building, 152, 159
Sniffen Court Historic District, 248
SoHo-Cast-Iron-Historic-District, 203
SoHo Museum Row, 204
Sollers, Philippe, 139
Solomon Guggenheim Foundation, 338
Solow Building, 297, 301
Sony Building, 102, 289
South St, 157
South Street Seaport, 172–5
South Village, 200
Spanish Institute, 310
State St., 138, 157
Staten Island, 28, 36, 43
Statue of Liberty, 138, 144–7
Steam Ship Row, 156
Stonewall Inn, 212
Stuyvesant, Peter, 31, 50, 224
Stuyvesant High School, 142
Sun Ra, 61
Sutton, Effingham B., 263
Sutton Place, 263
Swing St., 287
Swiss Center, 282
Synagogue Beth Hamedrash Hagodol, 195
Synagogue Khal Adath Jerushun and Anshei Lubz, 194

◆ T ◆

Tammany Hall, 40, 228
Tavern on the Green, 344
Taylor, Paul, 60
Temple Emanu-El, 311
Thames St., 154
Thames Twins, 154
Tharp, Twyla, 61
Thaw, Harry K., 211
Theater Alley, 170
Theodore Roosevelt Memorial, 347
Theresa Tower, 358
Thomas, Dylan, 215
Thomas Street Inn, 87, 219

Thurber, James, 55, 252
Tiffany, Charles, 296
Tiffany, Louis Comfort, 64
Tiffany and Co., 296
Tilden, Samuel J., 230, 252
Tile Club, 218
Times Square, 40, 170, 255, 257, 258, 299
Times Square (1), 255
Times Tower, 255
Tishman Building, 287
Titanic Memorial Lighthouse, 171
Tombs, the, 183, 196
Tompkins Square, 224
Tramway Place, 311
TriBeCa-West-Historic-District, 207
Trinity Building, 154
Trinity Cemetery, 361
Trinity Church, 31, 86, 138, 154–5, 158, 178, 208, 352
Troubetzkoy, A., 297
Trump, Donald J., 296
Trump Tower, 289, 296
Turtle-Bay-Gardens Historic-District, 262
Twain, Mark, 199, 226, 230
Tweed, William Marcy ("Boss"), 28, 40, 185, 228
Tweed Courthouse, Old New York County Courthouse, 185
"21" Club, 287
Twin Peaks, 214
Twin Towers, 138, 139, 140

◆ U ◆

Ukrainian Institute, 312
Union Club, 249, 309
Union League Club, 248
Union Square Savings Bank, 223
Union Square, 222
Union Theater, 228
Union Theological Seminary, 86, 356
Unitarian Church of All Souls, 312
United Nations, 29, 236, 263, 264–5
United States Assay Office, 161
U.S. Courthouse, 177, 183
U.S. Custom House, 142, 157, 160, 162, 168, 177
U.S. Post Office, 178
University Club, 288
Upper Bay, 42
Upper East Side, 26, 308–21
Upper West Side, 48, 342–8
Urban Center, 285

◆ V ◆

Van Eyck, Jan, 336
Van Gogh, Vincent, 291, 340
Vanderbilt, Cornelius, 36, 208, 236, 260
Vanderbilt, George W., 284
Vanderbilt, William H., 64
Vanderbilt, William K., 236
Vanderbilt Colony, 284
Vaughan, Sarah, 61
Vermeer, 323

Verrazano Memorial, 142
Verrazano, Giovanni da, 26, 42
Vietnam War Veterans' Memorial, 166
Vietnam Veterans' Plaza, 166
Village Community Church, 84, 219
Villard, Henry, 284
Vivian Beaumont Theater, 306

◆ W ◆

Waldorf Towers, 285
Walker, James, J., 213
Wall St., 27, 29, 38, 48, 85, 138, 154, 157, 160, 161, 162, 163, 164
Wall St. (63), 160
Wallace Building, 91
Warhol, Andy, 224, 248, 295, 327
Warshaw, Randy, 60
Washington, George, 27, 212
Washington Court, 102, 212
Washington Irving High School, 229
Washington Market, 207
Washington Mews, 216
Washington Square, 38, 198
Washington St., 140 162, 166, 169, 177, 199
Water St., 138, 166
Watson, James, 157
Waugh, Samuel, 148
Weinman, Adolphe A., 183
Welles, Orson, 57
Wesley, John, 158
Wesley Chapel, 158
W. 11th St. (18), 218
W. 44th St.,175–9, 214
W. 40th St., 48
W. 71st St., 345
West St., 140, 142
Westlake, Donald, 237
White, E. B., 51
White, Stanford, 259, 284
White Horse Tavern, 215
Whitney Museum of American Art, 104, 158, 217, 241, 320, 326–7
William St., 160, 166
William St. (20), 160
Williamsburgh Savings Bank, 160
Wilson, Woodrow, 158, 180
Winter Garden Theater, 258
Wolfe, Elsie de, 324
Woolworth, Frank, 97, 180
Woolworth Building, 17, 94, 161, 168, 177, 180–1, 234, 305
World Financial Center, 19, 103
World Trade Center, 19, 29, 138, 139, 152, 157, 177
Worldwide Plaza, 300
Wright, Frank Lloyd, 338

◆ Y ◆

Yale Club, 251
Yankee Stadium, 64
Ye Waverly Inn, 215
Yeshiva Chofetz Chaim, Yonkers, 26

◆ Architects ◆

Kahn and Jacobs, Egger and Higgins, 184
Babb, Cook and Willard, 91, 227, 320
Benjamin Wistar Morris, Burgee, John, 102, 289
Buchman and Kahn, 99, 163, 297
Carrère and Hastings, 92, 155, 309
Chanin, Irwin, 343
Cram and Ferguson, 354
Cross and Cross, 98, 160, 286
Da Cunha, George, 230
Delamarre, Jacques, 272, 345
Delano and Aldrich, 160, 214, 309, 310
Edward Larrabee Barnes Assocs, 289
Emery Roth and Son, 138, 261
Flagg, Ernest, 152, 206, 282
Foster, Richard, 201, 305
Franzen, Ulrich, 103
Greer, Seth, 84, 227
Gilbert, Cass, 140, 157, 177, 180, 183, 234, 312
Gilbert Cass, Jr, 183
Gordon, James Riley, 230
Graham, Ernest R., 153
Graves, Michael, 104 and Haggerty, John 178
Harrison, Wallace K., 305
Harvey Wiley Corbett and Charles B. Meyers, 183
Hastings, Thomas, 322
Hatch, Stephen D., 89, 208, 209, 234
Hood, Raymond, 99, 276
Hood and Fouihoux, 99, 254
Hood, Godley and Fouilhoux, 99, 256
Hunt and Hunt, 284
Hunt, Richard Moris, 142, 154, 204, 206, 328
Johnson, Philip, 100, 101, 102, 201, 286, 289, 292, 305, 311
Kahn, Ely Jacques, 98
Kohn, Robert D., 178
Kimball, Francis H., 154, 208, 309
King and Kellum, 88, 209, 230
L'Enfant, Pierre, 27, 32, 162
Lamb and Rich, 250, 313
Lamb, Thomas W., 156, 345
Le Corbusier, 155, 264
Loos, Adolf, 97
Mangin, Joseph F., 168
McComb, John, 142, 157
McComb Jr, John, 168
McKim, Charles, 93
McKim, Mead and White, 92, 96, 160, 201, 227, 249, 284, 288, 310, 320, 329
Meyers, Charles B., 184
Mies van der Rohe, Ludwig, 101, 286
Mould, J. Wrey, 347
Napoléon Le Brun and Sons, 184, 234

Pederson, Frederick A., 104, 225
Pei, I. M., 248
Pelli, Cesar, 103
Pope, John R., 322, 347
Portman, John, 257
Post, George B., 170, 303, 367
Raymond Hood Wallace and K. Harrison, 276
Richardson, H. H., 90
Robertson, R. H., 170, 171, 222
Robertson, Robert H., 309
Rogers, Isaiah, 160
Roth, Emery, 346, 347
Saarinen, Eero, 288, 306
Shreve, Lamb and Harmon, 242
Skidmore, Owings and Merrill, 100, 152, 153, 283, 286, 297
Sloan and Robertson, 155, 166, 272
Smith, Lyndon P., 227
Starrett and Van Vleck, 142, 282
Stone, Edward Durell, 100, 292, 304
Sullivan, Louis, 95, 227
Thomas, Thomas, 178
Trowbridge and Livingston, 162, 288, 347
Ulrich Franzen and Assocs., 240
Upjohn, Hobart, 312
Upjohn, Richard, 86, 218, 220, 368
Van Alen, William, 266
Vaux and Withers, 211
Vaux, Calvert, 87, 230, 329, 347
Walker and Gillette, 152, 296, 310
Wallace, Raymond Hood and K. Harrison, 276
Warren and Wetmore, 93, 229, 251, 260, 296, 302
White, Stanford, 230
Wright, Frank Lloyd, 227
York and Sawyer, 272, 303, 346

◆ Libraries ◆

Astor Library, 226
Avery Library, 206, 353
Butler Library, 353
Elmer Holmes Bobst Library, 200
Frei Bibliothek und Lesehalle, 224
Jefferson Market Courthouse Library, 211
Library and Museum of the Performing Arts, 306
Low Memorial Library, 93, 352
New York Public Library, 92, 236, 252, 306, 312
Pierpont Morgan Library, 93, 241
Schomburg Center for Research and Black Culture, 359

◆ Writers ◆

Adamic, Louis, 148
Auster, Paul, 47

Bellow, Saul, 347
Burroughs, William, 224
Céline, Louis-Ferdinand, 161
Cendrars, Blaise, 37
Charyn, Jérôme, 48
Chase, William Merritt, 302
Chesbro, George, 239, 267, 298
Chesterton, G. K., 118
Corso, Gregory, 224
DeLillo, Don, 117 .
Dickens, Charles, 115
Donleavy, J. P., 236
Dos Passos, John, 122, 177, 214, 284
Dreiser, Theodore, 116
Dwight, Timothy, 114
Faure, Élie, 178
Heller, Joseph, 123
Himes, Chester, 40
Hughes, Langston, 127
Irving, Washington, 154, 229
James, Henry, 117, 198, 199
Kafka, Franz, 45
Kerouac, Jack, 224
La Farge, John, 284
Lewis, Sinclair, 343
Mailer, Norman, 224
Mann, Klaus, 279
Mayakovsky, Vladimir, 120
Melville, Herman, 143, 199, 215
Mitchell, 124
Morand, Paul, 153, 233, 282, 302
Nash, Ogden, 126
O'Hara, Thomas, 141
O'Henry, 59, 229
O'Neill, Eugene, 199, 202
Poe, Edgar Allan, 199, 213
Sollers, Philippe, 139
Stevens, Wallace, 125
Strong, George Templeton, 119
Thomas, Dylan, 215
Trotsky, Lev, 126
Twain, Mark, 199, 226, 230
Updike, John, 128
White, E. B., 51
Wilson, Edmund, 121

◆ Civic Buildings ◆

3rd Ave. (1356–68), 312
1580 Broadway, 257
A. A.Low Warehouse, 173
A. A. Low and Alexander M. White Mansions, 368
Abigail Adams Smith Museum, 311
Academy of Music, 222
Actors Studio, 256
Alwyn Court, 303, 311
American Broadcasting Company Television Studios, 344
American Express, 141
American International Building, 159
American Merchant Mariners' Memorial, 142
American Radiator Building, 99
American Standard Building, former-American Radiator

Building, 99, 254
Appellate Division Courthouse, 234
Apthorp Apartments, 34
Ashcan School, 199, 21
Asia House, 311
Astor Court, 331
Avery Fisher Hall, 306
Banca Stabile, 196
Bank of Manhattan, 266
Bank of New York Building, 154, 161
Bank of the Manhattan Co. Building, 161
Bankers Club, 153
Bankers Trust, 97, 163
Bankruptcy Court, 157
Barclay-Vesey Building, 98, 140
Barnard College, 356
Battery Maritime Building 157
Bayard-Condict Building, 95, 227
Bemelmans Bar, 312
Beresford, The, 347
Bergdorf Goodman, 297
Bigelow Co. Pharmacy, 212
Birdland, 60
Bloomingdale's, 311
Bowery, 37, 45, 48
Bowling Green, 152, 156, 157
Brentano's, 282
British Empire Building, 275
Broad St. (85), 166
Broadway (1), 156
Broadway (29), 155
Broadway (165), 152
Broadway Dance Center, 61
Brooklyn Borough Hall, 367
Brooklyn Bridge, 186
Brown Building, 200
Bush Tower, 254
Cable Building, 227
Café Carlyle, 312
Café des Artistes, 344
Callahan's, 192
Carnegie Hall, 299, 301, 305
Cartier Inc., 287
Cary Building, 88, 209
Castle Clinton, 142
CBS Building. 288
Centre Street (240), 196
Century Apartments, 343
Century Building, 90, 223, 310
Chanin Building, 98, 272
Chase Manhattan Bank, 159
Chemical Bank Building, 261
Cherokee Apartments, 313
Chrysler Building, 29, 98, 139, 161, 236, 266
Chumley's, 214
Citibank, 160
Citicorp Center, 101, 286
City Center of Music and Drama, 300
City College of the City University of New York, 360
City Hall, 37, 46, 162, 168, 258
City of New York Office

Building, 184
Civic Center, 182
Cloisters, The, 362
Colonnade Row, 84, 227
Columbia University, 30, 93, 352–3
Commerce Street (39–41), 214
Community College, 209
Con Edison Building, 229
Cooper Union Building, 225
Cotton Club, The, 60
Croton Fountain, 170
Croton Reservoir, 34, 156, 170
Crown Building, 296
Cunard Building, 155
Cushman Row, 85, 220
Dakota Apartments, 346
David Brown Store (Thomas St. Inn) 87, 209
Daylight Factories, 205
De Vinne Press Building, 91, 227
Decker Building, 223
Delmonico's, 166
Diamond Dealers' Club, 299
Downtown Athletic Club, 142
Dyckman House, 82, 361
East River Savings Bank Building, 152
Edward Mooney House, 83
Empire Diner, 220
Empire State Building, 29, 139, 461, 236, 242–7, 266
Engelhard Court, 329
Engine Company no. 31, 184
Equitable Building, 39, 97, 153
Essex House, 303
Exchange Place (20), 160
Federal Hall National Memorial, 27, 85, 157, 162, 163, 168
Federal Office Building, 178, 184
Federal Reserve Bank, 158
Film Center Building, 99
Flatiron Building, 28, 96, 233
Fleming Smith Warehouse, 208
Flushing Meadow, 65
Forbes Building, 218
Ford Foundation Building, 101, 265
Fordham Law School, 304
Former Arnold Constable & Co, 232
Former Asch Building, 200
Former AT&T Building, 176
Former B. Altman Building, 249
Former B. Altman Dry Goods Store, 220
Former Bank of the Metropolis Building, 222–3
Former Bowery Savings Bank, 272

Former Coty Building, 288
Former Gorham Manufacturing Company, 232
Former Hugh O'Neill's Store, 220
Former James Brown Residence, 207
Former Knickerbocker Hotel, 254
Former Little Singer Building, 204
Former Lord & Taylor, 232
Former McGraw-Hill Building, 99, 256
Former New York Mercantile Exchange, 207
Former Paramount Building, 255
Former Seamen's Bank for Savings, 160, 161
Former Sieget-Cooper Dry Goods Store, 220
Former Standard Oil Building, 56, 156, 159
Former United States Appraisers' Store, 215
Former Vanderbilt Residence, 283
Former W. & J. Sloane, 232
Forward Building, 195
Fraunces Tavern, 166
Fred French Building, 252
Friends Meeting House, 230
Fuller Building, 296
Fulton Ferry Building, 366
Fulton Ferry Hotel, 172
Gainsborough Studio, The, 303
General Consulate of Italy, 310
General Electric Building, Former RCA Victor Building, 98, 261, 277, 278, 286
General Motors Building, 297
General Post Office of New York, 170, 249
General Society of Mechanics and Tradesmen, 250
General Theological Seminary, 220
German Poliklinik, 224
Gilbert Kiamie House, 91
Gilsey House, 88, 89, 234
Goethe House, 320
Gotham Book Mart, 299
Government House, 156
Governor Tilden's House, 87, 230
Gracie Mansion, 313, 321
Gramercy, The, 230
Grammercy Park W (3-4), 230
Grand Central Terminal, 236
Graybar Building, 272
Great Hall, 328
Greenwich House, 214
Grove Court, 215
Guggenheim Bandshell,

306
Hall of Records, 185
Hard Rock Café, 302
Harper's Bazaar, 55
Harvard Club, 250
Haughwout Building, 88, 94, 95, 204, 206
Hearst Magazine Building, 303
Helmsley Building, 260
Henry Villard Houses, 92, 284
Hewlett House, 334
House of Relief, New York Hospital, 209
Hudson Street Warehouse, 208
Hunter College, 310
IBM Building, 289
India House, 166
Inter-American Relations, Center for, 310
Italian Cultural Institute, 310
International Building, 281
International Center of Photography, 321
International Telephone Building, 163
Irving Hall, 222
Irving Place (49), 229
Irving Trust, 154
Jacob Javits Convention Center, 248
Jarmulowsky Bank, 194
Jefferson Market Courthouse, 211
John Ericsson Memorial, 142
Jones St. (26–30), 214
Juilliard School of Music, 306
Kaoshen Club, 192
Kent Garage, 305
King's College, 30
Knickerbocker, 310
Landmark Tavern, 256
Langston Hughes House, 88
Lescaze House, 100, 262
Lever House, 100, 286
Liberty Plaza (1), 152
Liberty Tower, 159
Liberty Warehouse, 343
Lincoln Building, 222, 250
Lincoln Center, 299, 304–6
"Little" House, 334
Lockwood De Forest Residence, 218
Lycée Français, 309
Macy's, 249
Main Building, N. Y. U., 200
Main Emigrant Landing Depot, 143
Maine Memorial, 174, 304
Maison Française, 275
Majestic Apartments, 345
Manhattan Life Insurance Company, 302
Marine Midland Bank, 153
Maritime Exchange Building, 166
Marshall Chess Club, 218
McGraw-Hill Building, 99

Men's Detention Center, 183
MetLife Building, former Pan Am Building, 237, 260
Metropolitan Life Tower, 234
Metropolitan Tower, 301, 310
Miller Building (1), 257
Mills House no.1, 202
Morgan Guaranty Trust Company, 162
Morris-Jumel Mansion, '82, 361
Municipal Building, 96, 168, 182
National Academy of Design, 320
National Arts Club, 87, 230
National Democratic Club, 240
Netherlands Memorial Monument, 142
New School for Social Research, 219
New York Athletic Club, 303
New York Central & Hudson River Railroad Freight Depot, 208
New York Central Railroad Company, 260
New York City Criminal Court Building, 183
New York County Courthouse, 183
New York Delicatessen, 302
New York Stock Exchange, 27, 156, 163, 164–5
New York Studio School, 217
New York Telephone Building, 140
New York University, 200, 216
New York Yacht Club, 65, 93, 251
News Building, The, 272
Northern Dispensary, 212
Old Merchant's House, The, 227
Olympic Towers, 283
Osborne Apartments, 302
Oyster Bar, 175
Pace University, 170
Parish House, 288
Park Row Building, 171
Peck Slip, 171
Pennsylvania Station, 29, 249
Pershing Square Building, 272
Pete's Tavern, 229
Philip Morris Inc. Building, 103, 241
Pier 15, 173
Players, The, 230
Potter Building, 90, 170
Provincetown Playhouse, 202
Public Shelters, 47
Puck Building, 227
Pulitzer Fountain, 297
Racquet & Tennis Club of New York, 286
Radio City Music Hall, 35, 277, 285
Realty Buildings, 154

Richmond Hill House, 202
River House, 262
Rizzoli Building, 288
Rockefeller Center, 29, 280, 282, 299
Roosevelt Building, 206
Rushmore National Monument, 178
Saks Fifth Avenue, 282
Salmagundi Club, 88, 218
San Remo, 346
School for Social Research, 219
Seagram Building, 101, 286
7th Regiment Armory, 310
Shea Stadium, 64
Singer Building, 152, 159, 206
Solow Building, 297, 301
Sony Building, 102, 289
Spanish Institute, 310
Statue of Liberty, 138, 144–7
Stonewall Inn, 212
Stuyvesant High School, 142
Swiss Center, 282
Tammany Hall, 40, 228
Tavern on the Green, 344
Theodore Roosevelt Memorial, 347
Theresa Towers, 358
Tiffany and Co., 296
Tile Club, 218
Times Square (1), 255
Times Tower, 255
Tishman Building, 287
Titanic Memorial Lighthouse, 171
Trinity Building, 154
Trump Tower, 289, 296
"21" Club, 287
Twin Towers, 138, 139, 140
Ukrainian Institute, 312
U.S. Courthouse, 177, 183
U.S. Custom House, 142, 157, 160, 162, 168, 177
U.S. Post Office, 178
Union Club, 249, 309
Union League Club, 248
Union Square Savings Bank, 223
United Nations, 29, 236, 263–4
University Club, 288
Urban Center, 285
Vanderbilt's Hudson River Railroad Freight Depot, 260
Verrazano Memorial, 142
Vietnam War Veterans' Memorial, 166
W. 4th St. (175–9), 214
W. 11th St.445 (18), 218
Waldorf Towers, 285
Wallace Building, 91
Washington Court, 102, 212
Washington Irving High School, 229
Washington Mews, 216
White Horse Tavern, 215
Williamsburgh Savings Bank, 160
Woolworth Building, 17, 94, 161, 168, 177,

180–1, 234, 305
World Financial Center, 19, 103, 141
World Trade Center, 19, 29, 138, 139, 152, 157, 177
Yale Club, 251
Yankee Stadium, 64
Yeshiva Chofetz Chaim, former Villa Julia, 348

◆ Religious buildings ◆

Abyssinian Baptist Church, 51, 359
African Methodist Episcopal Zion Church, 51
Brotherhood Synagogue, 230
Catholic Church of the Transfiguration, 192
Church of St. Ann and The Holy Trinity, 367
Church of St. Luke in the Fields, 215
Church of the Holy Communion, 86, 220
Church of the Unification, 51
Collegiate Church and Collegiate School, 348
First Church of Zion, 192
Grace Church, 87, 224
Grant's Tomb, 357
Islamic Center, 51
Jewish Theological Seminary, 356
John Street United Methodist Church, 158
Judson Memorial Church, 200, 201
Lady Chapel, 283
Mariners' Temple Baptist Church, 193
Most Holy Crucifix Church, 196
Old St. Patrick's Cathedral, 196
Pythian Condominium, former Pythian Temple, The, 345
Riverside Church, 356
Roman Catholic Orphan Asylum, 83
St. Bartholomew's Church, 285
St. James Church, 193
St. James Episcopal Church, 309
St. John the Divine, 354
St. Malachy Roman Catholic Church, 300
St. Mark's in the Bowery, 224
St. Nicholas Greek Orthodox Chapel, 140
St. Patrick's Cathedral, 50, 282
St. Paul Episcopal Church, 353
St. Paul's Chapel, 176
St. Peter's Church, 178
St. Thomas Episcopal Church, 86, 87, 288
Synagogue Beth Hamedrash Hagadol, 195
Synagogue Khal Adath Jerushun and Anshe Lubz, 194
Temple Emanu-El, 311

Trinity Cemetery, 361
Trinity Church, 31, 86, 138, 154–5, 158, 178, 208, 352
Union Theological Seminary, 356
Unitarian Church of All Souls, 312
Village Community Church, 84, 219

◆ Museums ◆

Abigail Adams Smith Museum, 311
American Fine Art Society, 302
American Museum of Natural History, 347
Audubon Terrace Historic District, 361
Chinatown History Museum, 191
Cloisters, The, 362–5
Con Edison Energy Museum, 229
Cooper Hewitt Museum, 132, 225, 320
Dia Center for the Arts, 220
Forbes Galleries, 219
Frick Collection, 309, 320, 322–5
Guggenheim Museum, 320, 338–41
Guggenheim Museum of SoHo, 204, 205
IBM Gallery of Science and Art, 289
Intrepid Sea-Air-Space Museum, 257
Jewish Museum, 321
Library and Museum of the Performing Arts, 306
Metropolitan Museum of Art, 161, 217, 320, 328–37
Michael C. Rockefeller Wing, 331
Museum for African Art, 204, 205
Museum of American Financial History, 156
Museum of Immigration, 148
Museum of Modern Art, 290–5
Museum of the City of New York, 321
New Museum of Contemporary Art, 204, 205
N.Y. City Fire Department Museum, 207
South Street Seaport Museum, 172
Temple Emanu-El, 311
Vanderbilt Colony, 284
Whitney Museum, 104, 158, 217, 241, 320, 326

◆ Parks, Gardens ◆

Admiral George Dewey Promenade, 143
Battery Park, 19, 138, 140, 142, 143
Battery Park Center, 29
Brooklyn Botanic Garden, 368
Brooklyn Heights

Esplanade, 368
Bryant Park, 39, 254, 297
Carl Schurz Park, 313
Castle Garden,143
Central Park, 22, 28, 32, 33, 99, 314–19
Central Park South, 303
Channel Gardens, 275
Chatham Square, 193
Christopher Park, 212
City Hall Park, 168, 170
Columbus Park, 190
Cooper Square, 224
Damrosch Park, 306
Duane Park, 209
Eastern Parkway, 33
Father Duffy Square, 257
Foley Square, 182
Gramercy Park, 87, 89, 230
Hanover Square, 38, 166
Herald and Greeley Squares, 249
Isham Park, 19
MacDougal Sullivan Gardens, 202
Marcus Garvey Park, 358
Paley Park, 288
Printing House Square, 170
Riverside Park, 348
Seward Park, 195
Sheridan Square, 212
St. John's Park, 208
Tompkins Square, 224
Union Square, 222
Washington Square, 38, 198

◆ Theaters ◆

Aerial Gardens, 258
Apollo Theater, 61, 358
Barrymore Theater, 259
Biltmore Theater, 258
Booth Theater, 258
Chanin's Theater, 258
Charles Ludbon Theater, 213
Helen Hayes Theater, 259
Juilliard Theater, 306
Lambs Theater, 259
Lucille Lortel Theater, 215
Lyceum Theater, 259
Lyric, The, 258
Majestic Theater, 259
Metropolitan Opera House, 305
Metropolitan Opera, the old, 56
New Amsterdam Theater, 258
New York State Theater, 305
Paramount Theater, 255
Shubert Theater, 259
Union Theater, 228
Vivian Beaumont Theater, 306
Winter Garden Theater, 258